THEO-DRAMA
Volume I

HANS URS VON BALTHASAR

THEO-DRAMA

THEOLOGICAL
DRAMATIC THEORY

VOLUME I
PROLEGOMENA

Translated by Graham Harrison

IGNATIUS PRESS   SAN FRANCISCO

Title of the German original:
Theodramatik: Erster Band: Prolegomena
© 1983 Johannes Verlag, Einsiedeln

Cover by Roxanne Mei Lum

CONTENTS

CONTENTS

II. DRAMATIC RESOURCES

PREFACE

This "Prolegomena" calls for an apologia on account of both its length and its contents. I am aware that I am grievously trying the patience of my theological colleagues, since the present work is not theology, properly speaking, but initially only the assembling of material and themes toward a theology. The book erects the apparatus, as it were, so that gymnasts may eventually exercise upon it. All the same, leafing through these pages, the sensitive theologian will anticipate the actual topics as they begin to emerge obliquely. All it needs is the magnet to align the iron filings and assemble them—into a Christology, a doctrine of the Trinity, an ecclesial and Christian doctrine of how to live.

But an apologia is even more pressing vis-à-vis men of letters. Out of the limitless literature of the stage I have selected only meager fragments; moreover I have not treated them from a literary point of view but have been obliged to select and present them for my theological purposes. This means that there is no formal aesthetic evaluation; the dramatists and works referred to are accepted as having literary significance; I make no attempt critically to justify it. The choice of a particular play depends on its theological fruitfulness—an admittedly one-sided approach. Greek drama, which was discussed, briefly at least, in *The Glory of the Lord*, Volume IV, remains in the background here. So does many an important work by *Shakespeare*, *Corneille*, *Goethe*, and many others that do not exhibit directly enough that theological significance which is evident elsewhere and which (it is to be hoped) will prove to have a seminal influence on a specialist theology that has been hitherto largely "epic".

What interests us here is the whole phenomenon of theatre: the sheer fact that there is such a thing as a structured performance and ultimately the actual substance of the play itself. Our aim will be to show how theology underlies it all and how all the elements of the drama can be rendered fruitful for theology. Of course it would be possible to understand theatre philosophically, starting from the way a child translates its world of experience into theatrical terms, conceives things, reacts to them, in speech and in all forms of play. On this basis one could go on to demonstrate that the theatrical is a primitive human instinct, more primitive, indeed, than our aesthetic needs.[1] Philosophy, like theology, has so far devoted no attention to the stage; it is as if the actor's banishment from Plato's *polis* has continued in force down the centuries. There are exceptions, and we shall mention them: *Hegel, Nietzsche, Simmel, Marcel, Gouhier,* and others have taken account of the philosophical aspects of drama, the phenomenon of theatre and, in particular, the actor. We shall discuss them to the extent that they reflect on the quasi-religious dimension of the stage, whose historical roots lie unequivocally in cultic activity. Even for *Diderot* the actor is a *prédicateur laïque.*[2] Theatre intends to be an interpretation of the world, in its "unreality" shining a ray of light into the confusion of reality.[3] Often actors themselves have been the most profound and existential thinkers about their unique profession, coming up with amazing revelations; like many poets (*Marcel,*[4] *Mauriac,*[5] *Hermann Bahr*[6]), they sense the uncanny nearness of

---

[1] P. A. Lascaris, *L'Éducation esthétique de l'enfant* (Presses Universitaires, 1928); N. Evreinoff, *Le Théâtre dans la vie* (Paris, 1930).

[2] Diderot, *Oeuvres* VIII, 392.

[3] "What we have here is a world (sic) mediated by creative, not ordinary, imagination. It creates the world anew, not a so-called fantasy world, i.e., not one lacking connection, but on the contrary one in which the connections are more visible than in the real world. Not a segment of this world, but a whole, complete world, that has all its conditions and consequences within itself. . . . A world that is midway between the objective truth in things and the law that our spirit is compelled to posit in them" (Otto Ludwig, *Schriften* V, 329).

[4] Marcel, "Reflexions sur les exigences d'un theatre chrétien", in *La vie intellectuelle* (Mar. 25, 1937): 460f. One can ask "whether the actor does not possess quite unique opportunities of grace, whether there is not something in his existence that can somehow attract God's favor. There is a word of scripture that, in its secondary meaning, can be applied to him: 'Ye are not your own.' He can only find himself if he is prepared to lose himself. Thus, pursuing his vocation, he can provide us, through his unusual life, with a metaphor of human life as it aims toward its supernatural goal."

[5] "How strange it is that this effort to 'dis-incarnate' oneself in the service of an imaginary story bears such a startling analogy to what the mystics are looking for, to that emptiness striven for by those who long to be overwhelmed by God" (Mauriac, "Le mystère du théâtre", in *Journal* III, 113).

[6] H. Bahr, *Schauspielkunst* (Leipzig, 1923), 45: "During the transformation he (the actor) remains its lord and master, . . . he, seized and wrenched from

the religious dimension: *Baty*, *Dullin*, *Ginsberg* and especially *Louis Jouvet* have discussed this in depth.

Gaston Baty, in an inspired book, has elucidated the relationship between the whole phenomenon of the stage and Christianity by reference to the medieval "mystery plays",[7] which he terms "cathedrals in dramatic form". Like the Greek stage, they were born out of the liturgy and became a movement involving the whole people.[8] Life itself—nature embedded in the supernatural—was acted out, and thus a "Catholic aesthetics",[9] for which Greek drama was obscurely groping, was brought to light. A non-Christian writer wonders: "Is there a relationship between Catholicism and the theatre? Does its objectifying of faith, its incarnation in things and beings, correspond to a giving and receiving of gifts, an exchange with the Divinity?"[10] It is enough at this point to have raised the question.

The reader will hardly need reassuring: we shall not be making any direct transition from the stage to theology. The world of the theatre will only provide us with a set of resources which, after they have been thoroughly modified, can be used later in theology. All the same, the model of the theatre is a more

---

himself, is at the same time in control of the power that overwhelms him—this is the absolute opposite of all hysteria." The actor "presents us directly with the ultimate mystery of human nature: i.e., that, when we have entirely overcome ourselves and totally ceased being ourselves, we then find our true selves and begin for the first time to be ourselves. The hysteria of the inexperienced actor leads directly to metaphysics."

[7] Gaston Baty, *Le masque et l'encensoir: Introduction à une esthétique du théâtre* (Paris: Bloud et Gay, 1926). Foreword by Maurice Brillant.

[8] In Rheims, in 1490, the crucifixion was performed before 16,000 spectators. Baty calls the *mistère* the "people's Bible". Through it, people became intimately acquainted not only with saving history, but also with the lives of the saints. Priests often took part as actors, often whole monasteries or cathedral chapters participated. The relics of the saint whose life was being depicted would be brought onto the stage. At the end all would sing the *Te Deum*; God the Father, the Mother of God, the devil, each in his costume, would join in (Baty, *Le masque et l'encensoir*, 235).

[9] As Baty says (see n. 7): "Although Aeschylus and Sophocles could foresee neither the dogma nor the ethics of the Gospels, they acted in accordance with a Catholic aesthetics" (319). See also M. Brillant's Foreword, 44ff.

[10] J. Auger Duvignaud, *L'Acteur* (Gallimard, 1965), 282.

promising point of departure for a study of *theo-drama* than
man's secular, social activity. For in the theatre man attempts a
kind of transcendence, endeavoring both to observe and to
judge his own truth, in virtue of a transformation—through the
dialectic of the concealing-revealing mask—by which he tries to
gain clarity about himself. Man himself beckons, invites the
approach of a revelation about himself. Thus, parabolically, a
door can open to the truth of the real revelation.

Hans Urs von Balthasar

I. INTRODUCTION: ORIENTATIONS

A. DRAMATIC THEORY BETWEEN AESTHETICS AND LOGIC

We have had to spend a great deal of time on *A Theological Aesthetics*, and its ecumenical conclusion still remains to be written. According to the original plan,[1] the *Aesthetics* forms the first part of a triptych. It describes the way we encounter and perceive the phenomenon of divine revelation in the world (in the manifold forms of its "glory" [*Herrlichkeit*]). If the two parties involved in the encounter are to do more than give a nod of recognition in passing, this first encounter must be followed by a conversation. Anyone who took seriously the encounter described in the *Aesthetics* was obliged to see that the phenomenon presented to him was one in which he had always been involved: "One man has died for all, and so all have died" and now "can no longer live for themselves but (only) for him who for their sake died and rose again" (2 Cor 5:14f.). Thus, right at the heart of the *Aesthetics*, the "theological drama" has already begun. "Catching sight" of the glory (*die Erblickung*), we observed, always involves being "transported" by it (*die Entrückung*). But this was all seen from within the aesthetic purview. Now we must allow the encountering reality to speak in its own tongue or, rather, let ourselves be drawn into its dramatic arena. For God's revelation is not an object to be looked at: it is his action in and upon the world, and the world can only respond, and hence "understand", through action on *its* part. Only after having examined this dramatic interplay can we properly proceed to the third and final part, which will have to reflect on the way in which this action is expressed in concept and word. In short, the three phases are these:

Theo-phany = Aesthetics
Theo-praxy = Dramatic theory
Theo-logy = Logic

These three parts cannot be totally separated from one another: the reason why the *Aesthetics* has taken up so much space is that

[1] *The Glory of the Lord* I.

15

it always had to show the encountered reality *at work*—as theo-praxy. The two volumes *The Old Covenant* and *The New Covenant*, in particular, largely anticipated the development of the drama of revelation and naturally enough employed concepts and words—theo-logy. What was utterly special about this encounter was that, by contrast with other religions and world-views (where it is a question of "envisaging" a divine ground for the world), here the divine ground actually approaches us totally unexpectedly, of its own accord, paradoxically, and challenges us to face it. And although this unique phenomenon was discussed in terms of "glory", it was increasingly clear from the outset that it withdrew farther and farther away from any merely contemplative gaze and hence could not be translated into any neutral truth or wisdom that can be "taught". What was manifest was a "light" that cannot be bypassed and yet is invisible; a word of incomparable precision, yet which can be expressed equally well in the cry of a dying man, in the silence of death and in what is ineffable—in religious rebirth, for example, and in the sense of oneness with the universe. If by "aesthetics" we are thinking more of the act of perception or its "beautiful" object, we are succumbing to a static view which cannot do justice to the phenomenon. Aesthetics must surrender itself and go in search of new categories. "Theology", similarly, can come to speak in static terms, but this can only be justified if it has previously experienced the dynamism of the revelation-event and is reborn by it in a form that is always new, not a dead "result". So we should not attempt to go straight from the "aesthetics" to the "logic", even if (as in the first volume of *The Glory of the Lord*) beginning with aesthetics were conceived as a deliberate protest against a theological rationalism. The "forms", "pictures", "symbols" which an "aesthetics" can present—and we put forward such "forms" in Volume II: Clerical Styles—are insufficient in themselves to interpret revelation in its absolutely unique, definitive form and in terms of theological "universal validity". This can only be done by the absolute commitment found in that drama into which the one and only God sets each of us to play our unique part. Death turns into life, and this is something that also takes place in our hearts so that, drawn into the action, they can look toward that center in which all things are transformed. But we have been appointed to play our part, and thus we share responsibility for our own understanding and expression of it. So it is incumbent on us to create a network of related concepts and images that may serve to hold fast, in some fashion, in what we think and say, to the singular divine action.

In other words, we are presented with the task of developing a theodramatic theory. As human beings, we already have a preliminary grasp of what drama is; we are acquainted with it from the complications, tensions, catastrophes and reconciliations which characterize our lives as individuals and in interaction with others, and we also know it in a different way from the phenomenon of the stage (which is both related to life and yet at a remove from it). The task of the stage is to make the drama of existence explicit so that we may view it. For the stage drama is the missing link: it transforms the event into a picture that can be seen and thus expands aesthetics into something new (and yet continuous with itself), while at the same time it is already translating this picture into speech. Of course there is also the pantomime, which entrusts all power of expression to the human body and limbs, but this complementary, substitute language cannot in the long run replace the free utterance of the audible word which, in drama, has its particular logic, a logic dictated by the course of the action. The action is not narrated; it takes place along with and in the words. The drama of existence is related in manifold ways to its presentation on the stage; these relationships are part of a system of dramatic categories; we shall have to unfold them at a later stage. It is important to note their existence here, for it shows that theo-drama can draw on a twofold, interrelated pre-understanding that is both existential and aesthetic. Nowhere is the character of existence demonstrated more clearly than in stage drama: we are drawn to watch it, and initially it is immaterial whether, in doing so, we are searching for or fleeing from ourselves, immaterial whether the performance is showing us the serious- or the play-dimension, the destructive or the transfiguring aspect, the absurdity or the hidden profundity of our life. Probably nowhere else but in this interplay of relationships (which is of the essence of the theatre) can we see so clearly the questionable nature and ambiguity not only of the theatre but also of existence itself, which the theatre illuminates. For the moment, however, it is not this ambiguity which is to the fore but rather the abundant wealth of material, relationships and connections; these provide a complete, ready-made set of categories—hardly noticed by theology up to now —which can be used to portray God's action.

Furthermore, the *Aesthetics* was essentially a doctrine of perception, and, however much the object of perception may have affected us ("transporting" us toward "him whom we have perceived"), there was always a boundary between object and onlooker. Dramatic theory (*Dramatik*) is concerned with what-is-going-forward (*Agogik*), and, as in the relationship between life and the stage, the boundaries between the two are blurred, so it is in God's dealings with mankind: the boundary between the actor or agent and the "auditorium" is removed, and man is a spectator only insofar as he is a player: he does not merely see himself on the stage, he really acts on it. True, in theo-drama it is God's stage; the decisive content of the actions is what he does: God and man will never appear as equal partners. It is God who acts, on man, for man and then together with man; the involvement of man in the divine action is part of God's *action*, not a precondition of it. Thus it is already clear that, while the conceptual categories of secular drama provide us with a preliminary understanding, they cannot offer anything like a complete grasp. They remain at the level of image and metaphor, as is clear from their ultimate ambiguity; here too, the greater dissimilarity in the analogy prevents us from using any terms univocally.

There is nothing ambiguous about what God does for man: it is simply *good*. Theo-drama is concerned with the good. What God has done is to work salvation, to reconcile the world to himself in Christ (2 Cor 5:19); he has taken this initiative out of love, which simply seeks to give itself. The good has its center of gravity neither in the perceiving nor in the uttering: the perception may be *beautiful* and the utterance *true*, but only the act can be *good*. Here, in the act, there is a real giving, originating in the personal freedom of the giver and designed for the personal benefit of the recipient. The *Aesthetics* has already uncovered the glory and hence the "beauty" of God's action, his

Covenant, the fulfillment of his covenant righteousness and his judgment as a function of this fulfillment. But in doing so it has also revealed the "goodness" of God's totally free love, without which his glory would not be beautiful nor his word true. So, ultimately, the good which God brings about can only be explained and demonstrated from within itself and will not allow itself to be drawn into the ambiguities of the "world theatre" (*Welttheater*)—the theatre of life and of the stage. Not ultimately. But penultimately? If God is to deal with man in an effective way and in a way that is intelligible to him, must not God himself tread the stage of the world and thus become implicated in the dubious nature of the world theatre? And however he comes into contact with this theatre—whether he is to take responsibility for the whole meaning of the play or is to appear as one of the cast (in which case one can investigate his connection with the other *dramatis personae*)—the analogy between God's action and the world drama is no mere metaphor but has an ontological ground: the two dramas are not utterly unconnected; there is an inner link between them. Theologically speaking, the ambiguity of the "world theatre" metaphor does invade the clarity of God's saving action, but how far is the latter obscured by the former? Or are we to say that when God's action submits to the rules of the world stage it becomes invisible and can no longer be verified as a distinct action? On the human stage he "plays" through human beings and ultimately *as* a human being; does that mean that he goes completely incognito behind the human mask? Is he only to drop this mask in death, when the play reveals who the actor in reality was ("This man was truly the Son of God" [Mt 27:54])? And surely only a human being can die; and if God was this human being, is not God really and truly dead? Thus, by entering into contact with the world theatre, the good which takes place in God's action really is affected by the world's ambiguity and remains a hidden good. This good is something *done*: it cannot be contemplated in pure "aesthetics" nor proved and demonstrated in pure "logic". It takes place nowhere but on the world stage—which is every living person's present moment—and its destiny is seen in the drama of a world history that is continually unfolding. What takes place, thus decisively, *for us* and *in us*, has

already been decided *in itself*; but, as a result of the contact
between God's drama and the world theatre, the "for us"
cannot be isolated from the "in itself". In the latter case ("in
itself"), the Victor only has to "wait until his enemies are made
his footstool" (Heb 10:13), whereas in the former ("for us"), the
Logos is always riding out to battle, his garments steeped in
blood (Rev 19:13). The *good* which God does to us can only be
experienced as the *truth* if we share in *performing* it (Jn 7:17;
8:31f.); we must "do the truth in love" (*aletheuein en agape*
[Eph 4:15]) not only in order to perceive the truth of the good
but, equally, in order to embody it increasingly in the world,
thus leading the ambiguities of world theatre beyond themselves
to a singleness of meaning that can come only from God. This is
possible because it is already a reality for God and through God,
because he has already taken the drama of existence which plays
on the world stage and inserted it into his quite different "play"
which, nonetheless, he wishes to play on our stage. It is a case of
the play within the play: our play "plays" in his play.

There is nothing unnatural about this paradox. Anyone who
knows anything about the theatre understands it as a projection
of human existence onto a stage, interpreting to itself that
existence which is beyond it. Since existence recognizes itself in
this interpretation, it can (in a privileged moment) realize that it
is playing a *role* in a larger play. Whether it can discern its
meaning is another matter; what is important is for it to realize
that in the very act of playing its role, even if it is a tragic one, it
transcends itself. In fact, theatre owes its very existence substantially to man's need to recognize himself as playing a role. It
continually delivers him from the sense of being trapped and
from the temptation to regard existence as something closed in
upon itself. Through the theatre, man acquires the habit of
looking for meaning at a higher and less obvious level. And at
the same time it dispels the disheartening notion that this higher
level is no longer dramatic but a static level where nothing
happens and which relativizes all events beneath and external to
it. In this way the theatre acts as a brake on all tidy philosophies:
it maintains the existential character of existence against all

attempts to relativize it; it shows that this existential character is a part of the all-embracing reality itself. How it does this, and with what result, is questionable, but at least it *holds fast to the question*. And so long as the question continues to be put, we can still hope for an answer. To that extent the theatre, in the background, is making its own contribution to fundamental theology.

If there is to be a biblical answer to this question, and if it is to be intelligible to human beings, it must show itself within the horizon of man's dramatic existence, with all its dubious facets. And let us stress once more, this means that the divine dramatic *answer* has already *taken place* in the form of the human dramatic *question*. This is something definitive, *eph-hapax*, not floating along with the tide of successive situations in world history, but embracing them all within its ambit, a horizon that is itself ultimately and eschatologically dramatic. The question becomes most acute in the cry of forsakenness that issues from the Cross. This cry is the very antithesis of that kind of religious resignation which surrenders to an undramatic, absolute horizon. From out of the silent horizon, the cry is answered by the lightning response of decisive action—Good Friday turns into Easter. The horizon replies in the form of event. The question is self-transcending; the reply too is transcendent, but it also answers the question of "death". Insofar as the answer is transcendent, and insofar as it responds to that cry (which sums up all our questionings), it is a definitive answer, *eph-hapax*, and no "play", either before or since, can match it. In fact the answer—covertly or latently—resides in the play's very essence; it gives it its horizon. The answer is relevant in all ages, being both the answer to *this* particular cry and ultimately, eschatologically, the answer to every cry. It cannot lose its relevance because it is itself entirely *act*, although it only shows itself to be such where people are themselves acting and questioning dramatically. The precise meaning of *eph-hapax*, then, is that there is a unique answer to all instances of the question. Not an answer definitively known and kept safe, obviating the question. Where there is no longer any sign of life, the horizon falls dumb and clouds over.

Thus it is a basic Christian requirement that existence should represent itself dramatically. Consequently many things are from the outset excluded: a dead faith, for instance, which has cut itself off from love and hope and become a rational system of truths to be believed, no longer yielding proof in terms of life. *Now* is the time for questioning and playing one's part; there *is* such a things as being "too late": "When once the householder has risen up and shut the door, you will begin to stand outside and to knock at the door, saying, 'Lord, open to us.' He will answer you, 'I do not know where you come from' " (Lk 13:25). But this also applies where there is mere contemplation of what has taken place, even if such contemplation *thinks* it is actually loving and hoping; if it only fixes its gaze on the event and fails to grasp it as the here-and-now, the dawn of the future, if it fails to come to grips with the secular "now" within the horizon of what has been achieved definitively, it will slip into unreality. We can say, "Lord, Lord!" in the depths of spirituality and mysticism, we can "eat and drink with him" sacramentally, but it is all in vain if we do not carry out the will of our heavenly Father. Furthermore, the mere proclamation of the word of salvation—which is incumbent upon us—will not elicit faith if the herald himself does not fashion his life into a dramatic word of testimony. Neither faith, contemplation nor kerygma can dispense us from *action*. And the libretto of God's saving drama which we call Holy Scripture is worthless in itself unless, in the Holy Spirit, it is constantly mediating between the drama beyond and the drama here. It is not a self-sufficient armchair drama; its very form shows it to be a multifarious testimony pointing to an action at its core that goes beyond all words. *Justin*, in his *First Apology*, sensed a mysterious apportioning of roles in the words which the Spirit, or Logos, puts into the prophet's mouth: "For sometimes he announces things that are to come in the manner of a prediction, sometimes, as it were, in the person of God, the Lord and Father of all things, sometimes in the person of Christ and at other times, as it were, in the person of communities making answer to the Lord or his Father. You may observe something similar in your poets: an entire work has a single author, whereas the persons he causes to speak are several."[2] It is not that different texts are given out for each role; the same text sounds differently at each point, it has perspective, speaks from different angels and in dramatic dimensions.

[2] *Apol*. I, 36: cf. *Dial*. 36 and 73–74. Also in Philo, *De Mose* III, 188: "The logia are in part spoken in the *prosopon* of God through the mouth of the prophet, partly revealed as the will of God in the form of question and answer, and partly uttered in the *prosopon* of Moses while he is under the influence of the spirit and 'beside himself'." Thus the same word of God originates in God (via Moses), in the dialogue (between God and Moses) and in Moses (in God). Cf. Epiphanius *Haer*. 48, 12: The exegete's task is to know which of the Spirit-inspired words are uttered by the *prosopon* of the Father, which by that of the Son, and which by that of the Spirit (Oehler I/1, 35). Origen says the same in *Redepenning* (1841), I, 256.

B. TRENDS OF MODERN THEOLOGY

We are proposing to use the categories of drama to illuminate Christian theology. On the one hand, the endeavor might seem abstruse, on the other hand, banal. It might seem abstruse, because here (as in the *Aesthetics* too, perhaps) we seem to be taking yet another byroad leading away from the main path, importing an element of play into the serious business of revelation and beclouding its clarity with the ambiguities of a parable—"world theatre"—which is of doubtful relevance today. It may seem banal, for we all *know* that biblical revelation concerns God's action and that the lives of Abraham, Moses, David, the Prophets, Jesus and his Apostles contain dramatic peripeteias of many kinds—and they are plain enough and need no assistance from secular dramatics. For the present we let both objections stand; we shall only know whether our "dramatic" approach is fruitful or not by actually going ahead with it.

However, in this introduction we *can* anticipate one argument in its favor. The shortcomings of the theology that has come down to us through the centuries has called forth new approaches and methods in recent decades. Disciples and opponents alike have been quick to narrow down each of these approaches to a slogan, a catch phrase, although originally they were often conceived in broader and deeper terms; and they have one thing in common. They all see theology stuck fast on the sandbank of rationalist abstraction and want to get it moving again. Each of these attempts contains something right, even something indispensable. But none of them is adequate to provide the basis for a Christian theology. Each needs to be complemented. In part they complement each other, but when juxtaposed they do not attain the methodological clarity and fullness that their object requires. If they are seen in their positive contribution as well as in their partiality, they can all be shown to converge on what we have called *theo-drama*. Here, each of them can find what it lacks.

Theology's turning-away from both a fundamentalist orthodoxy and an historical liberalism is characterized by the "event" principle. The real, which is theology's object, is not simply something that has taken place historically (a fact) or a string of data that can be enumerated; nor is it merely something supra-temporal to be abstracted from such facts, an idea that is somehow of importance for today, an "essence" or some "being" at rest in itself. It is utterly and completely an event, breaking vertically into the chain of facts which make up the world as seen from the inside and as such revealing both the living God's mode of being and his mode of acting. Thus he judges and saves the world by vertically breaking into time—simultaneously in act and word. Confronted with this active word—or coming to face it himself—the sinner is justified, the one who has fallen a prey to time is redeemed with a view to eternity, the deaf man becomes a hearer, the godless man a believer, the disobedient a doer of the word. There can be different, even opposite, emphases here. On the one hand, God himself is the (eschatological) event, the word-aspect of his act is the preaching of the gospel, and the acceptance of it is the "event" of transformation that takes place in man, in which man is crucified to the world and raised up by God and to God. Here, in the "now" of the kerygma, the event flashes like lightning between the hidden cloud where God is and the hidden heart of man. Alternatively, the lightning-bright word can be seen as attaining its full evangelical meaning in the Word-made-man, Jesus Christ: he is God's act, in him reconciling the world prior to any human activity; man *is seized* by the event, struck by the lightning, whether he knows it or not. And when he does come to know it and gives truth its due honor, he becomes a Christian. In both versions, horizontal history is pierced through vertically, its future has been inwardly anticipated and brought to fulfillment, and what seemed to be "past history" in the event has its center of gravity in each new "now" of present events.

Used in this absolute, straightforward way, the category of "event" has delivered the biblical revelation of God from the clutches of both orthodox and liberal rationalism—which, one way or another, got no farther than the historical fact. Of course, historicism could try once again to historicize the pure event-quality of the gospel and show it to be frustrated, with the help of the apocalyptic of the period and its expectation of the imminent vertical descent of the Kingdom of God (which failed to arrive). But the fact that Christianity did not collapse as a result of this alleged frustration but survived it[1] shows that it rested on different foundations. On the other hand, there is something timeless and context-less in this concentration on the pure event, which does not do justice to the genuinely historical nature of biblical revelation. This is clearest where it is a question of the relationship of Old Testament prophecy and New Testament fulfillment (a relationship which is anticipated in many ways even within the Old Testament itself), which requires horizontal time in which to unfold. In the Bible and in primitive Christianity (as opposed to gnosticism, which devalued the Old Testament) this horizontal relationship was the proof par excellence of the truth of the eschatological event that had taken place in Christ. But this relationship plays no part in the thought of the young *Barth* or in *Bultmann*; it was already obscured in the tragic Lutheran dialectic between "law" and "gospel". According to Scripture, however, there *are* "due times" appointed by God (*idioi kairoi*: 1 Tim 2:6; 6:15, Tit 1:3); there *is* such a thing as waiting for the proper "hour" (Jn 2:4; 7:30; 8:20), a waiting which includes salvific action in accord with God's intentions; there *is* such a thing as acting in the knowledge that the hour has come (Jn 12:23; 13:1). Finally, when the hour comes, it stretches itself out in a strange way which can only be expressed by a simultaneous future and present: "The hour is coming and now is" (Jn 4:23; 5:25; 16:32). It might be objected that the "future" aspect was something foreseen by Jesus prior to his Passion, and the "present" was the present of the evangelist in the church of his day; but this only shows how different horizontal points of time, different perspectives, are related to the event of the "hour". Time does not extend neutrally on either side of this event—the death and Resurrection of Jesus. Just as, before the death of Jesus, there

---

[1] O. Cullmann, *Vorträge und Aufsätze* (1966), 414ff.

was a "short *kairos*", which men could seize or fail to grasp—so long as it was there (Jn 12:35)—so, in the era of the Church, there is a "favorable time" (that is by no means timeless or permanently available), a "now", a "day of salvation" (2 Cor 6:2), a "today" (Heb 3:13ff.; 4:7), which may be followed by an ineluctable "too late" (Heb 6:4ff.). The Deuteronomists understood Israel's history as being entirely governed by this qualitative kind of time, consisting of offers of salvation that were accepted or—more frequently—missed, and of times when the people's response was relatively, or even absolutely, "too late". Paul's theology of history (especially Rom 9–11) reckons with events of salvation even after Christ; while they belong within the eschatological saving event and are determined by it, they do not simply coincide with it. You Gentiles have been converted, but take care: you can still fall away again; the Jews have been rejected, but this was for the sake of the conversion of the Gentiles, that is, on the basis of the saving plan of God, who will ultimately bring them, the Jews, home again. Here the vertical event has unfolded into a series of times of salvation comparable to the acts of a play. This does not mean that the vertical event-time has been dissolved into a merely horizontal time of successive saving facts, but it *does* mean that the vertical event-time overtakes and refashions horizontal time, using it so that the event may spread itself out in dramatic form. It is not as if there is *only* the fifth act, or even *only* the crucial scene of the peripeteia: God plays the whole piece right through with the individual human being and the human race.

2. *"History"*

A second watchword in modern theology organizes the material partly parallel with, and partly in opposition to, the first. It runs parallel inasmuch as, by contrast with a rationalist-idealist ethics of timelessly valid laws, the *kairos*, the situation, is elevated to be the guide for Christian conduct: what is valid, what is true, is what is required at each "now". Situation ethics leads by a straight path to situation theology: the Church's particular situation, with its urgent requirements but also with its historically distinct viewpoint, determines how precisely the absolute salvific event can now be validly lived and expressed. As is well known, the saving event itself found initial infrahistorical expression in the diverse traditions of the apostolic age, which were subsequently collected to form the corpus of Holy Scripture. They too are documents of their time, they are part of the stream of horizontal history, they are timebound and, in response to changing current modes of thought and expression, they continually need to be reinterpreted in order to remain relevant. In order to escape pure relativism here it is possible to affirm that the historical (in the theological sense) always expresses a permanent "transcendental" salvific will on God's part; the latter is present as such *in* these changing situations with their changing criteria, although they are no more than a formal pointer to it. God's salvific will can be seen as manifested once and for all (in its highest expression) in Christ, such that all historical situations, whether of individuals or of groups, are thought to contain a christological a priori, an *existentiale* or transcendental dimension; this would mark the most diverse, and externally perhaps contradictory, situations as "salvific" for "open" or "anonymous" Christians. In such an interpretation, while the historical aspect is certainly prevented from being pure flux in that it has an anchor in God, the individual moment is not brought out in its uniqueness. History, however, can also be identified with the innermost nature of man, insofar as he is freely self-determining; in this case he can be summoned continually to *choose* his own authentic being, which leads on to the question whether he can find this in himself or in others or in God.

But whether the historical is seen as rooted in God or in man, the mere category "history" is insufficient to grasp what is distinctive about biblical revelation, what sets it apart from all other forms of religion and world models. Now it is the horizontal that absorbs the vertical. The eschatological dimension, present in the early Church in the categories of apocalyptic and the expectation of an imminent Second Coming, is assimilated into the continuous stream of a time that is somehow "heavy with salvation", yet without leaving a recognizable trace in it. The form (*Gestalt*) which slowly arose out of the Old Testament and is brought to fulfillment in the event of the Cross, Good Friday and Resurrection is subordinated to the overall category of "history". Whereas, in fact, something has changed in salvation-time as it flows onward, something that makes it different from pre-Christian time: "If I had not done among them the works which no one else did, they would not have sin . . ." (Jn 15:24). A stumbling block for the fall and rising of many has been erected, one which did not exist before; all ages after Jesus will be marked (perhaps increasingly) by a Yes or No to him. That does not mean that his Kingdom and grace could not be latent prior to his coming (as the Church Fathers knew), as an *existentiale* or an historico-transcendental destiny. But this destiny comes from a point in history in which "God appears on the stage of world history." Cut loose from this dramatic context, the "historical" character of theology would dissolve, one way or another, into mere philosophy. Jesus himself has a unique and particular time,[2] and all time after him will be stamped by it in a special way. It is quite right to say that the death and Resurrection of Jesus inwardly affects all men of all ages since they share solidarity in a single history of mankind; but it is something else entirely to get personally involved with the "time" of Jesus, to "die" with him in transitory world-time and "rise again with him", and thus to exist at the mysterious intersection of the "aeons" of which Paul so often speaks. In one aeon the outer man dies daily, in the other aeon the inner man continually rises to new life; in the one he must stand guard, responsible for the destinies of the world, which has to prepare itself for the coming Kingdom, while in the other he has a hidden homeland—which seems to make him a foreigner in this world and a traitor to it. This dramatic tension between the times cannot be maintained using the mere category of "history".

There are further, more general considerations. The individual moment may involve a sharp conflict, but historically successive moments are even more full of tension with their

---

[2] On Jesus' "time": *Glory of the Lord*, vol. 7 (III/2 part 2), "New Covenant" (1969), 150ff.

clashes and confrontations. Given the multi-dimensionality of his "moment", can the Christian ever unequivocally define his standpoint in the total event? And if he cannot, how exposed he stands vis-à-vis other Christians and non-Christians, other historical situations, before and after him, which, seeing with equal difficulty in the same twilight, can misinterpret both him and themselves! And in fact all of them are inescapably related to each other, and in this relatedness all are obliged continually to judge, choose and move on this chessboard with its countless pieces! No one surveys the whole, and so no one can exhaustively define his own position or anyone else's. And yet every Christian looks toward the region of the whole, belongs to it and is meant to decide, when the historical moment calls for decision, on the basis of this belonging. Shall we succeed in making such decisions if we depend entirely on the light that comes solely from the practical decision itself? However, even this question is premature, if we consider what biblical revelation urges upon us and what the last question of a theodramatic theory must be: namely, What is implied by God's involving himself in the history of his world and, in becoming man, becoming a fellow actor with us in the world drama? Is the Absolute Spirit (*Hegel*), is Being itself (*Heidegger*), inwardly affected by history? And were not the myths correct, speaking of this as they did in their picture language? Does this mean that taking risks, being vulnerable, being uncertain about how things will turn out—that all this is ultimate? If the Creator gives his creature freedom, does he not become dependent on him? Or, as *H. Jonas* says, does this not mean that man becomes not only the "shepherd of Being" but also the guardian of God himself? But is God then still God?

3. *"Orthopraxy"*

Many people say that Christianity has for too long presented itself as a theory, a *doctrine*, a *theologia*. Without realizing it, it has betrayed the incarnate, crucified and risen Word of God to the Greek *logos* which seeks to encompass such historical "contingencies" and has transformed it into an ahistorical "doctrine".

This doctrine becomes more and more subtle; thus the divisive differences of opinion acquire an importance they would not have, given a different fundamental principle. Christendom, splintered as it is, seems unworthy of belief, both to itself and to the watching world. The scandal cannot be removed by further theoretical discussion but only by *praxis*, which is twofold: it is a decisive step into the future, beyond the baneful barriers set up by doctrine, and it is also a return to Christianity's authentic and original meaning: God shows his truth to us through *acting*, and the Christian (including the anonymous Christian, the Samaritan) likewise shows that he is following in Christ's footsteps by acting in love toward his fellow men. All will be judged by the way they treated "the least of my brethren", and the only way the Christian can commend himself to mankind today is through right action and determined commitment to the world in which he lives and to building the future. "What is Christian in the *church* sense", *Nietzsche* tells us, "is in fact anti-Christian: nothing but things and persons instead of symbols, history instead of eternal facts, nothing but formulae, rituals, dogmas instead of the practice of life. What is really Christian is total indifference to dogmas, cultic activity, priests, church and theology. The praxis of Christianity is no mere fantasy world any more than the praxis of Buddhism is: it is a means of being happy. . . . Christianity is a *praxis*, not a doctrine of faith. It tells us how we should act, not what we should believe."[3] "Go and do likewise",

---

[3] *Nachlass*. Schlechta III, 639–40. Cf. Der Antichrist, 39: "It is false to the point of absurdity to regard the mark of the Christian as 'faith'; for example, faith in redemption through Christ. Only Christian practice, a life such as was lived by him who died on the Cross, is Christian. . . . This kind of life is still possible today; indeed, for certain people it is even necessary: the authentic, original Christianity will be possible in all ages. . . . Not a believing, but a doing" (Schlechta II, 1200). "Blessedness is not promised out of the blue, it is linked to conditions: it is the only reality. . . . The result of this state is projected into a new practice, a practice that really corresponds to the gospel. 'Faith' is not the distinguishing mark of Christians: the Christian acts and distinguishes himself by a different kind of action. . . . The life of the Redeemer was nothing other than this practice." (*Ibid.*, 33; Schlechta 1195.) "What he bequeathed to humanity was a practice: the way he acted before the judges, henchmen and accusers, the way he responded to all manner of slander and mockery, his attitude on the Cross. . . . He pleads, he suffers, he loves together with and in those who treat him wickedly." (*Ibid.*, 35; Schlechta 1197.)

concludes the parable of the Good Samaritan. The New Testament is not a textbook but Spirit, a collection of occasional writings referring to Christ's exemplary conduct and indicating how Christians are to act. Were not the "saints" always aware of this, did they not act accordingly and thus merit their status as models?

The watchword "orthopraxy", however, while it drags Christianity out of the scholar's study and sets it on the world stage where it is to act and prove itself, abbreviates it to an ethics or a guide to human endeavor. It fails to preserve the distance between God's praxis which operates on man and man's praxis which takes its direction from God's. "God shows his love toward us in that, while we were yet sinners, Christ died for us" (Rom 5:8). This act is not only the first of a series; it comes from above, from outside and from below and makes the whole series possible. Otherwise we would have nothing but philanthropy. And for *Nietzsche*, and anyone else who is not entirely naive, philanthropy is only *one* role, *one* way of acting on the world stage. There are many other, opposed ways, and they are unfortunately indispensable: the struggle for survival in which the strongest or the greatest talent prevails; self-defense—both social and individual—against unjust attack now or in the future; the administration of justice with its sanctions, and so forth. Much of this can be said to be for the common good, that is, again, it is philanthropy, yet in quite a different sense from that indicated by God's primal act. As a result of this act on God's part, ethical orthopraxy finds itself in a field of tension in which its simple recipes are inadequate and which once more brings the Christian face to face with dramatic decisions. For what God's primal act in reality was, what implication it had for the world, is once again something that can only be accepted and pondered in a faith that precedes all personal initiative. Christ understood what he did as unconditional obedience to the Father. God acts through him and in him by giving his Only Beloved for the sake of the world. He does not do *something* for man, he does *everything*. Thus following Christ, which has become possible through his self-surrender, will not consist in doing *some right thing* but in fundamentally surrendering every-thing, and surrendering it to the God who has totally emptied himself, so that he can use it for the world, according to his own purposes. It is only in this framework—which we may call the practical self-surrender of faith—that Christians' individual ethical initiatives find their place and can be assessed. Once again, the field of play for Christian action is essentially more dramatic and full of tension than the formula of "orthopraxy" would suggest.

4. *"Dialogue"*

One of the most fruitful new approaches of Christian life and thought is to be found in the principle of "dialogue". Looking back over two thousand years of Christian theology, it is astonishing how little attention it has received until now. After all, at the very center of the biblical events lies the Covenant between God and man, in which God gives man, whom he has created and endowed with freedom, an area of independent being, an area where he can freely hear and answer and ultimately cooperate responsibly with God. There is not only the Word of the Almighty, to which we listen, prostrate and which we carry out as the Lord's servants; there is also the area of understanding, of taking up a position, of possible refusal. Of course, it is absurd to say No to truth, which is of its essence good; but God prefers to accept this absurdity rather than overwhelm his creature from the outside. His astounding masterpiece is to elicit the Yes of his free partner from the latter's innermost freedom. All the same, it takes all the mysteries of Christianity to achieve this: God must allow his Son to become man so that there may be a genuine dialogue between God in heaven and God as a human being on earth, where freedom, love and obedience can unite; God must send the Spirit of his Son into our hearts, crying Abba! Father! (Gal 4:6). This event opens up the perspective on both sides: on the one hand, it reveals the primal dialogue in God himself, which is the necessary, albeit unfathomable, presupposition for the Christ-event, and, on the other, it puts the internal human dialogue of mankind in an entirely new light. For from an earthly point of view, human existence is based on continual positive and negative interplay between people; various points of view address each other: often the exchange between them is neutral, mostly it is personally colored, hostile or friendly. People learn a great deal from each other, there is friction between them, they learn to go beyond their own point of view and assimilate that of others; things that were initially unintelligible or simply dismissed reveal an inner meaning, or at least become accepted as "a valid point of view"; teachers learn from their pupils, fathers from their sons. *What* people know is no longer a mere commodity, it is fused with the knowing person, people "communicate", "share themselves". All the same, the human dialogue remains one element of life among others. There is the inner mystery of subjectivity; it presuppposes that one is first "present to oneself" so that one can come forth to be present to others; and if this communication is to be a real gift, subjectivity must possess an inner wealth of character; moreover it must both possess and affirm a unique and solitary sense of vocation. And at the other end there is the breaking of the dialogue, at the point where no word is of any avail, no initiative succeeds, the bridges to mutual understanding collapse, where hatred, fanaticism, jealousy and ultimate alienation erect impassable ramparts and where one can only keep silent since all further speech would increase the alienation or act as a spark in a powder keg. Nowhere is this clearer than in the life of Jesus as the Fourth Evangelist describes it: there are many dialogues—or so it seems—but hardly a single one is genuine. The Word-made-flesh enters into a dialogue situation with his kindred, "but his own received him not". The two talk completely at cross-purposes. The Evangelist who writes these discourses down hears them all with hindsight, having witnessed the final act: the more the word of Jesus reveals its true nature—absolute divine love—the less people want to hear and understand it. This pseudo-dialogue ends before the Passion in a great monologue addressed to the—scarcely comprehending—"church" of disciples and finally concentrates all its attention in the vertical dimension of prayer. But this is not the end of the story; for John, as for the whole of the New Testament, the breaking-off of communication in the Passion of Jesus—both between him and men and him and God—signifies that the Word has penetrated the adversary's deepest and most secret dungeon (Mt 12:29, 40), so that a new wellspring of dialogue can burst forth out of the iron silence of death; here we have Easter and Pentecost in one.

This means that, although "dialogue" is a very essential facet of Christian reality, it is not its only category; and as a category it is inadequate to express the action taking place between God and the world, Christ and the Church, the Church and the world, man and his fellow man, in all its dramatic proportions. There can be no drama without dialogue; indeed, the dramatist shows his power most persuasively in the construction and clarity of his dialogues. But the action is not reducible to dialogue; not every plot is unravelled in speech and counter-speech; something that is beyond the speakers and governs them can make itself known, whether they are aware of it or not. The key to the protagonists' relationship can be some event of which they know nothing, of which only the audience is aware. Some decision, arrived at in silence, some unspoken deed can go beyond all that has been said and bring about the *dénouement*, unveiling the invisible starting point, uprooting all the apparently established trees and planting them in new surroundings. On the other hand, "dialogue" is never so subordinated to the whole as to be rendered obsolete. It grows up again elsewhere, at a new level. Today when we hear the word "dialogue" in theology and in the Church, more often than not it refers to the attitude that remains open to further listening, that allows the other his "otherness" even when there seems nothing more to say; it is the attitude that refuses to give up, that is, it is closely related to hope. At this point, however, the Christian must consider the *shape* of his hope: it is certainly not an infrahistorical horizon that is simply open to the future, according to which world history is hastening toward the "happy end" of a gradually emerging Kingdom of God—without having to go in its totality through the mystery of death and resurrection. The Christian's hope reaches beyond this death—for individuals as well as for the world as a whole—and in that sense may be more absolute than that of his dialogue-partner, who is equally concerned for the (earthly) future of man and humanity. Dialogue can achieve something when both partners are looking in the same direction. It can fail when the horizons prove to have no common ground at any point. In that case the Christian's last word in such a dialogue is the testimony of his existence—or of his blood.

5. *"Political Theology"*

If the "dialogue" principle is aimed at making the Church's kerygma, Magisterium and theology less of a monologue, the insistence that Christian involvement in the world and Christian theology have a *political* side is designed to deprivatize them. Once again we have a watchword which moves toward theo-drama from a different angle. Ancient drama was essentially concerned with the *polis*, particularly in its relationship to the religious dimension; it is no different in most of the plays of *Shakespeare* and *Schiller*. The great characters are not simply individuals, they carry the burden of the common good; kings, heroes, generals, statesmen, rebels either represent a supra-personal order or else they question it. When Jesus is tried, he is asked about his disciples and his teaching. His answer is: "I have spoken openly to the world; I have always taught in synagogues and in the temple, where all Jews come together; I have said nothing secretly" (Jn 18:20). The scenes of the Acts of the Apostles take place in the same public arenas, which is why both the trial of Jesus and the testimony of the Apostles become political issues. By opening up an horizon beyond the im-mediate horizon of the state, they indirectly limit the latter and subject it to an eschatological critique. A king who is not of this world but acts in utter seriousness on the public world stage is bound to be involved in the political drama. The only question is, in what sense? Does not Buddha too subject the whole theatre of the world and the state to a similar criticism, but in his case by projecting it onto an apolitical horizon? And as for Judaism and Islam, do they not push the political dimension beyond itself and dramatize it by infusing it with a messianic and eschatological motive power? Christianity stands strangely elusive between these two approaches, or beyond them both; this gives it a highly distinctive dramatic tension which is only inadequately expressed by the word "political". The Kingdom

Christ announces as the fulfillment of history stands at the door; both individual and community have to live with all their attention fixed on it, bending all their spiritual powers toward it, but it is from God that it comes; it does not emerge from within history as the result of human effort. Moreover, it comes about through Jesus' dying in expiation of the world's sin and being raised by God as the "first fruits of the dead"; the Kingdom becomes, in him, a hidden, transcendent *present* tense which will turn into a far more critical *future* tense for those who are still alive and know of him by faith. If we accept the Pauline picture of the Risen Christ as the Head of a Body which continues to exist on earth but is fashioned and animated by its Head and is growing toward its fulfillment, what a paradox human existence will be in such a Body! Negatively speaking, the Christian will be in a position to criticize every form of human community from the vantage point of an *eschaton* known to him and lived by him in faith. Positively (since "It is no longer I who live, but Christ who lives in me"), he will be aware of the basic lines of the coming Kingdom, to which he has to orient himself and his surroundings, without ever being able to implement it in the "old aeon" which "groans in futility". Should he attempt to erect a static copy of the Kingdom of God using the building materials of the old world, as the Constantinian and medieval, imperial theology tried to do? But static categories are Platonic; they lack the urgency which informs that "waiting" of which the gospel speaks. Or, on the basis of what he knows of the Kingdom's basic elements —"love", "righteousness", "peace"—should he make a serious endeavor to bring about a progressive and perhaps asymptotic realization of this Kingdom on earth? But in that case he will fall back into the Old Testament and surrender the boundary line established by Christ. He will change what Christ achieved by stepping over the boundary of death into a principle of movement to be manipulated along purely worldly lines. Or he will reduce it to the level of a harmless "salvific presence" which has no historical dimension, perhaps even conceived in "eucharistic" terms, or as an inbuilt *omega* that guarantees from within the ultimate emergence of the classless society, through human political action that strives for perfect organization. In Paul there is the startling idea that the last generation of world history will not have to die but will be taken to be with the Lord directly, just as it is; but, by way of balance, he adds that the generation of those who have died will take precedence at the resurrection of the dead (1 Th 4:15ff.). Transposed into an evolutionist context, this means that what is decisive is not the idea of a this-worldly approximation to the Kingdom but that separation of aeons which is made clear by Christ in his death and Resurrection. In this connection it is revealing that the life of Jesus—contrary to Jewish hopes, contrary to the messianic models of his time and contrary to the accusation which led to his death sentence—was devoid of any political claim to power, nor did it prematurely institutionalize features belonging to the *eschaton*. The Christian as such may be utterly deprivatized, commissioned to act publicly as an assessor on the world stage (1 Cor 4:9; Heb 10:33)—and in this sense he may be political: all the same, his existence cannot be classified in secular terms, and he himself cannot grasp it in its totality, and so the Christian cannot be simply put into the "political" pigeonhole. Politics concerns him: as a "member" under Christ, the Head, he is in profound solidarity with each of the Lord's least brothers and must realize that he has an inescapable responsibility for the conditions under which they live. In this more-than-human, specifically Christian responsibility, which is rooted in Christ's solidarity with every last sinner and poor man, there can be no self-complacent community of Christians, no closed Church. The Church is essentially planted in the field of the world to bear her special fruit in it and from it; she is mixed in with the world's dough to leaven all of it; but just as the Church can only be herself in going beyond herself to the world, so, on the other hand, the world is designed, retrospectively, from the *eschaton*, to transcend itself in the direction of the Kingdom of God (1 Cor 15:24ff.). At this very point the Church becomes the world's substantial pledge of a hope that bursts all bounds, although her leaven, which continues to ferment in society and presses for worldly power to be used in the service of justice and peace, is powerless in itself. Or, in Paul's paradox, it is only strong when it is weak (2 Cor 12:10). The impotence of the Crucified in death, which remains the inner shape of even the most vigorous Christian life, can never be manipulated to "amorize" mankind. The dramatic situation in which the Christian is consciously, and the world and its history are unconsciously, involved goes far beyond the category of politics. It complements the latter with a dimension which, depending on how one looks at it, can be described as ineluctably tragic or utopian (whether in a meaningless or meaningful sense) or as ultimately bringing reconciliation. If the "political" is to claim relevance to the issue of ultimate meaning—and it cannot do so unless it is prepared to give up applying valid norms even within the temporal sphere—it must consent to being taken beyond itself and set in relation to this dramatic dimension of human existence, which attains its highest tension only in the Christian reality.

6. "Futurism"

More than all the notions we have discussed so far, it is "the future" that attracts the creative energies of modern theology. We can say that the emotional associations of this term govern our generation in the way eschatology once dominated the theology of early Christianity and of a later period. The two are related; however, "eschatology" was marked chiefly by the sense of continually reaching the inner boundary (in the futility of individual and historical existence, destined for death) between time and eternity—something we did not refer to in our discussion of "event". "Futurism", on the other hand, while it does not entirely renounce all sense of the futility of the present, opens up a "flight into the future" as the only way out of the unendurable. In practice it presents itself as a shattered evolution-optimism—the lofty period of *Teilhard de Chardin* is no doubt past. People both see and fail to see that something is moving, and this motion, while it brings about some partial improvement, offers a greater threat when seen in its totality. Hence the somewhat forced undertones in eulogies of technological achievements; the latter interfere with the natural balance while holding out no hope that man will ever be able to gain control of the total range of forces. Behind this secular pathos there lies a theological one, which not infrequently sounds more naive than that of those with deeper knowledge and deeper concern. It draws its greatest strength from the following insight: Jesus himself was not deflected from living and working for the coming of the Kingdom. Also (though in a different way) the existence of the primitive Church was radically future-orientated. So Christianity today, borne along by the secular impulse to which it itself largely gave rise, has to live out in an exemplary way that fundamental dynamism which sets out to embrace the future that is in store for the world. In principle this is by no means a departure from Christian origins; it is one way of rediscovering them. But it does lead us straight back to fundamental biblical problems concerning the relation of the Old and New Testaments: To what extent do Jesus and his Church adopt the Old Testament expectation concerning the future, the active exodus out of the present into what is to come—and to what extent do they overtake or transform it? In a slightly different form, with Jews and Gentiles in mind, the question can be put thus: What right has the Church to adopt a futurism which was introduced into history by Judaism and use it to abolish a cyclic, futureless view of the world developed by the "nations"? Surely any such precipitation into the future has been rendered obsolete by the Fourth Gospel's radical reflection on the "realized" eschatology brought about by the Christ-event? Is this not a clear sign that we should at least proceed with caution? And if "realized" eschatology is absolutized and leads us back to a static-existential eschatologism, how can we discover the balance between the Christian "before all ages" and the "not yet"?

Clearly, the word "future" is closely linked to other, related watchwords of our time—*utopianism* on the one hand and *revolution* on the other: both reflect the broken and strained aspect of the world's situation with which Christianity finds itself involved. "Utopianism" suggests more the will to bring about, through freedom of the spirit, what is impossible in the order of nature, what in fact has no dwelling place within the world. "Revolution" looks for practical ways of implementing this "homeless" utopia through catastrophic changes of structures. It goes without saying that programs of this kind, placed with the utmost seriousness at the heart of human planning, exhibit a high concentration of dramatic aspects. A theology that is affected by this will never again be able to retreat into the "epic" theology of the medieval *summa* or the "lyric" theology of the spiritual treatises of the age of Bernard or Francis de Sales; it will be obliged to assume an inner dramatic form that has become an essential feature of mankind's existence, whether Christian or non-Christian. Using care, we can mention another key concept here, namely, *apocalyptic*, which is found both at the center of the Bible and in its immediate environs and signifies a special and extreme mode of presenting the drama of saving history. Mankind's situation today seems urgently to call for this particular form of theo-drama to be brought to bear once more in Christian reflection. This must be done critically, for the apocalyptic arsenal of images, with its action-packed and often breathtaking succession of scenes, itself needs to be "interpreted" (Rev 1:20; 4:5; 5:8; 8:3f.; 13:18; 17:9: "Here reason must be used, the reason that possesses wisdom."). But a critical approach does not mean doing away with the dramatic actuality by dismissing apocalyptic as an obsolete way of thought or even as a dream world of archetypes or of (para-)psychical or surrealistic motifs. It remains essentially the actualization of a drama between heaven and earth. The historical books of the Bible may seem to suggest that it is of a past age, but it is a dramatization of Being which, though it borders close on myth and gnosticism, is firmly rooted on the hither side of the border, in authentically Christian theological soil.

"Futurism", even when flanked by "utopianism" and "revolution", does not exhibit the wide range encompassed by the totality of theologico-dramatic aspects. It can only attain this breadth in the framework of the apocalyptic to-and-fro between world and God, heaven, earth and hell. Thus biblical apocalyptic, which addresses us in such a new way at this particular hour of mankind's history, is always to be seen as only the unveiled background against which the concrete biblical drama of salvation is played, in the midst of world history.

Next we must deal with two further, mutually related watchwords which have entered into general use through sociology and psychology and hence have acquired significance for theology: function and role.

7. "Function"

Just as, on the personal level, the "dialogue" principle opened up the subject (which had been somewhat closed and self-determining in Greek and Cartesian thought) and showed it to be rooted in interpersonal give and take, "functionalism" attempts to do the same on the sociological plane. Here it is not primarily a question of the spontaneous self-communication of free subjects but of the rules of reciprocity and exchange which arise from all social community. Thus it is concerned with structures which as such provide a presubjective "language" at all levels of social interaction—family, then the economic level and finally that of articulated speech. This is "structuralism", which (preeminently in *Claude Lévi-Strauss*) starts with a generalized theory of relationships between things and then moves on (influenced by the work of *Roman Jakobson*) to take linguistics as its basic model. The functional-structural "grid" which is laid over the contingencies of history to render them rationally accessible differs from the Kantian system of categories (which structuralists are at pains to avoid) in that no (absolute) subject is posited behind it. (These writers are closer to a Freudian or Jungian concept of the unconscious or simply to Marxist materialism.) Instead, the "grid" is held to be based on a priori reciprocities of the existing "subjects". Hence, from the outset, it already implies the whole tension between the simultaneously (timelessly) valid (the transverse axis of the "synchronic") and what is valid in its duration-in-changeability (the longitudinal axis of the "diachronic", in the terms of *F. de Saussure*), that is, between what is ordinarily called the ahistorical and the historical. There is something definitely undramatic, almost aesthetic, about a system of this kind which can even subordinate history to its categories. In fact, in *Lévi-Strauss* one is constantly coming across aesthetic and, in particular, musical analogies—that is, the "score" which, among other things, embodies the longitudinal axis of time. Similarly *Paul Claudel* was especially fond of the idea that every living thing in nature, with its specific differences, can only exist by virtue of its functional relationship to all other beings (that is, "genera" are seen as "nature's words"). On the other hand, the functional grid, already under pressure as a result of temporal succession and its implied transformations, is greatly overburdened in the effort to avoid a Hegelian dialectic of Spirit. This can have tragic consequences, as can be seen, for instance, in the work of *Michel Foucault*, where the tension between synchrony and diachrony is increased until it involves the necessary coexistence of meaning and madness.[4] *Lévi-Strauss* sought out primitive totemist cultures in order to apply his structuralist grid unmolested, which he would hardly have been able to do in historically sophisticated high cultures.[5] While, in contrast to *Lévy-Bruhl*, he did attempt to reestablish a unity in the structure of man and the world as seen by primitive and civilized peoples, this unity was an ahistorical abstraction covering the primitives' nakedness with the conceptual garment of modern functionalism (and cybernetics). And at the same time he would have preferred to dissolve modern civilization to the preconscious state of pure structure (in a paradoxical Rousseauism): "The ultimate aim of the anthropological sciences is not to construct man but to dissolve him . . . , to reintegrate culture in nature and finally to integrate life into the totality of its physico-chemical conditions."[6] No wonder that the total absorption of the free historical subject into the *code universel* leaves a residue of madness. The whole edifice is ultimately an extreme form of Neo-Kantianism in which the world of the senses (which can never be expressed in words) is now constructed by historical persons who resist being absorbed into the structure.

If we leave aside the systematic sclerosis of structuralism in its

---

[4] M. Foucault, *L'histoire de la folie à l'âge classique* (1961). He quotes Hegel's view (*Enzykl.* §408) that "madness reveals a depth that gives human freedom its whole meaning". It manifests, not "the abstract loss of reason" but "the contradiction inherent in reason as it currently exists". In fact, however, Foucault has something much more radical in mind, something that has more in common with Schopenhauer and Nietzsche: "Only in the night of madness is light possible, and the instant it scatters the shadows, it vanishes along with them. . . . The human being . . . is given a truth, his own truth, which is simultaneously offered to him and snatched away." Hence "*homo psychologicus* is a descendant of *homo mente captus*" (549–50).

[5] Paul Ricoeur, "Structure et Heremeneutique" in *Le conflit des interprétations* (1969), esp. 39, 48ff.

[6] C. Lévi-Strauss, *La pensée sauvage* (1962), 362–27.

obdurate claim to be totally scientific without having an identifiable premise (somewhere between nature and civilization,
idealism and materialism), the topic of "function" *can* be a
useful tool. Not only does it reveal the matrix of suprasubjective
social relationships, it also grasps subjects and their truth in the
light and in the exercise of these relationships: man cannot be
isolated from the goal and object of his action. His relationships
within the whole, the "body", determine his place and his
contribution as a part, a "member" of it, that is, in reciprocity.
Of course this immediately raises a crucial question: What *is* the
whole in which the "function" acquires its meaning? Is it, can it
be a "finite rational entity" like, for instance, "human society"?
But how could something finite come by its normative character
except by receiving it from another, superior finite rationality
or from some infinite and absolute factor implanted in its
functioning subjects? Otherwise we fall back into the base-
lessness, the indeterminacy of the structuralist code. At a certain
level it can be wholesome and sobering to think in terms of
"function", of the individual's service to the community; the
concept can also be applied to the realm of the Church, to
"debunk" the pseudo-sacral. In the secular realm, too, structuralism has an important task—as *Roland Barthes* has perceived[7]
—namely, to demystify things like technology, sports and the
cult of personality, which are continually being sacralized. Yet
this desacralization in the area of "finite rationality" can only be
meaningful (and without cynicism) on the basis of an overall
horizon of values; this will soberly allot the finite functions to
their area of service. For they all exist in an infinite context
which summons them, with great earnestness, to perform their
service, particularly in the realm of the Church, and thus endows them with a *genuinely* sacral character.[8] The apparently
finite realm of the Church, with its multiplicity of functions, is
always governed from a higher level, that is, the infinite presence of the incarnate Logos. On this basis, then, there is a
possibility that the structuralism which obscures all dramatic

[7] Roland Barthes, *Mythologies* (1957); *Système de la mode* (1967).

[8] This whole issue has been thoroughly analyzed in Heribert Mühlen,
*Entsakralisierung: Ein epochales Schlagwort und seine Bedeutung für die Zukunft der
christlichen Kirche* (1971).

aspects may yet make its contribution to theo-drama. The "functionalism" of the Mystical Body of the Church in Paul acquires its particular tension thus: on the one hand, the "charisms" of the individual members come exclusively from God (Rom 12:3) or Christ (Eph 4:11f.) or the Holy Spirit (1 Cor 12:8ff.); on the other hand, they are given exclusively for the benefit of the organism of the Church (1 Cor 12:12–30). Here we have the tremendous tension of the Christian life, whereby we are entrusted with an absolute mission and are immediately expropriated and absorbed into the mission's corresponding function, a function which has to operate within a structure (the Church) which is above the subject, partially constitutes him and demands service of him. If a functionalism adapted along Christian lines were to ignore this tension and—as often happens today in the secular field—present itself in purely finite terms, it would weaken the aspect of theo-drama, whereas if it were to develop *within* this tension, it would significantly promote that aspect.

8. *"Role"*

The problem of one's "role" and how to find it hovers back and forth between sociology and psychology and is clearly related to the foregoing topic of "function". A brief mention will suffice at this point, since we shall have to deal with the issue in detail later. The topic itself is as old as the metaphor that human life is a play; it implies all the problems suggested by this metaphor. Not only has the individual in the world theatre to perform the particular function allotted to him (by whom or what?—circumstance?—God?—himself?), he also, if he is to be really himself, has to identify himself with the role he plays, in spite of the fact that at some mysterious point he is *not* identical with it. Or, after all, should he rather *not* identify himself with it, ought he to maintain a distance between himself and the role, aware that "in principle" he could be someone else and that, to be himself, he must avoid losing himself in the role? This either-or will have to be decided before we can proceed to the modern

problem of the "search for identity".[9] Do I find my identity by
slipping into the role into which society has cast all *dramatis
personae*?[10] Looking back to what was said about "function",
one would be inclined to say Yes. For being oneself has the same
origin as being-in-relation, serving the "other", serving the
"whole".[11] But the proviso we have already made (that is, that
the tension between the finite order and the infinite must be
maintained) is even more relevant where it is a case of identifying the "I" with the role. Identification presupposes nonidentity and a bridging of the gap between the two; in the case
of the mentally healthy person this may be achieved almost
unconsciously and without friction, but it can prove extremely
difficult with the mentally sick and unbalanced; hence the interest taken by all forms of psychotherapy in the problem of role
and identification. The latter is perhaps to be attained in a
stepwise manner. But who can show me the role in which I can
really be myself? The question has as many layers as an onion;
what society offers, what it treats with acclaim on the one hand
and disavows on the other—all these things are only the outermost layers. Personal decisions of one kind or another may
perhaps be regarded as the middle layers, but what of the core
and what lies near it? Destiny can fundamentally change my
social role, not only on the basis of free decisions but even
more through the possibility of more and more thorough
"refunctioning" by society, by cybernetics, biochemical means,
and so forth. *Mann ist Mann* [—the title of a play by Bertolt
Brecht (1927) which raises the issue of such manipulation —Tr.].
There is an evident connection here between the notion of
"role" and functionalism/structuralism. In the latter, basically,
the important thing is that the function remain constant; it is
immaterial who performs it; the performers are interchangeable.
In the face of these technological changes, the question "Who
am I?" becomes far more pressing than the question which

[9] Anselm Strauss, *Spiegel und Masken: Die Suche nach Identität* (Theorie 2,
Suhrkamp, 1968).

[10] Peter L. Berger, *Invitation to Sociology* (Garden City, N.Y.: 1963).

[11] On the simultaneous development of the self and discovery of society cf.
George H. Mead, *Mind, Identity and Society* (Chicago, 1934).

produced the notion of the transmigration of souls. In the latter case, at least, there was a continuity of *karma*. The problem surely emerges in all areas of sociology and psychology and overflows into the sphere of theo-drama; by way of anticipation we can say that only in the theodramatic context can it find a satisfying clarification. Indeed, we shall see that no other theology but Christian theology can utter the redemptive word here.

9. *"Freedom and Evil"*

A final topic must be broached, one that has acquired an urgency today quite different from the urgency it had in primitive Christian and medieval theology. Naturally the problem of creaturely freedom, involving the possibility of evil, was always of current concern. How could it be otherwise in a theology of creation, providence, the Fall, redemption on the Cross and a judgment yet to come? How could it be otherwise in a theology that took shape at a time when late Hellenistic gnosis was locked in a life-and-death struggle with the question of evil, which ultimately led it to place responsibility for evil's existence on a subordinate "God" and, in Manicheism, on an "anti-God"? In spite of this, however, traditional Christian theology proceeds from the certain conviction that the God who created the world is good, that the creature's freedom remains subordinate to him and that evil is an instance of the privation of good. True, a definite consequence is drawn from the creature's genuine freedom, namely, the possibility and reality of eternal damnation; and this conclusion induces a sense of shock: people brood upon the obscurities of divine predestination, from *Augustine* and *Gottschalk* to the disputes on grace between Dominicans and Jesuits. Yet the spectrum of problems remains within the context of a certain paradisal naiveté; the concept of God is not essentially affected by these obscurities. God cannot be thought to be anything but good and just, even when we do not understand how.

The emphasis changes when, in modern times, the darkness and fragmentation of creation is projected into the divine ground itself (*Jakob Böhme*) and speculation discovers the element of absoluteness in human freedom (*Schelling* in his middle years, continuing the idea of autonomy in *Kant*). Now it is *God* who bears the contradiction (including hell) in himself, and in the same breath man, with *his* contradiction, moves over into the realm of the absolute. Here, as an equal partner with God, he can accuse the world of being contradictory and existence of being meaningless. Or, taking God's place, he can find meaning —as an *homme révolté*—in protesting against life's absurdity. C. G. *Jung* gives the potent expression of this new climate of thought and feeling when he calls for the Christian Trinity to be expanded into a Quaternity which would find a place for the opposition of good and evil, the good Son of the Father (Christ) and his counterimage, the wayward son (of the devil).

Modern man no longer wears those spectacles, lent to him by the Christian faith, through which the spectator once contemplated the world and saw it transfigured: God had pronounced the world "very good", perhaps in anticipation of the time when all its negative aspects would be balanced and cancelled by the Son's sacrifice on the Cross. But now man discovers the world's dark side: aggression, the will to power, reciprocal annihilation and, in the sphere of history, the tragedy of a civilization which seems to be proceeding toward self-extinction. A light has gone out; the landscape of existence seems drear and alien. At no point can sin's overthrow by Christ's sacrificial death be tangibly grasped; faith is impotent in the face of crushing brute reality. Just as the Christian has to struggle in a new way for the possibility of faith, the non-Christian is presented with this nagging question: Is there any other person or factor left to be blamed for the condition of the world (*Sigmund Freud* recognizes that there is no such person or factor and that man, wounded in his psyche, has to come to grips with everything, including himself, in silence), or must he regard evil as a mere force of nature? The idea that "Heaven and earth are full of the glory of God" and that such a world calls simply for praise and thanksgiving—such an idea causes even the Christian to doubt; his neighbor persuades him that he would be wiser to apply his efforts to changing this botched world.

The confrontation between divine and human freedom has reached a unique intensity; the contest between the two has moved into the center—the really dramatic center stage—of the problem of existence. The old theology recognized that God's noninterference in free human decisions implied the possibility of damnation, while making allowances for God's absolute freedom to bring a sinner to repentance through "irresistible" grace. Here also, however, the two things were juxtaposed in a certain naiveté. *Now* we have to look the question in the eye: What is the relationship between divine and human freedom? Should we suppose that God accepted some limit on his freedom when he created man, by whom his world could be brought either to perfection or to destruction? Is he powerless in the face of autonomous man's "No"? And how is this divine powerlessness related to the Godforsakenness of his Son on the Cross? Things that flitted like shadows at the periphery of the old theology now move into the center.

At this point we must break off. All these modes of approach seem to lead concentrically from the most diverse regions of contemporary thought toward a theodramatic theory. Until now, admittedly, theo-drama has been little more than an empty spot on theology's map. This space will not be filled by a mere combination of the aspects we have enumerated: in any case the list does not claim to be systematic and complete. Theo-drama will have to be built up from scratch, out of the confrontation between dramatic theory and Christian revelation. Yet, before we begin, we will do well to attend to a few warning voices.

C. OBJECTIONS

1. *Rudolf Kassner*

A first objection to the theodramatic enterprise proceeds simply by denying the analogy between the *dramatic*, or rather the dimension of the *theatre*, and *Christianity* and insisting that the two are totally opposed. We may take *Rudolf Kassner* as a passionate protagonist of this view, which runs through his labyrinthine work like a scarlet thread. Acquainted from his youth with all of Europe's great theatres and actors,[1] he observed the late, post-Christian blend of "personality" and "actor", that blending of the one-who-is and the one-who-seems; and since Kassner was, in fact and in intention, a physiologist, for him this "is" was not the "is" of hidden interiority but the embodied form familiar to and cultivated by pre-Christian antiquity and venerated by *Goethe*. But this same ancient world knows nothing of what will be achieved in Christianity, and more particularly in the "birth of Christ", namely, the shattering of the magical identity of the world's ground and the divine form which separates itself from it, the magical identity of utterance and counterutterance. Ancient tragedy springs from this split identity and essentially splits man into spectator and actor, while magically holding him together.

---

[1] Rudolf Kassner, *Bücher der Erinnerung* 2d ed. (1945), 96ff. However, as well as the admiring portrayals of Mitterwurzer, Duse and Wolters, note the malicious caricature, "Der grosse Schauspieler" (241). See also "Von der Signatur der Dinge" in *Physiognomik* (1951): Modern man has lost the ancient world's sense of the *typical*, and is also losing the *institution*, but (in the post-Christian world) he can no longer present a personal face to the world, he is "the man with the torn, split, gaping face, repressed, wounded. . . . Who, nowadays, has managed to *keep* his face, apart from the stage or film actor? And isn't that why so many people are only acting, i.e., acting a part until they drop, totally exhausted? —Because they have had to overstrain themselves, they have had to scream and shout, sell themselves, under- and oversell themselves. It seems to me that all institutions were covertly and profoundly hostile to the actor. Only the actor could gain from the decline and fall of most institutions" (42). Man "has lost his identity; now he is purely tentative, valid 'until further notice', inwardly an actor, a dilettante" (40).

51

This is the monism of the ancient world: the eternal "theatre of the world" which simultaneously plays and watches itself playing, in which Dionysos is torn to pieces and put together again—the *pais paizôn* of *Heraclitus*. True, part of this unity collapses in *Socrates*, who has "difficulties with the first person",[2] but he comes nowhere near the meaning which "I" and "person" will attain in Christ. For in Christ the magical sphere of the "world theatre" is broken through once and for all, in two directions at the same time, by what Kassner continually refers to as "conversion" and "sacrifice". On the one hand, this leads to the interiority which brings freedom from the powers of this world. On the other, it leads to perfect incarnation, that is, total concretion, unequivocal in time and history, overtaking all that is essentially ambivalent in the cosmic theatre and closed "causality" and introducing a clarity of "meaning"—which cannot be ascertained scientifically but only observed in terms of physiognomy.

Kassner can be accused of being arbitrary in the way he links Luther/Kierkegaard with Goethe. For him, the whole, healthy center of existence is the imagination which both sees and creates images, and in Christian conversion this is deepened to become a faith which, having attained an ultimate point of freedom, is able to let things "be", able to receive, to suffer and to endure. Only here can freedom be found, only here can it be a completely sound, world-transforming endeavor. Here the magical play is smashed: "I remain convinced that the God-man never, at any time, not even for a moment, however brief, saw or attempted to see his own face in a mirror."[3] He never "played a part"; incarnation is the opposite of all "disguise". Kassner regards the equation of freedom and incarnation in the God-man as an idea that springs from and was formulated by his Catholic inheritance.[4] Since Christ is "the

---

[2] Rudolf Kassner, *Geburt Christi* (1951), 20–38.

[3] *Ibid.*, 36. Cf. "Der Gottmensch und die Weltseele" in the volume of the same name (*Drei nachgelassene Essays* [1960], 83–129).

[4] "I am a Catholic, and was brought up a Catholic" (*Transfiguration* [1946], 36). In Kassner the concept "transfiguration" takes the place of the idealist transcendence.

epitome of all holiness",[5] the only figure of any consequence is the saint who tries to follow him; the artist is absorbed into the saint just as imagination is subsumed under faith and just as the magic identity is taken up into the unity of freedom and incarnation-in-the-world.

However, Kassner's total rejection of the metaphor of the stage is based on presuppositions that are themselves problematical. He puts forward this equation: magical world = the world of creation, with God as First Cause [*Ursache*, "primal thing" —Tr.] = the world under the sign of omnipotence, under the sign of Yahweh, "I am who am": these are "divine-magical tautologies, terrifying and demonic".[6] Turning from the magical/theatrical to Christianity is not only a turning from Greek ideas to Christ but also a turning from the Old Testament Father-God to the sonship of the New Testament. Thus the "God-man" has become the absolute center. The link between Father and Son is severed, and God and man are the two sides of a center which can also be occupied by the saint, the great "personality".[7] Man (in the God-man) becomes God's redeemer. This is gnosticism, somewhere between *A. Brock* and *E. Bloch*. The way Jesus understood himself as the one sent to reveal the Father is something that has been completely forgotten. From Kassner one can learn how the fulfillment brought by Christ far outstrips all dramatic polarities—person and role, actor and spectator, and so forth—but the manifestation of this fulfillment is distorted if it is alienated from the God of omnipotence and creation. Thus, contrary to Kassner,[8] it is *not* meaningless to speak of Christ's role or mission. In fact we need to ask in a new way whether and how far, in the Christian life, a deep and

---

[5] Rudolf Kassner, *Geburt Christi*, 68.

[6] Kassner, *Die Nacht des ungeborenen Lebens* (1950), 227–28.

[7] "God has created man, and man has created God. The God-man is the center of this circle. Without him it would have become a vicious circle or else it would have stayed at the level of idolatry" (Kassner, *Umgang der Jahre* [1949], 188). "The Son has broken through the circle, in which the Godhead circled around itself" (Kassner, *Geburt Christi*, 121). Cf. "Dionysos und Christus" in Kassner, *Die Nacht des ungeborenen Lebens*, 135ff.; "Pilatus" in *Umgang der Jahre*, 86ff.

[8] Kassner, *Geburt Christi*, 57.

Christian seriousness is compatible with a certain "play" dimension. In its seriousness, our life-decision aims to insert us into a particular field of "play", governed by rules of "play"; we are situated in a role, and hence we "portray" something. Here, in fact, "we have a structure that is rooted in man's enfleshed situation; it is fundamental and categorical" not only on the social plane but also on the religious plane, which presupposes the former.[9] It is not only a question of acquiring the habit (through taking our role seriously) of that reality of which *Kant* speaks so persuasively: "As a whole, the more civilized men are, the more they are actors: they adopt the appearance of inclination and respect toward others, of good manners, of unselfishness; nor do others find this oppressive—aware as they are that it does not in fact come from the heart—since it is an attitude with which they concur. Indeed, it is very good that things are so in the world. For, by playing this role, people are gradually aroused to a full exercise of the virtues whose externals they have cultivated for a space, and they acquire the disposition itself."[10] No. It is more: it is a question of affirming a "role" given to us in a religious context and of schooling ourselves to become existentially identified with it—something we shall mention again at the conclusion of this volume.

2. G. W. F. Hegel

a. Drama as the High Point of Art

Hegel's view of drama touches the nerve of our endeavor at a much more central point. Kassner simply denies outright that there is a serviceable analogy. In Hegel we find a far more nuanced analysis, but one which, whatever garments it may put on, finally reaches the same result. Anyone who allows himself to feel the weight of Hegel's critique will be forewarned about shortcuts here. Furthermore, this critique throws a revealing and troubling light on the topics we shall have to consider

---

[9] Helmuth Plessner, "Der Mensch im Spiel" in *Das Spiel, Wirklichkeit und Methode* (Freiburger Dies Universitatis), vol. 13 (1966) (Schulz, 1967): 9.

[10] *Anthropologie* (Weischedel, 1964), VI, 442.

next, namely, the problematical relations between the Christian Church and the stage from antiquity right up to modern times: does not the animosity, of which Hegel makes no mention, only reveal that deeper dubiousness which he ruthlessly exposes? All the same, Hegel's ultimate verdict depends on his view of Christianity which, like Kassner (whose ideas give the impression of being an intuitive and unsystematic repetition of Hegel), jettisons the very aspects which are of theological significance to us.

For Hegel, the drama is unequivocally the high point of all art. The archaic, symbolic age was dominated by architecture, "building a house for its god"; the classical period cultivated sculpture, "portraying him in bodily form as a *stele*"; the (Christian) romantic age excelled in painting and music—all it can do now is create a transfiguring halo for the "God-man" who has appeared in living form. Poetry, however, is equally present to all three ages, yet in such a way that first of all the spirit of the nation expresses itself predominantly in epic form, then an emergent subjectivity speaks in lyric terms, and then the drama rounds out and offers a transcending synthesis of both of them.[1] With evident pleasure Hegel dwells on his portrayal of ancient tragedy, of which he holds "Antigone" to be the ultimate expression.[2] In terms of world history, however, classical tragedy has a unique *kairos*: it becomes a possibility where two strands come together; it requires not only the subjective element of Greek culture as it crystallizes out of the Orient's monolithic, actionless truth-medium[3] but also the conjunction

---

[1] Hegel, *Ästhetik*, ed. F. Bassenge, 2d ed., 2 vols. (1965), II, 327, 401, 514–15. Hegel's other works are quoted according to the first edition of 1832–40, by volume and page number. "Drama must be regarded as the highest stage of all poetry and art since, both in form and content, it fashions itself into the most complete totality" (*Ästh*. II, 5, 12). With incomparable precision Hegel has condensed onto a few pages of his *Phänomenologie des Geistes* (2:527–61) all the essentials of his 1200-page "Aesthetics".

[2] "Of all the glories of the ancient and modern world—and I know more or less all there is of it; it is something one *should* and *can* know—the *Antigone* seems to me the most consummate and satisfying work of art" (*Ästh*. II, 568).

[3] *Gesch. d. Phil.* 13:137. As far as Indian drama is concerned, Hegel only mentions Sakuntala, of which he has a low opinion (*Ästh*. II, 530). He is unacquainted with the Noh plays.

of the Homeric epic and the ancient Greek lyric to form a living
and present action, represented by man himself. But this happens in such a way that the substratum of moral truth remains
present as the overarching and meaning-imparting horizon—
essentially represented by the chorus; the heroes, the agents,
detach themselves from it—representing the subjective and
self-conscious element—only as far as is necessary so that the
two poles form two sides, in dramatic tension, of the one
all-embracing truth.[4] This truth is divine; that is why classical
tragedy is related to the oracle, the *nomos*, to cult and the
mysteries.[5] The two sides are: "the unsundered consciousness
of the divine and the conflicting action which appears in divine
power and deed". The chorus is by no means "merely a reflecting
moral person like the spectator, external and uninvolved, . . .
but the real substance of moral, heroic life and action itself; over
against individual heroes, the chorus is the people, the fruitful
earth, out of which the individuals grow like flowers . . . from
their own native soil. . . . It can be compared to the archi-
tectural temple which surrounds the divine image, which here
becomes the operant hero."[6] To the extent that the chorus
essentially does not lend a hand in the action, however, and thus
lacks the power of the negative, "it cannot hold together the
richness and the colorful fullness of divine life and glorifies each
individual element as a particular god . . . in its hymns of
veneration." But when the chorus "senses the seriousness of the
concept as it treads upon these forms and smashes them", it will
not interfere but "calls to mind the alien destiny", which is the
gods' subjectless unity, "and utters the empty desire for comfort and the feeble talk of placation."[7] By contrast, the warring
heroes bring out the latent conflict in divine truth; they are
neither innocent nor guilty in the situation of tragedy;[8] in the
indissoluble unity of subjectivity and the will's content they
represent one, particular, limited side of the truth. They become
involved, in their "pathos that is full of collisions", in actions

[4] *Phän. d. Geist.* 2:533ff.
[5] *Phil. d. Gesch.* 9:240.
[6] *Ästh.* II, 562–63.
[7] *Phän. d. Geist.* 2:551.
[8] *Ästh.* II, 565–67.

that injure truth's totality. "Great characters have the honor of bringing guilt upon themselves":[9] this dictum, for Hegel, applies at this precise *kairos* in the history of Spirit, when tragedy's horizon is the closed *polis* and "the states are individual and small, unable to unite into a single whole"[10]—no more than the Olympian gods, whose unity is still spiritless: *fatum*.[11] For Hegel this is tragedy's unrepeatable point of origin. The true content of tragedy is "the eternal powers, what is moral in itself, the gods of living reality and all forms of the divine and the true; not, however, as it is at rest, omnipotent, but . . . in its communal aspect."[12] It is "the divine, as it enters the world and individual action, yet neither losing its substantial character in this reality nor finding itself turned into its opposite."[13]

In order to appear at this divine-heroic pinnacle, the tragic actor required the mask; he could not represent his own subjectivity. "The hero who appears before the spectator falls into two parts, his mask and the actor, the *persona* and his real self. The hero's self-consciousness must step forth from his mask and represent what it knows itself to be, namely, the destiny both of the gods of the chorus and of the absolute powers themselves, a destiny no longer separated from the chorus, that is, the common, general consciousness."[14] This is what happens in Greek comedy, where "consciousness exhibits a well-being and an acceptance of well-being that can no longer be found outside this comedy",[15] yet it takes place at the cost of the

[9] *Ibid.*, 566.

[10] *Gesch. d. Phil.* 13:175.

[11] "The gods are well disposed . . . , for they are spiritual natures; but *fatum* is the spiritless, it is abstract power, necessity, grieving because it lacks spirit" (*Phil. d. Gesch.* 9:249).

[12] *Ästh.* II, 517.

[13] *Ibid.*, 548.

[14] *Phän. d. Geist.* 558.

[15] *Ibid.*, 561. Cf.: "The comic requires . . . the infinite cheerfulness and confidence that come from being above one's own contradiction and not bitter and unhappy; it requires the sweet contentment of a subjectivity that, because it is sure of itself, can accept the dissolution of its plans and projects" (*Ästh.* II, 552f.). "Thus the true comic actor (of Aristophanes) finds *himself* comic" (II, 570); —he is not only comic to the audience, as in Molière (II, 583). "The whole tenor . . . is the unshakable confidence all these figures have in themselves, the more incapable they prove of carrying out what they undertake" (II, 572).

gods, who are now shown to be unreal; they reveal their impotence as the *polis* declines. But after all, in *Aeschylus'* trilogy, were they anything more than "factors", "binding together" the "real Athens" into a "complete, harmonious ethos"?[16] As he steps forth from behind his mask, the actor shows that he (with his destiny) is no different from what the spectator is and knows himself to be in his ordinary everyday life. Since "the gods have been removed from nature" and Olympus[17] in the "real, this-worldly divinity"[18] represented by tragedy, both actor and spectator are ultimately "at home in the same secular world".[19] This, however, signals the end of the theatre, and since drama was the epitome of art, Hegel can put forward the following formula: "Reaching this peak, comedy simultaneously leads to the dissolution of all art whatsoever."[20] He is quite serious here; he repeats this verdict many times.[21]

---

[16] *Ästh.* II, 569.

[17] *Ästh.* I, 561.

[18] *Ästh.* II, 547.

[19] *Ästh.* I, 527.

[20] *Ästh.* I, 585.

[21] The falling apart (in modern times) of the two sides "whose complete identity yields the authentic concept of art" produces "the collapse and dissolution of art itself" (*Ästh.* I, 551). "Our age cannot produce a Homer, a Sophocles, a Dante, Ariosto or Shakespeare. What has been so grandly sung and so creatively uttered, has *already been said*. These themes, these modes of viewing the world are already exhausted. Only the present is fresh; everything else is pale and bloodless" (*Ästh.* I, 581). He sharply criticizes Schiller, who, in his "Die Götter Griechenlands", had looked back with nostalgia and held Christianity responsible for the collapse of Greek beauty; at all events, Christianity cannot be to blame: "In Christianity there can be no question of celebrating a God who is enveloped in solitude, he cannot even be conceived as separated and cut off from a world that is now without gods . . . for God is immanent precisely *in* that spiritual freedom, that reconciliation brought by the spirit; seen from this angle, Schiller's famous line, 'When the gods were more humane / men were more divine' is utterly false." Rather, it is *one* feature of the Christian development, the Enlightenment, that is to blame: here "thought, reason, has suppressed the very element that art needs, i.e., God's genuine appearance in the form of man." *This* explains why "God is unknowable" and how "man is required to make the greatest possible renunciation, namely, that of not knowing anything of God, of not comprehending him" (*Ästh.* I, 487–89).

b. Christianity Abolishes Art

So we must ask Hegel what has abolished art and what has taken over from it. He does not give the answer we might expect (philosophy, *Socrates* and *Plato*)[22] but rather refers to three other phenomena. Drama, which, both in tragedy and comedy, presupposed the Greek manifestation of the divine in finite form as the principle of beauty, is dissolved into Roman utilitarianism: "This serves the ends of domination, and the god is that power which can bring such domination about."[23] The Greek gods are shipped to Rome in whole consignments: "This is the tolerance which Rome signifies. . . . Rome is a Pantheon where the gods stand juxtaposed to one other, cancelling each other out."[24] Now plays are nothing more than "the slaughtering of animals and human beings, the spilling of rivers of blood, life-and-death battles. They epitomize, as it were, what the roman can appreciate in terms of spectacle",[25] they are "a demonstration of the futility of human individuality". The only reality is the abstract power of the state, both as domination and as law. This "monstrous misfortune and universal woe", however, says Hegel, constituted "the birth-pangs of the religion of truth".

A second answer (in fact the central one) avoids this circuitous route via Rome and starts with the process whereby, in the comedy, the world is "deprived of gods" and the actor becomes human, leading directly to the principle of God's becoming man in Jesus Christ.[26] Here "anthropomorphism" is pushed "to the limit".[27] "The Greek gods are not to be regarded as human like the Christian God. Christ is much more a *human being*: he lives,

[22] The "history of philosophy" only indirectly indicates this transition in connection with Socrates (14:45ff.); even more strangely, where he deals in detail with Plato's philosophy of the state—"The state is the concrete form of the spirit"—he does not even mention the banishment of poets from the *polis* (14:269–97).

[23] *Phil. d. Relig.* 12:135.

[24] *Ibid.*, 141.

[25] *Ibid.*, 143.

[26] Esp. *Phän. d. Geist.* 2:561f.

[27] *Ästh.* I, 515. "The Greek principle was anthropomorphist, but only superficially so; not anthropormorphist enough, as it were. Christian anthropomorphism is the higher, for it has become aware that the human determines the content of the divine" (*Phil. d. Gesch.* 9:331).

dies and suffers on the Cross—which is infinitely more human than the human being found in Greek beauty." What we have here, in fact, is an affirmation of the element of subjectivity in God; God himself is portrayed as having appeared and died and as being now seated at the Father's right hand, in the man Christ.[28] Here, going beyond Socrates, there begins "the reversal of consciousness" in which two things are grasped simultaneously, namely, that "God is love" and that "God has died": "The most terrible thought that everything eternal, everything true *is not*; that negation itself is in God." But this idea, "the story of Christ", is told by people "on whom the Spirit had already been poured out", enabling them to see the two things together in a unity: "Infinite love is seen in that God has identified himself with what is alien to him in order to kill it."[29] Hence Christianity itself is now the absolute drama, the truth of both tragedy and comedy. Hegel does not put it like this because he is concerned to distinguish the absolute process *imaged* in the story of Christ on the one hand from the realm of art on the other.

From this vantage point we can see how problematical Hegel's third answer will be, when he has to accept the fact that post-Christian art persists, art of all kinds, including drama. This he calls "romantic" in contradistinction to classical drama. He has much to say about it: *Dante, Shakespeare, Calderon, Cervantes, Goethe* and *Schiller* cannot be ignored. Ultimately, however, his view is that this "romantic" art "in principle dissolves the classical ideal"; thus when romanticism itself disintegrates (conclusively in the nineteenth century), it is simply the manifestation of an intrinsic dissolution.[30] For Hegel, this is so because he has defined the entire Christian phenomenon as an "image" of the absolute process: as long as the spirit of a nation (primarily the Germanic spirit, but also that of the Romance and East European nations) was able to identify with it in faith, Christian art was possible; but once the "image" as such is seen—in the Enlightenment—to be part of the universal history of Spirit, that is, when religious faith and artistic inspiration part com-

---

[28] *Phil. d. Gesch.* 9:258–59.
[29] *Phil. d. Relig.* 12:246–51.
[30] *Ästh.* I, 568.

pany, such art is no longer possible: "We lack that innermost faith."[31]

Here we must examine Hegel most closely. He is making two assertions: (1) Christianity replaces art. Its content is not "invented by art", it is already there "on prosaic ground",[32] and moreover, in Christ, God's "externality is not *for himself* but for others; it is an externality made accessible and available to anyone and everyone . . . in the form of ordinariness."[33] It must immediately be added that this very surrender of the absolute subject is "experienced and perceived as deep feeling" in "devotion" by the "mind and heart",[34] and that this same feeling will become the starting point for a new, romantic art. Yet from the outset it is clear that this principle will never suffice to make the felt and perceived content adequately present (as art requires), with the result that "art, taken purely as art, becomes to a certain extent superfluous."[35] (2) But then comes the second assertion: what we have in the story of Jesus Christ is only the *image* of the absolute history of Spirit: "In thus going beyond itself . . . art equally signifies man's going back into himself, down into his own breast; here art brushes off anything that would limit it to a particular content and concept and makes the *humanus* its new saint: the depths and heights of the human mind and heart as such, the universally human quality of his joys and sufferings, his endeavors, deeds and destinies"[36]— these are now its subject matter. Both in its aim and its effect, Christianity is not only coextensive but identical with the human (which in turn is the manifestation of the divine).[37] Here again, as in Kassner, the identity of God and man is the point of

[31] *Ibid.*, 577.
[32] *Ibid.*, 486; cf. 507.
[33] *Ibid.*, 512.
[34] *Ibid.*, 519.
[35] *Ibid.*, 514.
[36] *Ibid.*, 581. The history of the life, death and Resurrection of Jesus has "the power of presenting to consciousness a *universally valid history* which repeats itself in each individual consciousness" (517). On religion as "image" see 11:79ff.
[37] Once man has achieved his goal of union with God, "he has become a free, infinite spirit. But this is only possible in so far as that unity (of God and man) is the primary reality, the eternal foundation of human and divine nature itself" (*Ästh.* I, 514).

absoluteness which interprets the whole process of Spirit; here too, though in a different manner, this identity causes the dramatic dimension to dissolve. Hegel may distance himself from the Enlightenment, which surrenders the "image" and hence surrenders the relevance of the historical tradition,[38] but he cannot avoid this conclusion.

c. Hegel's Understanding of Christianity

In fact, these two assertions crucially affect our projected theory of theo-drama. With regard to the first: Christian, "romantic" art is set forth by Hegel in three circles representing the factual historical developments. The first, purely religious circle is that of "abstract feeling",[39] which contemplates and represents Christ's redemptive history "and reveals the Absolute itself in what is initially a single existence".[40] "Divine love" is seen not only in the episodes of life of Jesus but also in that of his mother, Mary, in whom the deep feeling and pain of maternal love are made visible, and in that of his disciples and friends. Then comes the spirit of the community in which the negativity of Cross and death, and its transfiguration, are presented *directly*: in martyrdom, the inner renunciation of the world in penance and conversion and finally the utterances of the Spirit in miracles and legends, and so forth. Here, at all points, "romantic mysticism" remains at the level of abstract feeling "because, instead of permeating the worldly and taking it into itself affirmatively, it opposes and dismisses it."[41] The second circle of romantic art goes beyond this and aims to gather the world into itself: Hegel speaks of it as "chivalry" (*Rittertum*); its principle is that of objectifying the new absolute interiority and subjectivity in the secular world in terms of "subjective honor", "love" (of man and woman) and of "loyalty" (in friendship and between lord and servant). What is crucial to note here is that none of these themes, which, taken together, broadly constitute the medieval epic and largely the baroque drama too, succeeds

[38] *Phil. d. Relig.* 12:287.
[39] *Ästh.* I, 530.
[40] *Ibid.*, 513.
[41] *Ibid.*, 530.

in attaining the proportions in the world of art to which the Christ-event lays claim in the realm of prosaic world reality. The latter event is "revolutionary"[42] for the world as a whole and alters the world's very condition, whereas the personal life of the "chivalrous" man remains private, fortuitous and of no ultimate consequence. Hegel discovers this fortuitousness even in love, which now, in a Christian framework, can enjoy an infinite significance for the individual: "Necessity shows itself to be infinitely tyrannous in causing a man to prefer one woman and put her first absolutely on all occasions. . . . It is a merely private matter on the part of the subjective heart and a . . . peculiarity of the subject, as is the infinite obstinacy required to find one's life, one's highest consciousness exclusively in her."[43] This applies equally to Beatrice and Tristan, to Julia and Armida or Dulcinea, and so forth. Hegel's third circle, which he draws no doubt mainly for the sake of *Shakespeare*, essentially gets no farther than the second: it is that of the "autonomous" and "firm" subjective character who integrates an aspect of the world, like Macbeth, Othello and Lear. Yet they are marked by a (post-Christian) interiority which far removes them from the interiority of the dramatic heroes of antiquity[44] and, where the latter are directly imitated, reduces them to "mere personifications of particular passions".[45] The sphere of the objective Spirit, "fatherland, family, crown and empire", cannot be treated as such on the stage but only indirectly, as reflected in the peculiar character of the hero[46] (as in a Caesar, Coriolanus, the Maid, Mary Stuart, Wallenstein, Götz and preeminently—in Hegel's interpretation—in Hamlet, who, given to brooding as he is, is not equal to political action).[47]

Once we accept the force of this analysis of the post-Christian drama (given here merely in outline), we shall not be able to close our eyes to the disintegration which must follow from it. On the one hand, it is bound to fall into a prosaic realism of

---

[42] *Phil. d. Relig.* 12:242.

[43] *Ästh.* I, 544.

[44] *Ibid.*, I, 549–61.

[45] *Ibid.*, II, 576.

[46] *Ibid.*, 559.

[47] *Phän. d. Geist.* 2:554; *Ästh.* II, 575, 581.

ordinariness, "imitation of nature", of existence in its immediacy and fortuitousness, which "raises the question whether products of this kind can be called works of art at all".[48] In this context we continually come across the word "skill",[49] "virtuosity"[50] or, as we would say, technique; Hegel demonstrates it by referring to the Dutch genre painters. The (subjective) "adventure" of the courtly romance gives birth to the modern novel in which anything (and nothing) can happen. "No subject matter today can fundamentally escape this relativity."[51] Hence the backlash in the form of the irony and "humor" of Hegel's language, what we today would call "the absurd": forms that are deliberately unrelated to the given order, the "sheer subjectivity"[52] that unveils and "flaunts itself" as such.

It remains to mention the fact that Hegel, in order to deal with the persistence of drama in the Christian and "romantic" era, is obliged to contradict his own theory. He had asserted that the tragedy of antiquity was dissolved by comedy and that comedy itself dissolved into the prose of Roman culture on the one hand and of Christianity on the other. But he was forced to put forward a second theory, carrying little conviction, to the effect that the "play" should be regarded as the continuation of both tragedy and comedy. He does not dare to call it a synthesis; he speaks of an "intermediate thing", a "middle stage",[53] which consists, not in the reciprocal reversal of opposites, "but in their blunting each other and cancelling each other out",[54] that is, reaching "a lower level of interpenetration and hence also of importance".[55] The "play" is from the outset "less stable" than tragedy and comedy; it has the seeds of death within it and is always in danger of "slipping into the prosaic"[56] and seeking to "move", "entertain" or "morally improve" the audience.

[48] *Ästh.* I, 570.
[49] *Ästh.* I, 551, 570–71; II, 557, 584.
[50] *Ästh.* I, 571.
[51] *Ibid.*, 579.
[52] *Ibid.*, 574. Hegel deduces this—polemically and one-sidedly—from Fichte (I, 71f.). On the distinction between humor and irony see I, 75.
[53] *Ibid.*, II, 582, 546f.; an "intermediate species", 556.
[54] *Ibid.*, 555.
[55] *Ibid.*
[56] *Ibid.*, 556.

Whether justified or not in point of fact, this a priori de-valuing of modern drama is closely connected with the second aspect of Hegel's Christian and "romantic" dramatic theory, namely, the way he fits the Christian approach into an all-inclusive history of the human spirit: Christianity had to make its appearance at this *particular* point in the development,[57] however much it may remain its turning point and hence its center. The causes and effects of this kind of view of the Christ-event are obvious: reduced to the level of an "imaging" of the process, the recalling of this special event is in fact only "devotion" on the part of "mind and heart". It lacks two things it possessed in the New Testament and which it retains in Catholic dogmatics, namely, the real, active power of the life, suffering and Resurrection of Jesus on behalf of all men, which in turn grounds the active, real power of the exalted Christ to give men an inner participation in his universal mission. Christ does this by creating and animating, in the "body" of his Church, members who are filled with his life and Spirit and who carry out "what is still lacking in his suffering". Both these aspects, however, his action on their behalf and his mission, presuppose that the Lord who works is a person and remains this particular person after his Resurrection. Hegel, as is well known, regarded this as an inadmissible refusal to allow Christ's contribution to the total process to be subsumed into it. For Hegel, the aspiration to individual immortality (let alone the resurrection of the flesh) is egoism seeking to privatize every-thing.[58]

---

[57] It is well known with what determination Karl Löwith, in his *Welt-geschichte und Heilsgeschehen*, 2d ed. (1953), opposed such attempts to encompass Christianity within a system. On Hegel, 55–61. On Löwith's basic aims, cf. Jürgen Habermans, *Philosophisch-politische Probleme* (Bibl. Suhrkamp, 1971), 116ff.

[58] For Hegel, the Resurrection of Jesus is identical with the coming of the Spirit to the community (*Phil. d. Relig.* 12:257ff.). "The actual turning point in this life of God occurs when, in the Passion, he dispenses with his individual existence as *this particular man*" (*Ästh.* I, 517)—i.e., the Resurrection is not seen in personal terms as in the New Testament.

d. Catholicism Goes Farther

This provides us with a way of critically evaluating Hegel's dramatic theory as it affects our present project, which is to find and assess an appropriate analogy between the drama of worldly existence (which attains visible form in the theatre) and the divine–human drama (theo-drama). We are only interested in Hegel insofar as he is relevant to this endeavor. At the outset it must be said that no thinker before him more profoundly experienced and pondered Christian revelation in dramatic categories. It was precisely from the utterances and counter-utterances of the Old Testament and the synthesis of the New that Hegel read off his fundamental dialectical rhythms. From early days, futhermore, he had been interested in Greek tragedy;[59] as early as 1802 he wrote: "This is nothing but the performance, on the stage, of the tragedy which is latent in moral existence, the tragedy which the Absolute is eternally playing with itself: it eternally gives birth to itself in the world of objectivity and in this form delivers itself up to suffering and death, rising to glory out of its own ashes."[60] In tragedy, initially, we still see the Absolute at play with itself: in the Christ-event it will be seen to be a play in all earnest; but the framework in which the Christian reality is conceived (self-portrayal of the Absolute, in which the characters are only "masks" of the Spirit) is basically the same. Both tragedy and the Passion have the same basic nature: they are act. Reality is action, not theory. Hegel wished plays to be only performed, not printed to be read; they should only be kept in the form of stage scripts.[61] but this means that—however much mask and actor are identified in the new subjectivity—what takes place in Christ stays at the level of an "image". Here absolute Spirit simply contemplates its own being, namely, that of the self-alienated God who returns to his identity. Hence Christology has been superseded by philosophy (in a way that is both Nestorian and Monophysite, since the

---

[59] On the origins of Hegel's dramatic aesthetics cf. Wolfgang Schlunk, *Hegels Theorie des Dramas* (Diss. Tübingen, 1936), 9–23.

[60] "Über die wissenschaftlichen Behandlungsarten des Naturrechts" (1802/3) I, 386.

[61] *Ästh.* II, 538.

purely human is also the pure representation of God), and the doctrine of the Trinity is equally undermined (in a Patripassian and Sabellian sense). In the end, therefore, the difference between tragedy as play and the Christian Passion as seriousness is abolished: analogy, which is essential to a theory of theodrama, is absorbed in identity. The impersonality of destiny or of "moral substance" in tragedy predominates over the personalism of Passion and Resurrection; the "spirits of the race" (the biblical and Pauline "angelic powers") ultimately integrate into the total World Spirit. Whereas, theologically speaking, the Christian *person* has risen above all these powers.

At this point we must criticize Hegel's view of the possibility of a (post-)Christian, "romantic" theatre insofar as this is a representation (a play) of serious, Christian, dramatic life situations. We have already observed that, where the efficacy of Christ's Passion on behalf of all men is denied (as in Enlightenment thought) and where, therefore, as in orthodox Protestantism, there is no way in which the exalted Lord can give the Christian a genuine mission by enabling him to share charismatically in his saving act, all the Christian can do is cultivate "devotion in mind and heart". Effective action in the "secular world" remains extrinsic to this subjective contemplation. Thus, for Hegel, all romantic drama springs from the hero's interiority; his action does not penetrate beyond into the profane world. This, in turn, is dependent on the fact that he regards drama (*qua* theatre) as essentially bound to the pre-Christian classical period and has a particular interest in showing that the whole age of art has now come to an end.

But is he not basically right? There is much in us that would tend to agree with him. And in that case it would be anachronistic today, when drama is in decline, indeed may even have collapsed already, to write a theodramatic theory. Two questions need to be faced: Why is Hegel right? May it be because personalist Christology, with its notion of a real acting and being on behalf of others and of a real participatory mission, has dwindled to nothing (as a result of orthodoxy and liberalism) and is no longer a lived reality? And secondly, if it *were* to be genuinely lived, would not Christian drama (whether in terms of life or on the stage) be presented with quite different situations from those indicated by Hegel, that is, the mystery plays, "chivalry" and its disintegrated middle-class form? Indeed, would not this very tension between the total, secularized world and the universality of the Christian mission in this world—would this not keep alive a dramatic interplay? Would it not preserve us from the leveling-down of everything, Christian or non-Christian, under the universal, impersonal, dialectical law of "die and become"?

If we are to maintain this abiding tension, we need to base ourselves on the depth and breadth of Catholic dogma. Here is a brief resumé of the issues we shall have to examine in detail:

1. Mission, in the ecclesial sense, rooted in Christology and the doctrine of the Trinity, is neither "devotion" nor "character" but a reality. In "devotion" the Christian is meant to appropriate this reality; he is to make it his own subjectivity. His character is to enter into it and become absorbed in it. This subjectivity then, because it is centered in mission, is fundamentally world-oriented, world-embracing and universal (as is the *Catholica* as a whole).

2. At this point we encounter a distinction which had been presumed lost: that between the "substantial" nature of the Church as a whole and the particular vocation of the individual; the Church actually realizes at a higher level the role of the ancient chorus vis-à-vis the hero.[62]

3. Precisely because each Christian mission always has a universal content and yet in itself is particular (hence the body/members metaphor in Paul), when they meet there arises a genuine and unlimited richness of dramatic tensions, conflicts and collisions, both inside and outside the Church. Such missions, furthermore, may embody the objective spirit of an epoch (*Claudel's* trilogy) or even the spirit of a continent (*Claudel's Soulier de Satin*); in which case there can be a meeting and interplay both of Christian, ecclesial interests and of universal, historical ones.

4. Moreover, if every mission, in particular every highly nuanced[63] mission, is a participation in the whole mission of

---

[62] Of course, this does not justify the imitation of the Greek chorus as in *Die Braut von Messina*, and Hegel was right to reject it (*Ästh.* II, 563). But Eliot's *Murder in the Cathedral* would require special examination.

[63] In the sense used by Adrienne von Speyr.

Christ (which Hegel admits in his way), the drama of each particular Christian life can, in its own way, be a kind of reflection of the mission of Christ (which, with regard to the romantic drama, Hegel failed to see). This can show us for the first time the real significance of many of *Calderon's* chief works; but as we shall see, it also facilitates an understanding of *Shakespeare* that is totally different from Hegel's. Not only did *Calderon* succeed in reflecting the Christ-event back in time, into the dramas and myths of antiquity (which prepare the way for it); not only did he attempt to render this event credible as a here-and-now actuality in the most varied situations of his time; he also undertook to dramatize the theological epic: his relation to *Thomas* was to be like that of *Sophocles* to *Homer*. As for *Shakespeare*, he is still in the cultic mystery play's field of influence; it would be imprecise to say he secularized it; rather —in some of his greatest works—he conceived and fashioned the great destinies of the world as expressions and extensions of the Christ-event: it would not be in the least misleading to speak here of *(post-)Christian myth*, or, if this expression is felt to be too loaded, of a *"post-figuration"* of Christ, as *Albrecht Schöne*[64] and, more appositely, *Murray Roston*[65] have done.

5. Behind all this there is the basic problem of that theo-dramatic theory for which Hegel was ultimately searching and which forms the ultimate horizon of the present work: In what sense is the theological drama a drama of God himself? Does God enter into the action? And, in doing so, is he not down-graded into nothing more than an all-embracing dimension? Or, as in *Calderon's The Great Theatre of the World*, does he remain the sublime spectator? But is such a role worthy of him? (At all events there is no room for Christ in this play of *Calderon's*.) How is the immanent Trinity related to the eco-nomic Trinity? (For in Hegel, in the end, they coincide.) What is implied by the idea of God's *kenosis*? In what sense is God involved in the "world theatre"?

These theological questions are brought into the limelight by Hegel's philosophy. Where Hegel announces the *end* of drama

[64] A. Schöne "Figurale Gestaltung: Andreas Gryphius" in *Säkularisation als sprachbildende Kraft* (Göttingen, 1958).
[65] *Biblical Drama in England* (London, 1968), 69ff.

(albeit a drama seen chiefly in terms of "art" and "theatre"), new possibilities of drama open up from the angle of a Catholic theology. It may be the task of Christians to lay hold of drama's relevance and interpret it to the world, just as, elsewhere, we have enjoined them to shoulder responsibility for the philosophical task.[66] For the moment, however, we leave all this an open question.

3. *The Death of Drama?*

a. The Loss of the Framework

Does not the history of the theatre in the last one hundred and fifty years indicate, however, that Hegel is right? And as for the theological response we have outlined, is it any more than a shadow that will fade away in the light of the facts? Hegel, as a philosopher, announces the end of art and allots it to its relative place in the "system" as being on the whole a pre-Christian phenomenon that was bound to yield to the prosaic seriousness of real history. But, in doing so, has he not also undercut his own position? For philosophy remains speculative, whereas from now on—*Marx*, for example—the issue is one of changing the world. Thus the whole Hegelian horizon of absolute Spirit also disappears, which alone could provide a background for the theatre's action; it gives way to the horizon of human plans and designs that are only meaningful insofar as they can be implemented in practice. So not only theatre dies but also the precondition of its existence. *Must* there always be theatre, in particular "elevated drama"—which in fact scarcely existed after *Euripides* and prior to *Shakespeare*, and which many nations have only experienced in a diluted, ersatz form, if at all? The nineteenth- and twentieth-century stage still has the external pretensions of theatre's golden moments and continues to draw sustenance largely from the material of the ancient world, the Elizabethans and the Germanic myths. Such dramatists have been called "grave robbers".[1] But it lives on as a traditional and

---

[66] *Herrlichkeit* III/1, 980–83.
[1] George Steiner, *Death of Tragedy* (New York, 1961).

(more and more obviously) commercial organ of public entertainment: it lacks an ultimate raison d'être. The audience is no longer a society with a particular mental and spiritual horizon (like the Athenian *polis* or that of a court or town) but an amorphous and anonymous mass gathered together to watch something or other. *Pushkin* wonders how highly wrought, thoroughbred drama could be rerooted in its original soil: "The art of drama was born in the marketplace, as a popular entertainment. What does the populus like? What moves it? What language does it understand? *Racine* transplanted it from the fair to the court", and now we have to bring this institution that has become artificial back to the people.[2] But this was also what the dramatists of classicism (since *Lessing*) and romanticism (like *Shelley*) had wanted: instead of a court theatre they wanted a national theatre, educating the people toward an ethical consciousness (*Schiller*). This is no longer a serious proposition today, however, when we have come to think in terms of "one planet". This loss of an audience united in faith and *Weltanschauung* corresponds—we are deliberately avoiding the terminology of "cause and effect"—to the more or less evident disappearance from the stage of that spiritual horizon which, for Hegel, was still the precondition for a meaningful play, whether it was tragic, comic or simply dramatic.

"Tragedy", says Hegel, "consists in ethical nature detaching its unorganic nature, which it experiences as something adventitious, lest it become embroiled in it; it sets it up over against itself and, by acknowledging it in struggling against it, is reconciled with the Divine Essence which is the unity of both of them."[3] In this definition Hegel presupposes that there is a concrete, absolute (divine) idea of ethics, encompassing the community and the individual. Within it—because it is alive —identity has continually to reconstitute itself in the power struggle, and it does this precisely through the (loving) self-sacrifice of its distinctiveness vis-à-vis destiny (the adventitious), which it has itself posited as its opposite.[4] *P. Szondi* has shown

[2] A. Pushkin, *Essays and Diaries*.
[3] Hegel, "Über die wissenschaftlichen Behandlungsarten des Naturrechts" (1802/3) I, 387–88.
[4] "Der Geist des Christentums und sein Schicksal" (1798/9) in *Hegels theo-*

that behind this idea of Hegel's, which provides the foundation of all dramatic action, there is the New Testament and the Christian idea of the vanquished (Jewish) duality between man and (divine, alien) destiny. That is, for Hegel, both pre- and post-Christian drama is measured against the phenomenon of Christ: he is this distinctive individual who appears on the stage to take into himself, by dying on the Cross, the destiny of the world's guilt (which is not his) so that, transfigured, he can bring both back to the unity of the ethical.[5] In his aesthetics Hegel will say that "in tragedy the Eternally Substantial goes out like a victor, reconciling, sweeping aside what is merely the false one-sidedness of conflicting individuality and upholding the positive in its full affirmative form, no longer split. This, after all, is what the said individuality intended."[6] But precisely this framework, which can even embrace tragic death and which is presupposed by Christian faith and the philosophy which issues from it—and is also found in the Greek religious cult of Dionysos in tragedy and comedy—this framework can no longer be assumed to exist after Hegel's time.

The whole modern dispute concerning the *definition of tragedy* depends on this shattering of the framework; we cannot delay too long over it here, however, since at its core our topic is not tragedy but the dramatic and theatrical as such. Most writers make a polemical distinction between the tragic and the Christian,[7] indeed, between the tragic and anything that might bring about "reconciliation", whether in a philosophical or pedagogical

---

logische Jugendschriften, ed. H. Nohl (1907), 282–83 n.a.

[5] Peter Szondi, "Zu Hegels Bestimmung des Tragischen" in *Versuche über das Tragische* 2d ed. (Frankfurt: Insel, 1964), 20–29.

[6] (Berlin, 1938), X, 3, 533 (Bassenge ed. [1965], II, 551/2).

[7] "Christianity is an antitragic world-view. . . . Christianity offers man the certainty of a future security and rest in God" (Steiner, *Death of Tragedy*, 273). Karl Jaspers expresses himself similarly: "All man's basic experiences cease to be tragic once they are Christian. Guilt becomes the *felix culpa*. . . . Christ may be the most profound symbol of failure in the world, yet he is not tragic, since he perishes in the act of knowing, fulfilling and perfecting. . . . So there is no such thing as a real Christian tragedy" (*Von der Wahrheit* [München: Piper, 1947], 925). Of course, this fails to take account of two things: first, that Christ dies forsaken by God (i.e., *not* "knowing"), and that man's future, which depends on how his life will be judged, remains in doubt.

context. (Here we see the influence of *Rousseau* and again of *Marx*.) Then the Hegelian dramatic theory hardens inevitably into *Pantragismus*, that is, the objective and subjective world principles are irreconcilably opposed (*Büchner*, *Hebbel*), or the subject in his inner motions is hopelessly self-contradictory (*Bahnsen*). Subsequently tragedy either sinks to the level of the theatre of the absurd, where meaninglessness is no longer relativized by any framework and all action becomes impossible and self-annihilating, or else—as in *Schopenhauer*—tragedy demonstrates that there must be "a totally different existence, a different world, which we can know of only indirectly".[8] We are shown "life's terrible sides, nameless pain, the woe of mankind, the triumph of malice, the mocking sway of chance and the ruin of the just and innocent without hope of rescue". Here we see "the conflict of Will with itself, which is most completely developed here at the highest level of its objectivity, as it steps forth, spreading terror." In *Schopenhauer* (who here distorts Hegel) this is the framework that remains: "It is one and the same Will . . . whose manifestations tear each other to pieces." The purpose of the play is to deny this Will: "to surrender, not merely life, but the whole will to live".[9] Drawn into these terrible and contradictory motions, "we feel, with horror, that we are already in the midst of hell."[10] As a possible way out, a narrower framework of meaning than Hegel's can be adopted, not in the context of the World Spirit as a whole, but perhaps in that of "society". Thus the individual comes into conflict with society's laws or is destroyed by them. But since this framework is clearly still relative (even though it may be intended to be ultimate), the individual may be justly or unjustly crushed by it; thus, in perishing, he can open up a path to freedom, herald a new age, and so forth. Consequently such a process attracts

---

[8] "Zur Ästhetik der Dichtkunst" in *Die Welt als Wille und Vorstellung: Ergänzungen*, chap. 37 (*Werke*, Insel, n.d.), II, 1206.

[9] *Die Welt als Wille und Vorstellung* III (*Werke* I), 340–41.

[10] *Ibid.*, 343; cf. "Parega" II chap. XIX, §227 (*Werke* V), 480f. Schopenhauer ranks Christian tragedy higher (being a "joyful farewell to the world") than ancient tragedy (II, 1207), provided it does not "claim to be poetically righteous . . . as a cruely optimistic, Protestant-rationalistic or—one might even say—Jewish view of the world" (I, 341).

only limited interest. On the other hand, where this (social) framework is made absolute (that is, as a perfect social order of the future, which must and can be attained), interest in the individual's destiny crumbles, as we shall show later on.

Against all this, contrary to all objections and yet borne out by the facts, we must assert that dramatic action is ultimately only meaningful when seen against the background of a given, absolute meaning—albeit in the wake of Hegel such meaning can no longer be rationally adumbrated and demonstrated in concepts. In Christian terms such absolute meaning can only be grasped in the leap of faith, which is why many see drama inspired by Christianity as the only way out of absurdity (and hence the only way out of theatre's self-betrayal).[11] Other systems of meaning can vie with the Christian meaning—for example, that of *Lebensphilosophie* (since Nietzsche) or of communism—and this competition, to see which system of meaning is the more comprehensive and cannot be undercut, can act as a spur to new theatre and new dramatic approaches. We should note that, as Hegel rightly remarks, the frameworks of earlier tragedy and great drama always had considerable political implications: destiny that is purely private cannot aspire to be of *ultimate* interest. In Athens plays are performed in and for the framework of the *polis*; in *Shakespeare* they concern an empire, a court, a republic. In *Corneille*, long before Hegel, the *raison d'État* is almost the most concrete feature on stage: the whole weight of individual personality, together with his or her love, freely bows to it or is overpowered by it; or, by way of exception (*Surena*), it is the political side that capitulates. Even in *Lope de Vega's* serious plays the prince can be a scoundrel: his kingdom remains intact and often there is an *ex machina* conversion in which, in tears, he regains the dignity of his office. In *Racine* the power of Rome (which is no less majestic than in *Dante*) restrains the free play of the passions, which even in *Phèdre*, where the abyss of the underworld yawns, are im-

---

[11] For a rapprochement between Christianity and tragedy cf. H. Weinstock, *Die Tragödie des Humanismus: Wahrheit und Trug im abendländischen Menschenbild* (Heidelberg, 1953). Also J. Sellmair, *Der Mensch in der Tragik* (Munich, 1941); J. Bernhart "Der Mensch in der tragischen Welt" in *De Profundis* (Munich, 1952) and the entire work of Reinhold Schneider and T. S. Eliot.

maculately kept in check by the peristyle of the royal stage and the tapestry of the royal language. It is similar in *Kleist*, although here the restraint is less secure. Only where the absolute can no longer be discerned through and behind the political—as sometimes in *Schiller*—can the political be opposed as an ossified authority that ought to be overthrown in the name of either freedom or humanity. This opposition may still see itself as being a political system (*Tell*) or dream (Posa), but it can also be governed by the *daimōn* of anarchic power (*Fiesco*, *Wallenstein*). Existence must founder in the upheaval of revolution where there is no horizon of meaning (*Büchner's Danton*) just as, in the private realm too, when every protective norm is explicitly withdrawn (*Woyzeck*), existence is bound to perish. "Society" as such cannot replace the horizon of meaning: in fact, society needs to be nourished, renewed, justified—by the heart's blood of its tragic champion—if it has not already sucked him dry (as often in *Ibsen*). Hegel was right when he said that, without a political dimension—even a stylized one—the purely private is of little consequence.

There is no obvious reason, however, why the great political systems which wrestle with one another over the meaning and the riddles of existence should not join forces in their attempt to clarify the horizon. If meaninglessness, considered as a mode of action, has the last word, it annihilates itself and ends in *Beckett's* garbage cans. The alleged absolute freedom which can play the part of both God and the devil (*Sartre*) dissolves in pure *ennui*. The attitude of revolt (*Camus*) is absurd if it is absolutized, since, in order to survive, it must always presuppose whatever it is negating and thus entangles itself in the fatal contradictions of an Ivan Karamazov. Be the content of "given" absolute meaning never so hidden and ineffable—like the baffling figure of the one who judges between man and God in the ancient Book of Job—it must be *presupposed*, to form the framework within which drama can take place. And this "given" meaning is just as possible today as it was when the framework was fashioned in the categories of Athens or Rome.

b. The Loss of the Image

The hero of ancient tragedy, as a king, a son of a god or a titan, was a direct manifestation of the divine world, larger than life, buskined and wearing a mask. *Shakespeare's* kings and great lords reflect something of this mythical greatness, which is apparent particularly when they mix with the world of lesser people and fools. Like the heroes of French tragedy and those of *Calderon* and *Schiller*, they are "characters" in the Hegelian, and *dämonisch* in the Goethean, sense—a last reflection of the idea of the *daimōn* in the ancient world (from *Plato* to *Plutarch* and *Iamblichos*). Thus they are *images*.

But just as, earlier, the absolute framework of meaning of the *polis* was destroyed by a sociology which declared that models of society were mutable, so the image of the "hero" was eroded by psychology. What the behaviorist can analyze has already played its last role. To keep going at all, it has to borrow the aura of ancient myth: we are presented with yet another *Antigone*, *Medea*, *Electra*, another *Orpheus*, *Oedipus*, *Amphitryon*, another Orestes (even if he is disguised as discreetly as in *Eliot's Family Reunion*), an Achilles (*Kleist*), the Argonauts (*Grillparzer*), and so forth. *Giraudoux*, *Hofmannsthal*, *Shaw*, *Cocteau*, *Gide*, *O'Neill*, *Anouilh* adapt themes (including others such as Undine and Siegfried) to all styles, from "true tragedy" via parody to social criticism. The center is in fact occupied by *Freud*, this modern substitute for the ancient world's *daimōn*, since now the irrational dimensions of "destiny", which once burst upon the world from the intangible sphere of the divine and was often enough expressed as a sexual curse, breaks through from below and from within, from the vast, dark chambers of the unconscious, the "blood" and the instincts. But we *know* these causal connections, every child can have his Oedipus complex pointed out; the hero on the stage is only "a case of" whatever-it-may-be: his *daimōn* can be analyzed. "Consequently middle-class people lack the necessary height from which to fall",[12] they lack "the dignity of the *Fall*"[13]—in both senses [that is, *Fall*

---

[12] Schopenhauer, "Zur Ästhetik der Dichtkunst", *Werke* II, 1211.

[13] A. Lesky, "Zum Problem des Tragischen" in *Gymnasium Helveticum* 7 (Jan., 1953): 4.

= fall, and *Fall* = case, issue —Tr.]. So at best all we have is "inspired plagiarism".[14]

Nonetheless, once the subject's depth-dimensions have been opened up, questions arise which, while they cannot lead us back to the lost mythical world, do pierce the levels accessible to psychologico-rational explanation; going behind these levels, they enter a sphere of ultimate answers—whether the latter can be brought forward or not. Even if (like *Ibsen*) we know about the laws of heredity, we by no means know why they operate and cause problems for the human subject: the scientific explanations render the existential question more baffling than it was even in myth. Not only is freedom grappling with obstructions here; it can strike a level where guilt/destiny (or in Christian terms, the mystery of inherited guilt—"original sin") *has* to be held partly responsible for things of which I am unaware. *Pascal* considered this the most impenetrable of the Christian mysteries. And it may be that only the light of Christ, breaking forth from behind this darkness, enabling us voluntarily to accept partial responsibility, can point us in the direction of an explanation. In *T. S. Eliot's Family Reunion*, Harry succeeds in analyzing himself out of the inherited family curse, but only to take freedom upon himself as "a different kind of punishment from prison"—the acceptance of shared responsibility in atonement. In the *Cocktail Party*, the analyst shows man three paths: he can submit to false convention, he can turn aside into neurosis, but also—in rare cases—he can become a saint. Only in this third form is the absolute horizon glimpsed (by Celia) through the distorting mists of psychology and, in a final effort, attained. This breakthrough does not need to be formulated in specifically Christian terms. Without a doubt it also comes to light in the "inverted theology"[15] of a *Faulkner* in *Camus'* stage adaptation[16] or in the art of *Garcia Lorca*, who says of his figures: "The world is the battlefield not only of human but also of tellurian powers."[17] This also applies

---

[14] G. Steiner, *Death of Tragedy*.

[15] Claude-Edmonde Magny in *L'Age du roman américain* (Paris, Seuil).

[16] "Requiem pour une Nonne" (Requiem for a Nun) in *Théâtre, récits, Nouvelles* (Pléiade, 1962), 823–920.

[17] From an interview, quoted by Rolf Michaelis, *Garcia Lorca* (Friedrichs

to the drama of *Wedekind* as well as the modern myths of *Melville*, *Joseph Conrad* and *Thomas Wolfe*, where the most uncanny and unique interconnections suddenly become visible through the very ordinary foreground realism, restoring to the heroes that "height" of which psychology had robbed them. Once again, seen in this perspective, there seems to be no reason why theatre and drama should not continue to exist, albeit in new forms.

The basic position of *Peter Brook* is that theatre is by no means bound to appear in its traditional form, familiar to us from the rare and short-lived high points of the Greek, English, Spanish, French and Weimar stages. There have been long periods in between when it existed "only fragmentarily and in localized endeavors: one theatre is after money, another after acclaim, another after emotion, a fourth after politics and yet another after entertainment."[18] Wherever it pretends to be complete or is sure of itself, "it has already gone dead" (Rilke).

> Be it war or peace, the colossal stage-wagon of culture rumbles on, bearing traces of every artist to the ever-growing garbage dump. Theatre, actors, critics and audience are stuck in a machine that never stops, however much it may groan and creak. There is always a new season, and we are too busy to ask the one crucial question which puts the plumbline up to the whole structure: Why theatre? What is it for? Is it an anachronism, something unique and obsolete that continues to exist like an ancient monument or a bizarre habit? . . . Does the stage have a real place in our lives?[19]

But drama does not have to be written in five acts and in verse. It can take place on the market square and—why not? —experiment with new forms of expression in the cinema and television. "I can take any empty room and call it a bare stage. One man walks across the room while another watches him; that is all that is necessary for theatrical action."[20] Life manifests a fundamental urge to observe itself as an action exhibiting both

Dramatiker des Weltentheaters vol. 60, 1969), 79.

[18] Peter Brook, *Der leere Raum: Möglichkeiten des heutigen Theaters* (Hamburg: Hoffman und Campe, 1970), 55.

[19] *Ibid.*, 74.

[20] *Ibid.*, 27.

meaning and mystery. This urge is no more extinct in adults than in children. And so we are heartened to face the last objection.

c. The Overwhelming Weight of Material Reality

Does not theatre always presuppose the dichotomy between a life that cannot satisfy itself and its own self-idealization? And is it not, therefore, an illusion and an evasion? Is not *Kassner* right to summon post-Christian man to overcome this dichotomy? And as for post-Hegelian man, once he has perfected consciousness' speculative self-perception, has he any other choice but to move on to the task of changing the world?

In *Auguste Comte* positivism settled accounts with the theatre. According to Comte, intercourse between human beings begins with the communication of feelings rather than thoughts, and this involves the simple imitation of natural signs. The increasing sophistication of social life, and hence of thought, leads to the exchange of ideas, necessitating the creation of an artificial sign language. Art, too, begins with an imitation that is generally intelligible, but genuine knowledge of reality must first be "deciphered" from the representation. For *Comte*, theatre belongs entirely to the first phase of art: uttered speech is supported by gesture and mime, subordinate modes of expression. He is also aware of the theatre's sacral origins; it is a relic of mankind's "theological" period and thus cannot provide the true cultic celebration appropriate to today. It remains a hybrid phenomenon. "Positivism must once and for all extinguish the institution of the theatre, which is as irrational as it is immoral. It must entirely reorganize education and, through 'sociolatry', substantiate a system of celebrations designed to expose vain pleasures to universal ridicule." Today everyone can read and enjoy the dramatic masterpieces for himself. Performances should be prohibited. Theatre, as a whole, was only "a provisional stage in the development of humanity".[21]

---

[21] Auguste Comte, *Système de politique positive* (1851–) I, 286ff.; *Cours de philosophie positive* (1830) VI, 833; V, 124. In Eichendorff, *Dichter und ihre Gesellen* (Insel, 1941), II, 476f., Lothario says: "Poets must simply not give in,

Marx and *Engels* expressed themselves on the problem of tragedy when their friend *Lassalle* presented them with his tragedy *Franz von Sickingen* (written in 1857/1858), together with an accompanying essay on "the tragic idea". Here Sickingen is a spokesman of the Hegelian World Spirit, sent to urge human consciousness to take a step farther. He fails to bring the nobles with him, and the peasants' revolt does not begin until one year later. Sickingen's "guilt", according to Lassalle, is that he "lacks confidence in the moral idea", puts "excessive trust in unworthy finite means" and is involved in the "dialectical contradiction" which lies at the heart of all action undertaken anywhere between utopia and reality, inspiration and diplomacy: "*the* tragic collision of the revolutionary situation". But this was the very thing for which *Marx* had no use; Sickingen's "ruin" bothered him little, just as the individual's death is of no account, and nothing matters but the success of the revolution. *Engels* says that the really tragic element in Sickingen's fate is that the nobility were not prepared to go along with the peasants.[22]

In the drama of old, which was religious at least in a background sense, there was a real, absolute horizon (however hidden it may have been) which threw into relief the hero's actions, whether he eventually won or lost. This horizon has now disappeared, it has been swallowed up by the revolutionary process; what *seems* to be the latter's "ideal" goal is in fact *of the same order* as the present "real" or "material" state of the process and shares its necessity. Both differences disappear: the difference between material and ideal disappears because the ideal, insofar as it is not material, becomes simply the halo of the ideological superstructure. The difference between horizon (God) and actor (man) disappears because both are only real in the living totality of the human species. Thus, where it exists,

---

they must starve the theatres of poetry; they must let them gradually die of their own wretchedness and boredom, while, with freshness and impudence, they themselves dramatize the world."

[22] To Lassalle, Manchester, May 18, 1859. On this whole issue: Ludwig Marcuse, "Die marxistische Auslegung des Tragischen", in *Monatshefte für dt. Unterricht, dt. Sprache und Literatur* (1954): 214–48. Quoted from the reprint in: *Tragik und Tragödie* ed. V. Sanders, *Wege der Forschung* CVIII (1971): 99–108.

Marxist theatre is fundamentally antitragic and optimistic and fundamentally antiindividualist. Whether this meets Lenin's demand that "the really valuable part of the old culture, its insights and wealth of ideas, should be preserved and handed on to the masses"[23] is a moot point.

Counterbalancing the fundamental optimism of the Marxist view of the world, where no irreconcilable tragedies can be permitted, there is the monstrous weight of human suffering. In its absolutely terrifying proportions it simply cannot be idealized theatrically; it forbids us to act as distanced observers and commentators. No one can write a tragedy about Auschwitz. All there can be, at the most, is a "presentation of the facts" (*Peter Weiss*). *Karl Kraus* changed his *Die letzten Tage der Menschheit* from a tragedy into an operetta, as did *Brecht* with several plays, and *Dürrenmatt* followed him, with this rationale: "Tragedy presupposes guilt, necessity, evaluation, an overall view and responsibility. In our bungling century, in this last dance of the white man, no one is guilty or responsible any more. No one can do anything about it, and no one wanted it to happen. The whole thing runs on its own. . . . All we are left with is comedy. Our world has led to the grotesque, just as it led to the atom bomb."[24] All the same, operetta, comedy and the grotesque *are* theatre; in this form theatre is trying to express the age's dramatic tensions which, humanly speaking, can no longer be endured.

Let us therefore try to put forward a final rejoinder. Behind the Marxist radicalism, and forming its starting point, there is a biblical prophetism. According to *Marx* its Christian form, historically, has failed. He alleges that the prophecy can only be fulfilled—in terms of concrete, pragmatic love of neighbor—in its reversed, atheistic form. Marxism too, therefore, in the context of its origin, cannot be simply undramatic and untragic. It has been said that today the tragic has grown to such proportions that mankind "has experienced more *angst* and pain than can be portrayed on the stage" (L. Marcuse), that "where there is no world left, there is no longer anything to collide

[23] Michail Lifschitz, *Karl Marx und di Ästhetik* Fundus-Bücher 3 (Dresden: Verlag der Kunst, 1960), 11.
[24] Dürrenmatt, *Theaterprobleme* (Zurich, 1955), 47f.

with"[25] and that "language is stifled by the facts".[26] This being so—unless we are to escape to Nirvana—we are again left with the Christian approach, which cannot be disarmed by any horror and which can show us a way into the future. For Christianity, with its inner dramatic tension (which is not simply "theatre", to quote *Kassner*), can take all theatrical aspects into itself in even the darkest moments, cherishing them as the germ of new symbolic representation.

It is only possible to abolish the difference between material reality and the ideal if the material is seen as "alienated" by the ideological superstructure; where this structure is erected, it causes the meaning (which is identical with the material) to appear, and since material reality is a process, that meaning can be simultaneously a utopian one. But this introduces into the heart of material reality the whole gnostic (*E. Bloch*) contradiction, which *Nietzsche* unmasks in his two opposed formulae of the "Superman" (the coming truth of man) and the "eternal recurrence of the identical" (where the permanent lie is the truth). The "impossibility" of material reality being as it is causes it to jump into the realm of the ideal; if no room is left for this, it explodes into insanity and schizophrenia. But in the end the "impossibility of material reality" always founders on the suppressed question of the meaning of the individual's finite life (and death): in the optimistic realism of Marxism, as in the pessimistic realism of *Nietzsche's* faith, the individual and his question are mowed down. Privatized destiny no longer has any right to appear on the world stage.

Here, first of all, we should note the work of *Thornton Wilder*. Not so much because he completely clears the stage and needs no more than a couple of chairs to carry out his "experiment with life" together with the audience, but because he dispenses with the two pillars of classical drama, the "great personality", the "character", and the "significant action". *Wilder* takes *Hegel* literally when the latter says that art ends where the subject matter is "purely fortuitous and external". But contrary to *Hegel* he loves, not the idea, but the concrete individual human

[25] G. Anders, *Die Antiquiertheit des Menschen* (Munich, 1956), 217.
[26] G. Steiner, *Death of Tragedy*, 260.

being, however insignificant an example of this strange species he may be, inhabiting a star lost among millions in the universe. *Our Town* is a "very ordinary town, if you ask me", and it is immaterial whether Wilder's characters bear personal names or just typical ones ("Father", "Mother", "the organist", and so forth) or symbolic ones (Mr. and Mrs. Antrobus, that is, "Anthropus", the human being): they are all human beings, and each one is an individual, and it has become totally irrelevant to divide them into "significant" and "insignificant" people. Then there is the concrete action, the "daily round" in which very little happens, or at any rate little out of the ordinary, and then death. *Wilder* does not so much use life to illuminate death as death to illuminate life. In the third act the dead look back and see how the living spend their lives in a cloud of ignorance, blind to the depth of reality: "I never realized how troubled and how . . . how in the dark live persons are. . . ." Like *Rilke*, *Wilder* portrays the dead hovering between nostalgia and being weaned away from it, but this one moment of retrospect is sufficient for them to take in the whole dimension of reality: "I didn't realize. So all that was going on and we never noticed. . . . Oh, earth, you're too wonderful for anybody to realize you. Do any human beings ever realize life while they have it?—every, every minute?" The Stage Manager replies, "No. The saints and poets, maybe—they do some." As if with a telescopic camera, *Wilder* can view life from afar off, and again from up close, and he can symbolize the intervening space or time (in *The Skin of Our Teeth* it is the latter); but for him this extension of time never signifies an evolution. Whether it is the Ice Age, the Flood or the present, it is always the same basic tension, and this is where drama lies.

However, what will become of this modern idol, evolution? *Bertolt Brecht* takes seriously the tension between the solid weight of the individual life on the one hand and the aspiration to a redeemed humanity on the other. He does this first of all in the "only classical drama of communism to be found in all world literature, namely, *The Measures Taken*" (1930).[27] Here the

---

[27] W. H. Sokel, *Brecht gespaltene Charaktere und ihr Verhältnis zur Tragik* (1962), quoted in V. Sanders, *Tragik und Komödie*, 390. "The most important,

young comrade consents to his death at the Party's hands
because, contrary to the interests of propaganda, which called
for absolute ruthlessness in a particular operation, he continually
allowed himself to be moved to "humane" compassion, to
anger and indignation in the face of terrible individual suffering
and thus rendered himself unfit for communism's superhuman
work of salvation. *Brecht's* drama is one of absolute obedience,
and "it is interesting to know that *Lenin* learned Spanish specially
in order to read *Ignatius Loyola*, of whose writings he had a very
high opinion, in the original."[28] This tragedy succeeds (after
various preliminary attempts, like the *Didactic Play of Baden on
Consent* [1929])[29] because here the communist program is taken
seriously as the absolute horizon (like God's plan for salvation in
Christianity), and over against it there is a real, life-size human
being who has not been ideologized. The two things cannot,
however, be reconciled—like Christianity's absolute obedience
which goes to the lengths of Godforsakenness—and the young
comrade must die. He dies consenting to the program, just as
Jesus dies consenting to the "program" of his divine Father, but
the comrade's consent has to include a denial of his love for his
fellow men, a denial Jesus does not need to make.[30] For the
moment it suffices to indicate the parallels, as an example of that
welcome competition of horizons which we have proposed.
Measured against each other, both of these horizons are equally
relevant for today's drama. This is not altered by the fact that

---

though not the only, Bolshevist drama", according to Herbert Lüthy, "Vom
armen Bert Brecht" in *Der Monat* 44 (May 1952): 127. Similarly Reinhold
Grimm, "Ideologische Tragödie und Tragödie der Ideologie", in *Zeitschrift für
dt. Philologie* 78 (1959): 394–24 (quoted in Sanders, *Tragik und Komödie*, 237–78.)

[28] R. Grimm in *Tragik und Komödie*, Sanders, ed., 266, from W. Herzog,
Menschen, denen ich begegnete (Berne and Munich, 1959), 30. On this whole topic
cf. my essay, "Bert Brecht" in *Skizzen zur Theologie* III, *Spiritus Creator* (1967),
376–81.

[29] Ernst Schumacher, in *Die dramatischen Versuche Bertolt Brechts 1918–1933*
(Berlin, 1955), 320, speaks of "secularized Christian moral theology" in connection with this didactic play.

[30] From this point of view, not only is the situation of the young comrade
hopelessly tragic but so is that of the others involved, since, in obedience to the
program, they have to deny their own fellowship and intimate solidarity with
him. Thus they become fateful prototypes of that inhumanity which annihilates
human beings in the name of a program.

Brecht recognized the tragic character of *The Measures Taken*, rejected the play and subsequently attempted to avoid the inevitability of tragedy.

It is well known that, as far as the audience is concerned, the human tragedy of *Mother Courage* (1939) refused to fit into the moral Brecht wished to be drawn, that is, that the world simply must be changed and the Thirty Years' War abolished. And in *The Good Woman of Szechuan* (1938–1940) there is once again a contradiction at the very heart of the human being, which is so absolute that the good, directly helpful aspect (Shen Te) is only made possible, in continually new forms, by the presence of the wicked, heartless and calculating aspect (Shui Ta). The dialectical model is the same as in *The Measures Taken*. "Communists must hide their real 'I' and assume the mask of the ruthless, hardhearted intriguer in order to be able to carry out their wishes, just as Shen Te has to change into Shui Ta in order to get hold of the means of doing good."[31] Shen Te suffers profoundly from a schizophrenia imposed on her by life and is ashamed of whichever "I" is currently concealed. She justifies herself to herself by being harsh for her son's sake, so that he can grow up to be a hero and leader of mankind, knowing nothing of his mother's shame. The total picture she entrusts, in hope, to her son, rests on his ignorance of the real facts. What is important here is that, in unveiling this dialectic, Brecht is being neither flippant nor cynical; he is perfectly serious in struggling to find a life that is not fundamentally involved in contradiction. Again, as in *Wilder*, the dramatic dimension lies far less in the action than in the analysis of life.

Our interest in these things arises from the notion that, after Hegel, drama is bound to be destroyed, since all ideals will be absorbed into material reality and all tension lost in the "one-dimensional" world. The few examples we have chosen have already shown that this fear is groundless, however the continuing tension is interpreted—whether as a contradiction that must undermine existence itself or as a mystery that imparts meaning and inner satisfaction to what seems unimportant and even intolerable. It is enough that the horizon remains open and

---

[31] W. H. Sokel in *Tragik und Komödie*, Sanders, ed., 394.

thus leaves room for a Christian dramatic tension. We are not concerned to prove more than that.

So far (section 3.a above) we have not given a definition of what is tragic; the question of what is dramatic can likewise remain open for the present. In terms of world-view, *Brecht* and Christianity are in close competition; in both, life is seen as being full of tension, however different the two horizons may remain. Today's polemics against the middle-class, commercial theatre shows that people still expect the theatre to be a genuine laying-bare of existence. The fact that this is expected of the *theatre*, with its aspects of play and illusion, and that both *Wilder* and *Brecht*—to go no farther—use "alienation effects" (*Verfremdungseffekte*) and desacralize the theatre, manifests the theatre's intrinsic function, namely, to be a place where man can look in a mirror in order to recollect himself and remember who he is.

Functioning as a mirror, the theatre retains its ambiguity. It could emerge that existence, understood in Christian terms, cannot essentially be perfected, not just because of the world's implication in guilt, but simply by virtue of its creatureliness. In that case it would be necessary to look around for something beyond it that would bring it fulfillment. Cut loose from its origin and goal (which is "supernatural"), creaturely existence would be bound to appear tragic in its immanent structure, and the perfecting of the structure—in God's becoming man—would both set its seal on this tragic dimension and bring it to an end. *Erich Przywara*, in a perceptive analysis, has uncovered this essential relationship between the tragic and the Christian.[32] Equally, *Henri de Lubac* (*The Mystery of the Supernatural*)[33] has demonstrated the insoluble "paradox" of spiritual existence and distinguished it with great precision from contradiction and dialectic. Existence has a need to see itself mirrored (*speculari*), and this makes the theatre a legitimate instrument in the pursuit of self-knowledge and the elucidation of Being—an instrument, moreover, that points beyond itself. As a mirror it enables existence to attain ultimate (theological) understanding of itself;

[32] *Essenz- und Existenzphilosophie* (1939), reprinted in *Analogia Entis*, complete ed. (1962), esp. 231–46.
[33] 2 vols. (Einsiedeln, 1971).

but also, like a mirror, it must eventually take second place (and *Kassner* is right here) to make room for the truth, which it reflects only indirectly.

No wonder the debate between the Christian Church and the theatre has been a lively and sometimes stormy one! Before we proceed with our task of assembling the whole range of dramatic resources that will help us understand revelation, we must briefly rehearse the history of this debate between the Church and the theatre.

D. THE CHURCH AND THE THEATRE

1. *Criticism of the Theatre in the Ancient World and in Christianity*

The foregoing chapter was entitled "Objections". These objections arose in modern times, when a longstanding familiarity between Christianity and the theatre began to break up; increasingly, the two went their own ways, and it became apparent that they were perhaps fundamentally alien to each other. The aim of the present chapter is to unveil the tension between the Church and drama in the clash of its primal antagonisms. Antipathy and opposition to the theatre seem to be inherent in the Church; certain analogies may be drawn between the two, but the dissimilarity seems overwhelming. The Church Fathers and many councils were almost fanatically hostile to the theatre, and this hostility was like a dark cloud brooding over the history of the Christian stage. The struggle continued unabated right into modern times—*Bossuet* is one of the last prominent landmarks—exhibiting the whole scandalous contradiction between toleration and encouragement on the one hand and rigoristic condemnation on the other.

At a very early stage and with considerable application Christianity began to assimilate the *philosophy* of the ancient world in all its nuances; hence the question arises, was there nothing equivalent to be learned from *drama*? True, Plato had been acquainted with the loftiest masterpieces of the ancient stage and had nonetheless rejected it; he was concerned to replace its ambiguous, illusory world with the concrete state, the "imitation (*mimesis*) of the most beautiful and best life; this, in our view, is in fact the only true tragedy."[1] By the time Christianity arrived, there was little left but a noisy, popular entertainment; it was principally coarse and lewd and often cruel, so that even the pagans themselves turned away from it. All the same, at the time of Tertullian there was not only the

[1] *Nomoi* VII, 817b.

vulgar, unchaste *mimus*[2] but also the more humane comedy; tragedy still dealt with the ancient myths. *Cicero* had tried his hand at an *Electra*, an *Erigone*, a *Trojan Women*; *Julius Caesar* at an *Oedipus*; *Augustus* at an *Ajax* and an *Achilles*. But whether the passions were stirred up by nobler or more crude spectacles, whether it was artificial or real blood that flowed, the lower nature was unleashed. In the madding crowd only a stoic could remain unmoved, as *Epictetus* wished.[3] *Cicero*, *Tacitus*, *Seneca*, *Juvenal* and *Varro* complained about the disgusting aspects of the theatre; *Ovid* asked the Emperor Augustus to close these haunts of degeneracy.[4] Thus, in campaigning for a natural ethical dimension—inner peace of mind and spiritual discipline—the Christian writers are in fact continuing the expressions of protest voiced by pagans.

Of course, *Plato's* criticism of the theatre had different presuppositions from that of the Christians. But we ought not to miss the analogies. What *Plato* criticized in *Homer* and his dramatic derivatives was above all the ambiguity of the gods, which did not correspond to the "basic norms of theology".[5] The playwrights, with their ability to create illusions beyond the realm of good and evil, are led astray, along with the actors who perform their roles, into childish games (*paidia*)[6] unworthy of human beings. Genuine order in the *polis*, as well as a corresponding education (*paideia*), should be based solely on the imitation of what is immutably good and true; only in this way can man become a "divine marionette" in a new and positive sense,[7] which is "in his best interests".[8] For then he is no longer

[2] Hermann Reich, *Der Mimus* (Berlin, 1903), I, 1–2.

[3] "Frequent visits to the theatre are unnecessary. But if you happen to be there, do not show a particular interest in anyone other than yourself. In other words, let everything take place as it will; be glad at the victor's triumph, whoever he may be. In this way you will not become affected. Avoid entirely giving shouts of applause or clapping, or becoming excited. And when it is over, do not speak much about it", Epictetus, *Enchir.* 33.

[4] Texts in U. F. Stäudlin, *Geschichte der Vorstellung von der Sittlichkeit des Schauspiels* (Göttingen, 1823).

[5] *Politeia* 379cff.

[6] *Ibid.*, 602b.

[7] *Nomoi* 655d.

[8] *Ibid.*, 803d.

like the poet, a dilettante imitator[9] of the courageous earthly heroes whose praises he sings so inspiredly,[10] but receives from the gods themselves the gift of a harmonious rhythm of life. This is turn enables men to become attuned to the divine law of the cosmos, and so, in neighborly fashion, the gods themselves can join in the human dance.[11] Here *Plato* gives a decided "No" to the dubious myths of the gods and their self-transformations (first and foremost Dionysos, the god of drama). His commitment is simply to the "good" for which *Socrates* died and for which the just man should allow himself to be scourged, tortured "and, after all this ill-treatment, crucified".[12] This brings his ultimate concept of the "play" (with its whole spectrum of nuances, from the "blessed gravity" to the "marionette") mysteriously close to Christian grace and the whole tension in the life of the Christian, who, on the one hand, conducts his affairs with great seriousness and, on the other, calmly entrusts them entirely to God.

The greater the closeness, however, the more the difference becomes apparent. *Plato* can accommodate the "truth" of the quasi-historical Dionysian tragedy of gods and heroes in his ahistorical philosophy; but the latter is incapable of regenerating the stage, which goes on presenting the latest myths or occasionally mythologized history.[13] However, the biblical and Christian history of salvation was such a totally new beginning over against the mythical theatre that it was simply impossible to effect a transposition and assimilation, at least in the early stages. The mystery of God's stepping into the world had to be

---

[9] The accusation against poets (and sophist orators) in "Ion" and "Gorgias" was that they were dilettantes lacking in "technical" knowledge.

[10] Thus for Plato the ambiguity lies in the obscurity of the mythical concept of God as well as in that of the poet. To this extent his "inspiration" is incompatible with a practical-ethical attitude and ultimately leads to the catastrophic doctrines of pure power-politics (*Politeia* 1–2). Cf. Hermann Gunder, "Zum Spiel bei Platon", in *Beispiele, Festschrift für Eugen Fink zum 60. Geburtstag* (Den Haag, 1965), 188–221.

[11] *Nomoi* 653d–54a.

[12] *Politeia* 362a; cf. 612c.

[13] The titles of a number of dramas from the Roman period have come down to us, e.g., Pacuvius' *Aemilius*; Attius' *Brutus* and *Decius*; and Diomedes' *Marcellus*.

clearly distinguished from everything mythological. Only at a later stage of reflection, if at all, could this mystery be understood —primarily in its cultic side[14]—as the true drama. Later again, liturgy could once more give rise to theatre, and even later still drama's mythical themes could be seen as prefiguring and pointing toward the one true drama.

In Christianity this was a possibility right from the start. For *Plato*, the "celebration" he describes in his *Laws* is a serious "play", identical with human ethical and political existence; that is why it has left the theatre behind. No such identity can be asserted in the case of the celebration of the Christian cult. Though this celebration, for the Christian, is much more "serious" than any Greek initiation into truth, since here the death of Christ for me and for all men is realized and "proclaimed" through sacramental participation (1 Cor 11), yet the sacrament is not the whole truth of the Christian life, and the Church as represented by the clergy is not the whole truth of this Church. Priesthood and sacrament open out, inwardly, upon a larger and "truer" realm where Christ is embodied in terms of individual personal life and where the visible (clerical) Church transcends herself in the direction of the true Kingdom of God, of which she is an instrument.[15]

---

[14] As is well known, Odo Casel saw the Christian cultic mystery (*Das christliche Kultmysterium* [1932]; 4th exp. ed. [1960], quoted here) in terms of the *eidos* of the ancient mysteries, of which it formed the unique and transcending "divine crown" (77). In the *eidos* which is common to both, the divine actions (*dromena*) take precedence over the word (*legomena*). Both of these, however, are also a beholding of mysteries in "things shown" (*deiknumena*) (81); in both, the god's—God's—destiny (in which, perhaps, he suffers or is torn asunder and is subsequently healed or put together again) is made present, really yet in mystery, and this destiny is shared (perhaps through a meal) by the initiates. Just as, in the drama of the ancient world, "the gods, who were present, were the real actors" (190), "so we, as members of Christ, must make the Lord's gestures. We must be fellow actors, fellow players with him in the *mysterium*" (189). In 1918 R. Guardini had already anticipated something of Casel's ideas: cf. his *Spirit of the Liturgy*.

[15] The priestly, official side of the Church, as such, can only be portrayed indirectly on the stage, in the life of a person who "identifies" himself with his official mission (Eliot's Becket, Claudel's and Reinhold Schneider's popes, Raffalt's *Der Nachfolger*). The baroque theatre had good reasons for being reluctant to introduce the priest as a hero alongside the tragic king and the

This inner tension in Christianity between priesthood/sacrament—understood as a real "representation", effecting what it represents—and its perfected truth in concrete human life, lies at the root of all the problems involved in the Christian theatre. For on the one hand, it is logical that the liturgical (and hence clerical) side should press beyond itself in order to portray its truth, thus overflowing and creating the theatrical dimension. And on the other hand, everything "theatrical", since it is only the *visible presentation* of Christian perfection, is continually subject to self-criticism because the viewing of it is not the perfection itself. What liturgy brings forth is both more and less than itself, and this means that the theatre necessarily becomes a critique of the Church (thus it is largely anticlerical), whereas the Church must necessarily be suspicious of the theatre.

The original "No" to the theatre remains a burdensome legacy throughout Church history right into modern times; it weighs all the heavier since in part it had a theological basis (in the opposition of myth and revelation), and in part it arose out of the state of the theatre at that time, the social position of the actors, and continued the pre-Christian criticism of everything to do with the stage. We can only give a cursory look at these multi-layered historical problems, but even this will yield certain positive theological principles for the Christian theatre. This too, however, only helps us get a little nearer our central topic; for after all, what concerns us is the reverse, namely, how dramatic categories can be used to promote an understanding of revelation.

2. *The Unsolved Conflict*

a. Between Plaudit and Proscription

It may seem unfortunate that it is the rigorist *Tertullian* who begins the series of antitheatrical Church documents with his *Concerning Plays* (c. 197). Without taking any account—unlike the later puritans in Shakespeare's time—of the fundamental

---

martyr. The hiatus between office and person remains one of comedy's favorite targets, from the late medieval farces right up to Shaw, Anouilh, etc.

dramatic urge found in all peoples, he repeats the stoic objections to the arousing of the passions,[1] which indeed, in the
circus (according to *Horace*), rose to the level of "ravings" and
"madness".[2] With frightening realism he repeats and describes
the mixture of "obscenity" and cruelty; as far as he is concerned
this confirms that the theatres, dedicated as they are to Venus
and Bacchus, are inspired and maintained by demonic power.
Gladiatorial games and the dismembering of human beings by
wild animals reveal the demonic origin of the "offerings for the
dead" with their human sacrifices.[3] The mask and the buskin
are fictions insulting the Creator of Truth; to have men appearing
in women's clothes is forbidden by the law of God (Dt 22:5)[4]
Why not be satisfied with "the holy, constant, priceless dramas
of the Christians? If you want circuses, consider the way of the
world, . . . look forward to the turning point of perfection, . . .
glory in the palm of martyrdom. If the stage should attract you
on account of learning, then recall that we have enough literature,
poetry, proverbs, and enough songs too; only no fables, but
truths." The true wrestling matches are those mentioned by
Paul: "Behold, see how fornication is thrown down by chastity,
unbelief by faith, how brutality is flung from the field by
compassion. . . . And if you wish for blood, you have the

---

[1] "God has ordered that our intercourse with the Holy Spirit should be in
peace and gentleness: we should not discommode him through rage and fury,
anger and vexation (cf. Eph 4:30), since by nature he is sweet and sensitive. . . .
All plays, on the other hand, arouse strong emotions." An older, settled man
may decently enjoy a play, "yet even his spirit is not immovable; even he is not
without hidden passion in his soul" (Tertullian, *De spect.* 15). Cf. P. Wolf, *Die
Stellung der Christen zu den Schauspielen nach Tertullians Schrift De spectaculis*
(Diss. Leipzig, Vienna, 1897); A. Biglmair, *Die Beteiligung der Christen am
öffentlichen Leben in vorconstantinischer Zeit* (Munich, 1902). See similar passages:
Tatian, *Or.* 22–24; Theophilus, *Ad Autolyc.* 3, 15; Minucius Felix, *Oct.* 37, 11ff.
On the present topic see: U. F. Stäudlin, *Geshichte der Vorstellungen von der
Sittlichkeit des Schauspiels* (Göttingen, 1823); K. Hefele, *Beiträge zur Kirchen-
geschichte* (1964), I, 28ff.; Eriau, "Pourquoi les Pères de l'Église ont condamné le
théâtre de leur temps" in *Rev. des Fac. cath. de l'Ouest* (1913/14) (Paris, Champion,
1914). Joh. Stelzenberger, *Die Beziehungen der früchristlichen Sittenlehre zur Ethik
der Stoa* (Munich, 1933), 448ff.

[2] Tertullian, *De spect.* 16.

[3] *Ibid.*

[4] *Ibid.*, 12.

blood of Christ."[5] In conclusion there is the prospect of the eschatological drama, which is portrayed in lurid enough terms.[6]

Tertullian holds another strong trump card. Whereas actors were respected by the Greeks—the poets themselves often took the chief roles, and Philip and Alexander maintained actors at court—in Rome they had a low status (with the exception of the Atellana players) and, according to an old Praetorian law, were held to be below the level of citizens, dishonorable and infamous, like soldiers dismissed from the army and pimps (cf. *Digest* II, tit 2). Tertullian puts his finger on the "inconsistency": "The characters and actors of these spectacles, the charioteers, stage heroes, boxers and gladiators of which people are so fond, to whom men submit their souls and women even submit their bodies . . . are at the same time both despised and exalted; they are even condemned to infamy and denied the rights of citizens. . . . What perversity! People love them and do them harm, they dishonor them and applaud them, the artist is branded while his art is extolled!"[7]

In Tertullian's manner, *Novatian*[8] argues against those who use Scripture to justify the demonic and dissolute theatre and points Christians to the much more magnificent world theatre of creation[9] and salvation history.[10] Indeed, a few of the Fathers take up the metaphor of the drama to shed light on the christological event. Thus *Clement of Alexandria*: "Without divine providence the Lord would not have been able to complete such a gigantic task in such a short time; on account of his external appearance he was despised, but because of what he

---

[5] *Ibid.*, 23. Right into medieval times the liturgy of the Mass is represented as the true Christian drama: "Tragicus noster pugnam Christi populo christiano in theatro ecclesiae gentibus suis preasentat eique victoriam redemptionis inculcat" (Honorius of Autun, *Gemma Animae* I, c. 83 [PL 172, 570]).

[6] *De spect.* 30.

[7] *Ibid.*, 22. On the "infamy" of the players in Roman (pre- and post-Christian) law, cf. T. Marezoll, *Über die bürgerliche Ehre* (Giessen, 1824), 212ff.

[8] *De spectaculis* CSEL (Cyprian) III, 3 Hartel, 3–13.

[9] No. 9.

[10] No. 10. "Condigna fidei spectacula": the miracles of the Old and New Testaments. "Hoc est spectaculum quod videtur etiam luminibus amissis." Cf. Tertullian: "spectacula christianorum sancta, perpetua, gratuita" (*De spect.* 29).

achieved he was worshipped. . . . For neither did the message meet with unbelief when his coming was first announced, nor did he remain unknown when he adopted the human mask and clothed himself in flesh in order to perform the drama of mankind's redemption. For he was a genuine combatant (*agonistēs*), striving with his creature."[11] Or *Methodius of Olympos* lyrically affirms that, according to "the sons of the wise, our life is a festal celebration; it is as if we have come to the theatre to perform the drama of truth. . . . Those who fight against us are the demons." He is able to feel sorry for those who forsake "the theatre of truth" and no longer behold the heavenly drama.[12] But passages such as these remain in a literary context. When Clement speaks about the theatre as such, he expresses himself no differently from the other Fathers.[13] *Cyprian* repeats the arguments of Tertullian and Novatian and sets the dramas of the Christian life, which have God, Christ and the angels as spectators, against the devilish spectacles which have caused many a chaste virgin to lose her chastity before the end of the performance.[14] He refuses to countenance giving the Eucharist to theatre people.[15] *Lactantius*[16] and *Arnobius*[17] second him.

Augustine, having been once bitten, was bound to react with particular sharpness to the theatre.[18] He too recommends that actors should be excluded from baptism and the Eucharist.[19] It is forbidden to give them gifts.[20] We must inwardly overcome our sinful curiosity to see forbidden things, otherwise our whole existence will become a futile dream.[21] We should con-

---

[11] *Protreptikos* X, 110 (BVK Stählin I, 185).

[12] *Gastmahl* VIII, 1–3.

[13] *Paedagog.* III, 11.

[14] *De gratia ad Donat.* 8 (PL 4, 207ff.); numerous parallels in the notes.

[15] *Ad Eucracium*, ep. 61 (PL 4, 360ff.).

[16] *Div. Inst. lib* VI, c. 20 (PL 6, 705ff.; cf. 1074ff.).

[17] *Adv. gentes* I, 35 (PL 5, 1071ff.).

[18] *In Ps 102*, c. 13 (PL 38, 1327).

[19] *De fide et operibus* c. 18 (PL 40, 219).

[20] *In Joan. tr.* 100, c. 16 (PL 35, 1891).

[21] *De vera religione* 98 (PL 34, 165). Cf. the celebrated chap. 2 in the third book of the *Confessions*, where he refers to the illusory character of the spectator's involvement: compassion that takes pleasure in itself but must not go as far as real suffering. Here, Plato's basic view is confirmed by a personal life-experience which, while narrowing that view (for Augustine is not speaking about ancient tragedy), also deepens it (in the new, Christian awareness of life).

template the Christian dramas of our martyrs, which are much more exciting.[22] Not for nothing does Augustine often appear in medieval plays as the narrator and commentator.

The Church's *synods* had already given their verdict. Elvira (305) declared that "if actors want to become Christians, they must first give up acting." If they attempt to return to it, "they must be cast out from the Church."[23] Arles expressed itself similarly in 314.[24] The Apostolic Constitutions went into considerable detail: "Actors and actresses, charioteers, gladiators, runners, theatrical directors, Olympic competitors, players of flute, zither and lyre, and dancers—these should either abandon their occupations or be expelled from the Church; the same applies to those who are addicted to the madness of the theatre."[25] The Third Council of Carthage (397) declares[26] that an actor or dancer who has returned to his trade is not to be expelled provided he repents once more. The Fourth Council of Carthage (399) contents itself with the requirement that the newly baptized should stay away from the theatre at least for a time, and that anyone who neglects divine worship on a Sunday or feast day in order to go to the theatre should be excommunicated.[27]

H. Reich has shown that the conflict was not stirred up by the Church but by the theatre. Insofar as he was recognized as such, the Christian was the butt of jokes;[28] later, as the story of Genesius shows,[29] martyrdom was thoroughly parodied, the part of the pagan eager for salvation being played by the fool. Even prior to this, *Tertullian* writes: "We are bound to hate the pagan assemblies . . . since every day they call for us to be thrown to the lions."[30] And later, when the persecutions were a thing of the past, princes of the Church, particularly if they were involved in disagreements with one another, were obliged to

[22] *Sermo* 14, c. 3 and 17 c. 7 (Denis; Morin 57f.; 87f.).

[23] *Can.* 62.

[24] *Can.* 4.

[25] VIII, 32, 9 (Funk I, 534).

[26] *Can.* 35.

[27] *Can.* 88.

[28] H. Reich, *Der Mimus* I/1 (1903), 80–109.

[29] Besides Genesius, who is converted while acting a baptismal scene and himself becomes a martyr, there are several parallels: Reich, *Der Mimus*, 97, esp. 159.

[30] *De spect.* 27.

see themselves mimicked and laughed at on the stage. This happened to *Gregory of Nazianzen* when he was Patriarch of Constantinople, and no less to *Chrysostom*.[31]

We cannot set forth the latter's lifelong battle with the theatre or examine the writings of the other Greek Fathers.[32] More important for our purposes is Christian legislation. In the laws of the Christian Emperors the actor remained a "persona inhonesta". *Theodosius* only allowed plays on special festivals but not on Sundays.[33] "We only allow plays lest sadness result from imposing too great a restriction on them."[34] At the hour of death the actor was not to be refused the sacrament;[35] if he survived, he was not to be compelled (by theatrical directors) to take part in further plays. The decrees of *Justinian I*— whose wealthy wife *Theodora* had herself been an actress— go into even more detail. It was made easier for actresses to leave their dishonorable profession (in practice connected with prostitution), but neither Theodora nor Justinian were able to raise the status of the profession. This meant setting a seal, within Christendom itself, on that contradiction of which Tertullian had accused the pagan state, that is, of promoting an art—for enthusiasm for the theatre was particularly strong in Byzantium—whose performers were so absolutely exposed to disgrace that they had no way of acquiring an honorable reputation.[36]

---

[31] See H. Reich for the texts. Gregory refers to Paul's dictum: "We have become a new spectacle, not for angels and men like Paul, the noblest of athletes, but practically for the whole populus, continually, everywhere, on the market place and in the drinking bouts . . . and we have even arrived on the stage . . . and are made a laughingstock by the most shameless people. Nothing is as amusing to hear and see as the part of a priest in a comedy" (*2nd Oration*, 84 [PG 35, 489B]).

[32] Numerous texts in Reich, *Der Mimus*, 99–130.

[33] *Cod. Theodos.* XV, tit. 5, 5.

[34] *Ibid.*, XV, tit. 6, 2.

[35] *Ibid.*, XV, tit. 7, 1.

[36] We should note, incidentally, that the same thing applied to *dancing*. The exhaustive study by Carol Andresen, "Altchristliche Kritik am Tanz: ein Ausschnitt aus dem Kampf der alten Kirche gegen heidnische Sitte" in *ZKG* (1961), 217–62, shows that in post-Constantinian times dancing was one of those *adiaphora* ("things neither good nor bad") around which "pagan ways of life tend to crystallize" (226). There was also the connection with Judaism,

In the new empires, following the collapse of the Roman Empire, the actor continued to be outlawed. The Church assemblies of Mainz, Tours, Rheims, Chalon-sur-Saône (813) forbade bishops and other clerics to attend all plays whatsoever, upon pain of suspension; Charlemagne ratified the decree in the same year. The contradiction persisted in ever new and acute forms from the twelfth to the nineteenth century. Later, *La Bruyère*, thinking of Versailles, put it like this: "Is there anything more grotesque than a crowd of Christians of both sexes assembled on particular days in one place to applaud a troupe of players who have been excommunicated precisely because they provide this pleasure for the others, and are paid for it! It seems to me that one ought either to close the theatres or be milder in one's judgment of the actors' status."[37] In the twelfth century these "travelling people"—frequently accompanied by wandering clerics—went from village to village, castle to castle, showing their tricks and entertainments; they were treated with utter contempt by theologians, preachers and councils, citing the Church Fathers.[38] They were still refused the sacraments and told that they could not hope for eternal salvation. Clerics who did administer the sacraments to them continued to be suspended. A few theologians, including *Thomas Aquinas*, made

---

which had at all times been decidedly given to dancing and had "cultivated dancing both in its sacral form and as an art form and as folk-culture" (231). The pagan cultic dance lives on in the mystery religions; the gnostic "Acts of John" (§87–105) portray Jesus prior to his arrest as the leader of the chorus, with the disciples dancing around him and singing an "Amen" refrain in answer to his praise of the Father: here the cultic dance of late antiquity has been taken over. The Church resists assimilation of this kind with numerous synodal prohibitions (229, n. 34). The Church Fathers preach against folk-dancing at funerals (originally of Etruscan origin) as well as against the frequently wanton wedding dances; they try to replace the former with liturgical celebrations. Finally, the ever-popular ballet, which, in the form of the pantomime, had largely taken over from spoken drama, was condemned in the same terms as the latter. Professional dancers have no more rights than actors.

[37] *Les Caractères*, chap. 14.

[38] P. Browe, "Die kirchliche Stellung der Schauspieler im Mittelalter", in *Archiv für Kulturgeschichte* 18 (1928): 246–57. Browe shows among other things that, notwithstanding the precedent of the ancient councils, players in the middle ages were not regarded as excommunicated in the strict sense. But, like prostitutes, they were held to be public sinners.

allowances for them: if a person was able to ply his trade with decency, no sin was involved.[39] "Bards" who sang and declaimed the exploits of heroes and the lives of the saints were to be regarded as honorable. In the late middle ages, troupes of *jongleurs* joined together into guilds of a kind (under an overseer—*Spielvogt*) and often formed Church-based brotherhoods, in order to free themselves from "infamy". At the time of the Council of Basle individual troupes won privileges which would later be extended: they might receive the sacraments at Easter, but beforehand and afterward they had to refrain from exercising their trade for fourteen days (later five).

Gradually a normalization of the relationship between the Church and the theatre came about, but not without fierce battles and reverses. First, however, the ecclesiastical drama (followed by the secular drama) had to be totally reconstructed among the learned and the middle class—which again produced conflict with the Church, as we shall see—and in *Italy* the old *histrio* had to be resurrected in the new form of the *commedia dell'arte*, involving a mixture of the two social classes. In *England* the process was a dramatic one.[40] During the reign of Elizabeth I, protected by the nobility to whose households they belonged (without being paid), the players succeeded in asserting themselves against the united opposition of magistrates, the guilds and

---

[39] *S. Th.* IIa IIae, q 168, a 3. The preceding article discusses the necessity of recreation, amusement and humor, and the proper measure to be observed. And since "amusement is indispensable in leading a human life", and a special "*officium*" can be provided for it, "the office performed by the *jongleurs*, aiming to bring cheerfulness [*solatium*] to man, is not impermissible in itself, nor are they in the state of sin provided they keep a due balance in their performance." Consequently one can give them alms without incurring sin. Indeed, in doing so, one is paying them their due wage. Thomas restricts Augustine's words to those whose entertainment is "impermissible". In IIa IIae q 87, a 2 ad 2, the noun *histrionatus* (next to *meretricium*) must mean "procuring"; cf. Du Cange and the references in Urbain-Levesque (note 51 below), 235, note. Of course, the fact that the same word is used is highly revealing.

[40] M. C. Bradbrook, *The Rise of the Common Player: A Study of Actor and Society in Shakespeare's England* (Chatto and Windus: London, 1962); Russel Fraser, *The War against Poetry* (Princeton University Press: New Jersey, 1970), with a very extensive English bibliography; Thornton S. Graves, "Notes on Puritanism and the Stage", in *Studies in Philology* (University of North Carolina), 18 (Jan., 1921): 141–69.

ecclesiastical preachers. This took elemental strength, courage, cunning and stamina. One theatre after another was built outside the gates of London, and just as often closed for a time. In 1600 at least one actor, *Shakespeare*, was granted a coat of arms; but as the power of the theatre increased, so did the vehemently antitheatrical puritanism.[41] In his *Histriomastix* (1633), *William Prynne* produced a thousand-page *summa* of all the antitheatre passages to be found in the Church Fathers, pagan and Christian writers, councils, preachers and poets, and so forth. His book is itself in the form of a tragi-comedy, divided into acts and scenes. The year James I left London, 1642, the theatres were closed, and no plays were performed during the period of the Commonwealth. After the Restoration in 1660 the dispute went on into the following century.[42]

In *Germany*, after the Reformation's initially positive attitude to the theatre, it was primarily Calvinism and North German Lutheranism which undertook a campaign of annihilation against the stage.[43] In the Protestant towns of Switzerland they were successful, whereas in Catholic areas the Jesuit drama (the continuation of the learned, middle-class drama) was able to celebrate its triumph. The appearance of foreign companies of players (chiefly English) brought matters to a head at the end of the sixteenth century. Initially these players enjoyed protection at the courts of German princes, where they were honorably engaged, but later some of them degenerated and disintegrated. Here we have the same story as in England: proscription and

---

[41] Elbert Thompson, *The Controversy between Puritans and Stage* (New York, 1903); C. Cullen, *Puritanism and the Stage* (Royal Philos. Soc. of Glasgow, 1911/12), XLIII, 153–81; Wilson, *Cambridge History of English Literature* (1910), VII, chap. 14; William Haller, *The Rise of Puritanism* (1938; New York, 1957); P. Collison, *The Elizabethan Puritan Movement* (Berkeley and Los Angeles, 1967).

[42] Russel Fraser (*The War Against Poetry*) divides the objections to the theatre as follows: *philosophical*: drama is deception, the art of illusion, rejected equally by Platonists and the Calvinists and puritans of the later Renaissance; a *waste of time*: plays were performed in the afternoon and thus drew people away from their work; *financial*: actors, plying a trade that was not regarded as serious, earned more than workers belonging to a guild; the collection made before and after the performance was held to be begging; *religious*: the whole weight of the Church's antitheatrical tradition.

[43] Ernst Hövel, *Der Kampf der Geistlichkeit gegen das Theater im 17. Jahrhundert* (Diss. Münster, 1912).

renewed permission, inconsistently applied restrictions, ad hoc and largely obsolete arguments. Many of the official prohibitions and pulpit tirades evinced sheer jealousy of possible rivals. What *Prynne* did in England, *Schröder* did in Rostock; German pietism, headed by *Spener* and seconded by *Gottfried Arnold*, repeated the arguments of puritanism. Pastor *Anton Reiser* fought blindly and with malice against the Hamburg Opera. Actors were still being excluded from the Lord's Supper.[44] The problem of the actor's social position was still a serious one in *Goethe's Wilhelm Meister* and especially in the *Theatralische Sendung*: but here the theatre became a bridge between the middle-class world and that of the nobility. Again it was the clergy who zealously opposed the troupe's projects and whose prohibitions had to be circumvented.[45]

The position remained uncertain in the Catholic Church, and in Catholic *France* it became intolerable.[46] Italian players, subjects of the pope, seemed to be free from excommunication, even in foreign countries. Even so, many popes—Innocent XII, Clement XI, Benedict XIV, Clement XIII—sternly expressed their opposition to public performances. As late as 1702 the Archbishop of Toulouse forbade confessors, under threat of suspension, to absolve those who had attended the theatre against his prohibition. In Versailles, however, the whole problem broke out afresh in connection with *Molière's Tartuffe*, which, while it pilloried bigots, also exposed those close to the King engaged in intrigue.[47] The play was proscribed, then performed in 1664, then proscribed again. *Roullée*, of the Sorbonne, wanted to see *Molière* burn, *Boileau* defended him, as did *Chigi*, the papal legate, but the Archbishop of Paris forbade

---

[44] *Ibid.*, 101.

[45] "The hour of the performance was approaching when suddenly the disappointing news arrived that the new pastor . . . had had the play forbidden" (bk. 3, chap. 1). "The clergy grew attentive when they heard that the part of Daniel, the fourth of the main characters (in Wilhelm's tragedy *Belsazar*) was to be acted by a travelling player. They took the matter up with higher authority, and in the absence of the chief magistrate an instruction was issued to Madame de Retti not to perform the play" (bk. 3, chap. 13).

[46] Moses Barrer, *The Stage Controversy in France from Corneille to Rousseau* (New York, 1933).

[47] Paul Emard, *Le Tartuffe, sa vie, son milieu* (Paris: Libr. Droz).

the play to be either seen, produced, read or listened to, under pain of excommunication. When *Molière* lay dying, in 1673, he called for a priest; after two refused to come, a third came, but he was too late. The parish priest of Saint-Eustache refused to give him a Church burial; a petition from Molière's widow persuaded the King to order the Bishop to allow the burial; the latter gave his permission "on the condition that it take place without solemnity, in the presence of only two priests and not during the hours of daylight; and no public service is to be held, either in Saint-Eustache or anywhere else. . . ."[48] *Jean Anouilh*, in his *Mademoiselle Molière*, laid bare the poet's affairs on the public stage; and *Mikhail Bulgakov*, in the extremities of his last months, wrote a *Molière* in protest against the oppression of Stalinism; his play had to be abandoned after seven performances.

Passages from *Cyprian*, *Augustine* and the early councils were once again mercilessly applied to actors. To receive the last sacraments they had to repeat a formula, on their deathbeds, in which they renounced their occupation. This was to hold good even if they recovered. Many refused and stood by the honor of their profession, others said the words and, having recovered, no longer appeared on the stage.[49] Even in 1815, after the death of a famous actress, an incensed crowd had forcibly to exact a requiem from the Church of Saint-Roch. In 1691 the players of the Paris Comédie had addressed a petition to Innocent XII, asking him to lift the excommunication, but (and this happened to others later) the Pope referred them back to the Archbishop.[50] In 1735 Clement XII issued a brief ordering players to be admitted to communion, but in many French dioceses this fundamental reconciliation was not implemented. In 1694, in his *Maximes et réfléctions sur la comédie*, *Bossuet* pulled out all the stops of dogmatics, moral theology, Church history, scholasticism, patristics and even Plato and Aristotle to show that going to the theatre was incompatible with the Christian life.[51] His

---

[48] Albert Reyval, *L'Église, la comédie et les comédiens* (Paris: Spes, 1953), 83. Cf. Voltaire's biting remarks on the fact that the actress Adrienne Lecouvreur was refused burial: *Candide* chap. 22.

[49] Reyval, *L'Église, la comédie et les comédiens*, 98f.

[50] *Ibid.*, 100f.

[51] Urbain-Levesque, *L'Église et le Théâtre. Bossuet, Maximes et réfléxions sur la*

great ecclesiastical contemporaries, *Fénelon*, *Fléchier*, *Bourdaloue*, *Massillon* (to say nothing of the Jansenists), hardly thought and spoke differently.

Here, for the last time, the Church spoke on the basis of an unbroken, but also unreflected and uncritically accepted, tradition. Even in its origins, this tradition was a strange, timebound amalgam of Christian awareness, Hellenistic ethics and Roman social order. As we have seen throughout the whole tragic story, it was fundamentally illogical; here, as *La Bruyère* put it so cuttingly, was a Christian society promoting and admiring the work of artists whom, at the same time, it cast out from its midst.[52]

Can this dilemma be unravelled by evolution and reflection? When the Church lost her power in society, she came, whether she wished to or not, to accept the existence of the theatre; but in doing so, did she really overcome her former "complex" or merely repress it? Or does not this rivalry between the drama of the play and the drama of life, between man as "appearance" and man as "truth", perhaps express a fundamental problem? A problem that keeps emerging at ever-deeper levels and to which

---

comédie, *précédées d'une introduction historique et accompagnées de documents contemporains et de notes critiques* (Paris: Grasset, 1930). To understand Bossuet's attitude it is essential to read what the Theatine Fr. Caffaro has to say (67ff.) and Bossuet's self-defense (143ff.), even though this by no means excuses the Bishop's harshness.

[52] Bossuet sums it up like this (in Urbain-Levesque, *L'Église et le Théâtre*, chap. 11): "In ritual matters the decisions are clear, the practice is constant. Actors are refused the sacraments, in life and in death, unless they renounce their trade. They are passed over at the holy table as public sinners, and they are excluded from holy consecrations since they are dishonorable persons; and with infallible consistency they are refused a church burial." How far this practice was always carried out is another question.

Clergy continued to be forbidden to attend the theatre for a very long time. In the Synodal Statutes of the Archdiocese of Paris (1902), chap. 4, art. 224, we read: "Under pain of suspension we forbid all priests and ordained ecclesiastical persons to attend performances in public theatres, operas, balls, café-caberets and in a general any secular functions where the presence of a cleric could give rise to scandal. We regard it as unbecoming the dignity and reserve of a cleric to show himself at the circus, at public concerts and popular entertainments." The 1917 Code of Canon Law (§140) still said: "Spectaculis, choreis et pompis quae eos dedecent, vel quibus clericos interesse scandalo sit, praesertim in publicis theatris, ne intersint."

there is no final answer on earth? Is it not perhaps a *theological* problem, and did not the illogical situation result from an immature and premature attempt to answer it? Perhaps the actor actually does embody a dangerous temptation for all of us—that is, the possibility of not being ourselves, the temptation of having more than one "I". Perhaps the philosopher (*Plato*) and the Christian theologian have "projected" this possibility onto a particular profession in order to free themselves from it. For the moment we shall leave the question open and try another approach; by the middle ages, at least, theatre had once more evolved out of the Christian *mysterium*, as it had once evolved out of the myths of antiquity. To what did this lead? To a similar ambiguity?

b. From Mystery to Drama

In the West the cultic drama, the liturgy with the Eucharist at its center, unfolding through the course of the year and culminating in Holy Week[53]—which even today, in the Eastern Church, is the dramatic source of all Christian life—developed aspects of the theatre which helped to bring home the Christian reality. The clergy were divided into two alternating choirs, the plainchant texts were expanded with "tropes",[54] passages of Scripture were apportioned to different persons and made into little dramatic scenes; for example, the Marys at the tomb and the Foolish Virgins called forth the part of the spice-dealer or oil-seller. Advent (with the procession of the prophets who

---

[53] "Nos cérémonies (de la semaine sainte) sont le plus grand des spectacles et des drames" (Maurice Blondel, *Cahiers Intimes 1883–94* [Cerf, 1961], 200; Apr. 20, 1889). "Our entire Church calendar is designed to make people familiar, through dramatic, symbolic presentations and celebrations, with the few baskets of fragments which sacred history has gathered up for us, concerning that Hero who came down from heaven to earth and ascended back again, the eternal Father and Prince of Peace. These things are done as a memorial of him and as a sign of contradiction: he permits this contradiction against himself lest we grow weary and cease to have the courage to perform the 'deeds' appropriate to our following of him" (J. G. Hamann, *Konxompax*, Nadler III, 222).

[54] On the various forms of such expansion see U. Bomm, "Tropus" in LThK/2 10:375f. (with bibliography).

foretold it), Christmas and Epiphany, Passiontide and Easter were all developed in a visible manner. But the element of comedy and excitement entered in immediately: the earthy, the colorful and the comic made a space for themselves right beside the high seriousness, and both the clergy, playing their part in the sanctuary, and the spectators were amused by it; it was not long before grave admonitions were being issued.[55] The material grew and grew, the biblical episodes took on a life of their own, then came the legends of the saints; under the impetus of an inner logic and a delight in spectacles, there could be no stopping until gigantic performances were staged, lasting many days and involving hundreds of actors, illustrating the entire salvation history of creation, paradise and the Fall, right up to the Last Judgment; in the end these plays smothered in their own formlessness and died out. But this is not the place to describe them in detail. It is important to note, however, that this process became too big for the church building; the play was moved to the town square. Laypeople began to play roles; initially they were supervised by the clergy and then—in special guilds—they took over the production. Latin was replaced by the vernacular, and, unavoidably, a wealth of worldliness proliferated within the spiritual play. Even the clergy's preaching at that time employed elements of crudity, popular entertainment and tomfoolery in order to hold the listeners' attention; the spectacle lent itself even more to that kind of thing. In plays such as *The Prodigal Son*, *Joseph and Potiphar's Wife* and *The Wise and Foolish Virgins*, the "world" can claim half the scenes.

It must also be borne in mind that, in this theatrical presentation of the mystery of Christ, the real peripeteia—Christ's suffering on our behalf—could not be portrayed at all; consequently all the emphasis is on what is visible, namely defeat

---

[55] In 1244 Robert Grosseteste, chancellor of Oxford and bishop of Lincoln, tried to forbid his archdeacon and clergy from attending such plays. Earlier Gerhoh von Reichersberg spoke of monks who no longer took their meals in the refectory unless some play was taking place there (In Ps 132; PL 194, 890). According to him, the actors in the *Play of Antichrist* are doing the latter's work, to the immense scandal of the Church (*De Investigatione Antichristi*, tome I, cV, "De spectaculis theatricis in ecclesia Dei exhibitis", ed. Scheibelberger, [Lincii, 1875], 25ff.). Further examples in Hardin Craig, *English Religious Drama of the Middle Ages* (Oxford, 1955), 88–93.

(the Cross) and victory (the Resurrection). So the opponents and enemies became stylized, the devil on one side and the Jews on the other. If Christ is portrayed as the loser in the Passion play, it is followed by the *Vengeance de Notre Seigneur*, a light-hearted little history of the Jewish people in which the Victor visits just retribution and annihilates his enemies. Since the ancient world has a share in the promises—*teste David cum Sibylla*—its themes are instilled with new life, for example, the Trojan War, in the spirit of the courtly epics, although in other respects the chivalric world hardly had any influence on this entirely clerical and middle-class world of the stage.[56] Everywhere there was an admixture of the comic-grotesque, the cruelly satirical, that substratum of insanity which always comes to the surface where learning, scholasticism and incontrovertible authority pretend to truth.[57] The *Feast of Fools* was celebrated within the Church and outside her; here the Mass was parodied in all its parts, often obscenely, and the clergy, including the higher clergy, were ridiculed in all their weaknesses —political ambition, for instance. Is not every cleric, playing his sacred "role", inwardly a Tartuffe? Surely it is a work of truth and honesty to unmask him? It must suffice here to highlight a couple of instances. In the reign of Philip the Fair, a play of the Resurrection and the Last Judgment was followed by a "fox procession", a bitter satire against Boniface VIII. On Shrove Tuesday, 1511, *Gringoire*, in the presence of King Louis XII and to his approval, produced a play in which Louis appeared as

[56] It is possible that the Crusades introduced a knowledge of Byzantine Passion Plays, which were already in existence in the ninth century, into the West, thereby encouraging the development of the religious drama. The *Christos Paschon*, formerly attributed to Gregory Nazianzen (cf. the new edition by A. Tuillier in *Sources chrétiennes* 149 [1969], which attempts to reattribute it to Gregory), is dependent in terms of literary style on the tragedy of the ancient world. Thus the sorrowing Mary reflects Hecuba and Andromache; her lamentations are *a cento* from Euripides with borrowings from Aeschylus and Lycophron. In the East, too, it is possible that religious drama developed out of the liturgical hymn: M. Carpenter, "Romans and the Mystery Play of the East" (1936) Univ. of Missouri, Collection.

[57] This has been pedantically systematized by Michel Foucault *Wahnsinn und Gesellschaft: Eine Geschichte des Wahns im Zeitalter der Vernunft* (Suhrkamp, 1969). A lurid picture of the *Feast of Fools* in churches is given by a Petition of the Paris Theological Faculty requesting that it be abolished (PL 207, 1171).

"Prince of Fools" and the pope as "Mother Fool", the latter
dressed in full regalia, with his tiara, directing his prelates to
leave altar and church in order to attack the princes. Often
enough the official Church put a good face on it when presented
with the mischievous play. In the "spiritual" plays performed
by the citizenry, the world (with the whole range of worldliness)
was still at least formally within the ambit of the Church and
salvation history; thus the players could borrow the necessary
props from the sacristies. But the emergence of professional
actors in the sixteenth century awakened a more profound suspicion. The world's folly, pilloried by the Church's preaching,
was enthusiastically taken up and portrayed by the clowning
entertainers; the dialectical ideology of "folly", in humanism
(*Erasmus*) and in the Reformation, was played back and forth
between the Church and the world, Reformed and Catholic; in
the Christian sphere it became much more caustic than the
divinity-mocking comedies of the ancient world. For example,
in the play *Les Blasphémateurs* the main hero is a kind of atheistic
Don Juan who, with his women and drinking companions, is
trying to challenge God; during an orgy intended to insult God
in every imaginable way, the spirit of the Church appears with
the intention of moving the blasphemers to repentance, but it
meets with derision and is chased away; the orgy proceeds, but
then another pale spirit appears, Death, whose cold hand seizes
each one of them and hands them over to the devil. The play
continues in hell: Satan sends his henchmen into the world to
look for similar folk in taverns and brothels, to fill up his festal
table. The later *Don Giovanni* has its roots in this "religious"
play, which, in its ambivalence, contains both extremes. Should
the Church applaud (as Leo X applauded *Machiavelli's Mandragola*
and himself had it performed in Rome) or should she prohibit?
In fact, she did both by turns. The same play was permitted in
one town and forbidden in another. Things came to a head most
of all in *Spain*, Europe's classical country of the theatre. Here, in
the form of the *autos sacramentales*, the spiritual play lasted
longest and experienced the most profuse blossoming, while
wanton worldliness flourished in the comedies: the two were
united in the person of the stupendous theatrical genius, *Lope de
Vega*, who combined the life of the wildest adventurer with that

of a priest and (at times) penitent. (*Calderon* too was first a soldier, who had broken by force of arms into a nunnery whither his brother's murderer had fled; he had a natural son and was later ordained to the priesthood. Similar were *Tirso de Molina* and *Moreto*.) When *Lope* went too far with his plays, Philip II, in 1598, ordered the secular theatres in Madrid to be closed. But the poet was shrewd enough to go on offering spiritual plays, and after two years the theatres once more opened their doors. . . . How much here is worldly and how much spiritual? Both things go right through the heart of the poets, the plays and the Church they portray. When *Bossuet* launched his classical tirade against the theatre, he was parried by those who asked why such extravagantly rich prelates were fulminating against the poor people of the stage in the name of Christianity.[58] So the question arises: Has the Church ever become reconciled, inwardly, with the theatre?[59]

c. Precarious Neutrality

We can follow another line, a line reaching back into the middle ages but which only begins to thicken when the spiritual drama is fading away, namely, the learned drama. Taken up by humanism, it was mostly of a pedagogical nature from its inception. Strangely, indeed fatefully, it took up the tradition of *Plautus* and *Terence*, that is, that everyday milieu which *Hegel* held to be the end and dissolution of real drama. The only voice that comes down to us from the great silence between the fifth and twelfth centuries is that of the nun *Hrosvitha* in the tenth century, who wrote six dramatic legends in the style of Terence. There were a few attempts in the twelfth century: plays were performed by students;[60] clerics practiced their

[58] Urbain-Levesque, *L'Église et le Théâtre*, 278.

[59] P. de Parviller, "Vers la Réconciliation de l'Église et du Théâtre", *Etudes* (Jan. 20, 1931). A.-M. Carré, *L'Église s'est-elle réconciliée avec le théâtre? De Molière à Jouvet* (Cerf, 1956).

[60] E. Gilson asked why scholasticism, which after all was substantially based on Greek philosophy, was not quicker to promote Greek theatre as a Christian form. In fact, as Gilson demonstrates, the human figures seen on the grand stage of the sixteenth and seventeenth centuries are definitely in the classical mold.

Latin in writing comedies. In fifteenth-century Italy the Roman comedies were printed, explained, refashioned, performed and imitated. *Terence*, whether expurgated or not, was the pedagogue recommended by the Church: not only did he inculcate an urbane Latin (which is why *Erasmus* thought so highly of him), he also taught good manners (which did not mean morality). He embodied the practice of life as opposed to scholastic theory. He was performed by students and school-children; *Aeneas Silvius Piccolomini* recommended him and himself dramatized themes of the ancient world. For *Melanchthon* Terence was *orationis et vitae magister*;[61] *Luther* recommended the study and performance of Terence's comedies as a mirror to life,[62] which was able to keep young people away from "the unmarried state, celibacy and whoredom". Thus people attempted to create a "Terentius christianus", recasting the biblical drama into this form, which meant that the biblical figures became "moral examples" (which, according to the Bible, they are not); Joseph, Judith, Esther, and so on, became crypto-Christian heroes of virtue. *Gnaphaeus* wrote, among other things, his *Acolastus*, the story of the Prodigal Son (1529). His intention was *materiam theologicam komikos tractare*. This was a way of demonstrating both the Reformation and the Counter-Reformation teaching (the great Spaniards, Jesuit drama) in a practical and bodily manner. Indeed, praxis, the moral aspect, remained the common factor here. Consequently the plays of the sixteenth and seventeenth centuries illustrated themes from the Bible and the ancient world alternately and without any difficulty, in all camps, all countries and in the form of tragedy, comedy, drama, opera and ballet. It was secondary whether the virtue of steadfastness was demonstrated in a "stoic" hero of the ancient model or in a Christian martyr. With the printing of editions of *Seneca* and *Euripides*, the stream of subject matter and motifs began to swell; people debated the dialectic of representation and humanity, reason and passion, love and honor or political advantage, and the anthropological field of tension

---

The answer is that Aristotle only bequeathed a theoretical poetics to posterity; the plays he discusses had not yet been discovered. *Les idées et les lettres* (Vrin, 1932), 253f.

[61] *Corp. Reform.* 19:692.

[62] *Tischreden* (Table Talk) (Fördermann und Bindseil, 1848), 4:593.

expanded. In general, all this took place on the common, neutralized plane of respectable convention and Christian secularity, where good manners, edification and entertainment reciprocally stimulate one another—albeit the latter, while it may be allowed to arouse wholesome emotions, must not move people too profoundly.[63] The French Revolution interrupted this tradition of moderation by releasing a flood of rabid, antireligious and anticlerical plays, but tranquility was soon restored in the Empire; Weimar humanism, which was prolonged, watered-down, through the nineteenth century, already signaled its waning, and *Hegel* analyzed this long, tepid tradition, situating it in its context in an all-embracing history of Spirit.

Doubtless this whole epoch, whether it thrust forward from the realm of theological drama into the world of secular theatre or felt its way back from the theatre of life (*Terence*) to the Christian drama, was dominated by the tension that pulls Christian existence and the playing of roles back and forth. This was the case in *Shakespeare* no less than in *Calderon*, in *Racine* as in *Goethe* and *Grillparzer*, right up to *Hofmannsthal*. It almost does not matter whether this generalized, ethical wisdom still had a Christian face or not. The props can be Christian and even Catholic (often in *Schiller*), but what is being played is not faith but man: man in his loftiest, most enchanted moments, triumphing over others or over himself; man defeated, ultimately face to face with his limitation, death. *Everyman*, *Hecastus*, *Jedermann*, with roots in the legends of ancient India, could be played in every language, both as humanistic and as Christian drama; they could be taken to represent the Catholic "works" emphasis or (equally well) the Protestant "faith" approach. The same could be said of *Faust*. It concerns anyone who secretly longs to escape from finitude, like the old *Alexander* of the legend, and the even older *Prometheus*. Is there something distinctively Christian here, in the dramatic representation of the

---

[63] Cf. Bossuet again, in his theatrical maxims (in Urbain-Levesque, *L'Église et le Théâtre*, chap. 15): "It is wrong to accuse ancient tragedy (of frivolity); what has come down to us from the pagans of ancient times—and I blush with shame for my fellow Christians—is so far above us in earnestness and wisdom that our stage could not endure such simplicity." We are excluding, for the present, the few isolated masterpieces found in England, France and Spain.

human? Here too, ultimately, it remains an open question what significance this whole, highly intense history of the stage has for the Church and theology.

3. On the Theological Relevance of the Christian Theatre in History

Here we can only attempt a provisional answer to this bundle of questions, particularly since these problems are themselves preliminary to our actual topic. Everything said here is tentative and would require more thorough substantiation. Initially we are only concerned to establish a few points which will enable us to relativize the hiatus between Christian existence and the stage—a hiatus which lies at the root of Hegel's approach. We shall find that *Hegel* is right: the depth at which, in Christianity, the theological-dramatic plot thickens cannot be shown on the stage, nor can the decisive consequences of this event, that is, the transformation of the world's whole condition, the hidden advent of the New Aeon. In spite of this—and here we take up and expand what, at the end of our critique of Hegel, we saw to be "Catholicism going farther"—if there *is* such a thing as theo-drama (however intangible it may be at its core), and if it is fundamentally the event of God becoming man and his action on the world's behalf, there must be dramatic ways (legitimately so) of presenting it, be they ever so indirect, risky, precarious and ambiguous. And such forms of presentation, to which we now turn our attention, must yield conclusions with regard to the nature of this same theo-drama. We are faced with four elements of Christian drama, which can be distinguished historically and in terms of their content.

a. The Drama of Salvation Rendered Visible

The spiritual play which emerges from the liturgy of the middle ages[1] is initially a contemplation which renders the history of salvation visible and makes it live. We can see this from the texts

---

[1] G. Duriez, "La théologie dans le drame religieux en Allemagne du Moyen-Age", *Mémoires et travaux des facultés catholiques de Lille* (1914), 646.

of the Mass, from the wider context (the cycles of Christmas and Easter) and then from the Bible as a whole, which provides us with a key to an understanding of those episodes which continue the history of salvation (primarily the lives of the saints). This contemplation of something visibly presented to our gaze impresses on us the astonishing and paradoxical nature of this unique history that has really taken place; we are forcibly made aware of what *Kierkegaard* called "simultaneity", and on which the *Spiritual Exercises* lay such weight. To these two experiences, that is, "it is really true", and "I am there", the theatrical element adds a further, perhaps more hidden aspect: the thought that here something is being acted out for me awakens the deeper realization that everything that has taken place is "for me"; it happened on my account and so ultimately has a claim on me.

So much for the existential side. With regard to the content, "staging" the history of salvation will probably obscure certain of its aspects by moving them into the foreground, but it will also unexpectedly illuminate others, revealing their dramatic quality for the first time. Others, again, will remain unchanged in their content, unaffected by being rendered visible. We have already mentioned one example of how an aspect can be obscured: the oft-quoted disputes between the Church and the Synagogue never penetrate to the depths of the dialectic of Romans 9–11; interpreting them in the easy terms of gain and loss can only have a destructive effect on the theological issues. The Easter plays, however, are uniquely illuminating; naively portraying Christ's descent into the underworld, they mediate the awareness of an all-transforming action. Thus they continue the work of a theology that was alive in patristic preaching and in the frescoes and icons of the Eastern Church but which had been almost entirely stifled by the systematization of the scholastics.[2] It is significant that this play had been part of the Church's liturgy ever since the tenth century; from the eleventh century on it gradually became independent and was in fact the

[2] K. W. Schmidt, *Die Darstellung von Christi Höllenfahrt in den deutschen und ihnen verwandten Spielen des Mittelalters* (Marburg, 1915). J. Kroll, *Zur Geschichte des Spiels von Christi Höllenfahrt* (Vorträge der Bibl.: Warburg, Teubner, Leipzig, 1932). For editions of the many plays, with bibliography: W. Kosch, *Dt. Lit. Lex* III (1956), s.v. "Osterspiele".

fruitful seed from which sprouted the other spiritual plays. Its perspective was centered in the eucharistic mystery and at the same time in the whole drama of salvation. The consequences for theology of a genuinely dramatic grasp of the *descensus* are immeasurable; we shall continually be coming across them. It is from this center, insofar as they remain in contact with it, that the other episodes of the Old and New Testaments have their dramatic relevance; wherever they become independent units they are in danger of being merely episodic, moralistic or simply entertaining.

All the same, we can put in a word for the spiritual play which inflated itself to a portrayal of the whole history of salvation: it was a childlike way of seeing the whole ancient world (which lacked history) in historical terms; not only did it recount this history to itself in epic world chronicles like that of *Otto von Freising* or *Vincent de Beauvais*, it did this in order bodily to "be there". The aim was to make the individual's short span of life coextensive, for once, with the whole span of the life of the world.

We must mention another excerpt from the unshapely whole, namely, the Play of the Antichrist. This took shape as a legend from early times; it was developed in ample, Latin proportions in the *Tegernsee Play* (twelfth century) and was propagated in several European languages.[3] Naturally there is a danger here of naively equating the time of today with the time of the End; the danger arises through setting the play in the present or even of actually politicizing it (as occurs in the Tegernsee Play, where the "last" Emperor returns his crown and scepter to God, but they are snatched away by the Antichrist).[4] On the other hand there

[3] Text edited by Karl Schultze-Jahde in 1932. *The Play of Antichrist* from the Chester Cycle, ed. W. W. Greg (Oxford, 1935). For an early Italian play see A. D'Ancona, *Origini del teatro italiano* (1891), I, 141ff. H. Jellinghaus, "Das Spiel vom Jüngsten Gericht" in *Zft.f.dt.Philologie* 23 (1891): 426–36. K. Reuschel, *Die deutschen Weltgerichtsspiele des Mittelalters und der Reformationszeit* (Leipzig, 1906).

[4] Luther's description of the Pope as antichrist was dramatized in a very popular play by Naogeorg entitled *Pammachius* (1538). On the various "realizations" cf. H. Preuss, *Die Vorstellungen vom Antichrist im späteren Mittelalter, bei Luther und in der konfessionellen Polemik* (Diss.: Leipzig, 1906). On the genuine, current relevance of the theme cf. H. Schlier, "Der Antichrist" in *Die Zeit der Kirche* (1916), 16–29.

is explicit theological justification for making the eschatological character of "today" dramatically present—"now many antichrists have come" (1 Jn 2:18). The plays of the Last Judgment dramatize what was depicted in sculpture over the porches of the cathedrals: the gigantic process which is being realized right throughout world history in a way we cannot imagine. Indeed, drama can reveal aspects that the plastic and graphic arts cannot: what is the place of intercession in the Judgment? What will Mary achieve on my behalf with her Son? How deep go the mysteries of the "communion of saints" and the "transfer of merit"? Perhaps drama says too much about this, perhaps too little. But in any case it points to the Judgment as something that has the power to decide eternal destiny.

b. Centered on the Eucharist

Just as the plays of the middle ages take their point of departure from the celebration of the Eucharist, expanding from that center, the Spanish *autos sacramentales* take the whole panorama of salvation history and world history and lead it back to the eucharistic center. One can find fault with the literary genre as such and with the greater or lesser tastefulness of the individual production. Yet there is something astounding in the ability of these writers to take almost any subject matter—even the most worldly, for instance, Lope's drama of passion, madness and revenge *La locura por la honra*—and show it to be permeated with the eucharistic mystery; it seems to be on the borderline between theological second sight and writer's bravado. All the themes of ancient mythology are effortlessly rendered transparent to the central mystery: here Christ appears as the true Orpheus searching for Eurydice, the true Hercules, Jason, Perseus, the true Eros with his Psyche, the true god Pan, and so forth. The Old Testament prefigurations present themselves to the poet quite automatically. But, as we have said, even purely secular dramatic material is transformed into the spiritual, showing that it has an inner potential for spiritual interpretation that only needs to be actualized. On the stage, *Calderon* performs a genuine *reductio mythologiae in theologiam* that stands as an equal between *Bonaventure's* and *Schelling's* endeavor. True, many Corpus

Christi plays have no direct relation to the Eucharist and make explicit reference to it only at their conclusion, yet how magnificent this is, for example, in *The Great Theatre of the World*, where, after their lives' play is concluded, those found worthy are invited to the heavenly wedding table where chalice and host stand, and the Master of the world play says:

> Behold the wedding feast for you prepar'd,
> The Bread before which Angels bow the knee
> And anguish seizes all the Halls of Hell;
> Let him come forth now who may sit with me. . . .

Here the analogy of secular and spiritual, of the realm of nature and the realm of grace, has been made completely visible: each pole illuminates the other. Everything is founded on an unshakable faith in the Lord's eucharistic presence, which is the focus of the invisible presence of all Christian mysteries of faith.[5] And the eucharistic mystery shows its centrality by appearing as the universal consummation; temporally and objectively speaking, the interrelations of nature, of destiny, of the astronomical and historical elements of the world go beforehand; they have a certain autonomy, yet it is only poised in balance, for from the very outset they have been conceived and created with a view to this mystery. They possess a particular symbolism which, while it does yield an immanent, poetic system of relations, nonetheless remains essentially open to a superordinate meaning. When necessary, the *comedias* can be refashioned into *autos sacramentales* (but not vice versa: *gratia supponit naturam*); but in this case they must be totally melted down and recast; the floating plurality of meaning of the natural symbol must give way to the single meaning which man is both privileged and bound to take on in the light of God's Incarnation.[6] Thus at the end of the spiritual reworking of the play *Life Is a Dream*, the four elements of the world prepare the mystic meal for sinful

---

[5] Jutta Wille, *Calderons Spiel der Erlösung* (Diss. Zurich, 1932), is right at this point, although she finds this presupposition abstruse and narrowly Catholic, albeit simple and clear in itself. She is also right when she says that Calderon, particularly in his *autos*, can be effective only where his theological presupposition is affirmed by the audience.

[6] Max Kommerell, *Beiträge zu einem deutschen Calderon* (Frankfurt, 1906), esp. I, 16ff., 251ff.

and absolved man: the water of the Jordan washes him clean, the earth offers wheat and vines, air fashions the words of consecration, and fire is the event itself.[7] Here, basically, theatre is the self-actualizing analogy between creation and redemption; the analogy is discovered and beheld in the full seriousness of truth made manifest but keeps an awareness of the fluidity of meanings, an awareness that recognizes creation in its functionality (and to that extent its unreality), sees through it and allows it its limited validity.

c. Myth and Revelation

The Spanish theatre is able to deal with all historical subject matters, ecclesiastical, political and personal; but they never become real history on its symbolic stage. So over against this entire theatrical tradition another one must come into being which sets forth the sober toughness of an historical situation under Christian illumination. In principle such a form exists in the primitive martyr-play, and, whether it will or no, this play always takes place within a political framework, whether it is the Christian and the pagan cosmos, or the Holy Church and the resisting Christian state (Becket) or finally the personal struggle between Christians, where one has to stand for the values and duties of earthly Christendom and the other has to represent those of the new aeon (cf. the great dramas of *Reinhold Schneider*). In *Corneille's Polyeucte*, particularly if we see it with the eyes of *Péguy*, we have a martyr-play that implies the whole complex of problems existing between pagan civilization (where individuals may be highly civilized) and Christian resoluteness, with its culture of the heart under the influence of grace. The changing relations between the Christian and the world bring about untold and ever-new dramatic situations in which, while action occupies the foreground, the background shows a confession of faith in and through suffering. Increasingly, the direct can pass over into the indirect (*Eliot*); the boundaries between the person's own action and his allowing himself to be used can only be ascertained separately in each unique situation.

In his action, even if he is acting as a "hero" on the stage, the

---

[7] Calderon, Ed. Aguilar (1952), III, 1406.

Christian is always situated in discipleship to the Lord. More: insofar as the testimony of his Christian life is a dramatic mode of the presence of his Lord, who continues to act and suffer in his "Mystical Body", a new dramatic dimension comes into being— though it only attains fullness in the context of a Catholic concept of the Church. Here some momentous social or political situation becomes transparent: through it we discern the primal Christian drama that is played between God and the world in the central figure of Jesus Christ. We have already termed this a *postfiguration* in order to avoid the word (postchristian) "myth". Insofar as, in Christianity, the norm of Christian conduct is itself dramatic, we can glimpse from this vantage point a genuine, Christian dramatic genre which—given the right artistic *kairos*— can stand beside the classical tragedy of *Aeschylus* and *Sophocles*. As we shall show, certain of *Shakespeare's* plays attain this theological level. The connection with the primal image does not need to be made explicit, nor need the dramatist himself be aware of it: it is simply there, to the extent that the play is written from within a particular horizon of faith and consciousness. Naturally, if the work is to be objectively grasped, this horizon is just as essential as the reality of Zeus or Apollo or the Eumenides in classical tragedy. To attempt to abstract from this theological horizon and reduce it to the ordinary psychological categories of a "great character" is necessarily to misinterpret the core of the action. Both *Goethe* and *Hegel* succumbed to this in their interpretations of Hamlet.

Let no one say that after the Christ-drama everything has basically been said and shown, that drama is exhausted. No one knows all the implications of God's action which took place in Christ; the history of the Church and the world is there in order to bring them to light, not systematically, but dramatically. In the suffering of the God-man a role has been left for the believer, and evidently it is not a superfluous or dispensable one (Col 1:24); the action and Passion of Christ can rightly be termed "symbolic" (*Origen*) in view of the interpretation of this "symbol" by the body of Christ which is the Church. "Greater works than these will he do, because I go to the Father" (Jn 14:12; cf. 5:20). In this connection the question arises of the integration of Church history, and hagiology in particular, into the framework of an all-embracing theology. No doubt such a project will never be carried out except in a fragmentary way. Our approach presents no obstacle to such an attempt at an integration; the fictive works of art we have placed in the foreground here are only intended as a starting point; they are to yield a set of interpretative categories for a theodramatic theory that aims to do justice to concrete Christian existence in its personal, social and political dimensions.

d. The Christian, Ultimately the Only Partner Possible

There is one further confirmation (arising out of the very process of decline) of the interrelationship of Christianity and the dramatic dimension, or rather of the Church and drama, one that could even result in an unhoped-for rebirth. Over and above all revolutions and democratizations, the Church, both in her content and in her form, continues to represent the absoluteness of the eternal, divine plan; and this absoluteness, even where it is resisted and vehemently combated, remains the indispensable foil and counterpoint against which genuine drama can arise and catch fire. *Reinhold Schneider*—in deliberately anti-modern language—has put it this way:

> A tragedy can only take place where there are immovable laws, laws cast in bronze; . . . where there is no form, there is no necessity. . . . Thus all *Shakespeare's* royal plays end with the restitution and reconfirmation of the crown; its standing is beyond attack, whatever fortunes it may have undergone. . . . The tragic dramatist needs to show the highest degree of organizing ability, of inner order, and that means, quite simply, that he cannot be a revolutionary. Tragedy, . . . while it certainly sees revolt as an ineradicable feature of the world, does not regard it as absolute. There is no such thing as a revolutionary tragedy; the very term is a contradiction.[8]

This also applies to *Schiller* and those who followed him. We have already seen that Schiller in particular, wherever he is in revolt against "the crown" (*Don Carlos, Wallenstein, Wilhelm Tell*, not to mention *Die Räuber* and *Kabale und Liebe*), needs it as

---

[8] Reinhold Schneider, *Macht und Gnade* (Insel, 1946), 27–28.

a phantom against which the hero can try his strength. *Sartre* too, in *Le Diable et le bon Dieu*, needs such a phantom; in fact, every *homme révolté* needs it, lest his blasphemy should echo and die away in the void, merely shocking a few Christians (who have long since been written off anyway). Why does *Shaw* need to apologize in his long introductions, when he transports us to the period of Christian persecutions in *Androcles and the Lion* or presents us with a modern heroine fighting against reactionary forces in his *Saint Joan*? It is not worth going to the theatre to see a "strong character" or to be presented with a lamentable social situation that calls to be changed or, finally, to be confronted with the hopelessness and absurdity of existence or to see the audience heaped with abuse. If the theatre were played out, seeing no way back to the classical works of the stage and no way forward, *R. Schneider* would still cherish a utopian hope; let us allow him to express it in his language and categories:

> There is an essentially Christian dramatic and tragic dimension, and it is nothing other than the thousandfold and ever-inadequate reflection of the incomparable dialogue between the fettered King, who is Truth, and Pilate. The tragic explodes the boundaries of the earth. . . . For the Christian, there is both a tragedy under grace and a graceless tragedy. Tragedy under grace is what is experienced by the man who wants to do the truth and is brought down because truth cannot be done in this world; graceless tragedy is the lot of the man who does not want the truth. Hence, it is not correct to say that Christianity has abolished tragedy through its preaching of grace; at most it has abolished certain forms of tragedy. But perhaps it is only opposed to the misconception that tragedy is exclusively man's falling into the irrevocable abyss, man's *ineluctable* disintegration with the divine; for it would signify an untenable narrowing of ancient tragedy if the revolt or reversion which it portrays were thought to be *essentially immutable*. The converse is true: the ancient tragic dramatists always led us, by the power of the tragic itself, to that boundary where the tragic law no longer operates.
>
> The tragic relationship to the truth—and truth is always meant as something to be performed and can only be understood as such—is the nerve of the Christian drama. It follows from this that the drama becomes a judgment: it debouches into the Last

Day. The fire breaks out in the last act: the Judge is present, what is earthly is shattered as it meets the Truth. . . . This should make clear what the significance of drama is for our times; we can look to drama for something that no other poetic genre can supply, and there is no prospect of meeting the contemporary challenge with the means of art unless we have Christian drama. . . . But we are wrapped in such a twilight of uncertainty, so entangled in excuses, anxieties and halfheartedness—in short, we have sunk so low into the lie—that we lack most of all the tragic courage to say and do the truth. Truth does not offer protection, security or peace with the world: it calls for passionate conflict, for readiness to die, on the part of the man who is at peace in his spirit. While all the great dramatists of the Christian era were partly determined by the spirit of Christianity, we may say, perhaps, that the dramatic and tragic quality of Christian life and faith has not yet found an exhaustive expression. The fact that, at the time when the English, Spanish and French stages were at their most creative, drama (misunderstood as "theatre") was not recognized by the Church may have had much to do with this. In any case German poetry and drama developed too late. Our only hope is for an encounter between the Church and drama in which they would come to see that they have certain aims in common.[9]

Here we have arrived at the opposite pole to *Hegel's* theory of drama. We saw (above, C.2.d) that Catholicism "goes farther" than that "end" of drama indicated in *Hegel's* analysis. *Schneider* now takes this up and develops it. Without this continuance of the dramatic dimension beyond the "end" allotted to it by *Hegel*, even the post-Hegelian left's realism of world transformation—no longer on the stage, but in experienced reality—lacks a goal. Thus on the real stage of the world, too, there is an ultimate either-or, which *Schneider* clairvoyantly reveals as the alternative of tragedy under grace versus graceless tragedy: we are brought to ruin either by meaninglessness or by the God "who shatters kindly what we build and brings it down upon our heads" (*Eichendorff*). Where *Schneider*, in his historical interpretation, speaks of "the crown", we, in accord with his line of thought, can speak of the "fettered King before Pilate" as the

---

[9] Reinhold Schneider, *Rechenschaft* (Johannesverlag, 1951), 23–26.

"powerless divine power", the "mighty impotence of God" in the world. It may be that, today, the boundaries between the two forms of tragedy have become less clear: the Christian martyr is submerged in the tide of nameless martyrdoms, the voice of the Christian witness no longer penetrates the noise of the world of machines, and, to confuse the picture, many a non-Christian plays a role that is really intended for the Christian. We have come much nearer than *Calderon* or even *Shakespeare* to those hidden regions where the judgment of the world takes place. But no one, Christian or non-Christian, can live without undertaking the discernment of spirits. That is precisely why drama, as a representation of existence in its meaning (and in its *covert* meaning), is a possibility, perhaps even an urgent necessity for our age.

At the same time *Schneider* also shows the way out of the ambiguities which, historically, the stage could not shake off: when it was at its creative peak, drama was misunderstood as "theatre"—in a pejorative sense—and hence it was not acknowledged by the Church. We have to take account of man's ineradicable need to be entertained: theatre is not sinful illusion but the necessity of, and pleasure in, seeing oneself portrayed by another; in this "mask" the "person" both loses and finds himself. (Here *Hofmannsthal* has much more insight than *Schneider*.) Nor should we forget how much the scholastic drama of the Reformation and baroque eras and the drama of idealism were intended as a moral institution. *Schiller* was only bringing to fruition the *Sturm and Drang* efforts on behalf of a national stage. So too *Brecht's* "didactic plays" were explicitly intended as a school for living.

If the two things are held together, that is, the inbuilt need for play (which *Tertullian* and the puritans and pietists misinterpreted) and the serious attempt to discern spirits in the face of the veiled tragedy of existence, there need be nothing inevitable in the historical clash between Church and theatre; the stage need not necessarily profane the *mysterium*. However, our task here is not to justify the possibility of Christian theatre now and in the future but to reflect on the inner dramatic dimension of revelation which, at crucial points (C.2.d), *Hegel* failed to interpret correctly. The overwhelming weight of material reality (C.3.c) is no argument against the possibility of drama, let alone against the dramatic character of existence under revelation. But if revelation is the ultimate precondition on the basis of which existence (and its reflected image, drama) can experience genuine tragedy—and not a tragedy which dissolves in meaninglessness— the path is clear for us to get a view of the dramatic elements inherent in revelation itself.

E. THEOLOGY AND DRAMA

Looking back as a theologian at the thousands of attempts made since medieval times to present the dramatic content of Christian revelation on the stage, one cannot say that these efforts were in vain or that they produced nothing of theological consequence. On the other hand, it can be said without exaggeration that none of this has had a fruitful influence on systematic theology. No theological textbook has found it worthwhile to refer to the names of *Shakespeare* or *Calderon*. We have shown, however, that all of today's influential theological trends—aware of the inadequacies of systematics as practiced so far—converge toward a theological dramatic theory yet without being able to reach it; this is in part because they are not aware of their mutual convergence and often imagine that they can get along on their own, or in twos or threes. It is time, therefore, to attempt a synthesis: theology is pressing for it from within, and from outside—from drama—we have so much material at our disposal.

It is not a question of recasting theology into a new shape previously foreign to it. Theology itself must call for this shape; it must be something implicit within it, manifested explicitly too in many places. For theology could never be anything other than an explication of the revelation of the Old and New Covenants, their presuppositions (the created world) and purposes (its infusion with divine life). This revelation, however, in its total shape, in large-scale and in small-scale matters, is dramatic. It is the history of an initiative on God's part for his world, the history of a struggle between God and the creature over the latter's meaning and salvation. Immediately the question arises of whether the outcome of this struggle is predetermined or uncertain. Do we know how the fifth act will turn out? We are careful not to answer this question at present; it is enough to realize that it is there, for, once we have become aware of it, it will never go away: we shall encounter it everywhere. Everything depends on how it is answered, right back to the "It was very good" of the account of creation, to the problem of the "tree of the knowledge of good and evil", to the problem of the Law, which is said to be not difficult to keep (Dt 30:11ff.), and yet was promulgated to prove to man that he cannot keep it (Gal 3:19). The problem of redemption depends on it, whereby Christ has expiated all the sins of the world and yet will judge each individual according to his works; as does the problem of the "stripping of power" of all the cosmic powers which oppose God—which yet continue to dominate world history more than ever, continue to issue challenges to the Victor (Rev 9:11ff.) in spite of the fact that he has fought and won his final battle "once for all" and has "sat down at the right hand of God, then to wait . . ." (Heb 10:12f.). Theology will always have to reflect on all this, without ever coming to a finished conclusion; however much it tries to create a systematic presentation, it must leave room for this dramatic aspect and find an appropriate form of thought for it.

From the outset it has two faces: one is contemplative, turned inward to ponder what it has seen, which needs to be beheld anew each time since it exceeds the capacity of the human eye: yet such beholding is not enough, with the result that contemplation always draws the contemplative into action. This law is always at work throughout tradition, from the early Bible commentaries, via the Alexandrine, Cappadocian, Augustinian and Dionysian "mirroring" (*speculatio*), the monastic theology of the Syrian and Egyptian Fathers and through to medieval and modern times in the religious orders of East and West. Every contemplative, mystical speculation in Christianity has always had its active side, through which it participates in the Catholic struggle for the world's salvation.

Theology's other face is turned outward, in apologetics, criticism and, where necessary, polemics; it is essentially in dialogue with all those, whether near or far, who do not understand or who misinterpret what they have understood. Countless theological conversations have been going on since those of *Aristo of Pella* and *Justin* with the Jews, *Minucius Felix* with the pagans; there have been imaginary and completely real ones (like that of *Origen* with *Heracleides*); whole works (like *Origen's Contra Celsum* or *Augustine's* polemical treatises) have been written in dialogue form in answer to attacks formulated from outside. We also have examples of the dramatic monologue (*Augustine*, *Boethius*), of the imitation of the Platonic dialogue

or, in the *Symposion* of *Methodius*, of the oratorical contest.[1]
Medieval scholastic theology[2] still proceeds substantially by
way of the dialogue: the question (*quaestio*) stands in the center,
to the left are the reasons in favor of it, to the right those against;
sic et non, the answer is worked out, but even in its final form it is
flanked by the *objectiones* and *responsiones*. From such small
dramatic cells are the great organisms of the *summae* built up.
This literary genre remains intact up to the baroque period, even
if it becomes increasingly overgrown with the monologue
treatise. Indeed, from early times we find the concentrated
summary, the "traveler's guide" to the broad territory of theology—the "handbook" (*Augustine*, and then *Erasmus*, who, in
his introduction speaks in favor of a "short formula" of belief),
the *Itinerarium* (*Bonaventure*), the *Compendium* (*Thomas*); but
where the great theologians are concerned there is no danger of
this handy distillation replacing the proper and primary genre,
which is always questioning, open and searching. Nor could it
be otherwise at a time when theology and exegesis were so close
to each other (as was still the case with *Thomas*) and the interpretation of Scripture was always in touch with the drama of
revelation. But when exegesis begins to go its own way and
becomes "scientific", dogmatics increasingly becomes a "textbook", and only apologetics, placed before the other two,
retains an appearance of dialogue. Now, however, the latter, no
longer nourished by the drama of revelation, looks more like an
instruction manual for fencing or wrestling. The answers are
ready-prepared, the question is not allowed to present a real
challenge nor is the person of the questioner. Ultimately the
questioners become so insistent and their questions so clamorous
that no prefabricated answer is of any value. Then we have to
allow ourselves to be lured back by the questioners into the
original dialogue-world of revelation.[3] In the Gospels, we

---

[1] The Christian, apologetic and theological dialogues are listed and described
in *RAC* III, 945–55.

[2] M. Grabmann, *Die Geschichte der scholastischen Methode*, 2 vols (Freiburg,
1909/11).

[3] Augustine, in his *Contra epist. Manichaei*, n. 3, had proposed the following
method of disputation to his opponents: they should proceed together to adopt
the standpoint of that truth which, so far, had not been scientifically discovered,

cannot guess from the question what Christ's answer will be; almost every time the answer is so unexpected that it sounds like no answer at all. Or perhaps the questioner was asking the wrong question? All answering comes from the creative Holy Spirit. Of course, theology cannot think of competing with the word of revelation; but unless it too is inspired—in this here-and-now situation—it cannot interpret the word. The Spirit is empowered to utter a fresh and central answer in every situation: this produces not only the genuine pluriformity of theologies but at the same time their genuine unity—albeit not of the kind found in textbooks. Christ's Church is always and from the very outset the integration of these apparently irreconcilable elements.[4]

If theology, therefore, is full of dramatic tension, both in form and content, it is appropriate to turn our attention to this aspect and establish a kind of *system of dramatic categories*. Ultimately, the Catholic *"dialectic" between nature and grace* presupposes that such a system can be of use to theology:[5] a natural dramatic dimension is presupposed by, and prefaced to, the supernatural drama, which adopts it after having first clarified and transformed it and brought it to its true proportions. "Prometheus crucified" is a kind of prefiguration of the Cross of Christ, but it must be related to the latter if the ultimate meaning of this suffering is to be unveiled. This "dialectic" of nature and grace is based on the fact that man has been given freedom by his Creator and is thus equipped with a certain natural knowledge of his origin. Such knowledge can be obscured in myth, but it is always there in the background. Having

---

and should join in earnestly seeking it: "Ut autem facilius mitescaris, et non inimico animo vobisque pernicioso mihi adversemini, illud quovis iudice impetrare me a vobis oportet, ut ex utraque parte omnis arrogantia deponatur. Nemo nostrum dicat jam se invenisse veritatem; sic eam quaeramus, quasi ab utrisque nesciatur. Ita enim diligenter et concorditer quaeri poterit, si nulla temeraria praesumptione inventa et cognita esse credatur" (PL 42, 175).

[4] See also the method put forward in my book, *Convergences: To the Source of Christian Mystery* (Ignatius, 1983). In his *Paradoxes of Faith* (Ignatius, 1987), Henri de Lubac has created a methodological tool, using the concept of paradox, which embraces the dialogical dimension (*sic et non*) from the very outset without hardening it into a dialectic (which is prone to turn into identity).

[5] Cf. my book, *Karl Barth* (1962), 268ff.

given freedom to the creature, God, as Creator, is always "involved" in the world, and this means that there is always a divine-human dramatic tension. We must take notice of this in biblical revelation, for it is of theological relevance. Nothing else can be seen in this theological anteroom. It is not said that God's existence is identical with his initiative on the world's behalf, as idealism maintains, nor is it clear at this stage that the absolute source of all dramatic interplay between God and the world is the mystery of that life in God which is shared by the divine life-centers ("Persons"); this revelation—which is the final one—can only be made in connection with the unveiling of God's radical initiative on the world's behalf in the Christ-event.

But even before this final event comes to light, a play is always going on "in front of the curtain": this play is not a purely secular one and can only be played with one eye on the Absolute. Man is placed on the world stage without having been consulted; when the child learns to speak, it is being trained to perform its part: Is this role prescribed, or can it choose and fashion it itself? No one can respond to a question—a cue—without having identified himself, at least implicitly, with a role, a "prosopon", a "person". It is not the sphinx's "What is man?", but the question "Who am I?" that the actor must answer, whether he wishes to or not, either before the play begins or as it unfolds. Role/persona is a borderline concept in the dialectic of immanence and transcendence, nature and super-nature; as will emerge, it was a central concern of the ancient world (and of all Eastern civilizations and religions), and Christianity shows the direction in which the answer is to be sought. It becomes a crucial question, again, in modern socio-logy and psychology: the being or nonbeing of modern man and his society depends on the answer given. Can an answer be found in the anteroom of the "natural" relationship between Creator and creature (Absolute and relative)? Or must we step into the inner precincts of theology so that the darkness may lift, so that the actor on the world stage may know who he is—which is the first precondition for a "theatre of the world"?

We shall pursue the answer in two stages. First we shall examine what light is shed on it by the theme of the "theatre of the world" ~~form~~ *Plato* up to our own time; then, since the

from

multiplicity of ideas, mostly indirect, does not yield adequate clarity, we shall reflect upon the material directly. In this reflection, which is going on at an intense level in current anthropology, we discover the open question which human existence addresses to revelation, and hence the unmistakable point of connection between the Christian and the secular dramatic dimensions. The philosophical theatre of our time also raises this question—indeed exclusively so. Yet it cannot be answered in isolation but only in connection with the dramatic performance of existence. Thus arises our task, which is to draw an *instrumentarium*, a range of resources, from the drama of existence which can then be of service to a Christian theory of theo-drama in which the "natural" drama of existence (between the Absolute and the relative) is consummated in the "supernatural" drama between the God of Jesus Christ and mankind.

Initially, this *instrumentarium* can use the already-existing interpretation of the world as a "theatre", establishing the categories implied in it. But it will become clear that the "theatre of the world" theme ultimately reaches a level of reflection calling for special examination of the dramatic categories themselves. Only when this is done—the theatre and human existence ceaselessly and inseparably mirroring each other—can we go on to the second stage and turn specifically to the question of the role presented to us by existence, with which we shall conclude these Prolegomena.

The present work will enable us, in volume two, to embark upon Christian theo-drama and attempt to erect that framework for which, as we have indicated, the current trends in theology are calling. Two cycles of theme will emerge: on the one hand, we shall have to show the succession and interplay of dramatic aspects in the revelation-event, which is an action involving God and man, rooted in the history of creation and the world and prolonged in eschatology. In the midst of this, then, the second and final problem arises, namely, the involvement of God, who cannot lose himself in the world play and yet puts himself gravely at risk. Can we say that God has "staked his all" on this play? What is meant by "God's history", by his kenosis, by the death of the Son of God? What is the relation between the economic and the immanent Trinity in all this? And, since we

cannot avoid these ultimate questions which form the core of
theo-drama: Where is the path that leads between the twin
abysses of a systematics in which God, absolute Being, is only
the Unmoved before whom the moving world plays out its
drama, and a mythology which absorbs God into the world and
makes him to be one of the warring parties of world process?
The two extremes meet: they are both incorporated into the
gnosticism of the second century and once more in that of *Hegel*.
Will dramatic theory be able to yield a range of resources that
can avoid the dangers of gnosticism? Perhaps only at the price of
a reduced overall view, beause we are more deeply involved in
the play itself. In the end it is only by implementing this method
that we shall see what it has to offer.

II. DRAMATIC RESOURCES

A. THE IDEA OF THE "WORLD STAGE"

As it has come down to us, the idea of the "world stage"[1] is a product of the Western world, although originally it arises from an awareness of the world which is at least as Asiatic as it is European. Quite apart from the Greeks, countless other peoples have been acquainted with cultic and mythic drama: Egypt, Babylon, China, Indonesia and Japan with its Noh plays which survive to this day. But in the West we find the continual propagation of a tradition which hands on the stage image from *Weltanschauung* to *Weltanschauung*, changing, supplementing, enriching it—and sometimes also narrowing and curtailing it. This image is just as alive in today's theatre as it was in its origins. In the mythic age it is a *chiffre*, expressing in a single image what concepts could only present dialectically; in philosophy it is the one abiding metaphor, attracting to itself all the ultimate intimations concerning the meaning and structure of existence. When the ancient world's vision ebbs away, biblical religion takes up the image, to enrich it from within with a new dimension; the dramatic centuries of Christianity elaborate it in myriad ways, passing it on to idealism and finally to the modern stage, which, albeit often in unrecognizable forms, endeavors to extract the last drop of content from it.

1. *The Ancient World*

a. Mimesis

Here it all begins with the world drama on the Trojan strand, where the heroes, representatives of mankind, struggle for victory before the eyes of Zeus and the entire world of gods.

[1] Bibliography in W. Barner *Barockrhetorik* (Tübingen, 1970), esp. 42, nn. 25–29. Our project is substantially more limited than that of Margret Dietrich in her *Europäische Dramaturgie; Der Wandel ihres Menschenbildes von der Antike bis zur Goethezeit* (Sexel, Vienna-Meisenheim, 1952). She follows the leading theories of drama from Plato and Aristotle, via the Renaissance (Vives, Scaliger, Minturno, Castelvetro, Donatus) and the baroque, up to idealism; our

"Zeus never shifted his bright eyes from the scene."[2] As he looks, he ponders how he is to guide the mortals' destinies. The gods are primarily spectators, of course, but spectators who are very much involved. Many of them take an active part in the battles; all of them, and Zeus most of all, follow men's fates with their hearts in an indefinable mixture of divine superiority and compassionate concern.[3] And although this all-too-human sympathy on the part of the gods later fades away, absorbed by an abstract ideal which attributes a sublime passionlessness to them, the element of dramatic play before the eyes of the gods retains its vitality right to the end of the ancient era. It migrates via the tragedy and *Plato* to the diatribes of the stoics and cynics: the good actor, the wise man, is a sight worthy of the divine spectators. Concerning Cato's response to misfortune, *Seneca* observes: "Behold a play worthy that God, reflecting upon his creation, should watch it. . . . I cannot imagine that Jupiter should see anything more beautiful on earth."[4] We find similar expressions in *Sallust*[5] and *Epictetus*.[6] What is of interest is the hard, heroic situation: "I am not surprised that the gods occasionally feel the desire to see great men wrestling with some ill fortune." Even we human beings are excited to watch a young man fighting with a lion, although, of course, that is only mere "entertainment", of no interest to a god. "But this is a play worthy of the attention of a god who is absorbed in his work. Behold a couple worthy of him: a strong man locked in combat with an ill destiny, particularly if he has actually brought it upon himself."[7] *Paul* will have the same feeling when he sees himself and the other Apostles given the "last" and thus most difficult post, that of those condemned to death (that is, gladiators). "We have become a spectacle (*theatron*) to the world, to

---

topic is the idea of the world as stage, which we regard as offering a significant approach to the theological relevance of the theatre.

[2] Homer, *Iliad* 16, 644f. Cf. Plato, *Nomoi* 905a. In what follows I am partially indebted to an essay "Christ und Theater" that appeared in the collection, *Der Christ auf der Bühne*, eds. H. U. v. Balthasar and Manfred Züfle, Offene Wege 4–5 (Benziger, 1967), 7–31.

[3] Cf. *Herrlichkeit* III/1, 61f.

[4] Seneca, *De prov.* 2, 9.

[5] *Jugurtha* 14, 23.

[6] Epictetus, *Diss.* III, 22, 58.

[7] *De prov.* 2, 9.

angels and to men" (1 Cor 4:9), just as *Epictetus* had felt that "in all matters, but particularly in misfortune, the true philosopher is a spectacle to delight both men and gods."[8] However great the tragedy, it takes place before the face of God, even if Zeus only looks from afar at Prometheus chained to his rock, or even if Athene laughs at the horribly humiliated Aias; the hero's ethos is "to bear well (courageously) what is laid upon him".[9] In the tragedies the suffering man is lifted up like a monstrance and shown to the gods who, though invisible, are watching. And man acknowledges the necessity of this play acted before the gaze of the eternal ones; he does not seek to avoid it. *Marcus Aurelius* is well aware of this: "Drama in its earliest phase took the form of tragedy, which by its presentation of the vicissitudes of life reminds us how naturally things of that kind can happen and that, since they move us to pleasure on the stage, we have no right to be aggrieved by their occurrence on the larger stage of reality."[10]

A considerable philosophical development lies behind this utterance. The mythic sense of the world did not reflect on the distance between the divine spectator and the human actor (and *Pindar's Agone* are still very much part of that world), but in philosophy this distance is the subject of deliberate reflection and is interpreted as a distance between being and seeming (*Sein und Schein*). Thus there is a danger that the earthly events may sink to the level of a puppet play. Neither *Homer* nor the great tragic tradition was able to apply the metaphor of acting to world events. But the *Bhagavad Gita* could:

God dwells in the heart of all beings, Arjuna!
And his power of wonder moves all things—puppets in a play of
     shadows.[11]

Nor do we find the metaphor in *Heraclitus*; there is only the image of "time like a boy, playing, moving the pieces back and forth",[12] but connected with the old awareness of everything being laid bare to the eye of the Eternal: "How can a man hide

[8] *Diss*. II, 19, 25; III, 22, 59.
[9] Sophocles, *Oid. Kol.* 1694.
[10] *Meditations* (tr. M. Staniforth; Penguin, 1964), XI, 6.
[11] *The Bhagavad Gita* (tr. J. Mascaró; Penguin, 1962) 18, 61.
[12] *Diels Fr.* B 52.

from that which never goes down?"[13] Thus, for *Heraclitus*, the
two things become simply one, without any mediating link:
what, from God's point of view, is the most beautiful world
order can quite possibly be the very worst from the world's
point of view:[14] "The most beautiful world order like a pile of
refuse".[15] *Plato* introduces order into these contradictions (we
have spoken of this order earlier) by subordinating the human
politeia to a theologico-ethical norm: the divine is solely good; it
is unchanging and does not, as in the mythic drama, adopt all
kinds of masks to deceive men.[16] Man should imitate this
solely-good; he should not—as art does—take the mixed,
worldly events, composed of good and evil, and make them the
object of his imitation, in a dangerous mimesis of mimesis. This
is "playing about" (*paidia*).[17] By contrast, the ethical—which is
mimesis of the first degree—has all the seriousness of that reality
which poetry only reflects but cannot realize. "We're tragedians
ourselves, and our tragedy is the finest and best we can create."[18]
All the same, as the *Laws* (a late work) affirms, this seriousness,
compared with the one really absolute seriousness, that is, God,
is a "play" insofar as it is an imitation. Here, taking up the
metaphor of the puppet, *Plato* achieves a wonderful synthesis:
life is a play in the presence of God insofar as it is an education
according to the Muses and enters into the divine life-rhythm;
but at the same time this rhythm is a gift from God: God is the
real mover. Thus man moves in the proper order when he
allows himself to be moved as a "divine marionette" by God.
"Each of us living beings is a puppet of the gods. Whether we
have been constructed to serve as their plaything or for some
serious reason is something beyond our ken." But if the strings
are not to get tangled, they must be ruled by the delicate, golden
thread of reason, which in turn is held by the divine.[19] While we
do not know how serious the gods are about our existence, the

---

[13] *Ibid.*, 16.
[14] *Ibid.*, 102.
[15] *Ibid.*, 124.
[16] *Politeia* 379cff.
[17] *Ibid.*, 602b.
[18] *Nomoi* VII, 817b (tr. T. J. Saunders; Penguin, 1970).
[19] *Ibid.*, I, 644d–45a.

divine seriousness invests even its aspect of play and illusion with a reflection of that seriousness which is eternal. "I maintain that all men of good will should put God at the center of their thoughts; that man, as we said before, has been created as a toy for God; and that this is the great point in his favor."[20] It is not war and struggle—things we think of as serious—that are closest to the divine seriousness but "play and education", by means of which we enter into the divine dance. Philosophy, too, is "the playing of a laborious game".[21] In its totality, life is a celebration, a liturgy in the presence of God.

Can we say that the Platonic mimesis of God is the playing of an apportioned role?[22] Not in that clarity of outline which will soon appear. The pseudo-Aristotelian treatise *De mundo* goes no farther than the puppet metaphor:[23] here, God is the power which governs and animates the universe from the "summit of the world", which "needs no artificial means nor any external assistance. . . . God is like the puppet animators: by simply pulling a single string they can move the puppet's whole body— neck, hand, shoulder, eye—with aplomb." This treatise breathes a twofold spirit, both Aristotelian and stoic, and accordingly the God of which it speaks is both distant and (through that which it mediates) near at hand. In himself he is uniform, but, with "a single string", he brings forth a multiplicity of effects.[24] However, in this late, cosmic-theocentric text (first century B.C.),

[20] *Ibid.*, VII, 803c–804b.

[21] *Parmenides* 137b. On this whole topic: Hermann Gundert, "Wahrheit und Spiel bei den Griechen" in *Das Spiel, Wirklichkeit und Methode* (Freiburger Dies Universitatis) 13 (1966): 13–34, with bibliography.

[22] H. Koller, *Die Mimesis in der Antike* (1954).

[23] *De mundo* 398b (Bekker ed.; Lorimer, 1933).

[24] Full analysis by Festugière, "Le Dieu Cosmique" in *La Révélation d'Hermès trismégiste* (1949), II, 460–518, esp. 507, n. 3. Horace uses the puppet image incidentally (*Satires* II, 7, 82), but only for the sake of the simile of the "alien movement" of the wooden figure: "duceris ut nervis alienis mobile lignum". The slave, Davus, proves to his master, Horace himself, that the latter is not truly free (in the stoic sense) but the slave of his volatile passions, whereas he, Davus, is free because he is content—a remarkable anticipation of the Hegelian-Marxist master-servant dialectic. Diderot, in his *Neveu de Rameau*, will take up Horace's theme and transpose the dialogue between master and servant into the innermost level of his ego. Instead of the puppet play he will speak of the "pantomime", from which only the philosopher is "dispensed" (Billy [Pléiade,

the paradox prevents the central problem of role becoming an explicit object of study.

b. Ethics of the Stage

It is the Socratic *Bion of Borysthenes* (ca. 300–250 B.C.) who expressly introduces the concept of role, together with the idea of the "theatre of life (or of the world)". Characteristically he does so from the point of view, not of theology, but of anthropology and ethics. His discovery has come down to us through *Teles*, who shares his approach: "Just as the good actor must play well the part assigned to him by the poet, so too the good man must play the role allotted to him by the Goddess of Destiny. For, as Bion says, she too is like a poetess in that she gives men now the part of the principal actor, now that of the second; now the role of a king, now that of a beggar. Consequently, if you have been given the second role, you must not try to play the principal, otherwise you will create a fiasco."[25] We are not told here who this Goddess of Destiny is, what the relationship between role and person is, nor whether the role is an immutable fate. But the very metaphor of the actor implies a distance between the "I" and the apportioned role; it also implies that this distance creates freedom but at the same time calls for clean and decent acting. *Teles* underlines this distant, superior freedom vis-à-vis the role (and here he is doubtless reproducing *Bion's* view): "Just as the good actor plays superlatively not only the prologue but also the middle and the conclusion of the play, so the really conscientious man lives the beginning, middle and end of his life in a worthy manner. And just as I cast off a coat that has become threadbare and no longer wear it, so too, when life has become unbearable, I do not try to drag it out. I do not cling to life."[26]

Epictetus takes up the metaphor at a higher level and makes subtle distinctions: "Regard yourself as an actor in a play. The

---

1951], 471). Cf. E. R. Curtius, *European Literature and the Latin Middle Ages* (London, 1979), *excursus* XXV.

[25] Epiktet, Teles und Musonius, tr. W. Capelle in *Bibliothek der Alten Welt* (1948), 219.

[26] *Ibid.*, 224. O. Hense, *Teletis rell.* (Tübingen, 1909), further examples: CVII.

poet gives you your part and you must play it, whether it is short or long. If he wants you to play a beggar, act the part skillfully. Do the same if you are to play a cripple, a ruler or a private person. Your task is only to play well the part you have been given; the choosing of it belongs to someone else."[27] Who is this "someone else"? A fragment of the *Diatribes* tells us: "Perhaps you think that Polos (a famous actor) plays King Oedipus with a more beautiful voice or with more magic than the tramp and beggar of Colonos? Should the good man be shamed, then, by Polos? Should he not play equally well each role the Divinity allots him? Will he not rather imitate Odysseus, who shone no less in his rags than in his royal purple?"[28] Although in this picture of the world there is no mention of grace, humility or a sense of guilt, no personal immortality or any prospect of reward or punishment in a world beyond, there is a bond of mercy and gratitude between the divine Giver of roles and the human beings who play them. At the hour of death, *Epictetus* would aspire to be able to say to God: "Surely I have not overstepped your commands? Surely I have not misused the faculties you gave me? . . . Have I ever murmured against you? Have I ever complained of your ordering of events? I was sick when you so determined; so were others, too, but I willingly. I was poor when you wished, but poor with joy. . . . Now it is your wish that I leave the feast: I go, and thank you from my heart for having found me worthy to share with you in your feast, to behold your works and grasp your universe with my spirit."[29]

Here the stage metaphor is not a cliché as in the numerous popular diatribes,[30] nor is it simply an invitation to see life in terms of play and illusion, as the Egyptian *Pallada* suggests:

[27] *Handbook* 17 (Capelle 34). Pascal quotes this passage with approval (*Entretien avec M. de Saci* [Pléiade, 1936], 346).

[28] *Fragmente aus den Diatriben* II (Capelle 75).

[29] *Ibid.*, 90f.

[30] In his *Lucian und Menipp* (Teubner, 1906), R. Helm has made a great collection (pp. 43ff.) of passages by ancient authors, under four headings: the metaphor of the stage teaches men (1) that misfortune chiefly strikes the great and mighty (Epictetus, with a reference to *Diogenes* I, 24, 15, Dio Chrysostomus, Antisthenes, Aelian); (2) that each man must play his part well (Maximus of Tyrus, speaking of the philosopher, who must be able to find himself in any role; Ariston of Chios, Epictetus, Lucian); (3) that one must be able to leave the stage

All life is but a stage play; so learn how to act;
And put seriousness from you—or endure suffering.[31]

Instead, what we have is the lofty dialectic which already
enabled *Plato* to speak of a "tragedy and comedy of life".[32]
Epictetus wants life's play to be performed with deep seriousness, yet "the actors" must not think that "their masks, buskins
and garments are they themselves".[33]

Marcus Aurelius' imperial responsibilities ensure that this

---

at the right moment (Cicero, Epictetus, Marcus Aurelius, Seneca, Lucian,
Maximus of Tyrus); (4) that all outward magnificence is only superficial (Lucian
and Seneca refer to the petty fees received by the actors compared with the
wealth of the princes whose parts they play. See also the numerous passages
quoted by Helm, p. 53ff.).

See in addition the following well-known passages from Seneca: "Quomodo
fabula sic vita, non quam diu, sed quam bene acta sit, refert. Nihil ad rem
pertinet, quo loco desinas, quocumque voles, desine, tantum bonam clausulam
impone" (Ep. 77). But the stoic idea of freedom contradicts the Platonic
idea—e.g. Bion—namely, that God has given each one a role which he should
play properly from beginning to end. Seneca himself says: "hanc personam
induisti, agenda est" (*De benef*. II, 16, 2). He regards the theatre metaphor as
being the most suitable for elucidating the nature of life (Ep. 80, 7). The
appearance/reality topic is central: "Nemo ex istis, quos purpuratos vides, felix
est, non magis quam ex illis, quibus sceptrum et chlamydem in scaena fabulae
assignant: cum praesente populo elati incesserunt et cothurnati, simul exierunt,
excalceantur et ad staturam suam redeunt." This is heightened in Lucian: lofty
roles are acted on the stage, but after the performance one goes home to one's
wretched mediocrity. Elsewhere he says that the actor goes home hungry. Or
this: If an actor falls down on the stage, one can discern his head, all bloody,
behind the mask. There is a further aspect, however: the contrast between the
mask and the truth of the person: Petronius: "Vera redit facies, dum simulata
perit" (80). Similar are Lucian, Icaromenippus 29 and Themistius. All this has its
origin in the diatribe of the cynics. These moral considerations are transcended,
however, by the (Platonic) theological notion that God is the *poietes* directing the
drama of life (Epictetus, Maximus of Tyrus, Proclus, in *Tim*. 2, 305, 7ff.). But
in Menippus it is not God but Tyche who apportions the roles for the long festal
procession, and sometimes changes the costumes even during the procession
itself. God or fate? This question will continue to resound down the centuries.

[31] *Anthol. Palat.* X, 72.

[32] *Philebus* 50b. Cf. Letter 6: " The comic and the serious are brother and
sister" 323d). On the topic of comedy and seriousness in the ancient world and
Christianity see E. R. Curtius in *Roman Forschungen* 53 (1939): 1ff.; Heinrich
Weinstock, *Die Tragödie des Humanismus* (Heidelberg, 1953), 98ff.

[33] *Diatribes* I, 29, 31. Epictetus goes on to require the costumed player to
speak, so that it can be seen whether he is a real actor or a mere fool. Strip the

is no idle or self-cancelling dialectic. Like so many of his contemporary fellow Romans, he keeps his distance from the theatre as such. What is enacted there is always "the same sights", and precisely for that reason the theatre is a picture of life (VI, 46). He himself wants to be neither actor nor street-walker (V, 28a). But ultimately the stoic distance from life, the sought-for unity of alert attention and inner reserve (IV, 1), leads back to the stage metaphor: "An empty pageant; a stage play . . . puppets, jerking on their strings—that is life. In the midst of it all you must take your stand, good-temperedly and without disdain, yet always aware that a man's worth is no greater than the worth of his ambitions" (VII, 3). On the one hand, the Emperor repeats *Plato's* simile of the one, essential contact between the rational soul and God; compared with this everything else is merely "life's costume and scenery" (XII, 2), the twitching of irrational instinct (II, 2; VI, 16; VI, 28; X, 38); on the other hand, total commitment to one's fellow men (VIII, 12), who "exist for each other" (VIII, 59), forbids any form of flight from the world as cowardice (IV, 29; X, 25). For we are part of the "skein" and "web" of the "one whole" (IV, 40); our lot in society is "assigned", woven into our "particular web" (IV, 26): "Submit yourself to Clotho with good grace, and let her spin your thread out of what material she will" (IV, 34). ". . . Survey, as from some high watchtower, the things of earth; its assemblies for peace or war, its husbandry, matings and partings, births and deaths, noisy law courts, lonely wastes, alien peoples of every kind, feasting, mourning, bargaining—observing all the motley mixture and the harmonious order that is wrought out of contrariety" (VII, 48; IX, 30)—yet without behaving theatrically, particularly when death comes. (Here he takes a swipe at the Christians: death must be "a decision, not prompted by mere contumacy, as with the Christians, but formed with deliberation and gravity and, if it is to be con-vincing to others, with an absence of all heroics" [XI, 3].) One should not separate oneself from the organic whole but seek to play one's part in it (VIII, 34), or rather, since everyone has to

---

player of his costume and he remains; his speech will show who he is (42–43). Cf. *Diatr*. III, 8, 2.

play his part whether he wishes to or not, he should do so with appropriate seriousness: "All of us are working together for the same end; some of us knowingly and purposefully, others unconsciously (as Heraclitus, I think, has remarked that 'even in their sleep men are at work' and contributing their share to the cosmic process). To one man falls this share of the task, to another that; indeed, no small part is performed by that very malcontent who does all he can to hinder and undo the course of events. . . . Only, have a care that yours is not that sorry function which . . . is performed by the clown's part on the stage" (VI, 42). The stage is finite; no more than the erstwhile slave *Epictetus*, the Emperor has no belief in personal survival after death (VI, 24; VII, 50; VIII, 18). The limit is set by God, therefore we should make friends with death (IX, 3), and here and now, in finite existence, we should try to synchronize our breathing with the infinite breath of the world spirit (VIII, 54). *Marcus Aurelius* may despise the "applause of the shouting multitudes" in the theatre (VIII, 52), but he can find no other image but that of the stage to express this paradox between play and gravity, distance and commitment, as we read at the conclusion of his book:

> O man, citizenship of this great world-city has been yours. Whether for five years or fivescore, what is that to you? Whatever the law of that city decrees is fair to one and all alike. Wherein, then, is your grievance? You are not ejected from the city by any unjust judge or tyrant but by the selfsame Nature which brought you into it; just as when an actor is dismissed by the manager who engaged him. "But I have played no more than three of the five acts." Just so; in your drama of life, three acts are all the play. Its point of completeness is determined by him who formerly sanctioned your creation and today sanctions your dissolution. Neither of those decisions lies within yourself. Pass on your way, then, with a smiling face, under the smile of him who bids you go (XII, 36).

c. Metaphysics of the Role

However, this clearheaded attitude, which seeks to make friends with divinely appointed destiny and even tentatively recommends prayer in order to remain in contact with Nature's guiding (V, 7; IX, 40), has to leave one thing in the dark: the actual distribution of parts, the relationship between role and person. Only *Plato* had attempted, using the language of myth, to shed light on this mystery.[34] The concluding myth of his *Republic* sketches the basic plan of a philosophy of what, in the West, will be called "theatre of the world". Here the souls which are to enter existence make a fundamental choice; this is linked with *Plato's* teaching on rebirth (which is also the teaching of the East): those souls which come straight from "heaven" seize the outwardly most glamorous roles, "while those who came from earth had suffered themselves and seen others suffer and were not so hasty in their choice".[35] However, we can put to one side this part of the myth, which marks the introduction of the idea of karma into the Western world, and concentrate on the interplay between necessity and freedom in the spinning of the thread of life.[36] The souls which are to enter life first of all receive their destiny from the Parcae, the Daughters of Necessity. This determines the sequence in which they can seek, from among the many life patterns, that which is best suited to them; then they are given the freedom to choose one. "No guardian spirit will be allotted to you; you shall choose your own. And he on whom the lot falls first shall be the first to choose the life which then shall of necessity be his. Excellence knows no master; a man shall have more or less of her according to the value he sets on her. The fault lies, not with God, but with the soul that makes the choice."[37] These life patterns are of every conceivable kind: "For there were tyrannies among them, some life long, some falling in mid-career and ending in poverty, exile and beggary; there were lives of men famed for their good looks

---

[34] *Politeia* 614a–21a.

[35] *The Republic* 619d (tr. D. Lee; Penguin, 1955).

[36] *Ibid.*, 620e.

[37] *Ibid.*, 617d. The whole issue is rehearsed again in the "Laws", where the relationship between the free nature of the individual act (which is substantially influenced by the character, *ethos*, 862b) and responsibility for character (in the intelligible life-choice, 903d) is taken further than in the *Politeia*. It is the immanent law of correspondence between free choice and fate that enables the divine "draughts-player" (*petteutes*) to order and guide the ever-changing universe.

and strength and athletic prowess, or for their distinguished
birth and family connections, there were lives of men with none
of these claims to fame . . . wealth and poverty, health and
disease were all mixed in varying degrees in the lives to be
chosen. Then comes the moment, my dear Glaucon, when
everything is at stake." For from this variety of ethically in-
different earthly possibilities the soul must choose the one
which—according to the whole burden of the *Republic*—will
facilitate the ethically best life; it must be able, for instance, to
see "what effects, good or ill, good looks have when accompanied by poverty or wealth or by different dispositions of
character, and what again are the effects of the various blends of
birth and rank, strength and weakness, cleverness and stupidity,
and all other qualities inborn or acquired." Thus it does not
matter who chooses in what order, for the first one to choose
(who has the whole spectrum from which to choose) should be
as cautious as the last (who has to choose from what is left), for
even the latter can find a life "with which he may be well
content". To see these souls choosing their lives, the narrator
says, "was a sight to move pity and laughter and wonder"; here
again we see the influence of the idea of karma, which determines
souls to choose according to "the habits of their former life".
Yet here too freedom is involved: some allow themselves to
be determined by their habits, but others profit from their
experience; Odysseus, transfigured by suffering, is now free of
all ambition and, after a long search, chooses the life of a private
person, remote from all affairs of state—a life pattern that had
lain hidden in a corner, despised by all the others. Finally all the
souls appear, together with their chosen destinies, before the
Parcae and receive from Lachesis the particular genius which
goes with their destiny, "the guardian spirit to guide it through
life and fulfill its choice". The genius leads the soul to Clotho,
who fixes the destiny in the whirling spindle of necessity, while
Atropos "spins, making the threads of its destiny irreversible".
Thus the soul has made its fundamental choice in intelligent
freedom; once and for all it is welded to its role (however
mutable, from an empirical point of view, it may seem to be).
Henceforth its entire earthly life will be neither pure "fate" nor

pure freedom but a mixture of the two. It is *Plato's* genial hallmark that here, as elsewhere, he ascribes eternal individuality to the soul,[38] while distinguishing this individuality from the particular role adopted in each life (a role which, though it is suited to the soul, is not forced upon it but freely chosen by it). For *Plato*, this freedom, in the context of earthly existence, does not express itself so much *in opposition to* the role as *in* the role (which is guaranteed by the *daimōn* and unchanging). It all depends on how the role is executed—with a limited but real freedom—leading toward righteousness or away from it.

This is not the place to go into the very complex speculations of ancient philosophy, in the wake of *Plato*, on the vexed problem of necessity, providence and human freedom.[39] The topic once again raises its head in *Plotinus*, in magnificent and final form, in connection with the "theatre of the world".

Plotinus, in a philosophy of man's dramatic existence, unites the elements of ancient thought in a way that enables us to discern the boundaries of pre-Christian philosophizing. In the treatise on *Providence* (III, 2–3) he raises the question of "how the One distributes itself", how it is actually at war with itself in its parts, and yet this war is permeated and controlled by an all-embracing and all-infusing peace. The theatre metaphor yields a preliminary, "aesthetic answer": the constituent things must be unequal and graded if they are to form the most beautiful universe; otherwise one would have to criticize a stage play because not all its characters were heroes. A play also contains servants and people speaking boorish and vulgar

[38] *Timaeus* 41dff., Zeller; *Philosophie der Griechen* II, 1, 831f. We can leave aside the question whether Plato understands the soul's entry into corporal existence as being a primal fall (*Phaedrus* 246ff.; cf. *Phaidon* 80ff.) or not (*Timaeus*).

[39] Willy Theiler, *Tacitus und die antike Schicksalslehre*, Phyllobolia für Peter von der Mühll (Basle, 1945), reprinted in *Forschungen zum Platonismus* (Berlin, 1966), 46–103. This would be the point at which to trace the many transformations of the notion of genius in the ancient world; cf. part III below; Cicero, *De offic.* I, 114: "Suum igitur quisque noscat ingenium . . . ne scenici plus quam nos videantur habere prudentiae. Illi enim non optimas sed sibi accommodatissimas fabulas eligunt."

language, and if these inferior characters were removed it would no longer be truly beautiful, for they actually round it out.[40] Each soul, with its role, is "part of the world plan"; the fact that it is "fashioned with regard to the whole" and is incorporated in the play does not imply any diminution of its dignity: on the contrary, in this way it is "established in that place which is appropriate to its worth". Hostilities at the lower levels are simply the result of that individuation which is necessary in view of the whole and which manifests the latter's fullness: Why should animals not devour each other, since a term is set to their lives? By doing so they serve the continuance of life in its totality. "They are like an actor who is killed on the stage, changes his costume and appears again in another role." But what about the way human beings seek to destroy each other? Well, they too "show that earnest labor is only playacting"—as *Plato* knew—and "that death is nothing to be afraid of"—as the stoics insisted—and that, in dying, they are only handing back borrowed goods—as *Bion*, *Epictetus*, and *Marcus Aurelius* also said, using images from the stage. "And as for murder and violent deaths of all kinds, the capturing and plundering of towns, it must all be seen as on a stage: it is only a rearrangement of the set, a change of scene, accompanied by tears and lamentations. For in life too, with its vicissitudes, it is not the soul within but the outer shadow of the human being that sobs and moans and acts as if mad when men perform their play on that stage which is the entire earth. . . . It is idle sport [*paignia*, Plato's word]."[41] However, this harsh, aesthetic distance from the world's suffering is not *Plato's* ethos but that of the ancient world as it nears its end. By their manifold disciplines the cynics, stoics and even the Epicureans achieved a distance from even the most shattering scenes of life's drama. But can right and wrong be thus calculated out of existence as *Plotinus* seems to do? If all beings are well wrought, how then can they fail and disappoint? If they do no wrong, why are they unhappy? Can God burden a man with the role of transgression against the

---

[40] Harder (1960), V, 71. On this whole topic see Max Wundt, in *Plotinus* (Leipzig, 1919), 28ff. "Plotinus and the cynic-stoic diatribe".

[41] *Ibid.*, 79–81.

Divinity? "That would be like a playwright bringing an actor on stage to scold and revile the playwright himself."

Can *Plotinus* solve the questions he raises? Any attempt on his part will lie within the broad total framework he has sketched. Although the spirit of the totality "is hostile to itself in its partial manifestations, it is equally one with and in friendship with itself, just as the plan of a play is a dramatic unity while at the same time it contains many conflicts. For the drama holds the conflicting elements together in an articulated whole", just as music integrates "the clashing sounds" into a higher harmony. Within the total context of his dance, a dancer can adopt now a noble posture, now an ignoble one, "and such juxtaposition is right from an artistic point of view".[42] However, this does not get us beyond the aesthetic categories. What if the universal spirit which allots the roles were not, in fact, anything other than the individual spirits in the play? What if the assigning of places from above were *the same thing* as the individual soul's striving for a particular place? *Plotinus* has already said that "the souls too are, as it were, parts of the world plan";[43] initially, therefore, a distinction has to be introduced, as in the case of the stage play: "In some things the playwright commands the actors to act in a certain way, whereas in others he only uses their given characteristics. For the playwright does not himself create the principal, second and third actors, and so on; he only allots an appropriate speech to each one and shows him his place. Similarly, each human being has an appropriate place, one for good and another for evil; thus they both take the place they themselves have chosen."[44] "So they recite and act their parts, the one the infamous words and deeds of wicked men, the other the reverse, for prior to the performance the actors were of this kind; they bring their personal natures to the play."[45]

Thus, as there is a distinction in the drama between the poet's text and the actor's good or poor rendering of it, so there is a

[42] *Ibid.*, 87.

[43] *Ibid.*, 73.

[44] Harder: "The notion that personal choice is crucial, or at least has an effect, is a somewhat unprepared and Platonic idea at this point" (V, 356n.).

[45] *Ibid.*, 87–89.

distinction in the world drama between the destiny (*tychai*) assigned to the individual soul by the Creator-Poet (*poietēs*) and the way the soul "brings itself into harmony with it and enters into the action of the play". If the soul acts well, it simply accords with the overall plan; if it acts poorly, "it is dismissed by the poet and exposed to the ridicule it deserves" (as *Bion* had said), and—as we must interpret *Plotinus'* ideas here—this "punishment" is a restoring of balance within the overall plan, preserving its harmony. Here *Plotinus* is in fact only emphasizing *Plato's* notions (particularly adumbrated in the *Laws*) of the unity between the guiding divinity (and the play directed by it) and the individual players; for each of them is "created for the sake of the whole, not the whole for the sake of the part".[46] He also holds on to the Platonic idea of the intelligible prior decision; from the outset there is a reciprocal influence between two things: on the one hand, the constitution of the soul, which can freely[47] move away, farther or less far, from its origin and involve itself in matter and, on the other hand, the role allotted to it.[48]

Here we can fix the position of ancient metaphysics, located between the still untroubled ethics of the earlier *Diatribes* (which simply assert a certain freedom vis-à-vis the appointed role) and the later Christian theology, which will have to reconsider the problem of the role "woven" for the individual. It is characteristic that *Plotinus* (contrary to the later Christian thinkers) explicitly refuses to allow room for improvisation in the play: "No actor is to be brought on stage who recites any text but that of the poet. This would imply that the play were incomplete, the actors putting in what was lacking because the poet had left blank passages here and there. Such actors would be not simply actors but a part of the poet. (In any case he would already know what they would add to his script and thus be able to tie together, in a meaningful way, the play's subsequent action.)"[49] *Plotinus* speaks very cautiously here; in referring to this hypothetical adlibbing he seems to leave the way open for the concept

[46] *Nomoi* 903cd.
[47] Cf. *Enn.* III, 3, 4.
[48] Harder V, 91.
[49] *Ibid.*, 93.

of a (dramaturgic) freedom on God's part that can embrace creaturely freedoms. In his view, however, freedom can only be envisaged as a declension in the direction of matter; it is unthinkable as something ascending, as a counterpart to the Divine One.

2. *Christianity*

a. Athlete and Circus (Early Period)

If we wish to trace Christianity's entirely different attitude to the theatre image, we shall find it linked, not with the realm of Platonist metaphysics, but, on the one hand, with the privatizing of the idea of the "role" in the popular diatribe and, on the other, with that degeneration of the theatre into the circus which took place in late antiquity. These two factors hang together in pre-Christian times, for initially "theatre" does not mean the serious stage play with its own integrity but the entertaining of spectators (recalling what we have already said about the deity as spectator);[1] furthermore, the individual performer—be he athlete or gladiator, and so on—has to prepare and train himself all the more earnestly.[2] Strangely enough, this resulting tension between enjoyment on the one hand and grim seriousness on the other, in a fight for life and death that may involve torture, opens the way to the topic of "theatre" in the Bible.

Thus we find *Job* with his torments under God's impenetrable gaze: Does God enjoy the spectacle? God watches his misfortune (7:16–20; 10:20; 14:3), just as elsewhere he, the all-seeing (Ps 139:16; Jer 32:19), observes the punished Israelites: "I will set my eyes upon them for evil and not for good" (Amos 9:4). At

[1] Cf. Seneca, *De prov.* 2, 9–11, 12; Cicero, *Tusc.* 1, 45 (the delight of observing the earth from heaven). Further passages in Festugière, *Le Dieu cosmique*, 441–59. The roots are naturally there in Plato. Festugière, *Contemplation et vie contemplative selon Platon* 2d ed. (1950), 210ff.

[2] On these pagan parallels to the biblical images of the athlete and the stage: A. Bonhöffer, *Epictet und das Neue Testament* (Giessen, 1911); P. Wendland, *Die urchristlichen Literaturformen* (2, 31912), 357; M. Dibelius, *Die Geisterwelt im Glauben des Paulus* (1909), 28; A. Schweitzer, *Die Mystik des hl. Paulus* (Tübingen, 1930), 149.

the conclusion of the Book of *Isaiah* there is the spectacle, outside the gates of the eschatological city, of those who rebelled against God, now thrown into Gehenna for all eternity. The Hebrew reads: "And they shall be an abhorrence to all flesh" (RSV); the LXX: "And they shall be a spectacle for all flesh"; the Vulgate: "And all flesh will be satisfied with the spectacle of them." Again and again in late Jewish literature we read of the joy of the redeemed over the torments of the damned, whether at the more refined level (joy over the triumph of God's righteousness[3] or at the cruder level (the damned form a spectacle to delight the righteous).[4] This is explicit in the image of the arena in Enoch 9–12: in spite of intercession on the part of the mighty of this world, the Son of Man, as Judge, hands sinners over to the angels of punishment: "They will provide a spectacle for the righteous and his chosen ones; the latter will rejoice over them because the anger of the Lord of spirits rests upon them." This theme occurs throughout the Fathers right up to *Gregory the Great*: "The bliss of the blessed is not diminished by the sight of the torments of the damned. . . . They will come forth—not to a place, but in the spirit—to watch the torments of the godless; nor will this sight give them pain, but they will be full of joy, giving thanks that they have been spared the unspeakable misery of the wicked which they see before them" (Hom. In Evang. lib II, h 40:2, 7, 8). This text finds its way into the *Sentences* of *Peter Lombard* (lib 4, dist 50) and the commentaries of the great scholastics (*Bonaventure*, Quar. IV, 1049; *Thomas*, In Sent. ad loc. q 2, a 3, q 12; Suppl. 97,3).

However, this eschatological situation is only the reversal of that found on earth: here the righteous, either as individuals or as part of a community, are exposed to the gaze of the spectators, who enjoy the tragedy as if it were a comedy. The Jewish pogroms in Alexandria provide *Philo* with plenty of opportunity to use the metaphor of the theatre in this very tension between comedy and martyrdom (Flacc. 72), between the cheers of a

---

[3] Apoc. Abr. 31; Enoch 90, 18; 56, 8; 94, 10; Targ. Jes. 33, 17; 66, 24; Ps 49, 11; Book of Elijah 8, 6.

[4] Enoch 27, 3f.; Ezra 7, 93; cf. Enoch 5, 6. Text in Paul Volz, *Die Eschatologie der jüdischen Gemeinde im neutestamentlichen Zeitalter* 2d ed. (1934), 406.

boisterous audience and the bodily and spiritual torment of the victims (Leg Gaj 368). In the *Third Book of Maccabees* the entire Jewish population of the city is locked into the great stadium of Schedia, near Alexandria, to be trampled to death by elephants. The stadium "was huge and very suited to the purpose of making a spectacle of them" (3 Macc 4:11); the calamity is only avoided by miraculous intervention. The *Fourth Book of Maccabees*, with its lengthy praise of the seven martyr brothers and their mother, remains within the categories of ancient rhetoric when it says: "The tyrant was their opponent, the world and human institutions were the spectators, but the victor was the fear of God, which set the laurel on the heads of its warriors" (17:14–15).

In literary terms it is only a step from the Jewish "theatre" to the Christian, but theologically the step is a big one. Now the victims are not simply exposed to danger and death "for God's sake"; they undergo these things as followers of Jesus Christ and hence "with God". For now "the heavenly Word, the true contestant", has stepped onto "the stage of the whole world" to "receive the victor's wreath" (*Clement of Alexandria*)[5] Now it is no longer a question of the "true philosopher who offers a spectacle, particularly in misfortune, to delight both men and gods" (*Epictetus*),[6] but of the tension between comedy and tragedy, expressed in the decadent Roman circus but also in the rejoicing at the torment of the godless as found in late Judaism.

Paul (who calls his fellow Apostles "fellow players") bitterly compares his suffering-with-Christ with the comfortable spiritual well-being of the community: "Already you are filled! Already you have become rich! Without us you have become kings [in the Kingdom of God]! . . . We are fools for Christ's sake, but you are wise in Christ. We are weak, but you are strong. You are held in honor, but we in disrepute" (1 Cor 4:8, 10). This is biting sarcasm but at the same time an objective description of reality in the Church: the community allows its "father" (4:15) to suffer for it, ex officio; his suffering is on their behalf and

[5] *Exhortation to the Gentiles* I, 2, 3 BKV (1934), 73.
[6] *Diatr.* II, 19, 25; III, 22, 59.

overflows to the community. All the same, how dangerous it is to sit in the auditorium and receive so passively what is being won by someone else's suffering!

In the *Letter to the Hebrews*, therefore, the entire community is brought on stage as well. Here again the context is serious and admonitory, for the picture that is described already belongs to the past: "But recall the former days when, after you were enlightened [baptism], you endured a hard struggle with sufferings, sometimes being publicly exposed [*theatrizomenoi*] to abuse and affliction, and sometimes being partners with those so treated. For you had compassion on the prisoners, and you joyfully accepted the plundering of your property . . ." (Heb 10:32–34). The rare Greek verb here means "being publicly exhibited and exposed to the laughter of a (cruel) mob"—what *Bertolt Brecht* called the *Gestus des Zeigens*. *Thomas Aquinas* comments: "There is nothing evil in people laughing at a clown, even if the laughter is excessive; it is a serious matter, however, if a wise man is the butt of laughter. But it is exceedingly grave if, in addition, someone torments and mocks him. Thus we see the depth of their suffering: they were made a spectacle, and no one had compassion on them but rather took pleasure, along with the tormentor, in their torturing."[7] Here the community is being reminded of its solidarity; it seems almost immaterial whether those addressed are themselves martyrs or shared the martyrs' fate in their hearts and by giving aid: all are involved in the fate of those who suffered. The author may have been thinking of the persecution invented by the Emperor to entertain the populace, in which Christians were burned as torches (*Tacitus*, Ann. 15,14). It is not crucial to our argument here.

The image of the athlete in the arena is used frequently and as a matter of course.[8] On one occasion (1 Cor 9:24–27), referring to *Paul* and the community, it is developed more fully; here attention is focused exclusively on the gravity of the issue and the exertion that is necessary, without adverting to the audience at all. Everyone (cf. the *Diatribes*) is aware of the public character of the race or wrestling match and of the victor's wreath. The

---

[7] Commenting on this passage in Hebrews.

[8] Gal 2:2; 5:7; Rom 9:16; Phil 2:16; 3:13–14; 2 Tim 2:5; 4:7–8; Heb 12:1; Jas 1:12; 1 Clem 5:1; 7:1; etc.

dimension is theologically present in the entire New Testament. It is all "a spectacle to the world, to angels and to men" (1 Cor 4:9); and not only do the angels "long to look" at the spectacle of Christ's suffering and glory: men too will experience its public nature and will not be able to overlook it (Mt 10:27; Jn 18:20; Acts 4:20; Rom 10:18).

All this makes it clear how the motif of the "theatre of the world" could be used fairly casually throughout the course of Christian reflection without attaining particular intensity. But it also explains how, on occasion, when the theatrical aspect (and its inner, dramatic dimension) came to the fore, the metaphor could acquire a new depth and theological luminosity. Since the "circus" image of late antiquity kept in touch, through the stoic diatribe, with the earlier world of the theatre's greatness, the various layers of pre-Christian theatre could easily be rendered transparent, enabling the Christian reality to shine through.

b. Salvation History and Futility
(from Augustine to Calderon)

During that long period when the Church was divorced from the stage, the "theatre of the world" remained cryptic. Theatre signified a paganism that had slipped into the demonic; for Augustine it was even an anti-Church.[1] From time to time we hear the sound of motifs from antiquity: the image of the puppet

---

[1] For Augustine, in the final analysis, the theatre is an anti-Church: *"currunt illi ad theatrum, vos ad ecclesiam"* (*Sermo* 198, 2 [PL 38, 1025]). However, the two cities, the City of God and that of the world, are intertwined here on earth; as a result there are people who "in part join with God's enemies in filling the theatre and in part join with us in filling the church" (*City of God*, bk. 1, chap. 34; PL 41, 46). But the time of the "religion of the theatre" (bk. 6, chap. 5; PL 41, 182), i.e., the time of myths, is past (cf. bk. 4, chap. 10; PL 41, 121). The "theatre mob" is not summoned to the Church's celebrations (*Sermo* 351, 4; PL 39, 1600). People complain that culture fades with the advent of Christianity; for instance "because in practically every town the theatres disappear, these dens of vice which are a public profession of all that is scandalous" (*De Cons. Evang.* 32, 51; PL 34, 1068). "Empty spectacle, the manifold indecency of the theatre, the inanity of the circus, the cruelty of the amphitheatre . . . disputes about an actor, a pantomime player, a charioteer or a baiter of animals"—all this is the cult of demons (*Sermo* 198, 3; PL 38, 1026). On the opposition of the earthly theatre and the Christian struggle see Pseudo-Augustine, *De Symbolo* 5 (PL 40, 639).

theatre, illustrating the world's futility,[2] the image of the world
as a stage on which nothing is lasting,[3] the image of the world as
"God's plaything",[4] which, however—significantly—*Maximus
the Confessor* employs in the service of a theology of history: just
as we occupy children with nuts and flowers and pretty clothes,
whereas later, when they have grown somewhat, we accustom
them to more serious games (for example the study of literature)
until they reach a maturity of understanding, so God educates us
first of all using the picture book of nature; then, when we are
older, he uses the play of Holy Scripture to lead us to true
insight into the Divine.[5] And *Clement of Alexandria*, in an echo
of stoicism, says that the truly wise man "faultlessly plays the
role God has given him in the drama of life; for he knows what
he has to do and to suffer."[6]

There is an ironic passage in *Augustine* where he compares life
to a *mimus*,[7] but the stage metaphor remained foreign to him: he
was opposed to the whole business of theatre. He saw the

[2] Louis Lallemant, in his *Doctrine Spirituelle* V2, c2, a 2, 3, adduces a similar
passage from the sermon paraphrase of Gregory Thaumaturgus, which, however, is not to be found in Billius' edition (PG 10, 988ff.).

[3] Boethius, *Consol.* II, 3. The verses import human life's transitoriness into
the (thus imperilled) form of the universe. Cf. the *Song of Fortune* II, 1. John
Chrysostom employs the image of role and actor to distinguish a person's
apparent value from his true value: *De Lazaro* II, 3, VI, 5 (PG 48, 986, 1034–35).

[4] *Ambig.* PG 91, 1412B (*paignion Theou*, taking up an expression of Gregory
Nazianzen, *Carmina* I, 2, 2, 589f. (PG 37, 624A) and *Or.* VII, 19 (PG 35,
777CD). The play-aspect is interpreted (in a linking of Paul and Dionysius) as
"the folly of God" because of "the superabundant greatness of his wisdom"
(1409B). This folly, this "playing" on God's part, is ultimately his incarnation
(1409CD).

[5] *Ambig.* PG 91, 1413CD. This does not actually refer to the dramatic, but to
the symbolic, the aspect of transparence, which comes from the eternal world
and returns thither: "For this life, compared to the life which is to come, the
divine, true, and archetypal life, is only a child's game" (1416C). Maximus turns
the image of the divine play this way and that, interpreting it in various ways;
there is the aspect of play in God himself (in his "ecstasy" vis-à-vis creation), in
the various levels of the world (these are Evagrius Ponticus' three levels of
contemplation, which will recur in Calderon's Great Theater of the World as the
law of nature, Scripture, and grace); and there is the play aspect of the transitory
world as a whole.

[6] *Strom.* VII, 11, 65 (GCS III, 47, l.7–9).

[7] *Enarr.* in Ps 127:15 (PL 36,1686), possibly a reference to Horace, *Satires* I, 1,

struggle between the Church and the theatre as an illustration of the great conflict between the two principles of world history, that is, the City of God and the secular state[8]—principles that are intertwined and often hardly distinguishable. For *Augustine* there are "two ways of love", one open to God and the community and the other closed in on itself ("world"); for him, these two interpretations of life, competing for the ultimate horizon, constitute the dramatic tension of both personal life and life in community.[9] How can one know whether one belongs to the City of God or not? "Every state in the Church has its actors; I do not say that all are acting, but all states of life contain people who are acting a part", yet who will accuse everyone of wearing a mask? "You wretch, why do you keep silent about the good? You are quick to accuse those you could not bear, but you fail to mention those who put up with you, you wretch."[10] It is understandable therefore, that when the theme of the "theatre of the world" appeared anew in the sixteenth century, it could quote *Augustine* as its patron. *Otto von Freising's Chronik oder Geschichte der beiden Civitates* forms a transition here. In his preface addressed to the Emperor Frederick he says he wrote it "in bitterness of soul, not so much as a sequence of events as in the manner of a tragedy".[11]

Only the humanists, however, were in a position to bring the tragic-dramatic view of the world and history into contact with antiquity's metaphor of the theatre. *E. R. Curtius* has drawn attention to the significance of a passage in *John of Salisbury's*

18f.: "*Discedite . . . , eia, quid statis?*" We shall discuss *De vera religione* 76 (PL 34, 156) elsewhere.

[8] Cf. note 1 above.

[9] *De Gen. ad litt.* XI, 15, 20; *City of God* XV, 1; In Ps. 136:2; In Ps. 51:4.

[10] In Ps. 99:12f.

[11] SRG ed. A. Hofmeister (1912), 2–3; cf. *Prol. libri primi*: "Non tam historias quam erumpnosas mortalium calamitatum tragoedias . . ." (p. 7). His view is different from Augustine's: his ideal is the unification of the two civitates in the Constantinian era. When this unity collapses in the Investiture Controversy, he will see it as a sign of the imminent end of the world. Cf. Werner Kaegi, *Chronica Mundi: Grundformen der Geschichtsschreibung seit dem Mittelalter* (Einsiedeln: Johannesverlag, 1954), 7–23. On the transpositions undergone through history by Augustine's doctrine of the two cities, see Étienne Gilson, *Les Métamorphoses de la Cité de Dieu* (1952).

Policraticus (1159)[12] which quotes a verse from Petronius: "When the company plays on the stage, one acts the father, another the son, and the third a man of property. Once the comedy is over, the masks are cast aside; now we see the real face, and the painted face fades away."

However, the Englishman immediately complements this passage with Job's dictum that "man's life on earth is a warfare" (cf. Job 7:1); thus he erects two, if not three, stages. First, a lower stage on which the majority act, making life into a comedy rather than a serious war campaign. They become so absorbed in their comedy that they cannot extract themselves from their roles: "I have seen boys who have imitated stammerers for so long that, when they wanted to, they could not speak properly."[13] Then there is the small company of the Lord's chosen ones, whose "conversation is in heaven" (or, in Augustinian terms, who live according to the law of the City of God); they refuse to enter into this comedy. Between the two levels lies the "world" with its vanity, to which it is subjugated against its will, and on this stage all have to appear and then take their leave. Thus both comedy and warfare are transformed into tragedy.[14] The changing times cause the "play" to be divided into "acts", and the whole thing appears to be "fortune's jest". But there is no blind fate: behind is the all-seeing and all-governing God, and those who act their part in the play virtuously, refusing to play the comedian and despising fortune, will go to be with him; then, from heaven, together with God and the angels, they will watch the world's drama.[15]

This text—well loved and widely used—must suffice for a milestone. Not only does it once more relate the Augustinian

---

[12] E. R. Curtius, *European Literature and the Latin Middle Ages* (London, 1979). But cf. the severe censure of the actors of that period in the same *Policraticus*, bk. I, chap. 8 (PL 199, 405f.). We cannot follow Curtius' interpretation at all points.

[13] Bk. 3, chap. 8; 489B.

[14] *Ibid.*, 491C, 489C.

[15] *Ibid.*, 493D–94A. All the same, John does not see their destinies in a purely individual way: on the stage there is always a constellation of persons; if one drops out, it affects the whole: "Personae sibi invicem coaptantur, et si altrinsecus divertant, totius actus facies immutatur" (494AB).

world drama to the metaphor of the stage, and in a new way (yet without being absorbed by it); it provides a vantage point from which one can understand both what began in the middle ages as a Christian play, quickly expanding to become the world theatre of the great "mysteries", as well as existence itself, which, alienated in so many ways in the late middle ages, is able to move into the perspective of the theatre. In the late middle ages the play of human life is not only presented in a theological interpretation: on the one hand, it is heightened to the level of the *trionfi*;[16] on the other, it sinks into the gloom of the Dance of Death or the frivolity of the Feast of Fools, or else fades into nothingness.

These tensions are evident in the way both *Luther* and *Erasmus* experienced the world.

In *Luther's* case the ancient and medieval dialectic between God (providence) and fate (fortune) is dissolved: world history is nothing but God's mask (*larva*); the authority of parents, the secular authorities are his masks; he "conceals" himself behind them. The peasant who plows and sows is God's mask every bit as much as Alexander and Hannibal, the makers of history;[17] the entire course of the world is God's "mummery",[18] which implies both disguise and masquerade. Our actions are illusion, "shadowboxing"; what is real passes through us.[19] The Christian is a person who has come to see this.[20] Whereas, for *Marcus Aurelius*, the world drama is fundamentally pantheistic, for the Lutheran Christian it is ultimately "theo-panistic", even if this disguise is given a christological basis. Even as Creator, God

---

[16] W. Weisbach, *Trionfi* (Berlin, 1919); R. Alewyn, K. Sälzle, *Das Grosse Welttheater, Die Epoche der höfischen Feste in Dokument und Deutung* (Rowohlt, 1959), 19ff.

[17] On the following section and Luther's texts cf. Fritz Blanke, *Der verborgene Gott bei Luther* (Furche, Berlin, 1928); WA 30, I 136, 1.8; WA 46, 612, 1.9; WA 40, I 174, 1.5; 175, 1.17; WA 23, 8, 1.36; WA 16, 263, 1.4.

[18] WA 15, 373, 1.5. Erlangen ed. vol. 11:115: "All creatures are God's masks and mummery." But instead of the mask, God can also clothe himself with armor. We see him thus in the wars of the Old Testament and in the sword which authority still wields today.

[19] WA 16, 263, 1.4ff.

[20] WA 40 I 173, 1.5ff.

conceals himself to allow human beings a certain area of freedom—that is, in the final analysis he does this out of love;[21] but this concealment is made plain in Christ: without concealment there can be no revelation of the ever-hidden God and no faith which, in its humility, does not desire to "see". At a deeper level God, in his concealment, takes upon himself the sinner's alienness and opposed-ness;[22] Christ dies and descends to the hell of sinners,[23] and *this* "concealment under the contrary form" justifies all the other disguises on God's part. All philosophy is dissolved in the theological paradox.

In *Erasmus* "everything in human life shows two different sides". "What looks, at first, like death, turns out on closer examination to be life—and vice versa." Everything turns "unexpectedly into its opposite". But it is dangerous to want to look behind the mask: "If a man were to go up to actors on the stage and tear off their masks, revealing their real faces to the audience, would he not spoil the whole play and deserve to be thrown out of the theatre and be pelted with stones as a lunatic?" Or, in more general terms, "What else is the whole life of man but a sort of play? Actors come on wearing their different masks and all play their parts until the producer orders them off the stage, and he can often tell the same man to appear in different costume. . . . It's all a sort of pretense, but it's the only way to act out this farce." A wise man might drop from heaven and unveil the pretense, turning everything topsy-turvy, but what would he achieve except to expose himself before everyone as "a crazy madman"? A man would be ill-advised to ask "for the play to stop being a play".[24]

In *Luther*, as in *Erasmus*, there is ultimately no standard for judging between being and appearing, wisdom and foolishness. For *Luther*, God's grace can and must appear as "vain wrath",

---

[21] Blanke, *Der verborgene Gott bei Luther*, 8f; WA 15, 373, 1.5.

[22] *Commentary on Romans*, 219, 16ff.: "Bonum enim nostrum absconditum est, et ita profunde, ut sub contrario absconditum sit. Sic vita nostra sub morte etc." Cf. *ibid.*, 208, 1.4.

[23] *Ibid.*, 271, 1.21; cf. 1.5: "*Voluntas Dei abscondita sub specie* [the appearance of] *mali*." After the *Commentary on Romans* this idea has a constant and governing role in Luther's writings.

[24] Erasmus, *Praise of Folly*, tr. B. Radice (Penguin, 1971), 104–5.

his "faithfulness and truth must always first become a great lie"; "God cannot be God unless he first becomes a devil."[25] For *Erasmus*, the folly of the world and all its classes (including the croaking frogs of the stoics) is absorbed without residue into the folly of God and of Christ as found in *Paul*. He quotes the passages in full: "If any one among you thinks that he is wise in this age, let him become a fool that he may become wise", and "it pleased God through the folly of what we preach to save those who believe." The Cross is foolishness, and so it is right for this foolishness to be proclaimed by "simple and ignorant messengers". Finally, following *Plato* (and *Dionysius*), blessedness is extolled as a being "out of oneself", a "madness",[26] thus giving folly the last word about reality. No one asks whether this justifies the many pilloried instances of worldly folly. Accordingly all norms disappear in *Luther's* dialectical utterances.[27] But in both *Erasmus* and *Luther* the dialectic (which points toward *Hegel*) remains based in Christology, not philosophy. In Christ, God becomes the *Deus sub contrario absconditus*; in Christ, God, the absolute Wisdom, chooses foolishness in order to shame the wise men of the world. But in their extreme writings both writers absolutize this christological paradox, making it into a world formula no longer distinct from the natural order which is judged by it.

Baroque literature will not be able to outdo this absolute dialectic. On the contrary, by taking seriously the possibility of a representation, in this world, of the absolute, it will once more insert the backbone of a dramatic action into this dialectic, making it possible to impart a Christian meaning to the theatre metaphor of antiquity. *Shakespeare* will take advantage of this meaning: even when he gives Jaques his speech, "All the world's a stage" (*As You Like It*, II, 7), it is a world that has inbuilt categories giving order—as in *John of Salisbury*—to the various

---

[25] WA 31; 249, 16ff. (1530).

[26] Erasmus, *Praise of Folly*, 207–8.

[27] G. Ebeling, in his *Luther: Einführung in sein Denken* (Tübingen, 1964), 274, cautions us "not to succumb to the emotional power of such utterances". But they have their own intrinsic objective momentum, which will not stop even for Hegel. Sebastian Franck will term his *Weltchronik* (1536), "God's Shrovetide farce".

strata. As is well known, London's Globe Theatre, erected in 1599, sported an inscription from John of Salisbury's *Policraticus*: *Totus mundus agit histrionem*.[28] Here we have great drama that understands itself to be a world theatre, even if, as yet, it does not set out to fashion itself in that way.

Ronsard takes a more deliberate step than *Shakespeare* toward this project when, in 1564, in the epilogue to a comedy, he affirms with gravity and precision:

> Icy la Comedie apparoist un exemple
> Où chacun de son fait les actions contemple:
> Le monde est le *theatre*, et les hommes acteurs,
> La Fortune qui est maistresse de la sceine,
> Appreste les habits, et de la vie humaine
> Les Cieux et les Destins en sont les spectateurs.

Each one plays his part on the same stage, but no one, says *Ronsard*, can disguise himself to such an extent that an observer cannot discern his nature. They act as if they are content and yet are inwardly full of care.

> Qui fait que nostre vie est seulement un *songe*,
> Et que tous nos dessins se finissent en rien.

The good reigns in heaven, but on earth, deception and evil confusion:

[28] E. R. Curtius, *European Literature and the Latin Middle Ages*, 140, where he also refers to Ronsard. Vondel produced a corresponding epigram on the first Dutch National Theatre: *De weerld is een speeltooneel, / Elek speelt zijn rol en krijght zijn deel.* On Shakespeare's dramatic metaphors see A. Righter, *Shakespeare and the Idea of the Play* 2d ed. (London, 1964). In his *Apology for Actors* (published in 1612, written about 1607) the poet Thomas Heywood countered the constant puritan attacks on the theatre by stressing the continuity of the great theatre of antiquity and the Elizabethan theatre. He used the shape of the Globe Theatre to evoke the image of the theatre of the world, with God as spectator:

> If then the world a Theatre present,
> As by the roundness it appears to fit,
> Built with star-galleries of high ascent,
> In which Jehove doth as spectator sit,
> And chief determiner t'applaud the best,
> And their endeavours crown with more than merit,
> But by their evil actions dooms the rest
> To end disgrac'd, while others life inherit.

Quoted from M. C. Bradbrook, *The Rise of the Common Player* (London, 1962), 92.

Et, bref, tout ce monde est un publique *marché*
L'un y vend, l'un desrobe, et l'autre achete et change,
Un mesme fait produit le blasme et la louange
Et ce qui est vertu, semble a l'autre peché.

Heaven has linked reason and passion so closely together that
love vanquishes the spirit. But:

Tandis que nous aurons des muscles et des veines
Et du sang, nous aurons des passions humaines;
Car jamais autrement les hommes n'ont vescu.[29]

c. Theology and Metaphysics of the World Theatre in the Baroque Age

Ronsard's poem contains all the constitutive elements of *Calderon's*
theological drama: *The Great Theatre of the World*, *The World's
Great Fair*, *Life Is a Dream* (all ca. 1635). We can trace the
migration of ideas from France to Spain. A Frenchman, *Pierre de
Bovistuau* (called *Launey*), whose book was translated into
Spanish and was very popular at the end of the sixteenth and
beginning of the seventeenth century, wrote an ascetical work
on "the world theatre". As he said himself, his chief inspiration
was *Augustine's City of God*. As Sancho Panza's satirical speech—
in *Don Quixote* (1617) II, 12—shows, the theatre metaphor was
commonplace at that time. When Don Quixote utters it (in a
free rendering of *Lucian*), saying that life is a playing of roles and
death makes all men equal once again, Sancho Panza comments,
"a magnificent comparison—albeit not so novel that I have not
heard it before, many a time and oft". It is *Quevedo*, however,
who, going back to the great tradition of antiquity, gives a new
depth and richness to the metaphor. In his *Epicteto y Fociledes en
español con consonantes* (Madrid 1635), we read:

Life's a comedy, the world's a stage, men are actors, God is the
author. His responsibility is to allot the parts; man's is to act well.
    Remember that life is only a play. / The entire world is nothing
but the stage for a comedy / In which the scenery keeps changing. /
We are all simply actors upon it. / Remember that in this play it is

[29] Ronsard, *Pour la fin d'une Comédie* in *Oeuvres Complètes*, ed. G. Cohen
(Pléiade 1938), II, 472–73.

God / Who is the author and originator / And that what the play is about is beyond our ken. / If a man has been given a short part, / Let him play it as prescribed. / But he who is given a long part / Can only play it properly if his deeds are good. / If God requires you to act the part / Of a poor man or a slave, / A prince or a cripple, / Play whatever he has given you to play. / Only one thing matters for you: / To play your part perfectly / In all you think or do or speak. / But as for the part of allotting good fortune / And as for the length or shortness of your appearance on stage, / That is God's concern alone.

"There is a clear and indissoluble relationship between this passage from *Quevedo* and *Calderon*"[1]—even in the unlikely event of *Quevedo* having penned his lines under the influence of *Calderon's* play, and not vice versa. In paraphrasing his Epictetus, on the subject of God's authorship and assigning of roles, he brings Platonist and Plotinian themes more to the fore.

Calderon, however, lifts the metaphor out of triviality and, in his *Great Theatre of the World*, theologically deepens and broadens it. Now it confronts and has to come to grips with Platonist metaphysics. As in antiquity, the dramatic tension lies less in the horizontal course of human action than in its vertical implications: while the short play is not divided into acts, it clearly has a five-act form in which the first and fifth, second and fourth, correspond. The first is a prelude in heaven: God decides to put on a play, using the world; this primal action prior to the world's existence signifies both the origin of the stage, of the play as a structure and—the specifically Christian dimension— the unfolding of a theology of history applied to the concrete situation in which the play is being performed, namely, the temporal field of force of three laws: the natural law, the law of Scripture (Old Covenant) and the law of redemption (New

---

[1] Angel Valbuena Prat, *Calderon, Obras Completas* III, 201b. On the following section: A. Vilanova, "El tema del gran teatro del mundo" *Boletin de la Real. Acad. de Buenas Letras de Barcelona* 23 (1950): 153ff. J. Jacquot, "Le théâtre du monde de Shakespeare à Calderon" in RLC 31 (1957), 341ff. T. B. Stroup, *Microcosmos: The Shape of the Elizabethan Play* (Lexington, Ky., 1965). F. J. Warnke, "The world as theatre: Baroque variations on a traditional topos" in *Festschrift*, ed. F. E. Mertner (Munich, 1969), 185. W. Barner, *Barockrhetorik* (Tübingen, 1970), 86–124, shows the relationship of these individual studies to one another.

Covenant).[2] This means that biblical, Christian time has a directional inner structure, in contrast to the ancient world's time, which is a structureless, neutral milieu into which nothing lasting can be written. The second act is God's assigning of parts and the world's allotting of props: the players are equipped. The third act is the play itself, at the center of which is the peripeteia of the entire action. The fourth is the counterpart of the second: here the players, having acted their parts, are stripped of their effects in a powerful elegy on the theme of transitory life, very deliberately constructed by *Calderon*; it is the baroque form of the late gothic Dance of Death. The fifth act returns the entire action to its divine origin: the "Last Things"—the Judgment, with its fourfold outcome: purgatory, limbo, heaven and hell. The world is in no way reabsorbed into God: here we have a christological conclusion looking toward the messianic, eucharistic meal. Thus the play's central but invisible actor, the God-man, comes indirectly into view, just as he was the hidden presupposition of the play right from the beginning—as the "law of grace" with its "higher miracles" than the "world" can grasp.

In other *autos* by *Calderon* the part of Christ is much more strongly highlighted: in whatever role and mask he appears, he is always the one sent by the Father, his normative and ultimate representative. Thus the whole tenor of the role-topic changes: instead of being the mere donning of an ephemeral costume, as in antiquity, and although the theme of transitoriness remains, it acquires an eschatological emphasis: even when the players are stripped of their accoutrements, they still keep their "role", their "mission". This is a counterpart to the Platonic "karma", but without the notion of reincarnation; rather, it is the eternal, personal harvest of what has been sown in the temporal dimension. Accordingly, the transcendental point of exit must be different from that in *Plato*. The notion that experiences in earlier lives have influence on the choice of a future "life pattern" is jettisoned, as is the idea that souls without any prior experience, coming straight from heaven, seize the most glamorous roles.

---

[2] On this ancient *theologumenon* cf. my book *Kosmische Liturgie, Das Weltbild Maximus' des Bekenners* 2d ed. (1961), 288–312.

This idea contained a (more or less hidden) version of the souls' "fall" from the original vision of God (Phaedrus)—which cannot be sustained in a Christian framework. *Calderon's* characters come forth from the womb of God's thought; they have been "always at Thy service" and "in order to be present, each one, to Thine eyes, they do not need first to be born". Here they exist in complete indifference, as Beauty puts it:

> Only in Thy mind traced / We have neither life nor light, / We lack both hearing and sight; / Neither good nor ill do we taste. / But now we have come in haste / To this place our parts to play, / Hand out our roles, we pray; / And since we have no choice, / Bending our will to Thy voice, / We take them as best we may.[3]

But the characters which speak thus to God, as his thoughts, do have a kind of independence. The moment of creation is not portrayed (for these "thoughts of God" are already embodied on the stage), and so the instant they appear a dialogue can begin, involving even doubts (on the peasant's part) and bitter questioning (on the part of the beggar). God's answer is exactly the same as that of *Epictetus*: what counts is not what one plays but how one plays it; in the end king and beggar will be equal again. In this fluid transition from the idea in the mind of God to its first realization in life, *Calderon* leaves room for the creature to be somehow already there; that is, he allows for that intelligible prior decision which is stressed in *Plato* and *Plotinus*, though not attaching the same weight to it. The decision that counts is made in life, acted out on the world stage.

There is something else that clearly distinguishes the Christian playwright from the ancient philosopher. With the latter, the life patterns are set forth so that the soul may select one; this choice is made in interior freedom, guided by the soul's wisdom or goodness, and is then indissolubly welded to its appropriate *daimōn* by the Daughters of Necessity. In *Calderon* it is exclusively God's free will which apportions the roles and gives people their fundamental uniqueness. There is essentially no place in the allotted role for any initial cooperation or tentative willingness on the soul's part. It is the business of the "world" subsequently to provide the actor with the (as it were) "empirical" accoutre-

---

[3] *The Great Stage of the World* (Manchester University Press, 1976).

ments of his role: the actors are ready to step onto the stage, but the "world" detains them in order to provide them with their equipment. Fundamentally it determines nothing, unlike the Parcae, who "spin" destiny *Marcus Aurelius*) or at least "firmly bind" the *daimōn*. In *Calderon* it is the individual's mission that personalizes him for his life in the world, and this comes directly from the Lord of the play, God.

As for the horizontal action (the "third act"), it is practically nothing but a rehearsal, so frequently is it interrupted by the vertical dimension—the voice of God, the admonition of the "Law", the comments of the "world". The play begins, after Wisdom's extolling of God, with the characters presenting themselves; each takes his place in life—only the beggar has no place. Next comes the beggar's scene: Beauty does not listen to him, Wealth remains stonyhearted, the King bids him apply through official channels, the Peasant advises him to work, and only Wisdom gives him a piece of bread. Lastly comes the lyrical dialogue, continually interrupted by Death. The beggar's scene is the core of the action: it contains in a nutshell everything that *Hofmannsthal* will later develop from it. It is followed by a tiny excursus: Wisdom (faith) stumbles and the King helps her to her feet: the Spanish seventeenth century. But this throne-altar theme is only barely indicated. The entire gravity of the Christian play lies in the balance of the tension (a divinely instituted tension) between rich and poor, where "rich" means powerful, beautiful, industrious. Insofar as the "roles" are "commissions", they are neither private matters in mere juxtaposition (*Epictetus*) nor do they interlock to make a *politeia* (*Plato*); they are polarized by an active wisdom (and it was only Wisdom who gave the beggar the piece of bread), a wisdom which, on the basis of the law of the heavenly *polis*, eases the abiding earthly tension.

From *Calderon* to the present day the theme of the "theatre of the world" is turned this way and that in three sharply distinct variations: the baroque, the idealist and that newly fashioned by *Hofmannsthal*. Then, in a fourth form, it abandons its shape hitherto and—in *Pirandello* and his disciples—the theatre metaphor reflects upon itself. And this seeming disintegration will help us, in fact, to make a more precise analysis of the dramatic dimension, the dimension of the theatre.

It is possible to use the elements of *Calderon's* play to organize, to some degree, the many aspects of the "theatre of the world" as found in the baroque era. The play is performed within the clear confines of the stage; the action is limited in terms of time, space and characters. The stage is opened by the "world": thus it deals with appearances, being transitory; the theme of transitoriness is a major element of the action: the characters are summoned from the stage in the middle of the dialogue. Between God, the most high Spectator, and the world (Fortuna) there is a relationship, but their distinctness from each other is even clearer. Initially the roles stand in lonely juxtaposition, appointed from on high, but they only have meaning through their dialogue relationship. There is an abyss in the relation of the "I" to the role: an identity that is open, all the same, for reflection upon their nonidentity. The play is subject to the divine "law"; its kernel is the various attitudes to the beggar, that is, possession (of power, money, beauty, work) and the absence of such possession. Most important of all, "the baroque theatre was not a moral institution, nor an aesthetic one, but a direct parable, a true 'mirror'."[4] Life is *real* theatre; hence *Calderon's* play could have been written only in the baroque era. "Theatre" is the "key, the keyword" of the whole period, "the very element that shapes its style".[5] That is why the image is so omnipresent.[6] It brings the dramatic interpretation of existence very close to that of stoicism which—once all the waves of Neoplatonism have ebbed away, as far as *Ficino* and the Oxford school—experiences a vigorous revival[7] but essentially does not threaten the Christian distinction between God and man. Rarely was *theologia naturalis* built into Christian theology as intimately as here, with all imaginable transitions and tendencies, leaving us unsure— whether we are reflecting as Catholics or Protestants—whether

    [4] J. Rütsch, "Das dramatische Ich im deutschen Barock-Theater", *Wege zur Dichtung* 12 (Münsterpresse) (1932): 157 (hereafter abbreviated as "Das dramatische Ich").

    [5] P. Rusterholz, "Theatrum Vitae humanae", *Philolog. Studien und Quellen* 51 (1970): 10. Cf. Heinz Kindermann, "Das Theater als Paradigma der barocken Lebensform" in *Theatergeschichte Europas* (1959), III, 13–21.

    [6] Examples and bibliography in W. Barner, *Barockrhetorik*, 86–124.

    [7] W. Dilthey, *Weltanschauung und Analyse des Menschen seit Renaissance und Reformation* 3d ed. (1923), esp. 153ff.

so much stoicism is allowable or not in a Christian hero, king, martyr, and so forth.

The baroque theatre of the world differs in two ways from *Luther's* dialectic of the masquerade and *Erasmus'* universal folly: (1) There is a genuine representation of the absolute in world history: in secular terms, the Prince's court; in the spiritual realm, the hierarchical Church. (2) This genuine representation produces and governs a dialectic between role and person. But the spectrum of possible applications is so broad as to admit open contradictions.

1. The court is where the great theatre of the world really takes place:

No life presents a greater play and spectacle
Than theirs whose chosen element's the court[8]

Thus, in its great festivals, the court celebrates itself as representative world theatre.[9] As part of this celebration, the play in the narrower sense (with its limits of place, time and action) shares in the absolute validity of the framework. In *Racine's Phèdre*, for instance, complete chaos can be restrained in the completely restrained order of courtly language and the classical three unities. True, this court (or this "empire" which it makes concretely present) is in transition between the "mythic" court of antiquity and the representation exercised by the Christian Church; the absolutist court is in part the pre-Christian and anti-Christian absolute sanction (for instance, in the martyr-play), and in part it draws its nourishment from the Christian representation (as in the Spanish plays). But at all events the court is the world in miniature, the courtier is the "man of the world" who, with *Baltasar Gracian's Handbook and Criticon*, steps onto the *teatro de la Fama* to practice the *arte de ser persona*. First of all this means that the drama must take place no longer in the Augustinian panorama of world history but in a time and space that is condensed to the supposedly Aristotelian unities: it must

---

[8] Lohenstein, preface to *Sophonisbe* (Just 3, 249). Cf. Barner, *Barockrhetorik*, 117–124: the court as the perfect representation of the *theatrum mundi*.

[9] R. Alewyn, "Das grosse Welttheater" in *Das grosse Welttheater: Die Epoche der höfischen Feste in Dokument und Deutung*, Alewyn and Sälzle, eds. (Hamburg, 1939), 9–70, esp. 50, 34, 62, 66, 68.

be the destiny of some particular prince, tyrant, confessor, and so on, at a particular national court. There must be no departure from the ideal framework.[10] The absolute framework can be "Rome"—in *Shakespeare*, *Corneille*, *Racine*—with *Dante's* medieval interpretation in the background, as a symbol of all representation whatsoever, to which a man can only measure up if, in total renunciation, he grows beyond himself and into the superhuman role (thus *Corneille's Horace*, *Cinna*, *Pompée*, and *Racine's* Titus in *Bérénice*); or it can be some court dependent on Rome. Here, totally unlike the stoics with their emphasis on the private, the *raison d'État* has immense inertia: personal love shatters against it (*Nicodème*), occasionally triumphs over it (*Suréna*: "mon amour est trop fort pour cette politique")[11] or questions its legitimacy (*Sertorius*: "Je n'appelle plus Rome un enclos de murailles, / Que ses proscriptions comblent de funérailles. . . . / Rome n'est plus dans Rome, elle est toute où je suis").[12] However, *Corneille's* great political drama is directly transformed into a drama of martyrdom when Rome's hitherto legitimate, absolute claims clash with those of the new Christianity; now we have the Augustinian battle for the ultimate horizon, waged in perfect *noblesse* in *Polyeucte*.

This stage of the development raises all the problems connected with the representative function of the court. If (to be realistic) its greatness is based on power, not on right (as *Machiavelli* showed),[13] if the courtly role-play is an epitome of

[10] This was well observed by Walter Benjamin, *Ursprung des deutschen Trauerspiels* 2d ed. (1963), 71–73: in the period when Christianity exercised an unshakable dominion, "the medieval path of rebellion, of heresy, was hidden from it; partly because Christianity put forth its authority with considerable emphasis, but primarily because it was not even remotely possible for the passion of a new and secular will to express itself in the heterodox nuances of doctrinal and moral opinion. Thus, since neither religious rebellion nor religious submission were possible, the epoch's entire energy was directed toward the humane refashioning of life's substance while maintaining the outer form of Church orthodoxy."

[11] My love is too strong for these politics.

[12] I no longer call Rome a circle of walls
    That her proscriptions fill with funerals . . .
    Rome is no longer Rome; it is wherever I am.

[13] The Christian religion "causes us to place less value on worldly esteem

the lie (*Molière*, *Les Moralistes*: "nil hic ita cernis, ut est"),[14] the courtier will try to break out into the "truth" of a utopian shepherd's or hermit's existence;[15] if things become serious he may cleave to the totally different truth of Christian revelation by putting his existence on the line, perhaps in a martyr's death. Then the baroque *angst* which arises from the transitory nature of the entire world stage can get a firm foothold in the *angst* which comes from actual death; in turn, this fear overcomes itself when the whole center of gravity is shifted to unchanging eternity. Here we encounter *Gryphius* (*Catharina von Georgien*, *Carolus Stuardus*, *Papinian*) withdrawing from the "play of time": the players (who are themselves "played") recognize and see through themselves in their roles;[16] the (secular) "fall" from princely heights is seen to go hand in hand with an ascent, in terms of mind and spirit, into the eternal. The image of the King laying aside his garments and insignia always has the power to move us profoundly, from *Shakespeare* (*Richard II*) to *Bidermann* (*Cosmarchia*, which begins with this very scene), *Gryphius*

---

and thus makes us more gentle and mild. The ancients, by contrast, regarded this esteem as the highest good and were therefore bolder in their deeds and sacrifices. . . . The only men they regarded as blessed were those full of worldly splendor, like generals and statesmen. . . . Our religion calls for the strength to suffer rather than the ability to carry out a brave deed. Thus the world has become the prey of evil men who have an easy task of dominating, for, in their concern to get into paradise, people are more prepared to suffer mistreatment than to avenge it" (*Discorsi* I, 12). Only the *raison d'état*, with its realistic view of man as he has been and always will be, can educate him to exercise a genuinely political influence. "For those who act on the great stage of the world, that is, human beings, always have the same passions, and thus the same cause must always bring forth the same effect" (*Discorsi* III, 43).

[14] Moscherosch, "Gesichte usf." Kürschner, vol. 32 and the whole "other dimension", the world's being.

[15] M. Wehrli, "Das barocke Geschichtsbild in Lohensteins *Arminius*", *Wege zur Dichtung* 31 (1938): 32ff.

[16] This surrender is both stoic and Christian: "The free spirit, resting in itself, dead to the temporal and hence to all that is evil, liberates itself by recognizing that history has the quality of a stage play" (Rusterholz, "Theatrum vitae humanae", 50). "The only essential thing is the point of time occupied by the moment, the *kairos* of the decision, which aims straight at the eschatological/ futuristic vanishing point of eternity" (81).

(*Stuardus*) *Joseph Simon* (*Leo Armenus*, *Zeno*), right up to *Schiller's Maria Stuart*. *Papinian* departs with the words:

> Take back this cloak, these garments! When the play is ended
> Return the borrowed finery whence it was lended.

The final scene of *Cardenio and Celinde* is very similar. In *Calderon's Life Is a Dream* the theme of clothing-unclothing is brought from the (Protestant) eschatological world-view and placed at the center of the (Catholic) representational world-view.

The dialectic of "play" can degenerate and lose all shape in either Christian context. In Protestantism the "appearance" which plays between time and eternity (for all standpoints are merely "apparent" to each other) can lead to a demonic syndrome intensifying worldly power and desire, the more it knows itself to be futile (for instance, in *Hofmannswaldau's Heldenbriefen*, where we are shown "what monstrous games love serves up in the world"):[17] "It is not God who plays with the world: the world plays itself", and therefore man no longer possesses any particular, religious role; he now plays in an absolute sense. This, in the baroque age, is the deliberate embracing of "worldly wisdom".[18] In *Lohenstein*, who translated *Gracian*, it becomes wholly a masquerade of courtly life (for instance, in *Sophonisbe*, in deliberate and glaring contrast to eternal life, which only appears as an alienating (although unreal) alternative. Man is a "Proteus", a "Chameleon"; there is constant friction between power-politics, eroticism and religion. The great, all-embracing order of the world theatre, which in *Corneille* and *Racine*, set characters in opposition to one another to refine their ethical strivings, has no longer any function but that of a formal framework. The courtier can coincide with the saint, the anxiety-ridden tyrant with the martyr.[19] This destructive Lutheran dialectic is avoided, for the most part, in

---

[17] Kürschner, vol. 36, 5–79.

[18] Rusterholz, "Theatrum vitae humanae", 107–108. Klaus Günther Just, *Die Trauerspiele Lohensteins* (Berlin, 1961).

[19] W. Benjamin, *Ursprung des deutschen Trauerspiels*, 63ff., 93ff.

the Catholic milieu; but here the twofold earthly absolutes of throne and altar can lead to a hall of mirrors with no way out; all it needs is the addition of Jansenism—as in *Racine's Athalie*, where the court moves against the temple—for the demonic to show itself here too. This dramatic context only has a future where these two tightly entangled absolutes are carefully unravelled, that is, where it is reduced to the abiding Christian dialectic of Augustine's *City of God*, which is in the world and yet not of it.[20]

2. Where existence is directly interpreted as theatre, the "I" must be understood as the role.[21] The latter is bound to be hopelessly ambiguous, whether the world stage (the court, or even the Church in her representational capacity) is seen as the serious presence of a divine commission or as its symbolization, fraught with illusion: in the former case the "I" must insert itself entirely into the role (which may be superhumanly lofty and difficult) if it is to be itself; in the latter, it must see through it and place its center of gravity in the eternal, lest it succumb to the role. But the baroque theatre vacillates between the two aspects with the result that the relationship between the "I" and the role is never ascertainable and "our masks do not sit as we would like them to".[22] "Representation" means both showing and concealing; anyone who aspires to it must renounce his unique personality (if he is to be "The" Emperor, for instance). Such renunciation, however, can be ethical (stoic or Christian) or calculated (as in the lust for power). In both cases the baroque awareness of role seems to go about in mourning—however much it may be treated with burlesque. In both cases the dimension of acting is the key to interpreting the "I". "Life's a

[20] We need to see the great tragedies of Reinhold Schneider, but also those of Claudel (and Eliot's *Murder in the Cathedral*) as a continuation of the baroque tragedy.

[21] Heinz Otto Burger, "Dasein heisst eine Rolle spielen. Das Barock im Spiegel von Jacob Bidermanns *Philemon Martyr* und Christian Weises *Masianello*" (1961), reprinted in *Dasein heisst eine Rolle spielen: Studien zur deutschen Literaturgeschichte* (1963), 75–93.

[22] Hofmannswaldau, "Lust der Welt", in *Deutsche Uebersetzungen und Gedichte* (1700, 1710), 47. Kürschner 36, 88.

dream": a person can suddenly find himself placed in an entirely different role, totally alienated from himself;[23] thus the same material can be presented as a tragedy (*Calderon*) or a burlesque (*Shakespeare*,[24] *Hollonius*,[25] *Masen*,[26] *Weise*[27]). What is crucial is that the stage shows the spectator, who thinks he knows who the actor "really" is, that he does not know who he himself "really" is. One play by *Calderon* is entitled *En esta vida todo es verdad y todo mentira*.

In the Catholic world the theme attains its baroque crown in the form of the "actor acting himself": entering into an alien role (that of the Christian) at the level of the play, he finds himself transformed by grace[28] into its reality. The theme continually reappears in new variations, going back to three

[23] In his *Palaestra eloquentiae ligatae dramatica* (1683), Jakob Masen put the concept of alienation (*alienatio personae*) at the center of his dramatic program. This is analyzed in J. Rütsch, "Das dramatische Ich", 140ff.

[24] The "induction" of *The Taming of the Shrew*. This theme originally comes from one of the fables from the novel of Barlaam and Josaphat, the story of the *King for a Year*, which evidently has a Buddhist background. The *King for a Year* is a person placed temporarily in a ruling position; he shows his wisdom by taking thought for the time of need which is approaching. Jacob Bidermann shapes this material into his last play *Cosmarchia*.

[25] *Somnium vitae humanae*—as in Shakespeare, a drunken peasant is made into a duke for a brief period. He ends up in the ditch again and tells his friends of his experiences, thinking it all happened in a dream. The theme had already been treated comically by Macropedius in *Aluta* (1535) and by J. Ayrer in *Ein Possenspiel von einer versoffenen Bäurin*.

[26] *Rusticus imperans* (ca. 1650); the comic theme acquires a depth here: the peasant, acting as the duke, has to decide a case in which he (the peasant) was the guilty party, and afterward, once more a peasant, he has to make atonement. The mystery play and the Shrovetide farce are thus intertwined. The duke, finally leaving the peasant in the gutter once more, "*ex aula in caulam*", concludes from all this that life has a role dimension: "Quem nos hodie illo in homine lusum lusimus,/Deus ac natura ludunt nobiscum in dies./Personam tamquam in scenam agendam sumimus." The peasant "joco nos docuit, quod futurum serio/Aliquando sit mihi." In the play, however, the peasant had always been uneasy about who he was ("*mehercle iterum quis sim dubito*").

[27] *Ein wunderliches Schauspiel vom niederländischen Bauern, welchem der berühmte Prinz Philippus Bonus zu einem galanten Traum verholfen hat* (1685). Here the central point is a psychological one, namely, that "the 'I' will not take the step of committing itself to either of the two persons" (Rütsch, "Das dramatische Ich", 154).

[28] And not as a result of psychological training, as suggested by Kant (p. 170, note 10, above).

different sources:[29] the legends of Josaphat,[30] Genesius[31] and Philemon.[32] The more seriously the player acts his part (for now he has been converted and is identical with his role), the more he is applauded as an incomparable actor. The play rises above comedy and tragedy but finally also sloughs off the customary baroque uncertainty as to the standpoint of the true "I": what appears on earth to be an acted role (and remains a role, in the serious play, as far as the spectators are concerned) is filled with truth that comes from heaven: the concept of role shows itself to be analogical.

An ultimate clarity is attained at the level of the baroque world stage, yet, as in *Calderon's Great Theatre of the World*, it is held fast within the theatre metaphor. Even where the Christian dimension breaks through life's role-playing, the breakthrough itself is still described in the categories of the theatre. This is possible because, in the baroque age, the individual, whether in

[29] Leaving aside the rather different legend of Johannes Calybita or Alexius, the hermit who lives unrecognized in his ancestral home and only reveals his true identity on his deathbed, or puts it down in a document which only the emperor, or the Pope, or his erstwhile bride-to-be can remove from his stone-cold grasp. On the history of this theme and its various dramatizations see E. Frenzel, *Stoffe der Weltliteratur* (1962), 29ff.

[30] King Abenner wishes to induce Prince Josaphat, whom Barlaam has converted, to forsake his Christianity. He employs a certain Nachorius for this purpose; appearing in the form of Barlaam, he is to take part in a disputation and renounce Christianity. However, the prince sees through the trick and during the disputation the pseudo-Barlaam is himself converted and defends the truth of Christianity to the end. J. Müller, in his *Das Jesuitendrama in den Ländern deutscher Zunge vom Anfang* (1555) *bis zum Hochbarock* (1665) II (1930), 114, traces 28 performances between 1599 and 1750. These would also indicate different versions, including that by Bidermann (1619) and Jakob Masen (1647–48).

[31] The actor Genesius (Gelasius, Gelasinus) plays the part of an apostate Christian; during the performance he is converted and dies as a martyr. It has a precursor in the Old French *mistère* of "Saint Genis", in which, however, the stage theme plays no part. Genis, converted through a preacher, is baptized and subsequently, in a disputation with Diocletian, professes his faith and dies for it. In the baroque age the "acted" baptism on the stage turns into a real one, the play becomes serious reality, confusing both the other actors and the spectators: Genesius *is* what he is acting. The story has been dramatized by Lope de Vega (*Il Fingido Verdadero* 1622), Rotrou (*Le véritable Saint-Genest* 1647), Desfontaines (1645), Jakob Balde in a *Jocus serius theatralis* and Joseph Simon (see Rütsch, "Das dramatische Ich", 154ff.).

[32] Philemon, an actor, is prepared to sacrifice to the gods on behalf of the

176 DRAMATIC RESOURCES

the realm of the world or of religion, always plays a "typical" role. *H. O. Burger* rightly points once again to the myth at the end of *Plato's Republic*, where, prior to each return to earth, the souls "have to choose from a specific number of *paradeigmata*, 'life patterns' ".[33] The roles allotted by God on the world stage (the King, Wisdom, and so on) are all only typical roles. So in the whole of baroque drama there remains an unresolved residue indicating a profound uncertainty about the self's identity—at the penultimate stage. This stage of uncertainty is often simply skipped by miraculous intervention instead of being solved interiorly, which gives the baroque "theatre of the world" a somewhat triumphal and violent aspect; it overwhelms from without, ecstatically, rather than convincing from within.

We cannot bid farewell to the baroque drama without mentioning *Pierre Corneille's* brilliant comedy *L'Illusion* (performed in 1636), in which theatre and life are newly and triumphantly related to each other. As a result of his severity, a father has caused his son to leave home; the latter wanders through the whole of Europe, pursued by his remorseful father. A rich friend of the father's has a magician living in a grotto in his garden, who promises to reveal his son's fate. "Whatever presents itself to your eyes, do not be afraid; and above all, do not leave my cave before me, else you will die. Behold, already you can see, like two fleeting shadows, your son and his master." From the second to the fourth act, the play shows the son's increasingly unfortunate love affairs, with the anxious father commenting on them at the end of each act. In the fifth act

Christian, Apollonius, who lacks courage to be a martyr; on the way to the altar he is converted, and now the scene is acted out in all seriousness. Initially the prefect throws him in jail and sends for Philemon to make him give up his plan. Apollonius is discovered disguised as Philemon and unmasked. Philemon is similarly unmasked when he appears before the prefect for the second time; he is congratulated on his magnificent piece of acting, the trial is continued in jest, but Philemon answers the questions in all seriousness. The spectators are enthusiastic at such histrionic ability. In the end Philemon knocks over the god's statue. Apollonius is seized by remorse and wants to take back his Christian garment and release Philemon from prison. Both suffer a martyr's death and the prefect, Arrian, is converted. This is Jacob Bidermann's masterly version (1615), *Philemon Martyr*. It is published in Latin and German, tr. by Max Wehrli (Hegner, 1960).

[33] H. O. Burger, "Dasein heisst eine Rolle spielen", 86.

the lovers die and a curtain falls; the father is beside himself. But the curtain rises again to reveal the four characters involved, sitting at a table counting their money: the son and his friends had become actors, and the play the father saw was a "play within the play". The magician declares:

> Leurs vers font leur combat, leur mort suit leurs paroles,
> Et, sans prendre intérêt en pas un de leurs rôles,
> Le traître et le trahi, le mort et le vivant,
> Se trouvent à la fin amis comme devant.[34]

Since the father is appalled at his son's profession, it is put to him that acting is a noble art, and one that is currently delighting the whole of Paris: "à présent le théâtre / Est en un point si haut que chacun l'idolâtre." What in his time was despised is now "the favorite of all *bons esprits*", including the people, the nobles and "even our great King".

3. *Modern Times*

a. Idealism

In the baroque age the metaphor of the play covers the most contrary world-views: religious and areligious, ethical and nihilistic. It is epitomized in *Jakob Balde's* formula, "Eheu ludimus et ludimur" (comparing life to a game of chess),[1] which leaves it an open question whether the freedom and effort put into such playing is accompanied by the playing of a higher power or whether the actors are like puppets, overridden by it. And who is this superior power? God himself or blind fate?

---

[34] Their lines are their battle,
    their death follows their words,
  And without taking interest in even one of their roles
  The betrayer and the betrayed, the dead and the living
  Are friends at the end as they were before.

[1] "Ludus Palamedis" in *Dichtungen*, ed. and tr. Max Wehrli, lateinisch und deutsch (Cologne and Olten, 1963), 14. In the preface to *Sophonisbe* Lohenstein says: "In all things man is but a plaything of time. / Fortune plays with him, he plays with all things." This is still the case in Goethe's *Werther*: "I am playing with things, or rather, I am being played like a puppet" (20th January. WW edited by G. Gräf [Insel], 539).

Even Christian poets often leave us in some doubt here.[2] Man himself is incapable of providing the link between his super-human role and his experience of transience.[3] So he remains "Chameleon",[4] "Baldanders" (lit. "Quick-change"),[5] "Proteus".[6] He identifies himself with his role only too well, which makes the reflective observer somewhat uneasy. Two questions are never solved: How is the transitory role related to the eternal God (if, with *Calderon*, we regard God as the author)? And what is God's relation to the role-play? Is he merely its inventor, spectator and final judge? Such a view would be far inferior to that handed down in the Christian tradition. Indeed, it would surely be inferior even to the speculations of the Platonists and stoics.

The Enlightenment provides a pause. The "representational" model of the world gives way to that of reason, but, arising from *Descartes'* dualism of spirit and matter, the deistic model is in the ascendant. This presents us with a Divine Clockmaker, whose opposite number, in radical French materialism, is *l'homme-machine*, a later version of *Descartes'* animal machine. Thus we come back once more to the image of the *puppet play*.

On the other side, however, we find an ever-intensifying, contrary sense of existence, coming from the Platonic enthusiasm of the Renaissance (especially from *Bruno*), via *Shaftesbury*, to *Herder*. Here, man (and he may be an Enlightenment man too) experiences a free, enthusiastic oneness with the divine principle which permeates the universe (in a stoic-Plotinian sense); "reli-

---

[2] "One is dominated by the sense that man is entangled in a play, and God has moved to the very edge of the dramatic horizon, as in Czepko's great poem, 'Spiele wohl! Das Leben ist ein Schauspiel!'" ("Play well, for life's a play!") (ed. Milch I, 22). W. Barner, *Barockrhetorik* (Tübingen, 1970), 106.

[3] "To live does not mean self-realization; it is as yet (!) impossible totally to identify with one's self, in view of the supra-individual task laid upon us and as a result of the experience of our own weakness and transitory nature." Wehrli, *Arminius* 50.

[4] Lohenstein, *Sophonisbe* II, 262.

[5] The name of a character in Grimmelshausen. Cf. H.-U. Merkel, *Maske und Identität in Grimmelshausen's "Simplicissimus"* (Diss. Tübingen, 1964), 140ff.

[6] "Discreto Proteo: con el docto, docto, y con el santo, santo" Gracian, *Oraculo manual* no. 77 (del Hoyo, 173). W. Krauss, *Gracians Lebenslehre* (Frankfurt, 1947).

gion" means adopting this universal standpoint. "O mighty Nature! Wise Substitute of Providence, impower'd Creatress! Or (!) Thou impowering *Deity*, Supreme Creator!"[7] *Herder* characteristically translates *Shaftesbury's* exclamation thus:

Godhead's familiar friend, wise Regent
Of Providence, or—Creatrix, nay Creator?—[8]

But this "Nature" has "no apprehension at all of what it is doing, no Thought to itself. . . . And what is Nature? Is *It* sense? Has *She* Reason or Understanding? No. Who then understands for her, or is interested for her? No one; not a soul: But *everyone for himself*." And yet, just as bodies follow their center of gravity:

With what constancy all spirits pressed
Toward their goals! Yet, beholding chaos,
He whose singing harmonized the world
Will also sing these spirits to right order.[9]

Thus we see a new variation of the "theatre of the world" in the making, namely, the extemporized play. It was mentioned in *Plotinus*, only to be assessed and rejected. Now, however, the *hen-kai-pan* is that which fills all things, though it is only conscious in individual minds, and so the latter must act extempore in the play of the world. *Herder* seems to have been the first to approach this daring idea. To the Greek "drama" with its unity he opposes the Shakespearean "event", seemingly thrown together without any rule, consisting of many "pages from the book of records, blown about in the gale of the times", "the imprints of peoples, classes, souls", having a united effect on "the most disparate and far-flung agents"—which only the poet himself can grasp. The spectator lives through history as it takes place, "feeling the ongoing influence of all the forces that produce an event, each one in its place and extent, so that, partly by way of presentiment, partly through gradual experience, he sees and recognizes the result of these forces in the event." "Through the poet's creative power" the characters are "both

[7] Shaftesbury, *The Moralists* (London, 1709), 158.
[8] Shaftesbury, *Die Moralisten*, ed. Wolff (Jena, 1910), appendix III, p. 173.
[9] *Ibid.*, 176.

ends and means; themselves deliberately crafted, their action also contributes to the whole."[10]

Before we go on to trace the course of this variation, we must mention a third which begins with *Kant's* transcendental philosophy. When the mind asks how there can be an empirical "I" in experiencing, thinking and acting, it looks in the direction of an *intellectus archetypus*. The latter cannot be constructed, but its absoluteness guarantees man's freedom (which nothing can relativize). At the same time—since it is not the noumenal "I"—it points to a postulated God, whom reason, however, cannot conceive. The two converge to yield *Fichte's* "I", which attains its final form in late philosophy as the (Plotinian) life which is superior to all consciousness, expressed by its accompanying "world of spirits" of manifold dialogical character. But in idealist thought the rising problem of the absolute and the empirical "I" frightened an entire generation of poets and thinkers to death: *Herder* and *Hamann*, *Jacobi* and *Tieck*, *Jean Paul* and *Kleist*, *Wetzel* (the author of the *Nachtwachen des Bonaventura*), *Hoffmann* and *Büchner*. From the standpoint of the nonconcrete Absolute (they thought), the whole apparently concrete world must seem to be merely a spectral, macabre "play of ghosts" (*Geisterspiel*); madness seems to lurk at the bottom of every "I". The enthusiastic pantheism of *Herder* and the young *Goethe* could at any moment turn into an atheism casting gloom on everything. That is why, in the period between *Sturm und Drang* and *Biedermeier*, the baroque images of the world stage, particularly in its marionette theme, are found practically everywhere.[11]

---

[10] "Shakespear" in *Von deutscher Art und Kunst* (1773), Suphan V, 219, 244, 238: "Everyone is his own purpose and goal; only through the poet's creative power is he also a means, both a goal and a cooperator in the whole. Thus it may be that, at a higher level of the world, a higher, invisible life plays with a lower class of creatures. They all pursue their own aims, and lo! in doing so, without knowing it they are all blind instruments toward a higher end, contributing to the whole of an invisible Poet!"

[11] On what follows cf. Eleonore Rapp, *Die Marionette in der deutschen Dichtung vom Sturm und Drang bis zur Romantik* (Leipzig, 1924); R. Majut, "Lebensbühne und Marionette. Ein Beitrag zur seelengeschichtlichen Entwicklung von der Genie-Zeit bis zum Biedermeier" in *Germanistische Studien* 100 (Berlin, 1931, reprinted 1967). Also: K. J. Obenauer, *Die Problematik des ästhetischen Menschen* (Munich, 1933); R. Debiel, *Die Metaphysik des Schauspielerischen* (Diss. Bonn, 1951).

By comparison with the baroque, however—in spite of its deepened grasp of the problem—a new dimension was reached. It had already been there in the metaphysics of the role in *Plato*, *Marcus Aurelius* and *Plotinus*, but it could only attain its full dramatic scope in the milieu of Christianity, which pondered the relation of human freedom to absolute, divine freedom. This dramatic tension found expression in the great symbols of *Faust* (*Klinger*, *Lessing*, *Maler Müller*, *Goethe*) and *Prometheus*. Everything is there in embryo in *Goethe's* Prometheus fragment: man is as eternally free as the gods: "I last for ever just as they do. / We are all eternal!" Prometheus has Minerva as his *daimōn*: "Thus I myself was not myself; / A deity was speaking / When I thought I spoke; / And when I thought I heard a goddess speak, / The words were mine." At the very beginning stands the free act: "How much, then, is yours?" "The circle of my influence!" Finitude, death, coincides with the experience of the absolute moment: "When, stirred to the very roots of your being, you feel everything / And all your senses melt away / . . . then the human being dies."[12] Venerable Renaissance notions of the poet as creator (*poietēs*)[13] mingle here with the idealist motif, acquiring rights of citizenship in their new framework. Prometheus, led by Minerva to the source of life, is able to instill life into his clay figures without recourse to Zeus, who initially allows him to. He puts life into his puppet play so that it may become a theatre of the world.

In practice, however, in spite of its mystical enthusiasm and the "divine *daimōn*", this version is already anthropocentric,[14] suggesting that the poet is a quasi-divine author and stage director—a topic which will be the subject of explicit reflection only after idealism has come and gone. The idea of the extempore performance, which we have already mentioned, is now given a crucial intermediary role. In his *System des transzendentalen Idealismus* (1800), *Schelling*, continuing the line of *Shaftesbury*

[12] *Dramatische Dichtungen*. *Werke* ed. G. Gräf (Insel, n.d.) II, 327–38.

[13] E. R. Curtius, "Theologische Poetik im italienischen Trecento" in *Zft f. roman. Philol*. LX, 1940 (= 1941); André Chastel, *Marsile Ficin et l'Art* (Droz, Geneva, 1954). Accordingly, God appears as the Poet of the world (Chastel, 132). Cf. also Rolf Bachem, *Dichtung als verborgene Theologie* (Bonn, 1956).

[14] W. Barner, Barockrhetorik, 91f.

and *Herder* and developing *Fichte*, lends a new luminosity to the theme. Let us listen to the entire passage:

> If we think of history as a play in which each participant plays his part completely extempore and as seems best to him, we can only envisage this confused performance proceeding meaningfully if there is One Spirit giving utterance in all the parts, and if the Poet, of whom the individual actors are merely fragments (*disiecti membra poetae*) has from the outset harmonized the objective result of the whole action with the extempore acting of all the individuals so that, in the end, something intelligible must emerge. However, if the Poet were purely *external* to his play, we would be merely actors performing what he had written. Whereas if he is *not* independent of us but unveils and manifests himself only successively, through the play of our freedom—such that, if this freedom did not exist, he would not exist either—we are co-writers of the whole script, ourselves inventing the particular role we play.[15]

Here, in full seriousness and in the manner of *Kant*,[16] human freedom is made so absolute that the play's Producer only comes to be through the performance of it; he would only exist as the sum of all freedoms and their actions at the end of the play—if it could have an end. All the same, *Schelling* wants all

[15] Schelling, *Werke* (1858) pt. 1, vol. III, 602. This image must have been inspired by Tieck's *Verkehrte Welt*, which came into being two years earlier. In *Wilhelm Meisters theatralische Sendung* (bk. 3, chap. 8) Goethe had pleaded wittily on behalf of impromptu acting; every company of players should practice this at least once a week in order to keep themselves in good shape, so that they should perform well. "Extemporizing was the actor's school and touchstone. It was not a question of learning a part by heart and imagining that one could act it: what was necessary was the spirit, a vivid imagination, skill, knowledge of the theatre; the spirit would show its presence in the clearest possible manner at each step. Necessity obliged the actor to acquaint himself with all the theatre's resources; he should become thoroughly at home among them like a fish in water. And if a poet were sufficiently gifted to employ these instruments, a great effect would be made on the audience."

[16] Kant explicitly rejected the baroque idea of the world as a stage on which man played a part given to him by God, regarding it as unworthy of his view of freedom: "This would make man into a puppet, an automaton à la Vaucanson, put together and strung up by the Chief Master of all artefacts. He might be conscious, but his consciousness of being free would be 'mere self-deception' " (*Kritik der praktischen Vernunft* A181, Weischedel (1963), IV, 227.

the extempore actors to be animated by one Spirit, which is only conceivable if the Absolute is viewed as the supratemporal, objective convergence of all freedoms (their origin and end result) or as their totality (which, in concrete terms, is always in an historical process of becoming). Thus *H. Zeltner* is right when he says that *Schelling* shatters the very metaphor he uses.[17] The play's Producer drops out, as does the distinction between the role and the "I" (or freedom), for it is up to the freedoms themselves to invent their roles. The idea that, in spite of this, there is "one Spirit giving utterance in all", of which (of whom) the individual actors are fragments, can only be explained in terms of *Kant's* categorical imperative, which simultaneously represents the rule of active self-realization and social convergence. But the only way such convergence can take place in reality, that is, the only way the individual freedoms can be properly integrated, is on the basis of an undemonstrable pre-established harmony. According to the latter, history must be moving forward to a realm of reason, which would be reached "when all arbitrariness had disappeared from the earth and man, through freedom, had returned to the same point at which Nature originally set him, and which he left at the beginning of history."[18] This is the secularized form of the old theologoumenon of the wheel of history which, in its circling, once more comes round to paradise; it is the theme of perfect identity between freedom and nature (necessity) which haunts not only *Schiller's* dramatic theory but also, notably, the plays of *Kleist.*[19]

We must pass over the age's innumerable repetitions of the metaphor of the world stage and the puppet play[20] and go on to describe the effects of the new presuppositions. Rightly or wrongly, transcendental idealist reflection is understood as eliminating the distinction between the "I" and God and thus

---

[17] Hermann Zeltner, "Das Grosse Welttheater: Zu Schellings Geschichtsphilosophie" in *Schelling-Studien: Festgabe für Manfred Schröter zum 85. Geburtstag* (Munich, Vienna, 1965), 113–30.

[18] III, 589.

[19] Schelling's metaphor points far into the future, as is shown by a passage which Zeltner quotes from Marx's *Das Elend der Philosophie*: "Man is both the author and actor of his own drama" (1846–47).

[20] They are assembled by Eleonore Rapp and Rudolf Majut (see note 11 above).

becomes an intoxicated or progressive deification of the "I" or
replaces God with the "I" or subordinates the empirical "I" to
an egoless (and possibly demonic or nihilistic) Absolute. At all
events the lighthearted self-reflection of the "I" is metamor-
phosed into something dread and drear.

The idea that God is an artist and that the world is his artifact
is an ancient one, revived by the Renaissance, by *Bruno*,
Shaftesbury and *Herder*. But what if I look at the world from the
absolute vantage point of my reflection? Does it not become my
poem? And since I live in it, do I not become poet, actor and
spectator all at once? This is the hall of mirrors in which we meet
the heroes of early romanticism, *Jacobi's Allwil*, *Tieck's Lovell*
and many of *Jean Paul's* heroes. Poetry can "hover in midflight,
free of all real and ideal interest, on the wings of poetic reflection,
continually reactivating it and multiplying it as if through an
endless series of mirrors."[21] *Jean Paul's* Leibgeber-Schoppe has a
double consciousness, which logically leads to insanity. "He
was excited firstly by the feeling of a soul free from all relationships and secondly by the satirical feeling that he was making a
travesty of human madness rather than imitating it. In all this he
had the twofold consciousness of the comic actor and of the
spectator."[22] This gives rise to the borderline character of
Roquairol in *Titan*, for whom everything becomes an act and
who shoots himself, in a specially arranged play, during the
declaration of love to Linda, whom he has seduced; even his
death is an act. From here our gaze is drawn directly to
Dostoievsky's Stavrogin and Kirolov. The principle of reflection
("I did not merely enjoy but felt and enjoyed the enjoyment")[23]
obliterates any distinction between the play and life: "Then I
observe myself observing, which goes on ad infinitum. So what
is left?"[24] Even serious matters of life—that is, when Roquairol
becomes responsible for his sister's going blind—occasion in
him an "unlooked-for delight in the murderous tragedy".[25]

[21] Friedrich Schlegel, *Athenäumsfragmente* 116, *Kritische Ausgabe* II (1967),
182–83.
[22] *Siebenkäs. Werke* (1860), XII, 13.
[23] Friedrich Schlegel, *Lucinde. Kritische Ausgabe* I/5 (1962), 8.
[24] Jean Paul, *Werke* vol. XVI, 139.
[25] *Titan*, 32nd cycle, vol. XV, 154.

Jean Paul's problem, which is never solved, is that of trans-figuring the dreary, realistic, everyday world by means of "divine" imagination. Which are right, the heroes of the early novels, Wuz and Fixlein, who are happy in their illusions, or those of his mature period, where imagination's absolute ambiguity is always demonstrated by two opposite characters? Or is it the hero of the late work, *Komet*, for whom illusion once again transfigures everything *à la* Don Quixote? *Jean Paul* is aware that "if poetry were to become life in this mortal existence . . . our wishes would only grow higher and higher instead of being fulfilled, and the higher reality would only give birth to a higher poetry. . . . In Arcadia we would yearn for Utopia."[26] This is not only romanticism: it is an awareness of existence that must be the realist's too if he is to play his role properly.[27]

However, once there is this split in the "I" through radical reflection (and it begins as early as *Karl Philipp Moritz's Anton Reiser*,[28] proceeding via *Jean Paul*[29] to *Grillparzer*[30] and *Hoffmann*,[31] right up to *Hofmannsthal*[32]), consciousness is bound to vacillate between libertinage or self-identification with the Absolute and the sense of being subject to alien destiny. The puppet play provides a convenient symbol for the latter, replacing the image

---

[26] *Titan*, 45th cycle, vol. XV, 222. In the play, Roquairol really commits suicide; its mirror image is the feigned death of the advocate, Siebenkäs, by means of which he extracts himself from a real and difficult marriage and escapes into an "ideal" love.

[27] Thus the poet admonishes those who are coldhearted and calculating: "O Gaspard, are you sitting in a front box and not also standing on the stage? And are you not, like Hamlet, participating in a great play and at the same time watching a smaller one? Indeed, does not every stage ultimately presuppose a twofold life, a life that copies and one that is copied?" (*Titan*, 3rd cycle).

[28] Anton Reiser is alienated from his own empirical person; he feels that the people and things around him may be only the product of his own imagination. He runs away from this to the world of the theatre, for here everything really is what it represents (vol. II, 101). Moritz calls this fantasy the opium that makes it impossible for Reiser to distinguish between appearance and reality (II, 134; IV, 91). Roquairol enhances his own sense of existence by taking real opium (53rd cycle).

[29] Schoppe's madness (*Titan*, 137th–39th cycle).

[30] Cf. Majut, "Lebensbühne und Marionette", 106–7.

[31] Primarily *Prinzessin Brambilla* (1820) and *Die Elixiere des Teufels*.

[32] In *Andreas oder die Vereinigten*.

of the world stage. Quite early on, the puppet play was used to describe the unreality of court life,[33] and later it was applied in criticism of false social conventions;[34] now, increasingly, it expresses the feeling that our very existence has been rendered unreal by some unknown, uncanny fate that is pulling the strings—like the Hegelian *Weltgeist*, which cunningly uses individuals for its own ends.[35] Whereas the writers of classicism strive for a precarious balance above the abyss (*Schiller's* "urge to play" poised between the "urge for form" and the "urge for matter"),[36] *Kleist* dreams of a coincidence of the poles "Glieder-

[33] Liselotte von der Pfalz in a letter of Sept. 18, 1691 to the Kurfürstin Sophie: "I imagine that we are the Almighty's puppets, for we are made to go hither and thither and play all kinds of parts. Then we suddenly fall down and the play is over. Death is Polichinello, who gives everyone a kick and dispatches him from the theatre."

[34] Balder in Tieck's *William Lovell* (1795–96): "Often the whole world seems to me to be a dull, worthless puppet play. The generality of people are taken in by the appearance of life and are glad. But, having seen the wires which move the wooden figures, I am so depressed that I could weep for all who are deceived and are content to allow themselves to be deceived in this way" (I, 148–49).

[35] This is put most forcibly in Büchner's revolutionary drama, where the agent of the World Spirit, Danton, feels himself to be its puppet. "The Man on the Cross made it easy for himself: evil must come, but woe to him through whom it comes! —It must come, it must. Who will curse the hand on which the curse of this 'it must' has fallen? Who uttered this 'it must', who? What is it inside us that whores, lies, steals and murders? We are puppets, our strings pulled by unknown forces; we ourselves are nothing, nothing!—only the swords wielded by battling spirits; it's simply that we cannot see their hands, like in the fairy tales" (*Sämtliche Werke*, Bergemann [1922], 43–44). And earlier still, in a letter: "I studied the history of the Revolution. I felt crushed under the terrible *fatalism of history*. It seems to me that there is a power in human relationships that cannot be deflected; it is given to all and to none. The individual is only froth on the wave, greatness is mere chance, the domination exercised by a genius is a puppet play, a ridiculous struggling against a law of bronze. To acknowledge this law is our highest achievement, to control it is impossible" (530).

[36] *Briefe über die ästhetische Erziehung*. But Schiller knows that his aesthetic "center" does not have a single, clear meaning. For on the one hand, philosophically speaking, it is the beneficent equipoise of human powers, while on the other hand, seen in historical terms, it is a transitional stage between the religious (the "sublime") and the purely scientific (the "true"). This imparts a certain tragic ambiguity to his concept of the beautiful appearance (*schöner Schein*). Goethe's balanced life between poetry and (political and scientific) truth, the way his Wilhelm Meister passes through his "theatrical vocation" in

mann" and "Gott": "When knowing has undergone (as it were) infinite vicissitudes", it must rediscover the original "Grace".[37] And, since the entire idealist dialectic is an interlude between the *homme-machine* of late Enlightenment and the machine age of the nineteenth century, which is just on the threshold, the puppet image is set aside, with increasing consistency, in favor of that of the "automaton"; the robot, the modern *golem*, takes over literature.[38] The utterly demonic distortion of the world-stage metaphor is reached in *Wetzel's Nachtwachen des Bonaventura* (1804), a shrill, mocking indictment of the "insane creator of the world" who has "unleashed this tragi-comedy of world history, this ghoulish *mardi gras* in the madhouse", and who will settle accounts with man at the Last Day. "Devil take it", God says, "I should never have carved the puppet!"

Of course there are more cheerful marionette motifs (for instance *Brentano's Ponce de Leon* and the *Göckelmärchen, Büchner's Leonce und Lena*); there are strains of stoic resignation and composure in *Stifter*;[39] and above all there is the Catholic surmounting of idealist dialectic: thus *Görres* is able to insert the idea of the extempore play into the world of Christianity:

> The poet of this great dramatic action is the *Ancient of Days* who dwells in secret. The heroes have not chosen their roles themselves:

---

order to reach other and more serious things, Faust's migration from the Imperial Court to the world of Helen, to politics, war and technology—all show that it is impossible to maintain this equipoise except in a personal balancing-act that is never totally secure.

[37] "Über das Marionettentheater", *Sämtliche Werke*, ed. F. Michael (Insel, Leipzig, n.d.), 1142.

[38] Examples in Rapp and Majut (see note 11 above). In Jean Paul, automatons are used as frightening illusions of life, primarily in his satirizing of the Enlightenment; subsequently he uses them to illustrate idealism's decadent stage. In E. T. A. Hoffmann, however (*Die Automate, Der Sandmann*), they symbolize the bizarre, ghostly nature of existence as a whole. In Immermann (*Tulifäntchen*, with several preliminary stages: *Die Papierfenster eines Eremiten, Avertissement von kürzlich erfundener hölzerner Gesellschaft*) they are used in his polemics against the advancing mechanization of man and society.

[39] "People say that the world's carriage runs on wheels of gold. If people are crushed by them, we call it a misfortune; but God is watching, unmoved; he stays wrapped in his cloak and does not lift your body out of harm's way, for ultimately you yourself have put it there" (the beginning of *Die Mappe meines Urgrossvaters*).

they find everything already appointed, whether good or bad, when they step onto the stage. No written parts are distributed beforehand so that they can learn them; no cues are given. When the actor hesitates or is uncertain, the only thing that can help him further—if he will listen to it—is a voice, given to everyone, speaking in his breast. For the rest, everything is extemporized, depending on the succession of events, on destiny, insight, enthusiasm and passion. Mysteriously, from within, the play seems to be ordered, independently of the actors' collaboration and knowledge, according to that harmonious and essentially free necessity which comes from Him who has reserved to Himself the mystery of the dramatic action.[40]

Here we have an approach to a theology of the theatre that goes beyond *Calderon* without falling into *Schelling's* dilemma. But it was *Eichendorff* who, despite a deep acquaintance with the romantic "puppet" and "masquerade" experience,[41] knew how

[40] *Die heilige Allianz* (1822) in *Ges. Werke* (1929) XIII, 415. In his *Mythengeschichte der asiatischen Welt* (1810), Görres boldly traced the myths of all religions back to a single "primal" religion. In carrying out this synthesis he highlighted the Indian doctrine of maya—which he regarded as the "aesthetic" solution holding the middle ground between the Chinese teaching, which he calls "mechanical", and the Western teaching, which (from Zoroaster up to the Bible) proceeds "ethically" in the context of a dramatic dualism—as a game of love played by the Absolute: "Divinity wrapped itself in this maya, as in a veil, according to its good pleasure; thus it wove a sweet rustle of love around it." Maya is "appearance, illusion, but without pain or remorse; all is jest and play": (*Werke* [1935] V, 290). This is a very unhistorical interpretation; naturally it could not prevail against Schopenhauer, Nietzsche and Wagner.

[41] We find the theme of the *masked ball* everywhere (often mixed with that of the puppet play), as an image of the world's doings; in Jean Paul (where it appears as a "dance of the dead"), in Tieck (*Lovell*), Brentano, E. T. A. Hoffmann, Mörike, and in Schumann's genial carnival, inspired by Jean Paul: here we have both intoxication and the quality of the eerie, ghostly. In Eichendorff's *Ahnung und Gegenwart* (1815), Friedrich and Leontin, surrounded by night and solitude, look out from the crown of a tree and see the lively activity of a ball, without being able to hear the music of the dancing. They find it a "frightening and ridiculous stage play" as they "observe the many-hued pleasures of human beings without understanding their inner connections, watching them nod and bow to each other like puppets, seeing them laugh and move their lips, without hearing what they are saying. . . . And are you not presented with this play every day? . . . Do not all people thus gesticulate, toil and torment themselves, endeavoring to give an outward form to that particular, fundamental melody given to each one in his innermost soul? Some can express

to transform the theatre of spectres into a genuinely living theatre:

> The theatre's roof is lifted off, / The wings begin to stir / And stretch up to heaven; / The rivers and woods are making music! / Softly it emerges from the clouds, / Putting everything in confusion, / Something beyond the playwright's art: / People, princes, dryads. . . . / And of all the actors playing their parts, / None knows what the last act will bring. / Only he who beats time in the world beyond / Knows its ultimate outcome.[42]

Late romanticism was not in a position, however, to clothe this program in an adequate form.[43]

---

it more eloquently, others less, but no one can express it completely, as it is present to him" (*Werke* [Insel, 1941], II, bk. I, chap. 6, p. 71). Later (bk. II, chap. 1) he takes up the theme again: "The fair, with its strange jollity, was in full swing on both sides; merry, attractive and solemn images of life passed before him. . . . Countless mirrors were so placed that they multiplied life into infinity, confusing the figures with their reflections, so that his baffled gaze lost itself in the limitless remoteness of this prospect. These masks surrounding him filled him with horror." One high, slender mask dominated: Death (131–32). "Let man spread his wings, / Twist and turn about: / From this world of fools / He'll never get out" (312).

[42] *Dichter und ihre Gesellen* (1834; Included among the *Wanderlieder* as "Dryander mit der Komödienbande"). Cf. Lothario in the same novel: "The poets must not give in; they must let the theatres starve of poetry, they must let them gradually languish in their own wretchedness and boredom; while outside they themselves dramatize the world in fresh and bold ways" (bk. I, chap. 11, 476f.). For Eichendorff the drama of life is the theological drama, elevating the idealistic puppet play of destiny into its own truth. This is clear from his depiction of Calderon, for example in the *Andacht zum Kreuze*, where "the holy Cross, a Christian *fatum*" burns "grimly throughout the entire play, until finally, devouring and transfiguring everything earthly, it shines forth with a steady flame" (*Zur Geschichte des Dramas*, Cotta [1958], vol. 4:526).

[43] Before leaving this period, we must mention a further theme that continues one aspect of the idea of the "world theatre", namely, *the world as seen from above*, i.e., now seen from an airship. The gods of Homer and Virgil looked down from above on the world drama, and they were joined in this vision by the souls of the dead and of those in mystical ecstasy; the theme is commonplace in late antiquity (*Somnium Scipionis*) and even into the middle ages (Dante). Indeed, even in the ancient world it was possible for the scientist to look down on the littleness of the earth. Cf. Aristotle, *Metereologica* 352a: "It would be ridiculous to set the universe in motion for the sake of such trivial changes of extremely short duration (the raising up of land areas from the sea and the submerging of others); for in terms of mass and compass the earth is nothing compared to the

b. Disiecti Membra Poetae: Postidealism

We can see what replaces the "theatre of the world" in post-idealist drama by examining three cardinal writers of the century, *Grillparzer*, *Hebbel* and *Ibsen*. After them, it seems inconceivable that *Hofmannsthal* would still be able to write a "world theatre"; but he was writing on the soil of Austria, where there had never been a complete break with the baroque notion of empire and theatrical tradition. *Grillparzer*, the strange hybrid, will anticipate him here, mediating between the baroque stage and the postidealist theatre.

Consciously or not, the dramatist was bound to try to evade *Hegel's* verdict and occupy the vantage point from which Hegel thought he could evaluate "romantic" "characters" and their subjective limitedness. But the Christian idea of "mission", which was interpreted in the "theatre of the world" as a God-given "role", was no longer available. It alone could reconcile the finitude of a personal destiny with the infinitude of a divine commission: service and freedom. What replaces this role is yearning (*Sehnsucht*), intimations of totality, aspiration, the

---

whole cosmos." But the conjunction of the enthusiastic upward thrust and the detached overall view is modern. In the *Lusiads of Camoes*, Vasco da Gama sees the earth from above in a vision—in the service of Portuguese conquest. In *Primero Sueno* by the Mexican authoress Juana Inés de la Cruz, the world is seen from above in a dream, or rather, there is an attempt to see it in a single grasp; once more the dreamlike upward flight is combined with polyhistory. In idealism the airborne flight becomes the visible image of transcendental reflection. Jean Paul's Luftschiffer Giannozzo experiences the world below him as "the theatre of the world" (sixth flight): "On the surface, which flowed out into infinity on all sides, all the various theatres of life played at the same time with open curtains." Ultimately it makes him "wretched, empty and melancholy", but he will not let himself look up to God: in the infinite worlds above him things will be no different from what they are with us. Stifter, in his *Condor* (1840) also lifts the aeronauts into an intermediate state in which the earth is "no longer the familiar ancestral house" and, when we look up, the firmament is no longer there: "Our earth's beautiful blue bell had become an utterly dark abyss . . . , the sun a menacing star without warmth, without radiance, . . . gaping from the void with a destructive gleam." "Only a harsh light stared at the balloon and the ship, highlighting the machine in a ghostly fashion against the surrounding night and imparting a deathly glow to our faces." Saint-Exupéry's view of the world from his airplane brings this series to an end; no one writes poetry about the journeys to the Moon.

Platonic glimpse of God which strains toward the Infinite through the limitations of the finite. *Faust* is the perfect symbol of this totality which is both being and becoming, which cannot be narrowed down by any individual episode (Gretchen), and which is redeemable *because of* its striving (irrespective of particular actions: in the last act, world-conquering technology requires murder). Initially the Choirs of Spirits at the beginning of the second part were to "hymn the joys of honor, fame, power and dominion";[1] later they will sing of "compassion and the most profound mercy",[2] for now *Goethe* is making room in *Faust* for an "enjoyment of creation from within".[3] The play's framework, the Prologue in Heaven, comes from the "theatre of the world", but here it is nothing more than a horizon expressing totality. It is not an idea determining the action. According to *Goethe*, *Faust* has no such governing idea.[4]

Faust, together with Prometheus, is the genius of the century: the claim to totality. Such a claim can only be sustained philosophically on the basis of a *new monadology* in which every "I" or "self" (*Grillparzer*) knows itself to be a mirroring of the Whole or identical with it. (In its best moments it even *feels* this.) In such a context drama becomes a conflict between rival claims to totality. But the metaphysical-tragic conflict is sparked off, not only or initially by the clash of potencies, but even earlier, by the inner conflict within each individual potency between its ideal form and its actual self-realization on its course through the world. Of necessity, the synthesis of ideal and real dissolves into something inaccessible to intellect and action, something unconscious, which, in 1800, *Schelling* had described thus, in a formula that is very close to *Plotinus* and applies to the entire

[1] *Faust*, Paralipomenon 63.
[2] *Conversations with Eckermann*, fragment to part 4.
[3] Paralipomena, general outline, Apr. 11, 1800.
[4] "They come and ask me what idea I was trying to embody in my Faust—as if I actually knew or could put it into words! 'From heaven, through the world, to hell'—but that is not an idea: it is the course of the action. . . . That the devil loses the wager, and that a man who constantly strives to turn from a path of serious error and embrace better things can be redeemed—this is not an idea in the sense that it underpins the whole play and each individual scene in particular. . . . The more incommensurable . . . , the better" (*Conversations with Eckermann*, May 6, 1827).

century: the Highest itself can be "neither subject nor object, nor both, but only absolute identity. . . . This eternal Unconscious is like the eternal sun in the realm of spirits, concealing itself in its own untroubled light; although it never becomes an object, it imprints its identity on all free actions. It is simultaneously the same for all intelligences, the invisible root of which intelligences are only potencies, . . . the ground both of regularity in freedom and of freedom in the regularity of the objective."[5] In this definition (which *Schelling* expressed concretely in the image of the absolute extempore play), absolute freedom can coincide with absolute necessity (understood as "destiny"), which means, of course, that the tragic dimension makes itself absolute and in doing so abolishes itself. Looking ahead, we can see this standpoint leading to *Schopenhauer's* pantragism (with unconscious Will as ultimate), *Nietzsche's* strained affirmation of life and all later *Lebensphilosophie*, as well as *Freud's* psychology of the unconscious. Finally, too, it leads to a sociology that is made absolute, where the collective explodes the ossified, private "I"s and opens them up to the totality.

α. *Franz Grillparzer*[6]

is still operating in terms of the baroque "empire"; it experiences a resurrection in the emperors of his political dramas (and is passed on to *Reinhold Schneider*). But over against Rudolf of Habsburg with his humble superiority, *Grillparzer* sets his *Ottokar*, a man striving selfishly to attain totality. Rudolf II, in the *Bruderzwist*, embodies a totality that is disintegrating through the influences of the Reformation, Counter-Reformation and the coming Thirty Years' War. Ottokar desires the crown of Charlemagne (v. 610, 1184)[7] and thus stands "before an abyss": "Now, earth, stand fast by me; you have never carried a greater man!" (682). In the fourth act we have the baroque humiliation and ridiculing of Ottokar's arrogance, but, unlike *Shakespeare*, that is not the end; the last act once more brings us the now broken rebel, still philosophizing, even in his demise, about the human being, who is "a

---

[5] Schelling, *System des transzendentalen Idealismus* (1800) SW I/3 600.

[6] Franz Grillparzer, *Werke* in 16 parts, ed. Stefan Hock (Bong).

[7] "Yet perhaps I do not scorn to crown / The highest power with highest honor" (V, 1180f.).

goal, a self, a world within the universe" (835). He is contrasted with the true Emperor who has surrendered his "I" to the role: "I am not the man you once knew. . . . I have disrobed myself of what was mortal / And now am only the Emperor, who never dies." As the oil of consecration touched him, he had become "profoundly aware of the miracle" granted to him in his mission (1790ff.). In *Grillparzer's* mythical dramas this "miracle" will become "magic". The abdicating Emperor in the *Bruderzwist* is the last one to represent the totality, not "the half of a world" (360), unlike the Catholic Ferdinand, who accuses the Emperor of deep distrust "of your noble self" (353). Rudolf believes in God, not in the stars, "but yonder stars are also from God" and represent God's unchangeable, sacred order in the cosmos, that order which he, the Emperor, "a weak man with no gifts" (421) is supposed to uphold. Calmly and determinedly he shows what will happen if the imperial "representation" disintegrates, right down to the rule of the mob: "all will be equal indeed, equally base" (1286, 1492).[8] "The endless splintering will go on / In which God himself and his word are split."[9] Does the poet identify himself with this Christian baroque view? He is not a Christian but certainly believes in God: "Ultimately the historical tragedy . . . is God's work, . . . for only a higher Spirit, the *Weltgeist*, can guarantee events and underwrite the eventual outcome."[10] But what is the relation of this *Weltgeist* to individual freedom? Each "I" has by nature "a progressive and un-restricted urge to preserve and perfect itself", and "if two such un-bounded urges meet, they are bound to conflict, giving rise to evil. . . . For if there were a clearly delimited sphere, how could it . . . be reconciled with freedom?"[11] Thus, initially as a poet and subsequently in theoretical utterances,[12] *Grillparzer* approaches the notion of the idealist "I"-monad. The latter possesses its (unified) self in a "pre-existence" (mostly some mythical antiquity) and has to endeavor to preserve itself on entering the realistic period of history. Collapsing, it reveals its nobler descent (*Sappho*, *Medea* in the *Goldenen Vlies*, *Hero* in

[8] Cf. the emperor's reply to the petition of the Bohemian estates for freedom of religion (VIII, 1599ff.).

[9] Ferdinand, act V, 2618.

[10] *On König Ottokars Glück und Ende*, ed. Sauer, 20 vols., 18:188.

[11] *Studien zur Philosophie und Religion* XI, 28.

[12] "The Spirit is not anything at rest, but rather what is absolutely unresting, pure activity, the negation or the ideality of all fixed definitions of reason. It is not abstractly simple, but, in its simplicity, it simultaneously distinguishes itself from itself. It is not a being that is already final and complete prior to its appearance" (XI, 21, no. 33).

Des Meeres und der Liebe Wellen); or it succeeds in transforming itself but at the price of its original power (*Libussa*); or reality's inner possibilities are experienced as a "dream" and overcome on awaking (*Der Traum ein Leben*); or the hero, equipped with an idealist maxim, cuts his way through reality's web of lies as best he may and wins through (*Weh dem, der lügt*); or else, as a loyal servant, through suffering and loss, he holds to his maxim (*Ein treuer Diener seines Herrn*).

As if to give the lie to *Hegel*, who asserted that it was only in the mythical drama of antiquity that the hero could be totally identified with his destiny, *Grillparzer* always searches for a precultural starting point where man is still embedded in the totality (his "gods" are *daimōnes*, *elohim*,[13] they are *theion*, not *theos*) and can practice "magic", like *Medea* in Colchis[14], can "prophesy", as *Libussa* does to her virgin sisters; when, as a married woman, she tries once more to exercise her prophetic gift, her death is the result. As in *Schiller's* Johanna, virginity symbolizes existence in the ideal: *Sappho* is inspired so long as she is a virgin, *Hero* is expressly consecrated to the heavenly Aphrodite, not the earthly, and vows of a similar kind often govern the course of the action.[15] No more than in *Schiller*, this virginity is not fruitful in a Christian (Marian) way; it signifies "restricting one's life to itself, eschewing all else and preserving one's own meaning"[16] in order to "be a self, a being, a world".[17] Thus Hero's love for Leander brings a derangement that "alienates her from her own self" (1178), yet, when he dies, it admits her to the life of the universe, not unlike Isolde. All that remains "are only shadows; he disintegrates, a mere nothing. . . . / His life *was* life, yours, mine, / The life of the universe. Allowing it to

---

[13] XI, 46, no. 113. Hebbel and Wagner too, in their Nibelungen, like Ibsen in his Nordic plays, returned to an ancient Germanic age.

[14] Rachel too (in *Die Jüdin von Toledo*) practices "magic", fixing the King's picture with needles to the chair-back: "They say that the witches induce love by sticking needles, like this, in wax figures" (act II, 586). And the magic is effective: "Who are you, girl? Do you practice secret arts and crimes?" (V, 631).

[15] As with Fedriko (in *Blanka von Kastilien*), who has taken refuge "from the girl's enchanted circle" in the *Order of Santiago* (IX, 79); so too Margaretha, the wife of Ottokar.

[16] *Des Meeres und der Liebe Wellen* (vol. VI), act I, 165ff. The heavenly Aphrodite to whom Hero is "betrothed" (1223) is "sexless".

[17] *Ibid.*, 372. But Leander too, prior to his love for Hero, is to feel himself "a hero, a god, a man" (act II, 556). Grillparzer expressly traces this "self-seeking" virginity back to India (Naukleros speaks of the "insolent service of ill-humored slaves of Indus", 865): its aim is "recollection" (act III, 948), contemplation, as the explicit opposite of action ("Yet he whose striving leads within, / Where only *wholeness* brings full influence, / Let him remove his mind from outward struggle", 979–80).

die, / We died with him" (1972f.). *Sappho* is consecrated to art, and it is for the sake of art's ideal nature that she loves Phaon: "You adorn me with your own richness",[18] says the latter. But she is aware of the nonidentity of art and life;[19] identity was only there in preexistence.[20] When Phaon cries out in a dream, Sappho realizes that, unconsciously, he loves Melitta; she cannot find her complement in the "real" world: "Let not those whom gods have chosen for their own / Seek fellowship with citizens of earth" (948f.).[21] To Phaon, however, Sappho is "Circe", drawing her "circles of soft enchantment".[22] Having gone through all her jealousy, Sappho is purified to embrace her ideal existence: "I sought you and have found myself"; "she is encompassed by the radiance of the immortals"—as she dies.

Medea (a Brunhild who becomes a Kriemhild) embodies a mythical, primal totality; she is skilled in magic. She bears no guilt for the murder of Phryxus, though it is she who invokes the hereditary curse which confuses the world's justice; however, she falls victim to this same curse (in the *Argonauts*): while she is invoking the *daimōnes*, Jason jumps out from behind the statue of the gods and wounds her; she sees the God of Death in him, the "quiet god" (as *Hofmannsthal's Ariadne* calls Bacchus), and succumbs to the stronger enchantment of his love, in spite of her inner resistance.[23] But Jason too, originally a hero of the primal age, has "transgressed the bounds of life" and becomes alienated from himself because of this love: "I have become an object to myself; / One man thinks in me, but it is another who acts" (1196f.). It is impossible to unite barbarian and Hellene, as is underlined by the curse uttered by the father, who, dying with his son, foretells his daughter's fate in precise detail (1365ff.). This fate is fulfilled in the tragedy of *Medea*, where the impossibility of this love becomes apparent to Jason's self-seeking. He prefers the security of a concrete *polis* to perpetual banishment on account of his union with a barbarian foreigner and gradually pushes her back to her origins: "Go back to the wilderness which cradled you, / To the blood-drenched people to whom you belong, whom you resemble."[24] In this way he tries to extricate

---

[18] *Sappho* (vol. III), act I, 202.

[19] "Poor art's obliged eternally / To beg from life's superfluity. . . ." / "Let us endeavor then, dear friend, / To plait *both* wreaths about our brows, / Drink life from art's intoxicating chalice" (280–82).

[20] "Let me return to that time . . ." / "When love was still a magic land to me, / A strange and unfamiliar magic land" (385, 391–92).

[21] Once again like Phaon, act V, 1721.

[22] 1169; act V, 1665: "Then rage and kill, O treacherous Circe!"

[23] *Die Argonauten* (vol. IV) act III, 1011ff.

[24] *Medea* act II, 1057f.

himself from guilt: "I hand you over to your father's curse."[25] Quite logically, the encircled[26] and rejected woman, in the ultimate bitterness of her situation, finally embodies the curse she did nothing to deserve and kills her children. In truth, the curse is that impossible union which Jason has forcibly brought about, the attempt to seize the fleece: "Blindly you transgressed in reaching for the wanton, / though I cried out that you were courting death!" (2338). The play concludes with the Calderonesque image of life as a "shadow", a "dream".

What is the all-embracing totality in *Grillparzer*? It is the concept of destiny (*fatum*), which the poet has qualified both philosophically and theologically on many occasions. Even in his *Die Ahnfrau*[27] (which was prompted by *Calderon*) he wants to have nothing in common with the mechanical tragedy of destiny. In the background there is a negative theology which even Christianity could do nothing to change, for the links with the Absolute (which is itself only an intimation, even if it is termed "providence") are inaccessible to the human gaze; they are always felt to be a world of powers ("gods"), of impenetrable laws, involved in the actions of freedom.[28] In *Die Ahnfrau*, however, destiny reveals a totally disturbed world order that is endeavoring to regain its balance through expiation: both the Greek hereditary curse and the Christian hereditary (original) sin present only partial comparisons here. At all events "the intensified urge toward evil that can lie in the blood as an inheritance" does not suspend "the freedom of the will and moral accountability".[29] The atmosphere of ethical conduct is obscured; in *Die Ahnfrau*, as we often find in *Grillparzer*, there is an invocation of

---

[25] *Ibid.*, 1115.

[26] "Have you not so encircled the noble deer with the hunting nets of heinous treason that it has no way out" (act V, 2251f.).

[27] "Most probably there is in the divine a central core, a complex, indeed a regulating and creative core; and we may get closer to it by saying, 'There is no God', than if we were to say—according to our concepts—'There *is* a God' " (XI, 38, no. 95).

[28] Cf. the essay "Vom Schicksal" (1817) XII, 59: "Christianity has given us an omnipotent God who holds the foundations of all being in his hands and who is the originator of all change. That is sufficient to satisfy the spirit's presentiment. But is it enough to tame the brooding reason, the rioting imagination? The experience of 1800 years indicates the reverse. We know God as the *last* link in the chain of things, but the intermediate links are missing, and our reason always looks for a *series*." Grillparzer would like the concept of fate to remain so fluid that "it would never be entirely clear whether the poet shares this belief completely. In becoming concrete, providence automatically becomes a destiny [*Schickung*] indistinguishable from fate [*Schicksal*]" (XII, 62). The Introduction to *Die Ahnfrau* refers to Calderon in this context.

[29] XVI, 447.

the "fairyland" of childlike preexistence "Where, without complaint or wish, / Unacquainted with myself I lived / Hand in hand with innocence". Aroused to love for Jaromir, Bertha experiences the poison of eros: "Your love is transgression, / A fire odious to God".[30]

However, *Der Traum ein Leben* does give access to the innermost center. *Grillparzer* takes over *Calderon's* baroque motif, but he does not simply reverse it, as is often said. For Rustan's criminal dream-life is the development of a real, intrinsic possibility of his freedom: "Forget not: dreams create / No wishes, merely / Wakening those at hand; / And what is banished by the dawn / Lay in you, germ-like, hidden; / Beware. . . ."[31] The song of the Dervish at the end of the first act explains life's goods, its joys, words, desires, and even the emotion of love and the deeds of goodness, as "shadows", whereas only thought is true; this, together with Rustan's presentiment, in the midst of demonic doings, that the fantasy will soon be over and when he wakes up he will no longer be a criminal,[32] continues something of the "shadow" motif of the baroque theatre, even at the very heart of the idealist pre-occupation with the "I". In addition, however, these two features point ahead to the age of *Freud* and depth psychology. Where does truth lie: in the "dreamer", in the "unconscious" or in waking life? The question is soluble in neither world. In the end Rustan, at whose bedside Mirza watches,[33] is a pre-echo of Peer Gynt, whose solipsistic divagations are accompanied by Solveig.

In *Grillparzer*, the human being comes to grief in the anteroom of the unattainable "unconscious identity" of the ideal and the real (*Schelling*). This anteroom is felt to be haunted—a residual Christian feature—by guilt. Since man, free man, must forever strive toward the infinite, there is no longer an eternal Author to allot him a role. But *Grillparzer* holds back[34] from carrying the tragic dimension into the nature of the Absolute itself. *Hebbel* is the first to take this logical step.[35]

[30] (Vol. III) act II, 1529ff. Cf. Jaromir in act V, 2835ff. When Jaromir takes the dagger from the *Ahnfrau*, he has a déjà-vu experience of the crimes of the ancestors: "And I felt figures hovering round me, figures I had often seen, as if in a previous life. . . . And in the very depth of my bosom I seemed to find myself" (2132ff.).

[31] (Vol. VI) act IV, 2694ff.

[32] (Vol. VI) act IV, 2289–99.

[33] *Ibid.*, 2355–58.

[34] Apart from the final verse in *Des Meeres und der Liebe Wellen*, when Janthe takes the wreath from the statue of Amor, throws it toward the dead woman, and addresses the statue in these words: "You who promise so much, do you keep your word?" (VI, 2115f.).

[35] Between these two we must at least make mention of Christian Dietrich Grabbe (*Sämtliche Werke* 1874), who presents us in his plays with even more

β. *Friedrich Hebbel,*[1]

who was impressed by *Schelling's* philosophy of the world ages and of mythology—as mediated by *Solger*—took an abruptly contrary position, like *Grillparzer*, to the Hegelian theory of the demise of art. It would be possible for philosophy to overtake art if art were nothing more than "a comedy of characters, transposed (as it were) from the external theatre to the internal, where, now as then, the hidden Idea plays hide-and-seek with itself. . . . But art is not only infinitely *more* than this, it is something entirely *different*, it is *realized philosophy*, as the world is the *realized Idea*"; philosophy cannot represent the latter, "for it is only in art that the world is integrated into a totality".[2] This presupposes that the totality of the (Hegelian) Idea is no longer amenable to all-reconciling thought. In *Hebbel*, "God", the Absolute, retires into impenetrable mystery, being revealed solely in "the dialectic as it is transposed into life".[3] The poet, it is implied, renders this dialectic of life visible in symbolic forms, achieving the only possible reconciliation through the shipwreck of opposed characters. The individual "I" is guilty because of its "unyielding, self-seeking expansion" (not because of the "original sin of Christian teaching").[4] As to why the totality always presents itself with this primal fissure: "I have never found an answer to this question, and no one who seriously looks will find one."[5] All the same, *Hebbel* makes bold to say that the poet can unite "life in its brokenness" and the spiritual "element of the idea in which it redis-

---

isolated and metaphysically defenseless "ego-monads" than Grillparzer and Hebbel. But it is characteristic that these larger-than-life characters are set off—for the most part with some difficulty—against the background of a naturalistic, gaily colored and chaotic depiction of popular life. Grabbe's Napoleon (in *Napoleon oder die hundert Tage*) formally drowns in it, despite his grand utterances: "The Sun sank with me" (III, 65); "I am I, that is, Napoleon Bonaparte, who created himself in two years" (III, 131). To Cambrone: "General, it is my luck that is failing—I am not" (III, 249). In a similar way *Hannibal* towers in isolation above Romans and Carthaginians; he is betrayed by the latter and sacrificed to the economic "system" which cannot die (III, 486).

[1] Friedrich Hebbel, Tagebücher in *Werke*, 5 vols. (Hanser, 1966); 465–66; referenced in this section by volume and page number.

[2] Preface to *Maria Magdalene* in *Werke* I, 320–21.

[3] I, 313.

[4] *Mein Wort über das Drama* in *Werke* III, 546. "This guilt is a primal guilt, not to be separated from the concept of man; it hardly filters through into his consciousness, but is something given with life itself." The doctrine of original sin is "nothing other than a consequence drawn from it and modified in a Christian way" (III, 568).

[5] *Ibid.*, 569–70.

covers its lost unity".[6] Taking "the dualistic ideal factors which, when they clash, produce the creative spark which ignites the whole work of art, the poet [*Dichter*] can condense [*verdichten*] them into characters", representing "the inner event . . . in terms of external history".[7] Thus he must be presumed to *know* that unity which permits him to bring out the "subordinate elements" in such a way that "the superior elements devour them".[8] He must maintain the tension between life's two manifestations, being and becoming; only thus can the drama "illustrate the life process".[9] "The poet must show the process of becoming in its succeeding forms",[10] and so he must never let these characters appear fixed and final, for they only become themselves through tragic conflict with the Idea.[11] On the basis of his immutably tragic view of life, which excludes any progress through history,[12] *Hebbel* concentrates on the moments of collapse which signify the end of one era and the beginning of another; indeed these, and these alone, have always been the moments which produced great drama, that is, Greek drama and *Shakespeare*[13]—portraying the "shattering of a ring". Yet these historical crises are only "vehicles"[14] for him, enabling him to set forth what is perennially valid; only in this way can dramatic "art be the highest form of historiography".[15] Consequently he is suspicious of the socialist utopias of the *Junges Deutschland* writers,[16] and in his figure of Duke Ernst (in *Agnes Bernauer*) pays his tribute, like *Grillparzer*, to the old idea of empire.[17] From time to time he attempted a

[6] I, 312.

[7] I, 320.

[8] I, 319.

[9] III, 545.

[10] IV, 371 (no. 1471).

[11] III, 546.

[12] "[H]owever things may change around him, man, according to his nature and destiny, remains eternally the same" (III, 546).

[13] I, 309–10.

[14] III, 520.

[15] I, 322.

[16] I, 310.

[17] Though this play also expresses the Hegelian idea of the absolute subordination of the individual to society, of which "the state is the necessary formal expression" (to K. Werner, Feb. 16, 1852: vol. V, 709), Hebbel considers the tragic situation of Duke Ernst to be only a very extraordinary, "monstrous" one (to Euchtritz, Dec. 14, 1854: vol. V, 760). He did not wish to give allegiance to Hegel but to counter the spirit of the age: "For a long time I have felt the urge to erect a monument to the old German Reich" (to G. C. Gervinus, Dec. 11, 1852: vol. V, 746).

dramatization of the whole of world history on the basis of its periodic crises, but it was doomed to complete failure.[18] *Hebbel* the poet takes up a position from which he feels able to apply a "justice" (that is at least symbolic) to a theatre of the world that is no longer guided by any recognized, or believed-in, ultimate instance. Provided the poet "does not pettily and arbitrarily hide away in his own threadbare 'I', but allows the invisible elements to stream through him, elements that are in flux at all ages, ever fashioning new figures and forms",[19] he can be "confident" of being on the very spot where *Schelling's* unconscious World Spirit failed as director of the extempore play; the play, "as I construct it, in no way concludes with dissonance: for it itself dissolves the dualistic form of being."[20]

Two motifs strike us in the great tragedies: first of all the guilty attempt to lay hold of reality's sacred origin, mostly symbolized by the crafty seizure, on the part of masculine power, of woman's inviolate, veiled and sacred depths. This conquest dishonors the person's free and unfathomable integrity and reduces her to the level of a "thing". Thus, in *Judith*, she has been "murdered at her most sacred level" (I, 65), reduced to a "thing" (I, 67), and consequently thinks of nothing but revenge. *Genoveva* is presented as a "saint" (Epilogue v. 239), a "new saint" (V, 2899); in *Gyges und sein Ring* the veiled Rhodope is shown, unveiled, by her husband to his friend (who is invisible by virtue of the ring) and is thus "stained" (902); and in the *Nibelungen* the unapproachable Brunhild is subdued by Siegfried (wearing his cap of invisibility) and rendered amenable to Gunther; she is used as an object of barter for Kriemhild (1772ff.). In *Herodes und Mariamne* the King's sin is that he does not trust his beloved to kill herself if he dies but places her "under the sword" (50) and thus reduces her "to a thing" (2203); he thinks little of her (1624), dishonors the image of God in her (3107), "violates humanity" in her (1684f.). In the same way Gyges "destroyed the jewel of this world", not realizing what he was doing (1423f.) Kandaules expands the theme to cosmic proportions when he sees the ring as symbolic of the "entire world destiny": "The world needs its sleep" and its veil (1784, 1827), but there is always some cunning person to disturb, waken and unveil it. Such action once more sets history in motion; the latter's course is nothing but "retribution" or the ever-recurrent "revenge", restoring the balance by annihilation.

There is a second constant motif: *Hebbel's* heroes are all larger than

[18] The plans for *Moloch*, *Christus*, and for making *Judith* the high point of the Jewish, and *Genoveva* the high point of the Christian principle.

[19] III, 550.

[20] III, 569; cf. I, 319.

life. They are totalities which, under the conditions of finitude,[21] burst the bounds of what is human; they do this, not because of a mission they have received, but in virtue of their inner wealth and unfathomable depths. A king, Herodes says, should not submit himself to the lot of ordinary mankind. He "should not be bound, in his innermost self, to a being outside himself" (404ff.). The great characters all strut upon the buskin of their sense of self, that self which contains, intertwined, in embryo, the contradictions of hate and love,[22] and yet, as man and woman, they are as alien as stars to one another.[23] Characters like Rhodope, Mariamne and Kriemhild, on the basis of their fundamental identity of contradictions, can restore the metaphysical equipoise by taking "revenge" within love itself: when Herodes does not trust his wife to commit suicide, she takes revenge by compelling her beloved to condemn her to death and thus be unhappy for the rest of his life. *Hebbel* heightens his characters by showing them often in three dimensions: the "prehistorical and mythical"[24] (that is, the "demi-god", Holofernes; Gyges; the prophetic Valkyrie, Brunhild); the biblico-Christian, super-

[21] It is characteristic that, in *Herodes und Mariamne*, the whole "infinity" of love has to present itself within the confines of mortality, since immortality is explicitly rejected: (2979).

[22] *Judith* is a tangled confusion of love and hatred for Holofernes; her description of the act (I, 65) shows the identity of both. The crazed Golo in *Genoveva* recognizes the unity of love and death: "O love . . . / You are not life but death, death! / You are death's loveliest, highest form, / The only one who, in taking, gives" (300f.). Both Herod and Mariamne live and think in terms of this unity of love and hate. Herod: "I will escape from this whirlpool / Of hate and love, before I drown in it, / Cost what it may!" (2904ff.). Mariamne "now both hates and loves him" (940). On Brunhilde's relationship with Siegfried, Hagen says, "She is in his power, and this hatred / Is grounded in love . . . Yet it is not the love that binds / Man and wife together, . . . but some spell / By means of which her sex strives to maintain itself, / Driving the last female giant, without desire, / Without choice, into the arms of the last giant" (2161). Golo enunciates this identity most clearly in his description of a dream: "Now hatred and love were reconciled, / And hatred found in the wound it had inflicted / Its sweetest tomb, love, which in vain / Sought to heal what was incurable, / Dissolved in tears, and a higher emotion, gently binding the two, / Something primal, all-embracing, / Drew me down, as on waves, deep and deeper into night" (2053ff.).

[23] For Hebbel, sexual dualism is the clearest manifestation of the metaphysical. "When a man lacks nothing, he still lacks this: / To know woman as she truly is. / She forms something out of herself that he in vain / Endeavors to fashion from life's external matter" (*Genoveva* 154ff.). "Who has ever plumbed the depths of what is possible to a woman!" (2385f.).

[24] At the end of the list of *dramatis personae* in *Gyges und sein Ring*.

natural (Judith, Genoveva, Klara, Herodes, the Nibelungen); and the universally human, which includes, however, the abysses of the unconscious. The "mythical" and the "Christian" can no more be taken literally than reduced to "depth psychology": they are symbolic sounding boards, used to amplify the persons in their roles as "monads" and "totalities". This is clearest in *Genoveva*, where, on the one hand, perfect holiness is portrayed by continual comparison with the crucified Christ in his substitutionary suffering,[25] and, on the other hand, hell appears bodily in Margarethe, the witch and devil's bride, who finally reveals the whole immensity of Golo's crime.[26] Nor is this enough: the scene with the persecuted and tortured Jew expands the spiritual context by adding the eschatological dimension: the end of the world (656), the time fulfilled (865), the Last Day (1444), the humiliation of the Suffering Servant (874) and God's curse (916). However, Golo knows that no mercy can reach him any more (3375f.); he has a presentiment of "the most dreadful . . . highest court" (508f.) but at the same time wants to be "judge, plaintiff and spectator" (3547f.), and so, by overstretching the Christian categories (which envisage nothing of the kind), he drops out of them. The "Christian" element here is only the orchestration of the Titanic theme. The same can be said of *Maria Magdalene* (albeit it contains no Titans: here it is the pitiless middle-class milieu that ties the knot of retribution) and most definitely of the *Nibelungen*, where the Christian colors are only used as a foil in the heroic tableau.

The technique of mythical heightening becomes exhausted on the modern stage; the borrowed Christian form, lacking its content, must collapse. Both are absorbed by the psyche, whose proportions already determine *Hebbel's* work and will soon, in *Ibsen*, provide the field for the analyst. These psyches act on the world stage by representing fragmentary aspects of the whole; in decisions that are not the result of compulsion and yet are expressions of the hidden will of the whole, they execute world judgment, giving rise to something like reconciliation. In each case this becomes credible when the tragedian directs the play and mediates between the inaccessible ground of the world and his

---

[25] Genoveva is a bleeding icon (267ff.), a "holy of holies" (152), contemplating the sufferings of the Cross which obliterate the sin of an attempt to kill God (1197ff.); she forgives (Golo: 2112, Siegfried: 3285f.), and ultimately causes Siegfried to forgive Golo (Epilogue 281ff.).

[26] She brews the "satanic" plan (1685). The long sixth scene in act IV has all the paraphernalia of an invocation of the devil and demonic possession. Finally Margarethe wants to be absolute evil (2912ff.) as a foil to the absolute goodness of Genoveva. She ends by burning herself to death.

fragmentary images on the world stage. Thus the justice he creatively calls into being is a "poetic justice"; the spectator is free to be convinced or to reject it as a subjective construction. This brings into view the crisis of the "theatre of the world"; first let us see how it comes to a head in *Ibsen* before going on to face the inescapable alternatives.[27]

γ. *Henrik Ibsen*[1]

A school essay of the young *Ibsen* depicts a dream: an angel summons the sleeping boy to follow him. "I will show you a vision of human life in its reality and truth." They climb down immense rock steps into the inner regions of the earth, into a city of the dead, filled with countless blanched skeletons. "You see here", says the angel, "that all is vanity." There is a rushing sound like the start of a storm, like a thousand sighs, becoming a gale; the dead bestir themselves and stretch out their arms.[2] *Ibsen's* last play, his "dramatic epilogue", is called *When We Dead Awake*: it remains within the complete immanence of his childhood vision. Man is still the idealist monad, but now he is finally cut loose from the metaphysical background; Ibsen's two postulates, "freedom and truth", must verify themselves at the purely anthropological level. Now man himself is the audience before whom he acts. The playwright provides the situations in which man fails or proves himself. But what are the criteria of truth here?

His first play, *Catilina*, is meant to represent not only the "contra-

[27] This selection from the dramatists is only intended to provide examples. It is enough if it shows the outlines of nineteenth-century metaphysics—both of Schopenhauer and of Nietzsche, neither of whom, in fact, developed a fruitful theory of drama. Paths lead to them from both Hebbel and Ibsen: the post-idealist "monads" can be interpreted equally well as alienated forms of the unconscious, blind "Total Will" (in which they are destined to dissolve) or as stubborn expressions of the will-to-life or the will-to-power. Both are combined in the simultaneously pessimistic and *kulturoptimistisch* metaphysics of Eduard von Hartmann, whose deity is a "tragic hero" in Hebbel's and Ibsen's sense. From Hartmann the path goes on to Scheler. But the slide away from metaphysics and toward the depths of the psyche, which we have observed in Hebbel, will triumph in the drama: the sociological (G. Hauptmann) and psychological (B. Shaw) drama will become the dominant form, finally breaking the link with the old "theatre of the world".

[1] *The Complete Major Prose Plays* (New York, 1965).

[2] Roman Woerner, *Henrik Ibsen* 3d ed. (2 vols., 1923) vol. 1:23. This can be compared with an unwritten mystical prelude to *Emperor and Galilean*, in which we find the sentence: "The scene is the stronghold of the bottomless depths. . . . The spirits of the dead rise upward; the demons of the darkness hold them by cords; wearied, they sink back" (I, 319).

diction between strength and striving, between will and possibility",[3]
but, at a deeper level, the contradiction between guilt incurred in past
and future action. This contradiction is symbolized in the vestal virgin
Furia whom Catilina loves and who must hate him because he
has violated her sister. In this love-hate she becomes his "destiny"
(I, 184), his "nemesis" (192), a power arising from the realm of the
death on the yonder side of life.[4] In her love, Catilina's translucently
faithful wife Aurelia represents life. After the failure of the rebellion
due to a lack of material resources, Furia draws the defeated man down
with her to the realm of the dead, having described herself as "your
own eye, your own memory and judge" (196) and having garlanded
him with the opium of forgetfulness and persuaded him to kill Aurelia,
which he does, extinguishing all life, "all the beating of hearts" (199).
He himself is "a shadowy image, hunted by a thousand shadows"
(198). But instead of Furia and Catilina sinking together into Hades,
she remains alive, and it is Aurelia who dies with Catilina, proclaiming—
paradoxically enough—the triumph of love and light (201). The
clumsily constructed play fits the framework already mentioned; it
stakes out the area in which *Ibsen's* dramatic action will take place.

Like *Hebbel* and *Wagner* (since the early Greek tradition is too far
distant) he looks for the grand heroic ego in the Nordic sagas. There is a
powerful increase in intensity from *Lady Inger*—who stands "between
two hostile camps, both of which only half trust you" (I, 238) but
entangles herself in her own net and unknowingly kills her own
son—via Margit in *The Feast at Solhaug*,[5] who, like the later Nora, sits
"caged" in a loveless marriage (I, 320), almost murders her lover and
eventually, in penitence, enters a convent—to the superb Hjördis in
The Vikings in Helgeland. For once, in the prehistoric heroine and her
equally matched antagonists, we are given a convincing presentation of
that totality which later, translated into a modern setting, will only
appear in pathological distortion (*Hedda Gabler*). Hjördis' ferocious
pride cannot bear the thought that she was humiliated without realizing

---

[3] Preface to *Catilina* I, 124, "You must, you must!—a voice calls to me in my
innermost being; and yet I, I still hesitate." "O that once, for a split second, I
could flash and flame like a falling star through some lofty deed." Furia: "Your
heart is great, worthy of ruling Rome. . . . Oh, why do you hesitate?" (156).

[4] "I belong to the grave; that is my home. I am a fugitive fleeing from the
vales of death; by daybreak I shall be home again" (169).

[5] A stepping-stone, in milder vein, to the masterpiece which followed it, *The
Vikings in Helgeland*. This latter play, its theme taken from the Volsungen Saga,
was already fermenting in the poet's mind but had not matured; so the more
staid medieval story came before the wild saga of ancient times.

it when she was chosen as a bride: the warrior who wooed her in disguised form must be done away with: "Sigurd must die—or I!" (I, 409). They admit their original love to each other (421); since Hjördis wishes to be united to him, she kills him and then plunges into the sea, yet not without having heard that he has become a Christian and that therefore there is no prospect of reunion in the world beyond (436): this reverses the conclusion of *Catilina*. Next, after six years' work, comes *The Pretenders*, repeating the Catilina theme of the contradiction between ambition and inner resources in the figure of Jarl Skule, "God's stepchild" (II, 243); he is opposed by King Hakon, who stands for the same totality of representation we find in *Grillparzer* and before whom his rival finally capitulates.

Two years earlier, however, *Ibsen* had already moved away from mythical prehistory and shifted the problem of the personal monad into the present. Schwanhild in *Love's Comedy* is a totality of this kind, an embodiment of contentedly rounded life, which, for that very reason, eludes the young artist, Falk. For his part, he wants to "walk the path of truth" with her, away from the insincere philistinism that surrounds her (II, 86) . . . for one exhilarating summer ("You are the current of air that bears me aloft", 37). Who can guarantee a lifelong love? Schwanhild prefers to let this love die at its zenith, in its "truth", "today" (97). Falk says, "Only *thus* can I come close to you. As eternal day strives to emerge from death, so love only attains the dignity of true life when, redeemed from longing and desires, it arises to memory's home" (97). Now Falk is free to be a poet of love "with the courage of truth", "consecrated" to his life's work (98). She, however, will marry the solid merchant, Goldstadt. Thus the truth of poetry stands opposed to the truth of life, the ideal to the real. For the moment the mood is still lighthearted; later it will be ultimately tragic.

This means that the next two attempts to portray a "monadic" hero, *Brand* and *Peer Gynt*, are doomed to failure from the start. Even if *Brand* were not to negate himself, *Peer Gynt*, following his every step, would destroy him. They are the face and obverse of the same thing.

With his cry of "All or nothing" (II, 294, 299, 304, 306, 319, 414), *Brand* embodies the pitiless *will* that is aware that an equally "inflexible" (260) God has commissioned it to oppose every "cowardly compromise" (299), every dichotomy between life and teaching (260), both within itself and in others, be they family or nation. He speaks of God as the Lord (270) for whose cause he must give his life (251) and in whose name he will bury the middle-class God who is already dead and stinking (257); he compares himself with Abraham and his sacrifice (307), with Jesus on the Mount of Olives (299), on his Way of the Cross

(417) and in his sacrificial death (407). But he rejects prayer as an unworthy "begging for grace" and "Christ's mediation" (349), and his "readiness for sacrifice" that tips the scales is Pelagian (345). Here, therefore, *Ibsen* changes the picture of the ardent Christian saint who sacrifices everything for his mission to that of the absolute idealist, viewed from the *psychological* point of view. He portrays the actor on the world stage who now coincides with the playwright/director.[6] *Ibsen* asserts that the Christian element in *Brand* is inessential: "I could have gone through the same syllogism with a sculptor or a politician just as well as with a pastor." "The all-or-nothing demand applies everywhere in life: in love, in art, and so forth. I myself am Brand in my best moments. . . ."[7] Yet, although the poet rehearses similar syllogisms with different material, *R. Woerner* is right when he says that "the choice of the preacher was not entirely without significance."[8] Not only was there a Norwegian precedent (Pastor *Lammers*) and a Danish one (*Kierkegaard*, who had hardly any influence, however, on *Ibsen*): the only preidealist model for such an absolute identification of one's life with a divine commission is the Christian model. However, once robbed of its soul—faith and love—the latter can only yield a tragic caricature like Brand: "Too great, too great / Are your desires, your projects, your demands, / Your calling, your aim, your fate" (335). His watchword is "sickness" (414), his destiny futility, a falling into endless night (411); "All your suffering was dreaming and deception" (413), and the last word is "yearning" (415)—the desire for the impossible. Brand destroys the village church in order to build a bigger one, then he leaves the latter in order to obliterate the distinction between church and cosmos, life and worship (394f.); he ends in the "ice church", which, collapsing, buries him. The plot comes to a dramatic head when his identification with the absolute Will coincides with his marriage to Agnes. (*Kierkegaard* had escaped this dilemma by breaking his engagement and thus following the example of the great saints.) There is pathos in his having to "choose" between two absolutes (361–362); having sacrificed his mother, son and wife on the altar of his "self" (280–283, "living to oneself": 314), he too perishes on it.

Peer Gynt satirizes the Faustian German idealism. It is the first

[6] This is not contradicted by the passages in which, at "night", Brand haggles with God, nor by the final verses, when Brand asks God whether a "will *quantum satis*" is after all of no account, and is told that "God is *deus caritatis*"; this answer is demonstrably not the poet's but only the rejoinder designed to reveal the tragic dimension of an absolute will.

[7] From letters to G. Brandes, quoted by Woerner, *Henrik Ibsen* I, 175.

[8] *Ibid.*, 179.

"station drama" modeled on *Faust*, in which the "I", in continual monologue, reviews one situation after another as it takes place before him. *Strindberg* will perfect this form, which anticipates certain methods of the theatre of the absurd. It is no longer possible for a real Mephistopheles to appear, let alone a "master" (II, 579) of the play; occasional, indecipherable fragments and obscure symbols of the metaphysical flit past us. One central thing is clear: Peer, the "Emperor of Self" (541), intends to live unto and for himself (493), as "the world's God" (500), cutting a free path of his own choosing through this world's thousand snares (498), in order to bring "the caliphate of my being" (520) "through force of personality to the throne" (521). It is the fairly precise equivalent of *Kierkegaard's* "desperate desire to be oneself". The stages he goes through are like Faust's, except that right from the start Gynt "did nothing but lie and romance" (458). He traverses the subhuman dimension of the Realm of the Trolls (as Faust visits Auberbachs Keller and the Witches' Kitchen), proceeding via the betrayal of love (Gretchen) to exotic financial hijinks (Kaiserhof), to Anitra's prophetic phantasmagoria (Helena), the dream of cultivating the desert and the purely egoistic murder at the shipwreck (Philemon and Baucis). As an interlude there is the scene in the Cairo madhouse with its lampooning of *Fichte* and *Hegel*: "Absolute reason passed away at eleven o'clock last night." Here Gynt, who is always himself in all situations, has to be "so to speak beside himself" (534); the insane madhouse superintendent excuses him: "He's full of his ego; he has no room for anything else. He is himself in everything he says and does. Himself, because he is beside himself" (537). At the beginning, in the darkness, he encounters the "crooked man", who thrice identifies himself as "I-myself". Peer struggles with him yet cannot get a grip on him. But when he comes to the horizon of death, where "pathos and laughter are the same" (553), in the threefold encounter with the "button-caster" who wants to "recast" his utterly waste substance, it transpires that Peer, with all his clinging to himself ("I'm not going to give up a jot of myself"), is a man "who has never been himself" (571). The devil, in the form of a clergyman, tells him that it is only real, positive or negative characters that are of interest, whereas Peer is a "smudged out" photographic plate (584f.). The question "What does it mean: 'To be oneself'?" receives the paradoxical answer (which is intended neither in an idealist nor a Christian sense): "To be oneself is: to kill oneself" (578). And to the next question, namely, how a man can know what the master wants of him, comes the answer: "His instinct should guide him." *Grillparzer* would have agreed with this. Strangely enough, the Troll's advice, "Be thyself—Jack" (463), which

Peer rejects as intolerably subhuman (468) but which keeps occurring to him (510), ultimately reveals its profound ambiguity: "You've lived like a troll"—that is, egoistically (576). Nothing was enough for Peer, however; consequently he can find this "enough", he can find his truth and authenticity, beyond himself, in Solveig. She has waited all her life for the unfaithful Peer and ultimately it is she who opens up a sphere in which he can be himself. Peer: "Where was my self . . . the self that bore God's stamp upon its brow?" Solveig: "In my faith, in my hope and in my love" (589).

But this fixed point, which is able to revolutionize Peer's existence, proves insufficient to guide us through the sociologico-psychological jungle of the following plays. The first plays intend to unmask the tortuous insincerity of society and lead us to the "truth and freedom"[9] of the personality. But in the later plays this very truth and freedom are shown, by reference to their own history and their relation to society, to be questionable if taken as an absolute standard: "Nothing in this world can pass the test if one goes deep enough",[10] and not simply because it is finite but because no person can aspire to absoluteness—and this is the issue—without incurring guilt. In the end he takes the easier path of pillorying the social lie, "hollowness and corruption, . . . a whitewashed grave" (III, 443). In *The League of Youth* the egoistic opportunist Stensgård, is unmasked. In *Pillars of Society*, Bernik, the selfless social benefactor, is a person who is not afraid of lying (III, 496) or slander or, ultimately, of deliberate murder (520). He uses the social lie (536) to excuse his hypocrisy of a "clean conscience" (503, 515); circumstances finally oblige him to confess (546). But this trend goes too far in *An Enemy of the People*: Dr. Stockmann, having discovered that the wells have been physically poisoned, proceeds to a passionate denunciation and "disinfection" (283) of the moral poisoning (IV, 200); "standing alone" (298), he comes close to Brand's eccentricity, particularly when he would like to reform society using "the small number of spiritually superior personalities" (267). This utopian idealism is unmasked in *Rosmersholm*, where Rosmer, the correct man of honor (IV, 436), is drawn to his death by the stronger personality of Rebecca (the really guilty one): she made Rosmer's first wife commit suicide, "so you could be happy—and free . . ." (IV, 457). Rebecca's "courageous, free-born will" (507) was ultimately a "wild, uncontrollable desire" which did not scruple to use any methods and for that very

---

[9] "The spirit of truth and the spirit of freedom—these are the pillars of society." "I must really make myself snugly at home in the great world of truth and freedom that has now been revealed to me."
[10] III, 121.

reason failed to attain true freedom. *A Doll's House* (1879), like *An Enemy of the People* (1882), ostensibly works toward the emancipation of (woman's) personality from Helmer's evident egoism (IV, 43, 87)—which is a symbol, again, for society's lying corruption.[11] Both dramas take as their aim the perverse ideal of "self-education" and the "sacred duties toward oneself" (91). But in fact the point of departure is not a domesticated, subject woman but an accomplished "hypocrite, liar and felon" (83), who, naturally enough, contemplates suicide. Even before *Ghosts*, however, the theme of heredity played a part in several plays; the analysis of the guilty personality leads back to the guilt of others. Thus Osvald's propensity toward art, free love and the "sun" seems (and this, for *Ibsen*, is the ultimate possibility) to be the superstructure erected on a sick reality. (This will be *Thomas Mann's* starting point.) "I did not ask you to give me life", says the son to his mother (IV, 177).

The Wild Duck, a key play, asks whether there is any point or justification in unveiling the truth. Gregers, with his "moralistic fever" (IV, 402) and in accordance with his "summons to the ideal" (365, 401), wants to analyze his friend Hjalmar's marriage relationship. He blathers about "suffering and endurance" (395), but the cynical Relling tells him that the weak Hjalmar is not the kind of "personality" (401) to respond to such treatment; in most cases, in fact, "the life-lie" is "the animating principle of life", and "ideals" mean "lies" (403–404). In point of fact, the only thing Gregers achieves is the tragic suicide of the child, Hedwig, whereas the realistic marriage of the old sinner, Werle, and his housekeeper, a marriage based "on complete openness on both sides" (390), succeeds without complication. *The Lady from the Sea*, which, apart from *Little Eyolf*, is the only cheerful play of the late period, pursues the theme of the liberation of a person fettered by unrecognized passions. Ellida seems to be under the spell of an addiction (V, 39) to an old love which comes to tempt her again; she experiences this as pressure from her husband who wants to hold on to her. But in fact it turns out to be something in her own mind drawing and beckoning her (V, 84), a contradiction within herself,[12] ultimately "the hunger for the boundless, the infinite—the unattainable" (104). When her husband gives her complete freedom to choose, the spell is broken, and she can opt for him and her family. Here we see the reversal and overcoming of the rationale behind *Brand*. Something of it remains, however: only as a

---

[11] Nora: "I must find out who is right, society or I."

[12] Ellida: "He's coming to ask me . . . to start my life over—to live a life out of my own truth—the life that terrifies and attracts—and that I *can't* give up, not of my own free will!"

completely autonomous monad is Ellida able to commit herself once more to an interpersonal relationship. This topic serves as a prelude to the last plays, which are all tragedies of autonomy.

Hedda Gabler is the "desire for life" (V, 166) making itself absolute as the will to power (173), without love (164), even as a kind of sport (142). In a Dionysian manner she unlocks everything that has been carefully kept within limits and thereby destroys it. (Hedda gets hold of the erstwhile drinker Lövborg, makes him drunk and destroys his manuscript.) The "end in beauty" (193) is in reality ugly (208); having striven for full autonomy, she suddenly sees that she is "not free" (211) and kills herself. *The Master Builder* feels that he is one of the "chosen people" (275) who are to be assisted and served by those around them and who have the magical power to transform their wishes into reality (V, 232, 246, 275). He sees himself on a level with God (305), wrangles with him (312) because he is not God himself, builds "castles in the air", desires the impossible (298, 307ff.), but at the same time he is afraid of heights (302): his sense of autonomy causes him to feel guilt and hence *angst* (233, 251). When he himself wants to play the Judgment (233), he becomes a victim of "pitiless retribution" (281) and falls from the tower. The theme of total, autonomous idealism, erected on the foundation of guilty egoism, is carried through to the bitter end in *Ibsen's* two last plays. First, however, comes the intermezzo, *Little Eyolf*, linking up with *The Wild Duck*. It presents a strained totality in the form of the mother, Rita, who will not share her love for her husband with anyone, not even with her child (338f., 343, 358f.), not even in an imaginary heaven (359). After the child's death the play portrays the husband's equally strained totality (352, 379), but Eyolf's death—for which, again, the parents are ultimately to blame (361)—shows them that "being alone" is just as impossible as "not being alone" (370); they are opened up to each other by the "earth-bound" (383) "law of change" (386). *John Gabriel Borkmann* (a continuation of Bernik) is a "chosen one" (422), "Napoleon" (425), the identity of absolute idealism (using technology and trade to humanize the world: 439, 475f.) and the absolute lust for power (440) which grabs millions, heedless of whose they are (435, 439). When the collapse comes he wants to be his own prosecutor, defense attorney and judge (449) but, like Brand, dies in cold and lofty regions (479). The last play is *When We Dead Awake*, which goes back to the beginning, to the youthful essay *Catilina* and *Love's Comedy*. Rubek, the sculptor, is "dead", who once used Irene as a model for his masterpiece, the *Day of Resurrection*, rejecting her tangible love for the sake of getting his ideal form perfect. He, even more than Falk, is the egoistic artist for whom life is only the raw material of art. Consequently Irene too (who has been in an asylum) is now "dead" (V, 547). But a further consequence is that, since his masterpiece (which, in any case, he subsequently spoiled) his talent has dried up (526). Rubek's wife, Maja, succumbs to the crude sensuality of Ulfheim, the hunter of bears and women: she "wakes up" in naked disillusion. Both couples do not awake "from" the dead but *in* death, in time to see what they have lost: "We who are dead only see what is irrevocably lost . . . when we wake up. . . . We see that we have never lived" (537). "There will be no resurrection after our life together" (535). Once again both couples climb up to trackless heights and, like Brand, are engulfed by an avalanche.

This symbolic but futile and empty "upward" thrust is an *idée fixe* in Ibsen.[13] The mountain is both the metaphor of the ideal and the mount of temptation. Thus Maja says: "You said you would take me with you to a high mountain and show me all the glory of the world" (V, 489). This is a constantly recurring image.[14] The absolute nature of the ideal

[13] We find it in Frank, Brand, Solness, Allmers, Borkmann and Rubek.

[14] Rubek not only promised this to Maja; he had already said the same to Irene: "You enticed me up and promised me all the glories of the world if I . . . would follow you to the heights. And then I fell to my knees and worshipped you and served you." Falk, too, came to Schwanhild with "the gifts of this world". In *The League of Youth*, Aslaksen wanted to "share in everything that is glorious in the world". Bernik is "the first man of the town, in splendor and pleasure, in power and honor", although "this entire splendor is built on shifting, marshy soil". Helmer regards Nora as "all the glory I have". Hilde wants to take possession of "all the glory" that surrounds Solness; Borkmann says, "I wanted to subject all this land's sources of power to me . . . , I wanted to subordinate everything to me, taking power myself in order to create a good life for many, many thousands of others." Even as he dies, he says, "*My empire!* . . . My deep, unfathomed, inexhaustible empire! . . . I love you, you values that summon forth life—with all your brilliant train of power and splendor." And when Ella accuses him of having trodden underfoot her living human heart, he answers: "You mean, for the sake of the empire—and power—and splendor?" Finally, in *Emperor and Galilean*, Basilius says to Julian, "All the glory of the earth is laid at your feet". At the end of part 1, Julian's party and the choir of Christians clash in the church in Vienna. Julian says, "Mine is the kingdom!"—and Sallust salutes him with: "And the power and the glory!", while the choir in the church intones, "Thine is the kingdom and the power and the glory". In part 2, Julian tells of a dream in which he is lifted up by Minerva and the Sun—the king who rules the earth—"to the peak of a mountain . . . : they pointed into the far distance and showed him the inheritance of his entire race. . . . Then they announced to the young man that all this was to belong to him." Only he was to venerate the gods, remembering that his own soul was of divine origin and that he would be a god like them. Maximos advises Julian to

longing and the will to power thus remains profoundly ambivalent between good and evil (hence the inevitable reference to hidden guilt); the whole is embraced by the bounds of death. Since religion and metaphysics are of no account, the yardstick for both the longing and the urge has to be sociology and depth psychology, which cannot cope with the phenomenon.

Ibsen's only excursion into the realm of metaphysics is the work of his middle years, *Emperor and Galilean*, which he often referred to as his chief work. Its monstrous form, however, renders it a disaster in theatrical terms, and its contradictory and confused content make it ideologically a fiasco. Julian has been chosen by the "world will" to bring about the "third reich", going beyond both Greek antiquity and Christianity. This empire is to be "founded on the Tree of Knowledge and of the Cross" (III, 208). The idea that Christianity had been secularized and become unrecognizable under Constantius and Gallus and would be renewed as a result of Julian's persecution (303f., 317) is only a subsidiary topic. What is central is Julian's realization that the Galilean did not perceive and affirm the values of creation, the beauty of the world (163f., 187f., 281): in that case, how can Jesus be the Son of the Father who created the world? (383). In order to get beyond it in his synthesis, Julian must negate this negation on the part of Jesus; as Emperor, he must oppose the Galilean. He can embody this synthesis by freely affirming himself as the expression of the absolute, necessary and divine will: he is the Emperor-God, the God–Emperor, "He who wills himself" (371), who comes in his own name (385). His destiny is to found the empire; freedom and necessity coincide in his will (207). He is at the same time the total incarnation of the Logos and the unique spiritualization of the *pan*: "The spirit has become flesh, and the flesh spirit. Everything that is created lies in the sphere of my will and power" (406). He has no conscious hubris ("I have nothing to regret", for he was "an emanation of the divine", 435) and can thus call for divine honors and sacrifices (287f., 296). He "acts after consultation, so to speak, with unfathomable powers" (418). The first part shows Julian, who, as a pupil of the philosopher, visionary and magician, Maximus, has been initiated into the mysteries of his destiny, being carried up to the imperial dignity as if on the wings of these powers: "I bow to what cannot be averted" (250). He freely "chooses" (258) the destiny that bears him along. He hears voices urging him to "redeem Christianity" (190), and he does so by acting as both Emperor and Pontifex (278), reintroducing the old gods of creation side by side with the Christian God. The synthesis, theoretically impossible, would have

open men's eyes, like a doctor, "and then they will see you in your glory".

to be realized in his own person, as the third and final incarnation; his affirmation of the irreconcilable (in Christian terms) makes him the third "great acolyte of denial" (208), after Cain and Judas. For all three of them, obedience to an indivisible will coincided with a career of guilt. It is vain to look for some particular culpability on Julian's part, leading him to experience (392)—as a result of his attempt at a synthesis—the continuing vitality of the Galilean whose claim he contests (269) or for some reason why he must eventually end up as a man forsaken (419) and deluded by the gods (for example, his hesitation, a will that is not totally unconditional); his guilt lies in the very path he has taken. The goal of autonomy (in which freedom and necessity coincide), that is, of being God, is beyond finite man. Julian is a "victim to necessity" (437); "the world will has laid a trap for me" (434); he was deceived by the sun (436) but has no need to regret anything (435). And the third empire, which did not come into being through him, is projected into the future: "It may be after hundreds of years: I do not know" (370), but some day "it will come" (437). *Ibsen's* stance is optimistic: "I believe", he says in his Stockholm Banquet Speech of 1887, "that the teachings of science concerning evolution also apply to life's spiritual factors"; he avers that he is only a pessimist "insofar as I do not believe that ideals are eternal".[15] Not even "truth and freedom as pillars of society"? Contradictions become inevitable here, for he even surrenders the all-supporting tragic-utopian structure of the human being—Brand, Gynt—in favor of the future utopia of a third reich. If Julian was "both angel and serpent" (393) because he had to be God and man, free and necessarily guilty (and hence guiltless); if he was compelled to fail— what yardstick can there be for human action and for the construction of dramatic action?

Here the "world theatre" metaphor is completely dissolved in the idealist principle which had been established in *Goethe's Prometheus* and *Faust*, and which *Grillparzer* and *Hebbel* (two great spokesmen of the postidealist drama among many lesser ones) had attempted to carry through. From now on the stage will be dominated by the sociologico-psychological drama on the one hand and the utopian-absurd drama on the other—two forms of the same thing. Each of them lacks that dimension which can make the "world theatre" an arcane symbol of existence in its totality. Psychology and sociology stick to

---

[15] Woerner, *Henrik Ibsen* I, 283–84.

intramundane causalities and motivations; they assume that
changed social conditions will eliminate tragedy or that the problem of existence can be solved by embracing the proper social
"role"—and similar superficialities. The entire metaphysical
question of life's meaning is simply dropped. Conversely, the
so-called "theatre of the absurd" goes on asking the question, to
the exclusion of everything else, with the result that the empty
question gobbles up all immanent dramatic action.

Does this mean that the original "world theatre" notion,
familiar to the ancient world and to Christianity, is simply
obsolete? Or does it not keep turning up, of necessity, wherever
theatre is seriously performed, wherever the dramatic aspects
of existence are enacted before the eyes of the person who
experiences them? When all is said and done, are we not
constantly terrified and fascinated by the mutual "interference"
between what is enacted in the world and that contemplative
"viewing" of it which probes its ultimate meaning? Does not
this critical reflection accompany the action itself, imparting a
theatrical dimension to it? Is this not why we like to objectify
our human lives on the stage? Of course there is no way back to
the noble naiveté with which the stoics used this metaphor: the
path is blocked behind us; we cannot go back to a time prior to
the Christian question, "Who apportions the roles?" Nor is the
mythical answer of *Plato* and *Plotinus* available to us; for that
antenatal, intellectual choice in which freedom and necessity are
welded into a unity is only a projection of the paradox we
experience as the ground of our (dramatic) existence.

There seem to be only two ways forward. The first endeavors
to present modern man with the metaphor of the "theatre of the
world" as developed by antiquity and perfected by Christianity,
albeit taking account of the changed psychological and sociological perspectives: this is *Hofmannsthal's* lonely path. The
other reflects upon the content of the metaphor (a task long
overdue) by uncovering the metaphysical implications underlying its use. In this way it compels us to take the individual
elements of the "play" metaphor, which are always assumed to
be purely latent, and examine them separately. On the long
view this kind of work—which forms the second part of our
"Dramatic Resources"—will prove theologically more fruitful

than direct application of the metaphor of the "theatre of the world". *Pirandello's* most well-known play can provide a transition here, setting forth the various elements contained in the metaphor, ready to be submitted to systematic reflection.

c. Hofmannsthal: The Final Production of the "Theatre of the World"

The very fact that the "theatre of the world" could appear on stage again, in our century (and probably for the last time), is almost a miracle in itself, due to *Hofmannsthal's*[1] complex and unique personality and situation and his encounter with *Calderon*. *Hofmannsthal* sees himself as the heir and representative of a Europe that had its center in the Catholic monarchy of the Danube (in its organic relationship with Spain),[2] a Europe that, politically, was crushed by Protestantism (from *Frederick II* to *Wilson*) yet survived its own demise as a spiritual force just as, in the West, Hellas survived its material collapse.[3] In this European center the theatrical tradition of the people, a nonliterary tradition that united all classes, had always been alive. It had come down to the present untouched by the problems of the Weimar theatre and the consequences of *Hegel's* dramatic theory. The stage of both *Shakespeare* and *Schiller* (up to *Hebbel*) had focused on the "character", the hero and his fate; this became, in *Hegel*, the norm of the "romantic" (post-Christian) stage. In *Calderon*, however—and something analogous applies, at a lower level, to the Austrian popular stage—"man always acts within cosmic and religious relationships"; his destinies are interwoven "with

---

[1] *Gesammelte Werke* in *Einzelausgaben*, ed. H. Steiner, 15 vols. (1946–).

[2] E. R. Curtius, "George, Hofmannsthal and Calderon" in *Essays on European Literature* (Princeton, 1973), 149. Cf. *Ad me ipsum*: "A feeling of uninterrupted belonging to the Holy Roman Empire. Also to Italy" (*Aufzeichnungen*, 239). On the continuity of the Austrian folk theatre which, right from the baroque period, has handed down "tragedies of state in the grand manner, passion plays, plays of world judgment, German and Italian operettas, . . . legends . . . Shrovetide plays", etc., cf. *Prosa* III, 444–46.

[3] On the problems involved in this "representation" of a spiritual realm that no longer exists in the concrete, see Brian Coghlan, *Hofmannsthal's Festival Dramas, Jedermann, Das Salzburger Grosse Welttheater, Der Turm* (Cambridge/Melbourne University Press, 1964), 310–14.

the wheeling stars, with the poisons and healing saps of nature",
with the miraculous and magical; this play is cosmocentric
because it is ultimately "theocentric".[4] *Hofmannsthal*: "Anthropo-
centrism is a form of chauvinism."[5]

But *Hofmannsthal's* encounter with *Calderon* is not due to
some historically aware instinct for self-preservation. It takes
place in the postidealist era, when "Prometheus" has been
superseded by "Dionysos", the idea of a universal life that
imagines itself to be divine. This idea both presupposes and
postulates a vividly experienced totality; between presupposition
and postulate stands the riddle which is to be solved, namely,
the individual "I". The "I" senses that it comes forth from the
totality of living things (it is "preexistent" in that sense) and
belongs to it, and it tries to find ways of reaching beyond its
own boundaries and assimilating itself to the totality and hence
becoming "existent". To surrender oneself longingly to these
intimations of universal being is that "preexistence", that "most
enchanting dream" of all the *Kleinen Dramen* of the early years
up to the (commonly overstressed) crisis that breaks out in the
Lord Chandos letter of 1901. But even earlier we can see various
attempts to shatter the sphere of *homunculus* by allowing it to
collide with redemptive reality; for in *Hofmannsthal* it is never a
question of an aesthetic,[6] intoxicated "being absorbed into the
universe" but always of the ethical requirement, that is, the
performance of personal being on the part of a person in whom
the entire universe lies concealed and who is thus a riddle to
himself. *Der Tor und der Tod* (Death and the deranged) (1893)
gives judgment upon that aesthetic existence (preexistence)
which circles around itself, referring everything to its own
center; only when Claudio comes to die and has to lose his
mother, his beloved, his friend—people who are fulfilled in
themselves but suffer on account of the deranged character—

    [4] Curtius, "George, Hofmannsthal and Calderon", 160, 159.

    [5] "Buch der Freunde", *Aufzeichnungen*, 54.

    [6] Cf. Hofmannsthal's terrible judgment on Oscar Wilde: *Sebastian Melmoth*
(1905) in *Prosa* II, 133. But in his early period there are expressions of a purely
Dionysian philosophy of life: "The fundamental tragic rhythm: the world,
splintered into individuals, yearns for unity. Dionysios Zagreus wants to be
reborn" (*Aufzeichnungen*, 106).

does he discover that he has "trodden life's stage . . . as a mediocre actor . . . showing neither power nor value": "My life was dead; you then, death, shall be my life. . . . Now, dying, I feel for the first time that I *am*."[7] Long before *Hofmannsthal* took a serious interest in *Calderon*, he called another of his little plays *Das kleine Welttheater* (The little theatre of the world) (1897). Here we see characters walking, separated and isolated, up and down the bridge over the river of life; each talks about the way he is related to the whole. The poet constructs the "artefact of words that drip light and water", instilling into others a longing for the "burden of a life of which, as yet, we have only intimations"; the gardener, who was once a king, now sees in his flowers "the true paths of all created things" more clearly than in the business of politics; the young lord, to whom the puzzles of human destiny seem "like nets and fishhooks", trapping and entangling everyone, yet determines, "I will lend assistance to as many as I can". The foreigner, "maybe a goldsmith", looks into the enveloping waves with his urge to create: "Yet it is much too much and too true: / One thing must triumph, the others are scattered in the flood. / Only then shall I have fashioned this one thing / When I have wrested it from the great torrent." There is a girl in whom, as yet unknown, love is ripening; and finally there is the deranged man, always on the point of tearing open the last door, "Seeking a drastic path / To life's core": "Can you lead the whole, the real dance? / Do you grasp the meaning of this office?" On this occasion Dionysos has the last word; the disturbed man wants to throw himself into the river, but the attendant and the doctor gently restrain him; he mocks them: "Bacchus, Bacchus, they caught you too / And held you fast, but not for long!"[8] To the same year (1897) belongs *Der Kaiser und die Hexe* (The emperor and the witch). Here, the spell of preexistence, in the form of the witch, is confronted by the emperor, who sets "truth" against it: "Unless you're the same without and within, / Unless you strain to be true to yourself, / Poison will enter your senses, / You will breathe it in and breathe it out, . . . / You will hear the

7 *Gedichte und kleine Dramen* 290–92.
8 *Ibid.*, 373–94.

sound of truth . . . / Yet will not be able to respond to it." A condemned criminal is brought up; it transpires that his crime was the result of an injustice inflicted on him by the emperor; the latter admits it and makes the condemned man an admiral: "The man who has been / True to himself, at terrible cost, is beyond / The temptations of common men." Then, in the forest, he encounters his blinded predecessor, whom he has outlawed for three years: thus, by the very fact of birth, he is implicated, guilty yet innocent, in the fate of this man and of all: "All things are close to me; I must / Bear within me the light for him / Who on my account was blinded, / For I am the emperor." He lets the old man eat from his dish and lays him on his own bed. The witch, who has already been defeated once, approaches again to tempt him, but the emperor's encounters with truth have redeemed him: "Where I stretched forth my hand to feel you, / Mysterious doors opened before me, / Leading to true life and / Giving me back to myself."[9] Thus we have the three themes of *Hofmannsthal's* three inseparable major works: *Der Tor und der Tod* prefigures *Jedermann* (Everyman) (1911), *Das kleine Welttheater* prefigures *Das Salzburger Grosse Welttheater* (1922), and *Der Kaiser und die Hexe* anticipates *Der Turm* (The tower) (1925, 1927).

This external chronology is deceptive, however, for the last is the earliest:

1. It is very probable that, as a boy, *Hofmannsthal* saw one of the frequent performances of *Calderon's Life Is a Dream* in the Burgtheater.

2. From 1901 to 1904 he worked on a very free translation in trochaic verse of *Calderon's Life Is a Dream*. As both the text and his notes show, this anticipated crucial ideas of *Der Turm*, particularly the political ideas.

3. In 1905 *Calderon's Daughter of the Air* came into prominence, as a tragedy. Later (1908) an opera was planned, and in 1917–1918 *Hofmannsthal* took up the material again (*Zwei Götter*); much of which is incorporated into *Der Turm*. The two gods (Semiramis and her son Ninyas) are West ("power", "history") and East

[9] *Ibid.*, 329–72. "*Der Kaiser und die Hexe* is a pure personal confession", in *Ad me ipsum* (*Aufzeichnungen*, 240).

("cosmos", "nonviolence", "love"); Ninyas, another Sigismund, is imprisoned by his mother, then sacrificed, then elevated to divine status; she becomes his acolyte.

4. 1911 was the year of *Jedermann*, a re-presentation of the old English *Everyman*: a world theatre for the individual in the face of death, in which money determines personal attitudes and decisions. "What we should possess, possesses us, and what is the means of all means, money, becomes for us—in demonic perversity—the goal of all goals." "Man's relationship to possessions" is the "fundamental relationship in life".[10]

5. In 1918 *Hofmannsthal* promised to make one translation (either accurate or free) of a *Calderon* play every year for the Burgtheater. The first of these appeared in 1920: *Dame Kobold*.

6. Nineteen twenty-two saw the appearance, for the Drama Festival, of *Das Salzburger Grosse Welttheater*. The preface says that "the entire metaphor has been taken" from *Calderon*, namely, "that the world erects a stage on which the human beings perform the play of life in their divinely allotted roles. *Calderon* has also provided the title of this play and the names of the six characters who represent mankind, but nothing else."[11] But in adopting the characters, Hofmannsthal has also adopted their role-play, and, with it, a deeper reflection that goes back, behind *Calderon*, to its origins in the ancient world. There is something rather abrupt and incomplete about the central action; *Der Turm* attempts to rework it. The two symbols which are closely related in *Calderon*, namely, life as a play and life as a dream, become inseparable in *Hofmannsthal*.

7. *Der Turm* (first version 1923–1925; second abbreviated version 1925; third greatly altered version 1927) takes up the work of 1901–1904 and develops the themes which *Hofmannsthal* initiated there; but the figure of Sigismund is given a different rationale (primarily as a result of *Hofmannsthal's* experience of war and his deliberate turning toward Christianity in his seven last years).[12] Sigismund's apocalyptic battle with all the chaotic

---

[10] *Das alte Spiel von Jedermann* (1912) *Prosa* III, 115–16.

[11] *Dramen* III, 252.

[12] "The works of the last seven years of his life are Christian not only because of their symbolism, but because of the conversion of his heart, because of a great and silent *sursum corda*" (Curtius, "George, Hofmannsthal and Calderon", 167).

powers of hell (first version, fifth act) brings the motif of *Der Kaiser und die Hexe* to its fulfillment. The aim was to portray the whole reality of the age in its pitiless harshness. The work attempts to be a diagnosis, a myth and a prophecy, and to that extent it contains the "world theatre" and actually goes beyond it.[13]

Why did the earliest draft have to wait until last to find its full form? Because initially *Hofmannsthal* attempted to solve the question of the "I" versus universal life along contradictory lines, through a psychoanalytical entering into himself, into the infinity of life on the foundation of the "I"[14]—and by breaking out of the "I" (through action or sacrifice or the transformation effected with the approach of death) into the "other".[15] Descending into its own interior, the "I" that seeks itself not only discovers the entire gamut of possible "I"s,[16] from the

[13] "The individual and the epoch seen as myth, . . . Sigismund somehow mirrors the epoch's changed sense of the world since Kant" (*Aufzeichnungen*, 233). *Der Turm*: To show the pitilessness of our reality, into which the soul wanders, coming from some dark, mythical region" (242). Cf. the very late observations on the necessity of the "lyrical drama" and the "mythological opera" as "the truest of all forms" for today (*Die Aegyptische Helena*, 128 in *Prosa* IV, 459–60).

[14] In 1904 he asked H. Bahr for "the book by Freud and Breuer on the cure of hysteria through liberating repressed memories. . . . I know that I shall find things there which will help me greatly with *Das Leben ein Traum*" (*Briefe* II, 152). In the same year he writes: "I would like to ask you for something else, the *Maladies de la personnalité*. The theme which fascinates me most at present is *Das Leben ein Traum*, that is, going down into the deepest depths of the dubious cavern-kingdom of the 'I' to find either what is no longer 'I', or the world." (*Briefe* II, 155. The book mentioned is that of Théodore Ribot, 1884.)

[15] We can see from Hofmannsthal's scarcely decipherable *Aufzeichnungen*, *Ad me ipsum*, that these apparent alternatives were (even long afterward) no alternatives at all. The "basic theme" is "to find oneself" (*Aufzeichnungen*, 222); "Target idea: the higher life must be the heightening of the self, attained through finding what is right and proper to oneself" (220f.). "Intro-version as the path to existence (the mystical path)" (215). On the other hand: "The path to life and to human beings is through sacrifice. . . . Sacrifice as surrendering oneself" (217). "Transformation through action. To act is to surrender oneself." Yet again, "the essential thing is not the act, but faithfulness. Identity of faithfulness and destiny." Finally: "Transformation—but on the other side of life: Ariadne. Rebirth" (217). And a synthesis: "to change oneself (to seek one's destiny) through *action* (action in self-surrender)" (221).

[16] "Where did we learn to say 'soul' / For this juxtaposition of a thousand

highest to the most abject, from the divine to the animal,[17] it can also be schizophrenic (in fact, it must be) when it returns to the surface.[18] The boundary between the "I" and the world is eliminated, and the question of the nature and meaning of the "I" remains, a painful, open wound.[19] Sigismund is conceived according to this pattern in the early version, but so is Basilius, who abuses the imperial power and banishes the fate which threatens him—that is, his own son, Sigismund—to the deepest dungeon of his subconscious. There lies his fear, his bad

---

lives?" ("Gestern", *Gedichte und lyrische Dramen*, 223). "The accumulated energy of the mysterious pedigree within us, the layers upon layers of stored supraindividual memories" (Address in the home of Count Karl Lanckoronski. *Prosa* II, 30). The dramatist knows that he is pregnant with all the characters his play will contain: "There are so many of them in me; so many of them meet within me. Really and truly there are more beings living within each of us than we are prepared to admit" (*Shakespeare's Könige, Prosa* II, 154). Quite late he says that the poet "can give us an intimation of the vast medley which, through the mask of the 'I', becomes the person" (*Die Aegyptische Helena, Prosa* IV, 459).

[17] The Sigismund of the first version is an animal among animals, not only in "preexistence" but full of cruelty and lust for murder, in revenge for what has been done to him (*Dramen* III, 352), but also out of a "megalomania" which causes his person to seem nondistinct from the world: "Even his eating bowl, his bed straw, his lust for killing are now emanations of his divinity" (*ibid.*, 429).

[18] Hofmannsthal's explicit concern with a significant case of schizophrenia comes later (1907), when he had studied Morton Prince's *The Dissociation of a Personality* (1906). This gave him the dual character of Maria-Mariquita for his novel *Andreas oder die Vereinigten*. Cf. R. Alewyn, "Andreas und die 'wunderbare Freundin'. Zur Fortsetzung von Hoffmannsthals Romanfragment und ihrer psychiatrischen Quelle" (1955), in *Über Hugo von Hofmannsthal, Kleine Vandenhoeck-Reihe* 57 (1958): 105–41. But just as Freudian observations can be found in Hofmannsthal's jottings prior to his encounter with Freud, the problem of schizophrenia was already there, latently at least, before he read Prince. Just as the *wunderbare Freundin*, when Andreas possesses her totally, is complete, "*die Ganze*, neither Maria nor Mariquita but more than both of them—already belonging to God, sinning without sin—already part of the other world" (139–40), so the Sigismund of the first version is simultaneously a king's son and a murderous beast; the interchange of dream and reality now becomes a vicious circle. In his ego-transcending totality the changed Sigismund of the later versions will always carry the "other" within him. To the gypsy woman, an embodiment of chaos, he says: "You cannot shake anything from your womb, you black angel, but I would already be on intimate terms with it" (*Dramen* IV, 182).

[19] "That! I! Me! Why? Why? / Why, in coming into being, did I become this particular person?" (*Dramen* III, 350–51). "Am I in the world now? Where is the world?" (*Dramen* IV, 25; 335).

conscience,[20] thence comes total disorder in the entire empire.[21] However, as long as both the guilty and the innocent are modeled along the same lines (of *Lebensphilosophie* and depth psychology),[22] the actually intended opposition cannot come to light; the boundary between dream (play) and reality (seriousness) remains indeterminate—but not at all in the baroque sense.

Only the Christian view could provide a way out here by clearly distinguishing the two principles of universal solidarity— Adam and Christ. *Hofmannsthal* resisted the inevitability of this conclusion for a long time; when he finally opted for the distinction, it had, in his work, all the high drama of a peripeteia. The "Oedipus" plays make a last attempt to trace the "Sigismund" principle back to the "Basilius" principle, to trace Christ back to Adam, to identify the Christian insight into the atoning power of the Innocent with the Jewish understanding (from *Marx* to *Freud*) of man's solidarity in destiny, whether in the form of a dialectic of history (the son *must* kill his father, and so forth) or as the subpersonal totality of blood.[23]

[20] *Dramen* III, 357–68, 432.

[21] "This tower is the center of all injustice in the world; here terrible injustice is continually begetting demons" (*Dramen* III, 426).

[22] Elektra and Klytemnestra (*Elektra* 1903) are constructed according to the same model. The latter is the guilty woman who tries to contain and cover up the blood feud (=Elektra); the former the one who does not forget: "I do not know how I could ever die—except because you died" (*Dramen* II, 27). Thus, when Orestes has killed his mother, she breaks down in the midst of the victory dance.

[23] In *Oedipus und die Sphinx* (1905; *Dramen* II, 271–417) Hofmannsthal comes up against the absolute limit which causes him to turn around. Like Christ, Oedipus is "both priest and victim" (291), and this lifts him, together with his mother and spouse Jocasta, above the gods: "[W]e are more than gods, / We are priests and victims, our hands / Sanctify it, we alone / Constitute the world" (416). Oedipus knows that he is the world's center and principle: "I hold the world in my veins: no star falls, no bird topples from the nest without me" (390). But this is because he is pure contradiction: "I am a king and a monster. . . . No God separates the one from the other; kill me!" (405). This is because blood's abyss has opened up in him (a "dream", "blessing", "curse"), deeper than the sea, unfathomable (290–91): "O holy blood! / You do not know what a great river you are; / They can never plumb the depths of your life, / Where pain and illusion have died out, where neither / Love nor hate dwell, hunger nor thirst, / neither age nor death" (374). Oedipus has "plunged down" "in the night of sacrifice", seeking for "the source of the blood that is in me", and so his blood was hallowed "so that it might rise up of its own strength and confront God"

It is *Hofmannsthal's* own secret how in 1911, after years of silence, he came to that breakthrough which alone made the *"Welttheater"* possible. (Note, however, that as early as 1893 he had translated *Alcestis*, the play of pure and uncomplicated surrender.)[24] Now the first draft of *Die Frau ohne Schatten* (The woman without a shadow) came into view,[25] in which the

(289–90). In this abyss he dwells, along with the patriarchs (291), with their crimes, which remain latent in their children's children: "Like flowing water, the path leads on in and through my being" (300). Oedipus takes the guilt of his forbears on himself by *sacrificing himself*—and by realizing it in all its horror. He sacrifices himself, he surrenders his life in "uttermost loneliness", becomes "a companion of the mute animals", / "Then I will not need to lose my self / To the unutterable, the living death" (302). Thus his sacrifice is yet another flight from a deeper sacrifice. But he gives everything, and "it may be sufficient" (303). He gives up "father and mother, glory and world"; because he is a king, he must suffer (308). He does so as a "pure child" (299) who has never touched a woman (296–98); he renounces Sigismund's tower: "I had thought to ask my father for a tower, / A bed of straw and heavy chains— / But what good would that do us?" (301). He is ready "to humble himself day and night" (312). He is to "pay" the entire guilt of his ancestors (313). And in the final prayer of act I, Oedipus' gesture of surrender elicits an answer from the "voice" (of the ancestors): "Our struggling and grabbing have made him what he is: now let him pay us back" (307). In the spirit of this prayer he kills his father on the narrow path, and the latter's curse pierces his heart (314); the Sphinx crashes down on seeing him—he is the living contradiction of Being—and now the path leading to the kingdom and marriage with his mother, Jocasta, is clear. She receives the youth just as *Ariadne auf Naxos* will receive Dionysos: as Death, who is also the transforming god of intoxication. But what will be a weightless symbol in *Ariadne* is here weighed down with the whole contradiction of simultaneous guilt and atonement (362, 366, 378, 411–14). Hence the gods' complaint (399f.) about fate being unbearable, at the same time as the triumphal conclusion: the realization of guilt as the Dionysian redemption. Hofmannsthal's free rendering of Sophocles' *King Oedipus* (1906) does not alter this interpretation: here we have simply the unrolling of fate; the interpretation is given in Hofmannsthal's own play. Here "dream-life" (*Traumleben*) is an expression for the collapse of all things: "You cannot waken me now, / For everything dreams along with me" (280); "swept away is the boundary / Between sleep and waking, and soon that other one / Between death and life" (290). Oedipus dreams "the life-dream" (*Lebenstraum*)—to kill his father and marry his mother (292)—and thus the deed is already done in anticipation. The Sphinx, catching sight of him, "discerns my dream—ah, there is only one, / The dream of Delphoi, alas, the dream of father, / Mother and the child" (399). Creon's dreams (324–25, 328), the dreams of the two seers and of Jocasta (363) "all come true: that is the end" (363).

[24] But this *Alcestis* is still completely trapped in "pre-existence". Cf. the reference in *Aufzeichnungen* 129.

[25] *Aufzeichnungen* 162. The opera text dates from 1913, the musical setting

Empress of the Realm of Spirits, in order to become fruitful, humbly descends into all the humiliations of human existence; not only does she thus acquire children, she also redeems the Emperor from his egoism, the wicked Dyer-Woman (whose servant she is and who does not want children) and the bestially stupid Barak. As *R. Alewyn* says, she follows the advice Jesus gave to the rich young man—to "shed the load of his wealth". She "follows this evangelical counsel", she "puts us in mind of the Son of God, who took the form of a servant in order to redeem mankind".[26] Thus, in principle, *Hofmannsthal* had reached the christological vantage point. In the same year he wrote *Jedermann*, which is based on the same indispensable presupposition, though in reverse: the sinner, isolated from the community by death, is confronted with his solitary, personal responsibility and can only lay hold of it by accepting the offer of the Christian "faith", which, in turn, draws its entire power from God's redemptive act in the Cross of Jesus Christ. This is highlighted (to an almost exaggerated degree) right from the prologue of "God the Lord", who looks down on mankind (on "everyman"):

> Alas! I see at this instant
> They've quite forgot the Covenant
> I 'stablished once 'twixt them and me
> In shedding my blood upon the Tree.
> On yon Wood I hung in pains
> That they to life might gain entrance.
> From out their smarting feet the thorns I drew
> And on my head impress'd them as a crown so true.[27]

The motif cannot be overlooked; it recurs many times.[28] Dealing with this mystery, the poet turned to the mass audience for the

---

from 1915. The novel (published 1919) was written after the opera: *Prosa* III, 451f.

[26] R. Alewyn, *Hofmannsthals Wandlung* (1949), 158. Alewyn is right to say that at this point Hofmannsthal "broke out of the cul-de-sac of aestheticism", but it is premature to characterize his "metaphysical error" (which he now renounces) as the maintaining of a "dubious innocence by haughtily and fearfully ignoring the dark side of life". The "metaphysical error" was a far more wanton one: he wanted to identify innocence and guilt, prayer and crime, "Adam" and "Christ" in a magical, all-knowing naturalism.

[27] *Dramen* III, 10.

[28] In the mother's admonishment (*ibid.*, 31); where Jedermann conjures the

first time; the play was produced at the end of 1911 by *Max Reinhardt* in the Berlin Zirkus Schumann before an audience of thousands. Subsequently *Hofmannsthal* felt obliged to describe it as a "fairy tale",[29] even a "fairy tale that belongs to all ages, of universal validity",[30] "a human fairy tale . . . in Christian garb".[31] But he seriously appealed to the Christian tradition in the German people.[32] And in describing the effect of the premiere on the vast audience, he stressed the moment in the prologue when, in the above passage, God's powerful male voice suddenly acquired a "great gentleness", and "one realized that it was the Redeemer, the second Divine Person, who was speaking in the voice of the triune God; then the audience became noticeably quieter, as if they had grasped something."[33] But this is the poet's own project: it is he who takes responsibility for "having *given* something *back*" to the German consciousness, "something that, by rights, should never have been missing",[34] namely, by "showing things that are unutterably broken within the context of an unbroken understanding of the world—an understanding that, however, at its innermost level, is identical with the former."[35] This can only mean that *Hofmannsthal* regards the christological principle—God's death on the gallows for our sake—as underpinning the unutterable brokenness of the here-and-now. The principle is set forth, but the poet who sets it forth and thus comes forward to attest and guarantee it is thereby much more visible than in the time of *Calderon*. And he

---

Gesell to accompany him (58); in the profession of faith, which initially remains an external one (*Die zwölf Artikel*: "Of all faith that is the most pitiful part" 80); then in the entirely personal faith "in Jesu Christ, / Who came from the Father and was made a man like us . . . / Who in torment gave his life / For your sake" (81). Jedermann embraces this faith and has to be taught by it that he has the upper hand over his evil deeds. His simple prayer (83) to the "Savior" has been won for him by the sacrificial life of his mother (84; in an early draft it was through Mary's intercession).

[29] *Das alte Spiel von Jedermann* (1912) in *Prosa* III, 114.

[30] *Ibid.*

[31] *Das Spiel vor der Menge* (1911) in *Prosa* III, 64.

[32] "This eternally great legend is supposed to be of no concern to modern people, of no concern to five thousand, ten thousand Germans, members of a nation which owes its greatest spiritual inspiration to Christianity" (*ibid.*).

[33] *Das alte Spiel von Jederman*, 120.

[34] *Ibid.*, 62.

[35] *Ibid.*, 64–65.

deliberately offers his play as a "political" statement.[36] When his friend E. v. Bodenhausen expressed his dissatisfaction with the allegorical figures ("works", "faith", "devil") which left him cold, Hofmannsthal pointed out that it is the religious context which gives the play its invigorating third dimension, as was the case in ancient drama and in the mystery play of Faustus.[37]

Jedermann is a new Kleines Welttheater, but one where, as in Der Tor und der Tod, the action hinges on death. Here, however, though it is similarly a question of a wasted life that is judged and saved through the event of death, the governing system of coordinates is entirely new. For marking the horizontal axis are money, mammon, the symbol of power and possession, flowing to the advantage of "Jedermann" but being refused to the "poor neighbor" and the "bondservant". The central core is that "the means of all means, money, becomes for us—in demonic perversity—the goal of all goals". "The fundamental relationship in life, man's relationship to possessions"[38] determines the state of the world and hence of action within it. The poet wants to unveil the meaning of the age in which he lives: "The meaning of the moral and even religious revolution in which we seem to find ourselves may lie in getting beyond the monetary system."[39] This is a recapitulation, in realistic terms, of what he wrote imaginatively concerning preexistence as the interrelatedness of all destinies, as the emperor's responsibility for all the world's suffering. "Between these poor people and the rich man who hastens past them there is a commerce in which all rich men and all the poor are entangled. For the monetary system is a net that catches everyone, such that every rich man is the creditor and feudal lord of every poor man. The rich man thinks he does nothing, and yet day and night he sends hundreds into serfdom. . . . He prides himself on not knowing who they are; that is what distinguishes him from the slaveowner."[40]

Does this system of coordinates permit dramatic action? Not unjustly, people have doubted this.[41] Here the playwright in-

---

[36] Ibid., 62.

[37] Briefe der Freundschaft (1953) (Feb. 10, 1912 and Feb. 16, 1912), 136–38.

[38] Prosa III, 115–16.

[39] "Buch der Freunde", Aufzeichnungen 59.

[40] Prosa III, 124.

[41] B. Coghlan, Hofmannsthal's Festival Dramas, Jedermann, Das Salzburger

tends to be no more than an admonitory voice, a finger pointing upward and forward. Only *Das Salzburger Grosse Welttheater* manages to create a dramatic action, albeit in the only coordinate system possible in a revival of *Calderon*: the existing verticals— God apportions the roles, and the world determines their attributes in preexistence—make the horizontal action into a "stage play" and give it a depth which, compared with *Calderon*, is new. The penultimate act is almost identical in both authors, with the players being called away one at a time and the admonition on this transitory life.[42] The difference lies in the opening action, which takes place in the realm of preexistence; *Hofmannsthal* imparts a greater depth to his model, in both a Platonist and a Christian direction. Nor can it be said that his *Welttheater* is no more specifically Catholic than his *Jedermann* or that its fundamental subject matter is the glorification of our inner freedom as a reflection of the Most High Creator.[43] But this freedom is presented first of all in its antenatal form, as a life decision taken by the intellect, as in *Plato's Republic*. Once again the distinction between "destiny" (which is as far as the "world's" insight can reach) and divine grace (which imparts a luminosity even to the basest role, that of the "beggar") plays its part. The soul of the beggar initially refuses his role, which speaks only of distress, torment, loneliness and forsakenness. Beside the soul

---

Grosse Welttheater, *Der Turm*, 77f.: no climax, no genuinely ethical decision on the part of Jedermann, an all-too-easy substitution of remorse for the missing deeds, and a faith that comes from outside. The devil, a comic figure (as in the conclusion of *Faust*), is in no way convincing here. It is noteworthy that the first draft of *Jedermann* (1906) has only two main characters, Jedermann and Mammon, his servant, whose relationship is largely modelled on that between Faust and Mephisto: *Dramen* III, 439–46. This is important in that it shows us that Hofmannsthal allowed Goethe's world-drama to influence his play, but—far more markedly than Goethe (part 2, act I)—he placed "money", the economic and social factors, at the center.

[42] In Hofmannsthal this aspect appears somewhat abruptly, signalled (*Dramen* III, 315) by the change in lighting, the rushing of the wind as it blows the characters about. As for the "King's" hesitation to abdicate, the agony of "Beauty", on whose behalf "Wisdom" pleads, the arrogance and despair of the "Rich Man", the "Peasant's" hardness of hearing, the blithe resignation of the "Beggar-turned-hermit", and the appearance of all of them before God's judgment—including the eucharistic element found in the *autos sacramentales*— all this is simply an unrolling of Calderon's themes.

[43] *Briefwechsel mit Richard Strauss* (Zurich, 1952), 468.

stand the "angel" and the "adversary". The latter stirs him up to
contention, to "creative hatred".[44] "On behalf of this soul I
claim natural equality of destiny!" The "angel" persuades the
desperately resisting soul to accept this role by revealing that
"Your mouth speaks wildly, but inside you, like a miner's lamp
that burns peacefully in the deepest depths, there burns a
willingness to accept." The soul admits: "You hold out a bait to
me, and, truly, there is something in me urging me to swallow
it." So it is not "suggestion" but some absolute freedom
embracing all freedom of choice that is able to transform
suffering and nonaction into "creation upon creation". The
"angel" says, "Have you read these words: My God, my God,
why have you forsaken me? And these: Not my will, but thine,
be done?" Therefore, "Give in! How else should the ineffable
speak to you but through your shuddering fear?" And the soul
consents.

However, this prior decision means that the earthly play
already has a limited compass. The "adversary" has made a false
move right from the start, and the "beggar"—or, more clearly,
the proletariat, at the zenith of its revolt against existing
"tradition" and "order" (which are hymned by the "rich
man")[45]—characteristically rejects all-powerful "possessions"[46]
and, in demanding his "rights" and lifting his axe against
everyone, sweeps aside the adversary's promptings: "Enough! I
have my own speech, / And need no spokesman." The "adversary" keeps insinuating Marxist slogans ("work becomes a
servitude") and calls for "a manifesto!"; he came up with the
term "creative hatred". The proletarian can see no way out for
the entire world order; it must perish:

> The world's estate must go, a new one come to be,
> And if in going it must plunge into a sea of flames
> And perish in a bloody visitation,
> Such blood and fire is what we need.[47]

This circumscribed worldly fatalism permeates all the characters
so utterly that, faced with the raised axe, "all alike" cry out,

---

[44] *Dramen* III, 312.
[45] *Ibid.*, 294–95.
[46] *Ibid.*, 290.
[47] *Ibid.*, 294.

"Strike now and with one blow bring down the whole world."[48]
In "Wisdom's" prayer which follows we are shown the root of
this profound unanimity:

> Thou seest how, mysteriously,
> Injustice traps us all within its net. . . .
> Abruptly, with one frightful wave, thy hand
> Brings the command performance to an end.
> Behold us leaving, as we're bid, thy stage. . . .
> And he, dire messenger of the highest Will,
> Empower'd so awesomely to call us hence,
> His play too is done, in which so grievously
> He threatened us. . . .

The nearer the axe-man approaches "Wisdom", "the stronger
her voice becomes as she overcomes her deepest fear", and she
intercedes for grace on his behalf. What follows may seem
disappointingly naive: the "beggar" experiences a lightning
conversion, understanding that "Isaac's lamb" has taken his
place; the angel rejoices that "deed has replaced ill-deed"; and
the converted man resolves to go and work in the forest as a
hermit. But in this play *Hofmannsthal* is not concerned with
improving the world; the beggar knows that seizure of power
by the proletariat will not "turn the page":

> Were I to lord it in their place,
> It would make no great difference.

The playwright wants the christological and all-embracing
dimension of "yielding and cleaving to" the Father's will to
enter the world vertically, like lightning; he wants to show
blessed poverty in spirit as that which invisibly sustains and
transforms the world. Here is *Hofmannsthal's* "manifesto":

> We spoke of freedom, asked what it might be.
> . . . freedom is always close,
> Yet if you coarsely clutch at it, it shoots away;
> Gently yield, you'll find it's back at once. . . .
> It is a mystery that can't be named on earth.[49]

This clearly sets out the position: the new world order which the
proletarian intended to bring about by violent means is ac-

[48] *Ibid.*, 307.
[49] *Ibid.*, 314.

knowledged to be a transcendental future. "There must be a wholly new world order, / Else this life is but a wretched puppet play." A genuine anticipation of this is the disarming of money and possession on the basis of spirit: this is *Hofmannsthal's* Franciscan side.

This is not the last word, however. *Hofmannsthal* once more summons the image not only of the "play" but of the "dream". *Der Turm*, which goes back to the first *Calderon* adaptation as well as recapitulating everything written on the theme of pre-existence, forms the conclusion. Without sacrificing what is proclaimed in the *Welttheater*, this work gives a bleak portrayal of the conflict between "poverty in spirit" and the actual realities of power. There are two versions. In the first, Sigismund actively enters, to some extent, into the play of world powers, only to clash with the demonic per se and so perish: he gives way to a purely utopian figure, the Child King, who will refashion "swords into plowshares".[50] In the second, the embodiment of the demonic (the gypsy woman and her magic) and the utopian (the Child King) is dropped: Sigismund's fall comes about within a demonized power structure. At the level of ideas the difference is slight and should not be exaggerated. The fundamental structure is the same in both versions: the ramifications of the abuse of power. The King uses Julian to imprison Sigismund, the legitimate heir; Julian uses both Sigismund, whom he trains for his own purposes, and Olivier, the embodiment of crude force and naked incitement, in order to topple the King; but the tool, Olivier, wrenches himself from the hand that uses him and brings about the collapse of Julian as well as the others. This cascading collapse of power exhibits the sequence of forms of government found in *Plato's Republic*. Here, however, the King is unwise from the outset; hence the prophecy that his son—unblemished wisdom—will one day

[50] *Dramen* IV, 206. Cf. Hofmannsthal in conversation with Burckhardt: "Out of all these terrible aspects something reconciliatory, some future, must shine forth; only then does the really tragic have a genuine foundation" (*Hugo von Hofmannsthal: Der Dichter im Spiegel der Freunde*, ed. H. A. Fiechtner [Berne and Munich, 1963], 140). Originally, of course, Sigismund himself was to have been the child-king; cf. *Briefwechsel Hugo von Hofmannsthal–Carl J. Burckhardt* (Fischer, 1956), 70. The first four acts of *Der Turm* were written in 1920–21, i.e., before the completion of *Das Grosse Welttheater*. The first version of the last act was written in 1923–24.

bring him down. But Sigismund, misused by Basilius, Julian and Olivier, is anchored most profoundly right from the start in the principle of powerlessness and guiltlessness; this gives him an entirely different mode of solidarity with the totality of destiny, as compared with the others. Therefore, theologically speaking, he is bound to be a symbol of Christ. There are numerous allusions to this in the first version.[51] In the King and his entourage, the interlockings of destiny constitute "original sin", resulting in his Godforsakenness: "That hell grew quietly within you whose name is 'Forsaken by God'."[52] Sigismund's Godforsakenness is that of the Crucified, whom he sees, however, in the entire suffering world: "I cannot manage to separate the two, me with this (the crucifix) and me with the animal that was hung up on a beam, disembowelled, inside full of bloody blackness. . . . There is red fire and blackness in me. He must help me."[53] In this way the playwright put all the problems of his youth—his sense of involvement with all world destinies, the multiplicity of possible "I"s, from the purest to the most demonic[54]—into this character without touching what is "holy"[55] in Sigismund. We would fail to do justice to *Hofmannsthal's* intention if we were to interpret Sigismund's entrance (in the last act) into the world of politics as a besmirching contact with the sphere of power[56] or as his succumbing to the temptation to engage in self-seeking magic.[57] The principle he embodies (as its "postfiguration") does not prevent him from having both the simplicity of doves and the cunning of serpents. The final word of the fourth act clarifies everything: Sigismund is ordered by Olivier to follow him. He answers: "Whither we are going, obedience precedes command."[58]

[51] Jakob Laubach, *Hugo von Hofmannsthals Turm-Dichtungen* (Diss. Fribourg, 1954), 91ff.

[52] *Dramen* IV, 75.

[53] *Ibid.*, 88, cf. 87.

[54] *Ibid.*, 182.

[55] *Ibid.*, 27: The doctor: "Soul and torment without end." Sigismund: "There is a star inside me. My soul is sacred" (28). The doctor: "O more than dignity in such humiliation!"

[56] As K. J. Naef does in *Hugo von Hofmannsthal, Wesen und Werk* (Zurich and Leipzig, 1938).

[57] Laubach, *Hugo von Hoffmansthals Turm-Dichtungen*, 50.

[58] *Dramen* IV, 170.

Whereas in *Jedermann* the christological principle intervenes eschatologically (in the descent of faith upon the sinner) and in the *Welttheater* man-in-revolt is attuned to the principle before he is born, in *Der Turm* the principle is embodied in a whole living figure. Thus in the *Welttheater* the play motif acquires a further dimension, going beyond *Calderon*; the dream motif in *Der Turm* (which dominates the first version) loses its clarity: each of the two wrestling worlds is unreal as far as the other is concerned. In the end, in the apocalyptic battle between abysmal chaos and purity, *Der Turm* becomes a magical apparition: here ends *Hofmannsthal's* "most enchanting dream". Sigismund overcomes hell but only by dying of its poison. This is the "world theatre" of Holy Saturday.

d. Maschere Nude

As an alternative to *Hofmannsthal* we cited *Pirandello*, with his perverse "world theatre": perverse, because it contradicts itself inwardly and thus cannot be staged. Several times the theatre metaphor has reached this borderline of contradiction and self-dissolution. First of all with *Luther* and *Erasmus* and then again in romanticism. But for the most part people were only playing with the absolute contradiction; *Luther's* absolute point of reference was the God who could engage in "mummery *sub contrario*", *Erasmus* dissolved his total Play of Fools in Neoplatonist metaphysics, and the romantics acted out their play on the basis of an absolute "I" which could apply infinite irony and reflection to itself while still remaining itself. But where the idealist "Prometheus" world (of Absolute Spirit) submerges in the (meta-)biological "Dionysos" world (of life pure and simple, in the process of becoming), there is no standpoint left from which the masquerade, the role-play, can be evaluated and assessed.

α. Nietzsche,[1]

who does not say much about dramatic theory but devotes much attention to acting and masks, is well aware of this. Initially, of course, in his first period, influenced by *Schopenhauer* and *Wagner*, he takes a

[1] Unless otherwise noted, references are to Nietzsche's *Werke* in 3 vols., ed.

"dramatic primal phenomenon"[2] as his starting point, namely, the ecstatic Dionysian self-transformation which is fulfilled in the Apollonian vision (dream-vision). Here, in the tragic action, we gaze with redemptive effect on the "sufferings of Dionysos" (dismemberment or individuation), who is represented, under various "masks, in all the celebrated figures of the Greek theatre".[3] But then the same Greeks teach him that it is not a question of being redeemed from appearances by other appearances: "the 'apparent' is itself part of reality, a form of its being",[4] which is in fact no being at all but pure becoming. Life is "playacting" insofar as it invents and sets forth itself; but as such it is ambivalent to its very roots: it can be the naive, innocent self-presentation of one's own, victorious life power (which can both reveal itself or conceal itself behind the mask), or "the most adept, conscious hypocrisy", with a genius for self-mastery that aims at the conquest of others.[5] In either case *Nietzsche* needs to distinguish the actor from his mask—for his art is essentially that of "seeing through"—yet he cannot maintain the distinction because life is essentially a "seeming", and consequently "every opinion is also a concealment, every word a mask".[6] Are we to say that, in the "great comedy of the world and of existence",[7] it is only the man with "upward ambition", and whose mask has not yet become natural to him, who is "condemned to comedy"?[8] Does this mean that the Christian would be judged a (poor) actor and *Wagner* as the doyen of

---

K. Schlechta (Hanser, 1954). On this topic see also: E. Emmerich, *Wahrheit und Wahrhaftigkeit in der Philosophie Nietzsches* (Halle, 1933); Achim Fürstenthal, *Maske und Scham bei Nietzsche* (Diss. Basle, 1940); R. Debiel, *Die Metaphorik des Schauspielerischen* (Diss. Bonn, 1956).

[2] *Die Geburt der Tragödie* 8 (I, 52) [*The Birth of Tragedy*, London & Edinburgh, 1909].

[3] *Ibid.*, 10 (I, 61).

[4] III, 769.

[5] "Die Falschheit", in *Der Wille zur Macht* II, no. 379 (Kröner XV, 413f.) [*The Will to Power*, London & Edinburgh, 1909–10]. Since no one produces the blueprint of man but "life" itself, "person" designates the result, not the cause, of such production. Therefore: "We contain within us the *blueprints* for *many* persons. . . . Circumstances bring forth one of these figures, and if the circumstances greatly change, two or three figures will be seen" (XIII, 280). "Man is *unrecognized*, and what he does is *unrecognized*. If, in spite of this, we speak of human beings and acts as though they *were* recognized, it is because we have come to an agreement about certain *roles* which almost anyone can play" (XIII, 281).

[6] *Jenseits von Gut und Böse*, 289 (II, 752) [*Beyond Good and Evil*, London & Edinburgh, 1909]. "Every word represents a prejudice." *Der Wanderer und sein Schatten*, 55 (I, 903).

[7] *Menschliches, Allzumenschliches* II, 24 (I, 751) [*Human, All Too Human*, London & Edinburgh, 1909–11].

[8] *Jenseits von Gut und Böse*, 273 (II, 740).

actors "in every respect",[9] "acting out his own ideal"?[10] While, on the contrary, the rich man "at the zenith of his power", who could be liberal with his bounty, must don the mask for modesty's sake, as we frequently read in ever-new variations in *Beyond Good and Evil*: "Everything that is deep loves the mask. . . . Would it not be appropriate for the modesty of a God to go disguised under the *contrary* form? . . . There are actions of love and of extravagant generosity which are best followed by taking a stick and thrashing the one who has witnessed them, to confuse his recollection of the event. . . . Modesty is inventive."[11] There are people "who would rather become dumb than lose the modesty of moderation".[12] But how can we close the gulf between this consciously acted role, that is, mask seen as "good will toward the apparent",[13] this urgent need for the mask as a respite from existence's abyss ("Another mask! Give me a second mask!")[14]—and the determined effort to act out one's own ideal? "What is refined behavior? It means that one has constantly to represent oneself. It means looking for situations that constantly call for gestures. It means conceding happiness to the majority. . . ."[15] Does the refined person really need this attitude? Is there not something contradictory in the richly endowed man who can only express himself through masks, who has to have recourse to the same playacting as the poorer and weaker man who gets hold of a mask in order to seem greater than he is? Zarathustra's "Song of the Night"[16] sings of the rich man's tragic situation: "I no longer know the blessedness of those who receive. . . . My happiness in giving died even as I gave." So no one can play his role in truth, for the "appearance" side of the play is in any case a lie and a deception. It is no good talking about "sincerity"; that presupposes a foregoing truth: "In a world that is essentially false, sincerity would be a tendency contrary to nature: it could only make sense as a means to a particularly high degree of deceit."[17] In this way the higher person's virtues, which *Nietzsche* praises, are always self-contradictory. The higher man's "hovering" and "dancing" and his unquestioning "uni-

[9] *Nietzsche contra Wagner* (III, 1042).

[10] *Jenseits von Gut und Böse*, *Sprüche und Zwischenspiele*, 97 (II, 629).

[11] *Ibid.*, 40 (II, 603).

[12] *Morgenröte*, 527 (I, 1255) [*The Dawn of Day* London & Edinburgh, 1909].

[13] *Die fröhliche Wissenschaft*, 107 (II, 113) [*The Joyful Wisdom*, London & Edinburgh, 1910].

[14] *Jenseits von Gut und Böse*, 278 (II, 747).

[15] *Nachlass* (III, 796).

[16] II, 362f.

[17] *Nachlass* (III, 674).

versal affirmation" are always a "self-violation", making him "daily
more questionable", a hubris of self-experimentation: "We take pleasure
in inquisitively slitting our souls open in our living bodies":[18] the
higher man's asceticism and loneliness are incomparably harsher than
that of the Platonic or Christian backwoodsmen—which *Nietzsche*
unmasks as fundamentally insincere anyway. If "the character of
existence . . . is not true but false",[19] if "truth is a form of error"[20] and
if, therefore, "the nihilist does not believe in the necessity of being
logical",[21] the entire program of "revaluing values" cannot lead to any
new table of values. Life, striving upward and exercising its will to
power, can only produce naked and negating masks of itself; its
striving, as such, is decadence; its will to impress reveals its ennui. Thus
we can sum up *Nietzsche's* ever-deeper profundities in an aphorism of
his that is far less profound: "There is nothing more banal among men
than death. In second place comes birth, for not all those who die were
born. Next comes marriage. But these played-out little tragi-comedies,
in their countless and uncountable performances, are always played by
new actors, which is why they do not cease to attract an interested
audience; whereas one would think that all the spectators of the earthly
theatre would have hanged themselves on all available trees long ago,
out of sheer boredom. So much depends on the new actors, so little on
the play."[22]

Nietzsche's starting point (with its internal contradictions), that is, a
life that is continually going beyond itself and yet gets no farther,
provides the inner form of the wittiest and most effective dramatist
between *Ibsen* and *Pirandello*: *Bernard Shaw*. We cannot omit a glance at
his mediating role.

---

[18] *Zur Genealogie der Moral* (II, 855, 854) [*The Genealogy of Morals*, London &
Edinburgh, 1910].

[19] *Nachlass* (III, 678).

[20] *Ibid*. (III, 844).

[21] *Ibid*. (III, 670).

[22] "Der Wanderer und sein Schatten", 58 (I, 904). Fürstenthal endeavors to
show that Nietzsche was trying to work himself "out of the labyrinth of his
masked nature" which prevented him from making any unequivocal utterance.
But neither his middle period, in which the mask (covering the face of Dionysos)
is understood as an "instinct for moderation and measure" or as "the ability to
be silent" (74), nor his last period, in which he tries once more to affirm the
Dionysian element in its limitlessness (71f.), can provide a way out of the
self-contradiction which has been adopted as a principle.

β. *George Bernard Shaw*[1]

was described by G. K. *Chesterton*[2] as the Irish puritan whose philosophy could be "expressed as Schopenhauer stood on his head",[3] that is, in the courageous affirmation of the "man-trap" which this life represents. He is "a kind of believing and contented pessimist". Indeed, he carried out that transformation which incorporated *Schopenhauer's* pessimism into a positive view of the world, such as we find in Germany in *Wagner* and E. *v. Hartmann*, and even in *Nietzsche* and *Ibsen*. He went farther and placed the whole vision on the foundation of *Marx*. Simultaneously he studied *Das Kapital* and the score of *Tristan and Isolde*; when, later, he discovered *Nietzsche* and *Bergson's évolution créatrice*, the riddle of this simultaneity was solved: what *Shaw* was after was essentially a vantage point exalted above the immediacy of existence and its prejudices. That was his lifelong puritanism, to which he clung through all transformations. (*Nietzsche* never married, but *Shaw* lived from 1898 to 1943 in a marriage which, "as far as we know, was never consummated".)[4] This superior standpoint permitted him three most important attitudes, which roughly correspond to *Shaw's* three great creative periods. (1) From the superior standpoint of sociology (*Marx*) and psychology (*Ibsen*), one could look down and analyze, laying bare the implications of private and social existence. In this case the truth process would lie in the act of unveiling. (2) It was also possible, however, directly to illuminate the superior standpoint and show what real, synthetic, "spiritual" existence looks like; this would automatically unmask the false ideals of immediacy. (3) Yet, in the end, the mediation between "life" and "spirit" had to be exhibited, which *Shaw* undertakes to do in his ambitious quasi-philosophical superdramas. Only in the early phase does the Marxist analysis of society dominate (together with that of Ibsen, whom Shaw acknowledged as his master);[5] after the first plays this influence retires completely into the background.[6] Now

---

[1] *The Complete Plays of Bernard Shaw* (London, 1965), referenced in this section as *Plays*. *The Complete Prefaces of Bernard Shaw* (London, 1965), referenced in this section as *Pref*.

[2] G. K. Chesterton, *Bernard Shaw*. In his preface to *Three Plays for Puritans*, Shaw confirmed this view: "I have, I think, always been a Puritan in my attitude toward Art" (*Pref*. 743). He was so no less in his attitude to life.

[3] Chesteron, *Bernard Shaw*.

[4] Hermann Stresau, *G. B. Shaw* (Rororo, 1962), 83.

[5] In 1891, Shaw wrote "The quintessence of Ibsenism". In *Back to Methuselah*, "At the canonization of Saint Henrik Ibsen" a monument is unveiled "which bears on its pedestal the noble inscription, 'I came not to call sinners, but the righteous, to repentance' " (*Plays* 906).

[6] To have missed this is the mistake of the extensive dissertation by Friedhelm

it is the Nietzschean model of automatic superiority; the "superior man" (or "superman") gives the norm for true morality. Its "good" lies "beyond the good and evil" of the ordinary man, entangled in his prejudices. Since the "elevated" man quite naturally judges and unmasks the nonelevated world around him, the borderline between this and the first period is a fluid one: clearly, the ideal of the second is already present in the first. But where does he get his criteria for the "superior" man? The transition to the third approach is not a luxury, nor can it be attributed merely to *Shaw's* vain ambition to justify his often provocative plays by a profound philosophy; it arises from the matter itself. The horizon that comes into view is what *Shaw* himself calls "metabiological": the "life force" is a biological urge that goes beyond itself. It is only a "will to power" at the lowest level of evolution; at the higher levels of consciousness this power is so sublimated that it aspires to transcend all individual and social forms and institutions. The end of *Back to Methuselah* speaks quite clearly here. In a puritan vein, *Nietzsche* is left behind: the thrust is in a (Neo-)Platonic direction. *Shaw* had always rejected as irreligious the desire for personal immortality. Ultimately all the individual playing with particular forms—the form of a fellow human being in eros or the invented forms of art—is dismissed as of no significance: it is a "playing with dolls",[7] and in a far more negative sense than in *Plato's* late works. This kind of divine play—eros, dancing, art—(which is the "attempt to get into the rhythm of life")[8] is only permitted in the superman's earliest youth. Very soon it becomes pure boredom and is dropped; mature consciousness cuts itself loose from "this tyrannous body"[9] to become "pure intelligence".[10] The primitive, as yet unintelligent, attempts at civilization, where there were war, exploitation and state violence, are automatically eradicated through the rise of the superior men; but the latter, through their superiority,[11] assist the process; their very existence makes them "exterminators".[12] This is the only way in which such a walking contradiction as *Napoleon*, who can only achieve fame through murder but, through his victory, brings about "the demoralization, the

Denningham, *Die Dramatische Konzeption G. B. Shaws* (Bochum, 1969). Denningham tries to remold the whole of Shaw according to the categories of "social determinism" and quite clearly fails.

[7] *Back to Methuselah* in *Plays* 956.

[8] *Ibid.*, 938.

[9] *Ibid.*, 958.

[10] *Ibid.*, 962.

[11] As in *The Tragedy of an Elderly Gentleman*.

[12] *Back to Methuselah* in *Plays* 925; unwanted children and all life that is not valued is killed, 949. From the metabiological point of view it is a mere prejudice to make an essential distinction between animals and man.

depopulation, the ruin of the victors no less than of the vanquished",[13] can be overcome. *Shaw* himself, quite aware of what he was doing, an admirer of *Mussolini* and *Stalin*, became a spokesman for the new, deliberate and scientifically conducted campaign of extermination.[14] Here man consciously stages the world theatre of evolution.

Here is a rapid survey of the three periods in *Shaw's* dramatic work.
   1. The first task is to unmask the lie, using *Ibsen's* technique and on the basis of the Marxist analysis of society. Both in his first play, *Widowers' Houses*, and in the better-constructed *Mrs. Warren's Profession*, we have the initial revelation of scandalous immorality on the part of individuals (putting poor people into slums, keeping brothels), which is subsequently shown to be inextricably linked with the state of society as a whole, which relieves the guilty of responsibility and entangles the innocent who profit from these conditions without realizing it. The capitalist can "afford to be virtuous"—whether with a good conscience or not, is a side issue. Only later on do Trench in *Widowers' Houses* and Vivie in *Mrs. Warren's Profession* realize that they were involved right from the start. Vivie "raises" herself above her unsavory involvement by breaking both with mother and lover (who is implicated in the business) and wanting to live by her own work, remaining unmarried and knowing only "brotherhood". Thus she adopts a puritan and utopian standpoint over against the entire social and moral order. The figure of Vivie points forward to *Saint Joan*, but it is the whole stature of the latter that makes it a critique of secular and religious society. Shaw's most savage act of unmasking is *Major Barbara* (without which Brecht's *Johanna der Schlachthöfe* is inconceivable). Here the weapons magnate, Undershaft, because of his unlimited means, can provide far more for his workers than his daughter can through the Salvation Army. She can only distribute thin soup; people pretend to have Christian faith in order to gain access to her. Undershaft's motto is "Without Shame"; he sells his weapons to anyone who will give him a decent price for them, whether he be aristocrat or republican, capitalist or socialist, burglar or policeman. He sells to the highest bidder. He rules over war and peace. War, however, has the advantage of bringing in the cash with which, by way of amusement, he can build up those welfare structures which the Salvation Army cannot afford. He could even buy up the whole Salvation Army itself. "You cannot have power for good without having power for evil too", the power to "blow

---

[13] *Ibid.*, 929.
[14] Preface to *On the Rocks* in *Pref.* 353ff.

society up". Barbara is convinced: "There is no wicked side: life is all one. And I never wanted to shirk my share in whatever evil must be endured, whether it be sin or suffering." She transfers to the weapons factory in order to pursue her idealistic work more effectively on the realistic basis of society that has now been unveiled. "Then the way of life lies through the factory of death?—Yes, through the raising of hell to heaven and of men to God, through the unveiling of an eternal light in the Valley of the Shadow." This Nietzschean creed, which is perhaps *Brecht's* last in the *Good Woman of Szechuan*, anticipates Shaw's second and third phase. Beforehand, however, there are other unveilings to be made: there are the spurious, semidivine claims of science (for which medicine has to take the rap) in *The Philanderer* and *The Doctor's Dilemma*; the egoistic artist in *Pygmalion* who treats his "creature", the flower-girl made into a "duchess", as a robot, as an inconsequential pawn. Both these plays are closely related to *Ibsen*. There is the unveiling of the complacent pastor in *Candida*, who, asked to choose between the husband, full of himself, and the poor poet, chooses the former because, unmasked, he is the poorer; as for the poet, he must simply accept his fate of "living without happiness" as his "secret". There is the unveiling of the puritan in *The Devil's Disciple*, where Dick, who is branded as immoral, lets himself be taken in a trap instead of the escaped pastor, as a result of a confusion of identities he calmly allows to take place; in addition he loftily rejects the romantic love of the latter's wife. When asked why on earth he allowed himself to be taken, he replies, "Upon my life, Mrs. Anderson, I don't know." "I had no motive and no interest: all I can tell you is that when it came to the point whether I would take my neck out of the noose and put another man's into it, I could not do it." This is made more explicit in the related comedy, *The Shewing-up of Blanco Posnet*: Blanco's very questionable morality, when he gives the stolen horse to a poor woman to save her desperately ill child, is simply overplayed: "There's no good and bad, but by Jiminy, gents, there's a rotten game, and there's a great game. I played the rotten game; but the great game was played on me; and now I'm for the great game every time. Amen. Gentlemen: let us adjourn to the saloon. I stand the drinks." We find the same aimless and lofty passivity in another comedy of unveiling, which deals with Christian faith in the face of martyrdom, namely, *Androcles and the Lion*. Here, asked why she is prepared to die, Lavinia replies: "I don't know. If it were for anything small enough to know, it would be too small to die for. I think I'm going to die for God. Nothing else is real enough to die for." Naturally this presupposes the cynical psychoanalysis of Christian heroism in the face of death, demonstrated in

Ferrovius, who, at the last minute, instead of dying passively, slaughters everything in the arena. It also presupposes *Shaw's* elevation of one particular (and false) religion, that is, that of "the God that will be", to the level of a universal religion. Finally we must mention the light-hearted unmasking of suffragettism in *You Can Never Tell*, in which the entire dialectic of "family" and "antifamily" is dominated from above by the discreet figure of the waiter, who is in reality a lord. The "happy ending" of such plays, at their own (lower) level, is only a fortuitous reflection of that natural superiority which is the motif of the second phase.

2. Now it is no longer a question of unmasking but of an inner conquest which responds to the moralistic, idealistic and romantic knot of tensions (which originate, in reality, in the tangled sociologico-psychological situation) with its simple "It's not worth it." Its classical form is found in *Captain Brassbound's Conversion*, where the naively puritanical know-all, Lady Cicely, convinces the Captain, who is obsessed with revenge against his uncle for having unjustly treated his mother and himself, that revenge is simply not worth it. Brassbound must admit: "It seemed to me that I had put justice above self." It is characteristic of Lady Cicely, as of all of *Shaw's* subsequent "superior" people, that she is not unapproachable in a stoic sense. She admits, "I have never been in love with any real person" and says that she will never succumb to "that mad little bit of self in me"; yet, at the same time, she experiences anxiety for the first time in her life. *Shaw's* Caesar is humanized by his vanity, Bluntschli by his "huckster's soul" which is typical of the "Swiss national character", and Joan by her human fear of the stake which causes her, for a moment, to recant. Thus *Shaw's* "heroes" differ markedly from the martyrs and kings of the baroque stage. All the same we must ask whether these humanly softened supermen attain to full incarnation. Certainly not in the case of the strangely rapt hero of *Caesar and Cleopatra*, that play of great movement and color which ultimately refuses to yield its meaning. Caesar is a lovable, lonely superman (cf. his conversation with the Sphinx: "Sphinx, you and I, strangers to the race of men"; he is untouchable (or nearly) by the eroticism of the little viper, Cleopatra; he is above revenge, state duty, above the dialectic of power, fame and war. Above all emotional commitment ("Caesar loves no one"), he is in fact a Zarathustra in his seventh isolation; only his stupendous tactical skill connects him with the world. Less lofty is the "professional soldier" Bluntschli in *Arms and the Man*, a comedy designed simply to unmask the sorry romantic spell cast by war fever without preaching an

emotionally tinged pacifism. The debunking of the Bulgarian major is simply a foil for the elevation of the sober Swiss hotelier (who is acquainted with persecution and thus with genuine fear and accuses himself of attacks of romanticism) but who, like the old Swiss mercenaries, sees war as a craft and treats it professionally, not as a dilettante. Like Caesar he stands side by side with his role in a kind of Brechtian alienation: both share this puritan aspect. It is least evident in *Saint Joan* (the theme was suggested by *Shaw's* wife), in which, by way of exception, the poet clothes his superman ideal in the garb of a Christian saint, keeping the mask right up to the last word: "O God that madest this beautiful earth, when will it be ready to receive Thy saints? How long, O Lord, how long?" The fact that Joan is not susceptible to temptation shows her identity with her higher calling; this wholeness of hers makes her a walking utopia with her "head in the sky": "I owe everything to the spirit of God that was within me." Her imperturbable security ("I never speak unless I know I am right") enables her to perform "miracles" in the most natural way; things simply obey her. Like Vivian and Lady Cicely, she is unmarried, anticipating (in *Shaw's* sense) the eschatological state of the world. Like Zarathustra she is totally lonely and is very explicitly abandoned (in the fifth act) by all her supporters. Thus she is crushed between the cogs of the "political necessities" of church and state; *Shaw* depicts the whole trial and the forces at work in it with astonishing objectivity. When, in the epilogue, he celebrates the virgin's rehabilitation and tardy canonization, and all who betrayed and burned her pay her an almost liturgical homage, *Shaw* does not miss the opportunity of placing the gesture of betrayal at the end as something recurrent ("What? Must I burn again?"). The gap remains between sinners and saints, men and supermen.

3. The static dualism of levels of life raises a question which *Shaw* tries to answer with dynamic "metabiological" monism in his two monster plays *Man and Superman* and *Back to Methuselah*. The first goes back to the primal biological dualism of woman (the womb) and man (its fertilizer); man is an invention of the female life force. He is pursued, caught, domesticated and—according to *Maeterlinck's* model of bees and ants—killed when his duty is done. Thus the fleeing Tanner is pursued by Ann; she catches up with him in the Spanish sierra ("Hector: She is a regular Sherlock Holmes. Tanner: The Life Force! I am lost"). On this view, marriage is a "trap", something purely provisional; it is never ultimately fulfilling in *Shaw*. Lilith's original splitting (in *Methuselah*) into Adam and Eve has nothing in common with the splitting of the original hermaphrodite in *Plato's Symposion*; it is purely

a means adopted by the life principle for its own heightening, so that it may attain to "higher life". Thus, in the middle of the slight action of *Man and Superman*, in which (as *Chesterton* said) the mouse is pursued by the mousetrap, we find a mysterious interlude between Don Juan, Dona Ana, the Commendatore and the Devil. It takes place in hell.

Heaven and hell are recurrent symbols in *Shaw*.[15] Here, in the interlude, hell is everything *Shaw* abhors: blind pleasure, the satiated, unreal romanticism of beauty, happiness, ease, "virtue"; the devil is defined as the lack of all unrest.[16] In hell Don Juan finds everything that had disappointed him on earth, so he strives to escape. He symbolizes the unrest of the upward-reaching life force. The Commendatore, on the other hand, comes on a visit to hell because he is bored in heaven. *Shaw's* heaven is "reflection", "geometry" (we can see the origin of *Max Frisch's* Don Juan play here), the ever-growing power of self-contemplation for which the life force strives through systematic development of the brain. In short, "to be in hell is to drift: to be in heaven is to steer." What is remarkable in *Man and Superman* (as compared with *Methuselah*) is that the movement is in the opposite direction: Don Juan strives upward from below, the Commendatore wants to get down from above. The Devil says: "Men get tired of everything, of heaven no less than of hell"; and "all history is nothing but a record of the oscillations of the world between these two extremes." "Each generation thinks the world is progressing because it is always moving . . . reform, progress, fulfillment of upward tendency." But in reality it is only "an infinite comedy of illusion". Eternal recurrence envelops nature's irresistible urge to attain self-understanding and self-direction through the intellect; it is no accident that the Devil drops the name of *Nietzsche* here, the "German Polish madman"; even *Wagner's* Siegfried is honored with a mention as a superman. Tanner/Don Juan (the fleeing striving toward spirit) thus remains a function, a "prey" of creation's "blind madness", of the "boa constrictor", and marriage becomes the surrender of one's own self, "one and indivisible", "the most licentious of human institutions", a "limitless humiliation", although occasionally it may be unavoidable.[17] (This is the context for *Shaw's* continual flirtation with celibacy and

[15] Cf. Keegan in act IV of *John Bull's Other Island* or the dialogue between Joan and the down-at-heel English soldier who comes from hell.

[16] Cf. *Pygmalion*, act V, and the Preface to *Three Plays for Puritans*.

[17] *Getting Married*. The Bishop: "Marry whom you please: at the end of a month he'll be Reginald all over again." Leo: "Then it's a mistake to get married?" The Bishop: "It is, my dear; but it's a much bigger mistake not to get married."

with poverty as the elimination of private property.)[18] However, this contradiction between progress and eternal recurrence, which is the last word of *Man and Superman*, was too crass for *Shaw* the rationalist: he had to try to get beyond it in *Back to Methuselah*.

Here world process attains a single, "biological" direction: it is the life force's striving toward something transcendent ("metabiology"), once again called "consciousness", "contemplation", "thought": and "that will be eternal life". True, right at the beginning, with Adam and Eve, it is abhorrent to think of living eternally (that is, for an endless time) as the same individual; that is why the first human beings invented death as a means of "making room" for new life. But in the wake of this human invention of finitude—and through the "Cain" principle—come murder, war, eros, art, politics, heroism, romanticism and the dream of the beyond and of individual immortality. In fact, the dramatic peripeteia in *Shaw's* "theatre of the world" comes when life, in its striving for divinity, breaks through the tragic hold exercised by life's shortness. The foreground solution is an evolutionary leap to a life span of three hundred years; this enables man to shed the romantic childishness of his first hundred years and spend the rest of the time on the basis of the spirit, the real power. (Part of the program, as we have said, is the extermination of people with short life spans, who in any case mostly die of "demoralization".) Thus this quantitative prolongation of life implies something qualitative, namely, the overcoming of existence's pseudo-tragic dimension. The consequences are clearly drawn in the last play, *As Far as Thought Can Reach*. Eros (with its avowals of "eternal faithfulness") is the first to be dismissed as a childish game. Then comes art with its "playing with dolls". But finally he also dismisses the ultimate example of such playing, that is, Pygmalion's attempt to use technology to create artificial human beings, robots whose mechanisms harness the "high-potential Life Force", resulting in the development of "consciousness". The couple thus created are at the lowest level of human life: they see no farther than the notion that each individual is a "person", they are crassly egoistic and lying and finally murder Pygmalion. The animated puppets, who have "no self-control and are merely shuddering through a series of reflexes", are not viable; this gives rise to the idea that we must grow

---

[18] Soames: "My advice to you all is to do your duty by taking the Christian vows of celibacy and poverty. The Church was founded to put an end to marriage and to put an end to property . . . and to replace them with the Communion of Saints." Shaw's letters to the Abbess Laurentia of Stanbrook (published in 1956 by John Murray) show that these views of his were by no means simply eccentric.

beyond organic life's creative urge and discard "this body" as "the last doll", in order to reach an "eternal life" that is no longer limited by personal categories, a "perpetual resurrection". The final word is given to Lilith, primal Nature, who suffered a painful split at the beginning which yielded the duality of the sexes: matter has been made to serve life, but according to *Hegel* the servant becomes the master; thus matter has sublimated itself, heading for "a beyond" which Lilith (as the principle of evolution) cannot envisage.

From this last horizon, the little stage of life presented in *Shaw's* comedies seems to have been emptied of all meaning. At the level of existence which is here set forth, everything—personal being, love, marriage, economics, politics, death itself—is provisional, illusory, maya-like. Its intrinsic harshness is lightened only by a gleam of humorous, reconciling resignation that comes from the perspective of the "higher man". From his religious nirvana, where all the differences of the world religions are resolved,[19] from Zarathustra's seventh solitude or Joan's fiery death and transfiguration, *Shaw*, the master of the cosmic marionette theatre, animates his countless puppets. None of them may lay claim to personality—becoming spirit means losing what is personal—and each one has only the characteristics the playwright lends it. Paradoxically, the puppet, lacking all essential being, is completely one with the mask it wears, with the role it plays. "The poet does not dare let his characters take off on their own. He controls them with leading-strings."[20] Thus one path taken by postidealist drama, under the inspiration of *Nietzsche*, has come to an end. The theatre of the world can no longer produce a meaningful play, for what apportions the roles, the blind life force, does not know what it is doing. And the playwright, situated on a level above the dramatic action, pulling the strings and imparting a meaning to the play, can only do this insofar as he denies any meaning to the immanent action itself. So the last step brings us of necessity to *Pirandello*.

γ. *Luigi Pirandello*,

in his most celebrated play *Six Characters in Search of an Author* (1921),[1] reflected radically on the whole question of the possibility of dramatic construction. Through this play (which is concerned with the impos-

---

[19] Shaw was a passionate advocate for the unification of all religions and the abolition of all particular gods and cults (cf. the vicious satire, *A Black Girl Looks for God*, 1922). He regarded Islam as the best model, relatively speaking, for a religion for mankind.

[20] E. Brock-Sulzer, *Theater* (Kösel, 1954), 85f. (Reference to Shaw.)

[1] In *Three Plays* (Methuen, 1985).

sibility of its performance) *Pirandello* not only sounded the alarm with regard to the state of the modern theatre but also, at a deeper level, called for the critical dismantling of a hitherto unexamined "ideology" that had informed the postidealist drama. This had emerged most clearly in *Hebbel*, yet was not felt as a crisis: the old presupposition of the "theatre of the world", that God apportioned and took responsibility for the roles, had been given up; God was replaced by the human dramatist, who thus became the play's authority, creating its synthesis, bearing responsibility for it and bringing it to its conclusion. Playwrights have often expressed the idea that the characters they want to bring to life seem to acquire an independent existence in their imagination: *Pirandello* felt this most vividly: "It is a dangerous business, giving life to a character. These six, created by my mind, were already living their own life, a life that was not mine . . . like the figures of a novel, miraculously stepping forth from the page. . . . They took me by surprise . . . , tempting me to imagine this or that scene."[2] The playwright saw only one way of getting rid of them: he had to portray "the entirely new situation in which an author refuses to give life to some of the characters to which his imagination had given birth." "I took them as rejects and made them real." This is the start of the contradiction: "What was I denying them? Not themselves, clearly, but their drama, which interested them most." But in that case, how can they be themselves? For "every artistic creation must have its own drama if it is to exist, a drama in which and through which it is and becomes an acting person." These six characters appear in the middle of a rehearsal for a *Pirandello* play and ask the Producer (not the playwright—he has refused) to perform their drama; although they themselves have experienced this drama and it belongs to their past, "in itself" it has not taken place since the playwright has refused to give it reality. The only drama of theirs to be realized (artistically, by the playwright) is their demand to be performed and the impossibility of such a performance—which, of course, they cannot understand. "If anyone were to tell them, they would not believe it; it is impossible to believe that the sole ground of our life is the pain which seems unjust and inexplicable to us."[3]

The pain is not, in fact, the tragedy of the unperformed play but the

[2] Preface. "You've never seen it because an author usually hides all the difficulties of creating. When the characters are alive, really alive and standing in front of their author, . . . he must want them to be what they want to be. . . . When a character is born he immediately assumes such an independence even of his own author that everyone can imagine him in scores of situations that his author hadn't even thought of putting him in" (Father in act III, *Three Plays* 124).

[3] Preface. Whereas the characters are trying to have their play performed, "I

impossibility of finding the level of being on which this tragic play can finally be performed. Here the "world theatre" metaphor is used to stage its internal dismantling, right down to its metaphysical ground. There is a creator who causes characters to arise out of his mind and guarantees them a dialogue context—as we are shown when the missing seventh person, Madame Pace, suddenly materializes[4]—but at the same time denies them this context. So their drama, which they regard as their reality, will always be past; it will never become present on the (world) stage. The Producer, who at last decides to transpose the past event into the present, wants to see it as it really was, but the Mother refuses to acknowledge this eternal past as something that has come and gone. Producer: "But if it's already happened. . . ." Mother: "No! It's happening now, as well: it's happening all the time. . . ." Father (solemnly): "The eternal moment."[5] This refusal, which prevents the play from being performed, represents the creatures' response to the creator's refusal to write the play: for their part they refuse to enter into the "form" which "fixates" and thus falsifies real life. When the professional actors endeavor to imitate the roles of the six characters in a stage manner, transposing them into the stage milieu, the latter, highly indignant, protest that what they are doing is totally wrong and that everything was quite different. They protest that they *are* the characters;[6] the Producer wants to make them mere "material", "to which the actors give form and body, voice and gesture".[7] This twofold refusal (which is the play's real subject matter) indicates a twofold contradiction, with regard to existence (*Dasein*) and this particular mode of existence (*Sosein*).

Existence is negated. The ideal and the real radically cancel each other out as far as the existence of the six characters is concerned. For the reality of the characters is an idea in the author's imagination, containing all the vividness of personal exchange, yet he refuses to perform the transition into reality (as a stage play). The characters insist on this kind of reality and refuse to be trapped in a play which, while it

---

represent them as being part of another play; but they are not aware of this, with the result that their passionate emotion . . . is in a vacuum."

[4] "It is not a trick. It is a real birth, the new character is alive, of necessity." "Thus a hiatus has come about, a sudden change of the scene's level of reality, because a character can come into being in this way only in the playwright's imagination. . . . Using the stage itself, I have brought my imagination onto the stage at the moment of creation."

[5] *Three Plays* 118.

[6] *Ibid.*, 100.

[7] *Ibid.*, 101.

would bring this reality about, seems a falsification and an "illusion"[8]—although this realization is what they long for.[9] The conjunction of idealism and *Lebensphilosophie* (which regards "form" as ossified life) is bound to contribute to utter contradiction in the realm of being and hence also in the realm of truth: "But it's the truth" Producer: "The truth! Do me a favor will you? This is the theatre you know! Truth's all very well up to a point, but. . . ."[10] For a moment the Father sees this whole dialectic of contradictions: the Producer refers to the theatre as an "illusion of reality", and when the Father suggests that it is nothing but a "game", the Leading Actress is very indignant: "What happens here is serious!" Then the Father asks the Producer to "create the perfect illusion of reality" but bids him remember that "we have no other reality outside this illusion".[11]

This is the point at which the destruction of the particular mode of existence (*Sosein*) begins. For the six characters only possess an "I" within their role, that is, within their relationship with one another which arises in the drama of existence; but if the drama's level of existence cannot be defined, the "I" must also remain indeterminate. "Do you really know who you are? . . . A character, my dear sir, can always ask a man who he is, because a character really has a life of his own, a life full of his own specific qualities, and because of these he is always 'someone'. While a man . . . can be an absolute 'nobody'."[12] Pure existence in the flux of time makes what is real today an illusion tomorrow: "Don't you feel that not only this stage is falling away from under your feet but so is the earth itself. . . ?"[13] Existence only becomes a consistent, particular existence in the context of a role such as the six characters have, or rather might like to have. But since their play is not performed, they never get to play their parts, their roles, together; they stay in their monologues which lack relationship and hence reality.[14] This is capped by the Son, who has refused to cooperate right from the start, when, in absolute isolation, he says he will not act the crucial final scene: "And I'm doing what our author wanted as well—he never wanted to put us on the stage."[15]

[8] *Ibid.*, 122.
[9] Stepdaughter: "Now, now, I'm dying to do that scene!" (*ibid.*, 106). ". . . but I want to show you my drama! Mine!" (115).
[10] *Ibid.*, 115.
[11] *Ibid.*, 122.
[12] *Ibid.*, 123.
[13] *Ibid.*, 123.
[14] *Ibid.*, 115.
[15] *Ibid.*, 131.

It is sufficient to have demonstrated how the theme of the "theatre of the world" has eliminated itself in this one play of *Pirandello's*. His other plays deal with the same theme but from more partial vantage points. But *It Is So! (If You Think So)* (1917) also reveals the utter, unveiled contradiction in being itself, when, at the end, Signora Ponza embraces a double truth that cancels itself out;[16] this play, like *Six Characters* and *Cap and Bells*, ends with "manic laughter". In *Henry IV* (1921) it is the reciprocal questioning of insanity and rationality that reveals the obstructing delusion. In *Each in His Own Way* (1924) and *Tonight We Improvise* (1929)—pursuing farther certain motifs of *Six Characters*—the distinction between stage and reality (the audience) is obliterated, with the most cynical unmasking taking place in an exaggerated masquerade.

The identity-in-contradiction of the play of the world and its "metaphor", the "theatre of the world", seems to link up closely with tradition—one thinks, for instance, of the way *Plotinus* distanced himself from the genuine horrors of existence, which could only be looked at as if they were scenes from the theatre—and yet it is at the same time a radical break with this tradition. Tradition always rested on an analogy which assumed that God was the ultimate director who apportioned the roles; it endeavored to interpret the real events of the world in terms of the heavenly Dramatist. Now, however, the earthly dramatist has become the *analogatum princeps*, which, as *Pirandello* shows in his poetics (*L'Umorismo*, 1908), citing *Friedrich Schlegel* and *Hegel*, was a consequence of absolute idealism. Here the theatre is a "farce which, in representing tragedy, includes parody and caricature of that same tragedy, not as if they were elements added on but as the projection of the shadow of its own body." It is a "transcendental farce". The "I" can "laugh at the universe's vacant appearance: it can both bring it into being and suspend it; it cannot take its own creations seriously."[17] Through all the disguises, what looks out at us is wretched nakedness: *Maschere nude*.[18]

---

[16] Her being-for-herself is identical with her being-for-others, or restricted to it. Cf. the analysis of the play in Karl Löwith's *Das Individuum in der Rolle des Mitmenschen*, 2d ed. (1969), 84–103.

[17] Quoted from Renate Matthaei, *Pirandello* (1967), 23.

[18] Title of the complete edition of Pirandello's plays (Milan: Mondadori, 1958, 2 vols).

4. Conclusion: The Dramatic Resources of the "Theatre of the World"

In our attempt to provide dramatic resources for the use of theology we chose the "theatre of the world" because it contains, concentratedly and most abundantly—both widely scattered and in precise detail—the elements which, drawn from the dramatic process itself, facilitate a religious and ultimately theological interpretation of existence. *Seneca* considered this constantly recurring theme to be the image most apt for interpreting human life; *Maximus the Confessor* used the image of acting for the most diverse levels of theological interpretation of the world. Let us admit that *Kassner* is right when he says that the image, *qua* image, is ambivalent. But insofar as man the spectator, the audience, wishes to have the event of his own existence set before him in a clarifying form, in an attempt to understand himself better, it is evident that existence itself contains an accompanying reflection that is immanent in it and which the theatrical process only makes more explicit. In this regard, theatre—expressly seen as "theatre of the world"—is an image that is substantially more than an image: it is a "symbol of the world",[1] a mirror in which existence can directly behold itself. True, this relationship between the event and reflection upon it in life, a relationship which is reduplicated in the reflective spectacle of the theatre, exhibits a confusing ambivalence. But this is only the primary ambivalence of immediate existence itself. When existence beholds itself on the stage, it may be that the "game" aspect of existence, its irrationality, predominates, spilling over, as it were, from the stage into the audience. On the other hand, the seriousness of what is being enacted can be so overpowering that the spectator is seized by it and recalled to the "authenticity" of his own existence. We cannot reprove the theatre—as entertainment and as a moral and educative institution (*Schiller, Brecht*)—for its ambivalence, since the latter characterizes existence itself and its self-understanding.

Through all its variations, in the ancient world, in Christianity, and in modern times, the "theatre of the world" rests on four leitmotifs which together make it an arcane symbol of the

---

[1] Eugen Fink, *Spiel als Weltsymbol* (Kohlhammer, 1960).

dramatic dimension of existence, insofar as existence, in its metaphysico-religious self-interpretation, assumes a horizon of meaning.

a. The Distinction between the (Temporal-Spatial) Finitude of the Performed Play and Its Nonfinite Meaning

1. With its ineluctable finitude of action in both time and space—formalized in the classical "three unities"—the play mirrors the equally ineluctable finitude of human existence; moreover, even where no clear signal is given for the action to be broken off, meaningful acting is called for. In *Calderon's* "theatre of the world" this signal is given with a certain naiveté after the ("third") act—the reaction of the characters to what the beggar has done—in dialogue form, in a specific ("fourth") act: the summons confronts the King at the height of his power, just as he is on the point of expanding his rule; beauty, wealth and the peasant all attempt to resist the final signal which must come to "everyman". *Epictetus* (echoed in *Quevedo*) and particularly *Marcus Aurelius* were at pains to be prepared to leave in the third or fourth act, not necessarily in the fifth. This is a warning for all dramatic theory that would make the drama "absolute" and understand its temporal sequence as "an absolute succession of present moments", as "pure actuality": "It creates its own time."[2] A dramatic theory which assumes that the fifth act will be reached by some absolute necessity, as an unshakable matter of course (whereas *Molière* falls fatally ill while acting his *Malade imaginaire*) has forgotten one thing: the world theatre's time dimension has no intrinsic guarantee, and it is an usurpation on the part of the stoic who wants to end the play wherever he thinks best (*Seneca's* recommendation of suicide). The meaning of the "sequence of acts" (*John of Salisbury*) is immanent in it but only as a "nonfinite" meaning that also transcends it and which the actor, consequently, cannot grasp completely. Thus in *Plato*, implicitly in *Epictetus* and explicitly in *Calderon*: the spectator's ability to judge the meaning of a play and the quality of the acting is only a reflection of the transcendent act of

---

[2] Peter Szondi, *Theorie des modernen Dramas* (Suhrkamp, 1956), 15, 17, 67.

judgment which assesses the immanent, finite play of life after it has ended. This ability on the spectator's part is equally a warning to him: he too is subject to a transcendent evaluation. This is necessarily so if the time of the end is uncertain and yet what is enacted is capable of being faultless (*Bion*, *Teles*).

2. This distinction grounds the unavoidable ambiguity between the stage play's aspects of illusion and seriousness, frivolity and profound significance. In fact, the balance between these two poles cannot be found within the play itself at all: drama can justify both feelings at the same time—a sense of the radically illusory quality of all that happens on earth, with its pomp and circumstance, as well as the sense of the radical seriousness of what, on the surface, seems so frivolous (for the actor is answerable—to the audience or to the Lord of the play—for the most insignificant part just as much as for a major role). *Plotinus*, using the theatre metaphor, sees the dimension of illusion even in the most terrible tragedies of human existence ("man's outer shadow sobs and gesticulates as if mad"); in the baroque theatre the absolute point of reference is shifted from tragedy to the pure relation to eternity (*Gryphius*). This means that the "theatre of the world" will not let us step out of ambiguity; it will not let us dissolve the action into a pure, unreal illusion (*Schopenhauer*), nor, with all its deep significance, will it allow us to forget its ephemeral character. In and through the temporal "play" as such we can glimpse (but not seize hold of) an eternal meaning.

3. This brings us to a third element. Initially it emerged indirectly in the variants discussed (most clearly in *Calderon* and *Hofmannsthal*): the temporal succession of action may indeed contain factors of determinism, but they cannot vitiate the freedom in which meaning is imparted nor the freedom which is able continually to give new values to the whole play and even to those of its acts that are past and gone. When *Calderon's* "Beauty" concludes her role "well" since, in death, her heart is afraid ("because I did not succeed in doing better"), she thereby gives a new evaluation of her entire past. In the final analysis, however the play harmonizes the various accents, from determinism to freedom, it remains for its duration in a state of suspension (the noblest element of the dramatic tension) that

corresponds to the ambiguity between time and eternity and keeps the spectator's judgment hovering between the two.

b. The Distinction between the "I" and the Allotted Role

1. Historically this distinction, which is one of life's basic experiences, stands at the origin and at the demise of the "theatre of the world" as a symbol. It would be too simplistic to affirm a pure dualism, for at the heart of this distinction there is also a certain identity. In *Plato* this mystery is expressed in the myth whereby the "I" makes an intelligent, free, prior choice of its role and the two are welded together in preexistence. In *Calderon* the synthesis takes place in the mind of God but in such a way that, in the prologue, the "souls" are given their roles and appropriately equipped—to which some respond in an attitude of indifference and others with reluctance. Accordingly there is a disrobing in death and after death; here we see that the "I" is by no means unaffected by the role it has played: both in the Indian-Platonic doctrine of karma and in the Christian Last Judgment, the soul's reward depends on the way it has played its part. Beyond *Calderon*, however, there are further open questions in Christian theology, that is, what is the significance, from the standpoint of "heaven", of a role played "on earth" in the great theatre of the world, and what can such a role achieve?

2. At all points there is an awareness that the central task is to maintain identity while preserving distinction and distance. Wholehearted effort is called for to play one's role well from beginning to end (*Teles*), aware that the two, the "I" and the role, do not coincide—which is why an inferior role in no way harms the dignity of the actor. All the same, the "I" does not stand untouched behind the role: it acts out its own destiny in the role. It is in the role that it proves itself or fails to; this is where it freely acquires, or fails to acquire, its own shape. At a particular metaphysical point of departure it may have seemed that the role was picked by choice (the roles may even have been specially exhibited for such a choosing), but the next step is that of total affirmation and acceptance of the role. This, however, does not imply the loss of the "I" and its absorption into the role; rather, it guarantees that the actor can carry out the role in

lofty freedom. This mystery was grasped in such a profound and unprejudiced way in pre-Christian philosophy—which was not an ego-philosophy in the modern sense—that when Christianity shed ultimate light on the mystery by referring to the Person of Christ, it was able to link up with a serious understanding that was already there and in which it found a serviceable instrument. Both *Plato* and *Plotinus* know that they are approaching the boundaries of utterance when, in mythological and mystical terms, they try to speak of the relationship between the free person and the role allotted by destiny; they show clearly how close we are here to the mysterious well-springs of human nature, to a mystery that can only be penetrated by a word that comes from the source of being. Thus, in carrying out the role, we never surrender the freedom to shape it; in pre-Christian times this freedom may be viewed in somewhat narrower limits than in Christian and post-Christian times, when the role becomes more plastic (in the "extempore" play), but at no point is the original tension between "I" and role surrendered.

3. Above all this is the case because of the social involvement of each role with all the others, which *Marcus Aurelius* felt and expressed so forcefully: all are "born for each other", "interwoven and intertwined" in each other. As "Policraticus" says: "The roles are adapted to each other; if they go off on their own, the whole shape of the action is altered." This is the prime point at which the "monadic" theatre of postidealism failed; modern role-sociology is trying (albeit at too shallow a level) to recover the lost ground. It is here that *Claudel's* plays, informed by his metaphysics (according to which all worldly forms interpenetrate and determine each other) were able to instill new life into the perennial insights of the ancient world and of Christianity. There is a point of loneliness and incommunicability in every role; thus, in *Calderon*, the individual roles stand isolated and "typical"—like the angel species in *Aquinas*: "the" King is sharply distinguished from "the" Peasant, and so forth, just as each chess figure has its task and mode of movement; but, together, these solitary roles form a single game or play, and only within it do they receive their full meaning. This play rests on the presupposed tension between the "I" in its uniqueness

and the social context into which it must freely enter. The "I" with its freedom is designed for this context; only here can it implement its freedom for the good of all.

c. The Distinction between the Actor's Responsibility for His Performance and His Responsibility to a Director

1. The two prior distinctions point to an overriding identity, an origin, responsible both for the play within the finite compass of the stage and for the roles with their dialectic of freedom and manipulation, of person and social context. In the ancient world it was easy to speak of God as the dramatist, spectator and judge of the play, but the metaphor did not entirely succeed because God's free spiritual nature and his creative function were still obscured. All the same, this still-veiled apex radiated the individual aspects which point to it: the apportioning of roles, their meaningful interrelation and the sense of responsibility toward some higher instance than that of the play itself. In the Christian play these aspects were effortlessly related to the apex, now at last unveiled. Since, in all variants of the metaphor, the actors enjoy genuine freedom, they also bear genuine responsibility for their own performances; they are not slaves of the Most High Master of the Play, even if ultimately they must answer to him for the way they acquit themselves. Thus there is a distinction within the actor's unique responsibility, based on the fact that his freedom is not an absolute one but a freedom that is only realized in and through the distinction of roles, which, in turn, is part of an all-embracing social whole.

2. If the actor's responsibility is ultimately dependent on the play's Originator and Director; the latter, since he is responsible for the entire play, cannot conduct himself like a purely passive spectator. He is a spectator (and this is true in *Calderon* but also in the ancient world and in the Old Testament) insofar as the play is performed in his presence: he himself does not enter into it. But since he is responsible for the whole play, for the roles he has invented and allotted, for the freedom he has given to the actors, he cannot be a mere spectator. He is involved in the play, as we see clearly in *Homer*. In *Plato's Laws* the gods draw the human actors up into their higher play so that the universe is the

stage for a universal, divine-human drama. In *Calderon's* "theatre of the world"—in order to preserve the purity of the stage metaphor—the divine Director is represented only by the constantly resounding voice of Law (which not only presents demands but also brings grace), reminding us of his presence. But the eschatological meal to which he finally invites those who have acted well is the symbol of that much deeper involvement in human history on God's part, an involvement that is treated quite explicitly in many other *autos sacramentales*. The question that was equally pressing to *Plotinus*, to *Calderon*, to *Schelling* and his followers is further developed in the distinction of ultimate authorities, that is, the gods and Fortuna in antiquity, "Master" and "World" in *Calderon*, autonomy and destiny in the modern era. Within the stage metaphor itself a distinction is drawn between author and director (producer), which *Pirandello* made into an explicit theme. The next section of this book (on "dramatic resources") will have to bear this distinction carefully in mind. The stage metaphor preserves the relationship between God's transcendence and immanence vis-à-vis the play (cf. the treatise *Peri Kosmou*), which Christian theology will express in the concept of the economic Trinity.

3. Naturally the distinction between the "Master's" total responsibility for the performance and the individual actor's responsibility for his own acting encompasses the whole gamut of eschatological questions. How can the absolute freedom of global responsibility go along with the actors' partial freedom without vitiating it? And since this latter, genuine freedom can even embrace total refusal and rebellion, how can the play be performed according to the Author's intentions and brought to a meaningful conclusion? What kind of presence can the "Master" have in the events of the world play that will not threaten the actors' free responsibility within the performance? The problems raised by *Schelling* with his "extempore play", and which *Görres* attempted to develop further, will have to be taken up again (in the theological part of the present work), lest the whole issue become stranded in *Pirandello's* impasse, between the "author" and his "characters".

d. The Three Distinctions Give Rise to the Dramatic Tension

1. So far we have said nothing about the content of the play. In the "theatre of the world" the content cannot be just anything: it must arise from the distinctions we have enumerated. First and foremost the content can only be man himself, caught between his "I" and his role, between what he is and what he represents—though what he is cannot be totally separated from what he represents; indeed, his "I" must responsibly realize itself in this representational role. But this also has two sides: both as "I" and as a role he is responsible to the social context within which he acts, as well as to the Director who has cast him, as an individual, in the play. Nor do these two responsibilities necessarily coincide (as in the martyr-play, of which even the *Apologia of Socrates* is an example). The subject matter is human acts, intervening in the constellation of roles and exercising a creatively transforming influence; such acts have to render account, both to the world and to God, for the meaning (*Sinn*) or absurdity (*Unsinn*) they exhibit; they must be prepared to face the consequences of what they have initiated. Insofar as it has both a horizontal (infra-historical) and a vertical dimension (transcendent, open to God), and insofar as the meaning apparent to the individual role has to integrate itself into the web of meaning woven by all the actors together, there results a boundless multiplicity of plots, both comic and tragic. Both the revelations and concealments facilitated by the role-costumes, both the construction and dismantling of a role-personality (in order to bring out its "truth"), exhibit perspective: there seems to be no end of constellations and vistas, although the play will move toward a picture which—as a metaphor at least of the ultimate adjudication—must allow the plurality of standpoints to be integrated into a single and final one.

2. In this convergence toward an all-inclusive situation, the central question is always this: Where, in this network of roles, which as such are always engaged in "representing", can we recognize the authentic representation of ultimate authority—the Divine Will? We may expect to encounter the bitterest conflicts here, between a freedom that knows it has been given a task to perform and a representation of (maybe legitimate)

authority which the said freedom must criticize as unproven; between a personal love with its own center of gravity and the solemn dignity of an authority against which this love is dashed to pieces—if the latter does not actually inundate the former. In situations such as these, qualitative time, the threshold between aeons in the history of the human spirit (*Hebbel*), becomes important: things are intact within a value system on one side of the threshold but not on the other: this is the tragedy of *Socrates* and, in the transition from Judaism to the Church, the tragedy of Jesus. Quantitative time is an abstraction; time is essentially determined by the constellations and the sum of personal/social decisions, of which (indeed) only part is empirically ascertainable but which have an influence on the way in which a role is to be understood and responsibly exercised in a transcendent context.

3. Since man is always an "I" in a role (an exalted or lowly, powerful or impotent role), action on the world stage will always be determined in part by how the man in the lowly role is viewed. It is no accident that *Calderon* made the beggar's scene the central point and peripeteia of the play (and *Hofmannsthal* did the same with the proletarian who demands work). In the play of *Jedermann*, too, we see the mighty man suddenly bereft of all power in view of his imminent summoning from the stage. Both in the innerworldly, horizontal dimension and in the vertical dimension brought out by death, the master/servant dialectic automatically occupies the center of the play (where the latter sees itself as the all-embracing play of mankind). It need not be exclusively a question of material possessions; it applies to all forms of power and the way it is used in the social context. This dialectic can be demonstrated with the utmost light-heartedness in comedy, but at any moment it can pass over into tragi-comedy and tragedy.

These are the perspectives opened up for us by an historical survey of the motif of the "theatre of the world". Now we must go on to unpack, more precisely and systematically, the categories they imply. Only when we have done this shall we be in possession of adequate resources for our theological project.

B. ELEMENTS OF THE DRAMATIC

1. *Drama and the Illumination of Existence*

In the preceding section we were working on the basis of an understanding of the theatre that saw it as an illumination of existence, and a central one at that. We endeavored to identify the individual elements of this illumination: existence under the spotlight of the stage. Now we must go the other way, showing how the theatre springs from existence and is characterized by it.

Not all peoples are acquainted with the theatre in its full form as found in the West and the Far East (from India to Japan); in some places only certain elements of the theatre are present. Some peoples are satisfied with the aspect of masquerade and the play associated with it, or with the dance (which is often ecstatic and is always carried out with gestures), or with the dramatic presentation of a ballad, a myth, an epic story of gods and heroes, or with an exciting tale, told with such vividness that it does not seem to suffer by not being performed by one or more actors.[1] Originally, no doubt, the synthesis of the two elements (the individual's self-liberation from his own confines through the mask and the dance, and the presentation of an epic-dramatic mythical narration) was felt to be a monstrously risky undertaking: we can see this from the cultic drama performed annually

---

[1] Goethe and Schiller, "Über epische und dramatische Dichtung", in *Über Kunst und Altertum* (1827), vol. 6, bk. 1, set forth the relationship between the two poetic forms: "Neither form can arrogate anything to itself exclusively." "The great and essential difference between them, however, is this: the epic writer presents the event as something *complete and past*, and the dramatist presents it as *completely present*." Thus the epic poet "should not himself appear as a higher being in his poem; it would be best if he read from behind a curtain, so that the listeners could abstract from all personality." The actor, on the other hand, "projects himself as a particular individual" and must step forth "present to the senses"; "the senses of the listening spectator must be kept in a constant state of tension, and rightly so." On the other hand (cf. H. Reich and A. Kutscher, *Grundriss der Theaterwissenschaft*, 2d ed. [1936], 43, 61, 88) it must be admitted that the element of mimesis (the origin of all theatre) is present in all peoples, including those which have no developed theatre at all.

in Babylon (there were corresponding celebrations elsewhere too): it is a special religious event that involves the whole nation politically. The king is the meeting place of the two aspects: he represents both the people (as their macro-ego) and the gods, whose son and chosen one he is. The cultic origin of our theatre is beyond doubt;[2] the risky undertaking of a synthesis between the way man sees himself and his encounter with the divine myth as it manifests itself to him, between "Dionysus" and "Apollo",[3] takes place at the dangerous borderline where magic and revelation cannot be told apart. Like the Babylonian New Year play, the Greek tragedy (together with its accompanying comedy) takes place only once a year—on the occasion of the town's Dionysian celebrations, celebrated in the place called after Dionysus below the town fortress. By the time of Aeschylus the dancing area for the mimic chorus and the special raised stage "for the divine epiphanies" were separated from one another.[4] Yet the two belong to each other like question (or provocation) and answer. There is a certain hubris involved in showing the point of encounter between the human question and the divine answer in an event performed by human beings. This hubris will always be there in the background in all theatrical performance, awakening in the spectator a tense expectation that he will learn something revealing about the mystery of life.

However, if a tension of this kind is to be built into a performance, it must already be part and parcel of existence. Existence itself must give rise to a "faith" that its tentative projects will somewhere meet with a "seeing", a "solution" that will satisfy. Not in the form of an extrinsic "instruction"

[2] In spite of A. Kutscher's objections, which emerge for ideological reasons.

[3] For a synthesis of the two elements cf. A. Lesky, *Die griechische Tragödie*, 2d ed. (1958), 62ff. On the one hand there is the element of *ekstasis* and "transformation" "which alone can yield dramatic art, which is different both from imitation on the basis of the urge to play, and from a magical and ritual depiction of demons". On the other hand there is the mythical narration, which, "in the unimaginable wealth of its forms . . . is a reflection of human existence and human nature". It is "a view of the world exhibiting an unparalleled immediacy and richness", and to that extent goes far beyond the limited sphere of properly Dionysian myths.

[4] Karl Reinhardt, *Aischylos als Regisseur und Theologe* (Bern, 1945), 9f.

concerning life's meaning—in the form of the epic, the fable or of philosophy—but in the form of an action that presents life itself, in which question and answer coincide. The ambivalent "pleasure" of theatre-going (a harmless relic of the cultic age's hubris in being able to depict the "solution" of life's riddle at the peak of an orgiastic self-transformation) is a mixture of a vigorous delight in transformation and curiosity as to what may unexpectedly emerge from such transformation. This "pleasure" can also be described in terms of the "excitement" of the theatre, which is again composed of the synthesis of both elements: it is the taut expectation of existence itself—hoping to discover itself in this projected form, hoping to find its own tracks—and the excited anticipation of what may be encountered along this road, what will happen either from without or from above.

The "player" (*Schau-spieler*) or (as the Romance languages put it) the "actor" (*acteur*) is the place where this synthesis is carried out. On behalf of all the spectators, he performs the act of transformation by surrendering his "questioning" existence to "existence's solution"; by adopting the role, he can present this "solution" in a here-and-now, incarnate mode. He himself is the relationship established between the "reality of life" and "aesthetic reality";[5] the disguise (*Ver-stellung*) of the role ministers to the presentation (*Vor-stellung*) of that reality that can only enter the realm of reality through disguise. Thus the actor is seen to be the center of the encounter between two spheres of existence and truth. On the one hand there is the sphere of reality, embodied in the audience, to which the actor belongs by virtue of his humanity; and there is the sphere of an "ideality" that is not directly accessible to this reality and that is presented by the performed play, the drama as an artefact, a work of art, behind which stands its originator, the *author*. For some distinct authority must be responsible for the integrity of the successful "solution" that "presents itself" to the eagerly awaiting spectator, whether it is an individual poet, living or dead, or an anonymous collective that guarantees the transmission of an inherited myth. It can also be pure convention, as when we

[5] Dagobert Frey, "Zuschauer und Bühne: Eine Untersuchung über das Realitätsprinzip des Schauspiels", in his *Kunstwissenschaftliche Grundfragen* (Vienna, 1946), 151ff.

dwell upon the work of a particular author who presents his particular "solution" to an audience on a particular evening, for the important thing is that a horizon is opened up for "some solution or another", that is, the aspect of epiphany as such. The standpoint of the "author" (whoever he may be) is entirely filled up by the creative activity of a unificatory endeavor that sheds light on existence. For the performed drama should never be merely a poor imitation of life in the concrete with its unsolved problems. Even when showing life "as it is", the drama must show how it ought to be and why it appears in such a way, or why things are not as they seem. If the playwright constructs an ideal constitution of existence—that is, in the plurality of the characters who confront each other in the dramatic action— neither the individual actor nor the sum of individual actors will suffice to embody the indivisible unity of the play's ideal content. For this we need a new authority, creative in a different and unique way, to translate the ideal unity into real, concrete unity, namely, the *director*. His creative activity is clearly distinct from that of the author and the actor: his task is to transpose the play's ideal content as a whole into the reality of the performance as a whole.

Certainly, it can happen that these distinct authorities can coincide. There are great authors who have acted in their own plays and even produced them (*Aeschylus*, *Shakespeare*, *Molière*, *Lope de Vega*, *Goethe*, *Raimund*). Theatre is and remains a fluid reality, patient of many forms; its individual elements can vary from the fortuitous to deliberate and often pedantic nuances. We have already mentioned the form of the (partial or complete) improvisation, in which the "ideal" play is acted purely from below, on the basis of the transforming skill of the performers, as a spontaneous generation, a "happening". As in the commedia dell'arte it presupposes an instinctive mutual understanding among the actors, operating as a kind of collective and yet integrated and integrating author within the team. Mostly (and this is legitimate) it is one particular actor who takes the lead and functions as the core author. The aspect of direction also arises "of itself" here; its presuppositions are, for instance, the costumes and the role-types they suggest. In turn, these roles interact as a result of the energizing of the players' esprit de corps. In a "happening" of this kind there is no reason why the boundary between auditorium and stage should not be obliterated; the spectator may join in the action throughout or for part of the time, sharing in the "authoring" and introducing things he would like to see. At the other end of the spectrum there is the play that is designed to be read and that, sufficient unto itself, does not lend itself to adaptation to actual performance. In the former case the actor has absorbed both author and director into his concrete person; in the latter case the author commands the entire field and has absorbed actor and director into his ideal form. The director, too, can act as a higher instance, using the author's script as mere material that he refashions (adapting it to the times, the audience, external circumstances) and entirely subordinating the actor to his conception. Such a conception can be—and nowadays frequently is—foreign to the original *Weltanschauung* of the author; it may belong to a horizon that is different, wider or ideologically more specific. By being interpreted and played within such a horizon, the play sinks to the level of an almost fortuitous encounter between the audience's expectations and the particular ideology that is being put forward as the "only true solution". All these variations must be mentioned, however briefly, as departures from a norm that is implicit in the nature of the play as such.

The severe disruption of the norm that we find in *Six Characters* by *Pirandello* in fact only strengthens the normal system. Confusion arises because the author rejects the characters of his imagination (which represent real life), that is, he allows them to come into existence only as characters he has *rejected*, and so brings the whole world of performance (the director and actors) to a standstill. The characters *will not allow* themselves to be performed and thus attain reality on the stage, *nor can* the actors lend their real lives to these roles that refuse to accept the ideal form that the author wishes to impart to them. They assert that they already possess their entire ideality in their reality—and this refusal to be interpreted by others, although they do not know it, is only the converse of the author's refusal to give their ideality (their existence merely in the mind) a concrete aesthetic form on the stage. Thus they completely obstruct the work of the director and the actors, none of whom understand anything of the feud between the author and his characters. In fact, only the author is aware of it; the "characters" suffer it as an incomprehensible and insoluble tragedy.[6] The very disruption we find in this play uncovers the normal pattern that underpins it and to which we must now turn our attention.

We have already spoken of the twofold and intertwining "pleasure" found in theatre: the pleasure in self-projection (or delight in the possibilities of transformation) and the pleasure of being presented with a "solution". These two combine into a single pleasure that makes theatre-going "pleasurable" even when the stage's moral or didactic purpose is stressed or perhaps put at the center. This can only be so because the two pleasures —of transformation and of insight into a "solution"—are themselves grounded in man's performance of existence. Through the paradigm of life presented on the stage, the spectator is invited to fashion his life along the lines indicated by the play's solution; at the same time he is free to distance himself from it critically.

Everyone experiences the strange dichotomy between the core of his person (which is not immediately accessible to him) and the role he plays for himself and for society. He is hemmed in by this role and would often wish to break out of it, but he simply cannot; precisely because he is a person, he is *this* particular individual and will always have a *particular* mode of manifestation. But which is the right one, the one that fits his nature and his inalienable "mission"? It is not something he can produce out of himself *alone*; it arises in part from his reaction to his environment, from personal interaction. Is it dictated to him by society? His awareness of himself as a person resists such an interpretation; ultimately it also rejects the merely outward playing of a role, while he himself is inwardly completely different. He is familiar with both pleasures, the functional pleasure of *having to* play a role for the benefit of those outside him and the free pleasure of *being able* to change the "role", the

---

[6] Cf. the excellent analysis by Dietmar Schings, *Über die Bedeutung der Rolle als Medium der Entpersonalisierung im Theater des XX. Jahrhunderts: Strindberg—Pirandello—Brecht—Ionesco* (Diss. Munich, 1969). (In subsequent footnotes, title abbreviated as *Der Entpersonalisierung im Theater*.)

character, the phenomenal "I". The significance of the disguise and the mask oscillates back and forth between this "having to" and "being able to"; on the one hand there is the necessity of having to disguise oneself in order to appear before others, and on the other there is the playful exhilaration of being able to manifest oneself in different costumes without being trapped in any particular one. The stage play presents models of self-production within an interaction of persons; somehow these models are significant for the spectator, for through the medium of the play he can see himself in particular, unfamiliar roles, while at the same time he can look at them as in a mirror and learn how to mirror himself in life. Of course, the mirror that is held up to him in the complete model (that is, the play) is not a simple "result", the sum and constellation of characters. It is more than that: it has a "meaning" implanted in it from above, as it were (by the author); nor does this meaning emerge only at the end of the play: it dominates the whole constellation as it develops. To be presented with this meaning, to be able, as a spectator, to explore oneself within its context at one remove, is the second pleasure of the theatre: it grants us an insight, however limited, into the world's embracing horizon of meaning, within which a complex action unfolds, illuminated and judged by it. And this action is acted by real human beings lending their own reality to realize a fictional role, so that, through them, the embracing revelation of meaning may interject itself into the concrete world that unites both actor and spectator.

This latter aspect (which sets the theatre apart fundamentally from the epic and the lyric, as well as from the film or the sports arena) also brings the play very close—albeit in profound ambivalence—to (Christian) revelation: the aesthetic on-stage world provides us with an unreal—and yet enfleshed—model of that given meaning that revelation incarnates, no longer unreally but with utmost reality, in the reality of history. Here the extreme ambiguity of the theatrical mode is manifest: it offers a schematic model of historically incarnated revelation, but nothing more —even (and particularly) when theatre succeeds, through the special intensity and luminosity of a play of genius, in compelling the spectator to face the concrete dramatic dimensions of his own life. It can indicate these dimensions, but it is no substitute for them. For there is no going back to the theatre's cultic origins, where the meaning given from above was the original myth that, incarnated in the cultic play, also claimed to be the form that fashioned the *polis* or the Babylonian or Egyptian empire. All the same, the theatre cannot be dispensed from the task of indicating that which gives meaning in concrete reality; when *Samuel Beckett* describes a play's horizon as "meaningless", he is referring to "meaninglessness" in the real world. And when *Bertolt Brecht* proclaims a meaning on the presupposition that situations can be changed, the spectator is summoned to change the concrete situation. *Shakespeare's* historical plays, in their unreal stylization, stand as constellations ruling the vicissitudes of the history that, for him, is present. *Wilder's Our Town* aims to portray "daily life", but a daily life illuminated from a vantage point not normally attainable in life.

Its reference to life, which arises of necessity from the reality of performance, keeps drama from the temptation of being art for art's sake. Nor does it make drama serve alien ends; it does not automatically turn drama into personal or social edification. Only a purely rationalistic view of existence, in which everything could be manipulated, everything could be technologically and sociologically "changed", would threaten to degrade the theatre to a mere function of politics and economics (whether in a revolutionary or other context). And only a sophist would want to try to persuade us that the disinterested "enjoyment" of a work of art is compatible with the explicit goal-orientation of a "learning process". Drama, in presenting us with the right or perverse action of free human beings, will no doubt challenge our personal and social sense of "ought" through its positive or negative models. But in fact, the spectator's expectation is directed, not toward something that awaits creation, but beyond, to an order that freely bestows itself upon us and grants us ultimate meaning. All personal and social projects of self-realization need to be sustained and integrated by a revelation that comes to meet them. Here the given order provided by the author points of itself toward an element of grace that is hoped for, believed, and occasionally almost tangible in the world of concrete reality; ultimately every ethical endeavor and failure is encompassed by this grace. This "pointing" grounds the true self-sufficiency of art, which is particularly evident in the drama. It fulfills its ethical and social function most faithfully by refraining from exercising a direct regulatory influence on reality; rather, in its playful and "gratis" nature, art suggests that all-sustaining "gratis" of grace, the gift of life, which transcends the "utile" structure of reality as well as intractable destiny. So the author stays with his craft and does not mistake himself for worldwide providence; the actor remains an actor, incarnating, not some world-Logos, but only an aesthetic artefact; the director remains a director, not mistaking himself for the *spiritus creator* but simply producing a mere play, albeit in a convincing way. And as for the spectator's pleasure in watching this play, it remains a reference to that delight that underlies and sustains all life's seriousness, a delight in being privileged to share in existence. By preserving that distance from the theological realm that its nature requires, the aesthetic realm can come very close to it. "The outward appearance is aesthetic only insofar as it is *honest* (explicitly renouncing all claim to reality) and *independent* (doing without any assistance whatsoever from reality)."[7] For *Schiller*, it is only through this distance that the theatre can become a training in freedom: "True art is not concerned merely with some momentary illusion. Its concern is a serious one: it does not wish merely to transport man to a momentary dream of freedom, it wants to *make* him really and truly free, by awakening a power in him, and by exercising and shaping it, so that he may transform the world of the senses (which for the most part is merely raw material that weighs us down, a blind force pressing down on us) into a free creation of our spirit." In its unfettered self-presentation, art, which "changes nothing" in the real world, reminds us of man's true freedom and utters a challenge to it.[8]

This, then, is the perspective within which we shall be examining the categories of the dramatic. It is not a case of arbitrarily contrasting the stage and life, for the aesthetic illusion always *refers* to concrete reality and, by means of the performance,

[7] Schiller, *Über die ästhetische Erziehung des Menschen*, 26th Brief in *Sämtliche Werke*, ed. Fricke-Göpfert, vol. 5: 659.

[8] Schiller, *Über den Gebrauch des Chores in der Tragödie* in *Sämtliche Werke*, vol. 2: 815–16.

participates in it. But neither is it some kind of imperfect identity, for, if man, being the image of God (a "second God", an *imago exemplaris omnium*), is a creator, the world he creates (according to *Nicholas Cusanus*) is always only an ideal world that knows itself to be related to the real world, for the man who creates it is a "riddle" to himself, a riddle that God alone can solve.[9]

2. *The Three Elements of Dramatic Creativity*

First of all we shall discuss the three elements of creativity, the author, the actor and the director. But we must not give the impression that, in doing so, we have got to the heart of the event of theatre or have arrived at an exhaustive understanding of it. We shall see that this creativity only has meaning and a basis within a larger spiritual context: the performance takes place for the benefit of an audience, and the audience is not exclusively interested in this particular play (for in a large town there may be several performances to choose from), but in a something it hopes to encounter in this particular performance. All the same, the three elements of dramatic creativity possess a significance that has often been reflected upon; here we shall discuss them explicitly in their relevance for theology.

a. The Author

"The poet", says Julien Green—and here the distinction between the dramatic and epic poet is as yet immaterial—"is God the Father as far as his characters are concerned".[1] He stands at the point where the drama (which is to unfold between the individuals and their freedoms) comes into being as a unity,

---

[9] Cf. the relevant texts of Cusanus in H. U. von Balthasar, *Herrlichkeit* III/1 (Einsiedeln, 1965), 584–86; English edition: *The Glory of the Lord*, vol. IV.

[1] Julien Green, *Journal I* (Plon, 1938), 27. Two years later Green wrote: "Voici la vérité sur ce livre: je suis *tous* les personnages" (3). Cf. Henri Gouhier, *L'Essence du théâtre* (1943), 228: "L'auteur joue au Créateur, la comédie qui commence avec lui est l'imitation d'une Divine Comédie. . . . Une oeuvre qui imite la création du monde."

so that, via an arbitrariness that seems incapable of being co-ordinated, it may attain unity once more. This primacy of unity in the author is ontological. It leaves aside the fact that particular periods or peoples place the emphasis more on the actor or on the performance as such; nor does it question the fact that the author is not the epitome of the drama but brings it forth and causes it to be performed—thus the play designed solely to be read is a peripheral genre. (Accordingly there would no point in attacking the stress on the author[2] unless he were upsetting the balance of the threefold dramatic creation.) From time to time the author's primacy can be obscured by the strange success of extemporization on the part of a creative collective consciousness; but success of this kind remains fleeting, and soon there arises once more the desire for some antecedent context of meaning within which the individual actor's imagination can develop, unhindered. We see a direct attack on the author's primacy in the (nowadays quite usual) total reinterpretation of earlier plays by directors or secondary authors employed by them. If this is intended to provide a new interpretation of the play's entire horizon of meaning—involving the dismantling of

[2] Such as Gordon Craig demands for the sake of the visual performance: *On the Art of the Theatre* (New York, 1956). The multiplicity of literary forms must also make room for those plays which are written to be *read*. Even a great dramatic poet can have recourse to this form, as Lope de Vega did in writing his *Dorothea*, observing that the paper was a freer stage (K. Vossler, *Lope de Vega und sein Zeitalter* [1932], 175f.). So too Goethe, who did not care whether part two of his *Faust* could be performed or not, and Claudel, who, in his *Le soulier de Satin* blithely burst through the limits imposed by a performance lasting for a single evening. The subsequent stage version was adapted at the cost of heavy sacrifices. And yet these are writers who are very well acquainted with the realities of the stage, just like Schiller, who wrote his *Wallenstein*, Ibsen, who wrote his *Peer Gynt*, and Shaw, who created unperformable monster dramas. Having said this, however, Hofmannsthal is still right when he says that "poets of the theatre have always been involved with the stage. The two greatest dramatists known to us"—he is referring to Shakespeare and Molière—"were themselves actors. Countless others of second rank were attached to the stage all their lives or for a long period" (*Prosa* III, 60). This also applies to the "unplayable" plays we have mentioned: *Faust II* and *Le soulier de Satin* were written "conceived in an ideal relationship to the stage", a relationship which every writer involved with the theatre feels within him (*ibid.*, 115). Cf. H. Gouhier, "Le paradoxe du chef-d'oeuvre injouable", in *L'Essence du théâtre* (1943), 97ff.

practically the entire play and the recombining of its elements to construct a new edifice—it would be more honest to drop the original author's name. So we are only speaking of an onto-logical primacy of the author[3] over against the actor and director; later, in order to complete the hierarchy, we shall turn to the analogous primacy of the actor vis-à-vis the director, who is the servant of the production.

The poet fashions the interplay of his characters. His know-ledge of real life can and must serve as material, but the matrix, the unifying form, lies in himself. "Where did you get all these things?" "Where? From my imagination, which was like a living arsenal of puppets and silhouettes, constantly in motion."[4] But the poet selects what to bring forth from his arsenal in order to create a valid likeness of the world: *Schiller* demands "that he prepare us, on the basis of the harmony of small things, for the harmony of great things; on the basis of the symmetry of the parts, for the symmetry of the whole. He should cause us to admire the latter in the former."[5] By "submitting himself", as a "true realist", to nature, but "only to Nature in its totality", not in its "momentary urgencies", he also shows himself to be a "true idealist".[6]

Something apparently superhuman is required of him here: he is to enter into his, often antinomian, characters and guide their interaction, on the basis of an antecedent unity, toward a final unity. As the creator, he must stand in and above his play, "summoning beings and causing them to speak in the first person. One says, 'I', and yet he is not I. Think about this paradox for a moment. I call upon a character who depends on me, whom I have conjured up, who says 'I' and is not I. How can anyone fail to see that this kind of creation is like

---

[3] This primacy should not be misinterpreted as an aristocratic stance on the part of the poet, as if, from some lofty height, devoid of contact with the spirit of the people, he created culture. Cf. F. Gundolf, *Shakespeare und der deutsche Geist*, 2d ed. (1914), 279ff.

[4] Goethe, *Wilhelm Meisters theatralische Sendung* II, 3, Gräf edition (Insel), 191–92. "Le poète qui escrit les choses comme elles sont, ne mérite tant que celuy qui les faint" (Ronsard, *Franciade*, "Préface").

[5] Schiller, *Über das gegenwärtige teutsche Theater* (1782) in *Sämtliche Werke*, ed. Fricke-Göpfert, vol. 5: 815.

[6] Schiller, *Über naive und sentimentalische Dichtung* in *Sämtliche Werke*, 779.

that of a demiurge?"[7] But how can the characters be more than "puppets and silhouettes", how can they be genuine, free and "independent" of the poet? "There is no dramatic creation without a certain self-alienation on the part of the author for the benefit of the beings to whom he gives life."[8] As *Gabriel Marcel* goes on to say, the author must simultaneously "enter into each of them as deeply as possible, in order to appropriate their different, practically contradictory and irreconcilable ways of being, understanding and evaluating"—without coming down on the side of any one. In this way, as a dramatic writer, I can "liberate myself from my mortality, for a moment attain a higher justice that is related to selfless love and that allows me simultaneously to *be* the antagonists, to understand and transcend them, without necessarily being in a position to formulate this act of intelligible synthesis."[9] Earlier, *Maurice Blondel* had seen the particular delight in the dramatic performance in that "we can completely understand the events and characters, we can follow and explain the course things take; we have the satisfaction of looking down, from a position outside space and time, on the attitudes, concerns and uncertainties of the actors. From where does this feeling of dramatic beauty come if not from the prophetic vision that embraces the course of a life and a destiny, from the divinatory intuition that somehow initiates the actor into the mystery of eternity and God, from that 'pre-vision' that makes our reason into a kind of providence inherent in the logical course of deeds and passions?"[10]

Schopenhauer describes the power of self-alienation on the part

---

[7] Gabriel Marcel, "L'Influence du théâtre", *Revue des Jeunes* (Mar. 5, 1935): 355.

[8] *Ibid.*, 356. Yet this self-alienation does not go as far as the forfeiture of self, as Otto Ludwig rightly notes with regard to Shakespeare: "We are always aware that the poet himself does not share the emotions of his characters. . . . He is never on the side of a passion as if it were an absolute: he is always above the warring parties. Clarity of delineation is inconceivable apart from this coolness" (*Werke*, ed. R. Bartels, vol. 6: 74).

[9] *Les valeurs spirituelles dans le théâtre français contemporain. Orientations religieuses, intellectuelles et littéraires* (June 25, 1937): 788.

[10] *La Psychologie dramatique du Mystère de la Passion à Oberammergau* (1900), 36–37. The texts of Marcel and Blondel are quoted from Gaston Fessard, "Théâtre et mystère", the introduction to G. Marcel's *"La soif"* (DDB, 1938).

of dramatic authors: "They transform themselves totally into each of the characters they present and speak out of each one, like ventriloquists; now they speak in the person of the hero, now in that of the innocent young girl—with equal truth and naturalness. So it is with Shakespeare and Goethe. Poets of second rank transform their major characters into themselves, like Byron."[11] *Hegel*, who, on the basis of that mode of thought peculiar to him, must have been well acquainted with this process, describes it more from within: "The dramatic poet must not stay obscurely weaving in the depths of his mind nor must he hold on one-sidedly to some exclusive mood and limited partiality in perspective and *Weltanschauung*; he needs the greatest possible openness and breadth of spirit."[12] There is nothing arcane about this being immanent in all the characters; the aim is the openly spoken word, as *Goethe* illustrates magnificently in connection with *Shakespeare*: "Shakespeare makes himself the companion of the World Spirit; like it, he penetrates the world; nothing is hidden from either of them. But whereas it is the business of the World Spirit to preserve the secret prior to action (and often subsequent to it), the poet's aim is to let the cat out of the bag, to let us into the secret prior to the action or at least during the course of it. . . . The secret must come out, even if the very stones have to cry out."[13]

Balzac initially gives the impression of being the very incarnation of the World Spirit, going even beyond Shakespeare in entering into his characters; but *Hofmannsthal* has drawn a picture of *Balzac* that ultimately separates him from the dramatist. *Balzac* says,

> The characters in the play (are) nothing other than contrapuntal necessities. The dramatic character is a narrowing of the real. What fascinates me in the real is precisely its breadth. Its breadth,

---

[11] "Zur Ästhetik der Dichtkunst", *Werke* (Insel) II, 1205.

[12] *Ästhetik*, ed. Bassenge, 2d ed. (1965), II, 518.

[13] "Shakespeare und kein Ende", in *Schriften zur Literatur*, ed. von Bergmann and Hecker (Insel, n.d.), II, 488. In Goethe, no doubt, we can hear an echo of Herder's evaluation of Shakespeare. As early as 1774 (in his *Auch eine Philosophie der Geschichte der Menschheit*) Herder had likened the poet to a divinity in relation to his characters. The dramatist's plan of events is as unfathomable as the plans of Providence (Suphan V, 219ff.).

which is the basis of its destiny. . . . My human beings are only
the litmus paper that reacts by turning red or blue. What is alive,
great, real—these are the acids: powers, destinies. . . . To read
the destinies where they are written—that is everything. To have
the power to see them all, how they are consumed, these living
torches. To see them all at once, bound to the trees of the vast
garden that is illuminated solely by their burning: to stand on
the uppermost terrace, the only spectator, and to seek upon the
lyre for those chords that bind together heaven, hell and this
prospect.[14]

For this epic writer each figure is the whole under the sign of a
particular destiny; they are spiritual spheres that do not touch
each other, their music resounding together in the poet's ears. In
themselves, the individual figures are only protuberances of the
universal totality, which experiences them within itself in a
pantheistic simultaneity. This is not far from the portrayal of
the tragic artist in the young *Nietzsche*; "like a luxuriant Divinity
he creates his characters for individuality . . . , but then his
monstrous Dionysian urge devours this whole world of appearances, in its wake and through its destruction granting us an
intimation of a primal, a highest artistic delight in the womb of
the One."[15] The dramatic author, however, is not intent upon
such destruction. The play he brings forth from himself is, as a
cipher for the total meaning, ultimate. It is the poet's *word*, and
within the polyphony of the action it says precisely what the
poet has to say. *Schiller's* dictum on the poet who is close to
nature (*Homer* and *Shakespeare*) makes the point: "As the Divinity
stands behind the edifice of the world, so he stands behind his
work; *he* is the work, and the work is *he*; if we even so much as
enquire about the artist, we show that we are not worthy of the
work and do not measure up to it, or else are already tired of

[14] "Über Charaktere im Roman und im Drama", in *Prosa* II, 44, 55.
Intellectually this is not far from Strindberg's confession: "I live, and I live in
manifold ways the lives of all the people I portray. I am happy with the happy,
wicked with the wicked, good with the good. I crawl out of my own 'I' and
speak out of the mouths of children, women and old men. I am a king and a
beggar. . . . I have all opinions and profess all religions. I live in all ages and
have even ceased to be. This condition brings indescribable happiness" (W.
Behrendson, *Der Stand der Strindbergforschung* [1948], 13).
[15] *Die Geburt der Tragödie* (Schlechta I, 121).

it."[16] But how can the poet bring forth from himself this plurality of characters?

A. W. Schlegel wishes to describe the poet's fundamental quality as a "magnanimity" that gives room for the rich variety of forms.[17] Once this room has been provided they can appear "of themselves". "When I am writing a play," says *Bernard Shaw*, "I never invent a plot: I let the play write itself and shape itself, which it always does even when up to the last moment I do not foresee the way out."[18] And in *Faust*, *Goethe* says: "Again you draw near, figures that come and go, . . . and shall I try this time to hold you fast? . . . You press toward me! Good, then, the stage is yours."[19] *Claudel* has compared the emergence of dramatic characters in the author's imagination to the

semipassive state of mind when we dream, [when] the mind, contracted to the size of a tray, overflows with ghostly figures (whence do they come? not from the memory alone) that seduce us to collaborate with them to conjure up an event. Once the theme (and where does it come from?) has impressed itself upon us, the characters enlisted by some impresario in disguise keep appearing, to carry it through from exposition to dénouement. . . . There is an organic reciprocal influence here, like that between the embryo and the mother. The initiative comes from the stage, but what a chorus the audience makes! To say nothing of the pitiless critical reviews! . . . Confusion backstage, actors in a hurry to get

[16] *Über naive und sentimentalische Dichtung* in *Sämtliche Werke*, ed. Fricke-Göpfert (Hanser) V, 713.

[17] "The dramatic poet seems to have the ability to lose himself generously and magnanimously in other people; the lyric poet, in endearing egoism, draws everything and everyone over to himself." Athenäumsfragment no. 140, in F. Schlegel, *Krit. Ausgabe* (1967), II, 187.

[18] Epilogue to *"Back to Methuselah"* (London, 1921, 1931), 257.

[19] Goethe, *Faust*, Zueignung. Ionesco is even more explicit: "En fait, je ne peux rien opposer à ces . . . personnages qui sortent de moi. Ils font ce qu'ils désirent, ils me dirigent, car ce serait une erreur pour moi de vouloir les diriger. Je suis convaincu que je dois leur donner entière liberté et que je ne peux rien faire d'autre que d'obéir à leurs désirs. Je n'aime pas l'écrivain aliène la liberté de ses personnages. . . . La création ne ressemble pas à la dictature" (*Notes et contre-notes* [Gallimard, 1966], 274). In *Black Snow*, a theatrical novel (written in 1936–37, published in 1965), Mikhail Bulgakov delightfully describes how his characters came alive: "It was very simple. What I saw, I wrote down; what I didn't see, I left out" (chap. 7).

into their roles, and gradually, like an avalanche, enthusiasm carries the action forward with increasing tempo, creating its own laws and its own verisimilitude. Expression bubbles up literally under one's feet. . . . A single voice is not enough for the poet: he needs this group of interrelating people on the stage; and as for the audience that hungers for the Absolute and the true behind the everyday illusion, it needs this kind of sacrificial action on the stage![20]

As we have seen, *Pirandello* went farthest in making imagination's figures autonomous: they emerge in his imagination and he considers whether to lend them shape—too late! "One cannot expect to give life to a character and emerge unscathed. As creations of my mind these six characters were already living their own life and not mine; nor did it lie in my power to deny them this life." They "continue to live on their own initiative", coming closer "to lead me into temptation". The poet has no choice but to engage in the contradiction of accepting them as "rejected" characters and letting them play the tragedy of their nonacceptance.[21] However, this artificial dichotomy between matter and form—where the material fable is supposed to bear its "eternal form" within it[22]—is symptomatic of a profound dislocation in the modern relationship between the person and his appearance;[23] it drops away in *Hofmannsthal's* description of the creative process, in which the characters *appear*[24] to the poet together with their interrelated destinies; the poet is like a "bird-snarer" or a fisherman who wishes to cast his net out for

---

[20] "La Poésie est un art", in *Positions et propositions*, *Oeuvres en prose* (Pléiade, 1965), 53. In his *Le soulier de Satin*, Claudel most vividly presents the creative element on stage in the shape of the "irrépressible" (act II, scene 2). He has burst out of "the loft of the poet's imagination", where there is a whole army of characters held in reserve. For the duration of a whole scene he demonstrates his role as the performance's animating and organizing director.

[21] *Six Characters in Search of an Author*.

[22] *Ibid.* "Our (reality) doesn't change, it can't change, it can never be different, never, because it is already determined, like this, for ever" (act III).

[23] Cf. the analysis by D. Schings, *Der Entpersonalisierung im Theater*, 43–64.

[24] Letter to Fritz Setz, *Corona* X (1924–25), bk. 6, 796f. In a lecture on "Poetic Imagination and Insanity" (1886), Wilhelm Dilthey demonstrated analogous phenomena in Balzac, Flaubert and Goethe, clearly distinguishing them from insanity (*Gesammelte Werke* [1924], VI, 97f.).

the "vast shoals of great fish"; he feels the characters stirring behind his back. They speak to one another: "O that I knew whence! It is a destiny, / And somehow I am woven into it."[25]

This alternation of creativity from within and encounter from without, this gulf (albeit overcome) between allowing the characters to develop in their own way and guiding their interplay from a position of ultimate superiority—this is in fact the

---

[25] "Das kleine Welttheater", in *Gedichte und lyrische Dramen* (1943), 373–74. The great psychologist A. *Binet*, partly in collaboration with J. Passy, published several studies of the creative process in the work of dramatic poets: "Notes psychologiques sur les auteurs dramatiques", in *L'Année psychologique* (1895), 60–118; "Reflexions sur le paradoxe de Diderot", *L'Année psychologique* (1897); "La création littéraire: portrait psychologique de M. Paul Hervieu", *L'Année psychologique* (1904), 1–62. Of the authors discussed (Sardou, A. Dumas, A. Daudet, E. de Goncourt, F. Coppée) the case of *François de Curel* (1897) stands out (119–73). It is even stranger than Pirandello's Preface. After a period in which the poet gives birth, with much toil, to the dramatic characters, they begin to live a life of their own. "He let the characters he had created talk among themselves" (122). For him, inspiration is "the state in which one loses all sense of creating, because the invented ideas seem to proceed, not from the 'I', but from some other source" (127). "When I am writing, I am in no way absorbed; my characters speak for me. I am only there to decide questions of style and stagecraft" (133). "*I am there like a kind of providence that watches over its creatures without annihilating their freedom. . . .* All I have decided is the particular end to which they will come—which is the task of providence. From time to time I give them a little push, like the player who lets chance govern events until the time is right to steer them in the right direction" (135). When the play has come to an end, "I find it very difficult to kill my characters. They do not want to leave the stage and keep on talking" (140). This is strikingly close to Pirandello. Curel concludes, "I can say, therefore, that at certain moments my characters are really there and are really alive. Listening to them, I retain a feeble consciousness of my own self." But the actor who takes on a role of this kind "imparts a new existence to the character, by no means identical with the one the author gave it. Why, though, should this be any less true?"—for there are a thousand ways of "feeling oneself" into a role, whereas only one person, the author, "understands" it (141). Binet relates similar experiences on the part of Legouvé, Scribe (who writes while sitting in the stalls and seeing the play as a spectator) and Coppée. Binet makes a clear distinction between this form of creative imagination and the pathological schizophrenias. In his diary, Julien Green notes: "Did more work on my play. I discover the characters insofar as they speak, but often they speak too much. This reminds me of a young English woman who had been told she should write a novel. She had actually started it, and by the time she had reached page twenty she exclaimed, "These people keep talking and I don't know how to shut them up!" (1955, vol. VI, 44).

mystery of inspiration—calls for the theological model that *Green* had invoked at the outset. *Schlegel* had glimpsed it in his metaphor of the extempore play, but it slipped away from him because his Absolute was not a free God, who makes room for created beings endowed with freedom. On the one hand this freedom means that the characters do not always grasp the author's ultimate purpose,[26] and on the other hand it implies that the author does not approve of all his characters' provisional deeds and intentions.

> God [says *Kierkegaard*] is like a poet. This also explains how he puts up with evil and with idle chatter. . . . This is the poet's relationship with his work (which is also called his "creation"): he allows it to come into being. It is a mistake to think that what some individual says or does in a poetic work represents the poet's personal opinion. . . . No. God keeps his opinion to himself. But as a poet he allows everything possible to come forth. He himself is always there, everywhere, watching, continuing his work of poetry; in a way his poetical activity is impersonal, equally attentive to everything; and in another way it is personal, making the most terrible distinctions, such as that between our wanting what he wants and our not wanting what he wants.

Thus it would be impossible (like *Hegel*) to equate the true and the real, for that would be to "suggest that the words and actions of a poet's dramatic characters were his own personal words and actions". True—and here *Kierkegaard* makes way for the Christian *mysterium*, which alone can lift the veil that lies over the natural mystery of authorship—God does not pursue his poetical activity as a pastime: "It is a serious matter for him: to love and to be loved is God's passion, almost (infinite love!) as if he himself were subject to the power of this passion, almost as if it were a weakness on his part, whereas in fact it is his strength, his almighty love", which to that extent cannot be subject to any change.[27] This glance at the God of Christianity suggests that the dramatic author could never assemble his characters in a living play on the basis of a mere justice that

---

[26] "Nous sommes des personnages . . . qui ne comprennent pas toujours ce que veut l'auteur" (Julien Green, *Journal* [Plon, 1961], 775).

[27] Kierkegaard, *Diaries* (1854), trans. T. Haecker, 4th ed. (1953), 630–31.

apportions to each his own—and what might *that* be?—but by
virtue of his mode of being, which permits him to be (and to
work) completely *in* them and completely *above* them at the
same time. Naturally, the idea that the author—in whatever
way—could himself enter the immanence of the play in order to
guide it to its goal remains totally extravagant:[28] no one but the
actor should appear on stage. But the actor does not play
himself: he acts the role the author has assigned to him in his
play; the author has power to make himself present in the actor,
and *only* in him. The author remains hidden behind the reality of
the stage: "The concrete presence of characters and things causes
us to forget that of the author, who, like a creator, wishes us to
search for him", for "he has the privilege of disguising himself
as a creator."[29]

However, he does not leave his work as an unfinished draft or
a mere scenario or film script, to be completed by the director
and actor. *Hebbel* is right here: "To be dramatic, a poetical work
must be performable; if there is something that the actor cannot
represent, it means that the poet himself has not represented it,
and it has remained embryonic and schematic."[30] "The genuine
dramatic process of representation will, of itself, put flesh on
everything spiritual", it will "condense" [*verdichten*, compare
dichten, "to write poetry"—Tr.] the "idea-factors" into "char-

---

[28] With his burlesque humor, Claudel portrays the irruption of the God of
the Bible onto the world stage: "In my simple way I would like to compare the
good God to a dramatic poet who has hatched a plot, a beautiful, lengthy, subtle
and detailed plot, full of love. All that remains is to put it on stage. And now,
what a fiasco it is! A total sabotage! Who on earth has the author got to interpret
the play! There's the poor prompter who has lost his little book—where *can* it
have got to? And the worst thing is that the whole thing just won't stop. It's
much too long, much too tangled. And all these flour-sacks and poor devils who
don't know a single word of their lines! The author has a fit of rage. I myself,
God says, will take the thing in hand. It's high time. (Of course, this is the
rough-and-ready God of the Bible; the other one, the God of the philosophers,
has been so carefully purified of every relationship or similarity with his
creatures that we cannot really say in what sense he is Our Father)" (*L'Evangile
d'Isaie* [1951], 7). One will recall that at the end of his comedy *Scherz, Satire,
Ironie und tiefere Bedeutung* (*Werke* [1874], I, 470) "the accursed Grabbe" appears
on stage, making his way through the nocturnal wood, bearing a lighted
lantern.

[29] H. Gouhier, *L'Essence du théâtre* (1943), 228–29.

[30] Preface to *Maria Magdalene*, *Werke*, Fricke-Keller-Pörnbacher I, 318.

acters" and "render the inner event, in all its stages of development, visible in terms of an external history".[31] Consequently the author will not envisage the actor's and director's work as beginning where he leaves off; rather, he will need it throughout, he will guide and accompany it in its freedom and spontaneity. Furthermore, the author has already placed a particular perspective in the play: not only has he presented us with a precise constellation of characters, he also wants this constellation to be seen from the standpoint of a single, central figure (who speaks in the "first person"), without compromising the plurality of characters.[32] In everything it is the author's mind that presses toward embodiment, which means that we must consider all the processes and procedures of sense-presentation within his mind. This mysterious and continuing effect of the author upon his work (which extends to the sphere of the actor and director—not tyrannizing them but providing them with an area for creativity), while it influences each of them profoundly, it actually facilitates, in doing so, their creative activity. The author, with his shaping role, stands at the beginning of the whole production triad and ensures that it has an effect, beyond itself, on the audience; that audience which the author has envisaged right from the start and with whom, over the heads of the actor and the director, he has established an understanding. The constellation into which he draws the individual figures (*Gestalten*) of his play in order to make them into a whole (*Gesamtgestalt*) signifies the whole of reality in microcosm, and it is to this reality that the author wishes to direct his audience's attention. In giving the name "poetic justice" to this constellation or total figure (*Gesamtgestalt*), we are pointing to the unattainable metaphysical justice.

Stanislavsky is right, therefore, when he says that ultimately the actor is given not only the "task" of the role, but also the "higher task" of entering into the horizon of meaning that encompasses the role, for the latter is the author's final goal.[33]

---

[31] *Ibid.*, 820.

[32] Cf. also the subtle remarks of Etienne Souriau: *Les deux cent mille situations dramatiques* (Flammarion, 1950), 125–38, also 236ff.

[33] K. S. Stanislavsky, *The Mystery of the Actor's Success* [*Das Geheimnis des schauspielerischen Erfolges* (Zurich and Vienna, n.d.), 374ff.]. This "higher task"

This shows that while the role does, indeed, have a particular, given shape, it is in no way a limited one but an open one; it is all the more open, the more timeless and valid it is. It is precisely because of their openness that roles can be constantly reinterpreted, depending on the actor's creative power of entering into the "higher task". As André Bonnichon writes: "The author has not said everything about the life of his characters; the actor, keeping within the bounds of consistency, endeavors to discover what has so far remained hidden: he ponders inventively over the text and the event."[34]

From this point of view it is by no means absurd or reprehensible for an author to write a play for a particular actor who, he knows, will carry out the "higher task" according to his, the author's, intentions. Such plays are "made to fit" the actor; thus *Giraudoux* wrote *La Folle de Chaillot* for Marguerite Moréno. An interaction of this kind may produce much that is ephemeral and of poor quality, particularly if the actor is a "star" and the author merely ministers to his glamor. Yet we can conceive of the ideal case in which a writer is so fired by the performance of some artist that he creates a character and an action to be embodied specifically by him.

All the same, if the author is to be "God the Father to his characters", he must not ultimately allow himself to be governed by their interplay. He must love his characters, but for that very reason he must also cherish their autonomy. He owes it to himself, however involved he may be in the fate of his characters, to stand above them, so that in the very last analysis he can embody their destiny. "He must not fall victim to sentimentality. Therefore he will require a certain cruelty, a certain sarcasm, toward himself. The hardest thing is not to be overcome by debilitating emotion vis-à-vis oneself or one's characters—however much one may love them. Once the

---

is the purpose "for which the poet created the play and for which the actor creates his role; it is the scarlet thread which has guided the poet all his life." The examples given are Dostoyevsky's search for the divine and the devilish in man, Tolstoy's striving for personal perfection, and Chekhov's fight against stagnation in a middle-class existence and his dream of an authentic life.

[34] André Bonnichon (= A. Villiers), *La psychologie du comédien* (Mercure de France, 1942), 148.

author is in the power of his character, the latter will come to no good."[35] In one of *Arthur Schnitzler's* puppet plays, therefore, the poet can sweep his refractory actor back off the stage:

> That's it! The play is over! Such mischief!
> Who'll protect me from my own illusory phantoms?
> Away with you! Enough!
> How dare you act as if you did not depend on me?
> And if I've breathed into you so much soul
> That now you carry on your own existence,
> Is this most insolent and irrational uproar
> The thanks due to my creative power?[36]

b. The Actor

α. *Making it present.* The playwright's work is *potentially* drama: it only becomes *actual* through the actor. He lends a unique and incomparable reality to the dramatic idea. It is not the reality of everyday life—although as a human being he belongs to everyday reality—but that reality which *makes things present*: through his own reality he causes the idea to be embodied. It does not "appear", like a ghost, but is materialized in the realm of reality. *Georg Simmel* is one of the few to have glimpsed the whole subtlety of this process, formulating it cautiously in his essay "Zur Philosophie des Schauspielers".[1] The "truth" of what is represented can be defined neither as reality (the actor is not really Hamlet) nor as illusion (which presupposes a reality), but as a genuine making-present. "The actor's contribution makes the mystery of the theatre a mystery of real presence even before it is a mystery of transformation [*Verwandlung*, transubstantiation]." (Unlike the cinema, which always remains a picture.)[2] "Stage is absolute presence" (*G. Lukács*).[3] It is not as if the playwright's

---

[35] E. Ionesco, *Notes et contre-notes* (Paris: Gallimard, 1966), 180.

[36] *Gesammelte Werke*, part 2 (plays), vol. III (Berlin: Fischer, n.d.), 265–66.

[1] Simmel, in *Logos, Internationale Zeitschrift für Philosophie der Kultur* IX (1920/21): 339, 362. Cf. note 2 in the section below, "The Individual Law".

[2] H. Gouhier, *L'Essence du théâtre*, 5. Cf. 40: "Le réalisme dans la représentation ne rapproche pas davantage le théâtre de la réalité."

[3] G. Lukács, "Gedanken zu einer Ästhetik des Kinos", in *Literatursoziologie* (1961), 75–80. L. Jouvet, *Témoignages sur le théâtre* (Flammarion, 1952): "Le

work is in one place and its presentation is in another: the dramatic work is made present totally and exclusively in the performance. Put in an extreme form: "The dramatist is absent in the drama. He does not speak; he has created the means of expression. . . . The words uttered in the drama . . . must in no case be taken as coming from the author."[4]

And yet, if we can trace the art of the theatre back to the (panto-)mime of antiquity—"the actor is an elevated Thespian"[5] —it only becomes a complete work of art through the poetic word. However "eloquent" the body's expression may be, it remains dumb without speech, even if mere speech is never sufficient for a theatrical performance without the complement of gesture and only becomes action when it is integrated into it: "*Parler c'est agir.*"[6] Action arises directly from speech.[7] But according to *Hebbel* deeds become dramatic only in words and emotions.[8] The famous contest between *Cicero* and the actor *Quintus Roscius* to see which of the two could better portray a particular emotion—the one in words, the other in gestures—is resolved on the stage by uniting both.

Compared with the concrete, total reality of the performance, the author's work seems to be pale, schematic and preliminary —"the performance is the work of art, the text is only the foundation" (*Thomas Mann*).[9] So we are faced once again with

---

théâtre n'existe que dans l'acte du théâtre, dans cette fusion et cette effusion de la représentation, dans le moment dramatique" (192).

[4] Peter Szondi, *Theorie des modernen dramas*, 5th ed. (Suhrkamp, 1968), 15.

[5] Artur Kutscher, *Grundriss der Theaterwissenschaft*, 2d ed. (Munich: Desch, 1936), 88. Kutscher's entire theory of the stage, leading on from Reich, *Der Mimus*, and Hugo Dingler, *Dramaturgie als Wissenschaft*, is based on the idea that the theatre continues to be sustained by the universally human and universally understood art of mime, pantomime and expressive dance. This is a one-sided view. However, in saying this we are not questioning the possible perfection of an art that is pure mime. One need only think of Marcel Marceau, who makes his body into a perfect language-medium, seeming to express even things that cannot be uttered in sounds. Cf. Elisabeth Brock-Sulzer, *Theater* (Kösel, 1954), 25.

[6] Abbé d'Aubignac, *La pratique du théâtre* (Paris, 1657), 390.

[7] R. Rostowski, *Deutsche Dramaturgie*, 27ff.

[8] Hebbel, *Werke* I, 328.

[9] *Rede und Antwort* (Berlin: Fischer, 1922), 40. According to Thomas Mann the poet is present in the theatre only "as a guest", for the theatre's realm is an independent one. The poet often has illusions about this. Stanislavsky puts it

the question of the relationship between author and actor. Since it is the poetic work that is being performed, the author cannot be ejected from his prime position. "The master of the theatre is the author. The actor can do nothing but instill life into what the author has invented; the director cannot give life to any other play than the one envisaged by the author."[10] But this pre-eminence on the author's part cannot be expressed in terms of master and servant. We must reject any suggestion that would make the actor into the author's servant[11] and equally any that would degrade the author to the level of a mere cobbler of plays for the actor. We can say, indeed, that the poet is dependent on the actor,[12] but the converse is equally true. Their mutual

---

more moderately: "The literary work of a dramatist, . . . while it is in itself a complete poetic work, is not a complete stage work until it has been embodied in living terms by the actor on the stage. Just as mere musical notation or a score is not yet resonant music, so the written word is not yet a stage creation" (Stanislavsky, *Die Arbeit des Schauspielers an sich selbst*, in *Das Geheimnis des Schauspielerischen Erfolges*, 78).

[10] Charles Dullin in the Preface to Gouhier's *L'Essence du théâtre*, iv.

[11] Hegel for instance: "The poet [has] the right to require the actor to think himself right into the role he has been given, without adding anything of his own. . . . The actor must be as it were the instrument on which the author plays, a sponge, soaking up all the issues and handing them on unchanged." *Ästhetik*, ed. Bassenge, 2d ed. (1965), II, 541–42. Lucian had already given the actor this advice: "Adopt the hue of the sea-polyp, which in turn always takes the coloring of the rock to which it has attached itself." In Rudolf Borchardt ("An Max Reinhardt", in *Prosa* I [1957], 182) we read the extreme formulation that "theatre is a means of publication, a means of making public unpublished dramatic poetry"—but this view must be read in the context of Borchardt's many other observations on the theatre. Far more extreme are the attempts of Egon Vietta, allegedly basing himself on Heidegger and Indian theatre, to make the actor a pure medium of the cosmic word. Here "the actor grows far beyond a mere psychological instrument to become a medium of that (existential) level of language at which the real decisions are made". He utters the "eternal word" which "dwells in the ether and which man renders audible; yet man does not originate it: it comes to him." This presupposes that the actor or dancer is "egoless", that he can overcome the anthropocentric era and see himself as a medium of Ultimate Spirit. There is essentially no place here for an author; the actor becomes a kind of Christ-figure, a transmitter of the Word, albeit in a Monophysite sense, without having a creative human nature of his own. Cf. Margret Dietrich, *Das moderne Drama*, 2d ed. (Stuttgart: Kröner: 1963): 630–31.

[12] "The dramatic poet is not self-subsistent: he needs the actor" (Hans Wickihalder, *Grundzüge zu einer Psychologie des Theaters* [Diss. Berne, 1926], 64.

interdependence points to the unity of the work it brings about: "There are not two things, the script (the idea) and the performance; the two are profoundly one."[13]

Now, from the actor's perspective, we can arrive at the same point that was illuminated by the author's perspective: there is nothing mechanical about this making-present; it is a creative act for which the poet explicitly and necessarily leaves room in his work, both in terms of the depth of inspiration (the "higher task") and of the details of gesture, intonation, and so forth. The actor too, in recreating the author's character, is a free creator who, like the author, must conceive and execute his role on the basis of a single, unified vision. It is impossible for the two visions to be identical—as we can see from the diverse and often contradictory ways Hamlet or Othello is played (and rightly and convincingly played at that)—but there must be some inner analogy between them, an analogy that is realized, from the actor's point of view, as a result of the creative effort he makes to enter into and experience the author's vision. The actor, *Simmel* says,

> plunges into the ground of being from which the poet has created his character. . . . For him, unlike the reader and spectator, the drama is not something complete and finished. . .; he separates it into its constituent elements in order to fashion it anew, in and through its poetic form, into his work of art. . . . [He traces it back] to its core [and unfolds] the latent energies of this core in the situations as they emerge. . . . The actor's freedom is of the kind customarily described as ethical. . . . [He] must give the impression of *wanting* to do what, on the basis of the role, he *ought* to do; not as when, in the ethical realm, we obey a command that comes to us ready-made, as it were, from outside, but as when we spontaneously impose the imperative upon ourselves.[14]

This ethical freedom can occasionally oblige the actor to substitute his own inspiration for an inadequate inspiration on the poet's part; thus it often happens that mediocre plays are

[13] Hugo Dingler, *Dramaturgie als Wissenschaft* (1904–5), I 242, 272f. "Both artists, through their distinct talents and their distinct casts of mind . . . minister to the idea of the dramatic work of art as such" (Wickihalder, *Grundzüge zu einer Psychologie des Theaters*, 68).

[14] Simmel, *Logos* IX (1920/21): 360.

performed with great success by good actors. *Stanislavsky* expressly envisages this possibility: "He is free to supplement in his own way what the poet has provided",[15] indeed, he must "deepen" anything unsatisfactory in the author.[16] *Gottfried Keller* observed in a letter to *Hettner*: "The actor can bring dry material to life. He can present the work in a second nature."[17] He can be truer to the poet's original idea than the poet himself.

In this task of embodying, the actor is a mediator. He does not act for himself, but for the audience, on whom he is dependent in a new and different way. We shall discuss this later in "The Three Elements of Dramatic Realization", but something of it belongs here: the presentation or performance is addressed to a crowd (and only exceptionally to an individual) that accepts the "theatrical form" in its significance and affirms it in its reality. "*Un jugement d'existence*: that is the spectator's part in this 'realization', which is the dramatic performance."[18] This verdict is not that *Kainz is* Hamlet, but that he shall *stand for* Hamlet. This validity, this valid representation, is the actor's goal; he puts his own concrete existence at the service of this goal. And here he needs the cooperation of the audience: it must allow his representation to be valid. In this sense theatre rests on a "communion", as is evident again and again, not only from its origins but also from the way in which it has been renewed in diverse levels of society.[19]

β. *The psychologico-technical problem.* But what happens when an actor takes on his role? Since the eighteenth century few questions in the realm of art have caused more ink to be spilled than this one. Even before *Diderot*[20] the issue had been expressed

[15] *Die Arbeit des Schauspielers an der Rolle (Fragmente eines Buches)*. Compiled by J. N. Semyanowskaya, edited, annotated and introduced by G. W. Kristi (Berlin: Henschel, 1955), 131. (Hereafter referenced as *Arbeit an der Rolle*.)

[16] Stanislavsky, *Die Arbeit des Schauspielers an sich selbst*, 376.

[17] *G. Kellers Leben, Briefe, Tagebücher*, ed. Ermatinger-Baechthold, II, 229. Cf. Bonnichon, *La psychologie du comédien*, 148; also E. Brock-Sulzer, *Theater*, 204f.; A. Villiers, *La Psychologie de l'Art Dramatique* (Coll. A. Collin, 1951), 42.

[18] H. Gouhier, *Le théâtre et l'existence* (Aubier, 1952), 25.

[19] H. Gouhier, *L'Essence du théâtre*, chap. 10, I and II; cf. his "De la communion au théâtre" in *Théâtre et collectivité*, ed. A. Villiers (Paris, 1953).

[20] Rémond de St. Albine, *Le comédien* (Paris, 1747) required, as well as

in the alternatives of "empathy" (*Einfühlung*) or "technical
mastery": *Diderot* campaigned energetically against the former
and in favor of the second alternative.[21] His brilliant essay
adduces a number of convincing reasons: the play's repeated
performance; the necessity of rationally constructing the character out of details; the fact that older actors perform better than
young ones, that actors are capable of lucid reflection while apparently undergoing deep emotion and that emotions obstruct
the freedom of the artistic process. On the stage, according to
Diderot, emotions should come down from the mind, not rise
up from the heart.

We need not dwell on the numerous and in part passionate
objections voiced against *Diderot's* thesis by actors—and some
of them very great actors.[22] In *Diderot's* own case we must take
account of the background to his apparently extreme position,
namely, his campaign to free the French stage of unnatural
bombast and pathos (here he is a precursor of *Gluck*);[23] his
demand for a balance between *sensibilité* and *entendement*[24] because, according to his psychology, violent passions obscure the

---

"esprit", a true inner experience of the role on the part of the actor. A. François
Riccoboni published his *L'Art du théâtre* in Paris in 1750 (translated and annotated
by L. Schröder in *Vorschriften über die Kunst des Schauspielers*), and was of the
opinion that a person who himself feels the emotions he is to portray can never
act well. He must only *appear* to be totally immersed in what he is acting. The
problem had already been raised by Jean Bapt. Dubois, *Réflexions critiques sur la
poésie, la peinture et la musique* (1719).

[21] *Paradoxe sur le comédien* (1st version 1770, revised 1773, first published
1830. Quoted from *Oeuvres* [Pléiade, 1951], 1003–58). Exhaustive references on
the discussion of Diderot's work in André Bonnichon, *La psychologie du comédien*
(1942), 305–8. William Archer conducted a survey on the problem of "feeling or
not feeling", which appeared under the title of "Questions sur l'art du comédien"
in *Revue d'art dramatique* X (April/June 1888).

[22] Cf. Pierre Lièvre, *Supplément au paradoxe sur le comédien*, ed. du Trianon
(1929) and the book by the actress Madame Dussane, *Le Comédien sans paradoxe*
(Paris: Plon, 1933). Alfred Möller, *Der Schauspieler* (Karlsruhe, 1926); Günther
Knautz, *Studien zur Ästhetik und Psychologie der Schauspielkunst* (Diss. Kiel,
1934).

[23] "Le ton simple de l'héroïsme antique!" (Diderot, *Oeuvres*, 1044).

[24] Thus in the letters to Mlle. Jodin. Cf. *Essai sur la Peinture*: "J'exige ensuite
de la sensibilité. . . . (Mais) la sensibilité quand elle est extrême, ne discerne
plus" (Diderot, *Oeuvres*, 1169–70).

clarity of vision; and finally his strange "idealism" (not of a Platonic kind), which meant that he experienced the heroes of ancient drama as *fantômes imaginaires* and *spectres* of superhuman dimensions and thus required the actor to lift himself up to this idea and model his own spiritual powers on it.[25] The fact that the actor can abandon his own paradigms and adopt those of his role (and do so without any apparent hiatus) softens the inevitable alienation, "*cette incompréhensible distraction de soi d'avec soi*". If we interpret *Diderot* in this way, on the basis of the whole of his philosophy and aesthetics,[26] his paradox is considerably eased and shows a core that is of permanent relevance.

On the other hand those actors who put forward the view that the role must be "empathized" are not unanimous, indeed they often speak in paradoxes, particularly when describing their personal experience: even when carried away by their role they do not lose control of their performance.[27] Here, with *Baudelaire*, we can distinguish two sensitivities: that of the imagination and that of the heart.[28] But as yet it does not solve the riddle. The real paradox is that the dramatic art is precisely that: an *art* (and hence a technique); its material is the actor's entire physical, emotional and spiritual self. The actor puts himself and all the powers of his soul, including his emotions, at the service of the work of art, at the service of the part he is to play. This is what profoundly distinguishes his art from all the other arts that work with a nonhuman material. The actor is "his own sculptor, he is

[25] *Ibid.*, 1007, 1012, 1029, 1031, 1034 ("la grandeur d'un fantôme homérique"), 1053 ("Le comédien . . . se portera tout à coup et en plein saut à la hauteur du modèle idéal . . . n'étant jamais ramené au petit modèle qui est en lui").

[26] This is the merit of Bonnichon's thesis (= A. Villiers), *La psychologie du comédien*, 30ff.

[27] Lucien Guitry says both things at once: "Je me détache, *je perds la tête* . . . prêt è toute émotion et bouillant de passion et d'une *froide précision* . . . dans une sécurité réjouissante" (quoted by Bonnichon, *La psychologie du comédien*, 212). And Jouvet, who generally advocates that the role must be profoundly lived, does not dispense with the element of control: "Se mettre en état second et *contrôler* cet état quasi médiumique" ("L'Art du comédien", *Encycl. française* XVII, 17, 64ff.).

[28] "Il ne faut pas confondre la sensibilité de l'imagination avec celle du coeur" (*Variétés critiques* [Paris, 1924], II, 164).

both conductor and orchestra",[29] he is "a plastic artist working on himself. . . . The actor's personality is that of the craftsman, the technician, the artist."[30]

No one can have taken this simultaneity with such passionate seriousness as *K. S. Stanislavsky*,[31] wrongly held to be the opponent of *Bertolt Brecht*. (*Brecht* regarded *Stanislavsky* as the spokesman of "empathy" and saw himself in the line of *Diderot*, arguing for the essential distance between actor and role.) In a nutshell, *Stanislavsky's* method consists in a total dedication— encompassing body, mind and soul—to the role, a total mobilization for its sake. *Disponibilité*: here the whole human system is made available, beginning with relaxation exercises for every part of the body ("anatomizing")[32] so that it is ready for every possible gesture, observation exercises to overcome our everyday distractedness and semiattention, right up to the total activization of the imagination (starting initially with any object whatsoever, with a "suggested situation",[33] and going on then to concentrate on the role). This training aims at enabling the actor convincingly to embody the (poetic) reality of the role, to "substantiate" its "truth". The archenemy here is the stage cliché that is like an empty concept, devoid of substance, all merely cerebrally deduced ways of speaking and gesturing that are not believed in by the actor and hence not believable to the audience because they cannot inwardly "substantiate" the action on the stage.[34] A brief "feeling oneself into the role" is by no

---

[29] Bonnichon, *La psychologie du comédien*, 226.

[30] Erwin Reiche, *Siebzehn Kapitel von Schauspielern und vom Theater* (Berne: Francke, 1938), 11.

[31] Stanislavsky's works were planned to appear in four volumes: 1. *My Life in Art* [*Mein Leben in der Kunst* (Berlin: Henschel, 1951)]; 2. *The Mystery of the Actor's Success* [*Das Geheimnis des schauspielerischen Erfolges* (Zurich and Gallus, Vienna: Scientia, n.d.)]. This contains the following works which appeared in Russian in 1938: *The Work the Actor Has to Do on Himself; The Actor's Work on Himself in the Creative Process of Experiencing the Role; A Pupil's Diary*; 3. *The Embodying Process* (this never appeared); 4. *The Work the Actor Has to Do on the Role (Die Arbeit des Schauspielers an der Rolle)*. This remained a fragment and was edited as such by G. W. Kristi, see note 15, p. 285 above. In practice it is a workbook of rehearsals for *Othello*.

[32] Stanislavsky, *The Mystery of the Actor's Success*, 168.

[33] *Ibid.*, 38.

[34] *Ibid.*, 155, 185.

means enough; to act *within* the reality of the character embodied by the actor presupposes the highest degree of awareness and technical mastery. In everyday life we act from organic necessity and with mechanical logic; "on the stage this must be replaced by the conscious, logical and consistent *assessment* of each moment."[35] But this activity of assessment is also practical: "We are actors, not scholars, our sphere is activity, action; we steer by human experience."[36] It is only possible to live the role in a natural manner on the basis of deliberate physical training and psycho-techniques; the "subconscious" side is dependent upon the "conscious" side.[37] Of course, this *disponibilité* is not an inactive waiting; it is mobilized by *belief* in the *truth* (of the role): "The truth is inseparable from the belief, and the belief from the truth."[38] Since the task is that of embodiment, the actor is advised to begin immediately with the body; "a physical life" must be created that is a "favorable medium for the creation of spiritual life".[39] There is something sacramental about *Stanislavsky's* method.

Certainly, the actor's *disponibilité* for his role[40] can be experienced psychologically in the most diverse ways, and this can lead to opposing theories. Many actors feel that they are (passively) "indwelt" by the role,[41] others feel that they (actively) "inhabit" it; some experience particular emotions toward the

[35] *Ibid.*, 203. A subjective "living" of the role can be appropriate at a preliminary stage, and there can be an "echo" of it during the artistic run-up to performance.

[36] *Ibid.*, 218.

[37] *Ibid.*, 390, 403.

[38] *Ibid.*, 185f.

[39] Stanislavsky, *Arbeit an der Rolle*, 13. "My method consists in allowing the interior and exterior processes to deepen each other and in summoning a feeling for the role through the physical experience of the human body" (45). By experiencing the "tiniest physical truths" the actor arrives at a belief in the genuineness of his performance. "But if he wants to have violent emotions he will never believe in himself, and without this belief there can be no experiencing of the role" (71). Lessing, based more on Riccoboni and agreeing with Diderot, is largely at one with this method: appropriate bodily reactions can and should give rise to unconscious motions of the psyche (*Hamburgische Dramaturgie*, 3).

[40] See also Max Martersteig, *Der Schauspieler: Ein künstlerisches Problem* (Leipzig, 1900).

[41] Monet-Sully: "On se fait hanter par lui (le rôle)." Madame Dussane:

role—or coming to them from the role. But as we have said, this does not bring about a split in consciousness; the actor's dedication to his role will always be governed from a center of self-possession. "His aim is to be able to move freely in his chains: in spite of the real emotion that seizes the actor and could cripple him, he must have so much self-control that he is free, even while under the pressure of feelings, to channel his various spiritual emotions for the benefit of genuine expression" (actor, *Paul Mounet*).[42] The subtle middle position between identifying oneself with the role-character and remaining distinct from it can be described as the phenomenon of "acceptance",[43] or we can say that the actor has to concern himself more with the *issue*, the poet's idea, than with the character portrayed and that in this way no confusion occurs;[44] like *Simmel* we can be aware that the ability "to react to an invented character with one's whole personality" is naturally a limited one, for after all the actor does not play the role "like a marionette". Here, in the question of the role, we can discern a final boundary where the actor's faithfulness to the role and his faithfulness to himself cannot easily be reconciled. "Two loyalties are struggling with one another: loyalty to the poet and his work, and loyalty to one's own art and artistry. We can hardly conceive of them coinciding absolutely. . . . What is truth in the art of the stage? An honest struggle between the individual and his role."[45]

All the same, if the dramatic art really is *art*, it must—in the extreme case—exhibit the general paradox of art, namely, that the highest technique can be (and must be) surpassed under conditions of complete inspiration. So it is when Mozart is played by the Haskil or Haebler Quartets or conducted by Böhm; so it is when, on the basis of an almost inhuman intensity

---

"C'est bien plutôt le rôle qui se met dans notre peau" (quoted in Bonnichon, *La psychologie du comédien*, 197).

[42] Quoted in Madame Dussane, *Le Comédien sans Paradoxe*, 15.

[43] Alfred Möller, *Der Schauspieler*.

[44] Thus Walter Lammers, *Dramatische Wirklichkeit; zur Ontologie eines mythischen Raumes* (Diss. Kiel, 1937). W. v. Humboldt (writing to Goethe on the contemporary French tragic theatre, *Gesammelte Schriften* II, 390ff.) is of the opinion that the acting in the German theatre arises more from the *matter* itself, whereas in the French theatre it originates more in the gesture. Cf. also the journal *Propyläen* III, 1 (1800): 90.

[45] A. Kutscher, *Grundriss der Theaterwissenschaft*, 94.

of rehearsal, a scarcely hoped-for purity of human achievement is manifested. The actor may seem at a disadvantage here, since he must transform his own personality (and this is even less human) into the raw material of technique and training; but suddenly we see that he has a great and unexpected advantage, for the need to transform himself, and the delight in so doing— to be someone other than he is—is a most universally human trait.

> There is a primal histrionic attitude, [namely,] playing a part, not hypocritically or to deceive, but by pouring one's personal life into an [external] form of utterance that is somehow given and preexisting. This is one of the constitutive functions of our life as it is. . . . Man is meant to live out and represent a reality that is set before him, a reality that is different from the self-development he pursues by his own efforts; he does not simply abandon his own self, however: he fills this other reality with his own being. . . . This is the embryonic form of the dramatic art. . . . Somehow we are all actors, in however fragmentary a way.[46]

Thus *Erwin Reiche* is right when he takes this human basis as his point of departure and considers the genuineness of the human personality to be a decisive test of the genuineness of a dramatic performance: an immature man cannot play a mature one, and an insincere man cannot become a genuine actor. "The first and last criterion for the *actor* is the same as that for the *man* who happens to be an actor."[47] But when is man genuine if he is always an actor?

γ. *The existential problem.* Having said all this, there is still something left over. The way the actor puts his whole self into a role can be extolled as a great achievement of human truthful-

---

[46] Simmel, *Logos* IX (1920/21): 349.

[47] Reiche, *Siebzehn Kapitel von Schauspielern und vom Theater*, 16–17. Reiche puts in a nutshell what Stanislavsky says at greater length with regard to the interpenetration of the human and the artistic, the unity of feeling and technique: "One's own humanity, so to speak, is transformed into representational technique." The actor must "learn his own self", using imagination and dispensing with all the "waxworks paraphernalia". There is nothing unspiritual about perfectly mastering a mechanism. Cf. Goethe, *Wilhelm Meisters theatralische Sendung* II, 2: "No one can be really great on the stage or anywhere else unless he has a powerful vein in him."

ness: "Dramatic creativity means being true with body and soul. . . . The secret of dramatic creation lies in the gift by which a particularly favored human being can render his body transparent, allowing spiritual experience to pass through it in such a way that inner processes are manifested in facial expression, gesture, tone, bearing and movement—in a word, through *unmasking* rather than masking. In this sense the actor is truer than other people."[48] However, this truthfulness is only formal: a (perhaps) perfect correspondence between the role and its incarnation in the actor's whole being. Would it be right to attribute an ethical, or indeed a religious value, to this depersonalized entering-into the role (and reemergence from it), as *François Mauriac* seems to do when he suggests that man's self-transcendence in drama is close to mysticism?[49] Surely this is only one side of the total picture—and not a very realistic one at that.

First of all the question simply is: What becomes of the actor's sphere of personal intimacy when he is portraying a role? Is it reserved and veiled—or is it too used as material in his embodying of the role? At this point we can speak of two kinds of actors, referred to as "first person actors" and "third person actors". The former portray *themselves* in all their roles (like

[48] Friedrich Ulmer, "Die schöpferischen Kräfte der Schaubühne", in *Bavaria* I, 7 (May 10, 1930).

[49] "Le mystère du théâtre" in *Journal* III, 110f. It is worthwhile outlining Mauriac's whole train of thought. He observes that when actors leave the stage they have difficulty in finding their old "I", as if "some unknown soul were taking the opportunity of interposing itself, shining forth in the interval between the departure of the fictional personality and the return of the everyday 'I' ". It could be the light of the eternal self shining in this way, which we sometimes see in death masks. "It is somewhat disturbing that this effort of dis-incarnation in the service of an invented plot presents such a striking analogy to the object of the mystics' search, to that vacuum striven for by whose who wish God to take possession of them. There is something about the actor's work that frightens me. Perhaps it is the contrast between the aim in view, which is only a play (be it ever so brilliant), and the serious efforts in the spiritual realm which take place in the secret places of the soul. . . . A magnificent and dangerous profession, consisting in losing oneself and finding oneself again. . . . But between these two conditions some of them live in a third condition, perhaps without realizing it. Many of them do not suspect that, in pursuing the ridiculous goal set before them by dramatists, they come perilously near that terrible threshold which only the saints have crossed."

Talma, Kainz and *Moissi*), the latter *objectify* their "I" in their roles (thus *Duse* appeared as a different person in each part she played). Perhaps we should distinguish carefully between the typology of inborn ability and that of moral attitude, even if the typical inheritance can predetermine such an attitude to some extent. Both dispositions require the actor to portray himself; a certain *exhibitionism* goes with the profession. This ever-present relationship led to the (astonishingly widespread) low regard in which society held actors and their profession, of which we have already spoken. Not only in Rome but also in China, as well as in Tongking, in Vietnam, the actor was a person of low class; in India he belonged to an unclean and despised caste. The Chinese actress was officially treated as a prostitute. *André Villiers* has examined this relationship between the stage and prostitution,[50] and *Jean Auger Duvignaud* has adduced sociological reasons for it, to which we shall have to return.[51] Not only for Port Royal is the actor a "public poisoner" and "satanically possessed" (*Nicole*); the person of the actor continues to be despised even (as in the Grand Siècle) where the theatre itself is popular and highly regarded (compare *Grimm, Voltaire, Diderot* and naturally *Rousseau*, the enemy of the theatre);[52] even *Léon Bloy* considers the actor to be a member of a "shameful" class, and *Octave Mirbeau* describes the actor as a "subhuman being", as one of the "damned".[53] Unjust denigration of this kind generally comes from times when, because

---

[50] *La prostitution de l'acteur* (1946). Cf. A. Kutscher, *Grundriss der Theaterwissenschaft*, 77.

[51] Jean Auger Duvignaud, *L'Acteur: Esquisse d'une sociologie du comédien* (Gallimard, 1965). Cf. also his *Sociologie du théâtre: Essai sur les ombres collectives* (PUF, 1965).

[52] *Lettre à d'Alembert sur les spectacles* (1758). Here Bossuet's arguments are taken up once more, now in the name of social morality. More than 400 pamphlets attacked Rousseau.

[53] *Le comédien* (Paris, 1883), 8. The reason is the actor's *disponibilité*, which according to Mirbeau leads to the loss of personality and of every individual trait. Not only must the actor "stuff his ape's head full of all the ideas, feelings and experiences of his role, but he must also put on the appropriate clothes and shoes, etc." On this whole issue cf. the chapter entitled "Le comédien, personnage maudit" in Duvignaud, *L'Acteur*, 104–18. Rudolf Helfter, "Die moralische Beurteilung des Berufsschauspielers", in *Die Schaubühne*, 14 (Diss. Munich: Emsdetten, 1936).

of the way they were shunned by society, actors were forced into immorality and prostitution; naturally, the exposed nature of their occupation could render them particularly vulnerable here. For it is the actor's job to make himself entirely available, body and mind, for a fortuitous role and for the transitory pleasure of other human beings.

Thus the actor exists on a knife-edge; if fundamentally he has no shame he can be "somewhat exhibitionist" (*Louis Jouvet*);[54] but his surrender to his dramatic roles can also give him a unique, often unconscious and naive humility, which *Jouvet* has also expressed so well:

> How modest you *can* be. No one can do it better. Often you show a strange purity and selflessness. You do not live only on vanity and success. At every moment you show more love for the others than for yourself. It's just that you forget, you confuse yourself with them, mistakenly imagining that you are the central point from which everything comes forth. Then you become a mirror of their satisfaction. . . . Do not take yourself as the center but as the stimulus, the chance, the means, the filter, the communication wire. . . . Yes, there are actors whose humility (like in monasteries) and simplicity (like children) radiates from every gesture and intonation; you may laugh at them at times, but these pure hearts are the true actors, and in this resolute purity you once started to act and to live.[55]

Gabriel Marcel is convinced that "the selflessness of actors presents a challenge to metaphysical and religious reflection", and he boldly goes on: "I think we must discover in it something like that *initium caritatis* of which theologians speak."[56] *Marcel* is suggesting here that the actor's profession and life are the most transparent medium, showing us the mission and existence of Christ. For Christ's life is essentially a eucharistic existence for others, a humble, facilitating representation of the divine.

Let us prescind from all the personal, almost unavoidable vanity associated with this occupation, which requires a certain lack of inhibition and needs the crowd's applause. Then we shall

[54] L. Jouvet, *Le comédien désincarné* (Paris: Flammarion, 1954).

[55] L. Jouvet, *Témoignages sur le théâtre* (Paris: Flammarion, 1952), 14–15.

[56] "Réflexions sur les exigences d'un théâtre chrétien" in *Vie intellectuelle* (Mar. 25, 1937): 461–62.

see, in its professional objectivity, a humility, a willing to serve vis-à-vis the role, for the role is the most important thing to be shown to the audience. If this humility were to succeed—and it does not obstruct the entire creative interplay of physical and spiritual resources, in fact it calls for it—the actor would approach the ideal that *Kleist* and *Rilke* paradoxically realized in the marionette; not through some mechanical perfection that is no longer human, but because the person concerned would no longer be playing himself ("The man who can only play himself is no actor");[57] he would have put everything he is into the divine commission. Occasionally, by way of exception, the ideal does shine forth:

> The miracle happens: the actor forgets all his mastery of technique and becomes the person he is acting. It happens rarely. Here we are touching the deepest tragic layer of the dramatic art, which is a real reflection of human destiny. Here, without blasphemy, we can say, "Except ye become as little children." The path that leads through technical mastery must bring us back to what seems to be unconscious being, otherwise it was a false path. This is the tremendous demand made by every spiritual endeavor—even to *utter* it is asking too much. But perhaps we cannot define man and his most concentrated image, the artist, better than by saying that he is the only being of whom too much is asked.[58]

In support of this latter view we can recall the analysis of life in *Rilke's Malte Laurids Brigge*: "But deep inside and in your presence, my God—in your presence, spectator—surely we have no action? We discover that we do not know our roles, we look for a mirror so that we can take off our paint, take off the disguise and really *be*. But somehow or other some part of our make-up sticks to us, and we forget it. . . . And so we go round, a mockery, a half-thing, neither having real being nor being actors."[59]

This incompleteness of human existence is the ultimate reason for the actor's essential ambiguity as he stands between humility and vanity, between the power to mediate a higher truth of

---

[57] Jarno in *Wilhelm Meisters Lehrjahre*, bk. 8, chap. 5.
[58] E. Brock-Sulzer, *Theater*, 210. Similarly Jouvet, *Le Comédien désincarné*, 37.
[59] Rilke, *Sämtliche Werke* (1966), vol. VI, 920–21.

existence and the power to obstruct it through intrusive self-affirmation. This may be why—apart from the naive mystery plays—it is impossible successfully to represent the saint (who is unaware of his humility) on the stage unless he is shown in some unholy weakness, like Schiller's Jungfrau or Anouilh's Becket. The unity that comes down from "above" as a gift and a grace cannot be reached from "below".

The actor's twofold nature gives rise to the sociological fact that society responds to him with both enthusiasm and a certain reserve that may range from mistrust to scorn. This is evident, in the period of absolutism, not only in France but also, in varying degrees, in the other countries of Europe; people want to see their own greatness mirrored on the stage, and yet at the same time they cast aside the mirror as a vain and despicable tool. This changes, certainly, in the period of Liberalism; the official excommunications come to an end, but the theatre remains a kind of illusory paradise for the middle-class man, and the actor—particularly the star—becomes an idol from whom intoxicating experiences are demanded, even at the very heart of naturalism. The actor's life becomes an exceptional, fascinating one, and is once more distanced from society, albeit in a different way. People make an image of him by combining all the passions he portrays, all the vicissitudes he undergoes on the stage; he becomes a kind of *malédiction imaginaire*.[60] From here it is but a short step to regarding him as the *révolté* and entrusting him, the "committed actor", with the role of pioneer in "transforming society". In all ages, though differently, the actor is extrapolated from society; he is atypical, and to that extent is put under a visible or invisible ban. Without falling victim to an exaggerated sociological determinism,[61] we can say that the

---

[60] Duvignaud, *L'Acteur*, 162–64.

[61] Duvignaud deliberately follows this path to the end, unconcerned about the demonstrability of his theses. For him, the actor is "possessed" by his role; with his "otherness", his "mana" he is the destroyer of "social determinisms", blazing a trail to a new experience of freedom for particular groups (202). He is "the active revealer of the least admitted and admissible elements of human society, the obscene and sometimes frightening image of the determinism of the collective consciousness" (203). He "utters the innermost tendencies of the social organism toward change, tendencies which it hides from itself". The play becomes relevant to the spectator in that the actor makes his bodily existence

actor, through his professional activity, presents society with
possible models of freedom—embodied by him by way of
anticipation. He anticipates, and thus can be a pointer to something that, as *Mauriac* has shown, essentially transcends his
sphere.[62]

---

completely *disponible* and in doing so reaches down to a plastic zone that is common
to all men. (Cf. Merleau-Ponty's "intercorporéité" which was developed in
connection with Husserl, but see our earlier remarks on Stanislavsky.) In this
common human zone the ferment of society is producing archetypes (as yet
unknown) of new forms of freedom. This is the usual combination of Marx and
Freud (or Jung).

[62] H. Bahr, in his *Dialog vom Tragischen* (1904), 78, extolled the actor's art
of transformation as an educative factor. Here we have been considering the
actor only in his individuality. Naturally a great deal more could be said about
the social side of the actor's role-playing. Brecht sums it up in these pregnant
words from his *Kleines Organon*, no. 58: "The actor's learning must go hand in
hand with the learning of the other actors, as must the construction of his
character with the construction of the other characters. For the smallest social
unit is not a human being, but two human beings. In life too, we build ourselves
up together." On this basis Brecht calls for the actors occasionally to exchange
roles during rehearsal "so that the characters get what they need from one
another" (no. 59). Cf. also *Schriften zum Theater* I in *Gesammelte Werke*
(Suhrkamp, 1967), 15:401ff., 420ff. Finally we need to mention *Helmuth
Plessner's* essay, "Zur Anthropologie des Schauspielers" (Festschrift for H. J.
Pol, Amsterdam, 1948, now included in *Zwischen Philosophie und Gesellschaft.
Ausgew. Abhandlungen und Vorträge* [Berne: Francke, 1953], 180–93). Plessner
emphasizes the fact that the stage dualism ("I" versus role) has its basis in
everyday life. Man "presents" himself, and the basis of seriousness is his sense of
being committed to a role. Here the actor follows a creative aim according to
which his own feeling is only material for the fashioning of the particular
expression. The image he endeavors to bring into reality is one of the primal
forms of human existence, and it becomes clear, for example, where a "follower"
assimilates himself to someone who represents an ideal. If, in this discipleship,
he is "called by name" (188), he becomes himself *through* the other (190). By
analogy, the actor must *be* his role in a way that few people in ordinary life are
called to be. Such are priests and rulers, called to share the likeness of God; yet
they do so in a kind of distance from themselves. "The only thing that possesses
real dignity is a strength that has been broken, that fragile form of life that exists
between power and powerlessness." At this point Plessner's concept of human
"ex-centricity" leads him to see the actor as an anthropological model.

c. The Director

Between the dramatic poet and the actor there yawns a gulf that can be bridged only by a third party who will take responsibility for the play's performance, for making it present here and now. Since there is a multiplicity of actors, he must guide their ensemble and interplay—a difficult task and one that requires of him very specific qualities. There is nothing against the author himself taking on this role—and there are famous instances of this—or a particular actor doing so. But in the long run, in a normal theatrical organization, this mediating role has to be exercised by a distinct person.[1]

Considering the two ends that have to be tied together, namely, a stage script (not necessarily a printed one)[2] on the one hand and the available actors on the other, the director's creative achievement seems enormous. Performance requires that he come up with a unified vision embracing both the drama (with the author's entire creative contribution) and the art of the actors (with their very different creative abilities). It is mistaken, therefore, to say that the direction side is not a distinct art,[3] unless "distinct" is taken to mean totally independent.

Direction is, in fact, most profoundly dependent on the two extreme elements it has to integrate; its whole raison d'être

[1] For our purposes there is no need to go into the history of theatrical direction. It has always existed in some form or other, e.g., the *Frankfurter Dirigierrolle: Ordo sive registrum* for the medieval mystery plays. In modern times, however, and particularly in the twentieth century, the director's function has become considerably more specific. It will suffice to use the term "director" for the role of mediation between the dramatic text and the actors. It can stand for the various unifying and actualizing functions in the theatre, including that of the *Intendant* and the *Dramaturg*. The distinction between the *Dramaturg*, whose task is to prepare and adapt the texts and to execute the performance, and the *Regisseur* (and his assistants) is not a clear one: their roles interact. On the subject of *Dramaturgie* cf. Hugo Dingler, *Dramaturgie als Wissenschaft*.

[2] Insofar as drama is primarily designed for performance on the stage, Hegel (once again following a Greek line of thought) recommends that there should be no publication of texts: "In my opinion no plays should be printed. Rather, somewhat like the practice of the ancients, they should be written in manuscript and remain part of the stage apparatus. Only a small number of people should ever see them" (*Ästhetik* III, ed. Bassenge, 2d ed. [1965], 538).

[3] As A. Kutscher does.

consists in the way it mediates between them. It is a *puissance intermédiaire*,[4] a "power", which has to keep to the "hierarchy" of antecedent powers. "Without doubt, the first commandment for the director is obedience to the text",[5] which as such is the "primary" element (though not the only one) in the performance. However, as we saw in connection with the actor, the text is not something fixed and finished but something that needs to be understood and interpreted in a living and spiritual manner. "Putting on a play", therefore, while it certainly means illustrating it, translating it into three-dimensional reality, also implies penetrating the dramatist's mind and heart in order to prolong his thoughts and feelings over and above the words. There is the same "gap" between the play as written and the play as performed as "that between a piano reduction and the full score as performed by the whole orchestra".[6] Part of this task of bringing the play alive, making it present, is the question of how to make the issues it raises politically relevant here and now. We shall return to this question later. We already have a guideline in *Baty's* requirement of obedience to the text.

When it comes to the actors, the director's task is much harder, for they, since they are responsible for bringing their roles to life, can also claim a primacy over him. For his part, "together with the author", he has to keep before them "the creative goal that they all share",[7] not as something already complete, however, for the actors' imagination and creativity must freely integrate with it. *Stanislavsky*, himself a superb director, warns his actors against being overpowered by his imagination; they should develop their own imagination, "other-

[4] Seb. Mercier, *Essai sur l'art dramatique* (1773). Other texts in Kutscher, *Grundriss der Theaterwissenschaft*, 223. Reports reveal Brecht as a director of stature: his "direction was far more discreet than that of the famous directors. Those who saw him did not feel that he wanted to put over 'something he had in his mind'. . . . When he intervened, it was 'the way the wind was blowing' and so was practically unnoticeable. . . . It was like a child using a rod to steer some twigs from a riverside pool and cause them to sail out into the river" (*Schriften* 2, *Theater* 2, in *Gesammelte Werke* (1967), vol. 16: 759–60.

[5] Gaston Baty, in *Revue critique des idées et des livres* (Aug. 25, 1923): 479. See also Stanislavsky, *Die Arbeit des Schauspielers an sich selbst*, 79.

[6] Baty, 478.

[7] Stanislavsky, *Die Arbeit des schauspielers an sich selbst*, 80.

wise they will fall victim to directors, who will substitute their own imagination for that which is lacking in the actors."[8] It is a sad fact that in this century there are star directors who have forgotten their function of simply mediating and eliciting; they conduct themselves like virtuosos and act as if they themselves were the real creators of the performance. The director's book, which should be nothing more than a fluid collection of the most diverse notes, becomes a kind of full score. *Gordon Craig*, reacting against naturalism, stylizes the stage into a pure artefact of the director: "The actor will disappear, to be replaced by an inanimate figure—to be called, perhaps, a 'supermarionette'—until it has found a more splendid name";[9] he means an "ecstatic body with the power of symbolic expression". But the director is not a conductor and the actor is not a mere musical instrument. The director should devote his energies to rendering himself superfluous.[10] *Ionesco* puts it even more radically: "The director must let himself be led; he should not want anything of the play. He should annihilate himself, be a perfectly receptive vessel."[11] Above all he should know how to awaken the actor's creative energies (of which the latter may not even be aware) so

[8] Stanislavsky, *Das Geheimnis des schauspielerischen Erfolges*, 80.

[9] Gordon Craig, *On the Art of the Theatre* (New York, 1956). Cf. A. Villiers, "Le conflit du metteur en scène et de l'acteur", in *La psychologie de l'art dramatique*, 52ff. Antonin Artaud also denies the actor any "personal initiative" and wants him to develop an "athletic approach to the emotions".

[10] E. Brock-Sulzer, *Theater*, 178, following Dullin. The director should bring the imponderable into being: "proportion", "style" (*ibid.*).

[11] *Notes et contre-notes* (1966), 262. Similarly E. Brock-Sulzer, *Theater*, 142. It is quite different if the poet himself places the director on the stage and thus gives his drama that explicit "play" quality it had in the sense of the "theatre of the world", where "World" itself had appeared on stage as a kind of director/producer. Thornton Wilder introduced the character of the "stage manager" into several of his plays (*Our Town*, *The Happy Journey*, *Pullman Car Hiawatha*), indicating two things: first, the dreamlike evanescence of all life's events, and second, their importance vis-à-vis an invisible, higher instance. Here we look through the stage manager to divine providence beyond. Cf. Szondi, *Theorie des modernen dramas*, 144. The "Registrator" in Max Frisch's *Biographie, Ein Spiel* (Bibl. Suhrkamp, 225) exercises a purely impersonal role: he can cross out life that has been lived and give people a new chance, in the way a director stops a rehearsal and starts again from the beginning. However, none of these "stage managers" have anything in common any more with the director's real work.

that the characters really form an ensemble in the spiritual sense. As a figure he must disappear, as it were, in order to be a medium and an atmosphere present to all.

The rehearsal, then, is the director's proper sphere of work; by his patience, his shrewd leading and yielding, a unity gradually emerges, the unity that corresponds to the poet's idea but that, in concrete terms, is due to the director. The director has to show himself to be a "water-diviner", discovering springs of creativity in the actors and a mediator who can only achieve a synthesis through conflict and confrontation, through the "clash of the director with the dramatist, the director with the actors, the actor with the dramatist and the director, and between the actors themselves".[12] This is the place for creative compromise, which is no longer felt as such in performance. If the rehearsals are "a struggle for unity", there must be no perceptible sign of this struggle in the final result; there must be no sense of a violation, there must be no propping up of alien elements.[13] When it comes to the final result, the première, the director has done his duty and can go, leaving the actors behind and, through their play, the author.

In its première, the play enters into time as an event. It is so much an event, indeed, that the Greeks mostly eschewed repeat performances: historical events are unique. *Charles Péguy* showed a remarkable awareness of this. His *Clio, Dialogue de l'histoire et de l'âme charnelle*, speaks of premières in this way: "No play can ever recover from having found a scandalous echo in its cradle. A play should explode in the year of its birth." Other works of art can come into being secretly and gradually establish themselves, "but a stage play must be born publicly. It must come out or it will burst."[14] The play is performed at a particular time and this once more raises the question how a play from the past can be performed in the present. Neither the epic nor the lyric is ever rewritten; the reader himself must make the connection between then and now. The drama is itself a making-present,

---

[12] A. Kutscher, *Grundriss der Theaterwissenschaft*, 233.

[13] E. Reiche, *Siebzehn Kapitel von Schauspielern und vom Theater*, 38ff.

[14] *Clio, Dialogue de l'histoire et de l'âme charnelle*, *Oeuvres en prose* (Pléiade, 1957), I, 161.

however; it jumps over this distance: it speaks (and must speak) for today. The producer's or director's concern is to secure this actuality.

Now there are works—and these are the best—that stay alive and meaningful down the ages because they portray situations that are of permanent validity. In that case the art of editing will consist in highlighting those things in the old play that speak to the heart and conscience, without getting involved in the nonsense of artificial modernization. Naturally, *Racine* is played differently nowadays, with different costumes and gestures. This goes without saying. Often such transformations benefit the work in question: its essence comes out better on a simpler, more realistic stage than when wrapped in the bombast of a former age. But sooner rather than later we come up against the boundary between some past social situation, which provided the dramatic conflict, and the present situation. We can even wonder whether this earlier constellation of forces—for example, a feudal society and a monarchical power representing and making present a transcendent, divine lordship in the world —was not *the* precondition for genuine tragedy, no longer attainable in a purely democratic age. This was the view of *Reinhold Schneider*. We have said something about the truth and limits of this view in the section on the "death of drama". Here the question is, How far can we expect a modern audience to accept a particular social context that determines the dramatic action? Is it possible to perform the most grandiose plays of *Corneille* anywhere—except in the *Comédie Française*? Where is the audience that could be presented with a play by *Calderon*, who stands or falls by his theological implications? Does this mean, as *Bertolt Brecht* has suggested, that the classical dramas can only serve as a storehouse of dramatic fables that, now that they are in a totally new social order, need to be completely remotivated and reformulated? (Compare *Macbeth by Heiner Müller, after Shakespeare*.) *Stanislavsky* is surely right: "If you force contemporary reality on to an ancient, monolithic, classical work, you are putting proud flesh on a magnificent body and distorting it beyond recognition." If, on the other hand, a modern approach is prepared to insert itself organically into the "higher task" of the older play and thus enrich it, developing it inwardly in a particular direction, a valid *aggiornamento* can be brought about.[15] Here the director meets his hardest task: he must be committed enough to make the play relevant and at the same time civilized enough not to equate this here-and-now relevance with a narrow doctrine of society. The theatre *is* a political reality, in a lofty and noble sense, but it should not be misused for political party propaganda.

With *Siegfried Melchinger*, who wrote a "history of political theatre"[16], we can say "that propagandist theatre in the service of ruling power"—but why only here?—"should not be regarded as 'political theatre' ",[17] whereas all great European theatre was political insofar as it was concerned directly or indirectly with "public issues" and not infrequently engaged in criticism. This can quite definitely be demonstrated in the case of certain plays of antiquity—most notably, of course, those of *Aristophanes*[18] —and it can be shown or at least suspected in individual works of the tragedians;[19] in *Shakespeare* there is a constant interest in the use of power, but on the other hand few references to contemporary politics,[20] and in *Corneille* (alone among the great French dramatists) there are demonstrable references to the politics of *Richelieu*.[21] The eighteenth century remained middle-

---

[15] Stanislavsky, *Das Geheimnis des schauspielerischen Erfolges*, 388.

[16] Siegfried Melchinger, Velber: Friedrich-Verlag, 1971.

[17] *Ibid.*, 292. This restriction shows the tendency of this otherwise well informed book, which manages to say of Shakespeare: "The world is out of joint (as all his plays show) and must and should be transformed"(!) (170). In an even more crass example it speaks of the released crowd in Hofmannsthal's *Der Turm* as a "fascist horde" (372). His praise for G. Hauptmann's *Die Ratten* is also characteristic (309f.).

[18] Cf. primarily Victor Ehrenberg, *Aristophanes und das Volk der Athener* (1968), and see below, "Right and Judgment".

[19] On Euripides: G. Zuntz, *The Political Plays of Euripides* (1955). Apart from Aeschylus' *Persians*, Melchinger's theses, e.g., on *Antigone* and *Oedipus Rex* seem highly forced.

[20] Melchinger's remarks on Shakespeare are the least convincing of all. The fact that the poet avoided (132f.) the story of Henry II and of Thomas à Becket clearly shows that he steered away from contemporary politics. For him the stage was the world, not the state.

[21] *El Cid* provoked the cardinal's wrath, since it set personal virtues against the "abstract virtue of the 'state' " and unveiled the limitations of state power devoid of grace. In *Horace* the scene is moved to Rome, but the play portrays the

class and sentimental and the French Revolution produced not a single strong play; the Weimar circle (and particularly *Schiller*) kept a cautious, "ideal" distance from current events. In the nineteenth century there is only the occasional truly political play: not *Kleist's Prinz von Homburg* but *Büchner's Danton* (which, however, portrays "only a central problem of all politics") and his *Woyzeck* with its silent accusation against the social order, and, willy-nilly, *Gogol's The Inspector General*. The author, profoundly shocked by the political effect of his satire, fled abroad; all the same he understood that "originally, the comedy was a public and popular form. At least, that is how the father of comedy, Aristophanes, shows it to us. Only subsequently did it enter the narrow defile of private intrigue."[22] *Shaw's* first two plays, if not a critique of politics, are certainly a critique of the governing economic system. We find social criticism in *Ibsen, Strindberg, Wedekind* and many of the more modern writers.

All things considered, this is not a great deal. Dramatic poets were subject to censorship and were arrested (*Nestroy*) or kept in custody (*Wedekind*), but in this they were no different from novelists and journalists. It is openly admitted that, in political terms, the stage hardly ever achieved anything.[23] In general, while great dramatic writing addressed itself to the public, the *polis*, it did so in order to present models of what was ethically, and even metaphysically, right (*Shakespeare*); this could also involve the public pillorying of hypocrisy (*Molière's Tartuffe*, which caused a "political" uproar, and for good reason). *Goethe*

---

brutality that follows a preoccupation with renown. *Cinna* pleads for mercy on the part of the prince, where Richelieu was convinced of the opposite ("Il faut fermer la porte à la pitié", 187). *Cinna* was not allowed to be printed during the cardinal's lifetime. Melchinger is probably right when he says: "I am profoundly convinced that Corneille was a Republican; his models were Cato and Pompey" (188).

[22] "Bei Verlassen des Theaters nach der Aufführung einer neuen Komödie", *Werke* (Berlin: Aufbau-Verlag, 1952), vol. 5: 338.

[23] "Political theatre was seldom effective down through history" (Melchinger, 38). "When did political theatre ever succeed in influencing the wheel of history?" (*ibid.*, 62). "Basically—and this is a shocking realization—the theatre has achieved as good as nothing since it began to deal with politics two and a half thousand years ago" (*ibid.*, 418).

too, in his *Die natürliche Tochter*, was not trying to come to grips politically with the French Revolution but to establish a few broad guiding principles for the time he saw approaching. ("The ferment comes from below. . . . Coarseness affects the whole body . . . ; the bonds holding together the last form are loosed. The mass becomes absolute.")[24] Here *Goethe* anticipates the prophetic vision of *Jacob Burckhardt*: Great drama does not believe that man's fundamental nature can be changed; if it did, it would cut the ground from under its own feet. It appeals to the individual's ethical conscience, asking him to consider how mortal man (both as a person and as a community) can act and live according to his inner dignity.

The director who fails to recognize this fundamental impulse of all mainstream drama and tries to adapt it to political propaganda has in fact betrayed the dramatic dimension.

3. *The Three Elements of Dramatic Realization*

a. Presentation

The writing of the text, the staging, the rehearsals—all this takes place for the sake of performance. All the preparatory work is done with a view to people who are satisfied to know merely that it goes on; when the time comes they will also be glad to know the name of the play that is to be performed. In spite of this accidental remoteness, however, under favorable circumstances a substantial closeness and relationship can come into being, namely, when the theatrical people are able to count on a particular theatre-going public whose expectations coincide with what they have to offer. For the most part, felicitous constellations such as this belong to the theatre's historical high points: there was a passionate interest among the people of classical Greece in tragedy; there was an almost incomprehensible wave of theatre-madness at the time of Queen Elizabeth, and a similar one in Spanish classicism and in the Italy of the commedia dell'arte. Even the Viennese theatre still possessed a natural

[24] From the third draft of the continuation.

"unity between the three elements, drama, actor and audience", which, according to *Hofmannsthal*, "existed nowhere else".[1]

Whether the mixture be thicker or thinner, however, there must always be a "communion" between what happens on the stage and the audience if the play is to succeed. For the actor acts basically in front of and *for* someone. His achievement in existentially adopting a role that is different from his person only has meaning if someone sees it and acknowledges it to be substantial and successful. As we shall show, the audience's presence is not passive—quite the reverse; if the performance is to succeed, it must be active, a willingness to enter into the action. The necessity of this "communion" has actually been termed "ontological",[2] even though it is never automatic but always signifies a particular *kairos*, looks forward to it and helps to bring it about. The relationship can also be expressed (with *Jean Louis Barrault*) in erotic terms: "An act takes place between the stage and the auditorium that is symbolized by the sexual act, that is, by yearning and the self-communication of love." The auditorium is female, expectation; the stage is resolute aggression.[3] More moderately, the auditorium can be regarded as a resonating chamber (*Reinhold Schneider*): "In the face of genuine theatre the audience would become a single whole, heightening the artistic impression: it would serve as a sounding board for the melody played on stage."[4]

---

[1] Hofmannsthal, *Prosa* III, 431.

[2] "Le rapport, d'ordre ontologique, entre l'acteur et le spectateur est extrêmement important" (Villiers, *La psychologie de l'art dramatique*, 50; also his *Le Comédien*, 183f.).

[3] Jean Louis Barrault, *Le théâtre dans le monde*, 30.

[4] *Das Spiel vom Menschen* (Pustet, Graz, 1949), 6. Even phenomenological structuralism acknowledges that the closed form of the drama is open to the spectator: drama is the only poetic form that does not attain its full aesthetic unfolding in poetic medium itself, for the dramatic word is tied to public performance: Roman Ingarden, *Das literarische Kunstwerk* (1931), 329f. H.-G. Gadamer emphasizes that the spectator is integral to the play: "The play's openness to the spectator . . . is part and parcel of its concentrated form. . . . Indeed, it is the spectator who most authentically experiences the play; it is not the player, but the spectator, who sees the play as it is intended to be seen. In the spectator the play is elevated, as it were, to its ideal plane" (*Wahrheit und Methode* [1965], 104–5). Cf. 126 on the "communion" between stage and audience.

There are countless witnesses to the fact that the actor is dependent on feedback from the audience; here are two of them. *Madame Bartet*: "I communicate directly with the audience; I feel very clearly whether they are with me or against me. If I feel that they are not sufficiently on my side I exert myself to win them over, with an effort that seems almost physical. At an emotional climax the audience seems homogeneous, like a collective; whereas, if my role has only half taken possession of me, I am aware of the least movement in the auditorium."[5] *Louis Jouvet*: "You can have no idea of the warm, inner glow the actor feels when he hears the sound of the audience. You cannot imagine the shiver of delight, the surge of emotion, the excitement produced by an auditorium full of humanity when, silently, the curtain goes up; and who knows whether this feeling is one of affection or of fear?"[6]

With these great actors it is not simply a case of stage fright (although the term does come from the theatre); it is rather to do with the solemnity of what is going on (and here we are thinking of the highest theatrical endeavors, although there may be analogous feelings at a lower level), which, from the outset, is aimed at something that goes beyond the everyday life of both actor and audience. There is an obvious difference, for instance, between this and an event taking place in a sports stadium. True, the sports hero is also sustained by the sympathy of his supporters, who spur him on to ever-greater efforts; but he only puts forth his own strength and skill, whereas the actor allows something else to shine through him. For its part the audience also looks for the manifestation of this something else *through* the actor. It is not merely a display of dramatic art, however great and highly prized that may be, but, in and through the performance, a "revelation" is to take place. Audience and actors are not complementary and self-sufficient halves; both of them remain open, expecting some third thing that is to come about in and through both the players and the audience. The limitations of both of them open on to an unlimited horizon.

[5] In Binet, *Réflexions sur le paradoxe de Diderot* (1897), 293.
[6] "Les problèmes du théâtre contemporain", in *La revue hebdomadaire* (May 4, 1935): 15.

Here, according to *Hölderlin*, if the poet's word achieves in-carnation, the myth can rise again as the word of God, which takes place bodily in the face of the watching crowd.[7]

b. The Audience

We have already suggested, briefly, why human beings go to the theatre to watch plays (see the section "Drama and the Illumination of Existence"). We spoke of a twofold need and a twofold pleasure: we project ourselves onto an ultimate plane that gives meaning, and thus we are given our selves. It can also be described as the twofold need to see and to surrender ourselves to something that transcends and gives meaning to the limited horizon of everyday life. The dramatic presentation has to do justice to this "substantial pathos", as *Hegel* calls it.[8] In his *L'Echange*, *Claudel* has the actor look into the full auditorium and ascertain this substantial pathos:

> Do you know what theatre is? There is the stage and the audi-torium. In the evening, when all the shops are closed, people come here, sit together in rows and watch. And then the curtain goes up and something takes place on stage as if it were true. I look at them, and the auditorium is full of living, clothed flesh, and they stick to the walls like flies, right up to the roof. And I see these hundreds of white faces. The human being gets bored, and ignorance clings to him from his birth. He has no idea how things begin and how they cease, and that is why he comes to the theatre. Sitting there, with his hands on his knees, he looks at himself. And he cries and laughs and is reluctant to get up and go . . .[9]

This fascinated beholding of oneself is not a beholding of something long familiar and wearisome, but a beholding in the hope of learning something about beginnings and endings. And this comes about in and through the action presented on stage. For the action is on behalf of the audience: it must lend meaning to the activities of the human being, ignorant as he is from birth. As the action proceeds, man realizes his two inseparable func-

[7] Stuttgart ed. (1965), V, 293.

[8] *Ästhetik* II, 529.

[9] *L'Echange*, act I in *Théâtre* (Pléiade), I, 676.

tions, that is, being both a spectator and an actor in the play of existence.[10] This presupposes that he is unreservedly open, in principle, to everything the stage may offer him (thus he can go to the theatre without knowing what play is being performed this particular evening) and he must not watch it from an uninvolved vantage point but make the effort of entering into the action. The audience's indifference as to what is to be performed is not apathy; it is a taut, underlying disposition to respond to whatever comes. This tension on the part of the audience is its contribution to the tension of the dramatic action. Of course, the tension that lies in the action itself will heighten the audience's tension and make it specific; but it was already there in the first place, albeit in an open-ended and nonspecific form. *Goethe* speaks of it in this way: "The spectator's senses should be in a continual state of tension; he should not lift himself to the plane of reflection but should be passionately drawn along; his imagination is completely silenced and must not be engaged in any way, and even what is narrated must be *shown to* him, as it were."[11] However, if the performance is to win our unreserved involvement—for it excludes any neutral "observation"—it presupposes that we are unreservedly ready to be carried wherever it takes us, even "where you do not wish to go", into areas that are painful, disturbing and possibly unbearable.

On the other hand the audience's underlying, open readiness has certain expectations. It expects to be led "into the open" —and this must be made clear through the closed, finite action on the stage. This justified expectation means that, without diminishing its unconditional readiness, the audience has a criterion with which it can assess the performance; under certain circumstances it can refuse, wholly or partially, to go along with it. Whistling or lukewarm applause expresses the critical attitude that is part of the audience's readiness and that may put the author's and actor's work on the scales, as Dionysos does with the verses of *Aeschylus* and *Euripides* in *Aristophanes' Frogs*. *Goethe's* aforementioned dictum presupposes that both the play

[10] Cf. E. I. Watkin, *The Bow in the Clouds* (New York, 1932).
[11] "Über epische und dramatische Dichtung", *Über Kunst und Altertum* VI (1827). Brecht contradicts Goethe in the *Kleines Organon*, no. 50.

and the performance are perfect—in which case it would be wrong to question their authority. But what is human is seldom perfect. Often it can and must be taken as a passable likeness of something perfect that is aimed at but not attained and that needs to be supplemented. A mediocre play can be lifted above itself by a brilliant performance. Occasionally the spectator can be provoked to significant insights even by the mediocre performance of a mediocre work. Some question that touches profoundly on life can emerge even where it is given a superficial solution or none at all. The question bursts the horizon in which it is set; the question itself is a boundless light. This does not mean that the audience should simply put up with mediocre productions; it means that, as often occurs in the history of the theatre, things that in themselves are second-rate can have a lasting and not unjustified influence.

All the same, we expect to be presented with something more than the everyday world with which we are so familiar; the physical stage itself, whether within a proscenium arch or as an apron-stage, promises some "revelation" removed from the profane realm. The audience wants to be "transported", "carried away"—and this was precisely the danger which Christian critics of the theatre saw in it[12]—and the performance lets the audience participate (in some plays at least) in a way that seems to give it a sense of supernatural insight. It can observe characters when they are alone, it can even hear them utter their inner thoughts in monologues; indeed, the characters can even explicitly confide in the audience, speaking directly to it. In principle (though not perhaps in practice) the audience is allowed to know the course of the action in advance: it shares in the action as the "confidant" of the French classical stage. Thus the audience hovers in tension between knowing more and knowing less in a realm that is more than that of everyday, confronted with the open questions posed by life as a whole; it is this that creates the specific "pleasure"—even in tragedy[13]—

[12] Cf. Augustine, *Confessions* 3, 2; Bossuet, *Maximes et réflexions sur la comédie*, chap. 4: "On devient bientôt un acteur secret dans la tragédie, on y joue sa propre passion."

[13] Augustine's nuanced analysis (see note 12, above) does not simply reject the strange pleasure we take in tragic events in the theatre, but only in its

that, while it can exhibit different degrees of purity, is the fundamental reason why people go to the theatre.

Throughout the theatre's history people have tried to establish communication between the actors and the audience in new ways. There is the "path of flowers" in the Far East, in which the actors move from among the audience and proceed to the area which is cultically set apart; there is the chorus of the Greek theatre, in which (according to both *Hegel* and *Nietzsche*) the spectators see themselves represented, with their reactions and reflections, on the acting area (a technique frequently used in modern times);[14] and there is the medieval mystery play[15] and the tradition of stage managers communicating with the audience[16] (quite apart from the abuse current in the French baroque and rococo theatre, where privileged members of the audience were allowed to sit on the stage itself).

This communication rests on a convention, namely, that the stage represents the world, and that, through this serious play —"the play can only be wholly *play* if the playing is done seriously"[17]—we recognize that the poet's *Logos* has become incarnated, in the "nonserious" fiction that pretends to represent reality. We can never separate the essence of the performance

---

"aesthetic" isolation from the seriousness of existence: in the first place "the spectator is not summoned to give aid, but to view the suffering", and furthermore he is not educated to have compassion with those who are really suffering (and not merely acting it), in whom "there is no evidence of pleasure in pain". All this is quite apart from the indecency of the plays Augustine had seen.

[14] To name but a few: Racine in his two last plays, many baroque dramas, Schiller in *Die Braut von Messina* and *Demetrius*, Strindberg in his *A Dream Play*, Eliot in *Murder in the Cathedral*, Auden in *The Ascent*, Dürrenmatt in *Die alte Dame*, Frisch in *Biedermann*, etc. In opera the chorus becomes a permanent institution.

[15] Where "the whole town becomes a stage" (H. O. Burger, *Dasein heisst eine Rolle spielen* [1963], 82). In 1596 *Gottfried von Bouillon* (based on Tasso's *Gerusalemme Liberata*) was performed: "The prologue . . . endeavors to obliterate the division between stage and auditorium, the distinction between players and audience. . . . One is reminded of comedies of the romantic period or even of Bertolt Brecht's *Verfremdungseffekt*" (ibid.).

[16] H.-G. Gadamer, *Wahrheit und Methode*, 2d ed. (1965), 97.

[17] [L'univers de la représentation est essentiellement non sérieux, si tragique que soit l'action représentée.] H. Gouhier, *L'Essence du théâtre*, 38. Cf. Goethe, *Nachlese zu Aristoteles' Poetik* in *Über Kunst und Altertum* VI/1 (1827).

from this categorical convention. It is based, not on man's need for play and disguise, but, at a deeper level that is concerned with illuminating human existence; author, actors and audience are all involved with this level. This is what really fascinates us, and it is analogous to the sacral, just as the theatre is analogous to the realm of cult. But it is *only* an analogy and nothing more. We can see this most clearly, perhaps, in the fact that in the religious, cultic area, man must first "purify" himself before gaining admittance, before being allowed to participate in the sacred action and attain inner "enlightenment" and "perfection"—and here we are using the classical, Neoplatonic degrees that were so warmly adopted into the Christian scheme of things. In the ancient mysteries, "purification" (*katharsis*) was generally the necessary precondition, leading to the cultic action (*drōmena*, compare "drama") and perfect vision (*epopteia, teletē*). In the drama, this sequence of events takes place simultaneously: according to *Aristotle* the action itself carries out the catharsis (*drōntōn kai ou di epaggelias*)—whatever he understands by the term.[18] All the same, though the difference between cult and theatre seems greater than their similarity, we would not be justified in separating the two. For even the unpurified spectator, moved and carried along by the "purificatory" action, is drawn into a process of catharsis whereby, willy-nilly, he is placed before the same horizon as that to which the cult refers. This raises open questions to which we shall have to return.

So far we have understood the "audience" as a function of the theatre, in relation to the performance. However, there arises the disturbing possibility of isolating this function from the other elements and giving it independent existence. Of course this only makes sense if we can see through it to the concrete "theatre of the world", and then the question arises, as it does with uncanny insistence in *Ludwig Tieck's* short play *Ein Prolog* (1896, WW [1829] 13, 241–266), long before *Beckett's Waiting for Godot*: Will there be anything to see at all? For we do not know *what* will be played. *Will* anything be played? "Who can guarantee that we shall really see something here? In vain we hope at the end for light; perhaps there is neither director nor poet." This is

[18] *Poetics* 6.

countered by the fact of the audience's expectant hope: "Where would this longing come from, if there were no plays?" Just as shoes show us that there are such things as feet and legs, so man's yearnings lead us to infer that there is something that will fulfill them: "If we're patient and only hope, in the end the theatre will open up." But someone points out that no one has ever seen a director: "How then could a play come into being? . . . We . . . sit here and write, trying one thing or another, and that itself can be regarded as a play." If "there is no director *behind* the curtain", the play will be "performed *in front of* the theatre". Basically it is more amusing to watch human beings than to be a fellow spectator of a play on the stage. "What is the purpose of all this hoping and expecting? . . . Surely we ourselves are a sufficient comedy." The waiting audience becomes impatient, the theatre is in danger of emptying, and yet others keep coming in, with the result that the expectation is always fresh. A lamp cleaner asserts that he knows the director personally (this sounds like *Kafka*), and that if people are patient for a while they will "surely be amazed". An idealist ("Rüpel") is one of the waiting audience, and he claims to produce his entire external world; that is theatre enough for him. Someone else says: "When the curtain finally goes up we shall see what everyone experiences in his own home. . . . What a delight it will be to have our boring lives mirrored thus." Finally a buffoon tries to make a synthesis of all the different views, concluding: "And so it remains, my friends, / For us to hope (most strangely) for things / Which at the moment seem pure senseless fiction; / But we'll soon return to our former conviction. / This, I thought, to shorten the time / Would be the best pantomime." In these few pages *Tieck* produces a play with many aspects of meaning that is ultimately directed against the Christian hope of eternal life (as the beginning and end of the "world theatre") and that curtails the theatrical dimension of existence to life as it is here and now, with its hope, ennui, scepticism and disappointment. There is nothing to be seen but the hope of seeing something. This being so, people are right to say that the stage can show nothing but the boredom and lack of fulfillment that characterize everyday life.

c. Horizon

In our analysis of the aspects of dramatic production and dramatic realization, we kept finding a horizon within which the dramatic action takes place and to which the dramatist, the actors and the audience are all related. Naturally there are broad areas of the stage business where the only concern is the demand for and the supply of diversion, where the audience remains enclosed in its own amusement (*Brecht* referred to the "culinary theatre", particularly in connection with opera), laughing, chuckling or shedding a few tears at man's all-too-human nature. Or it may simply follow some train of events that could be read just as well in a weekly magazine. This is not something we need to criticize or despise. But for as long as theatre has existed, in all its high periods—which were clearly characterized by something over and above the business side of things—people have asked more of drama than this. People have sought insight into the nature and meaning of existence, things that cannot simply be read off from its immanent course but radiate from a background that explodes the beautiful and gripping play on the stage—which suddenly becomes inwardly relevant to the spectator—and that relates it to something that transcends it. *Julius Rütsch* has put it profoundly: the drama affirms that

> its closed world is an independent world; it tends to make the author into a myth, a strange, shadowy background against which his own, disembodied existence glows like a suspended sphere. And at the same time, precisely on entering into the dramatic "I", one realizes that to limit one's reflection to this "I" would render it fruitless. It would remain nothing more than a description that did not even do justice to the depth of the impression given by the performance; for in the performance the "I" of the stage blends with the "I" of the spectator, merging with the latter's living finitude. In this way it points in the opposite direction too, beyond itself.[19]

That is, it points toward the intention of the author, and beyond him to the horizon of all meaning whatsoever. The spectator, who has a general willingness to be impressed by the fate of the

---

[19] *Das dramatische Ich im deutschen Barocktheater* (Zurich, 1932), 19.

stage characters, is suddenly seized at a deeper level than he expected: he is no longer in charge of his own participation; he himself is called into question by his experience of the play; he is struck by "it".

This being "struck" is what *Aristotle* meant when he described the effect of tragedy as being in virtue of *phobos* (fear, horror) and *eleos* (heartfelt grief); the two concepts are related. According to *Aristotle* the first also contains *tarachē*: "a disturbing elementary emotion of direct power, called forth by the idea of the imminent threat of severe pain or annihilation".[20] Here we can ignore the fact that the ethico–humanitarian interpretation of *eleos* as "compassion" (current since *Lessing*) distorts the original meaning;[21] we can even leave aside the question whether the catharsis achieved by the two emotions is simply a purification in the sense of a more or less lasting purgation, a sense of relief at the tragedy's conclusion; it is enough if the object of this fear is the whole human condition, with the result that the spectator is frightened out of his spectator's vantage point and feels that he too is profoundly threatened. And if this is true of genuine tragedy, it applies no less to genuine comedy: by laughing at man's ridiculousness he is laughing at himself and allowing himself to be called in question. But what is the horizon within which this can take place?

We must also remember that theatre is something that goes on in public, even if in our time and in our countries the members of the audience sit next to one another related by nothing but the fortuitous buying of tickets. The interpretation of existence that is being presented is public, even in places where the religious dimension has been almost completely privatized. But it is precisely this public aspect that places a new question mark over the opening-up of an ultimate horizon. Can

[20] It is unnecessary to go into the original meaning of these two highly loaded words which, since Lessing, have been translated as "pity" (*Mitleid*) and "fear" (*Furcht*). Cf. the celebrated (but not unchallenged) treatment by Wolfgang Schadewaldt: "Furcht und Mitleid? Zur Deutung des Aristotelischen Tragödienansatzes" in *Hermes* 83 (1955): 129–71; also in *Hellas und Hesperien* (1960), 346–88, quotation on p. 349.

[21] Particularly his "Briefwechsel über das Trauerspiel" with M. Mendelssohn and F. Nicolai, ed. and annotated by J. Schulte-Sasse (1972), and numerous passages in the *Hamburgische Dramaturgie*.

a playhouse expect today's "privatized" audience to accept such an opening-up of horizons in public? Will this audience respond at all to such a suggestion? *Schiller* observed, "It will surely be difficult for the stage to shape [*bilden*] its audience before the audience is educated [*gebildet*] for its stage"[22]—although he later had a more favorable view of the audience.[23] Yet in the long run the will to embrace an open horizon seems irrepressible; the very fact of the theatre being conventionalized as a public institution automatically gives rise to protest. Such protest may come from a writer or a stage company or an audience, where people unite to demand something different, not content to be fed with *ersatz* horizons and not prepared to accept a conspiracy to abridge reality.

But what are the marks of this horizon, and how does it open up before us? Greek theatre was a dramatic presentation for the gods; they sat, invisible, behind and above the scene, and from time to time one of them could step forward or send a representative on to the stage. But we also know how torn this background was; it too was dramatically and even tragically rent asunder, as in Prometheus, the Titan who, in his struggle against Zeus, belongs entirely neither to the world of gods nor to the world of men.

This world of gods determines destinies; its highest name, embracing everything in unity, is Zeus, and yet it is men, poets, who are endowed with speech for this dumb world of gods.[24] Thus there arise figures from the mythical past, expressing their thanks to the poet; he gives them the final word in the name of the *polis*—as at the end of the *Oresteia*—but in reality it is he himself who utters them. Or (lest we oversimplify something

[22] Schiller, *Über das gegenwärtige teutsche Theater*, in *Sämtliche Werke*, 814.

[23] "It is not true, as is commonly said, that the public drags art down; it is the artist who drags the public down, and whenever art has declined it has been due to the artist. The public needs nothing but receptivity, and this it has. . . . It is able to appreciate the highest things" (Schiller, *Über den Gebrauch des Chors in der Tragödie*, in *Sämtliche Werke*, 815).

[24] On this issue see Hans Ehrenberg, *Tragödie und Kreuz*, vol. 1, *Die Tragödie unter dem Olymp* (Würzburg: Patmosverlag, 1920, subsequently Verlag der Arbeitsgemeinschaft in Berlin).

that is full of double meaning), he brings forth these words of his own innermost power, as "Athens", while at the same time gratefully receiving them from "Athene".

The borderline between men and gods remains opaque, like that between the gods themselves, whose fields of influence mutually restrict each other, always producing both trust and suspicion. This double relationship persists among the philosophers even after the process of demythologizing; the horizon remains split: on the one hand a quasi-personal "providence" (successor to Zeus and the personal and national tutelary gods), and on the other hand an impersonal and hence pitiless "fate" that somehow or other exercises a subordinate authority while having power over all that comes into being and passes away. The dualism between providence (*pronoia, providentia*) and fate (*heimarmene, fatum, fortuna*) remains open in the tragedies of *Seneca*, which transpose the Greek classics into a philosophical mode. And if the world of fate is experienced in countless death masks as a constant threat to life, the stoic can only take refuge in the authority of reason, which is superior to death and is simultaneously the highest and most divine and the most interior and most human.

In the ancient world, the spectator's gaze toward the horizon of tragedy must remain obscured: the whole realm of mortal man can provide a stage for great events and actions, but it contains no fixed point to which the heart might attach itself, where thought might come to rest. The crucial question remains: How far can "providence" make use of "fate" if we are to penetrate the foreground meaninglessness (ground that seems, at least, to be lost) and look for signs of a hidden meaning? However, an idea such as this will only be able to assert itself seriously where the ultimate horizon of "providence" is not only *understood* as almighty power in a state of repose, but also *believed in*, in an opening to the world that also takes initiatives in it: that is, in Christianity.

In the ancient world the horizon remained veiled because it had a twofold ambivalence; it was internally split and hence unclear in its relationship to man—Did it hold aloof from him, or was it on his side? Thus *Seneca's* attitude in his tragedies

remains ultimately dualistic: he arouses our interest by portraying terrible, destructive passion in the realm that is subject
to death, but passion can be overcome only through total
negation and flight into the undramatic higher world and the
world of interiority. The issue of providence versus fate is
continued in Christendom through the tremendous influence of
the idea of Fortuna (ever since *Boethius*) in the Christian middle
ages, and through *Seneca's* influence on Christian drama, which
began in the fourteenth century. Its effects are equally strong in
Shakespeare's histories as in the dramas and comedies of *Calderon*.
In both these Christian poets, however, pure dualism—which
as such can produce only "terror and grief"—gives way to a
mysterious interplay between the two spheres that allows us to
sense, behind fate's surface, something of that providence that
sight can never penetrate, namely, in the relationship between
guilt and grace. Grace, here, is the all-embracing alternative to
expiation, which could only mean a ruthless restoring of balance
within the realm of fate, or else man's own method of dealing
with guilt by his own power. Christian drama can represent the
interplay of the two spheres in very different ways: in *Calderon*,
for example, Fortuna can appear as a kind of unpredictable
"goddess", internal to the world, with her menacingly turning
wheel.[25] But the dominion she exercises, or her horoscope-like
determinism, can shatter as a result of the combination of
person ("free will") and divine providence, and be reintegrated
as one element in a higher context.[26] In *Life Is a Dream* we have

[25] One among countless examples: in the first act of *Die grosse Zenobia* the
vanquished Decius warns the rising Emperor Aurelian (whose successor he will
be): "Today am I scorned by all / And you have risen upon my fall. / Now I sink,
to rise once more, / You rise now, but your fall is set: / O be not haughty!" In act
III Aurelian holds his triumphal procession, with the conquered Zenobia in
chains at his feet, calling up to him: "For, weary of these plaudits, the wheel
could turn so easily / And I may see you at my feet / As you behold me now."
This does in fact come about. On the so-called tragedies of destiny, *Die Tochter
der Luft* and *Herodes und Mariamne* ("Jealousy, that greatest monster") see below,
excursus on *Fate, Freedom and Providence in Calderon*.

[26] "No power can conquer the freedom of the will" (*Das Schisma von
England*, act III). "Neither magic nor incantation / Can master free will" (*Der
wundertätige Magus*, act II). "Free will knows well how to guide the turns of

the most magnificent portrayal of the overcoming of fate.[27]
There are analogies in *Shakespeare, Corneille* and *Racine.*

Christian drama sets forth a horizon that, in virtue of its
clarified idea of God, has a more unified effect than that of the
ancient world, but at the same time its infinitely deepened
dramatic context (embracing man and God) is patient of hidden
and diverse interpretation. In Greek tragedy it was possible for a
god to step out of the invisible background of watching deities
and appear on stage; he could proclaim divine thoughts and
intentions, but only as an individual, not on behalf of the entire
divine world. Christ, the Son of God, is not just *any* incarnation:
he is the sole incarnation, revealing God's whole mind. God the
Father, who sends him, remains in the background as the real
"spectator" before whom "the great theatre of the world" is
performed; but since Father and Son are one, this role of
spectator on God's part cannot be separated from his entering
into the action on the stage. And when the Spirit proceeds from
the Father and the Son and is breathed into the Church of
Christ, something of God himself speaks in the mouths of the
actors. The ancient world's ultimately stoic and Neoplatonic
pact between what is most interior in man, on the one hand, and
the divine on the other, comes back again, now cleansed of
pantheism. Now, as before, the horizon within which the play
is acted out is by no means an uninvolved background that
relativizes the entire foreground play to the level of shadowy
futility (and this is what it was, ultimately, in the later ancient
world, where, as "providence", it offered a horizon of meaning
superior to the play of fate); now, with a dramatic dimension
that bursts forth from the Absolute itself, it comes to meet the

---

fortune / According to its own design. . . . There is no destiny where love rules"
(*Blinde Liebe*, act II), among others.

[27] In Calderon an apparently inevitable prophecy can ultimately be made to
serve at a higher level and be fulfilled in a way quite different from that expected.
In the *Constant Prince* the ill omens on the landing of the Portuguese army at
Tangiers (act I, scene 2) are dispelled by the martyrdom of Fernando, and
similarly the prophecy to the beautiful Phoenix, that she must be "the price for
one of the dead", is resolved at a supernatural level (act II, scene 1; act III, final
scene: "I am the price for one of the dead / According to heaven's decree"). See
below the excursus on *Fate, Freedom and Providence in Calderon.*

human play and imparts to it an ultimate destination, acting alongside man, from within. The uniqueness of the Christian conception of the horizon must be acknowledged: in it, and in it alone, meaning breaks forth (in a hidden manner, discerned by faith, in and through the stumbling block of Christ's Cross) from the depth of the horizon and informs the whole foreground action of the world play. For the present we leave aside the question of how far and how deeply this view was able to shape drama in a Christian way. We can surmise in advance, however, that a dramatic dimension that comes from God's horizon and is implanted in the world, comprehending and judging everything within the world and leading it toward its redemptive meaning, is so unique and exuberant that it can only be reflected in a fragmentary and broken way on the stage. Human eyes can never grasp as a whole the drama that unfolds from the horizon without falsifying the proportions; it does this in order to set up a serviceable standard for intramundane drama. *Calderon's* "Great Theater of the World" is played before a *Father-God* who watches the play and finally acts as judge; this end causes the Son's Eucharist to appear, but otherwise the Son plays his part invisibly on the world stage; true, his "Spirit" is expressed in the play's title (*Obra bien, que Dios es Dios*), and is recalled from time to time by the "Law", but it remains strangely external to the players. Against this we have the great martyr dramas of *Calderon* and the entire baroque theatre; their greatness lies in taking the element of *Christ's* dying as the focus of the horizon, but in doing so they run the risk of regarding this death as something that man himself can undertake (in a stoic vein). This is what happens in *The Constant Prince*; the prince has prior knowledge of his canonization and actually heralds it. In other words, the danger is that human death will be accorded the same significance as the unique death of the Son of God. Or the focus can be shifted to the Holy Spirit of Christianity; the danger here is that people can forget, to a greater or lesser extent, that in Christian terms the Spirit only becomes available to the world through the drama of Christ's death and Resurrection. *Lessing* says that the purpose of tragedy is to arouse pity in the audience (pity is for him the core of the humanitarian outlook); the classical, humanitarian drama of *Weimar* develops along these lines, eventually to be absorbed into *Hegel's* aesthetics (and his total system of "spirit"). Thus, as has been shown most penetratingly,[28] the whole horizon is incorporated into the subject, that is, into the total subject of the World Spirit, which affects and observes itself in its inner dramatic dimensions. In this total subject the difference between spectator, stage and horizon is submerged in identity.

For the Christian believer, the horizon opened up by God thus contains an unimaginable richness of different vantage points within unity, but this unity is never completely available to the dramatist because, essentially, it is *God's* unity, dramatically revealed. Christian drama, therefore, can only act *in the presence of* God, knowing that it is embraced by him; it can never allow the drama that flows from the horizon to be absorbed into the drama that presses toward the horizon. This is an almost unavoidable danger for the Christian stage; it is the reason for the splintering of drama in the post-Christian era, where the horizon's three interlocking foci fall apart, so far apart, indeed, that any idea of the play referring to a real, transcendent horizon becomes itself questionable. But it may be that this very fragmentation of the one (and triune) Christian horizon into various indispensable and yet irreconcilable pieces actually points to the unique horizon that man himself cannot construct. We shall come to this in the theological part of the present work.

All post-Christian drama can be regarded as a fragment of a drama that presses toward the Christian horizon. For now, as then, the drama is enacted in the face of an ultimate, supraindividual authority that judges between good and evil and is represented in man by the voice of conscience, even if the subject matter that exhibits this distinction is purely secular, entirely unreligious, and even if the horizon is cloaked in anonymity. Just such a fragment is that post-Christian drama that takes death as its absolute cardinal point, in whichever of its mysterious meanings (liberation, atonement, substitution, the ultimate act, the door into a transformed future, and so forth). It is not for nothing that the remains of idealism in *Schiller's* plays,

[28] Manfred Züfle, "Theater als weltlicher Ort", in *Theater als Aergernis?* (Münchner Akad.) Schriften 48 (1969): 41–66.

for instance (the belief that the empirical, mortal "I" can be overcome by the power of the ethical and intelligible), cling so closely to Christian themes: they provide the necessary resonance. Everything, in the end, must be regarded as a Christian fragment—perhaps hardly recognizable—that calls for the transformation of the hearts of individuals and of society and its conditions and structures. (This is the perspective of the Holy Spirit.) Thus the entire horizon toward which the dramatic action presses forward is shifted into a future that man must hope for and work for. This "horizontalizing" of the horizon is the consequence of that "absolutizing" of the perspectives of Spirit that comes down to us from the Enlightenment (*Lessing*) and *Hegel* and finds its logical continuation in *Marx*. The "Absolute" becomes an "ought" with which man's total consciousness must be inoculated so that it can practically set about bringing in this new reality. Critics of Marxism have always been aware that this view is only fragmentary and that, as such, it must show itself to be a utopian undertaking, that is, one that has no place in the real world and has a destructive influence on what *has* a place there. Such criticism (compare *Ionesco's* attacks on *Brecht*) is valid, even if the critics themselves have no more credible horizon to offer and positively refuse to put one forward (*Beckett*). Nonetheless, *Brecht's* outburst at the end of his *The Good Woman of Szechuan* with its shrill succession of question marks,[29] as well as the stifled absence of any human word and any meaningful gesture in *Beckett's* last plays, show clearly enough that, where there is no way out, there is still a horizon, emitting something like a light of meaning.

In the face of this fragmenting of the horizon in the post-Christian era we can ask this question: How can theatre, as a public institution, bring together people who hold different world-views? What is it (for surely it cannot be simply amusement) that unites these people who come with active expectation and a readiness to "enter into" the action? Under what denominator does it bring them through the performance? It is a

---

[29] "Do we need a different human being? Or a different world? Or perhaps just different gods? Or none at all? We have been *really* smashed to pieces, not just *apparently.* . . . Off you go, members of the audience, and find the conclusion for yourselves: there must be a good one there somewhere, there must, there must!"

very long time since the theatre had a homogeneous audience, such as the baroque theatre had and on which it could exercise a deliberately didactic influence (compare the "ruthless formative power" of French classicism).[30] Yet it still has the power to place man in acute, inescapable situations that strip him naked and confront him with the unavoidable question: Who is he, this being who exists in terrible finitude? His situation in the world is a dramatic one; even if he were to try to conceal it from himself, the stage would confront him with it. That is no small thing. It is not a cultic event, for the question "What is man?" does not oblige the spectator to give a definite answer. But it is a public act in which, through the participation of the audience, something like a "communion" is brought about. One could think of the theatre as a kind of ecumenical institution: it does not get too close to any particular denominational form, nor yet does it aim at a watered down common version; it points the different beliefs forward and up, toward a unity that is at present unattainable. This unity lies in the larger-than-life content of the performed play. "Freely consenting to the dramatic fiction, the various forms of belief converge toward the proposed universe, forgetting personal ideologies and opinions."[31] Moreover, "the equilibrium becomes possible only through a compromise with regard to the ambivalence of the stage event, in which the contradictory forces measure up to each other and achieve a floating balance."[32] They are by no means leveled out in the harshness and pluralism of everyday life; but here is a place where every proposal for a solution has to reexamine itself in the face of the publicly posed question.

We have indicated the Christian breadth and depth of the horizon, which shows that the post-Christian perspectives are only fragments of it. We can go farther and suggest that true ecumenism—however anonymous, unconscious or even rejected it may be—takes place within this most open of horizons.

---

[30] E. Brock-Sulzer, *Theater*, 215.

[31] A. Villiers, *La Psychologie de l'art dramatique*, 74.

[32] *Ibid.*, 78. Cf. H. Gouhier, "De la communion au théâtre", in *L'Essence du théâtre*, 215ff., where a clear distinction is drawn between the religious act and the theatre which is as such nonreligious. But the true stage poet "souhaite non la fusion mais la convergence des coeurs" (220).

Excursus: Brecht and Ionesco

In everything that we have said in the preceding two sections, the voice of *Bertolt Brecht* has been heard in the background like a radio-jamming transmitter. We have spoken as if his radical criticism of the middle-class theatre of escapism and illusion did not exist, as if he had never replaced the dramatic theatre with the epic theatre, resulting logically in his new theory of dramatic art (that is, that it no longer consists in the actor "feeling himself into" his role [empathy], but calls for a conscious distance between the two, so that the character being played is only "shown", and can thus be handed over to the audience for its critical appraisal).

The web that *Brecht*[1] so tirelessly spins consists of diverse strands that are hard to disentangle. We must isolate the most important of them if we are to assess the relevance of his critical objections. Like *Pirandello, Ionesco, Dürrenmatt* and others he finds that the world's situation has put a question mark over the whole theatrical activity. His suggestions as to how the crisis can be overcome sound more resolute, but it is precisely his best creative efforts that secretly or openly contradict his theory.

Whereas *Diderot* had objected to the actor's technique of "empathy" for purely aesthetic reasons, *Brecht* rejects it on the basis of a vehement critique of the (middle-class) audience's need for empathy: the audience wants to be "transported" into a state in which it "stares vacantly" at the stage as if "entranced"—a term that comes from the "middle ages of witches and clerics". It wants to "surrender to vague but powerful emotions",[2] to cast aside "all restraint",[3] using the theatre purely "aesthetically", as a "means of pleasure",[4] and looking for "illusions rather than experience, wanting to swoon rather than to be elevated, to be deceived rather than to be enlightened".[5] All this, according to

---

[1] We are not dealing thematically with the plays themselves. Cf. my essay in H. U. von Balthasar and Manfred Züfle, *Der Christ auf der Bühne* (1967), 137–82, reprinted in *Spiritus Creator, Skizzen zur Theologie* III (1967), 366–406 (abbreviated *Spiritus Creator*). Here we are concerned with his *Schriften zum Theater*, quoted according to the *Gesammelte Werke*, vols. 15–17 of the Suhrkamp Edition (1967), abbreviated here as GW. The *Kleines Organon* is quoted by number. Some passages are found in the *Schriften zum Theater*, "Über eine nicht-aristotelische Dramatik" (1962), abbreviated hereafter ST.

[2] *Organon*, no. 26.

[3] *Organon*, no. 72.

[4] *Organon*, Preface, 661; against the magical effect of the theatre and the trance: 341.

[5] 294.

Brecht, characterizes the end of a period and is symptomatic of resistance to the onset of the next. But we have entered the scientific age and are thus "challenged to adopt, not a passive stance that lacks will and rests on magic and hypnosis, but a critical attitude".[6] The dramatic arts may originally have come from cultic practice, but today they must "liquidate the vestiges of their cultic past that still cling to them from former times; they must also leave the stadium where they helped man to interpret the world and enter the stadium where they can help to change it."[7] Thus *Brecht's* program is already adumbrated.

It is based on the insight that science has given man power over nature, but that, so far, he has failed energetically to apply this power to the social conditions on which—whether yesterday, today or tomorrow—man's destiny depends. Furthermore, "the great themes of our time . . . the development of industry on a mammoth scale, the class struggle, war, world trade, combating disease" cannot be portrayed by the old theatre, "not, at least, in a fittingly great way".[8] To do this on the stage, both author and actor need a new technique, the technique of distanced and informative demonstration (= "epic theatre"),[9] and the audience needs a new approach, that is, reflection. Instead of the individualistic "theatre of amusement" we have the socio-didactic theatre.[10] It is no longer the feelings that are addressed, but the

[6] 223.

[7] 246. The modern theatre is precarious: the privatizing of the relationship between audience and stage has undermined the theatre's public character, with the result that the public has "no faith" in the theatre (329–31). There is no contact between stage and auditorium (83), no real appetite among the audience (125). There is a spurious cult of the "classics", whose social problems were entirely different from ours and whose solutions are no solutions for us. For Brecht the classics are useful only in providing "material" (106, 176–81). The "great individuals" of Shakespeare, for example, have developed into today's "capitalists" (127). In spite of his great veneration for Stanislavsky, Brecht takes him to task primarily for his sacral treatment of the theatre (380, 382).

[8] 236. Brecht sees a significant approach to this in Bernard Shaw (97, 101), whereas he regards the attempts of naturalism (139, 151, 169 [= 215], 201, 207 [= 214], 219) and expressionism (252, 292) as worthless. The former subjects man to determinisms of milieu, genetics, etc., and the latter, while it speaks of liberation, cannot bring it about.

[9] Because the subject matter is too "vast" for anyone to "feel himself into it" (186). Brecht is interested to hear "that Friedrich Dürrenmatt . . . has questioned whether the modern world can be shown at all by the theatre". He admits that this is "increasingly difficult" and sees epic theatre as the only solution, which can only describe the world by portraying it "as a world that can be transformed" (929).

[10] 143.

reason.[11] Nowadays man is risking everything. How could he possibly want to avoid commitment, and in the theatre of all places?[12]

We must acknowledge that there is much in what *Brecht* says here, particularly as he is always careful to restore the balance. Having rejected the theatre of pure euphoria (à la *Wagner*), he largely reestablishes the connection with the rational and also critical stance of the Greek and of the baroque audience, acknowledging that reason and emotion are not mutually exclusive and that noble, humane feeling is prompted by rational insight.[13] Nor is there any opposition, in principle, between the approach of the artist and that of the critic;[14] in this sense the theatre can also be called "a school of the emotions".[15] As far as the audience (and the whole theatrical process) is concerned, *Brecht* demands increasingly that "instruction" shall go hand in hand with "entertainment";[16] he stresses that, for *Schiller*, the theatre was indeed a "moral institution", a "place of edification",[17] but that he also saw it as "most certainly a pleasurable institution".[18] The reason why the modern theatre is so joyless[19] is that it contains nothing to learn, no distinctions to be drawn. On the other hand *Brecht* will not accept the objection that the actor's demonstrative function renders his acting unnatural or uncommitted and that he is simply juxtaposed to the character he represents, without emotional involvement. (For the actor is permitted to smoke whenever he has nothing to say.) Thus, in *Brecht*, *Diderot's*

---

[11] "The new aim is education" (198).

[12] "The spectator must not share the characters' experiences: he must reach decisions about them" (132).

[13] 242, 246.

[14] 377–78, 542, 919.

[15] 929.

[16] 285. He bases himself on the Enlightenment founders of stage aesthetics, Diderot and Lessing.

[17] 627.

[18] 270.

[19] 83. On humor in art: 120f.; on art's essential "superfluousness": 664; art provides instruction in the form of entertainment: ST 105; appendix to the *Kleines Organon*: 702. On morality and pleasure: 270; on the pleasure of learning: 267; theatre must always be entertaining: 663, 699. In agreement with Aristotle and Schiller, Brecht maintains that the enjoyment side of the theatre must persist through even the most terrible portrayals: "One of the actor's main tasks is to be attractive. He must carry out everything, especially the frightful things, with enjoyment, and he must show his enjoyment. If a person cannot teach while entertaining and cannot entertain while teaching, he does not belong on the stage" (411). It is Brecht's experience that "it is precisely the most rational form, the didactic play, that elicits the most emotional reactions" (242).

argument lives on ("Reason purifies our feelings", "the opposition between reason and emotion only exists in the minds of the unreasonable").[20] Nor will *Brecht* dispense totally with "empathy", particularly in rehearsal.[21] The actor must not become stereotyped, "he must not lose naturalness",[22] his acting must exhibit "full bodiliness".[23] In particular characters he can use "effects arising from empathy",[24] but "not for a moment must he allow himself to become totally transformed into the character"; he must not "simply live the character".[25] From very early on (1930), and increasingly over time, *Brecht* points to the Asian, and particularly Chinese art of demonstrative drama,[26] and also mentions—though only for the sake of its didactic aim—both "the medieval mystery play and the classical Spanish and Jesuit theatre".[27]

These references to history and this toning-down of a theory of drama that fundamentally places the actor *beside*, and not *in*, his role, cannot conceal the fact, however, that in *Brecht* this theory has a specific root, particularly as he himself senses "a certain *contradiction* here"[28] that he tries to resolve. It is not only the contradiction that the actor develops feelings that are not necessarily his (*Diderot's* paradox), but also that he "is not playing a role" only "giving instruction", "citing a character", "being a witness to a process". This is symptomatic of a whole complex of problems associated with the Brechtian theatre.

Quite simply, the basic contradiction is that *Brecht*, as a Marxist, believes in materialistic determinism, and yet at the same time he appeals to human freedom to decide to change the prevailing conditions. In his celebrated "two-column list", in which the dramatic and epic forms of the theatre are compared, the epic is said to "compel the spectator to make decisions" (instead of producing "feelings" like the dramatic theatre); but he also says that it shows "what man *must* do" (instead of "what man *ought to* do", as the dramatic theatre does). In the dramatic theatre "thought determines being", whereas in the epic "social being determines thought".[29] In spite of this "must", *Brecht* is continually summoning the spectator to make free decisions, and the

---

[20] 919.

[21] 52, 249, 342, 686; "Dramatic art does not need to dispense entirely with empathy, but it must also facilitate a critical attitude on the part of the spectator, and it can do this without losing its artistic character" (377).

[22] 370.   [23] 344.   [24] 314.

[25] *Kleines Organon*, no. 48.

[26] 202ff., 368, 424–28. But Brecht pays too little attention here to the fact that life that is shown forth (e.g., the making of tea), as well as the dramatic demonstrations in the Chinese theatre, have become conventions and rituals.

[27] 272.   [28] 351.   [29] 1009–10.

actor is supposed to distance himself from the character he is showing so that "the audience is left perfectly free".[30] The audience "must be able to interpose its own verdict",[31] because in the play it becomes evident that what is shown is not necessarily so. "The spectator of the dramatic theatre says: . . . Things must always be thus", this is eternally the human situation. "The spectator of the epic theatre says: . . . This must stop. The suffering of this human being moves me profoundly because there could be a way out for him."[32] And this is precisely what the actor must show: there must be "something concrete, something unique about the character he is playing, that would make him able, within particular sociological limits, to respond differently".[33] The actor should question, and have a critical approach to, the character he is playing,[34] and should show the nonnecessity of the character's actions, thus revealing in the background the other, opposite possibility as well.[35] The postulate that circumstances "must be changed" is so strong that it forcibly elicits the "can be changed", not only as far as present and future are concerned, but also in the past as portrayed. The purpose of all this, in *Brecht's* dramatic theory, is not to make the audience into a collective enjoying itself, but to bring the individual spectators to personal decisions: "It polarizes the audience."[36] It creates "conflict in the auditorium".[37]

At this point we must ask where *Brecht's* human being got this freedom, since, even before *Brecht's* communist period, he had been totally deprived of it in any personal sense, in favor of an impersonal chance. It was *Brecht's* fate to rescue himself and his human beings from all cultural addictions, but without having anywhere to go to. Violently he tears himself loose from a decaying bourgeoisie, to commit himself to a socialism that, with the onset of the Third Reich, once more makes him an alien and an emigrant; in his mature years he never totally identified himself with it. It is a negative freedom, resistant to all modern fascinations: the freedom of being at home nowhere.[38] His early plays had inflated man into a monster of total chance (*Baal*) or of amoral vitality (*Im Dickicht der Städte*), which was bound to collapse into the anonymity of Galy Gay in *Mann ist Mann*—who, since he is nil in terms of personality, can only too easily be revamped into a different role, even that of a Fascist war hero. It is well known that *Brecht* was

[30] 685.   [31] 694.   [32] 265.   [33] 405.

[34] 688, 690, 693.

[35] 363, 686; cf. 409: "the not-but".

[36] ST 39.   [37] 927.

[38] Jean Auger Duvignaud, *L'Acteur*, 263ff. The author rightly shows how, for Brecht, Hitler became the paradigm of the hypnotizing magician-actor.

later embarrassed by this play;[39] but he must have been even more embarrassed by another of his plays, *Die Massnahme* (*The Measures Taken*), in which he uses this negative chance (the fact that man is nobody) as a basis for the young comrade's absolute decision to accept the party line. The play, first performed in the Grosses Schauspielhaus in Berlin in 1930, split the working class among the audience. *Brecht* changed a few passages for the first publication,[40] and in all subsequent editions the text is "annihilated", remaining "a pitiful torso".[41] What was the thrust of the first version? It was that the party's concrete decision is a "summons" addressed to the individual; through it he becomes personalized, that is, rendered useful for the absolute norm of "changing the world":[42] the "nobody" becomes himself in and through this summons. Here, doubtless, we have the counterpart, created by Marxism's "atheistic theatre",[43] to the Christian relationship between the creaturely human being and the summons that comes to him from the personal God and endows him with a mission. The difference here is that the personal absolute becomes an impersonal order; the program does not rest on a historical fact (Christ) but in a future that is to be created; and the total obedience, which man has to give if he is to be a true person, is rendered not by a someone who has been created free, but by a "nobody", anybody.[44] The young comrade in *Die Massnahme*, however, does not simply carry out the order in a functional way, but acts as a free, responsible human being in deciding against it. Three times, while on his mission, he is overwhelmed by compassion, wrath and indignation in the face of blatant injustice toward the poor, and he takes their part. In doing so he transgresses against the party's cool directive, which takes the long view. The present suffering is "monstrous", whereas the "classics" (*Marx* and *Lenin*) speak of "methods

[39] "Bei Durchsicht meiner ersten Stücke" (951–52). Cf. D. Schings, *Der Entpersonalisierung im Theater*, the chapter on Brecht.

[40] In bk. 4 of the *Versuche*. The original draft is no longer available. On this whole issue: Reinhold Grimm, "Ideologische Tragödie und Tragödie der Ideologie", in *Zft. f. dt. Philologie* 78 (1959): 394–424, printed with additional material in V. Sanders, *Tragik und Tragödie* (*Wege der Forschung* 108), 1971, 237–78 (abbreviated here as "Ideologische Tragödie").

[41] Grimm, "Ideologische Tragödie", 277.

[42] Thus as early as the *Badener Lehrstück vom Einverständnis* (1929).

[43] 174.

[44] At this point R. Grimm points to the frequently noted parallels between Marxist and Jesuit obedience, adding: "It is of no small interest to learn that Lenin learned Spanish with the express purpose of reading Ignatius of Loyola, whose writings he much admired, in the original" (Grimm, "Ideologische Tragödie", 266).

that lay hold of misery in its totality". "Does that mean that the classics are not in favor of coming to the aid of each and every distress immediately?" "—No." "—Then the classics are filth, and I tear them up. For it is the living human being who is crying out, and his misery smashes through all the dams of doctrine." The young comrade announces that he is "totally in agreement" with it, in order to do "only what is humane". But previously he had agreed to the order that called for the obliteration of all personal features, and so ultimately he must also agree to himself being shot by his comrades as guilty and thrown into the lime pit.

Here we are shown an inextricable contradiction between two absolute values; *Goethe* and *Schiller* had seen this as the essence of tragedy. In this sense *Die Massnahme* is perhaps the only genuine communist tragedy,[45] which *Brecht* recognized, causing him to mutilate the play and prevent it from being performed again. There should be no pure tragedy anymore on the communist stage, for a way out is always in sight.[46] Thus tragic situations in the past must be explicitly "historicized"; it must be shown that the lack of a "way out" at that time was only relative. True, there is a tragic contradiction in *Mutter Courage* that cannot be solved by the characters, but it can be solved by society.[47] But how is the individual to act if, like the young comrade, he is confronted with acute distress and wants to respond effectively to it? *Der gute Mensch von Sezuan* (*The Good Woman of Szechuan*) responds with that schizophrenia that characterizes the plays of *Brecht's* maturity;[48] in order, as Shen Te, to be able to cultivate the joy of goodness, the same "person" must sometimes appear as Shui Ta, embodying harshness and selfishness. It is her "duty" to do so, for only in this way can she fulfill the conditions for her goodness. Shui Ta is the pitiless law embodied by the comrades in *Die Massnahme*. One year after *Der gute Mensch*, *Brecht* wrote *Puntila*, which shows the incompatibility of the two "I"'s in the opposite manner: the landlord would like to be good, but in sober reality he cannot; he needs the utopian unreality of intoxication. Here the absolute criterion of world-transformation disappears; we cannot see how Puntila could move toward a merging of his contradictory modes of appearance. And when, in *Der kaukasische Kreidekreis* (*The Caucasian Chalk Circle*), the dichotomy seems finally overcome, it is only because the whole story is taken as a fairytale. (It even

[45] *Ibid.*, 247–49.

[46] *Kleines Organon*, no. 33.

[47] *Mutter Courage*, presented in two forms: 895–96.

[48] Walter H. Sokel, "Brechts gespaltene Charaktere und ihr Verhältnis zur Tragik", in V. Sanders, *Tragik und Tragödie*, 381–96.

contains the interlude of "justice humiliated"—Azdok—reminiscent of the mystery play tradition.)[49]

We see, therefore, that in *Brecht* the Marxist dialectic came across a concept of the person that had already been destroyed; man's ability-to-be-anything, confronted with this dialectic, meant that he found himself defenseless[50] against this self-styled absolute criterion; he had to suffer from this dialectic externally and internally, resulting in schizophrenia. But this very definition of the subject renders the drama's original horizon dubious: this horizon was entirely immanent in the stage action, namely, a humanity obedient to the Marxist program and technically equipped to transform the world. What we earlier defined as horizon no longer exists at all. But now this purely "horizontal" horizon is called into question existentially by the schizophrenic characters: How do the comrades in *Die Massnahme* have the right to kill their compassionate colleague without submitting themselves to being questioned by him? "*Die Massnahme* only half realizes . . . the ideological tragedy; of the two tragic possibilities only that of the young comrade becomes a reality", and the tragedy of the agitators remains potential. Who knows whether the latter will not be turned into the "compliant dwarfs" (of the play of *Galileo*) who "can be hired to do anything"?[51] Here the party directive is criticized because it only points to the future, sacrificing to it all the tragedy of the present; if this existential critique of ideology were acknowledged, we should see once more, behind the horizon manipulated by human hands and projected into the future, the true, transcendent, vertical horizon. This is the authority to which the here-and-now cry of Mutter Courage and Shen Te appeals.

However, in that case, despite all *Brecht's* thought-provoking, foreground teaching on the new theatre, the ultimate ideological purpose of the *Verfremdung* (the "alienation effect", according to which the actor is prohibited from genuinely taking over his role) begins to totter; for the human person is neither a chance all-and-nothing nor a sick

---

[49] The most shattering document of this vulnerability is Brecht's *Galilei*, whom he wanted to make into an "epochal" character in Hebbel's sense, a man responsible for the rising technology that would transform the world. In spite of his three subsequent versions and interpretations he did not succeed in giving the play a credible consistency. The hero with the personal conscience, standing against the age in which he lives, becomes a criminal responsible for the atom bomb, and finally the cowardly egoist who prefers to keep his skin rather than persist in the truth. The ethical value of the action initiated is determined by its success.

[50] Cf. H. U. von Balthasar and Manfred Züfle, *Spiritus Creator*, 402ff.

[51] Grimm, "Ideologische Tragödie", 271, 275.

schizophrenic, but a person with genuine freedom who can take responsibility for himself and, without surrendering his self, accept a mission of service.

A fruitful comparison can be drawn between *Brecht* and *Eugène Ionesco*, no doubt the only modern dramatist in the same class as *Brecht*, and one who consistently opposed him. Starting from an opposite point of view, however, he too failed to reach the dramatic dimension.

Ionesco[1] is best understood where he is unequivocal, that is, in categorically rejecting not only the communist, but also every other ideology. This makes his plays of existential contradiction intelligible, even where they go right up to the limit of self-annihilation. At least occasionally, his dramatic technique comes through this process and attains an ultimate translucence.

Everything may be explainable once existence is accepted as a fact, but this fact remains the object of infinite wonder.[2] It is "the most improbable thing" there is, both in the height it attains above the void and in the way the void constantly threatens it from within.[3] What is most incomprehensible is that *I* am, that I am *I*,[4] in the face of the certainty of death, which, though it brings me to an end, can never obliterate the fact that I did exist.[5] Externally everyone is replaceable;[6]

---

[1] Quoted according to the four-volume edition of plays (referenced in this section as I–IV) published by Gallimard (1954 to 1966). Also, in separate publications: *Jeux de Massacre* (1970); *Macbeth* (1972); *Notes et contre-notes* (1966; referenced in this section as N). Cf. Reinhold Grimm, "Brecht, Ionesco und das moderne Theater" in *German Life and Letters* XIII (Oxford, 1960), 221f. Further references in Ernst Wendt, *Ionesco* (1967).

[2] IV, 41f. A constantly recurring theme: N, 179, 225. This "wonder" is the common, super-temporal basis of all true thought, i.e., of mysticism, philosophy and poetry (N, 65).

[3] "I look around me, I look inside me and mutter: That is impossible, it's too improbable, it's not true, it cannot last. And in actual fact it will not last, either" (N, 296). "I am amazed that I exist . . . , amazed to be amazed, . . . amazed to be" (I, 212). "Astonishment is the fundamental tenor of my existence. I don't find the world tragic, but strangely comical, yes, and ridiculous. All the same, if I look at it for any length, I do feel a certain pain; something tears me. And this pain is a further source of astonishment, this tearing puzzles me" (N, 295).

[4] N, 17; "I feel uneasy in my existence . . . I cannot get used to myself. I do not know why I am" (IV, 23).

[5] I, 198–99; cf.: "You (the dying king) have been written eternally into the register" (IV, 55). But subsequently this is corrected: "You will be preserved in a mind that has no memory" (IV, 71).

[6] I, 322.

inwardly everyone is unique.[7] Everyone is alone in the face of his death, in the fear of it: *that* is what is common to man.[8] Only at the last level is the external, social dimension what is common; what is much more profoundly common to all is the nonsocial dimension.[9] Existence itself is the real drama, for it calls into being two states that alternate without warning: a state of overwhelming fullness, presence, floating bliss and lightness—and a state of emptiness and threat, which announces itself in the midst of the former floating state, turning it into an inexplicable deadweight.[10] The two extremes are always related: the longing (*Thirst and Hunger*) for the airy is bound to be experienced as a loss of substantial weight, and existence in this heavy, dull, everyday world becomes unbearable because of the urge toward freedom and fullness. Initially the pole of "ecstasy" is represented in terms of upward flight (*Victim to Duty*,[11] *Amédée*, *A Stroll in the Air*) or "light",[12] "ineffable euphoria",[13] equipoise, happiness beyond under-

---

[7] "They can be treated at the level of the mass and yet, at the same time, at their deepest level they are all individualists, all individual souls" (N, 292).

[8] "Man's fundamental constitution is characterized by loneliness and, above all, fear" (N, 123).

[9] N, 196: "It seems to me that what is fundamentally common to all is the nonhistorical" (N, 167); "I think that *all* society alienates, socialist society in particular. . . . Wherever man is regarded as a social function, there is alienation (for the social is the organization of functions). . . . But man is not only a social function" (N, 103); "So-called realism misses the deepest human realities: love, death, wonder, pain, the dreams of our extra-social hearts" (N, 274).

[10] "All my plays spring from two basic states of consciousness; sometimes one dominates, sometimes the other. . . . These are: volatility and heaviness; emptiness and a surfeit of presence; the world's unreal transparence and at the same time its opaqueness; light and profound darkness" (N, 230–31). In *Chairs*, for instance, we are presented with "the unreality of the real"; the two characters (who are themselves unreal) serve to identify a "world condemned to disappear" (N, 268). In *Victim to Duty* the dimensions ("at the bottom" and "at the highest level") are set forth: having reached the top, Choubert declares: "a happiness . . . a pain . . . a being torn . . . satisfaction . . . fullness . . . emptiness . . . a desperate hope. I feel strong, I feel weak, I feel bad, I feel well, but above all, I still *feel*" (I, 204). The policeman rebukes him for this: "You forget your duty. That is your mistake. You are too heavy; you are too light" (I, 213). "He is heavy when he ought to be light, too light when he ought to be heavy. He has no balance, he does not adapt himself to reality" (I, 215). In the interlude in *Amédée* the two characters represent the extreme tension: "Amédée, II: 'house of glass, of light', Madeleine, II: 'house of iron, house of night' " (I, 281).

[11] "Il va s'envoler" (I, 210).

[12] "Cité radieuse" in *Tueur sans gages*.

[13] II, 77.

standing,[14] the recalling of things forgotten[15]; but as *Ionesco's* work proceeds, the more clearly does this "upward transcendence" show itself to be an illusion. In *A Stroll in the Air*, from the loftiest heights, Bérenger observes the whole apocalyptic horror of the world, and in *The Killer* the "city of light" has already been laid waste by a senseless killer.[16] What remains is transhistorical: "No society has been able to annihilate human sadness, no political system can free us from life's pain, the fear of dying and our thirst for absolutes."[17] Note this latter expression: right through the contradictions of existence and unquenched by it runs the thirst for the Absolute. Conceptually we can distinguish two stages. First, the quality of existence on the edge of the void: "The world's extreme fragility and questionability: as if it all simultaneously existed and did not exist, hovering between being and nonbeing. This is the origin of my tragic jests."[18] They cannot be described as "absurd": "And yet, and yet: we exist. Perhaps there is a reason, beyond our rationality, for our existence: that too is possible."[19] The insubstantiality of reality prompts our thirst, "the search for a substantial, forgotten, unnamed reality".[20] But then, particularly when we realize that we have to die, an element of falseness shows itself: "Do we not have the impression that reality is false, that it does not correspond to us? That this world is not our real world? . . . Were we not made to understand everything, and yet we understand only very little? Were we not made to live together, and yet we tear each other to pieces? We do not want to die—so we must have been made to be immortal. But we die all the same. This is hideous and cannot be taken seriously."[21]

For *Ionesco*, existence is a contradiction.[22] In the end, when Bérenger

[14] "I would be less happy if I understood" (III, 157).

[15] III, 155.

[16] That is, the idea of evading the terrible nature of existence gradually fades: "I have no other images for the world but those which express its transience and harshness, vanity and anger, the void and the repulsive, senseless hatred. . . . What else have I to say?" (N, 220). He openly acknowledges the increasing tendency toward horror in N, 231f., 296, 335.

[17] N, 143.

[18] N, 196; including the feeling that "everything is threatened by some imminent, noiseless fall into I know not what abyss, somewhere beyond day and night" (N, 224). Everything is "the fruit of the void" (N, 285).

[19] N, 230.

[20] N, 261. On the futility and emptiness of existence: II, 89, IV, 42.

[21] N, 166.

[22] "Loneliness oppresses me. So does conviviality. . . . Life is something abnormal" (IV, 24). And when the logician has "proved" something, Bérenger

succeeds in following the clues that lead to the "murderer" who kills senselessly at the heart of the world, he cries out for "some common point, some common language",[23] for some kind of agreement, however precarious. But there is no such thing. The play ends with despair concerning "life's meaning", and in "pure contradiction". "Perhaps the world as a whole is meaningless, and perhaps you are right to want to blow it up." Existence, *experienced* as contradiction, is now *conceived* and explained as contradictory. "What a contradiction! What a dissonance between thought and life! Between me and me!"[24] It may be that the contradiction is between different strata of consciousness,[25] but they are nonetheless all within me: "I see myself torn by blind forces that arise out of the depths of myself and struggle together in a desperate conflict, with no way out. I seem to identify with one or the other, although I know that I am not entirely either of the warring parties—What do they want from me?—for I cannot know who I am, nor why I exist."[26] For *Ionesco*, however, this is what produces drama: "These contradictions violently rend each other and thus bring the drama into being."[27] "We must develop a twofold mode of thought involving an intention and its opposite, aware that, when we desire something, we also (and most of all) desire its opposite; we must adopt [*installer*] this whole complex with its inner contradiction."[28] As far as drama is concerned, it follows that the author cannot and may not engage in any instruction,[29] but must give a testimony, and a contradictory one at that: "The more contradictory his testimony is, the truer it is."[30] "The contradictions must be allowed to develop quite freely; the antagonisms will probably confront each other automatically and thus form a dynamic equipoise."[31]

It is clear, therefore, that *Ionesco* propounds a purely vertical drama, contrary to the purely horizontal drama of *Brecht*. What is really dramatic (indeed, the only thing that is so) is existence itself in its primal state, torn between opposites. Whereas for *Brecht* everything depended on the fable, *Ionesco* is not interested in any "intrigue, any

---

retorts, "I can see that, but it does not solve the question" (IV, 42). In another play he says: "If there is no complete agreement between my interior 'I' and my exterior 'I', what we have is the ultimate catastrophe, the universal contradiction, the absolute hiatus" (II, 73); cf.: "You must feel this contradiction" (II, 78).

[23] II, 167.   [24] IV, 115.   [25] N, 18.   [26] N, 224.   [27] N, 227.

[28] N, 317. As applied to death: "I am afraid of death. I fear death, probably because unconsciously I want to die. What I am afraid of is my longing for death" (N, 321). So Ionesco turns against the psychoanalysts who would attempt to eradicate contradiction from the psyche in IV, 168–69.

[29] N, 127.   [30] N, 185.   [31] N, 173.

individual story. . . . The aim is to produce the dramatic tension without bolstering it up with any genuine intrigue or any particular content. . . . In its limited meaning, a dramatic intrigue obscures its real application."[32] What is left is "a rhythm, an abstract progression".[33] "Pure theatre is this: the mutual confrontation of antagonisms, dynamic oppositions, the groundless clash of opposed wills."[34] Drama must "be purified of all logic in its conflicts", leaving us with pure tensions "as in a piece of music".[35] This is polemics, for the differences in people's experiences of existence are, after all, part of the content, and it is the latter that yields the dramatic dimension. Contrary to *Brecht*, *Ionesco* asserts that "the theatre cannot be epic, precisely because it is dramatic. . . . The play consists of a series of conditions or situations of consciousness that intensify, deintensify, and then engage, either to disengage or to end in an unbearable tangle."[36] *Ionesco* is well aware of his similarity with *Strindberg*,[37] and particularly with "*Beckett*, that contemporary Job".[38] "In certain aspects" his work belongs "to the existentialisms" and earlier expressionism.[39]

Indeed, the power of expression is everything for him; in its uniqueness, in its originality, it is the criterion of poetic truth. "What is original is true."[40] The regurgitation of what has already been thought and said is untrue.[41] "The profoundest subjectivity will ultimately break through to the objective."[42] That is why the genuine work of art cannot be used in the service of any ideology.[43] Since it is an "expression of life, or is life itself, the ideas come *from it*; the work of art is not an emanation of an ideology",[44] but discovers and prescribes its own rules. This sounds like the poetics of *Sturm und Drang*, but it is not: the originator is not genius but the loneliness (common to all) of "existence in death". This primal reality can only express itself by continually demolishing the hermetically sealed shells with which men surround themselves, by bringing down the ostensibly protective walls. Walls are always being razed (*Délire à deux*),[45] holes appear (*Exit the King*), streets, houses, "entire towns, entire civilizations" submerge.[46] The first play, *The Bald Soprano*, tears aside the veil of language, to find nobody behind it; it is "the tragedy of language";[47] the figures "are

[32] N, 254–55.   [33] N, 258.   [34] N, 314.   [35] N, 298.
[36] N, 329.   [37] N, 134.   [38] N, 223.   [39] N, 332–33.
[40] N, 26.   [41] N, 104.

[42] N, 30. Ionesco points out that, for him, Benedetto Croce is the master. "Croce taught me that substance and form are one and the same in expression" (*Découvertes*, in the collection *Les sentier de la création* [Geneva: Skira, 1969]), 19.
[43] N, 27.   [44] N, 86–87.   [45] III, 201ff.
[46] IV, 79.   [47] N, 131; cf. N, 234, 252.

dehumanized, emptied of all psychological content, because they have no inner drama";[48] nor is this comic, for instead of human beings expressing themselves we have "figures without character, straw puppets, beings without faces" on the stage, and the author comments: "It is not easy to be oneself, to play one's own role."[49] We shall have to ask whether he is able to create a character at all. In *The New Tenant* modern man is stifled under all the objects of modern comfort.[50] In *Jacob* we are shown the omnipotence of an empty tribal tradition and a compliant eros. In the continuation, *The Future Lies in the Eggs*,[51] the idol of "production" (in the sexual and technological senses) is unmasked. *Victim to Duty* is even more radical: life is ideologically and morally obligated to search, between intrinsically impossible poles, for something that cannot be found (Mallot, compare *Beckett's Godot*).

The fight against ideologies[52] becomes theoretical and is radicalized in stage plays, as two masterpieces, *Rhinoceros* and *Thirst and Hunger*, show. *Rhinoceros* attacks the fascination of the Nazi ideology and endeavors to "demystify" it (a word often used by *Ionesco*, mostly satirically), but takes the opportunity of this crude and obvious case to attack every ideology (for example, that of communism). All the characters apart from Bérenger become infected, the logician, the ambitious man (Jean), the journalist (Papillon), the average conformist (Dudard), the socialist (Botard) who claims the right to develop himself[53] and finally Daisy too, the girlfriend, who wants to be in harmony with her environment, with the majority. There is only one person who, even in the insecurity of his existence,[54] "will not accept" false security[55] and takes his stand on the truth of absolute loneliness. Bérenger: "You know that I am right." Daisy: "There is no absolute right. It's the world that is right, not you or I." Bérenger: "No, Daisy, I am right, and the proof is that you understand me . . . Love." Daisy: "I'm a little ashamed that you should call this morbid feeling, this weakness on the part of man and woman, 'love'. It cannot be compared with the intense heat, the unimaginable energy of all these beings around us."[56] Here too, as in *Le tueur sans gages*, Bérenger is totally alone in the face of the world's superior power. But what does *Ionesco* regard as ideology? Everything that "sets limits", that "blocks the horizon",[57] by providing a ready-made formula that renders life's riddle harmless: "morality, theology, politics",[58] and also "sociology",[59] history revamped as futurology[60] and all fanaticisms[61] that devour each

[48] N, 175.   [49] N, 255.   [50] II, 177ff.   [51] II, 207ff.
[52] N, 274–75.   [53] III, 98.   [54] III, 23–24.   [55] III, 89.
[56] III, 113.   [57] N, 126.   [58] N, 38.   [59] N, 31.
[60] N, 326.   [61] N, 125.

other in their intolerance.[62] Every genuine work of art can be interpreted according to any ideology; it can be "explained in Marxist, Buddhist, Christian, existentialist, psychoanalytic terms",[63] but in doing so we fetter its "absolute freedom" and "creative power",[64] for it arises from an "original intuition" of the imagination[65] that owes nothing to any fashion;[66] "and yet it has a unique contemporary relevance, constantly tearing aside the veil of appearance and destroying everything that lifts itself up."[67]

This explains *Ionesco's* dogged opposition to the "Brechtian barracks",[68] against the "two-dimensionality", the "lack of depth", the "simplism" of *Brecht's* characters.[69] Thus he attacks *Brecht's* ideological reaction (because it is dated)[70] and the way he changes "the actor into a chess piece, a tool without life, fire, personal involvement or imagination"[71]—and on the basis of a theory of alienation that is inimical to the theatre.[72] In *Ionesco's* view, *Büchner* is much more contemporary than *Brecht*.[73] Every ideology is *petit bourgeois*, and this applies to the conformism of the left just as much as to Nazism;[74] evidently, no social revolution can change the hopeless *condition humaine* in the least;[75] in fact, it is a sign of a hatred of the latter.[76] Even a philosophy like *Sartre's* (who writes plays to illustrate it) belongs with the ideologies.[77] They are all "prisons",[78] they are "abstract", whereas the experience of existence is concrete.[79] Ideologies show how unjust[80] they are when they assert themselves by annihilating all the others[81] and thereby cause existence to seem absurd. All ideologies alienate man from himself; the task of drama is continually to demythologize them.[82] Both the bourgeois and the communist theatre are "cut off from the deep sources of the human soul. . . . They express nothing but their own schizophrenia."[83]

What, however, will *Ionesco* be able to show on his own stage? Nothing but the fundamental contradiction of man's consciousness of existence in the empty void, alone in the face of death. He had to

---

[62] N, 229. Christianity is pilloried here for having been "against God, killing people in God's name, and torturing people in the name of love".

[63] N, 144.   [64] N, 182.   [65] N, 127.   [66] N, 158.

[67] N, 197; cf.: "Le renouvellement de l'expression est destruction des clichés, . . . (il) résulte de l'effort de rendre l'incommunicable de nouveau communicable" (N, 188).

[68] N, 51f.   [69] N, 194–95. [70] N, 64.   [71] N, 51.

[72] N, 279, 299.   [73] N, 94.   [74] N, 142, 291, 299.

[75] N, 220, 305, 319.

[76] N, 230. On the definition of the *petit bourgeois*: N, 109, 129, 253.

[77] N, 178.   [78] N, 184.   [79] N, 310.   [80] N, 314.

[81] N, 318, 324; III, 126.   [82] N, 170.   [83] N, 299.

destroy the horizontal interconnecting action (the "intrigue"), but he has also destroyed the *person* by going behind everything that "character" once signified in order to search for the identity of existential consciousness (which is "always mine").[84] Nicolas d'Eu proclaims his manifesto: "I shall bring contradiction into the realm of noncontradiction, and noncontradiction to what, in the commonsense view, is contradictory. . . . We abandon the principle of the identity and unity of the characters in favor of movement and a dynamic psychology. . . . We are not we ourselves. . . . Personality does not exist."[85] As a result, the figures move simultaneously in the direction of a super-Shakespeare (where the characters would disappear)[86] and of a Punch-and-Judy show, which had enthralled the poet since childhood.[87] The two characters in *The Lesson* are pure dynamics: one, the teacher, swells from pianissimo to fortissimo; by comparison the other, the schoolgirl, shrivels up. The clearest sign that the person has been destroyed is that ethics has been superseded. Fear still exists, along with anxiety, cruelty, incomprehensible death in all its forms; and there is still that worthless tool in the attempt to overcome it and heal man's existence, namely, ideology. All the same, in the contradiction of existence there is really neither good nor evil. The three acts of one of the central plays, *Thirst and Hunger*, first of all show domestic love's inability to survive its low points; for Jean, Marie-Madeleine's faithfulness is nothing but a fetter, and in a surrealistic gesture full of pathos he tears the wild rose of love from his heart, dabs away the drops of blood and vanishes. The second portrayal shows him in the airless heights of ecstasy, longing for his beloved who fails to come to the rendezvous. The third brings him to a quasi monastery, where, in the face of reality in the form of a bowl of soup, the opposed ideologies are shown to cancel each other out: the clown Brechtoll, an atheist, is persuaded to pray an Our Father, and the clown Tripp, a bigot, to deny God. Jean sees his wife and daughter through the grating in the monastery door, but stays imprisoned within. This is a tragedy of existence beyond good and evil; reality is "hunger and thirst for the Absolute".

Unlike Sartre, however, hunger and thirst are not themselves equated with the Absolute: the contingency of this incomprehensible existence remains related to something beyond itself. "I believe that there is a

---

[84] Once again D. Schings in *Der Entpersonalisierung im Theater*, 87ff. has proved this in a penetrating analysis, even though he does not do justice to Ionesco's ultimate positive aims.

[85] I, 226.

[86] This is clearest in *Macbett*.

[87] N, 53. Certain scenes are to be played as "guignol tragique", e.g., IV, 25.

pole star that can help us find our bearings. But it is far above the floods."[88] *Macbett*—dramatically a failure—is similar here, in practice taking Hegelianism to absurd extremes.[89] Macbett is by no means the traditional scoundrel, no more than the other puppetlike figures (who are in part confusingly similar and deliver pages of identical tirades); the witches keep prompting and "predestining" them to their evil deeds so that in the end they carry them out. The characters' attributes are not combined in "tension": they are simply incompatible. Thus King Duncan is simultaneously an egoistical blackguard and an anointed and sacral personage who heals rows upon rows of sick people by the ancient royal charisma. The action is governed by the demonic principle; the witches (of whom Lady Duncan is temporarily one) have lifted the lid of Pandora's Box.[90] They regard guilt feelings as a mortal disease to be guarded against.[91] In order to heighten the tension between the contradictions, *Ionesco* introduces the dimensions of the sacral (the reception of Holy Communion)[92] and the satanic.[93] At no point is there an opening in the horizon in this tangle of contradictions, except the demonic itself, which hacks all the "characters" to pieces and renders every series of actions arbitrary. The end of *A Stroll in the Air* (which explicitly poses the question of transcendence) is also radicalized: beings from the "counterworld" (of which there may be many, all interpenetrating and being reerected in the ruins of our world)[94] step over the boundary into this world; Bérenger makes bold to "transcend" and is carried up, borne aloft by "his certainty", but all he can see from the ultimate heights is the world's apocalyptic horror, endless calamity.[95] Joséphine: "Fly away with us, beyond the beyond, beyond hell." Bérenger: "Oh, I can't, my dears. There's nothing beyond them."[96] But the whole thing concludes not with a certainty but with a "perhaps". "Perhaps it will come right. . . . Perhaps the flames will die down. . . .

[88] N, 318.

[89] With reference to the countless guillotinings, Candor makes the following speech: "It is a great pity I did not win this battle. The course of history was against it. Objectively speaking, history is right . . . and always follows the stronger. . . . The logic of events is the only valid logic. . . . No transcendence could impugn it" (36).

[90] 82.   [91] 60.   [92] 73f.

[93] "Satan": 91. Spitting out the host, throwing down the cross, etc.: 85.

[94] III, 152.

[95] III, 190, 195 (in Ionesco's view the smallest quarrel goes on and on unabated till the end of the world: *La Colère* III, 295–304).

[96] III, 197.

Perhaps the ice will melt. . . . Perhaps the abysses will be filled in. . . . Perhaps the gardens . . . the gardens."[97] For *Ionesco* does not want to engage in metaphysics. The theatre must not try to be didactic.[98]

We can understand, therefore, that the author devotes himself increasingly to his own most distinctive theme and, in doing so, creates at least two masterpieces of the modern stage. A prelude to this is *The Chairs*, which is on the subject of absence. A whole crowd of absent people are treated as if they were present, thus giving a plastic form to their absence ("It cannot be an illusion," says Bérenger on one occasion, "because I feel this absence so terribly").[99] We are shown "the emptiness of reality, of speech, of human thought", and the stage must "be more and more crowded out with this emptiness", revealing "the holes in reality" ever more clearly. The two real characters must only speak from within "the presence of this absence".[100] The theme, according to *Ionesco*, is "ontological emptiness",[101] the continual disappearing of this world.[102] This is a prelude to death. "I have been obsessed by death for as long as I can remember. Since I was four years old and discovered that I would die, this fear has never left me. . . . My writing, too, is a crying aloud of my fear of death, of my humiliation by it."[103] In the first two acts of *Amédée*, death is something both horrifying and fascinating (a growing corpse that finally fills the whole house, emitting green light from its open eyes and compelling people to watch and attend to it), and then, in the last act, it turns into a fantastic parachute bearing Amédée away.[104] Here death is only one pole; there is still the other. In *The Killer*, death becomes a principle immanent in existence as such, the negation with which, right to the last, no agreement can be struck; as the curtain falls, it kills the living.[105] *Exit the King* takes the risk of making the sole subject of the play the slow,

[97] III, 198.

[98] The theatre "proves" nothing (N, 198). It is at a different level from that of instruction (N, 185). It is under no circumstances didactic (N, 127). But it should grip the audience (N, 282f., again in opposition to Brecht), and the spectators should identify with what is being shown (N, 303) and discover in it the universally human, the nonsocial (N, 287, 303).

[99] N, 264.   [100] N, 264.   [101] N, 266.   [102] N, 268.

[103] N, 309. "I am crippled, for I know that I shall die", says Bérenger (III, 128).

[104] He is a writer who wants to write a play against death but cannot make any headway (I, 300). He is also (and the ethical significance of this is completely passed over—being mentioned incidentally only once) the murderer of the dead man who was allegedly his wife's lover (I, 265).

[105] II, 171.

inevitable death of the king, who, in his regal assumption that he can move things, and in identifying himself with the universe, stands for all ego-consciousness.[106] Of course the king knows in theory that he will die, but he does not want to die yet,[107] it strikes him as unnatural.[108] Since his ego is his universe, he gets into a dialectic of contradictions: Will everything disappear with him—or will it remain?[109] He "cannot" die, he feels like a schoolboy in an examination who knows nothing, who has not learned his part.[110] He must be helped to set himself loose, but he keeps on loving himself ("*je m'aime*") and stammering "*Moi. Moi. Moi*".[111] He is told to make himself light; invisible cords holding him to the world are cut, and sacks weighing tons are lifted from his shoulders. "The dreamer is withdrawing from his dream." He is told to go beyond sound, beyond color; he is to go past the burning, circling wheel (a Buddhist image); he is not to be drawn into compassion for the beggar who seizes his hand; he is not to bend, to climb, to look into the imageless mirror or surrender his limbs one by one: "Look, now you'll see: you don't need words any more. Your heart doesn't need to beat. There's no point in breathing any more. All the hurrying was a waste of time, wasn't it? Now you can take your place."[112] *Ionesco* reaches his meridian in this drama of the shedding of the ego; and at the same time, beyond contradictions, beyond the anti-ideology, he attains a different, ultimate singleness of meaning, albeit—for the veil of *maya* is rent[113]— one that situates him close to Buddhism or to some other mysticism of unbecoming.

This astonishingly strong "everyman" play is the only play in which *Ionesco* unfolds any kind of a plot, and characteristically he stretches the vertical dimension into the temporal plane. This shows that *Ionesco's* drama—as opposed to *Brecht* and in spite of his dramatic gifts—does not succeed in setting forth genuine persons in genuine, finite time. On its own, the pure vertical, even when transposed into the temporal plane, cannot produce a plot. Indeed, *Ionesco* explicitly rejected the idea. After this play, which examines death in slow motion, there was only one other possibility, namely, the play that portrays death as a ceaseless guillotine, chopping horizontal time into mincemeat: *Jeux de massacre*. Death has broken out among men like an "epidemic" and "for no reason";[114] "we are the victims of an absurd disease that has no

---

[106] IV, 40, 64.   [107] IV, 20f.   [108] IV, 46.   [109] IV, 55.
[110] IV, 32.   [111] IV, 56, 70.   [112] IV, 74.

[113] "On brise la croûte de l'actualité superficielle" (N, 221). "C'est dans l'irréel que plongent les racines du réel" (N, 221).

[114] He himself lists the names of Solomon, Buddha, Shakespeare and John of

ethical significance of any kind."[115] One person locks himself in and seals up all the cracks against the outside world, but in vain. A patient in the clinic suddenly dies, but not from his illness. Someone collapses in the street and the passersby say that he died of the disease. The prison is opened, but it is the man who escapes who dies. The epidemic is interpreted ideologically: death is demystified,[116] some people call for action, revolution; others promise, not that the evil will go away, but that it will be reinterpreted.[117] They preach against the authorities, who are said to be "obsessed by the compulsive neurosis of death".[118] A council of doctors is convened to discuss the necessity or nonnecessity of death and the power or powerlessness of science. Someone puts forward the view that death is reactionary: it ought not to be allowed to obstruct the forces of progress; another suggests that people die through ignorance or ill will. When one of the doctors dies, another says, "I am not surprised", and a third says, "His belief in death killed him."[119] In between come scenes of lovers parted by death and crowd scenes in which people cry out for help from their windows and then fall out of them dead. Finally it is announced that the epidemic is lessening; during the ensuing celebrations, fire breaks out and surrounds everyone, leaving no way out. The whole thing becomes a dance of death, illuminating death's inroads from every angle. *Ionesco* even goes as far as explicitly to envisage the interruption of the stage play: the announcer begins his address to the audience, cries out and is overwhelmed by death; the curtain opens behind him to reveal a table bearing the coffin, in which he is carried away. The menace of death has finally triumphed over the action; now existence can only appear as something that has been terminated.

4. *Finitude*

a. The Time of the Action

We can use the opposition between *Brecht* and *Ionesco* to define the drama's mode of time. It can be neither pure horizontality,

the Cross when it comes to this "vision of death" (N, 221). "King Solomon (as the author of the Book of Ecclesiastes) is my master" (N, 197). "King Solomon is my guide" (N, 223).

[115] N, 23, 37. [116] N, 101. [117] N, 73. [118] N, 75.
[119] N, 79.

in which "the fable is everything" and the "I" and death nothing,[1]
nor an expression of pure verticality in which "the fable is
nothing" and death everything.[2] The characters of the drama
are limited, mortal beings, locked into a finite time-span within
which a meaningful dialogue-action must take place horizontally.
But this does not go on without the constant vertical presence,
veiled or manifest, of human finitude—and it is this that renders
the timebound play properly human, that is, human existence in
an abbreviated and condensed form. The time-horizon is short
and finite; this compels us to make final decisions and grounds
the dignity of the mortal human being, who must live his life in
the face of the a priori reality of death.[3] Drama, with its
horizontal-temporal restriction that calls for the action to be
meaningfully brought to a conclusion within it, provides a
metaphor of the dimension of meaning in all human finitude,[4]

---

[1] Of course Brecht stands here as the representative of a whole tendency that
sees the "unredeemable I" as an antimetaphysical principle (Ernst Mach, *Analyse
der Empfindungen* [1886]) and assumes that drama has a generic or "cosmic"
breadth right from the very beginning. For example, Hermann Bahr in his early
theatrical writings: *Dialog vom Tragischen* (1904), and *Dialog vom Marsyas* (1905).

[2] It is impossible to discover how far, for Ionesco, the "I" is the abiding or
evanescent factor in death. The young Lukács anticipated Ionesco's idea in his
"Metaphysik der Tragödie" in *Die Seele und die Formen* (1911) and his *Zur
Soziologie des modernen Dramas* (written 1909, published 1914): the soul's loneliness in the face of death constitutes a limitation of existence that imparts
meaning; it gives the soul its distinctive self-consciousness and, at the same time,
its absolute value and absolute context in destiny. By virtue of this constitution,
existence itself is pure tragedy, for tragedy "only knows of the dimension of
height, in which the intensive totality of substantiality manifests itself" (Dietrich
Mack, *Ansichten zum Tragischen und zur Tragödie* [Munich: Fink, 1970], 99). A
similar view is to be found in T. Spoerri, *Das Problem des Tragischen* (1947), who
regards the vertical dimension as the really tragic one. Lukács is influenced by
Paul Ernst's *Der Weg zur Form* (1906), where existence is determined by the
(empirically unfulfillable) claim of absolute ethical action—that form which is
tragic because it cannot be fulfilled. Reinhold Schneider will define and shape
tragedy in the same way.

[3] Georg Simmel, "Zur Metaphysik des Todes", in *Logos* I (1910–11): 57ff.
Max Scheler, "Tod und Fortleben" (begun ca. 1911–12), *Gesammelte Werke* X,
Schriften aus den Nachlass I (Berne: Francke, 1957), 16–36.

[4] "Why do men expect any end to the world? . . . Because reason tells them
that the continuance of the world only has validity as long as the reasoning
beings in it are in tune with the final goal of their existence. If this were not to be
reached, creation itself would seem purposeless to them, like a play with no

and hence it also allows us to discern a (vertical) aspect of infinity.[5]

This is why *Aristotle* demands that the drama should be the "imitation of a complete and entire action", "of a specific duration" and should thus have "a beginning, a middle and an end",[6] and that the action, and not the character, should be the determinant. For human beings "do not act in order to display their characters, but the characters are contained within the action" and refer to the goal (*telos*), which alone is important.[7] In the context of *Aristotle's* metaphysics we can say that the existing being has its goal within it (*entelechy*) and only reveals itself as a character by pressing toward this goal and in the tension that this creates.[8] All mere actualism destroys the human being, who has a built-in thrust forward. The actual (the here and now) makes sense only as the "now" of something that is moving toward its goal (and hence toward its self).

Whereas the lyric "recalls" the world and things, and the epic "makes them present" and "fixes" them, the drama "projects" them:[9] "Its existence strains toward its goal", which it thus "evaluates" by "contemplating a thing by referring it to a pre-supposed order. The expression 'referring it to' well sums up all the possibilities of dramatic action, from that which merely questions to that which expresses itself in passionate struggle."[10] The frightening side of dramatic, "futurist"[11] existence is that, within a finite period of time, an "ultimate meaning of existence"[12] is to be presented, in the form of a model that is verified through

---

outcome and giving no evidence of an intelligible plot": Kant, "Das Ende aller Dinge", Weischedel VI, 179.

[5] What Paul Valéry wrote concerning the work of art applies particularly to the drama: "Ce que nous appelons un 'Oeuvre d'art' est le résultat d'une action dont le but *fini* est de provoquer chez quelqu'un des développements *infinis*. D'où l'on peut déduire que l'artiste est un être double, car il compose les lois et les moyens du monde de l'action [which is finite] en vue d'un effet à produire l'univers de la résonance sensible" ("Pièces sur l'art", in *L'Infini esthétique, Oeuvres* [Pléiade], 1344).

[6] *Poetics* 7.   [7] *Ibid.*, 6.

[8] Hegel agrees with this in speaking of the goal-orientation of the dramatic action: *Ästhetik* II, 533.

[9] Emil Staiger, *Grundbegriffe der Poetik*, 3d ed. (Zurich: Atlantis, 1966), 217.

[10] *Ibid.*, 219.   [11] *Ibid.*, 171.   [12] *Ibid.*, 175.

action, contested through various encounters, and re-won or even surpassed, perhaps through suffering and death. Thus the drama's tension is an objective tension, intrinsic to it, and the spectator's subjective excitement only follows from it.[13] The objective tension lies in the inner transcendence of a strict immanence, in the justified expectation that the necessarily closed framework[14] will—equally necessarily—be exploded by the intrusion of an absolute meaning. It does not matter if chronological time continues after the conclusion of the dramatic action, as at the end of *Hamlet* or *Macbeth* and in *Shakespeare's* histories; the dramatic action as such has reached its end, and insofar as this action was a concentrated form of the overall, total meaning, the world too has come to a conclusion. All genuine drama is a kind of "man-trap": its space and time are absolute[15] and this means that, once the action has started, under given conditions, it must be played out to the end.[16] According

[13] Peter Pütz, *Die Zeit im Drama. Zur Technik dramatischer Spannung* (Göttingen, 1970), 11.

[14] There is a certain justification in distinguishing between plays with "closed" and "open" form (Volker Klotz, *Geschlossene und offene Formen im Drama*, 4th ed. [Munich, 1969]), i.e., those that draw all preceding time into the time of the drama and direct it toward the final tension, and those that go beyond the time of the drama and select individual tensions that, when relaxed, call forth further tension. However, this does not affect our fundamental view. Cf. the distinction between "extension" and "concentration" in A. R. Thompson's *The Anatomy of Drama* (Berkeley, 1946). Oppositions of this kind are always part and parcel of an overall dramatic form, which, as such, must always be absolutely or relatively "closed", absolutely or relatively "concentrated". Cf. the antinomy pointed out by E. Brock-Sulzer, that many plays compress the world onto the stage whereas others are able to open up the stage to the world (*Theater*, 95). Accordingly, the strict, imprisoning "four walls" of the stage can be rigid, as in a Renaissance play or a French classical drama, or as in Lorca's *The House of Bernard Alba*, Camus' *L'Etranger*, Claudel's *L'Otage*; but it can also expand into infinity as in Wilder, it can rock and sway, and, as on Piscator's stage, the ceiling can be lowered, confining the world within a tiny room, or it can be raised, "expanding its narrowness into the dimensions of a world" (Piscator, in Szondi, *Theorie des modernen Dramas*, 110).

[15] The drama's finitude produces the "classical three unities", however broadly or narrowly these are construed. In particular it produces the unity of time, which, chronologically, can even extend beyond a single human life span in cases where the destiny of a whole family is concerned, with its interwoven fabric of personal decisions. Cf. the excursus (below) on *The Drama of Generations*, pp. 408ff.

[16] On this cf. Peter Szondi, *Theorie des modernen dramas* (Suhrkamp, 1956), 14–19.

to *Souriau* the dramatic man is put into a "straight jacket": his whole destiny (which contains that of the world) is brought into a narrow place; he is set upon a road and must walk along it whatever the cost; he is thrust into making a free decision. For he is not only "caught" in the situation, he is also pronounced responsible in it.[17]

Time in the drama is the normal time of the action that takes place within it (which naturally does not have to coincide with the time-span of the performance);[18] however, as *Goethe* says, the essential action must be concentrated, abbreviated or epitomized within a narrow time-compass, attaining a "compactness that is improbable, if not impossible, in real life, weaving together threads that lead backward and forward".[19] Not only in the sense of a well-constructed internal dramatic plot, but more especially as a recapitulation of the past that is *not* dramatized and as an anticipation of an open future that is not limited to the play's final act. Above all else, action is the run-up to a future that is not predestined, but is indicated in various ways. Thus we have the characters of the *dramatis personae*, their plans and latent conflicts, a task to be performed (such as the Ghost gives to Hamlet, or as the Master of the World Theater gives to the souls along with their roles), the making of vows, predictions, prophecies, omens, wagers, trials, intrigues, dreams, complex tangles, disguises, mistaken identity, and so forth. All these attempts lead toward an open future, they adopt a direction without any certainty as to how things will turn out. And even if the outcome were known, the spectator's undiminished excitement would consist in not knowing *how* the goal was to be reached. But since the hero's destiny is indivisible and does not begin from scratch when the curtain rises, there is always need for a recapitulation of the past, initially in the exposition[20] of the opening scenes and often, too, in later references to the past; it is indispensable if the progress of the action is to be made intelligible. Ultimately, for example—in the analytical plays of

---

[17] Souriau, *Les deux cent mille situations dramatiques*, 41, 69.

[18] Petsch, in *Wesen und Form des Dramas*, distinguishes between the time of presentation (the performance time) and the sequential time (the time embraced by the dramatic action).

[19] P. Pütz, *Die Zeit im Drama*, 17.

[20] *Ibid.*, 168f., 197f.

Ibsen but also in *Oedipus*—the progress of the action consists in an increasing unveiling of the past. However, the past can be made present in the drama in the most diverse ways: it can be an inertia that hinders the forward movement or the precondition for a transformation, for example, through forgiveness, repentance,[21] right up to the limit where what has been is obliterated, or where an entire life is fashioned in terms of atonement.

These anticipations and recapitulations fill the particular present with a wealth of tension that gives it its exemplary meaning and re-presents in it a content that transcends the temporal. The wealth of tension contained in each moment flows on into succeeding moments, pregnant with the future, facilitating various forms of dramatic intensity. There is always the forward impetus that *Schiller* terms "precipitation",[22] but from time to time it is held back by delays, blockages and the torment of excitement sustained, or else it is hurried along in the tempo of cascading events. "Both tempi, both acceleration and delay, can create tension. Neither of them takes precedence over the other. . . . It is in the nature of tension to be nourished both by the imminent approach, and by the postponement, of the future."[23] For the most part the flow of the dramatic tension converges on one or more central scenes where it reaches its greatest density; then it expands and relaxes again as light is shed from above; many of *Shakespeare's* plays are built around a single scene on which everything hangs. *Aristotle* speaks of the two main elements, the "turning" (*metabole, peripeteia*) and the discovery (*anagnorisis*), as the turning from ignorance to knowledge: "this discovery is most beautiful when it coincides with the peripeteia."[24] The poet is sovereign in his fashioning of time. He never shows on the stage everything that happens; he lets many things, even important ones, happen behind the

---

[21] On the transformation of the past cf. Max Scheler, "Reue und Wiedergeburt" in *Vom Ewigen im Menschen: Gesammelte Werke* (1954), V, 27–59.

[22] Schiller to Goethe (Oct. 2, 1797).

[23] P. Pütz, *Die Zeit im Drama*, 55, 57. Cf. the debate with Ferdinand Junghans, *Zeit im Drama* (Berlin, 1931) and Eberhard Lämmer, *Bauformen des Erzählens*, 2d ed. (Stuttgart, 1967).

[24] *Poetics* 11.

scenes or between acts, "condensing the time, leaping over it and stretching it"; techniques that *Shakespeare* "employs in a sovereign manner".[25]

The thrill of a play, in which the eternal destiny of man is set forth within a finite time-span, is quite different from that of a detective thriller. It is worth reflecting that we can keep returning with renewed excitement to great dramas in spite of the fact that we know the story and its outcome. We can make a legitimate distinction here between the external events, which take place in a linear manner on the stage, and the inner action, which manifests itself *in* the external events as an essential condition of the world, freely and aware of its own situation.[26] Of course, there is very often a difference in the drama between what those on stage know and what the audience knows; the audience knows more as a result of the monologues, asides and addresses *ad spectatores*; or else it knows less (as in the analytic drama); and this difference heightens the tension. But once we have seen or read the play several times, this too fades. On the other hand, the excitement with which we follow the *Oresteia*, *Othello* or *Maria Stuart* is quite different in kind. The latter draws us into the tensions of existence as such that are always there and can never be overcome, and that now appear—with sovereign freedom—in *this* particular dramatic form. Something of this freedom is communicated to the spectator: he already knows the decisions that will be made because he has seen the play before, and yet each time he enters into them anew in their contingent form; profoundly moved, he thinks Hamlet's thoughts, pondering why he will not and cannot kill the king, deep in prayer. "It is almost as if, in entering into a play, we put ourselves back into a state of ignorance. In the same way, the child allows itself to be fascinated each time by the same thrilling story, the same puppet play; indeed it will protest at the slightest deviation from

---

[25] Wolfgang Clemen, *Vorwort zu Shakespeares Komödien, Werke* (Munich: Winkler, n.d.), I, 19. Cf. Claudel, *Le soulier de Satin*, act II, scene 2: "On the stage we treat time like a concertina, just as we like. Hours last forever, and whole days disappear without trace. Nothing is easier than to have several different times running in different directions at the same time." Cf. E. Staiger, *Die Zeit als Einbildungskraft des Dichters* (Zurich, 1939).

[26] Petsch, in *Wesen und Form des Dramas*, 63–66.

the familiar story. Thus repetition does not destroy the excitement."[27] In fact, the feeling that something is coming that (theoretically and in the abstract) could still be averted heightens our excitement as we look toward the impending conclusion.[28] A comparison with music suggests itself: music's present moment is nothing apart from its tension vis-à-vis past and future; each note played only has significance insofar as it successively interprets, unveils, justifies the past and anticipates what is to come. And what is to come cannot be constructed out of the present (even in the case of strict fugue). The present moment —in a Mozart symphony, for instance—is so full to the brim with tension that the genuine listener has neither time nor inclination to think of the past, let alone anticipate the future. With the passing of each note we sense the presence of the whole, which simultaneously comes into being in time and—in some incomprehensible supratemporal realm—always *is*.

This yields two opposite recommendations for performance. According to *Stanislavsky*, the "stage form only comes into being during the course of the performance, before the eyes of the audience, and must be shown in the process of its formation and development. . . . In order to show the suffering Othello, terrible in his jealousy, at the end of the performance, the first act must show him as happy as possible, quiet and contented. The form only takes shape as a consequence of the life lived out on stage."[29] But the same *Stanislavsky* has also continually insisted that every moment of the play must bear within it its entire past and future,[30] and *Brecht* too, in his *Kleines Organon*,

---

[27] P. Pütz, *Die Zeit im Drama*, 14.

[28] On p. 14 Pütz quotes the excellent formulation by A. R. Thompson: "Suspense does not, like surprise, depend on the spectator's ignorance of what is to follow. It is strongest when the spectator knows or at least suspects the outcome, as when we see a swimmer helplessly drawn to the brink of a waterfall" (*The Anatomy of Drama*, 146). Also Ernst Howald: "Ignorance of the course and outcome of an action is only part of the experience of tension, indeed a relatively unimportant part of it": *Die griechische Tragödie* (Munich and Berlin, 1930), 11. Also Arnulf Preger: "What a wretched drama it would be that could only bear being seen once, because after that we would already know the plot" (*Grundlagen der Dramaturgie* [Graz and Cologne, 1952], 67).

[29] Kristi, in Stanislavsky, *Die Arbeit des Schauspielers an der Rolle*, 162–63.

[30] "The direct linking of the character's present with his past and future

can demand that it should be "quite evident" from the actor's performance "that, right from the beginning and in the middle, he knows the end".[31] He must master the fable in its entirety: "Only then, on the basis of the clearly defined total event, can he arrive with a single leap, as it were, at a final figure that integrates all individual traits".[32] It would be wrong to say that these two demands contradict each other: the conductor of a symphony too must have the whole work in his head in determining the significance of a particular passage, and yet he does not allow this overall view to distract his full attention from the detail.

These apparent paradoxes arise out of the nature of dramatic time. What is played is a unique event and yet as such it is a revelation of something timelessly valid, a metaphor, a parable. So the dramatic reality is not upset by the presence of an interpreter or narrator side by side with the unfolding event, commenting on the action from a contemplative distance. Such is the old poet John Gower in *Shakespeare's Pericles* or the Chorus in his *King Henry the Fifth*, or the figure of Time in *The Winter's Tale*, or the two commentators in *Britten's Lucretia* or the singing narrator in *Brecht's Caucasian Chalk Circle*. In a way, figures like these embody the audience's contemplative awareness, into which the temporal sequence of events is inscribed. In *Sakuntala* and *Faust* the Director speaks the prologue and then leaves the play to itself; but in *Thornton Wilder's* work, the Stage Manager takes an indispensably active part in the play: in *The Happy Journey, Pullman Car Hiawatha* and *Our Town* he is the all-embracing power who controls the play both from without and from above and provides the props, but he is also always intervening in the action and addressing the characters. Occasionally he even takes on the role of a character. As *Wilder* says, the Stage Manager directs the whole like an orchestral conductor. He is above and in the play like a providential divinity, intimately involved in the life, the emotions and the

---

condenses the essentials of the life of the portrayed person and provides a justification for the present" (*Ibid.*, 107).

[31] Brecht, *Kleines Organon*, no. 50, in deliberate contradiction of Schiller (to Goethe, Dec. 26, 1797).

[32] Brecht, *Kleines Organon*, no. 64.

sufferings of the characters, but at the same time he simply presents them like precious and dearly loved puppets. He follows them in their journey through time, but is himself so distanced from time that he can also let the characters die so that they may at last understand life. ("Now I understand everything", says the dead Harriet.) This life is once-for-all, we should not cling to it: so the dead Emily in the last act of *Our Town* must be weaned from the earth, and in tears she turns to the Stage Manager: "Do any human beings ever realize life while they have it?—Every, every minute?" Stage Manager: "No. (Pause) The saints and poets, maybe—they do some." It is true that, with his Stage Manager, *Wilder* is accentuating a very particular world-view; that is not the important thing here, however, but rather the particularly successful way he shows the interplay of time's horizontal and vertical dimensions. The horizontal has genuine tension only within the accompanying vertical dimension. It is the vertical that makes the horizontal into an irreversible movement and gives the decisions that are made within it both meaning (*Sinn*) and direction (*Sinn*).

Max Frisch, in his *Biographie. Ein Spiel*,[33] has attempted to remove this meaning and direction by regarding the individual's freedom (55, 119) and personal qualities (30) as "given", but the concatenation of his decisions as purely contingent ("It had to happen like this. . . . It can never be proved, but it can be believed. . . . Destiny. Providence" [102]). "The play shows . . . the way things could have been different in life. . . . Rather like a game of chess, when we try to reconstruct its decisive moves, curious to know whether, where and how the game could have been played differently." Kürmann gets into a cul-de-sac; he retraces his steps and is able to choose (*küren*) another variant; but, significantly, no scene seems so apt to him "that it could not have been otherwise" (119), and consequently none yields a meaning that is even half satisfying. "I refuse to believe that our biography . . . could not be otherwise"(29), "I

---

[33] Max Frisch, *Biographie Ein Spiel* (Bibliothek Suhrkamp, 1970), 225. Similar problems are raised by Armand Salacrou in *Le pont de l'Europe* (1927), where Jérôme acts out his possible lives on his private stage, which leads his true "I" to insanity, and in *Patchouli* (1936), where each life choice shows its inherent limitations.

refuse . . . ; we give things a spurious meaning once they have happened and because they have happened, because they have become history, irrevocable"(52). The purpose of this refusal is simply to show that *all* choice and variation are meaningless; they are a perversion of the idea of freedom, which aims to create meaning and take responsibility for it as something freely chosen. Nor, in his play, does *Frisch* make freedom absolute, able to do both the best and the worst (*Sartre*). All he does is deny, by way of experiment, that temporal decisions have a meaningful sequence; they are all "comedy"—and this destroys all drama whatsoever. He has seen quite clearly that, deprived of that vertical dimension that takes human beings at their word, the horizontal dimension robs temporal life of all meaning. Furthermore, the individual (who, like "Everyman", stands for all people) remains, with his freedom, in complete isolation; the constellation of human beings, which includes him, is determined solely by him; this means that no drama is possible, only an experiment with ideas.

b. Situation

Dramatic action is possible and meaningful only within a given situation or constellation. This is its point of departure, which is changed through the action, yet in such a way that the changes are variations of a theme. We can attempt a crude classification of the dramatic situations,[1] if we wish, and no doubt many of them are so similar as to seem practically identical, but the uniqueness of each human being, acting together with other unique human beings within a never-recurring constellation of destiny, renders all such pigeonholing highly questionable. The

---

[1] Gozzi, who revitalized the commedia dell'arte in the eighteenth century, was prepared to admit only thirty-six dramatic situations. Goethe quotes this opinion, approvingly, to Eckermann: "Schiller thought there were more, but he did not even manage to find that many" (Feb. 14, 1830; similarly to Soret, Feb. 14, 1830). M. G. Polti, in his celebrated book on the "thirty-six dramatic situations" (Mercure de France [*Die sechsunddreissig dramatischen situationem*], 4th ed., 1934) took up the same view once again. Etienne Souriau endeavored to explode this narrow view in his *Les deux cent mille situations dramatiques* (Paris: Flammarion, 1950), and, with the help of astrological combinations employed only for symbolic purposes, he arrived at the precise total of 210,141 situations.

elements to be combined are innumerable: most of them can be
defined only in an approximate way. Where something does
emerge from the blurred and obscure medium and show a clear
outline—which is essential for dramatic action—the relationship
between the determinants and the freedom that operates in them
(whether triumphant or vanquished) remains open and new at
every moment.

A first dimension is the field of tension that is divided up
among human beings with their free decisions. They live
together and clash with one another, continually influencing
each other, in the dialogue of words and the diapraxis of deeds, a
constellation that is constantly changing as a result of every
move in the common game of chess, yet always within the same
match. However, this dimension can make itself felt only within
a second dimension, which situates every acting character, and
the totality of characters, within the framework of humanity as
a whole with its problems. Moreover, this second dimension
directly poses the question of the individual's meaning within
this totality and the totality's meaning within Being (and hence
the meaning of Being as such).

We could imagine a static model of the world with an ordered
nature as its umbrella, allotting each part its function in such a
way that this part, freely and responsibly exercising its function,
would embrace and fulfill the situation that nature gave it, even
in the human and political arena. This is the grandiose panorama of the *Republic* of *Plato*, where everyone "does his own
business" (433B) and performs "justice through possessing and
administering what is his own" (434C). It is a view that is still
cherished by Denis the Areopagite,[2] and there are signs of it in
Paul (1 Cor 7:17, 20, 24), though here the function allotted by
nature is replaced by "the call of God". Initially the latter is a call
to an earthly state of life (whether "circumcision" or "uncircum-
cision", "freeborn" or "slave"), but it can be extended to
entirely personal vocations such as Paul (and, by analogy, every
person possessing a charisma) has. Even for the Greeks, however, the all-embracing natural order could be broken through

---

[2] "Everyone should be in his own order [rank: *taxis*]" (Ep VIII, PG IIIm,
1093). Cf. René Roques, *L'Univers Dionysien* (Paris: Aubier, 1954), 89.

by personal vocations, for example, the *daimōnion* of *Socrates*, which had an analogy in the destinies of the great tragic heroes. Oedipus, Heracles and even Prometheus explode the whole Platonic convergence of nature and function, of *physis* and *polis*. A light shines into the world from a higher region and anchors itself deep in the heart of the man who is called; as a result, he will not allow himself to be integrated seamlessly into the social edifice.

The metaphor of the body with its members determined by their function within it, which we find in the ancient world and in Paul, is expanded as a result of this intervention from above (whence come all personal vocations: Rom 12:3, 6; Eph 4:10f.) and acquires a more complex structure. In the organism of the "body", be it Church, state or humanity, there is an interplay of free human beings, all of whom can claim to have received an absolute commission even if there is mutual opposition and contradiction between them. What authority lies behind these commissions is as yet undecided: it can be the inner consciousness of a special mission, of a task that goes beyond the laws of humanity and the "world powers"—and here *Goethe* speaks of the "demonic", whether it be beneficent or destructive; it can be on the basis of a real or alleged harmony with the "world powers" (*Wallenstein's* belief in the stars); it can arise from an even more profound sympathy with Being in its totality (as in *Kleist's* heroes with their "unconscious feeling"); it can be the summons addressed to a latent noble nature (*Schiller's Warbeck*) or the bond with the Universal Spirit that transcends all individuation (*Hölderlin's Empedokles*).

However, this inner freedom of vocation has to play against powers, at whatever level, that fetter, obstruct, cripple, retard, contradict and challenge it. First of all there is the particular cast of mind of the man to whom the mission has been entrusted: a contemplative, essentially hesitant man is obliged to act (Hamlet); a man bearing a burden of inheritance has to free himself (Osvald in *Ghosts*). Most importantly of all, a man has his own past that clings to him and predetermines his actions (*Rosmersholm*). There is the invincible power of a milieu, for example, social misery and limitation, whence no escape is possible (*Büchner's Woyzeck*; the tragedies of *bürgerlich* life, where pregnancy out of wedlock is the ultimate catastrophe: thus *Wagner's Kindsmörderin*, Gretchen in *Faust*, *Hebbel's* Klara in *Maria Magdalena, Hauptmann's Rose Bernd*). Finally there is the kaleidoscope of difference between person and role (be the latter genuine or imaginary): perhaps the role was an adopted mask that a man must give up to attain truth (*Eliot's* society dramas); perhaps it was held to be a man's genuine mission, which, when stripped from him, causes the framework of his existence as a person to collapse (*Schiller's Demetrius*); and perhaps the role, once adopted, has to prove itself through extreme temptation (*Calderon's Sigismund*) or even through an unsuspected reversal (*Kleist's Prinz von Homburg*). The person and his vocation may be confronted with superior social forces against which it is not possible "to win, only to resist" (*Claudel*), but this resistance, which outwardly ends in defeat, may blossom into an unlooked-for blessing: "There is surely no higher catharsis than 'Oedipus at Colonos', where a half-guilty criminal plunges himself and those who are his into the deepest, most irretrievable misery and is elevated to kinship with the gods and made the beneficent, tutelary spirit of a country, worthy to receive sacrificial offerings" (*Goethe*).[3] Or he may be called to maintain ethical integrity in a situation of social disintegration (*Goethe's Natürliche Tochter*), to confront and resist the fascination of an ideology (*Ionesco's Rhinoceros*). In situations like these we do not have an intact hero versus a corrupt and tempting society; the antinomy makes itself felt in the hero himself, who must be inwardly tempted and torn by it. Such a hero can be a chess piece, while simultaneously being the chess player, who knows how the pieces are related to one another; in a situation whose constituent elements can scarcely be brought within a single view and organized, he must create a form that manifests unity, a form in which he, the sole figure, can survive, whether he is victorious or falls in the attempt. We have spoken of middle-class (*bürgerlich*) ethics; the ethos of a hero can be, and mostly is, influenced by tribal or group modes of thought, by a social morality. No baroque tragedy is conceivable—whether Spanish,

---

[3] "Nachlese zu Aristoteles' Poetik" in *Über Kunst und Altertum* VI/1 (1827).

French, German or English—apart from the aristocratic ethics of representation (and hence of "honor"). It takes a concept of honor that has been absolutized into a fetish to produce situations like those in *Calderon's The Physician of his Honor*; and only a notion of obedience to the party exaggerated into inhumanity could result in the situation in *Brecht's The Measures Taken*.

How far freedom is unquestioningly guided and predetermined by models of this kind and how far it consciously and personally submits to them after a struggle with conscience are different from play to play.

However, situation is essentially determined by antinomies between different persons and their free decisions, made on the basis of how they see the world and their individual vocations. Both ideals or potencies can have their justification, in the abstract: the concrete situation may necessarily result in the choosing of the one and the rejecting of the other, depending on whether personal considerations or considerations of the times (the historical epoch) are paramount. The conflict may be between *raison d'état* and the ethical ideal of freedom (*Don Carlos*); between conscience and the use of power (in the great plays of *Reinhold Schneider*); between the impurity of political and the purity of ethical action (*Wallenstein*); between political reason and personal love (many of Corneille's plays, *Racine's Bérénice*); between active and contemplative existence in the creation of culture (*Goethe's Pandora*); between sober, concrete planning and the unreality of the poet's existence (*Tasso*); between personal love and the love of art (*Grillparzer's Sappho*); between positive action and—when it is too late for this—acting through renunciation (*Goethe's Natürliche Tochter, Claudel's L'Otage, Hofmannsthal's Der Turm*); between endeavors to change the world and the realization that such activity will never change things fundamentally (*Büchner's Danton*), and so on.

In all this we must not lose sight of the fact that no dramatic situation is immobile and fixed, but develops through the course of the action; the alteration and qualification of points of view can change, confuse and just as suddenly disentangle it. "The same thing can be experienced as unnatural or natural, depending on the different circumstances in which it finds itself.

For the nature of a developing thing is different from its nature when it is complete."[4] Thus love can manifest ardent passion at first, leading us to sense a future alienation, though we cannot tell whether it could be avoided or not (*Grillparzer's Medea* trilogy); in *Strindberg's* and *Heiberg's* tragedies of married life this alienation becomes inevitable because of the inconsistency of the characters and their vulnerability to every attack from others.

It seems that these conflict situations could all be explained at the horizontal level, by history, psychology and anthropology. But the very fact of coordinating two antinomian free decisions—neither of which can be dismissed as superseded and unsustainable—calls for some authority superior to both that is able to judge and recognize or reject them. The volatile names given to it in dramatic theory—"fate", "nemesis", "providence"—are more ciphers than definitions, for this factor that embraces situations is something hoped for and felt rather than something known. The subject that lies behind such appellations remains unnamed, expressly so: it is an "operant power" (or powers?), a "guiding force". Generally speaking, in the drama, the name "God" is not to be uttered; it has an extravagant ring to it. Frequently drama is content to address a question to this overarching dimension by stripping the veil from what, in everyday life, is covered up and by fomenting turmoil. It always takes some kind of *faith* to see the emergent form, the constellation-in-destiny.[5] This faith reaches backward and forward for an ultimate horizon of meaning that is not accessible to rationality. Such questionings and intimations are always remnants of a religious view of the world; high drama like that of Greece, the Elizabethans and German idealism arose at a time in history when the great conflicts between human beings took place within a horizon of the divine that, though increasingly obscured, was still recognizable as such. As we have yet to show, where this horizon still seemed unobscured, as in French and Spanish classicism, it continued to hover between the "powers"

---

[4] "Uni et eidem rei est aliquid contra naturam et secundum naturam secundum eis status diversos; eo quod non est eadem natura rei dum est in fieri et dum est in perfecto esse" (Thomas Aquinas, *De veritate* 13, 1 ad 1).

[5] R. Petsch, in *Wesen und Form des Dramas*, 37.

and the "almighty power", between Fortuna and *providentia* or between the world's tragic situations, deepened by the religious aspect, and their redemption. However, if a time should come when all divine visibility in the world should cease, when all questioning of God—even in the form of revolt or despair—should fall absolutely silent, drama would have lost its most essential dimension.

Furthermore, where "destiny" is a power that simply hovers above the characters and plays with them, a "fate" imposed on them from above, or where it is reduced to the level of mere sociological or characterological determinants, here too it would cease to be of any interest. The "ought" that burns in the hero's heart, that for which he must freely strive, is not some categorical imperative that threatens him from above: it must indwell him most intimately as his most personal task, which he carries out at the risk of sacrificing his entire empirical individuality. This sounds like *Schiller*; but in this context, in order to attain certainty beyond *Kant, Schiller* refers to the Christian dimension, the infusion of God's transcendent will into the heart of the believer by the gift (to him personally) of the Holy Spirit. As he wrote to *Goethe*, "As for Christianity's distinctive trait, which distinguishes it from all monotheistic religions, it lies in nothing other than the *suspension of the law* or the Kantian Imperative; Christianity wishes to replace this with a free inclination. In its pure form, therefore, it is the representation of ethical *beauty* or the incarnation of the holy, and in this sense it is the only *aesthetic* religion."[6] We need not take this to mean anything more than that the "power" must be operating *in* as well as above the hero and the other characters, so that the just order established at the end of the action ("poetic justice") is shown to come from within no less than from above. It is at the delicate point of encounter between what is profoundly and most humanly right and the law that summons man to renunciation (compare *Goethe's* dramatic *Elective Affinities*), that the decisive dramatic situations and decisions take place (for example, of Rhodope in the final act of *Gyges und sein Ring*). This point is what every genuine drama, including Greek drama,

---

[6] Schiller to Goethe, Aug. 17, 1795.

aims for.[7] The so-called "drama of destiny", in which an external, mechanical fate unwinds, which is nothing other than a "personification of natural necessity, of the external circumstances that are independent of our will", a "supplement to the gods" (*Grillparzer*), fails to reach the level of drama. Or at least it can do so only if man's "succumbing" to these impersonal forces is interpreted theologically as a "secularized notion of original sin": "The abandoned ego, rejected by God, wants to return to the sacred order rooted in God, but it finds its path cut off by the hereditary (original) sin of existence and the urgings of blind instinct. All it can do is cry out in *angst* and misery to a Divinity that no longer saves: 'Protect me from myself!' "[8]

Whether this existential experience of being the prey of forces of destiny is understood in pagan terms (as a belief in fate, *heimarmene*, or the hereditary curse) or Christian terms (as original sin, the *servum arbitrium*), it only becomes dramatic where it is dialectically opposed to the possibility of liberation, where it is related to some saving factor. This is at its greatest in the *Eumenides* of *Aeschylus*, but we can also sense it in the lost conclusion of the Prometheus trilogy. Liberation may come through the breaking of the curse on the demise of its bearer (*Die Ahnfrau*) or by the curse-bearer, through some high endeavor, spiritually overcoming the demonic element that lurks within him (thus *Goethe's Iphigenie*, who, like Orestes, is under the curse of the fallen Titan, Tantalus; compare the *Parzenlied*). Initially the model of the world to emerge from a dialectic of this kind looks suspiciously gnostic. It manifests two spheres, one above the other: that of "fate" (which has the upper hand over freedom) and that of a gracious "providence"—if we may give this abstract name to the saving factor that is in communication with human freedom. We must beware, however, of branding this dualism as an inadmissible gnosticism. For it can equally be found in late Jewish apocalyptic and even in the New Testament

[7] "Chez Homère, les Kères, les Daimones, les Erinnyes sont à la fois des êtres individuels et des forces intérieures qui existent au coeur même de la vie des hommes. La Moira est à la fois une puissance cosmique néfaste et une forme de la conscience de l'individu": Jean Guitton, *Le Temps de l'eternité chez Plotin et S. Augustin*, 3d ed. (Paris: Vrin, 1959), 320.

[8] Benno von Wiese on Grillparzer's *Die Ahnfrau* in *Die deutsche Tragödie von Lessing bis Hebbel*, 7th ed. (Hamburg: Hoffman und Campe, 1967), 387.

teaching of the two aeons between which the Christian lives in a period of transition, paying tribute to the old but living "liberated to hope" unto the new, which, though hidden, is already genuinely present. What has Paul to say with regard to the drama of existence? "If Christ is in you, although your bodies are dead because of sin, your spirits are alive because of righteousness" (Rom 8:10). And John says: "He who believes in me, though he die, yet shall he live, and whoever lives and believes in me shall never die" (Jn 11:25).

While the two aspects of the vertical that codetermine the dramatic situation are most definitely incarnated in the given horizontal conditions (those that prevail between human beings and within the individual's soul), they are not completely identical with them. Only thus can human destiny, even the most tragic, avoid seeming completely meaningless and therefore of no interest. Even the *homme révolté* only has meaning if there is a hidden, elusive authority against which he is in revolt. *Goethe's* Prometheus (in the fragmentary drama) may revolt against the tyranny of Zeus and appeal to a "destiny" beyond the gods; but this, again, is seen to be "all-powerful Time" and "the life source", to which the Titan's creativity has an affinity. The young *Goethe* (and many later writers) were in danger of equating this "life source" beyond the gods with the creative wellspring in the human heart. The mature *Goethe* rejects this; he acknowledges that, even in the "pure breast" (*das Waltende*), "the power that is at work", however mysterious he continues to find it, is more than human.[9]

Excursus: Fate, Freedom and Providence in Calderon

Without doubt the greatest expansion of the horizon within which and before which man plays his part is to be found in the dramas and *comedias* of *Calderon*.[1] For the present we must put his *autos sacramentales*

[9] In the Prologue to the opening of the Berliner Theater, May 1821, Goethe describes the modern attitude as a "delicate" unity of the Greek belief in destiny and the Christian belief in providence: "Destiny and faith can share no common ground, / All salvation's in the pure breast to be found; / In all events, whate'er the story, / A God is close to us and deep inside. / Where earth and heaven salute and bless, / Man, wondering, is faced with glory" (*Dramatische Dichtungen* III [Insel], 1086f.).

[1] Quoted according to the *Obras Completas*, 3 vols. (Madrid: Aguilar, 1956)

to one side. The net within which man acts out his life is never drawn pitilessly tight around him, but it always remains elastic enough to allow him, with his power to choose (*albedrio*), to make his distinctively human contribution. There was a time when *Calderon* was interpreted one-sidedly and put forward as the progenitor of the modern German drama of destiny, but this view clung only to one side of his model of the world, namely, that which shows him to be the authentic heir of the ancient tragedy of destiny and which also corresponds to the Reformation idea of the *servum arbitrium*. While there is something of both spheres in *Calderon*, he cannot in any way be restricted to them.

In the first place *Calderon* is different from classical antiquity in that his "destiny" is not a specific divine curse affecting a dynasty but a sphere that embraces the whole world, subsequently embodied in highlighted figures of destiny (like Semiramis, the *Daughter of the Air*). This sphere, and hence the life course of the individual, is governed by astrological and horoscopic laws even more than in the *heimarmene* of the ancient world. On the other hand it would be a mistake to understand this sphere of "fate written in the stars" in *Calderon* in a gnostic, dualistic sense, as if it corresponded to a demiurge independent of the Most High God or hostile to him. In fact it is subordinate to the will of the Most High God (analogously to classical tragedy): "The destinies prescribed by heaven, / Once written by God's finger / On azure tablets, / Never deceive and never lie."[2] All the same the sphere of destiny does acquire a relative autonomy that, in *Calderon's* theological view of the world, is best explained by creation's falling a victim, against its will, to *vanitas* (Rom 8:20), or what, as far as man is concerned, is the same thing, to original sin.[3] In this way the playwright seems to approach the contemporary Protestant sensibility; but

---

and the German translations by A. W. Schlegel, Gries, Malsburg, Eichendorff, Schack, Lorinser, Pasch and Martin. *Life Is a Dream* and *Daughter of the Air* have been translated into German by Max Kommerell, *Beiträge zu einem deutschen Calderon* II (Frankfurt: Klostermann, 1946). Kommerell's first volume contains some of the most balanced observations on the poet ("Etwas über die Kunst Calderons"), which form the basis for much of what is said here. It is clear that Calderon cannot lay claim to any special originality at this point. We have already become acquainted with the speculation regarding "providence" and "fate" (see above, p. 144ff. and p. 319ff.); it is the result of intensive study of ancient philosophy (Pseudo-Plutarch = de Fato, Calcidius, Nemesios, cf. Praechter, *Die Philosophie des Altertums* [Berlin, 1926], 555), emphasizing the conditional nature of *heimarmene*.

[2] Sigismund in act III of *Life Is a Dream*.

[3] That (and only that) is why Sigismund can say right at the beginning of the play that man's greatest guilt consists in the fact of being born.

·

in spite of an unmistakable affinity he puts the accents elsewhere. As we see quite clearly in the *autos*, he leaves man free under certain circumstances to burst through the sphere of destiny, for instance, in an attitude of self-conquest and renunciation. This, he shows, is only possible on the basis of a prevenient grace offered to man from the sphere of God. The *comedias* remain within the worldly sphere, and so they can refer only peripherally to this opening to heaven that heaven itself creates. The *autos* view reality from the perspective of Christian revelation and show the mutual relation of the two spheres in cross section, as it were: (fallen) nature and divine redemptive grace.

According to many of the Church Fathers, man's position in the cosmos is that of a recapitulation at a higher level: he is the epitome of all intramundane powers. Thus the playwright can often analyze him into his separate faculties. "Will", "reason", the "five senses" and so forth, appear as powers that are only integrated, more or less harmoniously, in the dramatic argument. Man is shown in his twofold nature of body and soul, which is compared to a "marital dispute". It is not an ontological, but an ethical dualism. The body's concupiscence pulls downward, the soul's constitution pulls upward, and death initially concludes the marriage litigation in favor of "separation", while granting a final prospect of reconciliation between the part that is transcendent and the part that is immanent in the world.[4] Man's mystery, for *Calderon,* is that, being a "microcosm" of the world, he has the ability to transcend; furthermore, not only has man a potential *knowledge* of everything in the universe: essentially he *is* this recapitulation of everything—including the galaxies. His very being possesses a receptivity for all the analogies present in nature, on which the poet can play as on a resonant harp. "A thing's place in the cosmic network is established by a poetical calculation."[5] Man, a knowing being, can be initiated into cosmic algebra: Cipriano, the *Wonder-working Magician*, is initiated by a demon, like Faust. In *Love's the Greatest Magician*, the enchantress, Circe, "Medea's kinswoman", learns mathematics, philosophy and astronomy from a great magician so that she can read the alphabet of the stars and understand the sounds of animals

---

[4] When the soul is accused at the Judgment it responds in a way that is both Platonizing and biblical, quoting Ps 142:8 ("O Lord, rescue my soul out of prison") as well as Augustine's gloss, namely, that the dungeon of the body is the scene of this captivity. Job, Jerome, Paul (Rom 7:24) and Gregory Nazianzen are all cited, as well as Christ's redemption of the woman who was a sinner (Lk 7:36ff.): *Autos* in *Obras* III, 89, Eichendorff, *Der Ehezwist* in *Werke und Schriften* III (Cotta), 982f.

[5] Kommerell, *Beiträge zu einem deutschen Calderon*, I, 19.

and the colors of flowers; she has studied chiromancy, geomancy, pyromancy, necromancy and so forth. This mythical knowledge of nature reveals man's dimensions as a natural being. This explains the poet's inexhaustible store of horoscopes and oracles, which are retailed to indicate the cosmic sign and constellation to which the hero belongs, the field of force or grid within which his destiny will unfold. We must realize, of course, that in *Calderon* such astrological scenarios are often used simply as props, particularly in those plays that are customarily dismissed as the worst possible mechanical "dramas of destiny". This is the case, for instance, in the magnificently constructed drama *Herod and Mariamne* ("*El mayor monstruo los celos*"). Here, although there is the unavoidable fulfillment of a double prediction (when Herod vainly tries to get rid of the curse-bearing dagger), the play's real spiritual center lies elsewhere, namely, in the way Mariamne carries out her promise at the end of the second act concerning Herod's jealousy: "As a princess I forgive; as wife I shall take revenge." Thus her womanly heart, which swings "from one extreme to the other", is satisfied in every way, but also, even within her specific destiny, she can cause "the conflicting duties to have a moderating influence on each other".[6] On this central plane *Calderon's* play is in no way inferior to *Hebbel's*.

Horoscopes can be dramatic in themselves when two opposite poles are struggling for mastery. Since astrology designates these forces with the names of the planetary gods and *Calderon* interprets the ancient gods as symbols of the energies of the world,[7] the destiny of many a hero is outlined, right from the outset, by the struggle of two gods or goddesses. This is so most clearly and consistently in the *Daughter of the Air*, whose birth is due to the violation of a vestal virgin (the Diana principle) in the Temple of Kypris (the Venus principle), which thus gives rise to an "eternal feud" between the two goddesses. At the end of part one, when the blinded Menon predicts that Semiramis will murder her husband, Ninus, she recalls her natal chart: "Venus and Diana now avenge old jealousies; for what was lifted up by the help of Venus will be brought down by Diana's grudge." At the end of part two, when the queen, at the end of her hubris that knows no moderation, collapses, wounded, she comes to a realization: "After all, Diana, you triumphed finally over Venus! You let me live only to see the unfolding of ruthless destiny, which had threatened me with signs and wonders. I was to be cruel, proud and tyrannical, and, stained with the guilt of murder, I

---

[6] Cf. the entire concluding monologue of act II.

[7] Ludovicus Enius describes in detail how these forces operate, by way of explaining his own evil horoscope, in his long speech before the king in act I of *St. Patrick's Purgatory*.

should receive death after being cast down from the heights." At this point we can interpose a significant word from Astolf in *Life Is a Dream*, which illuminates *Calderon's* idea of fate: "Fate seldom lies when heralding pain; as dependable in evil as it is unreliable in good." Another example of warring constellations is Odysseus, who since the fall of Troy is pursued by Venus and protected by Juno. In a complex dialectic Odysseus triumphs over Circe's cosmic magic by means of the eros-enchantment of Venus, but then—after unspeakable toil on the part of his companions (in the end, even the dead Achilles has to appear)—he is shaken out of the "highest enchantment of love" and escapes to pursue his own destiny.[8] The problem is interestingly posed: we can discern three stages: "eros", the "highest enchantment", overcomes Circe's intracosmic magic, and she falls vanquished into the void. Yet eros too represents bondage; the twig that Juno sends to her protégé to foil Circe's magic can work only "provided love has not fettered you", and he finds it hard to extricate himself. This renunciation in the mythological *comedia* is the symbolic reflection of what, in the Christian plays, will be liberation from the bane of destiny itself. Before sinking to oblivion, Circe says, "Since I see that love is superior to my magic and that he whom I failed to enchant has succumbed to love, I wish to die."

This presents us with the question as to how, according to *Calderon*, man is to face a destiny that seems to be unavoidable. Initially, viewed as a cosmic constellation, fate is not the actual event itself, nor does it contain the latter mechanistically, as in a materialistic and deterministic model of the world: it is potentiality. A great number of *comedias* (and *autos* based on the same material) begin in a "cave"; the hero or heroine is "clothed in skins" and lives in a kind of dreamlike preexistence. (In the *auto Life Is a Dream* this cave existence represents man's preexistence in the mind of the Creator.) Thus Sigismund dwells in his "tower" fashioned like a cave, and Semiramis is imprisoned in a cave because her horoscope (like Sigismund's) promises things that are too terrible. In a similar state are the following characters: Achilles in *The Garden Monster*; Heraclius, the emperor's son, in *In This Life All Is Truth and All Is Deceit*; Mafisa in *The Fate and Proverb of Leonido and Mafisa*; and Clymene, who is brought up in isolation because of a prediction that must not be allowed to come true (in *Apollo and Clymene*). This condition of preexistence is the person's "endowment", even before it

---

[8] The same theme occurs again in the eclogue *The Gulf of the Sirens*, which is a continuation of the drama of Circe. There is another battle between Venus and Diana in *Loved and Rejected*, and another between Pallas and Minerva in *The Statue of Prometheus*.

is tested through the use of freedom, albeit an endowment that exhibits the common "fallenness" of all creatures and often enough the guilty *flight* from destiny. The "cave" imprisonment is meant to prevent people from suffering the fate in store for them.

But this endowment of potentiality, whatever the oracle says about it, can only incline (*inclinar*) people in a certain direction, it can never force them (*forzar*).[9] Thus, in principle, free will is capable of lifting itself above fate, or at least of molding it so that it is fulfilled in a larger and unforeseeable context. Like everything else in *Calderon's* great hall of mirrors, this allows of analogous forms and stages,[10] but at the decisive level, the Christian level, all ambiguity is shed. Ultimately the *Daughter of the Air* is a great tragedy of destiny only because Semiramis is resolved from the outset to allow herself to be pushed in the direction of the demonic *inclinacion* that is part of her endowment. She is the clearest paradigm of the pagan, unredeemed world under the power of original sin. She says to her guardian, Tiresias: "Today, through your

---

[9] We have already demonstrated this (above, p. 319ff.). There are countless such texts. In *The Miraculous Magician* the demon says, "Y inclinarlos podré, si no forzarlos", for he cannot force Justina's will (*Dramas*, 1088). In the speech of King Basil, in which he announces the reason for Sigismund's imprisonment, he confesses his grievous error, namely, "to have regarded foretold destinies as fixed and inevitable. The blood of a prince may incline him to fall, yet it is possible for him to continue to stand. It is true that a harsh destiny, wayward blood and a baneful planet can bend their influences upon the free will, but they can never force it." Similarly at the beginning of act II: "For man is more than the stars" (*predomina en las estrellas*). And when Clotald tells the prince that he has been transferred to the royal palace: "Yet be assured that you will learn to master the star's influence, for never did a lofty spirit submit to the stars."

[10] Thus Odysseus' overcoming of Circe's enchantment is attributed to the *albedrio*, as he explains to her toward the end of act I, although this does not mean that he has attained full liberty (from the magic of eros). Mariamne also tells the Tetrarch that the diligent man can be "the lord of the stars by the strength of his active will, preparing himself for danger and even fashioning evil into good" (act I). Aurelian says the same to Zenobia: "All the fire of the passions will not compel me to love, if I will not love" (act II). The most potent example beside *Life Is a Dream* is *The Miraculous Magician*: all Cyprian's demonic magical power cannot compel Justina to yield, tempted as she is from within and without. Cyprian knows this from the outset, just as Faust knows that Mephisto cannot satisfy his urge toward the infinite, and makes the contract with the demon under an unfulfillable condition: "What you offer (the seduction of Justina) is not within your power, for I know that neither spell nor enchantment can master the free will" (act II).

confining will, my stubborn pride shall break", because, as she says, it is "folly" to fear destiny. "Take precautions, and let that be enough." She wishes the lightning to strike her dead. But she emphasizes her freedom, her self-conquest: "I go forward of my own free will, lest anyone should compel me" (I, 1). Indeed she knows, at the end of the great explanation of her origins, "that heaven never acts contrary to divine nature, never violates our power to choose". Stubbornly she asks Menon, "Is my will unfettered or am I a slave? What power has destiny over me, what right of tutelage?" (I, 2). As her influence expands, her subjects split into a Fortuna party and a party of *justicia* or *razon*: Semiramis is Fortuna incarnate, basking in the euphoria of power and doomed by the wheel's continual turning: she thought she was free, but she was merely being driven.

Sigismund fights the decisive battle between "right" and "happiness" (or "power") within himself; consequently he is in a position to give the most profound advice as to the attitude to be adopted to destiny. The plot is complex in that King Basil, in himself a kind man, puts his son (who has a terrible horoscope) into the tower in order to resist fate. This very intervention, however, makes the son into an "animal" brutal enough to put his foot on his father's head. Sigismund's own power to decide is so vitiated by this intervention that he can call the king the *"tirano de mi albedrio"*. Thus Sigismund's preexistence is not at all the pure, naturally given potentiality prior to the freedom "test" that is designed to show what kind of man he is; he is already at a disadvantage because of the king's guilt. The king tries to disguise his act as an attempt "to see whether the wise man can win mastery over the stars". He arranges a test in which Sigismund is allowed to reign for one day, "to see whether heaven (which cannot lie) may not eventually moderate its hostile stance and finally, conquered by resoluteness and insight, abandon it altogether" (act two). Of course, under these conditions, Sigismund cannot pass the test. "My inclinations are the test of what is right": *justo—mi gusto*. However, he is persuaded that it was all a dream. Subsequently, in a real dream, he reproduces the scene, wanting to take his revenge "on the vast stage of the world theatre" and place his foot on his father's neck; here the difference between the significance of reality and the significance of the dream has evaporated. This distances him, and out of this distance, in an almost Buddhist manner, arises true ethical freedom, which calms "the raging of wild ambition" (end of act two). Then, set free by insurgents and put at the head of the army "of the nameless and rejected", he is concerned only to *"obrar bien"*: he has "seen through" everything else ("*ya os conozco,*

ya os conozco"), he has become "sober" (*desengañado*). From this distance
he can both forgive his father and fall at his feet, and renounce his
(instinctual) love for Rosaura.

From this vantage point he can also formulate *Calderon's* final norms
as to how the horoscope should be approached. The first rule is this: do
not flee from destiny; take no measures to escape its nets. The king
himself formulates this, in falsely fatalistic mood:

> There's no escaping what must come,
> And rash is the desire to see the future.
> Hide you may, t'will find you all the same;
> If it's to be, your protection's all in vain.
> A sudden fall, an abrupt end, the baneful sign appears!
> Flee the danger and you'll find it about your ears!
> Vainly I sought security by my own hand:
> Instead I wreaked ruin upon myself and my own land.

So it was foolish to hide Clymene away in the attempt to keep her from
having the son of whom disaster was foretold: Apollo himself will
make her pregnant. Similarly, it was foolish to keep Achilles in the
cave, for he will pursue his hero's path, and so forth.

More important than the first principle of not opposing fate is the
second principle: the horoscope should not be "used impurely"; man
should not "intrude into its mystery" (as Basil did) but approach it with
"reason", "moderation", "humility" and "wisdom", by submitting to
the test to which it puts man. "There's no protection nor safety to be
won / In counteracting danger ere it come." Only *in danger itself* can
humility offer any protection; there is no way of avoiding it (Sigismund's speech to the king in act three). This humility is expressly
referred to as wisdom, which alone can triumph in destiny. In the final
scene of *Saint Patrick's Purgatory* there is also the confident hope that the
guilty man, whom the demons are already taunting with the certainty
of his being lost, will not be abandoned by God.

However, this has taken us over the borderline and into the area of
Christian theology, with which the *autos* specifically deal. Here self-
conquest, freely undertaken, which (from below) was seen as "humility", "wisdom" and "renunciation", is described (from above) as the
operation of grace. This makes it finally clear that, for the Christian,
Calderon, there is no neutral "destiny" but only an either-or: either man
is enslaved in original sin, to what Paul calls the "powers of the
universe", or he lays hold of redeeming grace in a humility that accepts
the external fate of death but, by so doing, inwardly transcends it.[11]

---

[11] Kommerell sees this clearly: "In the case of the Christian, destiny enters

Calderon took renunciation (supported by grace) as the cardinal theme of his plays on countless occasions. One only has to think of *Prince, Friend, Wife* or the Alexander play *Darlo todo y no dar nada*, to say nothing of the martyr plays.

The play entitled *Meditation on the Cross*, so often wrongly misunderstood as an unbearable drama of destiny, stands on its own. Here the theme is not destiny at all but the omnipotence of grace. The man whom grace has specially chosen cannot escape: it will overtake him in full flight. This play is like an echo of the celebrated disputes on the question of grace at the turn of the century. Clearly, when these presuppositions are not held, the play is easily misconstrued; *Grillparzer*, for instance, took the inspiration for his *Die Ahnfrau* from it.

c. The Theme of Death

Ultimately, drama is thus severely restricted in terms of space and time because behind the finitude of the action there lies the finitude of life and its decisions, that is, death. Death stands, unuttered, behind every play, and often enough it becomes its explicit subject matter, and not only in tragedy either. The view has been expressed that Greek tragedy arose entirely out of dealings with the dead, that it came from "the act of transforming a soul from the realm of the dead into an active, living being".[1] Be that as it may, the realm of death must intrude into

---

into two relationships which reveal anxiety: with sin on the one hand, particularly original sin . . . and with grace on the other hand" (*Beiträge zu einem deutschen Calderon*, 51). On the difference between this and the theme of destiny in the ancient world see above, p. 196. On the philosophical problems involved in freedom and destiny (which, however, Calderon always deals with and solves in a theological way): "By 'predisposition' we mean man as he is, 'nature' in the Christian sense, that is, vitiated by evil influences. The will, too, does not come forth from man as his dynamic personal disposition, purified in consciousness; rather, it is closely bound up with grace, making it possible for man to be a supernatural being dependent on God" (203–4).

[1] A. Baeumler, introduction to J. J. Bachofen's *Der Mythus vom Orient und Okzident* (Munich, 1926). Naturally we cannot go into the philosophy of death. Cf. on the subject J. Choron, *Der Tod im abendländischen Denken* (Stuttgart, 1967); Anton Hügli, "Zur Geschichte der Todesdeutung" in *Studia Philosophica, Jahrbuch d. schweiz. Philos. Gesellschaft* XXXII (Basle, 1972): 1–28.

life as a confining element, exhibiting the irreducible ambiguity that arises from its proximity to life. For it is simultaneously the unavoidable end to which all are obliged to come, and the concluding event that a man can arrange—in suicide—and shape in manifold ways. The dying man can make his death the highest expression of his existential will, as in the case of the martyr or the person who sacrifices himself for some lofty ideal. By means of this final act, whether he suffers it or seeks it out, he can imprint a meaning, retrospectively, on his whole existence. Thus in the drama it is generally only the last act that rids the preceding one of its fluid and provisional character and confirms the entire action.

So, paradoxically, death can change from being a radically passive event, which, even if we try desperately to flee from it, will eventually overtake us, to become a highly active event, deliberately chosen and shaped as to its when, where and why. This presupposes a mysterious preknowledge of death, which comes not only from familiarity with dying in the human milieu, but from the fact that death is immanent in every temporal moment. The time within which we live contains this paradox in itself: it is evanescent, it is ceaselessly running out, and at the same time it continually offers us the opportunity of a new beginning; what has been is removed out of range of our freedom, but this only serves to make room for the further exercise of freedom. The final moment of time thus presents two sides: it is man's ultimate humiliation, striking him down and changing his organism into corruption, and at the same time it is something most precious and noble if he accepts it as the total offering and final form of his existence. On the one hand it is society's *pudendum*. This is increasingly so as society sees itself more and more as a mere collective. Then all open encounter with death is avoided; in the theatre it is laughed at in all kinds of grotesque forms, for example, Dürrenmatt's *Meteor* (1966), where the comedy lies in the fact that every "final" death keeps turning out to be premature: "When shall I finally kick the bucket?"[2] and *Jack Gelber's The Apple* (1962), where, again, death (both real and supposed) is the subject of comic-grotesque

[2] *Der Meteor*, comedy in 2 acts, 2d ed. (Zurich: Arche, 1970), 71.

play. On the other hand people *do* wish to see this final point, for
without it, life as it is experienced seems to have no meaning at
all. But the question is, Can this moment carry such a weight?
Can it be expected to give meaning to the meaningless when it
itself seems to be the most meaningless of all? Death is thus
either man's worst enemy or his best friend; it is either an
expression of the essential law of all nature or something absolutely unnatural. Furthermore, it is independent of a person's
age; for instance, death is not the enemy of youth and a friend to
age. Neither is it dependent on sickness and health; it cuts right
across such foreground aspects. It is possible for a life that is on
the decline somehow to reach out organically for death because
it feels profoundly unworthy of life (*Chekhov*),[3] but even this
raises the question of an appropriate manner of death. Conversely it is possible for a life in full bloom to be inwardly ready
and willing for death, if some great cause beckons (*Kaiser's Die
Bürger von Calais*, 1914).

The aspects are many and mutually opposed, yet they are not
ultimately to be separated from one another. Even when a death
is freely chosen it is still a making-present of that death that is
our destiny; even when it is unwanted and resisted, in the end it
must be affirmed. And it is this mysterious paradox that imparts
ultimate meaning to the play of life, or denies it any meaning.
This being the case, we are obliged to examine those aspects of
death that play a crucial role in drama.

α. *Death as destiny*. The play may consist in a living person
being chased and driven into the arms of death. In the plays of
antiquity it can be the gods who carry out this chase. Thus
Athene pursues *Sophocles'* Ajax ("The goddess . . . is tormenting
me to death");[4] Hera brings madness upon the Heracles of
Euripides as he returns from the underworld, making him kill his
own sons.[5] In the modern drama it is human beings, occasionally
of mythical dimensions, who hunt their fellow men. This is the
case with *Dürrenmatt's* ruthless *Alte Dame* who gives a billion to

---

[3] *Ivanov*, *The Seagull*, *The Churchyard*. Here the tragic is fashioned as a
comedy; the dramatist himself understood the work as a pure comedy.

[4] Sophocles, *Aiax*, 401–3.

[5] Euripides, *Heracles*, vv. 831ff.

her impoverished home neighborhood, thereby buying justice for herself:[6] in exchange, someone is to kill Alfred Ill, who has denied fathering the child of Claire (an "arch-whore"). "With financial muscle like mine it is possible to buy an entire world order."[7] Money is the new god, chasing people to death. Ill refuses to kill himself: "You *must* be my judge now, . . . I cannot relieve you of your task."[8] It is for this "justice" that Ill is killed. In *Max Frisch's Andorra* (1961) it is the anti-Semitic ideology that chases the young Andri to death. Though not a Jew, he is thought to be one, and in the end he faces up to the role that has been forced upon him: "My grief raises me above you all, and so I shall fall."[9] Between the images, the individual characters take their stand in the witness-box and profess their innocence; at most they are victims of circumstance. "They do not ask which of *them* is the murderer."[10] In a similar way, in *Peter Weiss'* Auschwitz Oratorio, *Die Ermittlung* (1965), no one will admit to being the murderer. Again, in *Arthur Miller's The Crucible*, John Proctor is the victim of mass hysteria; like Andri, he refuses to buy his freedom by a confession that would have violated his conscience (namely, that he had communed with the devil). In *Dürrenmatt, Frisch* and *Miller*, as in the drama of antiquity, the individual, out of his inner freedom, raises himself above the mob. (*O'Casey* shows us a comic-grotesque witch-hunt in his *Cock-a-Doodle-Dandy* of 1949.)

But it can also be that death itself, in person, as it were, steps forward as the alien enemy of life. Here the essential tragedy can be that life that is happy or vigorous suddenly finds itself face to face with the abyss of "thus far and no farther". In the fourth chapter of his *Laokoon*, with reference to *Sophocles'* Philoctetes and the dying Heracles, *Lessing* had already opened up the stage to the lamenting hero, comparing him to someone physically ill whom no one helps and who cannot help himself: "We see before us nothing but despair in its most terrible form." *Goethe's*

---

6 Dürrenmatt, *Komödien* I (Zurich: Arche, 1957), 282.
7 *Ibid.*, 315.
8 *Ibid.*, 328.
9 Frisch, *Stücke* II (Suhrkamp, 1962), 274.
10 *Ibid.*, 297.

Egmont does not go quite this far; but the whole play (if we set aside the Netherlands' struggle for freedom from servitude under Alba, which is not central) is nothing other than life's struggle with a death that, through cunning, conquers life from outside. Egmont is the darling of the people, secretly in love with Klärchen; he is carefree and hence, in spite of Oranien's warning, he is essentially unsuspecting, carrying his head as high "as if majesty's hand were not poised above it". He feels as *Goethe* does in *Schwager Kronos* and *Faust*: "Should I not enjoy the present moment?" "As yet I have not reached the peak of my growing, and when I stand upon it, I want to stand there firmly and without fear. If I am to fall, let a thunderbolt, a hurricane, throw me back into the depths. There I should lie with many thousand others." He aptly compares himself to a "sleepwalker" perched dangerously on the ridge of a roof; no one must call out to him. He is youthful vitality at all levels of his being, and so he falls into Alba's net. Death suddenly stands before him, "terrible". Until now, in battle, he had overcome it, but "now death has found his mark in me". In vain he asks Ferdinand for a way of escape. The terrible thing is that life must die. "Sweet life! O beautiful, familiar habit of being and doing, am I to part from you? . . . Life is coming to an end for me. Yet I have lived." The final word is "destiny": "Man thinks he directs his own life . . . but what is deepest in him is irresistibly drawn to his destiny."

Closer to *Lessing's* thought is *Kleist* with his *Robert Guiskard*: here the mortal enemy no longer confronts the hero; it is within him. The plague he wishes to turn away from his army, which is lying outside Byzantium, is eating his own life away. His lofty plans of gaining the Byzantine crown and settling the feud in his house are undermined and brought to ruin in his own heart. He believes he has the royal charisma of being able to touch the sick, immune to disease: "Even if 'twere plague I tell you this: / On these bones it would gnaw itself to death." But the enemy within him is stronger, and "the sentenced man has no resurrection". A similarly high-flying hero is *Grabbe's Kaiser Heinrich der Sechste*; "high up on Mount Etna", in the very bloom of his power, he is struck down by death: "Crying out, Woe! / What

struck me? What's that knocking?—not my heart— / Death!
—The dog!"[11] Even *Gerstenberg's Ugolino* (1768) was nothing
but a huge, terrible, physical dying, a stylized scene from the old
Dances of Death that have been resurrected in our century by
Leo Weismantel (*Totentanz*, 1921), *W. H. Auden* (*The Dance of
Death*, 1933), *Michel de Ghelderode* (*Le cavalier bizarre*, 1920; *La
ballade du Grand Macabre*, 1936), right up to *Ionesco's* headlong
Jeux de massacre (1970). In *Le Roi se meurt* (1966), an individual's
act of dying fills out a whole evening. In *Arthur Schnitzler's Zum
Grossen Wurstel* (1904), real actors appear as puppets, their limbs
suspended from strings. At the end the Unknown Man appears
in a blue coat and "severs all the strings at a stroke. The puppets
collapse on to the floor"—including the playwright. Speaking
to himself he says, "I am terrified by my own power! / Is what I
write truth or darkness? . . . / Is it me—or only a symbol?"
"Yes, were my sword held less tightly, / I know how many a
one who prides himself, in pain and pleasure, / on his highly
questionable reality, would—(to the stalls:) What would have
become of you, for instance?"

It is the act of self-surrender, performed perhaps at the end of
a period of desperate resistance. In *Georges Duhamel's Le combat*
(1913), the consumptive youth's fight against certain death
becomes "a genuine school of the heart". In *Thornton Wilder's*
three-minute play *And the Sea Shall Give up Its Dead* the only
issue, in the face of the Last Judgment, is that of self-surrender.
The empress observes that we keep clinging to our selfhood as if
it were something of value; Horatio Nissen is terrified of having
to give up himself ("Oh God, don't let people think I'm a
Goy"), and Father Cosroe beseeches God to let him keep his
special mind, avid for knowledge, and all he has filled it with.
But then the anxious souls reach the ocean surface, and the
momentous business of the Last Judgment is over in a trice. In
his play *The Living Room* (1932), *Graham Greene* portrays the
senseless attempt to escape death: after all the rooms of the house
in which a person has died have been locked, those who are
trying to avoid death are finally struck by a ray of grace: they
will be allowed to die there once the rooms have been unlocked

----

[11] Grabbe, *Sämtliche Werke* (Detmold, 1874), vol. 2: 503.

again. In *Maxim Gorky's Igor Bulitchov* (1931), the man dies an "untimely" death of cancer in the midst of the whirlpool of a collapsing middle-class society, while the Revolution is starting; death renders both past and present meaningless: "Where is the court to which I can appeal against my sickness? Against my untimely death?" "I have lived and lived, and I ask myself, Why do you live? . . . What does death mean to us, Pavlin?" "I don't live in the right street. I have fallen among strangers; for thirty years I have been living among nothing but strangers." Death is the other, the alien, that which disorients. In *O'Neill's* one-act play *Bound East for Cardiff*, it is symbolized by fog: a sailor dies, embarrassing his fellow sailors, for he had wanted to be buried on dry land, but it will be a week before they reach Cardiff. "I shall be buried at sea."

β. *Death as the interpreter of life.* Even in some of the plays already mentioned death throws light, retrospectively, on life. It puts life on the scales and ascertains its specific significance. In *Hofmannsthal's Der Tor und der Tod* (1893), death is the first genuine reality, showing Claudio how all his prior encounters were unreal and governed by aspects of preexistence and ego-centricity. Death gives him everything by withdrawing it from him: "Since my life was dead, you, O Death, shall be my life!" "Only now that I am dying do I feel that I *am*." *Büchner* put this even more forcefully in his *Danton*: the hero has been flirting with death for a long time ("it is quite delightful to make eyes at him from a distance through a lorgnon"), and now death draws closer and closer to him, the one reality in the face of which everything that has been is mere play-acting.[12] Here, however, death is so much the one concrete reality that, by contrast with transitory life, it will never pass away. "If a man could believe in annihilation there would be hope for him", but the dying man "cannot die". *Büchner* gives a metaphysical gloss at this point: "All is chaos. The void has killed itself; creation is its wound; we are its drops of blood; and the world is the grave in which it is

[12] "[W]hether they die on the guillotine, or from a fever or from old age. . . . That's just fine and suits us; we are still on the stage, even if, in the end, we too will be given the knife" (*Sämtliche Werke*, ed. Bergemann [Insel, 1922], 34).

decaying."[13] Death unveils existence—in a Buddhist or gnostic sense—as the result of the void's sinful fall.

Wilder has fewer metaphysical pretentions, but in his *Our Town* (1939), the dead Emily looks back over her life but is told by the dead not to cling to what has been; she must look to what lies ahead and get ready for it. Having been allowed to relive one of her earthly days, she has to admit that, in those earthly moments, nothing has been really lived out. "Things go too fast. We don't even have time to take a look at ourselves." This retrospect is similar to that of *Shaw's* Joan in her nocturnal conversation with the king. Everything is put to rights.

But the retrospective view may also show that the lived experience is unique and unrepeatable, with the result that all attempts to rerun it are doomed to failure. So it is in *Pär Lagerkvist's The Man Who Lived Again* (1928): as soon as the hero plunges into life's murky air once more, he succumbs to crime again. So it is in *François Paliard's* one-act play *X Lives Again*, though here the hero is so bound by his constitution that he keeps failing. So it is, too, in *Jean Paul Sartre's Les jeux sont faits* (1947): man only has a single opportunity of making a decision about himself. The same theme is found, lightly clad, in *Ferenc Molnar's Liliom* (1909).

Death is seen as the harsh light illuminating the life that precedes it; it can light up everything, right from the very beginnings. *O'Neill*[14] has most movingly turned this searchlight onto the past, again using his fog motif in *A Long Day's Journey into Night* (1940): the journey into night is the journey farther and farther back into one's own past. Eventually Mary, having gone back as far as her childhood, succumbs to insanity; this is the same as *Büchner's* view of tragedy. Similar is *André Obey's Revenu de l'étoile* (1939) (that is, from the Monument to the Unknown Soldier), where the lonely woman's memories go back farther and farther, right to the birth of her children, but ultimately the present comes back again. The theme is caricatured in *Jardiel Poncelas' Quatro corazones con freno y marcha atrás* (1936, *Four Hearts with Brakes and Reverse Gear*), where time glides by

---

[13] *Ibid.*, 65.

[14] O'Neill dealt grotesquely with the theme of the return from the dead in *Lazarus Laughed* (1928).

while, for the "four", it stands still, so that in the end they find themselves going to school with their grandchildren.

There is another way in which death illuminates life, that is, when, at the moment of passing over, a person's entire past life is brought before his consciousness. Thus *Pär Lagerkvist*, in his *Den svara stunden* (1918), unfolds a single second (which is all it takes to die in a railway accident) and shows the dying man his life's guilt. In another one-act play he shows the realization, in death, of having failed in life. In a similar way *Armand Salacrou* in his *L'Inconnu d'Arras* (1935) unfolds the second taken by the suicide's bullet as it penetrates his brain in order to confront him with his views, his attempts to find a meaning to life, a single good deed he has performed, but primarily with his decision, his affirmation of freedom. All masks fall away in the face of death.

γ. *The immanence of death.* Those who flee from death as something alien, in fact carry death within them. "Life carries a law of bronze inscribed upon it and everything has its price. Love involves the pains of love, success is inseparable from the infinite weariness of the journey toward it, and the warmth of emotion is matched by the horrors of desolation. The price of our entire existence is death."[15] So life is "saturated with death" (*Tennessee Williams*). This very experience is the content of the plays of the young *Maurice Maeterlinck* (*L'Intruse, Les aveugles*, 1890; *L'Intérieur*, 1894). Here *Maeterlinck* ultimately portrays a condition, not an action (he calls his plays *drames statiques*), the condition of man, defenceless in the face of death. Characteristically, it is blind people who are most aware of the approach of death.[16] In *Les aveugles*, death has long been among them: the old priest, for whom the twelve blind men are waiting, lies dead in their midst. But: "It seems as if we are always alone. . . .

[15] Hofmannsthal, *Der weisse Fächer* in *Gedichte und Lyrische Dramen* (Fischer, 1946), 316–17. This was written before Georg Simmel produced his essay "Zur Metaphysik des Todes" in *Logos* I (1910/11): 57ff., in which, like Scheler and Rilke later on, he describes death as a reality inherent in every living being, giving shape to it and leading it to maturity.

[16] In *L'Intruse*, too, it is the blind grandfather who has profound understanding of the mother who is dying in the next room.

One must see in order to love."[17] The theme is distorted into the grotesque *tragédie bouffe* in *Maeterlinck's* fellow countryman *Michel de Ghelderode* (*Le Cavalier bizarre*, 1920); a "spy" describes the arrival of death for the benefit of geriatrics in a hospital, but in the event death arrives not there but next door. In *Maeterlinck's* *L'Intérieur*, while the "old man", who knows about death, is holding a conversation with a stranger from his window, his daughter's corpse is brought into the room.

Following *Maeterlinck* many philosophers have described this immanence of death in life, the awareness of its presence, as a boundary situation (*Jaspers*). We have already encountered the young *Georg Lukács*; for him, the reality of death in life is the precondition of that boundary that gives meaning, of ethical and aesthetic form.[18] Close to him are *Paul Ernst, Arnold Gehlen* (for whom death is the central locus of tragedy)[19] and finally *Ernst Bloch*: "Death is thus simply the making visible of a form that is essentially there; in the same way, for instance, that Michelangelo saw the statue in the block of stone: his chisel only had to chip away the superfluous material around it."[20] *Gabriel Marcel* expressed himself similarly, before climbing to a higher level of reflection, which we shall shortly discuss.

A great number of classical and modern plays could be mentioned here insofar as they presuppose and progressively demonstrate the all-powerful presence of death, which is ultimately only the explicit implementation of something implicit: the situation was ripe for it. To this category belong *Shakespeare's* *Hamlet* and *Julius Caesar*, *Racine's Phèdre*, the tragedies of *Gryphius*, *Lessing's Emilia Galotti*, *Schiller's Maria Stuart*. In others—*Grillparzer, Hebbel, Ibsen, Chekhov*—the unavoidable moment is central at some point or other. Or else a murder has been decided upon, and the only question is the identity of the wretched man who is to come under its law, as in *Camus' Le malentendu*.

The theme can be coarsened and changed into a living person's

---

[17] *Théâtre* I–II (Brussels, 1910), 104.

[18] *Die Seele und die Formen* (1911); *Zur Soziologie des modernen Dramas* (1914).

[19] "Die Struktur der Tragödie" in *Neue psychologische Studien* XII, 3 (Munich and Berlin, 1934).

[20] *Das Prinzip Hoffnung* (Frankfurt, 1959), 1375.

encounter with his dead self, as staged for instance by *Calderon*.[21] In an even more grotesque form the same person can be brought onto the stage in four ages of life at the same time.[22] But it is also possible to disperse the theme throughout the whole play, like an atmosphere; this is often the case in *Pirandello* and even more so in *Tennessee Williams*, albeit the omnipresent fear of death also manifests signs of a neurotic fear of life (particularly in *Camino Real*, 1953).

However, what if death's immanence refers not (only) to oneself but primarily to a deceased loved one? If one has genuinely and definitively given oneself to another, it is not something that can be revoked or broken off because of this person's death. At this point, which is central to both the philosophy and dramatic theory of *Gabriel Marcel*, the surviving partner becomes aware of something eternal at every second of his existence, precisely through this earthly absence. Ultimately *Marcel's* intuition goes beyond spiritism (to which it is close); it is a genuinely metaphysical intuition that definitely presupposes a free choice—that is, the eternal value of love.[23] Thus the locus of communication with the deceased loved one becomes the most prominent locus of transcendence; through the essential renunciation of any awakening from the dead it becomes a hope reaching into eternity. The first person to dramatize this idea was *Marcel* in *L'Iconoclaste*,[24] in which Abel despises Jacques' love for the dead Viviane as sacrilegious and tries to destroy it, but finally has to acknowledge its validity while at the same time liberating Jacques from a desire to cling to her at the level of the senses. He must make room for the mystery, otherwise life cannot breathe. In *Le fanal*,[25] it is the dead woman whose invisible presence governs everything, bringing back the unfaithful husband and restraining the son who wanted to marry a

---

[21] In *St. Patrick's Purgatory*, Enius encounters himself as a dead man. There is a similarity between the scenes in which, in both Calderon and Gryphius (*Cardenio und Celinde*), the lover embraces, not the beloved, but her skeleton. Cf. C. F. Meyer's poem "Begegnung".

[22] Peter A. Ustinov, *The Photo Finish* (1962).

[23] Texts and discussion in Roger Troisfontaines, *De l'existence à l'être, La philosophie de Gabriel Marcel* I–II (Louvain and Paris, 1953), 141–71.

[24] *Trois Pièces* (Plon, 1931).

[25] In *Supplément de "La vie intellectuelle"* (1936).

divorced woman against his mother's will. The absent person, the apparently powerless person, is the strongest: death itself, which takes part of the living over into the eternal realm, is the signal (*fanal*). This idea leads *Marcel* further to the theme of substitutionary death, to which we shall have to return.

δ. *On the borderline*. If death is part of life, does not this mean that, however mysteriously, life participates in death, and that what is dead can manifest itself in life? *Marcel* has dealt specifically with this active presence. It is hard to draw the boundaries here between mythical or literary conventions that allow dead people to appear among the living (from *Aeschylus' Persians*, via *Shakespeare*, to *Grillparzer's Die Ahnfrau*), or the living to walk the paths of the dead (the ceaseless variations, right up to the present time, of the themes of Orpheus and Alcestis, whom Heracles brings up from Hades after a struggle with Death). In this context we are leaving to one side the drama of spiritism, although it is well known how much *Strindberg* is indebted to it—his *Blue Book* is dedicated to *Swedenborg*—as well as the drama of anthroposophy, which shows us the soul's path of guilt and purification as it goes through many lives and traverses many cosmic regions. Nor shall we deal with *A. Mombert's* dramas of the universe with their lyrical pathos.

There are plays, however, in which man is open to an invisible, supramundane reality and where the dramatic plot arises from the fact that the hero is explicitly addressed by this reality. In the *Women of Trachis* of *Sophocles* it is a dead man who finally brings Heracles to death according to the oracle (1159–1163). In *Shakespeare's Hamlet*, we cannot dispense with the ghost of his father and replace it with Hamlet's conscience, for instance, after he had learned of the committed misdeed. It is crucially important for the entire course of the action that this ghost should make its appearance from purgatory: "Cut off even in the blossoms of my sin, . . . / No reckoning made, but sent to my account / With all my imperfections on my head" (I, 5). The ghost in *Giraudoux' Intermezzo* is equally indispensable. The girl Isabelle is open to the realm of the dead and to a sense of something universal embracing both life and death; the play concerns her transition to a middle-class, adult existence in which death is nothing but life's "normal" end. Everything remains in a state of flux (similar to *Rilke's* Elegies): as far as Isabelle is concerned, there is nothing abstruse about believing in ghosts. "What I think is not normal is this indifference of the living with regard to the dead. Either we are all hypocrites, and millions of Christians (who affirm that the dead have another life) do not believe what they say. Or else, as soon as they speak of the dead, they become self-seeking and shortsighted."[26] But then, as a result of the intervention of authority, this "invisible friendship" becomes a public affair: what brings the girl out of the danger zone,[27] what the ghost says about those who have died young (II, 6), what Isabelle suspects about the "mission" of the deceased, her "confidant", and her own responsibility toward the dead—all this clouds over in the uncertainty as to the boundaries between the living and the dead[28] and results in the ghost being driven out by Isabelle's future husband, who invites her to walk along "the only normal path toward death and the dead".[29] So the ghost parts from the girl and leaves her to her husband "who will keep you turning back and forth between your two ideas of death".[30]

It can be the gods, rather than the dead, who tear a hole in men's *lebensraum* and profoundly undermine it. So Jupiter in the Amphitryon plays (*Molière, Kleist, Giraudoux*), and in *Sartre's Les mouches*, or Apollo in *Thornton Wilder's Alcestiad*. Or angels may intervene in the fate of the world (*Giraudoux' Sodome et Gomorrhe, Dürrenmatt's Ein Engel kam nach Babylon*). Or, as in *Ionesco*, anyone at all may come into our world from the antiworld and open up unsuspected dimensions to the person who takes a *Stroll in the Air*.

New psychologies (*Freud, Jung*) facilitate new interpretations of the descent into hell, that is, into areas where the "I" is dissolved in the collective and what is alive here and now is dissolved into the potential. It is even possible to descend to

[26] *Intermezzo* II, 3, in Jean Giraudoux, *Théâtre*, 4 vols. (Grasset, 1959), vol. 2: 50.

[27] "Their game [the dead] is well known. They get hold of one of the mortals and separate him from the crowd" (*ibid.*, 54).

[28] Cf. what the druggist says in III, 2 (*ibid.*, 77).

[29] III, 3 (*ibid.*, 81).

[30] III, 4 (*ibid.*, 90).

regions where "what is frightful bears a smile" (*Cocteau's Orpheus* film). New philosophies that maintain man's freedom to make a once-for-all choice can present us with a hellish other world in which no change is possible: locked in iron selfhood and hatred, everyone is eternally alien to everyone else. So it is in *Strindberg's Dance of Death*, where the reactions of hate between Alice and the captain operate purely mechanically, and among the old people in the *Ghost Sonata*. So too, finally, in *Sartre's Huis-Clos*, where people are no longer able to be alone or relate to others. Inès: "I shall burn, burn, and I know that there will be no end."[31] Garcin, too, drumming on the barred door, is prepared to endure all the torments of the old hell if he can thus escape the unendurable torments of this new one.[32] Suicide no longer offers a way out.

We need not delay over plays that deal with what comes after death, like *J. B. Priestley's Johnson over Jordan*,[33] but we must mention plays in which some fatal deed is appointed to be carried out; fatal, because from the outset the deed itself is one that transcends the human and thus necessarily destroys the doer. Thus it is in *Albert Camus' Les justes* (1949),[34] which deals with the assassination of the Grand Prince Sergei by terrorists in 1905. Kaliayev, arrested for the assassination, is in conversation with the grand princess, who, as a Christian, would like to forgive the murderer. Here the absolute quality of Christ's act is pushed to one side as unworthy of belief: "The Church has kept grace to itself and left us with the task of exercising love."[35] Now it is the passion for absolute justice in the world that calls

[31] Jean-Paul Sartre, *Huis-Clos*, Collection Folio (Gallimard), 65.

[32] *Ibid.*, 85.

[33] More plays in M. Dietrich, *Das moderne Drama* (Kröner, 1963), 531. Brecht's *Lukullus* belongs here. There is also the grotesque alternation of life and death: in *Piétons de l'air* Bérenger's father is supposed to be dead, but is alive and may have risen from the dead. "Resurrection announcements" are distributed. In Dürrenmatt's *Meteor* the fact of imminent (and overdue) death is continually postponed, with the result that Schwitter, to his annoyance, attains the odor of someone who has miraculously risen from the dead, whereas all the subordinate characters die or otherwise decline.

[34] In *Théâtre, récits, nouvelles* (Bibl. de la Pléiade, 1963), 301–93.

[35] Before going out to do this deed, Kaliayev crosses himself before the icon. "Does he believe?—he doesn't practice—and yet he has a religious soul. . . . For

for the absolute commitment of one's life. If possible, "killing and dying" do not need to balance each other: it is better to die for the alleged crime in a personal and justifying act. "We pay more than we owe. That means dying twice." For Stepan, the unscrupulous terrorist, there is no problem: "I do not love life; I love justice, which is more than life." He would even have thrown the bomb among the children sitting in the carriage. The others are ground to pieces by the contradiction between love for the concrete human being and love for abstract justice. On the one hand there is compassion (for the children); on the other there is the "honor of the revolution". Is it possible personally to love the impersonal? Is it possible to be a pure exponent of the party? Yes, if one calculates backward from death: "We are not of this world: we are just. There is a warmth which is not for us. . . . Ah! Mercy for the just!" Can a man die impersonally for justice in the world? "If death is the only way out, we are on the wrong track. The right track leads to the sun. . . . The others, our grandchildren. . . . Yes. But Janek is in jail, and the rope around his neck is cold. He will die, perhaps he is dead already. So that the others can live. Ah! Borya, what if the others *won't* live? What if he dies in vain?" It remains an open question, an open contradiction. It is the same contradiction as in *Brecht's The Measures Taken*. Again we have the confrontation with Christ: "We have taken the world's misfortune on ourselves. That's what he did. What courage! But it often seems to me to be a kind of pride, which has to be punished." The answer comes: "We pay for this pride with our lives. No one can do more." And again the question raises its head: Perhaps other murderers will come, taking us as their precedent, yet not prepared to pay with their lives? Dora, who asks this, shares *Camus'* realization: "It is easy, so much easier, to die from one's contradictions than to live them." This play is far more profound that *Sartre's Les mains sales*, to which it is a reply.

This strange anticipation of death, which is supposed to justify criminal action on behalf of abstract justice, contains a kind of perversion of the mythical descents into Hades. In the

---

us, who do not believe in God, there must be complete justice, otherwise there is only despair" (*ibid.*, 355).

latter, however, while love involved renunciation, it was a love without contradictions. Only by renouncing immediate happiness was Orpheus able to wrest his Euridice from death. Only on the basis of a supreme renunciation of immediate love is it possible for Alcestis to go to death for her husband's sake and ultimately return to him from death.

The mature *Shakespeare* plays with this borderline in quite a different way. He takes the risk of portraying the return from the realm of the dead as a pure gift to those in mourning. In these self-contained plays the Christian resurrection from the dead becomes the reappearance of those believed dead. In *Pericles* —the eventful romance with its many journeys, shipwrecks and other happenings—the prince receives back both his daughter, Marina, whose tombstone he has read, and ultimately his wife too, who had been committed to the tempestuous sea in a coffin. It is even more splendid at the end of *The Winter's Tale*, when the statue of the dead Hermione comes into sight, the guilty Leontes stands thunderstruck before the "masterpiece" that seems to breathe, and Paulina promises him even greater things if he will rouse up his "faith"; the statue descends, alive, from its pedestal, and Perdita, the lost daughter, is rediscovered. The audience too had thought Hermione to be dead and experiences her "resurrection" as profoundly as Leontes.

Neither the Pygmalion motif (bringing the statue to life) nor that of Alcestis is sufficient to explain *Shakespeare's* action. In the remote background there are the Christian miracles of the medieval mystery plays. But *Shakespeare* performs a "post-figuration", transforming the Christian elements into a fluid, elusive metaphor for the grace of existence. We can hardly say whether he is fired more by themes of antiquity or by Christian themes; the atmosphere is inconceivable apart from the Christian background, but this background only diffuses an anonymous light over the miracles of earthly love.

ε. *Death as atonement.* Once again *Camus* has already made the transition to the new interpretation of death. Death, in its active-passive ambivalence, can be understood as atonement (freewill or imposed) for a shipwrecked, guilt-ridden existence. This interpretation goes through all the various layers, from the unreflected, common human awareness that it is meaningful to deprive a person of life for grave crime, to the intermediate position that grants that, in insolubly confused situations, suicide can bring light and air, to various metaphysical views that regard death as expiating the guilt of earthly, sense-bound existence.

In *The Quare Fellow* (1958) by the Irishman *Brendan Behan*, we are shown that the ethical dimension exists even at the lowest level: the execution of a criminal can make an entire prison hold its breath and provide the man's comrade with the opportunity of a noble death. Finally, thanks to his pitiable beggar's state, even the greatest criminal of the ancient stage, Oedipus, attains the dignity of a royal death that brings salvation in its wake. The complex action of one of *O'Neill's* masterpieces, *The Iceman Cometh* (1946), ends with two suicides and someone else giving himself up to justice. Hickey, who wants to bring the decaying characters in Hope's pub out of their daydreams and back to a real life, finally has to give an example himself: he accuses himself of murdering his wife because he could no longer stand her constant forgiving of his infidelities. The young Parrit, who has betrayed his mother, draws his conclusions and jumps off the fire escape. Larry, the philosophical grumbler, likewise ends his life, and the others subside into alcohol again. Here self-execution is the way to truth for a life that has been a lie.

The theme recurs in the *petit bourgeois* setting of *Arthur Miller's Death of a Salesman* (1949), where suicide is the only remaining way in which Willy Loman can redeem the failure of his life and at the same time give his family a new start—with the insurance money from his car "accident". Here, death is a way of silently making room for others, similar to Hedwig's suicide in the *Wild Duck*. The same theme emerges even in such a subtle play as *Hebbel's Gyges und sein Ring*: only Rhodope's death can atone for the misdeed and break through the tissue of lies. Similarly Don Cesar in *Schiller's Braut von Messina* must kill himself. "Only death, freely willed, can smash the chain of destiny." This destiny may be seen in stoic terms, as fate, from which there is no escape except through individual freewill action, or in a Buddhist or idealist sense, where no solution can be found at the level of the senses and the only way out is upward, through

a vertical opening. This is how it is in *Richard Wagner's* dramas
of redemption, and even in *Schiller's Jungfrau von Orleans.*
"Reconciliation" of the antagonistic forces—rather than "atonement"—is the aim of all idealist drama. The hero must be
reconciled not only with destiny but with his concrete opponent:
"The enemy who is merely *thrown down* can rise again, but the
reconciled enemy is really vanquished."[36] *Kleist* continues the
theme, on the basis no longer of idealism, but of unprotected,
pure humanity.

In *Kleist's Prinz von Homburg*, the hero has to undergo all the
phases of the process of dying, in expiation for his military
disobedience. First he manifests disbelief in the sentence of
execution, then shock and fear on seeing the open grave; then he
forfeits all dignity as he pleads for pardon. Next the prince-
elector appeals to his "feelings": "If he can view this verdict as
unjust, / I will cancel it and he shall go free" (IV, 1). Homburg:
"Unworthy man that I am, / I cannot stand against one so
worthy" (V, 4); and he declares himself guilty. At this point the
prince-elector can allow mercy to take precedence over justice.
Mentally and spiritually Homburg has undergone death in its
entirety; he has been totally humiliated by it and has finally
consented to the intolerable. Not only has he atoned, he has
gone through death and attained freedom, a freedom that is the
real blueprint of that "preexistent" security in which he sleep-
walks through the early scenes.

Almost inaccessible, beyond both Weimar and *Kleist*, there is
Hölderlin's Tod des Empedokles in its three versions. The theme
here is self-sacrifice, "through a death freely undergone, according to divine law".[37] Ultimately its task is not so much to
expiate the hero's personal guilt as to reconcile the "great
quarrel"[38] between "nature" (the cosmos, saturated with
Divinity though unconscious of it) and "art" (reflex thought,
culture). Consciousness' original unity—we should not forget
Hölderlin's pietist sources—that is open to the divine and that the

---

[36] Schiller, *Über Anmut und Würde*, in *Sämtliche Werke*, ed. Fricke-Göpfert
(Hanser), V, 465.

[37] Hölderlin, *Sämtliche Werke*, ed. Beissner (Insel, 1961), 880.

[38] *Ibid.*, 891.

poet calls "interiority" (*Innigkeit*) must collapse; the human spirit cannot cope with being in direct contact with God, for this is an "overpowering interiority".[39] Reflection associates the divine self-communicating with the "I": "The gods had become / Of service to me; I alone / Was God and said as much in insolent pride."[40] "You have brought it upon yourself, wretched Tantalus, / Violating the sanctuary and / Arrogantly tearing asunder the fair covenant."[41] The guilt (word-guilt) incurred by uttering the ineffable is only the extreme instance of reflection under the aspect of culpability: it always refers the eternal grace dimension to its own self. The gulf cannot be bridged by "song" or by active "deed" (which never "reveals the whole man"), but only by "a sacrifice". This is the only way to overcome a situation in which God is remote. All the pain of this antagonism must be borne within the soul; the whole man must offer himself, in death, to the divine. But *Hölderlin* always stresses that this tragic gulf is that of the present times, in which religion is monopolized by the priest and the world of culture is handed over to profanity. So Empedokles (in closest proximity to Christ) atones on behalf of the age, although in the third version he has to prove to Manes that he is the "Chosen One", the "new savior", in order to be able, as man, to perform the reconciling sacrifice that the divine "Lord of Time" requires at this particular moment. That is why Pausanias, the "all-sacrificing heart", cannot "follow his master below": for he is not the "Chosen One". We might suspect Empedokles of seeing his sacrificial death as an instrument he himself wields to achieve union with Divinity, but in the end the idea breaks through that such a person must be *chosen*: he has been selected to endure to the very end, in his own person, the quarrel between heaven and earth that characterizes history. This spells his death. It is in the act of dying in pain and surrendering his own self that he overcomes this quarrel. We must leave the questions open whether *Hölderlin* understands this event eschatologically or in a chiliastic sense.[42] Two themes in his

---

[39] *Ibid.*, 885.   [40] *Ibid.*, 783.   [41] *Ibid.*, 781.

[42] On this whole issue: "Guardini, Hölderlin, Weltbild und Frömmigkeit",

Empedokles bring us to the next two aspects of death to be discussed: death and love, and death on behalf of someone else.

ζ. *Death and love.* Inevitably, these two come close to one another. The Greeks knew this with with their eros-thanatos, and the Song of Songs expresses it thus: "Love is strong as death, jealousy is cruel as the grave" (8:6): love can attain a power and finality that rival those of death. Love's finality, which is called into question by death, can actually use the finality of death to show its own credentials, unmoved by the contradiction that death puts an end to it. "Essentially the only problem", says *Gabriel Marcel*, "is that posed by the conflict of love and death. If there is an unshakable conviction in me, it is that a world abandoned by love must sink into death; but that, where love persists, where it triumphs over everything that would desecrate it, death is ultimately vanquished."[43]

---

in H. U. von Balthasar, *Herrlichkeit* III/1 (Einsiedeln, 1965), 644–82; English edition: *The Glory of the Lord*, vol. 4.

[43] Cf. "Valeur et immortalité" in *Homo Viator* (Aubier, 1944), 189–214; "La fidélité créatrice" in *Du refus à l'invocation* (Gallimard, 1940), 192–225. Fridolin Wiplinger, *Der personal verstandene Tod* (Freiburg and Munich: Alber, 1970) has pursued this train of thought further: "Death is separation from what we love" (45), and, quoting Augustine: "Life that had become one out of what was mine and what was hers (his mother) was torn apart" (*Confessions* 9, 12). If, in love, I experience my self-being only as being-with-another, this must come to an end, whereas I am still alive physically. "Or has it *simply become transformed* into a transcendence, my own 'real' death having brought me completely, and for the first time, into this transformation?" (51). "That is why love, by its very nature, is 'love unto death' " (64); precisely because it is always "embodied". "Accordingly, the meaning of time and temporality is to be ascertained *on the basis of the meaning of dying and death*, and not vice-versa" (85). Therefore, as long as this decision has not proved itself in the face of death, "there is no such thing as 'person' (for it has not been realized)". "The unconditional nature of personal love in the purity of its altruism, as the highest goal of the life decision . . . ultimately demands that 'everything', i.e., the whole of life, shall be seen in the context of this rationale, shall be squandered, offered, and—under certain circumstances—surrendered for it" (88–89). Here, by contrast with idealism, this transcendence remains outside the sphere of our "manipulation", which means that we may not frivolously seek death or play with it. True, it can be seen as a returning home to our most authentic being, yet it is an experience of a "radical break, a necessity laid on us . . . . a bitter fate"; love itself must view it "as a humiliation and a curse, as something contrary, against which we must protest". We must hold fast in this paradox, however, in all its sharpness, for

World literature is full of the theme of lovers dying together or not being able to survive each other. There can be many variations, and all testify to the same paradoxical law that once a "we" has come into being and is willed by both parties to last forever, it cannot fall apart into a separate "I" and "thou". From antiquity (in the fourth book of *Ovid's Metamorphoses*) we have the story of Pyramus and Thisbe, who, though forbidden, communicate through the separating wall of their adjoining houses. At their first rendezvous a lion frightens away the waiting Thisbe and stains her garment with blood; Pyramus, who finds the veil, stabs himself, and when Thisbe returns she follows him to death, pleading that they may share the same grave.[44] *Maeterlinck's Pelléas et Mélisande* (1892) is quite close to this naive version; here Pelléas is killed by his brother Goland, the husband of Mélisande, although his relationship with his beloved is an innocent game; she follows him and embraces death. With the ancient Irish saga of *Deirdre*, dramatized by *Yeats* and *Synge,* we enter into the realm of love as experienced passion. Deirdre has fled to Scotland with her lover, Naoise, in order to escape from the wooing of King Conchobar. After seven years of blissful love they are promised that they can return without punishment, but the king hangs Naoise. Deirdre promises to follow Conchobar provided she can take leave of Naoise; she kills herself beside her lover's body.

Then we come to *Shakespeare*. In his first important tragedy, *Romeo and Juliet*, death overtakes a youthful, blossoming love; in one of his last—at all events one of his most glittering—tragedies, *Antony and Cleopatra*, he sends a mature, voluptuous, self-tormenting, demonic passion to its dual death. These pairs of lovers by no means resolve to bid farewell to life together. Romeo mistakenly thinks that the poisoned Juliet is dead; he takes poison and dies, whereupon Juliet, awaking, kills herself

---

only thus shall we see what death is (94–95). For Marcel the ultimate, all-embracing background is the death and Resurrection of Christ, to which all these personal aspects are related. Wiplinger, in a more polemic vein, wishes that Christians would extricate themselves from impersonal Greek metaphysics, "and then they might get a view of man's personal being and a personal grasp of his life, dying and death in and through that same Jesus Christ" (116). Cf. also Arnold Metzger, *Freiheit und Tod*, 2d ed. (Rombach, 1973).

[44] On the various dramatizations and Shakespeare's parody in *A Midsummer Night's Dream* cf. E. Frenzel, *Stoffe der Weltliteratur* (Kröner, 1962), 531–33.

with his dagger. The later play is much more rhetorical: Mark Antony "falls between two stools" as both general and lover, for he is angry with Cleopatra for leaving him at Actium but immediately succumbs to her enchantment once again. Cleopatra is divided between being a genuine queen and being a cunning "jade". The entire play represents the Roman hero slowly and inevitably declining into oriental sensuality. When Octavian is victorious in the last naval encounter, Antony curses "this foul Egyptian" and "monster". But when the queen, in flight from Caesar, takes refuge in her tomb and puts it about that she is dead, he commands his boy, Eros (whose name is continually heard in the play), to kill him. Eros, however, falls on his own sword. Antony wants to do the same but only succeeds in wounding himself, then asks to be carried to the queen. He dies in her embrace. She puts the two asps to her bosom and arm in order to escape Octavian's triumphal procession in Rome: "And make death proud to take us" (IV, 15). "Where art thou, death? Come . . . and take a queen worth many babes and beggars!" (V, 2). Her kiss kills her attendant, Iras, and then she herself dies. Caesar gives orders for the two lovers to be buried together.

In this apotheosis of eros-thanatos we can already hear the sultry enharmonics of *Wagner's Tristan*. It is as if Antony has already drunk the "love potion" that changes eros into the dark enchantment that, at least since *Gottfried von Strassburg*, is part and parcel of the story. In *Gottfried* the "love-grotto" was a sacral area and a sacral action, consciously modeled on the Christian and sacramental mystery of love and death, with the Song of Songs as its text. Now, however, the same Song of Songs that prefigured the mystery of Christ, when taken as a postfiguration, becomes a blasphemy. Now eros, deliberately bypassing Christian marriage (King Mark), is made absolute, imparting an unpleasant aftertaste to this love-death.

Only with difficulty does *Paul Claudel* escape this problematical situation in his *Le soulier de Satin*. Prouèzes, having abandoned her marriage with Don Pelayo for the sake of her beloved Rodrigue, expiates her action by separation and by being transferred by the Spanish king to Mogador, where a second marriage becomes necessary, for state reasons, with the unbelieving traitor Don Camille. When Rodrigue wants to rescue her from the latter's clutches, she blows up herself and the castle. In this death, for Rodrigue, she is transfigured into a star, purified by an angel of all sensual love. However, the "death" that Rodrigue will have to die is one in which he is progressively stripped and humiliated. (Another, closely related problem is the absolute quality of eros on the entire human plane, which will not fit into the Procrustes' bed of [bourgeois] marriage and, because it cannot be lived, calls for death. So it is in the plays of *Heiberg*.)

But the topic of death and love, which, in tragedy (and particularly in post-Christian tragedy) often seems a little forced, is countered by those dramas in which life has the upper hand over the notion of death. After all these deathly serious issues they seem like the playing of Satyrs, and yet they have a logic—irreconcilable with the dramas of death[45]—which sets limits to man's absolutizing of love and at least regards it as an exception. *Hofmannsthal*, who was after all the author of *Jedermann*, often dealt with this theme, from *Der Weisse Fächer* (1897), in which two young people, recently widowed, meet at the gravesides and get to know each other, via *Der Abenteurer und die Sängerin, oder die Geschenke des Lebens* (1899), up to *Ariadne auf Naxos* (1912/1916). In *Ariadne*, the *bourgeois gentilhomme* wants *opera seria* (Ariadne abandoned on her island by Theseus) and *opera buffa* (the scantily clad Zerbinetta with her companions from the commedia dell'arte) to be performed at the same time: while Ariadne waits for the god of death, Zerbinetta sings and dances for her on the theme of life's transformations. "The new god came, and silently I surrendered" —and she is right, for the god who comes is not the god of death but Bacchus: in her readiness to accept death, Ariadne is translated into the new love. One degree more frivolous is *Christopher Fry*, who adapts the old theme of the "widow of Ephesus"[46] in a most light-hearted piece of verbal fireworks.[47] Here the widow, Dynamene, wants to starve to death in her husband's tomb, but

---

[45] To the chagrin of F. Wiplinger, Eugen Fink, in his *Metaphysik und Tod* (Stuttgart, 1969), insists that "not only must the two be played out against each other, but the twofold aspect of man's death must be brought into view"; i.e., the perspective of the dying and that of the surviving, without giving precedence to either (36–38).

[46] For other adaptations cf. M. Dietrich, *Das moderne Drama*, 572.

[47] *A Phoenix Too Frequent* (1948), in *Plays* (Oxford, 1969).

Tegeus, the soldier guarding the bodies of six hanged men nearby, engages her in a conversation that grows warmer under the influence of wine. Whereas at the beginning the servant-girl, Doto, had asserted, "But life and death / Is cat and dog of this double bed of the world", the widow initially reacts to Tegeus like Ariadne: "It is possible he has come to show us the way / Out of these squalid suburbs of life." When she insists that she wants death, not him, Tegeus replies: "I'll answer to anything. / It's desire all the same, of death in me, or me / In death." In the end the dead husband's body is hanged up in place of one of the corpses (which has been stolen): "He can be the other body. . . . He has no further use." It is better to hang the dead man than to let the living man be court-martialed.

It is surely right that there should be this light-hearted foil to the serious play, lest people should think that "Man and woman, woman and man / Reach as far as Divinity can", lest they imagine they could attain immortality by force, through the seriousness of their love. *Marcel* is right: the death of the beloved *is* a threshold, *the* threshold. But we ourselves cannot cross it.

η. *Death on behalf of someone else.* Death is passive but can be active. The most exalted way to make it active is to die on behalf of someone else. This is something rooted in our common human condition. One man can provide bail for another (*Schiller's Die Bürgschaft*); a person can sacrifice himself for the good of society. Two forms of this sacrifice are well known since *Euripides*, and often they intermingle. In *Alcestis* it is personal sacrifice for the beloved; in the *Heraclides*, Makaria sacrifices herself of her own freewill for the common good, as does Menoikeus in the *Phoenician Women*. In *Iphigenie in Aulis*, stress is laid on the freewill of the one on whom sacrifice has been forcibly imposed.[48]

Alcestis undergoes many transformations down through the centuries. The theme is taken up in the operas of *Lully, Handel* and *Gluck*, and by *Herder's* musical drama *Admets Haus oder der Tausch des Schicksals* (1803) and is passed on to *Hofmannsthal*

---

[48] On other plays of Euripides (partly lost) cf. H. U. von Balthasar, *Herrlichkeit* III/1, 135ff. (*The Glory of the Lord*, vol. 4).

(written in 1893, performed in 1911) and *Thornton Wilder* in his *Alcestiad* with the farce *The Drunken Sisters* as an epilogue (1955). Whereas *Hofmannsthal* stays in the realm of the symbolic fairy-tale, in *Wilder* the Christian background shines through every-thing. In the first scene there is a meeting between Apollo and Death: Death has been given a lesson and his rigid law is to be broken through. At the conclusion, Apollo tells Alcestis (who is dying in misery) that, while the grave signifies an end, she will have no such end; she is the first of a great number who will not have such an end. On her wedding day Alcestis, who wanted exclusively to serve God at Delphi, beseeches him for a sign; she can see no life meaning in the coming marriage. "We do not know why we live and die, or why hundreds of thousands live and die." Now, however, a message comes from Tiresias: Apollo will dwell incognito among men for one year, in Admeta's house, as one of the four dirty, boorish and mostly drunk shepherds. "If the gods wanted to show themselves to us in all their glory, they would kill us." Admeta pleads with his bride not to leave him on the wedding day: "I am only a quite ordinary man, but the love that fills me is no ordinary love. If such a love does not find love in return, life itself is a delusion." This, and the god's hidden presence, elicits Alcestis' answer: "Summon me to live for *you* and for *your children* and *your people*—to live for you as if I were ready to *die* for you at any moment." Twelve years later this has serious consequences. Admeta is mortally ill from a wound and the oracle gives this condition for his recovery: someone else must die in his place. Many offer themselves, but Alcestis demands to be allowed to be the victim because it is hardest for her. Furthermore, "This must be a work of love, Shepherd; a work, not of expiation, but of love." But the shepherd explains that there are two kinds of death. One is an end, and the other is "a going forward . . . full of what is to follow. It is part of something greater that we cannot see." Admeta is brought outside the house and Alcestis says: "Did I ever tell you that I love you more than my life?" At this moment *she* has the wound and its pain and dies of it. Admeta is cured. There follows the traditional scene with Heracles, who brings Alcestis back from the underworld. Another twelve years go by. Admeta has been killed; the city, ruled by King Agis, is infested with plague, and Alcestis, a slave in rags, is held responsible: "She *is* the disease. . . . She was already dead. . . . And she has brought death with her." In an interlude, Apollo explains to Death that he can only bring back from the dead those who have given their lives for others. "Did you repair the wall that Heracles broke through? . . . You will have to accustom yourself to some changes. . . . *One* shaft of light has already penetrated into your realm." *Wilder* includes the Orestes motif at this point: one of Admeta's banished sons returns home secretly to kill Agis, but his mother, who finally recognizes him, forbids him. Once upon a time she was privileged to receive a great happiness, and "everything that has happened since then has come from the same hand and is part of a whole. It is simply that I cannot see it." She tells the king that the plague has been sent "to open our eyes". Apollo shows her the way "through the gate".

Wilder's play is paradigmatic; we can deal more briefly with other plays, some of which are better constructed. We find the genuinely Christian peripeteia in *Paul Claudel's L'Annonce faite à Marie* (1912). Here the dead child of her demonic sister, Mara, is raised by a miracle, which is effected by Violaine catching leprosy from Pierre de Craon. Through her perfect willingness to let it happen—*fiat mihi*—Violaine is drawn into the miracle of the Christmas night; then, blind, she is pushed into a sand-pit by the jealous Mara and nearly buried alive. Pierre brings her home, where she dies, and the whole thing ends in a paean of praise, celebrating the fruitfulness of the earth and of heaven.

As early as 1896 (the year he translated the *Agamemnon* of *Aeschylus*), during his first visit to China, which deeply impressed him with its ancient culture, the poet wrote a kind of liturgical drama, *Le repos du septième jour*. Its central point was the emperor's descent into the realm of the dead on behalf of his people, to save them from strange misfortunes visited on the living by the dead. *Claudel* is not afraid to use the ordinary human notion of substitution in support of the Christian notion; thus, when the emperor returns, his imperial sceptre buds on either side to form a cross. Nothing could moderate the severe visitation of the empire, neither sacrifice nor magic. The empire's first founder, Hoang-Ti, when asked, "Who will tell us what to do to be saved?", replies: "He who went down to the dead and came back from thence." Thereupon the emperor, as the shepherd responsible for his people, resolves to undertake the journey to the underworld: "I will not let my people die. . . . I will question the underworld [enfer] and find out what it has against us." He descends, and in act two becomes acquainted, not with the pagan Hades, but with the depths of the Christian hell. He is shown the various degrees of human sin right up to the most fundamental denial of the light that comes from heaven, which changes it into an ever-watchful self-reflection: "a fire without flame or smoke". Then the "angel of the kingdom" tells him how man has to live so that the nether realm will not gain the ascendancy on earth: he must live in a God-given freedom as "priest to the world" that he cultivates. But on the seventh day he must lift his hands to heaven, whence comes blessing. This act closes with the Advent prospect of Chinese/biblical wisdom, looking toward a redemptive incarnation of God. In the third act, the emperor returns to his empire to find it shaken by revolt. The court and the crown prince desire to see his face; he lifts the golden mask: "His face has disappeared, his eyes are nothing but bloody holes, only his mouth is still not leprous." That is the price of the testimony he can now give to the people and that will restore order to the cosmos. He institutes his son as his successor and disappears into the mountains, to be nothing more than an intercessor.

The instances of self-sacrifice on behalf of others are more discreet and more muted in *Gabriel Marcel*. In his *Le monde cassé* (1933), for instance, Christiane loses her young man when he becomes a Benedictine; in despair she turns to a wanton life that brings her to the brink of suicide. But then she learns that the monk understood her love and sacrificed his life for her, aware that he may have plunged her into spiritual darkness. She discovers the laws of the "communion of saints" and succeeds in setting her life to rights. In *Le dard* (1936/1950), a twofold sacrifice bears fruit. The musician Werner Schnee has left Nazi Germany for the sake of his companion, the Jewish Communist Rudolf Schönthal, whom he has left behind, dying, in Switzerland. Werner draws sustenance from the latter's renunciation. In Paris, where he lives with friends who take him in, he strikes up a friendship with Beatrice, the wife of the jealous Eustache. Werner resolves to return to Germany, in danger of his life; his renunciation of love will provide the power to reunite the estranged couple. "You will think of me, as I think of Rudolf. Later I shall dwell in you, as Rudolf dwells in me."

William Faulkner's Requiem for a Nun, dramatized by *Camus* in 1956, takes as its starting point the conviction of the black servant-girl Nancy, who has strangled her employers' second child. Slowly it goes on to reveal that Temple (who, like Nancy, was once in a brothel) wanted to break out of her marriage with the vain Gowan and that Nancy could find no way to stop her and protect her from the blackmailer, Peter, other than by killing the child. For four long months she waits to strangle the child, and now she is purified in her innermost self; not only can she calmly wish to die "on behalf of" Temple, she actually brings the spouses together on the night before she is to die. Her transfigured wisdom is a Christian wisdom; she speaks of "our Brother", by which she means Jesus: "I will settle all that with my Brother . . . the Brother of prostitutes and robbers, the Friend of the murderer. They killed him the same time as they killed them. I don't understand everything he says. But I love him because they killed him." As the months went by she still hoped. Now she has nothing but faith. "Believe." She tells Temple, who does not know how to go on living: "Trust in him".

Georg Kaiser's masterpiece *Die Bürger von Calais* heightens the theme of substitutionary death. The king of England stipulates that, if the town is to be spared, six citizens must present themselves the following morning, dressed in shirts of penitence and with ropes around their necks. The heroic defence of the town is given up and the path of self-sacrifice, of humiliation, is adopted as the harder and morally better path. The first to offer himself is Eustache de Saint-Pierre, followed by six others. The volunteer victims take leave of their families and eat a last meal. They will draw lots to find out which of the seven shall go free. But Eustache postpones the decision until the next day because there is still too much pride in the volunteers: the last one to appear shall go free. Next day the six assemble; Eustache has killed himself to demonstrate the necessity of sacrifice. A son is born to the king, and he pardons the town.

The significance of bodily death on behalf of others is primary here, although the spiritual sacrifice is not absent. But there are plays that highlight the spiritual sacrifice, right up to the paradoxes that are only possible and meaningful within a Christian framework.

William Butler Yeats makes a Christian "Faust" of his *Countess Cathleen* (1892). In order to avoid the threat of famine in Ireland she gives away more than her entire fortune: she meets two demonic figures who are going through the land offering people bread and money for the price of their souls and she sells them her own soul for fifty thousand crowns, on condition that all the bartered souls will be given back. Her beloved offers his soul for hers, but to no avail. But, beside her dead body, he has a vision telling him that Cathleen is saved.

What is kept at the distance of legend in *Yeats* is brought realistically and psychologically close in *Paul Claudel's L'Otage* (1911).[49] Here we have a Christian sacrifice that stretches the sacrificed and sacrificing victim beyond the limit. In 1812 Sygne de Coûfontaine, the daughter of an old, noble family, is obliged to marry the unbelieving and cynical Turelure, a former Jacobin, now a Bonapartist baron, in order to save Pope Pius VII, who has been rescued from prison and hidden by her cousin Georges. (Turelure knows of this.) In doing this she saves the head of the Church, but the sacrifice has consumed all her spiritual strength, so that she is incapable of seeing herself as an instrument of divine grace. The sacrifice that the Curé Badilon persuaded her to make has shattered her. During the whole of the final act she has "the nervous tic of slowly shaking her head from left to right like someone saying No". She dies, having thrown herself in front of Turelure to shield him from Georges' bullet, still making her "No" gesture: "*Tout est épuisé.*"[50]

Graham Greene goes one step further in his play *The Potting Shed* (1958),[51] which combines many of the fundamental themes of his novels. James, who has suffered from amnesia going right back to some particular episode in his youth, is prevented from

---

[49] Claudel, *Théâtre* II (Pléiade, 1948), 190.

[50] *Ibid.*, 209. In the second version, when Turelure scornfully proclaims the war cry, "Coûfontaine adsum", the dying noblewoman tries to raise herself but falls back, dead.

[51] Graham Greene, *The Potting Shed* (Penguin, 1971).

being present at the death of his father, a well-known atheistic writer, from whom he had hoped to learn the truth. The truth comes out during the play: as a young boy, James had been initiated into the mysteries of Christianity by his clergyman uncle, but his father's ridicule had so undermined his conviction[52] that the boy tried to hang himself in the potting shed. The gardener freed him and the clergyman, clasping the boy to him, had offered himself in place of the dead child. "It was as if I were the one who had been strangled . . . then your breath came back, and it was as if I had died in your place. . . . I said: Take from me what I love most, take it, take it." James: "Take my faith away and let him live." Uncle William lives for thirty years as an unbelieving priest, drinking and performing his duties mechanically. Was it a miracle? "How could that be? If you had been dead it would have been a miracle, and then God would exist. That horrid image (the crucifix) would have a meaning. But if God exists, why does he take my faith away? I have served him well. And I will go on serving him. The saints may experience dark nights, but not for thirty years." Following this conversation William gets his faith back. It transpires that his brother, the atheist, stopped writing after the event in the potting shed. James: "I don't need any other proof for God than the fact that he was not there. I saw the traces his feet left as he departed." Here, as in other works by *Greene*, one wonders whether such a redrawing of the "dark night" of the saints is sustainable on Christian terms.

Georges Bernanos' Dialogues des Carmélites[53] (1948–1949) forms the conclusion and high point of this series. Here he takes *Gertrud von Le Fort's Die Letzte am Schafott* (1931) as his basis, but he greatly develops it. Blanche de la Force has been born under the sign of fear; during pregnancy, in pre-Revolution times, her mother had been profoundly shocked by a street scene. For the poet, this fear is not merely psychological: "Despite everything, fear is a daughter of God, redeemed on the eve of Good Friday.

---

[52] "I had taught you about the Virgin birth and he cured you with physiology" (*ibid.*, 72).

[53] Georges Bernanos, *Oeuvres romanesques* (Pléiade, 1961), 1562–1719. Albert Béguin rounded out the author's posthumous manuscript and subsequently made it into a stage version. The original was planned as a film.

She is not beautiful; people mock her, curse her, everyone denies her. But make no mistake; she sits at every deathbed, interceding for men."[54] For *Bernanos*, fear and courage are equal; in the face of the threat of martyrdom his Prioress Lidoine says: "Looking at it (fear) in the perspective of the Mount of Olives, where all human fear was divinized in the most adorable Heart of the Lord, it seems to me that the distinction between fear and courage practically collapses."[55] The courage of the sub-prioress, by contrast, is unproblematical; in the absence of the prioress, and contrary to the latter's wishes, she requires the community to take a "vow of martyrdom". As a punishment, she is the only one not permitted to go to the scaffold.[56] Is Blanche's determination to join the Carmelites an escape? Her father warns her and her brother visits her in the convent in an attempt to persuade her to go home to her lonely father. Her reply to her brother is, "Where I am, nothing can reach me."[57] But the time itself is saturated with fear. "Everyone is afraid. They all catch fear from one another as in an epidemic of plague or cholera."[58] Blanche had been accepted by the old Prioress Cressy, who had warned her that the convent was not a place of escape and that in the first instance each sister had to pray and suffer in loneliness.[59] Only after that could they "pray for one another".[60] But when she learns that Blanche is asking for the same name she herself once bore, "Sister Blanche of the Agony of Christ", the gravely ill prioress "takes her over" and says that she is ready "to give my own poor life" to protect Blanche from the threat that hangs over her.[61] She is taken at her word, frighteningly so. Instead of dying the edifying death the community expects, she dies in the most terrible mortal fear. "As if the good God had given her the wrong death, as one gets one

---

[54] From *La Joie*, which the poet placed as a motto at the beginning of the *Dialogues*.

[55] Bernanos, *Oeuvres romanesques*, 1653. Moreover: "In the Garden of Gethsemane Christ has no power over anything anymore. Never did human fear attain such heights. It will never reach this level again. It obscured everything in him apart from that extreme point of his soul where the divine 'Yes' had taken effect" (1668). "The martyrs were sustained by Christ, but he received help from no one, for all help and all mercy come from him" (1668).

[56] *Ibid.*, 1578.   [57] *Ibid.*, 1632.   [58] *Ibid.*, 1661.   [59] *Ibid.*, 1584.

[60] *Ibid.*, 1586.   [61] *Ibid.*, 1600.

coat from the cloakroom attendant rather than another. . . . We
do not die for ourselves; we die for one another."[62] Blanche is
terribly frightened by the revolutionaries' house-searches: she
can still be "reached", even here. She hides in a shed and then
runs away home. But her father has been guillotined and she is
ill treated by the servants. The sub-prioress wants to bring her
back. Blanche says: "I was born in fear, have lived in fear and
still do. Everyone despises fear, so it is right for me to live a
despised life."[63] In the end she is nothing but a woman haunted
by fear, but when she sees her sisters mount the bloody structure
she pushes through the crowd of spectators and is the last to
mount the scaffold, singing and free from all fear. The sub-
prioress, denied the opportunity of this sacrifice, feels that she
has been "dishonored". The priest who hears this is satisfied:
"That is what I wanted to hear. . . . In your case it really is the
cry of nature in agony. That is the blood that God demands of
you; you must pour it out."[64] In *Bernanos'* most mature work,
the theme that *Greene* distorted is presented in its proper proportions. Blanche's fear, which is first of all a natural fear, is
underpinned from the outset by the supernatural fear of the
Mount of Olives and embedded in the mystery of the communion of saints, where it belongs.

θ. *The unmaking of kings.* Here we can include this final motif,
which we have already encountered in the context of the baroque,
because in classical drama the pathos of the king who falls from
power (to humiliation, prison or death) is a far more impressive
theme than the portrayal of a private destiny. This is because the
king represents the divine order and authority in the world. It is
a favorite subject of *Shakespeare.* It does not matter what mistakes the king has made when at the height of his power;
deposing him is sacrilege, and by descending into the deepest
dungeons of the world he acquires an inner dignity: as he goes
through humiliation and moves toward death, the radiance of

---

[62] *Ibid.*, 1613.   [63] *Ibid.*, 1702.

[64] *Ibid.*, 1718. Finally we ought to mention Bela Just's *La potence et la croix*
(1954), in which a young prison chaplain who, accustomed to accompany
condemned men to their execution, exchanges clothes with a convicted but
innocent man, helps him to escape, and takes his punishment on himself.

majesty intensifies.[65] *King Lear* is the prototype here, of super-human dimensions. At the beginning, when he divides his king-dom, he is foolish and irascible, rejecting Cordelia, banishing Kent and clinging to Regan and Goneril, his two demonic daughters; but in his growing humiliation, which leads him to madness, he increasingly becomes someone to be revered. His fate is amplified, as it were, by other characters; for example, Edgar is rejected by his father, Gloucester, and later Gloucester is blinded and supposedly brought to the Cliffs of Dover by Edgar, whom he does not recognize. These three, together with the Fool, constitute a kind of chorus of humiliation in various forms of real or pretended insanity. Lear is Job: "I am a man more sinn'd against than sinning" (III, 2). He is "as poor as the King" (I, 4), "your slave, a poor, infirm, weak, and despis'd old man" (III, 2). He is naked too, for he tears his clothes off (III, 4) and sinks so low as to lose his identity: "Who is it that can tell me who I am?" (I, 4). And if Gloucester dies " 'Twixt two extremes of passion, joy and grief" when Edgar reveals the truth to him, Lear does the same when confronted with the dead Cordelia: "Break, heart; I pr'ythee, break!" (V, 3). But right to the end Lear is "anointed flesh" (III, 7), and those who oppose him—Goneril, Regan and Edmund—are the forces of sacrilege and plain guilt.

Lear's superhuman figure stands outside history. In the his-tories, however, the cardinal character is *Richard II*, *Shakespeare's* first great tragic figure who is not a scoundrel. According to *Shakespeare* his deposition by Henry Bolingbroke is *the* guilty act that goes on reverberating through the two tetralogies. It is

---

[65] At the very peak of his insanity, "fantastically dressed up with flowers", Lear utters his "Every inch a king" (IV, 6). "I am king, my masters, know you that" (IV, 6). Shakespeare's potent model was Christopher Marlowe's *King Edward II* (ca. 1589), who, like Shakespeare's Richard II (but even more so) is a guilty king and an unworthy one because of his blind love of court favorites (Gaveston, and then the younger Spencer). But then he is taken prisoner, mocked, compelled to abdicate—the scene in which he plays with the crown anticipates Shakespeare—and is finally kept in the filthy depths of the castle's sewer, with the drums beating incessantly to keep him awake. He is put under a board and is crushed by people trampling upon it: in all this his suffering becomes sublime: the sufferings of lesser men are soon healed, but not that of kings (V, 1).

continually cited as the origin of misfortune.[66] Initially he too is someone who has failed, who is deceived by sycophants, who has exploited the land. There are all kinds of premonitions, for example, on the part of the queen (II, 2) and Salisbury (who sees Richard's glory "like a shooting star, fall to the base earth from the firmament" [II, 4]), and these come true when the banished Bolingbroke returns and his power grows. *Shakespeare* slowly traces Richard's decline: "Down, down I come; like glistering Phaeton" (III, 3). He himself goes to meet it and speaks of the death of kings and of how they are all mown down and ultimately have nothing to "bequeath, save our deposed bodies to the ground". "I live with bread like you, feel want, taste grief, need friends" (III, 2). Initially the usurper offers allegiance on condition that his lands are restored (III, 3); but Richard yields to force. "Depress'd he is already; and depos'd 'tis doubt he will be" (III, 4), and he is actually compelled to abdicate by Bolingbroke—an invention on *Shakespeare's* part (IV, 1). There is a wealth of allusions to Christ's Passion here. There is mention of Judas' kiss, of Pilate, washing his hands and delivering the prisoner to be crucified. The king asks for a mirror, so that he may once more see the "brittle glory" that shines in this face, and then smashes it. He is dragged off to the tower, and rubbish is thrown at him from windows as he goes (V, 2). In prison, his last "station", he reflects on the many roles he had to play:

> Sometimes am I king; / Then treason makes me wish myself a beggar, / And so I am: then crushing penury / Persuades me I was better when a king; / Then am I king'd again: and by and by / Think that I am unking'd by Bolingbroke, / And straight am nothing:—but whate'er I am, / Nor I, nor any man that but is, / With nothing shall be pleas'd till he be eas'd / With being nothing.

There follow the famous lines on music and the measurement of time, and the observation that "I . . . for the concord of my state and time, had not an ear to hear my true time broke" (V, 5). He is killed by a hired murderer. The play closes with a schizo-

---

[66] *Henry IV* part one, I, 3; III, 2; IV, 3: part two, I, 1; I, 3; III, 2; IV, 1; *Henry V* prays prior to the battle for the repose of Richard's soul: IV, 1. In *Henry VI* part one, II, 5, the entire hereditary curse of the Mortimers is once again described, and in part three, I, 1, the original event unleashes the Wars of the Roses.

phrenic speech by the new king, approving of the deed but rejecting the murderer as another Cain. The bishop of Carlisle had previously urged the king's inviolability: "What subject can give sentence on his king? . . . And shall the figure of God's majesty, his captain, steward, deputy elect, anointed, crowned, planted many years, be judg'd by subject and inferior breath. . . ?" He predicts the coming civil war (IV, 1). Richard: "You may my glories and my state depose, but not my griefs: still am I king of those. . . . With mine own tears I wash away my balm, with mine own hands I give away my crown, with mine own tongue deny my sacred state, with mine own breath release all duty's rites" (IV, 1).

A whole procession of disempowered princes makes its way through the royal dramas. *King John* constitutes a prelude. He is the lawless king who dies both physically and spiritually poisoned (V, 7). *Henry IV* fights in both dramas against conspirators and is oppressed by anxiety on account of his son; he feels his illegitimacy (part 1, IV, 3, V, 1). He is sick and cannot sleep (part 2, III, 1). In *Henry VI*, during the Wars of the Roses, a "feast of death" is celebrated (part 1, IV, 5). In part two the duchess of Gloucester, who has allegedly insulted Queen Margaret, appears "in a white sheet, and a taper burning in her hand"; she goes into exile exposed to the gaping eyes of the "giddy multitude". Later the king is humiliated by York: "King did I call thee? No, thou art not king" (part 2, V, 1), and in part three this humiliation is complete when the king finds York sitting on his throne and refusing to get down (I, 1). York, now a prisoner, is humiliated in turn by Margaret: she mocks him by putting a paper crown on his head and has to listen as he rails against her (I, 4). All three parts of the drama are a preparation for the deposition of the king, which takes place at the last. The king is supplanted by Edward IV, who will not allow him to speak (II, 2) and seeks him out in his hiding-place in the northern forests (III, 1), while the king dwells on the burden of the crown and his loss of royal power: "O God! methinks it were a happy life to be no better than a homely swain" (III, 5); "Thy place is fill'd, thy sceptre wrung from thee, thy balm wash'd off wherewith thou wast anointed" (III, 1). The keeper asks him, ". . . thou talkst as if thou wert a king", and the king replies, "Why, so I am—in mind; and that's enough." He "humbly yields" to God's will. He is accused of being too "calm" (II, 6, compare IV, 8); in weakness he gives way to the monster, Richard III, just as Pope Celestine yielded to Boniface VIII. There are continual humiliations under Richard, who brings this series to a close. The worst is that of Elizabeth (I, 3), and again in act IV, scene 4, where Margaret calls her "A queen in jest, only to fill the scene"; "For queen, a very caitiff crown'd with care". As for the king, he cannot be humiliated any more, only continually cursed and execrated. He is a man who has broken faith, whose oaths are worthless (IV, 4), a man afraid only of himself, who loves, nay, hates only himself (V, 3).

Then we have the strange epilogue, *Henry VIII*, a kind of spectacle full of murders. Its sole subject-matter is the demise of one person after another at the king's behest, occurring at regular intervals as if controlled by some inexplicable superior power. First there is Wolsey's magnificent engineering of the fall of Buckingham, who could not keep a guard on his tongue. He is arrested for high treason and is condemned to death despite Queen Catherine's intervention. Like so many before him his last journey to the place of execution is accompanied by the spectators' commentary: we hear how he was seized by mortal terror on hearing the verdict, but subsequently attained "a most noble patience". The executioner appears, holding his axe with the edge toward the prisoner; he stops, forgives his judges, asks for prayers and declares his mind (II, 1). Next it is the queen's turn. Henry wants to marry Ann Boleyn, and Catherine, humiliated by the court's decision, manifests her greatness of soul:

> My lord, I dare not make myself so guilty
> To give up willingly that noble title
> Your master wed me to: nothing but death
> Shall e'er divorce my dignities (III, 1).

We see her in the end, sick, dreaming of a blissful transformation, like Egmont in his prison cell; then she makes her will. Finally Wolsey himself, his plotting unmasked, is overthrown. "And from that full meridian of my glory I haste now to my setting: I shall fall" (III, 2). He dies "fearing God" (IV, 2). Cranmer, close to being indicted by the Privy Council (" 'tis a cruelty to load a falling man", V, 3), is rescued by the king.

Looking at *Shakespeare*, one is struck by the relentless succession and variety of deaths on the stage, whether received in battles, dungeons or armchairs. Far from being spared death, the spectator is inoculated with it. Death brings impotence, whether it is the slow individual death or the apparently senseless heaps of dead in *Titus Andronicus, Lear* and *Hamlet*. The poet who can speak so crudely of begetting and giving birth in no way softens the crudity of death. Indeed, death can be shown in its harshest light at the fall of the great.

Shakespeare has said almost all that there is to be said on the subject. What remain are simply variations of it. Thus in *Gryphius* the theme of the rise and fall of the great is central and the idea of the wheel of fortune is more prominent than in *Shakespeare,* but here there is the possibility of a "paradoxical identity of the earthly fall and a religious and spiritual ascent".[67] So it is in *Leo Armenius* (1650), where the sacredness of the emperor's office is not brought into question by the evil deeds of the one who holds it: the emperor's demise leads to the rise of the insurgent Michael Balbus. In *Die Ermordete Majestät*, the poet portrays the indictment of King Charles I by the English Parliament and his public execution at Cromwell's instigation in 1649. (The play was written in 1649–1650.) The king allows himself to be despoiled in conscious imitation of that king "who ascended a cross".[68] In *Catharina von Georgien* (1657), which also deals with an event of the recent past, we have a drama of martyrdom. The queen, unabashed and steadfast, is tortured and then burned alive. Shortly before her death we have the theme of the distribution of jewels that points back to *Shakespeare* (compare the scene with the crown between the young Henry V and his dying father), but even more strongly points forward to *Schiller's Maria Stuart* (1801). Even more than many of *Shakespeare's*

[67] F. Rusterholz, *Theatrum vitae humanae* (Berlin: E. Schmidt, 1970), 54.

[68] On the development of this theme between the first and second drafts cf. A. Schöne, "Figurale Gestaltung—Andreas Gryphius", in *Säkularisation als sprachbildende Kraft* (Göttingen, 1958), 29–75. In the second draft the role meanings are modeled even more clearly after Christ's Passion, as "postfiguration".

kings, Mary has a dark past. When the two queens meet, Elizabeth taunts her with it, whereupon Mary calls her a bastard. The imprisoned Mary is already condemned to death; here she attains an earthly, tangible greatness that then, in the final act, when she is totally at the mercy of death, passes over imperceptibly into a spiritual greatness. Mary forgives her rival (V, 8), gives away her treasures, receives the solemnly administered last sacraments and walks toward her death, royally attired and with the diadem on her head and the crucifix in her hand. "Fear not! Mary Stuart will die as both queen and heroine" (V, 1). "Once more I feel the crown upon my head, the noble dignity within my soul" (V, 6). This is a far cry from *Shakespeare*: it is German idealism, where dignity (*Würde*) contains lofty grace (*Anmut*) within it.

Leaving aside *Grillparzer's* two great imperial dramas depicting the collapse of Ottokar and the Emperor Rudolf, we come to *Frank Wedekind's König Nicolo oder so ist das Leben* (1901),[69] whose tragic-grotesque scenes distantly recall *King Lear*. In the prologue the king speaks thus to his daughter: "Now let us plunge into the abysses of the soul, explore the dark recesses of human nature." Alma: "Then *you* will sense the exhilaration of playing ball with *freedom, nobility, majesty* and *renown* as if they were golden apples." Nicolo too is deposed because of his unworthiness, his daughter refuses the hand of the new king's son and follows her father into exile from Perugia. The king observes that if he could manage to denigrate his own past he would probably be able to find a victualled table once again. "For when a pig-butcher is elevated to the throne, the state has no position left for the king but that of a court fool."[70] And that is what happens. He looks for work as a herdsman, becomes a tailor, is treated shabbily ("A curse upon the king who prevents me being a man like any other!"),[71] has to defend himself in court against a charge of lese majesty and in doing so points out the invulnerability of God's divine majesty and of the royal majesty that approximates to it most closely. "God has walked on earth in lowliness, and *low humanity*

[69] *Gesammelte Werke* (Munich and Leipzig: Georg Müller, 1919), vol. 4: 99–181.
[70] *Ibid.*, 118.   [71] *Ibid.*, 128.

thought it could bring him to his death. Just so, *low humanity* may think it can expel the king, but he will remain where he has always been."[72] Consequently, as the unacknowledged king, he cannot be sentenced by any court. He is banished from the city for life and he and his daughter end up among circus people, where he sings the ballad of his tragic fate and is engaged as a "magnificent comedian". The troupe comes to Perugia and the king, in the role of a clown, tells the true story; he and his daughter play the farce of the "abased king". The new king is moved; Nicolo explains that it is simply the harmless comedy of "That's life". He is appointed court fool and reveals himself to be King Nicolo. No one believes him; Nicolo is believed dead. Nicolo dies, since he cannot adduce any proof of his identity. "I abdicate, not as king but only as a human being."[73] In *Wedekind*, according to the prologue, the theme is the inextinguishable royal dimension in man, even in the deepest humiliation.

Probably the only writer of the second half of this century to attempt to create a great royal tragedy of Shakespearian dimensions was *Christopher Fry* in his *Curtmantle* (1961),[74] the story of the fall of Henry II. Unlike *Eliot* and *Anouilh*, *Fry* takes the king, not Becket, as the main character, a man with elemental powers for good and ill, possessed by the wish to give his country good laws, yet himself unable to control his urges, his anger and desire for pleasure. The queen remonstrates with him: "You who so struggle for order everywhere except in your own life" (53). In appointing his friend Becket as archbishop, he has the idea of an amical unity of Church and state, "one justice, not two" (14), but: "Can you draw lines in the living water?" (47). Becket immediately sees the conflicts threatening and accepts them. He is warned by the king, the court and the bishops. In a fit of rage the king asks who will rid him of this "turbulent priest". Four nobles slip away. The king, having cooled down, tries to catch up with them, but the murder has already occurred. The third act shows the consequences. First we see the king, fasting and penitent, at Becket's tomb, then we see him scourged by the monks of Canterbury (his son says scornfully, "I saw him whipped like a

---

[72] *Ibid.*, 131.   [73] *Ibid.*, 180.
[74] Christopher Fry, *Curtmantle* (Oxford University Press, 1961).

boy" [78]). Queen Eleanor, a French woman who bore him four boys (apart from the bastard, Roger, who will remain loyal to him), turns his children away from him. The heirs, Henry and Geoffrey, die; Richard (the Lionhearted) demands the kingdom, which is denied him; he goes to France, to Philip II. Finally, when the king succumbs, the fourth son, the landless John, goes over to them. Henry's native city, where he had taken refuge, goes up in flames; an old woman drags his dirty mattress out into the open country and the mortally sick king is laid on it. Richard and Philip find him. The latter compels him to stand up and pay him homage, which he does, "now that his greatness has been so humbled" (88). The terrible curse he utters against God ("I will wound you in the heart of your love, just as you have done to me") is again only a momentary outburst; he takes it back, asking for a monk to give him absolution. While Roger is away looking for one, the king's body is looted and left naked. He is covered up and carried off; the old woman keeps dragging his mattress along. So ends the hope of a triad: the state, the Church and the French wife who embodies the French fiefs. Henry's demonic personality has destroyed this dream, again due to a kind of hereditary curse: "My father is only / Demon by descent. But he made the most of it" (90). Yet he wanted the best for his country. The dying man wonders anxiously whether the laws will hold, and, as he dies in agony, cries out, "It is all still to do!" (97).

Excursus: The Drama of Generations

Atoning death on behalf of someone else has shown us that, while dying is the most personal, most solitary act, it is by no means a private act. *Ionesco* saw a profound social dimension precisely in this total loneliness. Life, with its interrelated destinies, bursts through the "three unities" of classical drama. *Shakespeare* is very often at pains to show that, after some great tragic action, life goes on; for example, Fortinbras in *Hamlet*, Malcolm in *Macbeth*, the birth of Elizabeth in *Henry VIII*. A hermetically closed action would be abstract if it were not typical of much that is human. *Wedekind's* subtitle was, *So ist das Leben (Such Is Life)*. No man is an atom; he is a living cell within an organism of destiny. It is arbitrary to chisel his circumscribed form out of mankind's total destiny, or even, perhaps, out of life itself. It is quite legitimate, therefore, in seeking to understand a dramatic sequence, to look further than the realm of a single, individual existence.

It is possible to compress the constellation of events, the game of chess of an epoch, into a single play, as *Schiller* did in *Wallenstein* and *Reinhold Schneider* did, on a larger canvas, in *Innozenz und Franziskus* (1952) and *Der Grosse Verzicht* (1950). With even greater daring it is possible to make the characters into symbols of whole continents and fit the entire Earth and its dynamic interrelations into four acts, as *Claudel* does in his *Le soulier de Satin* (1924). Such plays, however, cannot be performed on a single evening. Of themselves they generate a dramatic cycle in which a *single* destiny is lived out through the various phases of the cycle. Antiquity blazed the trail here with its trilogies; the uniting factor was often the hereditary curse that worked itself out in a dynasty. So it is in *Aeschylus'* Tantalus trilogy. But this was by no means conceived as an oppressive fate that diminished man, for things happen "as Zeus determined, he who moves and perfects everything. For what could take place apart from Zeus? And as for this that has happened, is it not God's doing?"[1] Furthermore, what happens is more than a family tragedy. In the *Eumenides* the play witnesses a change that marks off the mythical from the ethical epoch, very remotely comparable to the change from the Old to the New Covenant. The same thing must have happened in the Prometheus trilogy; it must have represented the change from the titanic dimension to the human.

We have already referred to *Shakespeare's* histories. They are substantially looser in construction than those of antiquity, and the poet wrote later parts earlier than the earlier ones. In *Henry V* he gives himself a breathing space, making it into a brilliant, patriotic festival drama. But, apart from this intermezzo, he is almost pedantic in the way he sees the long drawn-out sequence of the eight dramas as originating in the episode of the deposing of Richard II. This illuminates and precipitates everything. "To the third and fourth generation . . ." This is the place to mention *Wagner's* tetralogy, which, in a much more confused manner, deduces everything from the curse issued at the violation of the sanctuary.

The French Revolution undoubtedly signifies the change to the modern era. Three cycles of dramas by great writers are based on it. The first remained unfinished: *Goethe's Die natürliche Tochter* is the only complete part of a triptych now lost. It is concerned with the danger to which a nobly born soul is exposed and the sanctuary it finds in the new bourgeois age; instead of the flight to the convent we have marriage

---

[1] *Agamemnon* 1486–88.

with a husband from the middle class. This is a "sacrifice" in an almost Christian sense. Its consequences are hidden from us.

Romain Rolland worked practically all his life on a dramatic epos laid out in twelve parts. It begins with a prologue, Pâques fleuries (1927), and moves on to the storming of the Bastille in 1793, which culminates in a gigantic popular festival (Quatorze Juillet, 1902). Its central events are the fall of Danton in 1794 (Danton, 1900), the noble demise of the Girondists (Le triomphe de la raison, 1899) and the fall of Robespierre (Robespierre, first performed in 1952). Two plays are rather more in the nature of episodes: Les loups (1898), which takes place in the siege of Mainz in 1793 and shows the revolutionaries devouring each other, and Le jeu de l'amour et de la mort (1925), which portrays the heart-rending episode of the outlawed Girondist Claude Vallée, who traverses the whole of France and returns to Paris, to the lion's jaws, in order once again to kiss his beloved, Courvoisier's wife. Courvoisier sends the two lovers on their way to the frontier with passes intended for him; he embraces death. In the epilogue to Les Léonides (1928) the former enemies meet again twenty-five years later, reconciled, in Switzerland. As Rolland has said several times,[2] his aim was to show the elemental forces that open up all the human dimensions, arousing superhuman heroism and wickedness, for the sake of a utopian ideal of freedom. This ideal may cause heroic and bestial men to devour each other, but the poet takes it seriously. The pathos of this new notion of freedom migrates eastward, to Germany and Russia. (Rolland welcomed the Russian Revolution.) Freedom, in Rolland's sense, is the world's freedom.[3]

Paul Claudel's trilogy, L'Otage, Le pain dur, Le Père Humilié (written in 1910, 1913–1914, 1916, respectively), while it is more tightly knit, is still not completely perspicuous. It provides a number of cross sections through the later phases of the Revolution, the thirties and the years 1869–1871. These portraits of a century are the only thing in French

[2] Primarily in the Preface to Le jeu de l'amour et de la mort (Paris: Albin Michel, 1925).

[3] "I can already see the ground trembling beneath our feet. . . . The nations embrace each other. Like streams joining together to become a river. We are the river, sweeping everything away": Le 14 Juillet in Théâtre de la Révolution (Paris: Ollendorff, 1909), 72. Danton, certain that he will fall: "So, then, the Republic will appall the world by the noise of its collapse" (193). Robespierre: "All friends, from the smallest to the greatest, will work together on the sublime task, namely, the freedom of the world" (198). But the utopian side plainly emerges at the end of "Danton": Vadier, mocking, says, "The Republic will only be free, only be pure, when there is no more Republic." Saint-Just: "Ideas have no need of men. Nations die so that God shall live" (271).

literature, according to *H. Gouhier*, to match the "Henrys and Richards of Shakespeare".[4] In the first play a pope appears as a "guarantor" or "pledge", the only person beyond the mortal struggle between the old and new regime. In the last play another pope, Pius IX, is deprived of his Church-State as a result of the unification of Italy and has difficulty in accepting his new role. In the first play the Church extricated itself from the grasp of both imperial and feudal power; in the last play it is liberated willy-nilly, by political intervention, from a directly political role. In *Sygne*, *L'Otage* portrays the ultimate victim of feudalism, though it is hard to say whether the presentation is thoroughly Christian; *Claudel's* heart beats for the new age and for the vigorous ruffian, Turelure. Turelure and his son will adapt to the changing forms of authority—Napoleon, Louis XVIII, the July Monarchy, Napoleon III, the Third Republic—although the Revolution's original idealism cannot survive these compromises. *Le pain dur* is the loveless harshness of early capitalism with its colonial expansion, the partition of Poland (which had a special and painful significance for *Claudel*) and Jewish emancipation. These are forces that continue to operate through the century, so that the third play, *Le Père Humilié*, which outwardly is concerned with the unification of Italy, is inwardly more like a lyrical sum total or distillate of the modern era. Orian's love for the blind half-Jewess, Pensée (the daughter of Sichel and the younger Turelure), remains unfulfilled despite their child growing within the girl. Orian is killed in the Franco-German War and his brother Orso marries Pensée. This child, a synthesis of the Christian and Jewish principles, was to have been the center of a fourth play, which *Claudel* glimpsed only once in a flash of intuition. It must have been an eschatological panorama, hardly performable on the stage. *Le Père Humilié* remained "enigmatic" even to the poet himself. The trilogy "could only end with a further opening".[5]

Can drama be expanded even further than such cyclic portrayals of a whole epoch? Why not, if the stage's raison d'être is to present existence, "the world"? The medieval mystery plays set forth the whole of world history from paradise to the Last Judgment. If, in modern times, something of the kind is attempted in an individual play or a dramatic cycle, the aim is either to focus on the efforts made by humanity as a whole—seen optimistically as progress or pessimistically as futility—

[4] "La Trilogie", in *Entretiens sur Paul Claudel sous la direction de Georges Cattaui et Jacques Madaule*. Décades du Centre culturel international de Cerisy-La-Salle, nouvelle série 11 (Paris and Hague: Mouton, 1968), 215.

[5] Letter to Georges Cattaui, in G. Cattaui, *Le Père Humilié, loc. cit.*, 225.

or else to show the typical as it is embodied in each new, personal phenomenon. *Imre Madach's The Human Tragedy* (1861), in part based on *Goethe's Faust*, begins with the Lord's conversation with Lucifer (who is "the original idea of negation" and as such was implicit in God's plan of the world), the tasting of the apple and Adam and Eve's expulsion from paradise. Lucifer causes them to sleep and shows them how they will be transformed through the course of future world history: every great idea is doomed to disintegrate, to choke to death in the filth of the real world. The vision concludes with images of capitalism and collectivism, of the "brave new world", of space travel and finally of the world enveloped by ice. Adam has seen enough; he wants to wake up and take stock: perhaps it would be better to forestall God's plan and take his own life. Eve stops him from doing this by telling him that she is expecting his child. The Lord appears and Adam asks him what is the meaning of history: "Is this straitened existence all I have, purifying my soul through struggle" and making of it a wine that God pours into the earth, "or is the noble sap designed for better things?" Is it simply the case that the animal walks round and round in circles, driving the mill, or can "my race draw near your throne"? The Lord forbids man to investigate this riddle any more closely. By grace it remains hidden. Man's greatness is his faith, his trust, his will to go on living despite all the forces that would drag him down. Endless is the realm that demands that man labor, and beside Adam stands Eve, who causes what is impossible in the long run to seem meaningful at any particular moment. Trusting, Adam sets off on the hopeless path, only to be shattered by the collective.

We need not devote any more space to the optimistic version in *Shaw's Methusalem* and his glorification of the "life force". Far more humane are the two plays of *Thornton Wilder* that portray life's stream in such a way that the individualities it contains lose nothing of their sharpness of outline. In the one-act play *The Long Christmas Dinner* (1931), the author deals with the time-span between 1840 and 1930. On the left side of the stage is the brightly decorated door of birth, and on the right the black door of death. Ninety Christmas dinners are summed up in this one, the generations and their characters change, the children grow up, the old pass away, but it is all the same life, trivial but irreplaceable. *The Skin of Our Teeth* (1942) depicts the history of the Antrobus family from the Ice Age onward, and "the end of this play has not yet been written".

It is also possible to draw together the whole of world history, nonchronologically, at a particular historical point, as *Max Frisch* does in his *Die Chinesische Mauer* (1947). This play is enacted both in the past, in pre-Christian times when the sublime emperor, having achieved all his victories, erects the Great Wall (to shut out the continuing march of historical time), and in the present. From the standpoint of this present, "modern man" looks back over world history, which is embodied in a whole series of famous historical figures like Napoleon, Pilate, Columbus, Don Juan and so forth—all speaking in the style of their period. The series concludes with the invention of the cobalt bomb. The play remains just as dialectically open as *Madach's*: the future that brings the bomb must not be allowed to happen. Thus the Wall is right; and yet time does not stand still: the Wall has long been rendered obsolete.

It is good that these diverse forms of the drama of generations, with few exceptions (*Shaw*), do not overstate the death of the individual; thus, in manifold ways, they respect the laws of the human dramatic situation. Such laws are only disregarded where a "purely horizontal", communistic or evolutionist theory of drama prevails, which would allot small significance to personal death and see mankind only as a historical or biological collective. This would spell the end of the dramatic dimension of human existence. At best, the stage would be a medium of propaganda.

5. *The Struggle for the Good*

a. The Good Slips Away

We have seen that drama is essentially human action, action as a way of imparting meaning to existence in its search for self-realization. The dimension of this search is the future: existence (which contains its past and present) interprets itself with a view to the future. This activity is fundamentally different from a purely biological process. It is based on the spiritual freedom that, as we saw in *Brecht*, must be postulated dramatically even where a particular *Weltanschauung* would deny it. Drama is concerned about change, whether it is change of man himself or of his environment, and for this purpose it presents us with themes and counterthemes, forces and counterforces that freedom alone is able to assess and evaluate. We have already seen that drama's tension lies in the ambivalence of the present situation (together with the past that is stored up in it). The responsibility of this free, future-oriented decision is to lead the future out of its fluid indefiniteness of meaning toward a firm outline; however, as long as the action lasts, the firm definition thus achieved will always contain within it a new fluidity to be overcome.

In every case the goal of the decision is the Good. As long as we are in the flesh, however, the Good exhibits gradations. It has a vanishing point that, itself unattainable, is the absolute Good indicating the direction in which we are to strive; and it has a concrete stopping point on the way, namely, our best course of action under the circumstances. Only in the catastrophe of tragedy are these two points brought to coincide; that is, in the martyr play, where the total witness of a life coincides with death, which, for the believer, always leads directly to union with the Divinity. It also occurs, however, in non-Christian plays—as in Camus' *Les justes*—in which some ideal is taken as absolute and is affirmed and vouched for by the prior acceptance of death. (We have drawn attention to the inherent contradiction in this, as in *Brecht's Good Woman of Szechuan*.) By its very nature, comedy deals with attaining only a relative happiness that, at best, can symbolize the absolute Good and testify to a belief in it. But precisely this reveals the questionable nature of the Good that can be attained on earth.

Every good for which man strives as a feasible possibility is surrounded, attacked and relativized by other goods and values. We do not need to set forth a philosophical ethics beforehand in order to grasp this. Values that are posited as absolute can refute themselves during the course of a dramatic action—thus Tellheim's concept of honor is shown its limits by the sure hand of Minna von Barnhelm—but they can also show themselves to be unrealizable by the ruin of the hero who pledges his life on their account. This offering of a person's life always bears several interpretations. It can be the stubbornness that beats its head against a wall or the hubris that thinks it can demonstrate an absolute value through its own demise; it can also be the straightforward answer (in Christianity) to the absoluteness of God as it penetrates into the human realm.

For the most part, man finds himself in a thicket of relative goods and values and tries, with the aid of an internal compass, to find his way to the Absolute. First of all, objectively speaking, there are many layers, many choices between emphases in life.

There is the private realm or the public arena, the small circle or the large, politically significant group; there is visible success or the paramount importance of the invisible, the religious; one can opt for vitality or economics or aesthetics, or morality in the narrower sense. We have to decide how far it is worthwhile investing ourselves in this or that value, and determine when such investment begins to threaten the balance of our own spiritual housekeeping. This objective plurality of layers, which is embedded in every human life, only becomes dramatic because of the subjective freedom we have to change our perspective on the objective world of values, moving this good into the foreground to make it more desirable, moving that one farther back to deprive it, at least for a time, of its power of attraction, "suppressing" it in favor of some other value. If man is to live, surrounded as he is by a press of possibilities, he is obliged to choose; yet, provided he is not totally overwhelmed by necessity, he is free with regard to his fundamental decisions —which may be very deeply hidden.[1] This freedom not only concerns the ability to choose but also the right or wrong choice, which presupposes the existence of clearly perceptible criteria. Such criteria are grasped, not in the either-or of a purely objective and purely subjective scale of values, as if man were able abstractly to choose either the "good-in-itself" or the "good-for-him", but in that intertwining of both points of view that arises from fellowship with other human beings, from the dialogue-character of existence. For no one can wish to realize the good-in-itself without immediately encountering the limitations of human freedom and human attitudes; similarly, no one can strive for the good without trying to implement it either together with his environment or in opposition to it. At all events he must become aware of the value systems of others, either like a spy who gets to know a foreign territory for his own advantage, or in open exchange, with the aim of personal enrichment, or perhaps in the hope of being of service to the other world of value and of sharing in it, if it seems to be a larger and more significant world. In either case, the subject "gains" as

[1] H. E. Hengstenberg, *Philosophische Anthropologie*, 3d ed. (Kohlhammer, 1966), 40ff.: "obligation to freedom", "freedom within obligation".

a result of the dialogue. In the first instance he gains egoistically, annexing the other world as part of his ego, and in the second instance he gains altruistically: the other world is enriching precisely insofar as it is *not* his own. However, even this self-transcendence is ambivalent, for it can be sought as the enjoyment of an adventure ("To surrender oneself is a delight": *Goethe*), or as the selfless offering of oneself for the sake of a cause that is greater than one's own sphere, be it a personal or a political cause. Moreover, a process that began under one sign can change over to a different sign—often without anyone noticing.

Pure egoism in the unmasking of hypocrites like Richard III and Tartuffe is rarely taken *ad absurdum* on the stage. What is more common is the conflict within a person between his self-assertion and his desire to devote himself totally to a cause (as in *Schiller's Fiesco* or his *Demetrius*). Even more common is the conflict between different forms or levels of dedication, for instance, personal love and political obligations (*Racine's Bérénice*), or personal love and honor (*Corneille's Le Cid*). In the latter case Rodrigue is torn between his love for Chimène and his duty of avenging his father; subsequently Chimène too is torn between her love for Rodrigue and the obligation to punish him as her father's murderer—a theme taken up hundreds of times in Spanish comedy. There is also the conflict between a persecuting love and the lover's personal attachment, as well as the violation of one value by another (as where politics attempts to use love for its own purposes: in *Corneille's Nicomède* [1650], *Sertorius* [1662], or where love triumphs over politics in his last play, *Suréna* [1674]). In *Camus' L'État de siège* the conflict between personal love and the love of humanity is heightened to an abstract and radical level at which Diego is compelled to sacrifice his love for Victoria for the good of the town. In doing so he gives life back to the mortally ill woman, but he himself dies: "I am no longer a man and it is right that I should die."[2]

But the conflicts can also take place entirely on the political scene, and we know how difficult it is here to assess the greater good and take necessary action against the evil. This is the place

[2] Camus, *Théâtre, Récits, Nouvelles* (Pléiade, 1963), 297.

for plays dealing with revolution and the assassination of tyrants, from *Shakespeare's Julius Caesar* to *Schiller's William Tell* and *Weiss' Marat/Sade*, although in the older plays it is not so much a question of the success of the new regime as the legitimacy of the old: when does the latter become so lightweight that it justifiably tips the scales of revolution? *Schiller*, the author of *William Tell*, also wrote *Fiesco* and *Wallenstein*, and in the latter play emphasized the demonic self-consciousness of the traitor, whereas the question of the legitimacy of the emperor in Vienna remains obscured; nor, in *Don Carlos*, is it resolved unequivocally in favor of the Marquis Posa. The overthrowing of a legitimate authority or of an unbearable tyranny to achieve a state of freedom can contain elements of personal drama,[3] but objectively speaking the conflict of values would only be decided if and when the new realm of freedom actually managed to prove itself. *Romain Rolland*, in his revolutionary cycle, was objective enough to keep showing the questionable nature of this freedom and to let the final result remain utopian. *Camus'* great drama of liberation, *L'État de siège*, in which one person makes the ultimate sacrifice in order to overcome the "plague" (the deadening tyranny that characterizes the total rationalization of modern life), ends with the unavoidable return of all the powers that had been confronted: "They come back, the previous powers, the powers of yesterday, of all times, ossified, calming, comfortable . . . tradition. . . . Governments pass away, the police remains. So there *is* a justice."[4] But this justice is not the good for which Diego died.

As world history moves on, and with the increasing rationalization of existence and the increasing concentration of technological and political power, so the conflict between justice, which compels everyone to be given what is his, and freedom, which resists any leveling-down or leveling-up, becomes more problematical. The modern plays that call for "world transformation" are naive insofar as they do not see this dilemma;

[3] Walter Benjamin, in his *Ursprung des deutschen Trauerspiels*, rev. ed. (1963), 60ff., has pointed out the inherently dramatic quality of those baroque tragedies in which the tyrant, in his fall, is also revealed as a martyr, because the fall from greatness is understood in an entirely formal way.

[4] Camus, *Théâtre, Récits, Nouvelles*, 299.

others see it but can only portray the individual's *angst* in the face of its intractability. Drama is always concerned about the individual: How is he to survive and take responsible action, surrounded as he is by ever more gigantic forces and institutions? This is the growing difficulty of the serious stage. But "circumstances" never dispense anyone from taking personal decisions. Human existence, even where it is stripped of all power, is still able to bear witness to the Good that has been glimpsed in and through all the conflicts.

This makes two things clear. In the first place, the purity of conscience is not fundamentally affected by the harshness and gigantic dimensions of the available alternatives. True, drama can do nothing with manipulated, technologically clouded consciences (if brainwashing of this kind can succeed without the victim being at fault). The stage can present characters who have become so fixed as a result of habit and tradition, whose better nature has been so stifled or become the prey of patently false ideologies, that they are obliged to oppose any person who manages to see through this fog; they may perhaps be converted to his view of things and throw away their masks, but equally they may crush him under their superior weight. There must be *one* clear conscience on the stage—or at least *one* which deliberately renounces the acknowledged higher value—so that the spectator can grasp the hierarchy of values. (Compare the final version of *Brecht's Galilei*.) Even if the author himself seems to be unsure about his hero's conscience, he must ultimately reveal the norm, in the hero or in some other character, according to which the spectator can get his bearings (compare *Schiller's Wallenstein* again). Objectively speaking the choice between the conflicting values can be so difficult as to be almost impossible, but the decision that is finally to be made in subjectivity must be free and responsible: *this* is the compass direction—in the primal forest that is the world—in which the invisible and absolute Good is to be sought.

Other conclusions follow. The Absolute does not make itself present simply, in a bodily way: it announces itself only in the relative goods and values, but eventually it does this so clearly that no further hesitation is legitimate. The choice itself can be clouded by passion, led astray by deception; it can subsequently reveal itself as a total mistake that calls for the chooser's self-destruction (*Othello*); but at the moment in which it was taken it seemed right. At the crucial moment, at a level that, as far as the spectator (and often the actor too) is concerned, is deeper than psychology can reach, there takes place an act of obedience or disobedience to the light. Such moments can be rare—and for long periods the decisions taken can go on operating almost mechanically—but their existence is indispensable if we are to call an action genuinely human. Often the light, which is always sufficient for the making of the decision, is so bright as to transcend all rational assessment. Thus *Goethe's Clavigo* knows what his conscience is impelling him to do, in spite of the plausible reasons to the contrary presented by his friend Carlos. But the old Duke Ernst, too, in *Hebbel's Agnes Bernauer*, can face his conscience when he pronounces the death sentence over the middle-class girl his son has married. Decisions can be fraught with tragic implications that keep the claims of the countervalue at a distance: this is part and parcel of the dramatic tension; but it does not mean that clarity cannot be attained in the decision itself.

All the same, we must take a step back from what we have said so far. The ethical dimension is thickly clogged with elements of psychology and sociology, and the limitations of these fields are sometimes like a miasma obscuring the ethical light. *Hegel* saw the strength and weakness of the modern drama in the "character": the character lives as a kind of microcosm, following the laws of its own nature and confusing its own inner light with the light of the Absolute. *Shakespeare* has portrayed such characters with the limitation that clearly clings to them: *Coriolanus*, for instance, who equates his own proud honesty with the Roman *virtus* and draws disastrous consequences from this premise. Or *Timon of Athens*, who identifies all virtue with his magnanimity, and, when his former friends betray him when he cannot pay, rails against the world order.

There is a fluid transition from figures such as these to less powerful characters whose spiritual horizon is restricted or distorted by passion or what nowadays is called ideology. They make their choice and are convinced that they are acting in accord with conscience, but the latter is governed by some ideal they have accepted, provisionally at least, as an absolute light. *Ibsen's Brand*, his *Enemy of the People* and particularly his Gregers in the *Wild Duck* and his *Julian* too are trapped in their ideologies, which are mostly characterized by a rootless idealism, but occasionally by a narrow realism (Bernik in the *Pillars of Society*), a forced realism, used as a pretext, like Wallenstein's. In *Shaw* the whole play often consists in balancing out the psychological standpoints, behind which the real ethical decision threatens to disappear. It can also happen, however, that the conflict of opposed forces remains unsolved, leading to that schizophrenia that goes right through *Brecht's Good Woman of Szechuan*. As for crude naturalism (which sees man absolutely controlled by his environment, to such an extent that there can be no such thing as a free decision) we need not dwell on it here, but it is worth mentioning the plays of *Chekhov*, in which a kind of fate hands over the period, inclining all the characters to ruin, like trees bent by the ocean wind. There is still room for personal stances in this overshadowing fate, but all are affected by the general atmosphere.

Thus the whole horizon from which the light of decision was to break forth can be obscured. The scale of values can seem to be destroyed, or its distortions can result in it being the butt of mockery; all compasses can seem to lead astray. We see this in *Shakespeare's Troilus and Cressida*, where Ulysses solemnly speaks of the existing hierarchical world order and scale of values (I, 3), but immediately goes on to show how it can be corrupted: if "degree" is taken away, "Force should be right; or, rather, right and wrong, / Between whose endless jar justice resides, / Should lose their names, and so should justice too. / Then everything includes itself in power." The order has been destroyed because the Greeks are fighting for an unworthy object, the voluptuous Helen, and Troilus is made a fool of by the faithless Cressida. The Greek army is torn by dissension and Hector, who is initially in favor of letting Helen go (II, 2), debates with Troilus about the objectivity of values:

> Troilus: What is aught but as 'tis valued?
> Hector: But value dwells not in particular will;
>   It holds his estimate and dignity

> As well wherein 'tis precious of itself
> As in the prizer: 'tis mad idolatry
> To make the service greater than the god.

When Cassandra foretells the collapse of Troy, Troilus insists on the unconditional value of defending it: success does not determine whether an action is right or not. Hector gives in, against his better knowledge, when renown beckons ("Mine honour keeps the weather of my fate" [V, 3]), and goes to the battle, and is treacherously killed by Achilles after he has laid aside his weapons. Troilus however, for whom loyalty is the highest good ("While others fish with craft for great opinion, I with great truth catch mere simplicity" [IV, 4]), refuses to believe Cressida's faithlessness, which he has seen with his own eyes, because if he did, his whole house of values would collapse and rend his own heart:

> If there be rule in unity itself,
> This is not she. O madness of discourse,
> That cause sets up with and against itself! . . .
> Within my soul there doth conduce a fight
> Of this strange nature, that a thing inseparate
> Divides more wider than the sky and earth; . . .
> Cressida is mine, tied with the bonds of heaven: . . .
> The bonds of heaven are slipp'd, dissolv'd, and loos'd (V, 2).

While the collapse of values seems normal on earth (Thersites: "Here is such patchery, such juggling, and such knavery! . . . [A]nd war and lechery confound all!"), Troilus longs for death (V, 6): "I . . . dare all imminence that gods and men / Address their dangers in" (V, 10). What makes the play so significant is that it expresses both aspects at the same time: the hierarchy of values and its practical unfeasibility.

In *Macbeth* it is demonic powers[5] that becloud his horizon: the witches greet him as the Thane of Glamis, of Cawdor, as the future king: if the first comes true immediately, must not

---

[5] Cf. primarily Hecate's speech in III, 5:

> And that, distill'd by magic sleights,
> Shall raise such artificial sprites,
> As, by the strength of their illusion,
> Shall draw him on to his confusion:

Macbeth, for the sake of the prophecy, cut a path to the last? Banquo: "And oftentimes to win us to our harm, / The instruments of darkness tell us truths" (I, 3). Like the witches in *Macbeth*, the "stars" in *Wallenstein* stand between the hero and his conscience; but in both plays they cannot ultimately mask it. For a modern example, we could mention two plays by *Wedekind* (*Der Erdgeist* and *Die Büchse der Pandora*) in which Lulu is a demonic power expressly referred to as the "earth spirit": the poet regards her as an "authentically tragic" character.[6] There is something analogous to *Troilus and Cressida* in *Schiller's Die Räuber*: a world order, acknowledged as valid in the background, is relentlessly subjected to doubt. In a way this doubt is prior to both heroes, for it is a doubt about the validity of the Enlightenment's interpretation of existence. Franz Moor embodies the dismemberment of this interpretation at the hands of *Voltaire*, Karl Moor embodies *Rousseau's* critique of it.[7] Both of them act freely while at the same time they are driven by a destiny associated with the period in which they live. Both of them are utterly unabashed in executing their plans and finally recognize that it has not been what they wanted. The humiliated father, the innocently suffering Amalia, represent the real order behind the order that is distorted; this real order can assert itself only by destroying the other (in the demise of Franz Moor), leaving it an open question whether, for *Schiller*, the villain's fear of hell has any theological weight or is only an effective stage motif for the sake of the audience.

The vault of heaven is present, overarching, in many plays of the modern period, but it is an obscured, distorted, ultimately powerless,[8] annihilated heaven, misinterpreted as man's demonic

---

He shall spurn fate, scorn death, and bear
His hopes 'bove wisdom, grace and fear:
And you all know, security
Is mortal's chiefest enemy.

[6] Preface to *"Die Büchse der Pandora"*, *Werke* (1910), III, 105.

[7] A. Rousseau, however, who is compelled (because of Karl's activity as a robber) to contradict himself, only expressing himself in Karl's nostalgic effusions "in the region of the Danube" (III, 2).

[8] In W. Borchert's *Draussen vor der Tür* (1947) God is an old man who weeps because he can do nothing to help. "I am the God in whom no one believes

antagonist. Modern heroes do not seek an absolute Good above them, they only ask the God who dwells in their own breast. As with *Schiller's Demetrius*, it can happen that they collapse in midcourse, or have to cut a path through the impenetrable undergrowth of a hostile existence that is too much for them, as in *Büchner's Woyzeck*. Or else, like Oreste in *Sartre's Les mouches*, in order to guarantee their own freedom, they have to imagine a hostile God who is allegedly in competition with it and who humiliates them by holding them down by force. This convulsive gesture of absolute self-determination ends in the hell of *Huis-Clos*; man's conscience must be in touch with things as they are: the two poles, personal inwardness on the one hand and relation to one's environment and one's fellow men on the other (the poles of conscience and norm), are necessary if we are to have a starting point indicating both the imperfectibility of all intramundane Good and the direction in which we must seek the transcendental, absolute norm. In modern drama the latter is mostly shown as a blind feeling around for something beyond the attainable world, as the impatient urge to change the fundamental conditions of existence, or as the attempt to contemplate existence from a lofty (Buddhist) vantage point and see it as the realm of pure futility: *Strindberg's A Dream Play* is the most beautiful and moving play of this kind.

What we have said here about the Good "slipping away" seems to end in open contradiction. Certainly it is not a contradiction that can be arbitrarily closed. For at the moment when decisive action is taken, the Good shines forth, providing us with the opportunity of ethically evaluating such action, of "judging" it. On the other hand the horizon of the Good can be obscured in various ways, preventing us from "judging" clearly because, subjectively or objectively, the norms may be distorted

---

anymore." Beckmann: "We have bellowed for you, wept and cursed for you! Where were you then, dear God? Have you turned away from us?" God: "My poor boy, I cannot stop it . . . no one listens to me anymore. You make too much noise!" Beckmann: "Or is it that you are too quiet, God? Perhaps you have too much ink in your blood, God, too much theologian's ink? Away with you, old man; they have walled you up in the church, we can't hear each other anymore" (*Gesamtwerk* [1949], 148f.).

or displaced. Perhaps drama can and should evoke both at the same time; that is, that there is an ultimate light by which human action will be judged, and that it is no man's place to make such judgment.

b. Tragic, Comic, Tragi-comic

These three words raise a vast host of questions of *Weltanschauung* and dramatic practice, questions with a confusing plurality of aspects. It would be impossible to go into them in any depth here. We shall only deal with them insofar as they come within the spiritual ambit of this chapter and particularly as they relate to the problem raised at the end of the preceding section. What we have already said in "The theme of death" is relevant here: death is an event that is given a meaning from many angles, but this partial meaning can never cover the entire phenomenon of death. It would be *hubris* for a man to claim knowledge of a meaning embracing the whole of existence. At best, in happiness or misfortune, success or failure, he will feel his way toward this all-embracing meaning, he will tentatively exercise faith in it; or, on the other hand, having established tiny islands of meaning, he will see them founder in an infinite ocean of meaninglessness. The three words of our heading are concerned with the question of *meaning*, a question that goes through them all. There can be tragedies depicting the fall of the hero within a horizon of meaning or meaninglessness, just as there can be comedies in which the partial reconciliation takes place either as a symbol of a belief in total reconciliation or, on the contrary, as an element of lightheartedness against a background of horror. Finally there can be tragi-comedies that observe the events (which have a simultaneously tragic and comic effect) either with conciliatory humor or with grimness.

This overlapping arises from the fact that, in the historical origins of tragedy and comedy (tragi-comedy belongs to the modern era), there is no clear distinction between what we call tragic and comic. In Greek theatre there are many tragedies that have a conciliatory ending. Moreover, the concept of the tragic as applied to tragedies from antiquity to the present time exhibits an inner multiplicity inimical to clear classification. The first observation shows that it will not do to see tragedy as the opposite of comedy; there must be room for the overlaps that have emerged quite normally over the last centuries. The second observation calls for an elementary clarification of concepts on the basis of the relationship of the tragic (and analogously the comic) to the horizon of meaning.

In this connection the most fruitful distinction is that drawn by *Albin Lesky*[1] between three modes of the tragic. The criterion here is the concept of reconciliation. First of all *Lesky* discusses the *tragic situation* in which a man cannot find any way out between conflicting influences and "sees his existence handed over to annihilation"; but this situation is not final: "the clouds, which seemed impenetrable, part, and from a cheerful sky the light of rescue illuminates the stage". Orestes' conflict in *Aeschylus'* trilogy is "unimaginably terrible"; yet in the end it admits of the reconciliation of the warring powers. The second possibility is that of the *closed tragic conflict*. This is what *Goethe* understands by the tragic: "Everything that can be called tragic depends on some irreconcilable *opposition*. Tragedy disappears if there is accommodation or the possibility of it."[2] Here there is no way out of the tragic situation at its own level, but the latter "is not the whole of the world"; "from the overarching totality", "on a higher plane than that on which this conflict had a fatal issue", meaning can shine through. This is how it is in baroque drama and in idealism,[3] and even in *Hebbel's* pantragicism, where the

---

[1] Lesky, "Zum Problem des Tragischen", in *Die griechische Tragödie* (Kröner, 1958), 11–45. See "The Death of Drama?" pp. 70ff. above, for an initial analysis of the tragic dimension. There are apposite remarks on tragedy, comedy and tragi-comedy in Eric Bentley, *The Life of the Drama* (London, 1969).

[2] Goethe to F. v. Müller on June 6, 1824 (Biedermann III, 1, 697). Cf. *Conversations with Eckermann*, Mar. 28, 1827: "It is simply a matter of the conflict which admits no solution. This can arise out of the clash of any relationships whatever." This is a polemical formulation directed at the Hegelian Hinrichs who wanted to assert that the only essential conflict was that between the family and the state.

[3] Formulated most clearly by Solger, *Vorlesungen über Ästhetik* (1819, published 1829): "Where the totality of reality, understood as the representation and manifestation of the Idea, seems to contradict itself and to submerge into the

tragic "extends deep into the being of God" and "is inherent in life itself", but the hero's tragic situation, placed as he is between "equally valid opposites", by no means appears meaningless, for even in the midst of collapse it is the path to reconciliation. It is only the third possibility, the *closed tragic world view*, that denies any overarching meaning to the tragic action. Here the structure of the world is seen as ultimately one of antagonistic and mutually annihilating forces and values. Tragedy in this sense is absent from even the most sombre plays of the Greeks; it is the Nietzschean Yes to the world's ultimate contradiction, a Yes uttered, with many implications, by *Max Scheler* in his essay "Über das Tragische" (1914).[4] Logically, however, this absolute "tragicism" leads to the self-abolition of the tragic, because a scale of values that is inwardly at war with *itself* (and lacking a governing highest value) makes the conflict seem meaningless, along with man, caught in its toils. Thus *F. Sengle*

Idea, this is the tragic principle" (309). "It is through annihilation that tragedy manifests the Idea as existing. For by annihilating itself as existence, it shows itself to be present as Idea, and the two are one and the same. The demise of the Idea as existence constitutes its revelation as Idea" (311). Existence appears as a "worthless life" that only acquires value if the divine Idea manifests itself in it; but at the same time it is not strong enough to sustain this Idea, and can only proclaim it as something doomed to fall. According to this view of the world, "the concrete, in which the divine must appear if it is to be beheld", actually involves "the annihilation of the divine", which is turned into its opposite (P. Szondi, *Versuch über das Tragische* [Frankfurt: Insel, 1961], 29f.). Formulations such as these would suggest, however, that this concept is inevitably drawn beyond itself toward Lesky's third category. This category is advocated by Schopenhauer, for instance, and Julius Bahnsen, *Das Tragische als Weltgesetz und der Humor als ästhetische Gestalt des Metaphysischen* (1877), but also by P. Szondi himself, who regards the constitution of being as essentially dialectical and "the tragic" as "a mode, a particular manner, of that annihilation that is both imminent and already carried out, namely, dialectical annihilation" (60).

[4] There is a connection between Lesky's distinctions and Alfred Weber's studies on *Das Tragische in der Geschichte* (Hamburg, 1943), which distinguishes the "tragic situation . . . , together with its first symbolization in myth" from the "elevation of this tragic situation into the central theme of the whole of existence". Similarly Benno von Wiese in *Die deutsche Tragödie von Lessing bis Hebbel*, 7th ed. (Hamburg, 1967); von Wiese's subtitle, "tragedy and theodicy, tragedy and nihilism", actually indicates the transition from Lesky's first two categories to his third.

and K. Jaspers insist that a relation to a nontragic Absolute is the indispensable precondition of the tragic.[5]

First of all we can deduce from this, again with Lesky, that genuinely tragic situations are possible for Christians. This is something that many deny, George Steiner,[6] for instance, and paradoxically K. Jaspers too.[7] Some Christian writers also reject

---

[5] Lesky draws attention to the important essay by F. Sengle, "Vom Absoluten in der Tragödie", in Deutsche Vierteljahrschrift 20 (1942): 265ff. In opposition to the post-Hebbel tragicism that sees the world "as the meaningless conflict of equally valid forces" the author calls for "the tragic dimension to be linked to the Absolute . . . as an essential element". He asserts that great tragedy never ends in "discord and doubt, but rather in a word of transcending faith that affirms the fate portrayed in the drama and the constitution of the world, shot through with suffering as it is". Similarly Karl Jaspers, in the section "on the tragic" in his book Von der Wahrheit (Munich: Pieper, 1947), 917–60, requires transcendence if the tragic dimension is to exist at all: "The tragic cannot exist without transcendence. Even in the stubborn resistance of mere self-assertion, in the face of ruin at the hands of gods or of destiny, there is a transcending: here man transcends toward Being, toward what he really is, toward what, even as he is being overwhelmed by his fate, he knows himself to be" (925). "To us it seems absurd to say that the Ground of Being is tragic. . . . This is not genuine transcendence, it is a narrow pseudoknowledge that absolutizes something that belongs to the world. The tragic resides in the appearance. The tragic allows Being to shine through; through it speaks something else, something that is itself no longer tragic" (955). Indeed, according to Jaspers, it is even improper to speak of man's worth and nature as "tragic". To do so would be "the most sublime error of a tragic Weltanschauung". For "man presses toward redemption from the terrible realities which are his, which are devoid of any tragic 'lift' " (958). "The merely tragic is apt to serve as a veil to conceal the void in cases where the absence of faith would like to give itself some shape" (959).

[6] The Death of Tragedy (London, 1961). Tragedy is antibiblical (4). He regards "Christian tragedy" as a paradoxical concept. "There has been no specifically Christian mode of tragic drama even in the noontime of the faith. Christianity is an antitragic vision of the world" (331).

[7] In Von der Wahrheit (919), Jaspers says of Calderon and Racine that "tragic has been extinguished" by the tensions between grace and condemnation, and by the awareness of God and a fallen world (due to original sin). There is no such thing "as a really Christian tragedy, because in the Christian play the mystery of redemption forms the basis of the action and the sphere in which it takes place; there is always a prior knowledge of the liberating effect of grace, which perfects and saves" (924). Others who dispute the possibility of tragedy in Christianity are Hermann Weisser, Calderon und das Wesen des katholischen Dramas (1926); J. Körner, Tragik und Tragödie (1931), 274ff.; H. Hefele, Das Wesen der Dichtung

this, for instance, *Theodor Haecker*, who equates the tragic with
"tragicism".[8] D. Mack is right to point out, with regard to
those who reduce Christianity to "an unclouded harmony of
God, the world, and man", that "antiquity's *Nemo contra deum
nisi deus ipse* found a parallel in the New Testament in Christ's
anguished *Eli, Eli lama asabthani*; the Christian realm still contains the possibility of the most profound doubt, the greatest
failure, suffering and conflict, unbelief, the baffling nature of
existence this side of the grave and apparent meaninglessness.
The Christian is not automatically an optimist; he is exposed to
the risk of freedom and hence to the danger of tragic failure."[9]
Mack quotes *Wilhelm Grenzmann* as a witness,[10] for whom the
tragic dimension lies in man's antithetical, paradoxical relation

---

(1923), 103ff.; C. Janentzky, *Tragik und Tragödie* (1942), 6ff.; B. von Wiese, *Die
deutsche Tragödie von Lessing bis Hebbel*, 7th ed. (1967), 14: "It is necessary to hold
fast to the fundamental separation of tragedy and Christianity. For it is of the
essence of tragedy that the divine is drawn into its problem, indeed, into its
desperation." Von Wiese qualifies his approach, however, on pp. 15ff. Cf.
Dietrich Mack, *Ansichten zum Tragischen und zur Tragödie* (Munich: Fink, 1970),
127ff., n. 243 (hereafter referenced as *Ansichten zum Tragischen*). H. G. Gadamer,
Wahrheit und Methode, 2d ed. (1965), 125, also has the same reservations about
Christian tragedy. The opposite line is taken by Oskar Walzel, "Vom Wesen des
Tragischen", in *Euphorion* 34 (1933), who is anxious to distance himself from
Scheler (whose concept of tragedy, he asserts, cannot in any case be reconciled
with that of antiquity).

[8] In *Was ist der Mensch?* (Hegner, 1933), Haecker disputes Nietzsche's and
particularly Spengler's view of man. According to Haecker the Greeks found no
ultimate solution in the tragic catharsis: the laughter of the satyrs covers up the
unsolved area, "the insolubility and impenetrability of the tragic". In Christianity
"persisting tragic elements were drawn into the mystery of the Incarnation,
subjected to the law of freedom . . . , illuminated by the revelation of righteousness and mercy" (105–6). Eventually there was a loss of power in Christianity
and "the old pagan order" returned: "The insolubly tragic dimension", preeminently in Nietzsche's *amor fati*, came back and then, "in the forms of the farce
. . . openly objectivized the meaninglessness of existence and organized the
flight into the void"; the result is so chaotic that tragedy intermingles with the
play of satyrs (107–8). Cf. also T. Haecker, "Wandel im Tragischen", in *Brenner*
(1920).

[9] Dietrich Mack, *Ansichten zum Tragischen*, 128.

[10] "Über das Tragische", in *Gedenkschrift für F. J. Schneider* (Weimar, 1956).
Reinhold Schneider was of the same opinion: "It is incorrect . . . to say that
Christianity abolished tragedy by proclaiming its message of grace": "Zeit und
Drama" in *Rechenschaft*, 23.

to his God (that is, which can only be understood in religious terms). Man, and the Christian in particular, is placed in the tension between election and rejection; as a martyr, he takes on himself the tragic destiny of proclaiming salvation in this world, or else is involved in the battle between faith and unbelief; he finds himself in the contradiction between the divine law and the human desire for self-affirmation; he is exposed to evil. In addition to *Grenzmann* we should mention *Reinhold Schneider, Erich Przywara, Heinz Flügel*[11] and *Josef Bernhart*.[12] Here, however, we are entering a region that cannot be discovered fully within the scope of these prolegomena. The words used by *Mack* such as "doubt" and "unbelief" should not be applied to the abandonment of Jesus on the Cross (which can show certain parallels in the destinies of Christians and human beings generally: "being handed over to evil"),[13] even though this abandonment is more profound than anything we can imagine and, according to the Christian understanding, underpins everything in the world that can be termed "tragic". This mystery eludes all literary categories and relativizes them: we shall discuss this at a later point. It is clear from the start, however, that this overarching Christian reality (God on the Cross abandoned by God) goes way beyond the problems of the mere opposition of human and divine freedoms. In this context such problems are only superficial. Modern dramatists like to represent man's freedom as his personal possession, which God cannot touch. We hear "God can do nothing, and man is free" in *Salacrou's L'Inconnu d'Arras* (1935), and similar sentiments in *Ernst Barlach's Die Sündflut* (1924) and in *Camus*, to say nothing of *Sartre's Le Diable et le Bon Dieu* and *Les mouches*: Jupiter's powerlessness in the face of Oreste's freedom. *Stefan Andres*, in *Gottes Utopia* (1950), overcomes this false opposition: Consalves discovers

[11] *Tragik und Christentum* (Berlin, 1941).

[12] *De profundis* (Munich, 1947). For Bernhart, the tragic is rooted in the structure of the creature, in which there is a "battle between a finite and an infinite power"; in the external defeat of the higher value it becomes possible to penetrate and see inside the power that opposes it. "Thus the tragic dimension seems to contain its own abolition" (178). In this sublimation—as in Jaspers—the light of transcendence breaks through the world's tragic being. Cf. also J. Sellmair, *Der Mensch in der Tragik* (Munich, 1948).

[13] For example, the novel by Georges Bernanos, *La joie* (Paris, 1929).

real freedom by allowing God's freedom to operate within him. But such things can only be explained with reference to the heart of the Christian mystery.

It will suffice if we have shown that tragedy, shorn of transcendence, shorn of "faith", annihilates itself.[14] At this point, however, if we look back over the three categories, a serious question raises its head: What about the second level, where the hero on the earthly stage necessarily perishes, while we sense a reconciliation at a higher level? Is it the upward flight of the ruined man's freedom that renders this higher level visible (and actually constitutes it), or does this level exist in its own right, embracing and protecting the doomed man? Is "transcending" to be equated with transcendence, or is it transcendence that enables man to transcend? This means that, in the end, this second category must join the first or third category. If the doomed hero, in his exaltation, is *the* meaning of what seems meaningless—whether he produces this meaning out of himself or is given it by the dramatist—what we have, willy-nilly, is the *closed tragic world view*. But this does not mean that the spectator can view the tragic destiny from some secure superior and external vantage point: rather, he too must experience all the severity of the conflict in its earthly inevitability. Then, from within, in the ruin that directly concerns him as a human being—*tua res agitur*—he may have the courage to throw a glance of faith and hope toward something or someone who can save him. This is the proper place for an aesthetics of empathy (*Theodor Lipps, R. Müller-Freienfels, Johannes Volkelt*): by sharing in the experience of human pain we become existentially aware

---

[14] In addition to F. Sengle, "Vom Absoluten in der Tragödie", cf. Wolfgang Kayser, *Das sprachliche Kunstwerk*, 8th ed. (1962), 371: "Tragedy takes hold of the tragic dimension in such a way that it becomes the organizing central point. . . . On the other hand it fashions the course of the action as if it is necessary, so that we can sense a meaning in it." Kayser views the tragic element in life as a meaningless loss, to which tragedy imparts an intimation of meaning; in this case the creation of meaning cannot be an aesthetic *creatio ex nihilo*, but must be the uncovering of some objective meaning that is at least possible. Also Christian Janentzky, "Tragik und Tragödie", in *Blätter für deutsche Philosophie* 16 (Berlin, 1942): "We can only understand tragedy threatened by nihilism if we recognize that it preserves certain characteristics of its former religious origins, even in a world rid of gods" (quoted by Mack, *Ansichten zum Tragischen*, 96).

of the power of the Good of which man is capable. This provides a rationale for our "pleasure in tragic objects". Furthermore, this shared experience actually brings into view the objective structure of the world, be it (*Dilthey*) the structures of the human spirit[15] or (*Scheler*) the value structures of being itself.

Two questions must be faced here: How deeply has Being been disturbed? And how is guilt related to such disturbance? Discussion of the second, extremely difficult question will come in the next section, although the first question cannot be fully illuminated without it. But it is certain that the tragic cannot be reduced to the interplay between (personal) guilt and expiation, which is what Christian tragedy often and expressly has been. Nor is the ideal of tragedy the hero's inner mastery of the tragic dilemma, his being lifted into the sphere of reconciliation; for the Christian play has also tended in this direction, following *Seneca*,[16] particularly the baroque drama, but also the idealist drama. One thinks, for instance, of the end of *Oedipus*, which *Aristotle* had in mind in his discussion of *phobos* and *eleos*, grief and horror. And as for the family curse that gives shape to the fable, it is more a symbol of the disturbed world order than a cause in the narrower sense. Darkness moves in on the primal origins to such an extent that the divine cannot be allowed to hover, uninvolved, above the grief of tragedy; particularly if we are concerned to avoid the meaninglessness of the contradiction in Being itself. So the interpretation of the tragic comes within a

---

[15] The tragic has "its origin in the nature of the human spirit, which is always the same. It is a form of dramatic presentation arising from it necessarily" (Dilthey, *Die grosse Phantasiedichtung* [1954], 142) in which "the highest utterances of life and their transfiguration . . . are made visible in suffering" (Mack, *Ansichten zum Tragischen*, 77).

[16] But Seneca is only drawing the stoic consequences from the principles established by Plato. In Seneca the sufferings and passions of the dramatic characters are observed with equanimity by the wise man; the hero, in his virtuous victory, inspires admiration, not horror and grief. "With Plato's grandson and pupil, Polemon . . . tragedy, in a grotesque exaggeration of the Platonic attitude, becomes a means of practicing *apatheia*: people frequent tragic performances with the deliberate intention (in spite of listening attentively) of being in no way moved or affected by the tragic action (cf. Diogenes *Laert.* IV, 3, 17 18)." K. von Fritz, "Tragische Schuld und poetische Gerechtigkeit in der griechischen Tragödie", in *Studium Generale* 8 (1955): 204.

hair's breadth of the third of the categories mentioned, while remaining just as clearly distinct from it. *Erich Przywara's* insight is correct here when—albeit in a very condensed survey—he sees tragedy as arising "twice out of religious mystery": first there was the transformation of the ancient Dionysus cult into the classical Greek tragedy, and then came the development of the medieval and modern tragedy out of the dramatic presentation of Christ's Passion in the Church's Passiontide liturgy. "The eye-to-eye confrontation of 'Dionysian passion' (the god of life's pleasures is torn to pieces and comes to life again) and 'Christian passion' (in the Cross and Resurrection of the God who gives himself in love), this eye-to-eye encounter, which, for *Nietzsche*, is reinterpreted as a rebirth of the Dionysian, is actually there at the origin of tragedy and thus characterizes the 'pure style' of the tragic." From *Aeschylus*, via *Socrates* to *Euripides*, the sacral is increasingly secularized, but since this sacral dimension was "of the lower gods", *Przywara* can say that "the apparent decline seen in the secularization of the sacral" was "in reality the ascending movement of a sublimation of the life forces". After the period of Catholic drama, and as a result of the destruction (by Protestantism)[17] of the theory of "representation" it set forth, this sublimation of vital forces resulted in a return of "the ancient world's secularization of the sacral, albeit on a different plane". *Aeschylus'* theme of wrestling with God is revived in the figure of Faust,

> which is at the bottom of all modern tragedy: it is a secularization of Christ's (and the Christian's) wrestling with the Father's will —for the Christian is a "member of Christ". *Sophocles'* tragedy of destiny is the hidden form in the "objective mediation" of Shakespeare's tragedy: it is the secularization of Christ's (and the Christian's) succumbing to the "night of the cross". *Euripides'* tragedy of "destiny seen as character" is resurrected in the principle of the "inner tragic necessity" in Hebbel's more psychological and Paul Ernst's more mythical tragedy of the "pure man": it is the

---

[17] With its "contradiction (within the confines of temporal existence) between a remote and solely operative deity (in the metaphysical distance of the wrathful *Deus absconditus*, and the historical distance of the reconciling *Deus revelatus* in the purely once-for-all, historical Christ) and an immanent profane reality in competition with God."

secularization of Christ's (and the Christian's) entering into and submitting to "ordinary human nature". . . . Modern tragedy becomes a rebirth of ancient tragedy, parallel to Christianity's regression to the Dionysian[18]

—but insofar as the distance (in antiquity and nature) between the divine and the human becomes, in the post-Christian era, an identity-in-contradiction (where there is no "distance" at all), the formulas of pantragicism emerge, which, as we saw, cancels itself out. Having reached this point we can say that "all formulations of the 'tragic', from *Schelling* to *Nietzsche*, are aware of a necessary split (a 'rent', a 'dichotomy') in the nature of the universe ('God', 'Idea', 'Will'); they all sense a dissonance inherent in 'morality' (*Hegel*), 'freedom' (*Schelling*) or 'will' (*Schopenhauer*)."[19] Put in another way: "The hero's ruin is tragic only if it arises out of the unity of opposing forces, if it results from one pole changing to its opposite, from dichotomy within the self. But it is also only tragic provided that this loss *ought not* to be, provided that, in the wake of this loss, the wound does not heal. For the tragic contradiction must not be subsumed into some superordinate sphere, whether it be immanent or transcendent, and there annulled."[20] Christian theology alone can prevent the tragic dimension from this self-destruction and from being absorbed and nullified in stoically conceived transcendence, in the passionless sphere of a "God of the philosophers";[21] it can do this because it combines God's ultimate initiative on behalf of the world and his free creature with the *gratis* and unmerited quality of this loving self-gift.

[18] *Analogia Entis*, 2d ed. (1962), 251–53.
[19] David E. R. George, *Deutsche Tragödientheorien vom Mittelalter bis zu Lessing.* Texte und Kommentare (Munich: Beck, 1972), 311.
[20] P. Szondi, *Versuch über das Tragische* (Frankfurt: Insel, 1961), 60. M. de Unamuno, in *Das tragische Lebensgefühl* (1925), indulged in similar formulations. "We live only by contradictions. Life is a tragedy, and tragedy is a constant battle without either victory or hope of victory: it is just a contradiction" (19). But this description of existence refuses to draw God into the contradiction, no more than Kierkegaard or Pascal did, who influenced it.
[21] For example, those dramatists who want to get beyond tragedy: Hermann Bahr, *Dialog vom Tragischen* (Berlin, 1904), 23f., who regards the tragic as an obsolete category; the goal is not the pathetic but the civilized, the strength to be unclassical. Maeterlinck is similar insofar as he attempts to replace the area of

Tragedy has always called for a certain "dignity" in the doomed character; he must fall from a "significant height".[22] This arises less from the character's status than from his closeness to the religious origin of the tragic. In the Greek myth this was naturally guaranteed symbolically and visibly by the heroic quality of the persons on stage.[23] Most closely related to this are *Shakespeare's* royal characters and, most of all, those of *Corneille*: because of their representative character and their ethical tenor they can permit themselves only the purest motives and sentiments. In *Corneille's* heroes, probably better than anywhere else, we can see what *Ignatius Loyola* meant by "*grande animo y liberalidad*" (*Exercises*, no. 5)—naturally in relation to God. "Corneille released an influence capable of molding heroic souls" (*Goethe* to *Eckermann*, January 4, 1827). The "status clause" contained in all older tragedies was undermined in the Enlightenment and with the rise of the tragedy of common life (the *bürgerliches Trauerspiel*) and particularly where the plot involved a struggle between classes: henceforth the inner stature and distinction of a soul would replace external status, however silted up this inner quality might be, and however indirectly it might shine through life's humiliations (*Woyzeck*). So long as the inner nobility of particular people is recognized and acknowledged (and they manifest only the nobility of man as a whole), tragedy remains possible.[24] *Jean-Marie Domenach*, in *Le*

---

destiny by "wisdom": *La Sagesse et la Destinée* (1898). Dehmel can also be mentioned in this context. Brecht's attempt to get beyond tragedy is, however, another story.

[22] Lesky, *Zum Problem des Tragischen*, 21–22.

[23] So much so that Walter Benjamin regarded the myth alone (and not the story) as able to sustain the tragedy.

[24] Cf. Emil Staiger, *Grundbegriffe der Poetik*, 3d ed. (1956), 152. In her *Widerhall*, Letzte Erzählungen (DTV, 1968), Tania Blixen sees how the tragic is threatened: "It is easy to banish the tragic element from life. . . . I can see a society like ours a hundred years hence. . . . They will be able to fly to the Moon, but they will not be able to write a tragedy to save their lives." She attempts to explain this: "For tragedy is very far from being the result of the Fall. On the contrary, it is the strategy man has adopted against the vile, hideous effects of the Fall. . . . By a sublime effort of his humanity he has created tragedy. This was a surprise to delight the heart of the Lord God. 'This creature', he exclaimed, 'was really worth creating, . . . for he makes things I

retour du tragique,[25] is of the opinion that the collapse of tragedy, our theatre "without heroes, without a plot and without a solution only demonstrates the contemporary riddle all the more clearly: at the limit, people are prepared even to accept the disappearance of the theatre as an organized dramatic institution, whereas it would continue to survive in political assemblies, law courts, parliaments and family gatherings. One can pick up a novel and put it down again, but one can never get away from theatre", particularly its high point, tragedy, which "elevates and lays bare the *condition humaine*".[26] It is true, of course, that neither the middle class with its concern for well-being, nor socialism, which dreams of building a future ("and the future will not be tragic"), is able to create tragedy. While the novel, from *Dostoyevsky* to *Faulkner,* from *Kafka* to *Malraux*, exhibits the continued existence of the tragic dimension, it so wallows in fatality that it "lacks the detachment necessary for theatrical presentation". But a time is coming when man will penetrate beyond ideologies: "Unrest and doubt arise once more as to the reasons for living and dying. Having done so much killing, people wonder what is the point of it. . . . Then tragedy can reemerge. I think we have reached the edge of this new era."[27] We still have to get beyond the modern "anti-tragedy", however, which contains merely the clash of vacuums, voids, nonvalues and absurdities, and which puts a question mark over freedom.[28] And by "getting beyond it" we do not mean that man must lift himself up out of his humiliation; rather, *in* his humiliation he needs once again to encounter the mystery of the mighty God whose love was not able to answer his Son when, on the Cross, he cried out for him. Man needs once again to encounter the mystery of an incomprehensible but ever-present guilt in the relationship between heaven and earth.

---

would never have managed without him'. . . . All tragedies . . . are based on the idea of honor; it does not rescue mankind from its suffering, but enables it to write a tragedy" (197–99). "Honor" here means the sense of man's nobility.

[25] *Essai* (Paris: Seuil, 1967).

[26] *Ibid.*, 13.

[27] *Ibid.*, 70–73. Cf. Alfred Simon, "Le degré zéro du tragique" in *Esprit* (Dec. 1963).

[28] *Ibid.*, 265, 268.

We have not space here to do justice to *comedy* and its manifold derivatives. It will have to suffice to define it by reference to tragedy. This can be done simply and briefly by using *Lesky's* three categories. There is nothing fortuitous about the relationship between comedy and tragedy, as *Socrates* (whom *Aristophanes* so ridiculed) knew well: at the end of *Plato's Symposion* he puts a speech into the mouth of the drunken companion of which the narrator, unfortunately, understands only a fraction. "For the most part, he said, the upshot of it was that Socrates had forced them to admit that the same poet should be competent in the writing of both tragedy and comedy; the accomplished tragic poet needed to be a comic poet also. While he was obliging them to agree with him (and they were unable to follow him entirely), they had nodded off. In fact it was Aristophanes who fell asleep first." This theory is vindicated by the three great tragic dramatists, also by *Shakespeare, Corneille, Lope* and *Calderon, Lessing, Goethe* and *Kleist,* but hardly by *Schiller, Grillparzer* and *Hebbel.* From romanticism onward greater significance attaches to a mixed genre, the tragi-comedy. It had long been prepared for, but now it was demanded by a new *Weltanschauung.* We shall have to devote some attention to it: it certainly did not belong to *Socrates'* horizon.

Laughter is as much a part of life as weeping: the lighthearted game, the acted or narrated jest, the joke, good humor, poking fun at misconceptions and inappropriate conduct, the delight we take in the unexpected and unhoped-for that falls into our laps as a gift. Countless comedies, rooted in the popular, earthy farces, pranks and saturnalia, in increasing degrees of refinement yet without losing contact with these roots, correspond to an elementary taste and need for entertainment on the part of human beings of all cultures. They possess a certain foreground quality, a certain immanence: according to *Goethe,* the poet (and this applies particularly to the comic poet) needs "a certain good-humored limitation that is in love with the material world and behind which the Absolute lies hidden. The exigencies that come from above destroy that state of innocence and productivity."[29] But if, according to *Socrates,* the dramatist should be

---

[29] Goethe to Schiller, Apr. 4, 1801 (no. 810 of the Tempel-Ausgabe).

competent in both genres, we cannot avoid the question as to the common background of both tragedy and comedy. We cannot say that tragedy alone opens up a perspective onto transcendence whereas comedy, by comparison, remains within the relativities, subjectivities and illusions of immanence. We have already noted that comedy is rooted in the life of the "people" (not for nothing should the characters of comedy, according to the classical definition, belong to the lower classes). This shows clearly that comedy is sustained, not merely by coarse and earthy aspects of life, but equally by a mother wit that is not attenuated by any schooling of the intellect, by an imagination that is not merely animal but also spiritual, and that always has a sense of the quality of life as a whole. Where it is directly accepted and not given an ideological tint, this quality, which makes room for the comic element and justifies it, is an equally valid approach to the unfathomable meaning of the "Whole", no less than tragedy. Each has its rightful place next to the other, not one within the other. It is beyond man's competence to dissolve one in the other or to cause the two to coincide. "There is a time to weep and a time to laugh; a time for lamentation and a time for dancing" (Qo 3:4). Both point in the direction of an Absolute, but man cannot see where their lines intersect in infinity.

We saw that the middle of the three categories of the tragic remained ambivalent: the reconciliation at a "higher" (ideal, transcendental) level of what is insoluble at the immanent level can either be drawn into the first category, if this level is part of a picture of the world familiar to the spectator (like "eternal life" in the case of a Christian watching a mystery play); or it can be incorporated into the third category ("tragicism"), in which this transcendence consists in nothing more than the freedom of the doomed hero. But we have established that tragicism in an absolute sense (which reduces the Absolute to a single formula) actually destroys meaningful tragedy. It will suffice, therefore, to compare comedy with the first and third forms of tragedy.

Comedy, doubtless, should be situated at the heart of the first category. Human weaknesses, limitations, rigidities, perversities are portrayed, or there are confusions, comic contrasts of sit-uation and tricks played by chance; we laugh at them, albeit harmlessly,[30] on the basis of an overall experiential knowledge of life's "normal" conditions. For our laughter to be appropriate, the comic figure must appear as a type, not as a pitiful individual; he must exhibit that rigidity that makes the type out of harmony with the flowing, organic nature of life.[31] Once we move over the borderline from the typical (and the lack of feeling with which it is possible to treat it) to the psychological, comedy itself can become questionable. Thus it is in *Molière's* greatest character plays or in *Kleist's Amphitryon*.[32] It is hard to define the proper locus of comic art, for it has one foot in real, social life and for the most part shows a not "disinterested" tendency, while it has its other foot in the field of art, the object of which, according to *Kant*, is beauty beheld with disinterested delight. For this reason *Kant* decidedly leaves the comic outside the sacred precincts; but he equally decidedly undervalues it, attributing merely physiological significance to laughter over comic subjects.[33] In saying this he is surely not doing justice to the spiritual content of the comedies of *Aristophanes, Menander, Terence, Shakespeare, Calderon, Corneille, Molière* and *Goldoni*. The enjoyment that is produced by higher comedy in particular is a fundamental resonance of existence, and the spectator can feel attuned to it with a good conscience.

But the question will not go away: What is the relationship between this sphere of enjoyment and the all-embracing horizon of being? Just as the modern era has tended to elevate the inescapably *tragic* dimension of life into a universal principle, there is also a contrary and related tendency to make the *comic* the ultimate, overall principle. We shall see that the two attempts run parallel and become interchangeable, which leads to one

[30] Aristotle, *Poetics* 5: "Comedy is . . . the imitation of baser things, but not of everything that is bad, only what is ridiculous, which forms part of the odious. For what is ridiculous is a failing and a disgrace, but one which does not give pain and does no damage, like a funny mask, for instance, which is hideous and distorted, but does not pain us." This "harmless" quality of comedy can best be seen in Don Quixote, the prototype of the ill-adjusted comic figure.

[31] Cf. Henri Bergson, *Le rire. Essai sur la signification du comique*, 23d ed. (1924).

[32] Goethe's diary, July 13, 1807.

[33] *Critique of Judgment*, note following section 53.

cancelling out the other.[34] Two connected trends come together in German philosophical idealism and the (contemporaneous) poetic romanticism: the "I" and the world are subjectivized, going beyond *Kant*, and comedy is included (contrary to *Kant*) in the realm of the "beautiful", in which the (absolute) subject comes to grips with the "non-I" and identifies itself with it. *Schiller* blazes the trail here with his discussion of the place of comedy: people argue about the relative status of tragedy and comedy; "If they are simply asking which of the two deals with the most important *object*, there can be no doubt that the former takes precedence; but if the question is, which of the two calls for the most important *subject*, we may opt for the latter. In tragedy very much is dependent on the object, whereas in comedy nothing depends on the object and everything on the poet."[35] The same status issue is discussed in a posthumous fragment: "In general we can say this: comedy puts us in a higher condition, tragedy in a higher activity. In comedy our condition is peaceful, clear, free, lighthearted, we feel neither active nor passive, we are onlookers, and everything remains external to us; this is the situation of the gods, unconcerned about anything human, hovering at will above everything, untouched by fate and compelled by no law."[36] A superior, godlike standpoint of this kind, where the subject's relation to the world, nature and necessity was simply that of a spectator, would constitute the ultimate, eschatological synthesis: "Comedy would be the most perfect of all poetic works of art" (*F. Schlegel*).[37] For *Schelling*, too, comedy is "the fruit of only the highest education".[38] In *Hegel* we encounter *Schiller's* mode of speech again: "It is the laughter and bliss of the Olympian gods, their

[34] On what follows cf. primarily: Fritz Güttinger, "Die romantische Komödie und das deutsche Lustspiel", in *Wege der Dichtung*, vol. 34 (Frauenfeld and Leipzig: Huber, 1939); Helmut Arntzen, *Die ernste Komödie. Das deutsche Lustspiel von Lessing bis Kleist* (Nymphenburger Verlagshandlung, 1968), with references.

[35] *Über naive und sentimentalische Dichtung*, in *Sämtliche Werke*, ed. Fricke-Gopfert, V, 724.

[36] *Ibid.*, V, 1018.

[37] "Vom ästhetischen Werthe der Griechischen Komödie" (1794), in *Pros. Jugendschriften*, ed. Minor, I, 17.

[38] *Philosophie der Kunst, Werke* I, 5, 716.

untroubled equanimity, that has come home to man and is able to deal with everything."[39] For *F. Schlegel*, comedy—the ultimate form of romantic, progressive "universal poetry"—"may possibly achieve its aim in some remote future . . . when the observance of rule becomes freedom."[40] *Fichte* too, who has no great opinion of comedy, can describe the spirit's sudden insight into "the Whole" as "positive wit" (*Witz*).[41] For *F. Schlegel*, "wit" is one with the freedom of the "I" that plays with everything, including itself; it explicitly equates this freedom with "arbitrary will" and "caprice". *Tieck* moves in the direction of this pancomic total work of art (*Gesamtkunstwerk*), this "comedy of humanity", in his fantastic comedies. So does *Brentano* with his *Ponce de Leon*, which leads to *Büchner's Leonce und Lena* (influenced by *Musset*).[42] *Hebbel* makes the last, doomed attempts; he too regarded the question of comedy as the most important issue in modern drama.[43] Since the "play" is supposed to be the spirit's playing with itself, romanticism sees the

[39] *Ästhetik* ed. Bassenge, II, 572. Hegel is thinking primarily of Aristophanes, whom he regarded as the necessary end of classical tragedy. "Aristophanes introduces us to this absolute freedom of the spirit, fundamentally at peace, right from the outset, about everything to which man puts his hand; he shows us this world of subjective lightheartedness. A person who has not read Aristophanes can hardly be aware of how the human being can experience utter well-being" (571).

[40] F. Schlegel, "Vom ästhetischen Werthe der Griechischen Komödie", 17.

[41] "If he (the philosopher) succeeds, in the end, in grasping the Whole in its absolute unity in a single shaft of light which illuminates it like lightning and isolates it, so that every intelligent listener or reader is obliged to cry out, 'Indeed, so it is! *Now* I see it!' this is the representation of the posited Idea in its immediate visibility, or its representation by the wit [*Witz*], in this case the direct or positive wit" *Grundzüge des gegenwärtigen Zeitalters*, ed. von Medicus, vol. IV, 469.

[42] These are only a few of the most important references. A great many more are in Güttinger, "Die romantische Kömedie und das deutsche Lustspiel", 114–16.

[43] Preliminary note to *Diamant*, *Werke* (Hanser) I, 221. "It is quite evident that the pinnacles grow out of the whole building and that comedy, if it is to be truly such, must embrace all elements of the world just like genuine tragedy. For initially comedy wishes to be the equal of tragedy. But eventually, if comedy wants to surpass tragedy, it must do something further. What can it be? It attains a freer overall perspective, resulting in a greater indifference toward all individual factors. Whereas the tragic actor weeps to see them shatter, the comic

comic dimension in the boundless confusion occasioned by freedom (*Ponce de Leon*), in the destruction of the theatrical illusion, for example, as the "play within the play", whereby theatre overthrows itself (*Tieck*).[44]

Alternatively, comedy is seen in the destructive rage that expresses "pure joy";[45] in such a case the entire play becomes *transcendental bouffonnerie* (*F. Schlegel*). In the perspective of idealist philosophy, which suddenly shows itself to be close to the Buddhist view of the world, human finitude as such seems comic, ridiculous, grotesque. So it is, not only in *Schlegel* but

---

actor laughs as he himself shatters them" (remarks on *Der zerbrochene Krug* in *Werke* III, 640).

[44] *Schriften* V, 281. Naturally, this romantic use of the "play within the play" is only one of many possible instances. As early as the Renaissance, and very frequently in the baroque period, we see on the one hand the audience being drawn into the play and on the other hand the stage being turned into an audience for another play. The most important example is the play set as a trap within *Hamlet*, and the comic performance of the Pyramus tragedy within *A Midsummer Night's Dream*, which underlines the latter's dream quality. Tieck uses Shakespeare's technique in the service of romantic ideology; Pirandello, who read Tieck during his time in Bonn, uses it for the purposes of his new, ghostly comedy, which, however, can clearly be traced back to romanticism. On the various uses made of this technique cf. Max Dessoir, "Das Schauspiel im Schauspiel", in *Beiträge zur allgemeinen Kunstwissenschaft* (Stuttgart, 1929); Joachim Voigt, *Das Spiel im Spiel: Versuch einer Formbestimmung an Beispielen aus dem deutschen, englischen und spanischen Drama* (Diss. Göttingen, 1954); Erich Proebster, *Theater im Theater* (Diss. Munich, 1955); R. J. Nelson, *Play within Play. The Dramatist's Conception of His Art: From Shakespeare to Anouilh* (New Haven, 1958); Wolfgang Iser, "Das Spiel im Spiel. Formen dramatischer Illusion bei Shakespeare", in *Archiv* vol. 198 (Braunschweig, 1962): 209–26. Jörg Henning Kokott, *Das Theater auf dem Theater im Drama der Neuzeit: Eine Untersuchung über die Darstellung der theatralischen Aufführung durch das Theater auf dem Theater in ausgewählten Dramen von Shakespeare, Tieck, Pirandello, Genet, Ionesco und Beckett* (Diss. Cologne, 1968). Of course the direct addressing of the audience, of which Tieck makes liberal use, is a widespread way of destroying the theatrical illusion. Tieck, *Schriften* V, 281: "The development of the theatre also leads to the practice of making fun of the theatre."

[45] F. Schlegel, "Vom ästhetischen werthe der Griechischen Komödie", 18, on Greek comedy: "pure joy . . . , the highest degree of life's vitality, must have its effect, must destroy. And if it finds nothing outside itself, it turns inward to a beloved object, itself, its own work, and wounds in order to provoke." Cf. the end of Tieck's *Prinz Zerbino*.

also in *Jean Paul*[46] and *Hebbel*: "Individuals are comic as such."[47] The absolute standpoint reveals the finite in its worthlessness. We already saw that, in romanticism, man understood himself as a puppet: "The puppet theatre is the real comic theatre" (*Novalis*).[48] "Life has become a world of shadows and night, and only on the yonder shore dawns the eternal day of real existence" (*A. W. Schlegel*).[49] This not only renders comedy a solipsistic monologue, but also empties it of content.

The final result of the idealist and romantic standpoint is the dialectical identity of tragedy and comedy: both rest on the contradiction within the subject between finite and infinite. *Schelling* treats this explicitly:[50] comedy "arises simply through the inversion of tragedy".[51] His pupil, *Solger,* systematizes the idea,[52] and thus has an influence on *Hebbel*. *Hebbel* regards the humorous as the "feeling of complete contradiction in all things",[53] the "dichotomy that is aware of itself",[54] which takes up an earlier theme of *Tieck*: "the comic stage is based on the dichotomy, the twofold nature of the human spirit".[55] This identity of the comic and the tragic (identity through contradiction or mirroring) brings us to the very same point at which tragedy, made

[46] *Vorschule der Ästhetik*, sect. 29, "Humoristic totality". "Humor", which characteristically takes over from the comic in romanticism, "is the sublime turned on its head; it does not destroy the individual thing, but the finite thing, by contrasting it with the Idea. It knows neither individual folly nor fools, but only folly in general and a mad world" (*Vorschule der Ästhetik*, sect. 29, "Humoristic Totality" [1804]), I, 175.

[47] "Die moderne Komödie", *Werke* III, 123.

[48] *Schriften*, ed. Minor, III, 300.

[49] *Wiener Vorlesungen*, 3d ed. (1846), I, 16. Güttinger quotes similar views by Schleiermacher, Hegel and Schopenhauer: 178f., 180.

[50] Schelling, *Philosophie der Kunst*, 711.

[51] *Ibid.*, 693.

[52] Both tragedy and comedy arise from the eternal contradiction between the divine and its temporal manifestation in existence. If this transition is thought of as an act "in which either the appearance disappears entirely in the idea, or the idea is dissolved in the appearance", we have the "opposition between the tragic and the comic": *Vorlesungen über Ästhetik* (Leipzig, 1829), 92. Stefan Schütze, in his *Versuch einer Theorie des Komischen* (1817), shows how not only tragedy, but comedy too, arises from the "clash" of the individual and fate.

[53] Hebbel, *Briefe*, ed. Werner, I, 191.

[54] Hebbel, *Tagebücher*, no. 1566.

[55] Tieck, *Phantasus* II, *Schriften* V, 281.

absolute, had cancelled itself out. Now comedy does the same. This resulted simply from romanticism's inability to construct a stageable comedy on this theory. The few performable comedies, *Lessing's Minna* and *Kleist's Der zerbrochene Krug*, keep their distance from speculation and stand in the great tradition of genuinely interpersonal conflict. The theorists might look down on that tradition as a mere preliminary stage, yet they continued to yearn for it as for a lost homeland, that is, the spectacle, close to the people, the traditional Viennese farce. Naturally *Schelling* is aware that "the principle of the modern drama" is based on "the mixture of opposites, that is, preeminently the tragic and the comic";[56] but such a mixture is possible only provided that the tragic and the comic have not been previously identified with one another within the context of absolute spirit.

It would not have been necessary to give special attention to this subsidiary development in the history of comedy, had it not thrown light on the "theory and form" attributed to "the modern tragi-comedy".[57] We have already seen how many layers are to be found in the concept "tragedy",[58] and the same is true of comedy. Not every dramatic sequence in life, or on the stage, can be fitted into these two categories. Many plays touch on the tragic or comic, or both, during the course

[56] Schelling, *Philosophie der Kunst*, 718. Similarly Novalis: "Both comedy and tragedy gain a great deal if they are combined delicately and symbolically. Indeed, only then do they become really poetic. The serious side must have an airy quality, the humorous side must manifest a certain seriousness" (*Fragmente der letzten Jahre* no. 2860, in *Gesammelte Werke*, ed. Carl Seelig [Herrliberg-Zurich: Bühl, 1946), IV, 257. Novalis sees this requirement realized in the Christian religion: "It is tragic and yet infinitely tender, a genuine drama: a mixture of comedy and tragedy" (no. 2865, p. 259).

[57] Karl S. Guthke, *Die moderne Tragikomödie: Theorie und Gestalt* (Göttingen, 1968), with references. Also his *Geschichte und Poetik der deutschen Tragikomödie* (Göttingen, 1961). Hildegard Mahler, *Das Tragische in der Komödie* (Diss. Munich, 1949). On the history of the concept: Marvin T. Herricks, *Tragicomedy, Its Origin and Development in Italy, France and England* (Urbana, Ill., 1955).

[58] According to Aristotle (*Poetics*, chap. 13) tragedies may sometimes have a happy ending, as numerous examples of classical tragedy show, particularly in Aeschylus and Euripides (e.g., *Alcestis, Andromache*, the two *Iphigeneias, Helen, Ion*). In the sixteenth century Giraldi Cintio called his plays "tragedias di lieta fin", but also allowed them to be called "tragi-comedies".

of the action—indeed, this is usual—but have their center of gravity elsewhere. Theoreticians of the eighteenth-century *comédie larmoyante* referred to it as a third type. From the fifteenth to the seventeenth centuries the tragi-comedy or comi-tragedy (depending on whether it had a happy or an unhappy ending, according to *Jacob Masen*), a mixed form, was usual. It was based on a remark in *Plautus*,[59] historically justified by the mixed form of the medieval plays, and offered a wide variety of possibilities depending on which criteria were employed.[60] Those who advocated the strict classical distinction were unsettled by the gigantic example of *Shakespeare*, who deliberately alternated the comic and the tragic (*Voltaire*, *Wieland*).[61] There were isolated precursors, like *Dryden*,[62] but it was *Lessing*, most importantly, who at least on one occasion discussed the possible simultaneity of comic and tragic in the "nature of our emotions and faculties of the soul".[63] Here *Lessing* takes a first step toward the idealist-romantic subject, in whom the two aspects coincide.

[59] In the prologue to *Amphitryon*: "si voltis faciam ex tragoedia / comoedia ut sit omnibus iisdem versibus." "[F]aciam ut commixta sit: sit tragicomoedia" (vv. 54f., 63).

[60] Mainly four: (1) The difference of class, i.e., elevated or ordinary people; (2) the resultant difference of style; (3) the criterion of the "matter" (as defined by Martin Opitz, *Buch von der teutschen Poeterey* [1624], chap. V); and finally (4) the happy or unhappy ending.

[61] Yeats even remarked that "Shakespeare is always (!) a writer of tragi-comedy"; *Essays* (New York, 1924), 297.

[62] Whereas the classical theoreticians primarily based the distinction between the two genres on the idea that the corresponding emotions have a reciprocally weakening effect on each other, Dryden, in his *Essay on Dramatic Poetry* (1668), puts the contrary view into the mouth of his Neander: "Why should the soul be more lethargic than the senses? . . . *Contraria iuxta se posita magis elucescunt.*" Englishmen should be proud to have discovered a more agreeable way of writing for the stage, "which is tragi-comedy". Later, in 1695, Dryden rejected his earlier statements and returned to the view that the comic and the serious are mutually injurious to one another. Cf. Guthke, *Die moderne Tragikomödie*, 42f.

[63] "Only when one and the same event, as it proceeds, takes on all the nuances of our interest, and they do not merely follow one after another but each arises of necessity from the other; when gravity produces laughter and sadness produces joy so immediately that it seems impossible to abstract the one or the other: in such a case we do not look for them to be abstracted in art either, and art knows how to use this impossibility to advantage": Lessing, *Hamburgische Dramaturgie*, 70.

Only on this basis can tragi-comedy be conceivable at all as an identity of the tragic and the comic. As we have shown, *Schelling* can proclaim the mixture of heightened opposites as the principle of the new drama. *A. W. Schlegel* deems the tragi-comic to be the most faithful expression of modern man's mentality, and this will be repeated continually up to *Dürrenmatt* and *Ionesco*. In France, *Victor Hugo* advocated the idea in the preface to his *Cromwell* (1827): for him, Christianity, with its twofold view of man as body and soul, the senses and the spirit, is the true source of the *"féconde union du type grotesque au type sublime"*: as a body, man is comic; as a soul, tragic.[64] And since, from the standpoint of idealism, a total reversal is always possible, *E. T. A. Hoffmann* can say "that the greatest tragedy must be produced by a special kind of jesting",[65] and *Christian Morgenstern* can say subsequently that tragedy is "the highest form of comedy".[66] *Harold Pinter* says that "the greatest earnestness is funny; even tragedy is funny", which is based on the absurdity of all human action and conduct.[67] This sequence of quotations demonstrates the decline from the idealist absolute that treated comedy and tragedy indifferently; the loss of the metaphysical dimension puts a question mark over both tragedy and comedy and leads to the modern obliteration of the distinction between them.

Special mention needs to be made of *Sören Kierkegaard*, who used the romantic identification of tragedy and comedy in order to get beyond it. In order to understand his remarks in *Stages on Life's Way* (1845) and his further commentary in the *Concluding Unscientific Postscript* (1846), we must take it that the "humorist", Frater Taciturnus, is making an "experiment" with a "Quidam" who, roughly speaking, is in the same situation in life as Kierkegaard himself: it is a case of the passion of an "ethically religious" man for a girl of a similar nature, yet whose love is

---

[64] *Cromwell*, ed. Nelson, 21.

[65] *Prinzessin Bambilla*, chap. 4 in *Späte Werke* (Munich: Hanser, n.d.), 267.

[66] *Stufen* (Munich, 1918), 56.

[67] Quoted by Guthke, *Die moderne Tragikomödie*, 125f. On p. 73 he quotes J. Loewenberg to the effect that every tragedy is comic at its deepest level, and on p. 176 Thomas Hardy: "If you look beneath the surface of any farce you see the tragedy; and, on the contrary, if you blind yourself to the deeper issues of a tragedy you see the farce."

"aesthetic"; the relationship shows itself to be inherently impossible and is dissolved. The one conducting the experiment,
however, is at a "lower level than what he produces" and
"discovers and demonstrates the higher".[68] He can achieve the
romantic identity; in contrast to Quidam he can say of himself,
"Things are quite different in my case, for I sit, in the best of
spirits, at my calculations and observe both the comic and the
tragic at the same time."[69] But as for Quidam, "he himself is the
unity of the comic and the tragic; yet he is *more* than the unity,
for he comes *after* it."[70] Kierkegaard takes as his starting point the
everyday experience that, just as a man has two legs with which
to walk, seriousness and humor, so the tragic and the comic are
"necessary extremities of mobility for the man who wishes to
exist in the power of the spirit." "If a man is to walk properly he
must have the appropriate balance between the comic and the
tragic."[71] Now there are "many situations in which one does
not know whether to laugh or cry. This is the tragi-comic. . . .
In the comi-tragic both are present, and the spirit that has
dialectically been rendered infinite perceives both of them, at the
same time, in the same instance."[72] Then comes the significant
statement: "Paganism comes to a peak in that strength of spirit
whereby both the comic and the tragic are seen in the same
instance."[73] Similarly he sees "humor" as a *confinium*, a "last
boundary mark with regard to what pertains to the Christian
religion", situated outside the latter's gates.[74] Or else it is
"speculation" that wants to go beyond faith and so introduces
"a general confusion". To overstep this *confinium* is to leave the
romantic tragi-comic realm behind, even if *Kierkegaard* expresses
this step in the old categories: "The same man who, with his
reason, sees the comic, also suffers the tragic; out of the unity of
the comic and the tragic he chooses the tragic."[75] He selects the

---

[68] Kierkegaard, *Concluding Unscientific Postscript* I (1846); abbreviated hereafter, *Postscript* (Düsseldorf: Diederichs, 1957), 286.

[69] Kierkegaard, *Stages on Life's Way* (1958), 477.

[70] Kierkegaard, *Postscript* I, 287.

[71] Kierkegaard, *Stages on Life's Way*, 449.

[72] *Ibid.*, 447.

[73] *Ibid.*, 449.

[74] *Postscript* I, 287.

[75] *Ibid.*, 286.

Christian seriousness from the idealist unity of seriousness and humor; he will not allow "the comic, lightly armed, to pass by the ethical in its search for the carefree atmosphere of the metaphysical, for by revealing the contradiction it would serve only to provoke laughter".[76] He opts for the Christian distinction between the tragic and the comic and thereby leaves romantic indifference behind him.

Here too *Kierkegaard* remains the exception; he is bypassed by the "modern" trend, which endeavors to abolish the difference and make the "contradiction of existence" absolute with the result that the tragic and the comic coincide. Even the robber, Karl Moor, regards "life's colorful lotto" as "a play, brothers, that will draw tears from your eyes when it tickles your sides".[77] *Büchner's* comedy lifts itself to a realm devoid of air; from this vantage point all that is comic and tragic on earth seems to coincide. In *Grabbe's Hannibal*, Scipio the Elder says, "What is tragic is also amusing, and vice versa. I have often laughed at a tragedy and have been almost moved in comedies."[78] On several occasions *Thomas Mann* has suggested that "the achievement of the modern artistic spirit" consists in that "it no longer recognizes the categories of the tragic and the comic, that is, the theatrical forms and genres of tragedy and comedy, and regards life as a tragi-comedy".[79] As we have already seen, *Ionesco* speaks with ultimate clarity when he avers that he never understood the distinction between tragic and comic.[80] He also denies that the two elements can form a synthesis: by rejecting, criticizing and refuting each other, each illuminates the other and creates the dynamic balance, the tension of existence.[81] *Bertolt*

[76] Kierkegaard, *Stages on Life's Way*, 466.

[77] *Die Räuber*, act III, scene 2.

[78] *Werke*, III, 409. Cf. B. von Wiese, *Die deutsche Tragödie von Lessing bis Hebbel*, 457, 462. "The tragic turns into the grotesque and precisely in doing so attains ultimate horror" (496).

[79] Preface to the translation of J. Conrad's *The Secret Agent*, quoted by Guthke, *Die moderne Tragikomödie*, 102, cf. also 120. On Richard Dehmel's theory that the tragic dimension (which presupposes some yonder, absolute power) is disappearing and that tragi-comedy is a possible form for the future, cf. his *Tragik und Drama*, in *Gesammelte Werke* (Berlin, 1909), vol. 9.

[80] Ionesco, *Notes et contre-notes*, 61.

[81] *Ibid.*, cf. 176, 219. Existence is an "insoluble unknown", an "indescribable

Brecht finds tragi-comedy in *Shakespeare*,[82] in the simultaneity of the tragic and comic; he wonders, of course, whether it is not precisely the contradictions of existence that make the world transformable.[83] *Ionesco* denies this: the world is both unbearable *and* unchangeable.[84]

Here the tragi-comic arises from the nature of things; in *Hebbel's* oft-quoted introduction to his *Trauerspiel in Sizilien* it is governed by time and situation. "Tragi-comedy . . . arises wherever a tragic fate appears in a nontragic form: on the one hand, for instance, we have a man struggling and going to his ruin, and on the other, instead of the authorized ethical power, we have a morass of unwholesome conditions that strangles thousands of innocent victims. I am very much afraid that much that is going on at the present time, however important it may be, can only be presented dramatically in this form."[85] It is *Dürrenmatt*, with his previously quoted manifesto on the subject, rather than *Brecht*, who follows this line of thought to its conclusion. *Dürrenmatt* generalizes *Hebbel's* approach: "Tragedy presupposes guilt, necessity, the large scale, a horizon, responsibility. But there is no guilty person, no one responsible left in our muddled century, in this trash can of the white race. No one can do anything about it; no one wanted it to happen. . . . Everyone is dragged along and eventually gets impaled on some spike."[86] The modern world is shapeless, but "the task of art is to create shape, concrete form." *Dürrenmatt* is of the opinion that tragi-comedy,[87] since it is a "paradox of the senses", could

---

confusion", "plunged in contradiction. It may seem tragic, it may seem comic, or both at once; but I cannot distinguish the one from the other" (226). Cf. also E. Souriau, *Les deux cent mille situations dramatiques*, 51ff.

[82] Vol. XV, 310.

[83] Vol. XVI, 924, 940.

[84] "On ne peut trouver de solution à l'insoutenable et seul ce qui est insoutenable est profondément tragique, profondément comique, essentiellement théâtre" (Ionesco, *Notes et contre-notes*, 7).

[85] Hebbel, *Werke*, I, 388.

[86] Dürrenmatt, "Theaterprobleme" (lecture, 1954/55) in *Theater-Schriften und Reden*, 2d ed. (Zurich: Arche, 1969), 122. Cf. 90–131.

[87] He does not use the word directly: "Tragedy and comedy are formal concepts . . . invented by aesthetics; they can be describing one and the same thing" (*ibid.*)

become the form of something formless, the face of a faceless world. It could be the comedy that essentially creates distance and so gives rise to tragedy. But this tragic dimension should be genuine; it should show the alternative to despair: "It is still possible to portray a courageous human being."[88] So, after all, out of this "muddle", the individual emerges to take a personal, ethically responsible attitude toward it. To that extent "the comic" can be "recognized as the dangerous, revealing, demanding, moral dimension"[89]—which it was in *Ionesco's Rhinoceros*—and in this sense the tragi-comic would be a valid way of summoning to reflection people today, on their "insane journey" without a driver's licence. In doing this, however, it would have emancipated itself from its romantic origins and presuppositions.

By affirming the ethical (in *Dürrenmatt* and *Ionesco*, and in a different manner in *Brecht*)[90] but rejecting the metaphysical, tragi-comedy hovers between despising and accusing God[91] and accepting that the world has a hidden meaning. This creates an insecurity[92] that makes so much noise precisely because it

[88] *Ibid.*

[89] *Ibid.*, 128.

[90] "Brecht is ruthless in his thought because he ruthlessly avoids thinking about many things" (*ibid.*, 124).

[91] The God who allows this insane world must himself be either insane or sadistic; this theme, found in *Die Nachtwachen des Bonaventura*, survives to the present day in Wedekind, Strindberg, Salacrou, Pirandello. After the first performance of Jarry's *Ubu roi* (1896), Yeats was convinced that the image of the "savage God" would dominate the whole of future European literature (Guthke, *Die moderne Tragikömodie*, 105, 170).

[92] M. Dietrich is right to say, in *Das moderne Drama* (1963), 556–57: "The existential dilemma should not be equated with helplessness, nihilism and despair. For the dilemma only becomes a possibility if people perceive that life has value." Adopting a stance vis-à-vis the ungraspable, the absolute dissonance "creates a sense of present reality which, in the archaic myth and the cultic play, was ascribed to magical power. Strange and incomprehensible it may be, but the fashioned form, seen with one's very eyes, makes acceptance and orientation possible." To which situation, however, in "archaic myth", does this refer? There was a period of faith in the divine or fate, but this was followed by the tragedies of Euripides and the comedies of Aristophanes, which exist in a similar twilight and conduct the same kind of "double entry bookkeeping" (Otto Weinrich) as the moderns. Euripides accuses the gods (*The Trojan Women*) and raises doubts about the authority of their decrees (*Orestes*); on one occasion Aristophanes can accuse Socrates of dissolving the gods into clouds, and

wants to provoke an answer to the question of existence. However, the demanding and challenging attitude with regard to the
metaphysical (that is, God, if there be a God) is always an
expression of foolishness. In presupposing a God against whom
he can rebel, the *homme révolté* is a fool who does not know what
he is saying and doing. And if God is a mere taboo who does not
exist, he can only rage against himself, against his own being,
which, in its fundamental structures, is probably not transformable (as *Brecht* hopes) but identical with the being of man
and the world (*Ionesco*).

In speaking of the "courageous human being" who can still
be portrayed today, *Dürrenmatt*, like *Kierkegaard* with his option
in favor of ethico-religious seriousness, indicates the way out of
the cul-de-sac of the idealist dialectical theory of identity. We
can certainly admit that the classical division of drama into
tragedy and comedy is inadequate and has been largely over-
taken by historical developments. Nonetheless, the phenomenon
of the tragic and the comic (in *E. Staiger's* sense) is still found
undiminished in life and in its poetic representation, and hence
in drama. If we look more closely at a human life, we often find
that the two aspects lie very close together, and whether a
situation seems more comic or more tragic can be simply a
matter of lighting.[93] It may be true, furthermore, that the
political and historical preconditions of the traditional pure
comedy are disappearing,[94] and it is surely right to introduce the
concept of the "serious comedy". Let us conclude by referring

produce pious hymns by way of contrast, while at another time he can cause the
god Dionysus, in whose honor the comedy is being performed, to soil himself in
sheer fright. There is an analogy between that era and our own that cannot be
lightly dismissed.

[93] Cf. Helmut Arntzen, *Die ernste Komödie*, 11. He points out that the value
of a comedy does not depend on the funniest comic writing; in fact "the
momentary nature of all comic humor" is "opposed to the comedy as a dramatic
form". Hildegard Mahler, *Das Tragische in der Komödie*, 66ff., inclines to the
view that the tragic element is essential to high comedy. She argues "that the
basis of all comedy is a tragedy, and that the perverse, the contrary, which is part
of all comedy, is essentially something very tragic. Indeed, only comedy can
present the whole tragic dimension of life and the world, provided we look
behind the comic play" (74). That is why comedy should show us types, rather
than individuals.

[94] Mahler, *Das Tragische in der Komödie*, 19.

to what must be the most subtle and balanced comedy of this century, *Hofmannsthal's Der Schwierige*. Here we are presented with the final moment of a disappearing social class that no longer exists today (which may mean that this play can no longer properly be performed). In addition the apparently "shapeless" aspect is transferred to the hero himself, a man who, in his "difficult" manner, is yet decidedly courageous. He has seen through the surface issues of the social situation (compare his war experience) and, with his ethical instinct—as against the total lack of instinct of the "world-mastering" German baron —finds his way through all the confusions, supported by a spiritually congenial woman. This is a resurrection of *Molière's* comedy of character and *mores*, now sublimated and transferred to our situation of endangered social relationships. It is also the most natural and delightful blossoming of the old Viennese comedy tradition that comes via *Grillparzer, Raimund* and *Nestroy*.[95] This aspect of "courage" can no more be accused of moralism here than in the great comedies of the traditional stage.

It is not only in tragedy, but in comedy too that people act humanly, that is, responsibly, in all the vicissitudes of destiny. Otherwise the audience would not be interested. That is why this whole reflection on the nature of the tragic, the comic and the tragi-comic has been placed in this context, between two questions: on the one hand, How can the Good appear on stage if its ultimate criteria seem to be slipping away? And on the other hand, How can the stage become (as it must) a place where a verdict is reached, a place of judgment?

c. Right and Judgment

Drama means action, and human action is governed by a goal considered to be desirable, by what seems right to the agent in his situation. The concept of "right" implies that of "meaning", and if we pursue it "energetically, it leads on and on and will not

---

[95] Note how, in *Der Rosenkavalier, Cristinas Heimreise, Arabella* and *Silvia im Stern*, the element of seriousness, bordering on the tragic, is drawn into comedy, without our needing to speak of "tragi-comedy".

rest until it finds some ultimate meaning in existence". It "will not rest until everything is gathered up in the single idea, points toward it and becomes perfectly clear and transparent in its light". To that extent the poet (who after all is "God the Father to his characters") is like "the judge to whom a case is submitted for judgment" and who selects the material so that it "helps him to come to a just verdict". "Thus drama tends, of itself, toward the external form of the court process" (*E. Staiger*).[1] Most of the great dramatists have used this form at least once, often quite explicitly and often by allusion, for instance, the three Greek classical dramatists, *Aristophanes, Menander (Epitrepontes), Shakespeare, Corneille, Calderon, Goethe (Götz), Kleist, Gogol, Brecht (Lukullus, The Caucasian Chalk Circle)* and many others. What is crucial here, however, is not this external clarification but the fact that each play encourages the spectator to make a decision as to whether, in this particular course of events, the right thing has been done; or whether (which comes to the same thing, since attention is focused on it) it has *not* been done.

What we have just said goes beyond the question whether or not the theatre must necessarily have a political, or at least an ethical tendency and whether its scope is restricted (after the manner of the Enlightenment) if it is seen as a "moral" stage with primarily educative goals. We know that the theatre was "moralized" (as can be seen from the way the Aristotelian *eleos* and *phobos*—"terror" and "grief"—were reconstrued as "pity" and "fear") and that this had a feedback effect on the interpretation of the great Greek tragedies, eventually provoking a vehement protest against such misguided treatment.[2] *Aristotle*, it was said, had prescribed that the tragic hero must not be completely wise but fallible like ourselves ("or somewhat better, but no worse"); he must not be a villain, for then his punishment would elicit no *eleos* or *phobos*, but must get into misfortune as one "who did not deserve it" (*anaxios*); this should come about as a result of some *hamartia*—which should be translated, not as "guilt" or "sin", but as "mistake", a "faulty attitude",

---

[1] *Grundbegriffe der Poetik*, 3d ed. (1956), 175–77.

[2] Cf. primarily Kurt von Fritz, "Tragische Schuld und poetische Gerechtigkeit in der griechischen Tragödie", in *Studium Generale* 8 (1955): 194–239 (abbreviated hereafter, "Tragische Schuld und poetische Gerechtigkeit").

even a "great mistake" (*hamartia megale*).[3] In some of the greatest tragedies this error cannot be shown to be a subjective sin; thus in the cases of Oedipus or Antigone, for instance, but also with Orestes, who kills his mother on the express command of the god Apollo. Their situations or deeds are terrible, objectively speaking, but they themselves are not subjectively guilty, which is why the court pronounces Orestes innocent; yet he is not "forgiven like a Christian sinner".[4] "The goal of ancient tragedy is not merely *not* the so-called poetic justice: it actually excludes it. Thus it is profoundly different from other forms of the drama that emerged only later in the West."[5]

This overlooks one fact, namely, that the peoples of early civilizations do not make a clear distinction between objective and subjective guilt. This is clear in the Old Testament, up to the change that comes in Ezekiel 18: the fate of the individual can be sealed by some overall objective wrong due to the guilt of earlier generations or even simply through a "sullying" of the land (the miasma in *Oedipus* and *Antigone*; compare Dt 21:1ff.). Oedipus and his daughter Antigone are situated within the objective context of the guilt of the Labdakides dynasty, just as Orestes and Elektra are within an analogous context of guilt of the house of the Atrides. The background of all ancient tragedies is some *dike* that often goes beyond the human horizon. As in the trilogies of *Aeschylus* (the *Oresteia*, *Prometheus* and the *Danaids*), this *dike* only arises through the introduction of a mythical dichotomy; or, as in the trial in the *Eumenides*, through a profoundly significant event of institution whereby divine law comes to apply to earth as well. In the tragedies of *Sophocles* the emphasis is placed on the hidden and ineluctable quality of divine justice: essentially, man is the sufferer of this divine justice (*Elektra*, *Deianeira*), but he is often shown to have subjective guilt, *hubris*, as well, which must be expiated by some penalty imposed by the gods. Thus, in *Aias*, the hero puts an end to his disgrace by dying. Apart from this, in the case of both tragic dramatists, certain inalienable human rights apply, like the right of sanctuary and the right of burial, which also in-

---

[3] *Poetics* 1453a.

[4] Von Fritz, "Tragische Schuld und poetische Gerechtigkeit", 198b.

[5] *Ibid.*, 220b.

fluence the progress and goal of the action. In *Euripides* the overarching, objective norm of right conduct becomes questionable: gods can push human beings into a culpability in which they would perish, were it not for some chance intervention from above. This is clear in *Orestes*: whereas in *Aeschylus* he is acquitted by a just court of law, here, by contrast, he is condemned by the Argives,[6] not protected by Menelaos, and driven to desperate acts (taking hostage) from which the god saves him at the last moment. In *Herakles* and *Ion*, too, the question of what is genuinely just is posed with profound scepticism: in *Ion* it is accepted that the solution proposed by the god may involve deception. In the *Trojan Women*, *Euripides* is quite unequivocal: this is a case of blatant injustice. Tragedy questions the fundamental criteria of justice; the fact that the question is increasingly wide open does not mean that it is not being asked.

Comedy has an easier task. In *Aristophanes* it inclines in a socio-ethical direction. It does this so boldly that the poet openly boasts of his daring: "No wonder that the confederates . . . are full of longing to see the splendid poet who dared, with great danger to himself, to tell the Athenian people what is right and true."[7] He compares himself to Hercules, cleansing the Augean stables of the polis. In the débâcle of the Peloponnesian War he writes three comedies for peace: *The Acharnians*, in which a shrewd Attic peasant hits upon the idea of concluding a separate peace with Sparta—pouring scorn on the militarists; *Lysistrata*, which puts its lascivious content at the service of peace; and *Eirene*, in which people (on a gigantic flying dung beetle) search for peace in heaven, and, not finding it, eventually pull it up out of a deep, stone-filled hole with ropes and windlasses. Even more daring are the direct attacks on the ruling former tanner, Kleon, and his powerful assistants Demosthenes and Nikias in the *Knights*, against Kleon's pernicious new legal

[6] Orestes himself is highly uneasy about the divine command to murder (vv. 962–87).

[7] *The Acharnians*, 644–45. Cf. the verses in the *Frogs* which reveal a fundamental view on the part of Aristophanes, even if it is not totally consistently applied: "The poet should carefully veil the scandalous; he should not bring it out into the light of day, let alone on to the stage: for what the teacher is to boys, fashioning and guiding them, the poet is for grown adults" (1052–54).

methods and the general taste for denunciations and litigation (in the *Wasps* and at the beginning of the *Birds*). Social inequality and material distress are the theme of the *Ekklesiazousae* (which, however, takes the countermeasures to absurd extremes); *Pluto* is concerned with the unjust distribution of wealth; *Clouds*, with the education of the younger generation (here Socrates appears as a sophist, understandably enough for someone rigidly clinging to the tradition); and the end of the *Frogs*, with the common good. The poet also raises the question of the position of woman in these plays, and also in the *Thesmophoriazousae*. It is significant that, in the background, this dramatist who is often so wanton and frivolous is always dealing with the theme of justice (like *Molière* or even *Nestroy* later), a symbol of which is the frequent motif of the arbitration court. Thus in the *Knights* the court is to decide who is the more base, Kleon or the sausage dealer; in the *Wasps* the Athenian legal practice is itself brought to the bar of the poet (with the splendid parody of dogs' trial); and in the *Frogs* Dionysos, having descended into the underworld, personally becomes the judge who puts the verses of *Aeschylus* and *Euripides* on the scales: Which of the two poets does more to further the common good? In the *Clouds*, too, the sophist debate between the *logos dikaios* and the *logos adikos* is naturally a judgment scene.

It was necessary to spend some time with the ancient world in order to counter a twofold prejudice. On the one hand it was said that the moralization of drama was a postclassical innovation (stoicism,[8] *Seneca*, Christianity), and on the other that the question of the "right", of justice, was identical with the question of morality. While we cannot deny the ethical dimension in *Aristotle's Poetics*,[9] what he means by "noble" in tragedy goes beyond what is moral in the narrower sense and heads toward a more all-embracing (transcendental) concept of the right or the

[8] The theme of the "theatre of the world" emerges with stoicism. Together with this concept (of the role properly played) the question of the ethical arises naturally and explicitly.

[9] It is already present in the distinction between the "noble characters" of tragedy ("nobler people imitated the deeds of the great and noble") and the "ordinary" or "base" characters of comedy (chap. 4).

Good. It is true that, from the perspective of *Euripides'* question (and he had heard *Socrates*) the question of personal responsibility acquires an urgency in Platonic and stoic philosophy, and most of all in Christianity, that it had not exhibited in ancient tragedy. So the impression can arise that all postclassical tragedy is alienated from its origins by moralism. This view lacks the necessary nuances. Christianity too is acquainted with an all-embracing world situation that has something to do with the phenomenon of guilt and hence with the guilt of the individual: the individual is in solidarity with all other guilty men; his guilt and atonement cannot be neatly isolated from the common human destiny. The sole Judge of the world acknowledged by Christianity is One who expressed his solidarity with all sinners, though innocent himself, and who could proclaim his truth in no other way than by undergoing a criminal's death. In *Shakespeare* —particularly in *Hamlet*, who cannot cope with a world that is "out of joint" except by dying—and in *Racine* (where Jansenism brings the world's guilt to light), in *Calderon's* fate-providence complex, and even in as non-Christian a pure tragedy as *Kleist's Penthesilea*, we sense something akin to ancient tragedy.[10]

All the same, as we have said, in the Christian ambience personal responsibility comes into the foreground, and on the other hand ethical norms acquire such a clear profile from revelation that serious drama—not the kind of comedy that merely aims to entertain[11]—can dare to show real court scenes

[10] One really ought to make a special study of this. To what extent does the concept of justice and injustice penetrate here? Cf. the comedies of confused identity (Plautus, Shakespeare), farces such as *The Merry Wives of Windsor* or *The Taming of the Shrew*. To what extent (e.g., the Paris boulevard play) does a certain healthy moral instinct make itself felt in opposition to the alienated inherited tradition (albeit this morality may not always be easy to distinguish from immorality)? On the other hand, where man has become a pure dancer of the spirit, a puppet (Büchner's *Leonce und Lena*), we are outside the sphere of personal responsibility. There are analogies to responsibility and judgment, as for example in Schikaneder's and Mozart's *Magic Flute*: the "verdict" on Tamino is quite different from that on Papageno.

[11] Here we cannot deal in any more detail with the idealist theories of a split in the ethical substance, as in Hegel (and its antecedents in the dialectic of freedom and necessity in both tragedy and comedy in Schelling). Essentially these theories are based on Greek tragedy, although Hegel, in his "Der Geist des Christentums und sein Schicksal", in *Hegels theologische Jugendschriften*, ed. Nohl

on stage, pre- or postfigurations, as it were, of that "Last Judgment" that was the ultimate reality illuminating the Christian play in the middle ages.[12] It is hard to say how far the poets were aware that (as *Ibsen* observed) to pursue their craft is to hold a "day of judgment" on themselves. *Shakespeare*, the author of *Hamlet*, knew it, as did *Calderon*, who wrote *Life Is a Dream*. Others simply look straight ahead at a justice that must be reinstated at all costs. Thus in Christian drama there can be no tragedies of pure revenge, like *Kyd's Spanish Tragedy*, the whole of which is played before two invisible spectators: the ghost of the murdered Andreas, who thirsts for retribution, and the ghost of revenge, who assures him, from act to act, that he will soon be granted his desire. At every minute we hear the words "revenge", "nemesis" and "retribution". And although, in the prologue and at the end of the play, the world of the dead is painted in the ancient colors of the underworld, what is meant is

---

[1907], 241–342, wants the Old Testament alienation between the God who commands and man who obeys to be overcome in Jesus, who places love above "morality" and through whom destiny is reconciled (283). Following on from Jn 3:17, therefore, he says: "Judging is not an act of the divine. . . . To judge is to evaluate, to decide what is equal and what is not, to recognize what is a unity in the mind or an irreconcilable opposition. The Son of God does not judge, separate, divide, does not hold things apart and opposed; when the divine utters, when it stirs, it is not promulgating laws." We can speak of "saving" insofar as "the saved person is removed, not from his essential nature, but from his former condition" (310). While Hegel correctly describes the way the Old Covenant is transcended, the uniqueness of Jesus disappears in his dialectical process. Later this complex of biblical problems is projected back in time onto ancient tragedy: Kreon will represent the Jewish principle (of external law), Antigone the principle of love. (Both of them will also exhibit the opposition of man/state and woman/family.) Hegel's interpretation of Antigone has rightly been rejected: Kreon is a tyrant; he has "neither consulted the people nor made any attempt to acquire sacral authority; the senate is summoned to receive his commands; the representative of the priesthood, Tiresias, will appear in the name of the Polis to oppose the usurper" (Melchinger, 51). For Schelling too, Greek tragedy, at its most perfect, proclaims the highest ethical standard: I, vol. 5, 714.

[12] H. Jellinghaus, "Das Spiel vom Jüngsten Gericht", *Zeitschrift für dt. Philologie* 23 (1891): 426–36. Also *Le Jour du Jugement*, ed. E. Roy (Paris, 1902); K. Reuschel, *Die deutschen Weltgerichtspiele des Mittelalters und der Reformationszeit* (Leipzig, 1906). Other themes, such as that of the Antichrist or the Wise and Foolish Virgins, lead in their own particular ways to the play of the Last Judgment.

"the eternal tragedy" of the Christian hell. It is a usurpation of the "Last Judgment": in the final scene the ghost of Andreas says: "O sweet revenge, let me be judge and damn them to eternal pain." Judgment is made present in a different way if some authority appears on stage, accredited to represent and exercise divine justice. In *Aeschylus* it was Athene herself. In *Hamlet* it is the hero's father, languishing in purgatory, who calls for retribution less on his own account than in the name of the realm beyond. In the *Spanish Tragedy* the king is God's representative: by means of severe judgment in which mercy has no place, he can restore the world, which is out of joint, to its proper alignment. A few examples must suffice: in *Calderon's Las tres justicias en una* (*Three Retributions in One*) the king cannot bring himself to believe that a son has boxed his father's ears. In disguise he goes to the mother, Blanca, and learns that the alleged son is not her own but the child of her sister, Laura, and another man, Chief Judge Mendo, who did not marry the deflowered girl but left her in the lurch. According to the principle that secret guilt should be expiated secretly, the king himself strangles the son in prison before his kin can free him. Thus the son's trespass against his father, Mendo's faithlessness toward Laura and Blanca's deception of her husband are all expiated. The same principle is applied in *A secreto agravis secreta venganza* (*Hidden Vengeance for Hidden Offence*) and also in *Un castigo en tres venganzas* (*One Punishment in a Threefold Vengeance*), where a duke of Burgundy learns that among his four advisors there is a traitor who has banished three innocent people; later he realizes that it is the one remaining advisor who is the traitor; he kills him, and the latter, dying, confesses his threefold guilt, which is expiated by the one punishment. In *La niña de Gomez Arias*, the eponymous hero has thrice handed over his lover, Dorothea, to an inhuman monster each time he has become tired of her; Queen Isabel condemns him to death although Dorothea pleads for mercy on his behalf.

Here judgment is given by kings who are representatives of God. Something similar must be said of the duke in Shakespeare's *Measure for Measure*, which is a transparent allegory of God, initially observing the world incognito and then emerging visibly to judge it. The fact that in this case the majority are pardoned is something to which we shall have to return. In *Lope de Vega's* terrifying play *El castigo sin verganza* (*Punishment without Vengeance*), the duke of Ferrara punishes his young second wife and his son, between whom a relationship has developed, not in revenge but so that they can expiate their wrong by penance. He shows the unsuspecting duchess the document proving her adultery; she faints, he ties her to a chair and gags her to stifle her screams, then covers her with a sheet and summons his son to pierce the veiled traitor with his sword. Federico obeys after some hesitation, then lifts the sheet, recoils in horror and is struck down by the guards.[13] Going down the class ladder we come to an important play, *Calderon's Alcalde de Zamalea*, in which the poet masterfully completes an unfinished draft of *Lope's*. Here Crespo, the rich peasant, has just been nominated village judge when the Captain Alvaro de Ataide, who has been billeted with him, violates his daughter and refuses to marry her. First the father kneels before the guilty man and pleads like a man ("*como un hombre no más*") for the restoration of his daughter's honor. Then, when he gets nothing but mockery, he throws the captain in jail without any consideration for his high birth and the fact that he is subject to military justice. The general, who in vain demands the return of the captain, commands the village to be set on fire. The king, who happens to be passing by, adjudges Crespo to be in the right, but he requires the prisoner to be released. However, when the jail is opened, the captain is found strangled. Crespo defends himself thus: "The justice of the realm, while it has one body, has many hands." The king confirms him in his office for life.[14] This play has nothing to do with revolt of the lower classes against the higher; the borderline on which the plot stands is acceptable to Spaniards because they approve of the private restoration of injured honor, as we see in numerous plays, that we would find intolerable. Thus in *A Physician of His Honor* (a reworking of

[13] Summary in Karl Vossler, *Lope de Vega* (Munich: Beck, 1932), 257.

[14] In Lope de Vega's *The Burning Village*, a grandee misuses his power by chasing women. One girl escapes and summons the village to stand up to him. He is murdered. King Ferdinand and Queen Isabella instigate a search for the guilty person, but the name is always given to the judge as the name of the village: Fuente Ovejuna. The village is pardoned by their majesties.

Lope de Vega's play of the same name), *Calderon* has a husband kill his wife on the basis of a mere (unfounded) suspicion. Similarly, in *A Painter of His Own Shame*, a husband regards his wife as guilty on the basis of false evidence. *Lope de Vega, Tirso de Molina, Francisco de Rojas* and others treated the same theme. In this radical form it constitutes a Spanish specialty.

At the lowest level, as we already noted in the chapter on death, we find the hero judging himself. This is how countless tragedies end: a man can find no other way of reestablishing the balance of justice but through his own death. There is an unbroken chain of such plays from *Aias*, via *Othello* and *Antony and Cleopatra* to *Die Braut von Messina, Penthesilea, Sappho* and so forth. Occasionally a (Christian) path leads out of this self-sentencing, as in *Tolstoy's The Power of Darkness*, where Nikita, overwhelmed by the weight of his guilt, wants to hang himself, but the drunkard, Dimitritch, shows him that a man need not fear other human beings; he resolves to confess and gives himself up. Sentencing oneself is a desperate attempt to heal a violated world order on one's own. The robber, Karl Moor, knows that this attempt is foolish, he who "dreamed that he could beautify the world by means of atrocities and uphold laws through lawlessness. I called it vengeance and justice. . . . Have mercy, have mercy on the boy who wanted to usurp *thine* authority: vengeance is *thine* alone." He knows that a sacrifice is required, but he refuses to regard "a mortal sin" as "the antidote to mortal sins" and freely gives himself up to the law.

Can human judgment be anything more than a necessary evil? Can it be more than an indispensable symbol for the existence of a higher order of justice, an approximation that, for the sake of the public good, maintains a moral order without which no people can live? Surely it cannot claim to make any judgment about the innermost conscience of the guilty person, and, since every court is composed of culpable people, must not human judgment submit itself to an invisible, higher court? If drama is necessarily judgment, the dramatist himself must submit to it. "This ethos of self-accusation, self-rejection is the only thing that qualifies the author to criticize the world. Just as, here and now, he and all his characters stand before the judge, so too the world will one day stand before him. In its profound essence the stage is a tribunal. . . . Every drama leads on to the the the Day of Judgment."[15] It is hard for the playwright to live up to this requirement. Does *Bertolt Brecht* do this when, in his plays on the theme of justice, he adopts the standpoint of the absolute program without fear of being judged by it, for instance, in the *Badener Lehrstück vom Einverständnis* (1929), which calls for "cruelty" to be applied to those who are failures, in the *Massnahme* (1930), in the *Jasager*, in *Simone Machard*, in *Das Verhör des Lukullus* (1939; later *Die Verurteilung des Lukullus*), where the court finds the great general to be too easy and condemns him to the void? Only in *The Caucasian Chalk Circle* (1944–1945) does *Brecht* portray a weak, venal but ultimately humbled judge who is able intuitively to come up with the right judgment.

The theme of flawed, fallible judgment is a necessary corrective to our first theme (judgment as representing absolute justice). Two of the greatest comedies of the nineteenth century are *Kleist's Der zerbrochene Krug* (1811) and *Gogol's The Inspector General* (1836). In both cases the deception practised by the corrupt judge takes place in the face of a higher juridical authority: in *Kleist* it occurs in the presence of Justice Walter, who presides over the increasingly hopeless muddles and self-incriminations of Judge Adam; in *Gogol* it takes place in the presence of the real inspector general, as yet invisible (but known to the audience), who materializes on the stage in the final scene. A third play critical of judgment is *Ugo Betti's* masterly *Corruzione al Palazzo di Giustizia* (1949), which reveals the fallibility of justice in all problem situations. All judges are affected (they are looking for the "guilty" man, but none of them can say that they themselves are not guilty) and some people are affected more particularly. Cust, the guilty man, accuses the aged president, driving him and his daughter to their deaths, while the elder judge, Croz, dying, accuses himself of guilt—but in jest, for he does not believe in any justice; Cust, now elected as the new president, cannot bear the thought that

---

[15] Reinhold Schneider, "Zeit und Drama", in *Rechenschaft* (Einsiedeln, 1951), 24.

nothing is left of truth, of the difference between right and wrong, and accuses himself.[16]

Great tragedies witness the fragility of human justice. In *Shakespeare* a kind of hereditary curse clings to the English royal succession because of the fraudulent condemnation of Richard II. To say nothing of the baroque martyr dramas. What kind of judgment does Elizabeth give in *Schiller's Maria Stuart*? Or what of the verdict on Joan of Arc in many plays, right up to *Péguy, Shaw* and *Brecht*? At this point, however, we must raise a further, more weighty theme that leads right into the heart of theology: What of the amusing judgment scene in *Shakespeare's Merchant of Venice* when Portia, disguised as a judge, leads the Jew, Shylock, by the nose? Who is not moved by Portia's speech on that mercy that is more than justice, that is of the New Testament, which has crossed the threshold of the letter and the rigid law to which Shylock clings? Who is not uplifted by the music that sustains the entire play, whereas the Jew is "The man that hath no music in himself" (V, 1). One could go further: who can fail to see that *Shakespeare*, influenced by *Marlowe's Jew of Malta*, which portrayed the latter as a mere monster, attempts to bring out psychological nuances in the character? But does not this make the issue even more embarrassing? For now it is not merely a question of the taste of the period, but of justifying it. Shylock's harshness in demanding his "equal pound / Of your fair flesh, to be cut off and taken / In what part of your body pleaseth me" if he does not get back within three months the money he has lent to Antonio—this harshness he depicts as the result of the harshness of his Christian opponents.

> Shylock: Signior Antonio, many a time and oft,
>   In the Rialto, you have rated me
>   About my moneys and my usances:
>   Still I have borne it with a patient shrug;
>   For suffrance is the badge of all our tribe:
>   You call me misbeliever, cut-throat dog,
>   And spit upon my Jewish gaberdine,
>   And all for use of that which is mine own.

[16] Ferdinand Bruckner treats a different theme in *Die Verbrecher* (1928), namely, the powerlessness of human justice to deal with crime in the world. Five court proceedings take place simultaneously on the one stage.

> Well, then, it now appears you need my help:
> Go to, then; you come to me, and you say,
> *Shylock, we would have moneys:*—you say so;
> You, that did void your rheum upon my beard,
> And foot me as you spurn a stranger cur
> Over your threshold. . . .

Antonio: If thou wilt lend this money, lend it not
As to thy friends (for when did friendship take
A breed for barren metal of his friend?)
But lend it rather to thine enemy,
Who if he break, thou mayst with better face
Exact the penalty. . . .

Shylock: O father Abraham, what these Christians are,
Whose own hard dealings teaches them suspect
The thoughts of others! (I, 3).

And later: "If a Jew wrong a Christian; what is his humility? Revenge. If a Christian wrong a Jew, what should his sufference be by Christian example? Why, revenge. The villany you teach me I will execute . . ." (III, 1). And again, to Antonio: "Thou call'st me dog before thou hadst a cause: / But, since I am a dog, beware my fangs" (III, 3). What can one say of the moving speech, "The quality of mercy is not strained . . .", which is designed to soften Shylock, particularly as immediately afterward, when the Jew has been outwitted, Portia shows herself to be satanically cruel? When his goods are forfeit, he has to implore the doge's mercy for his life. Doge: "That thou shalt see the difference of our spirit, / I pardon thee thy life." Antonio also suggests "that for this favour, / He presently become a Christian" (IV, 1). The final act shows the lovers in bliss in Belmont.

This unbearable play is an extreme case of the problems involved in earthly justice. *Lessing's Nathan der Weise* attempted to set a few things to rights, but at a level that neither will nor can tackle the theological (and not merely historical) issue between the Old and New Testaments. All the same it is good that *Shakespeare* has so crudely portrayed the obscuring of right and wrong; it warns us against all simplifications, against transposing absolute justice into the relations between human beings. "Judge not, that ye be not judged."

Having said this, we are still commanded to recognize the tree by its fruit, to cultivate the discernment of spirits. The Christian message, which calls for forgiving love seventy times seven in a single day, is also acquainted with a limit; at this limit judgment must be left to God to carry it out. There is an irreducible residue that we may call "Judas". And in the classical "drama of justice" there is the axiom that a traitor or hired murderer cannot claim payment. The axiom is a kind of minimum, inadequate and symbolic, showing that absolute justice does shine through earthly justice.

In *Calderon*, Prince Sigismund expresses the principle: "The traitor's not required once the treason's done" (in the final scene, when a soldier who rescued him from prison during a rebellion looks for a reward). It is the same in the *Great Zenobia*, when she talks to Livius in act two, and once again in the final scene, when Livius and Irene, who, dressed up as peasants, intended to murder the Emperor Aurelian, are condemned by the new emperor: "Quickly put the heads of these two peasants on two poles." We find the same in *Marlowe* when, after the gruesome killing of King Edward II, the murderer, Lightborn, boasts of his deed, and is given his "reward"—he is stabbed to death (V, 5). In *Shakespeare* too, when the hired murderers of Richard II demand their payment from Bolingbroke, insisting that they acted on his command, they are given this answer:

> They love not poison that do poison need,
> Nor do I thee: though I did wish him dead,
> I hate the murderer, love him murdered.
> The guilt of conscience take thou for thy labour,
> But neither my good word nor princely favour:
> With Cain go wander through the shade of night,
> And never show thy head by day nor light (V, 6).

So too in *Corneille*: Perpenna, who has killed Sertorius, announces the achievement to Pompée: he has established peace and rid him of his wife's lover; but for his pains he is sent to his death as a "traitor" (*Sertorius*, V, 6-7). Caesar acts similarly when King Ptolomey offers him the head of Pompey; he is spared for Cleopatra's sake, but his fellow conspirators are killed and he drowns himself (*Pompée*, III, 2). Another, similar theme goes through the plays: men who have violated a girl are compelled by law to marry the girl and are then hanged or beheaded. So we read in the forty-seventh *novella* of *Masuccio*, which served as the original of *Lope de Vega's Judge of Zamalea*; in *Masuccio* the two guilty men are hanged, in *Lope* they are beheaded. So too in *Calderon's La niña de Gomez Arias*[17] and at the end of *Shakespeare's Measure for Measure*, where the king pardons all except Lucio, who mocked the king's majesty: it shall be proclaimed throughout all Vienna:

> If any woman's wrong'd by this lewd fellow,—
> As I have heard him swear himself there's one
> Whom he begot with child,—let her appear,
> And he shall marry her: the nuptial finish'd
> Let him be whipp'd and hang'd (V, 1).

Excursus: Shakespeare and Forgiveness

The "right" is the goal of human action. This "right" can be the justice that tries to balance accounts, but it can also go beyond this. In the world A.D., in what we have called the "postfiguration" of the gospel, the possibility of allowing mercy to take the place of justice (a universally human possibility, already found in the ancient world in the concept of "sanctuary") can become a major dramatic theme that also brings ancient motifs into the brighter light of Christianity. So it is in *Corneille's Cinna ou la Clémence d'Auguste* (1643), where Octavian pardons his counsellors who have been plotting against him.[1] We have already met a purely Christian portrayal in *Hebbel's Genoveva*; but we could also cite the end of *Schiller's Kabale und Liebe*, *Kleist's Prinz von Homburg* and many ideas in *Grillparzer*, who leads his heroes to mercy through the severity of judgment, and finally there is *Goethe's* refashioning of the Faust theme.[2] The motif of mercy keeps cropping up everywhere, even in Spanish drama with its preoccupation with justice that often verges on fanaticism; we find it in *Moreto's El valiente justiciero* (*The Severe Judge*), to quote only one example, where Doña Leonor pleads with the king (III, 1) in a speech that extols mercy as the brightest jewel of justice, all the more so because the king is "God's image" and "mercy lifts justice to heaven".

---

[17] Further historical examples in the introduction to this play in *Calderons ausgewählte Werke*, ed. W. von Würzbach, vol. 6: 198.

[1] There is a similar story in Pietro Metastasio's *La Clemenza di Tito* (performed in Vienna in 1734), which provided the theme for Mozart's opera.

[2] Cf. pp. 359–60 above.

But the real dramatist of forgiveness is and remains *Shakespeare*. The transition from equalizing justice to mercy is one of the innermost motive forces of his art. A single tragedy of vengeance, *Titus Andronicus*, remains within the sphere of justice; it is evidently deliberately constructed as such under the direct influence of *Kyd* and *Seneca*. As in *Kyd* we have a figure—in this case the evil Empress Tamora—who is the personification of "Revenge, sent from the infernal kingdom", and her two sons present themselves to the supposedly mad Titus as "Rapine and Murder" (V, 2). Titus, in desperation on account of the wrong he has suffered, had wanted to dig down into Pluto's realm and bring justice forth; now he turns to heaven:

> And, sith there is no justice in earth nor hell,
> We will solicit heaven, and move the gods
> To send down Justice for to wreak our wrongs (IV, 3).

But even in the reworking of *Kyd's Hamlet* (which, no doubt, was also constructed as a tragedy of revenge), *Shakespeare* takes quite a different course, as in *Coriolanus*.

If we wanted to divide *Shakespeare's* work into periods with regard to the theme of forgiveness (pardon, mercy, indulgence, grace), the following scheme would emerge. In the first period the emphasis is on the mercy and grace that comes from human beings; thus in *Two Gentlemen of Verona*, the royal plays and up to *"All's Well That Ends Well* and *Measure for Measure*. In the second period of the great tragedies the theme recedes, even though it is still there in *King Lear, Macbeth, Antony and Cleopatra, Timon of Athens* and particularly in *Coriolanus*; in fact, none of the tragedies are without some conciliatory prospect. In the final period, that of the so-called "romances", it completely dominates; here human forgiveness becomes so transparent, revealing the underlying quality of grace in of Being as such, that occasionally (in *Pericles*) thanksgiving takes over: there is nothing more to forgive. At the same time the poet is aware of the cost of forgiveness, which is a kind of miracle in our life; indeed, it *must* be a rarity if it is to have its full effect. This is expressed in *Measure for Measure*,[3] which has the Old Testament concept of justice in its title: death for death, love for love, hatred for hatred, like for like, measure for measure; but its whole thrust lies in the fact that it goes beyond this level. Everything depends on this costliness; it is this that imparts weight to the theme, rather than

[3] Escalus to Angelo: "Mercy is not itself that oft looks so; / Pardon is still the nurse of second woe" (II, 1).

the poet's frequent references to the transient, dreamlike, stage quality[4] of existence, which would seem to imply that justice is, as it were, not worthwhile.[5]

We begin with the histories. *Richard II* opens with the dispute between Bolingbroke and the duke of Norfolk, in which the king pleads for mutual reconciliation: "Forget, forgive; conclude, and be agreed" (I, 1), but then, when the pair show themselves irreconcilable, he seals his own fate by banishing them both. When Bolingbroke returns and topples him from his throne, obliging him to abdicate, Richard, soliloquizing upon his misery, has this word for the new king: "God pardon all oaths that are broke to me! / God keep all vows unbroke that swear to thee! . . . God save King Henry, unking'd Richard says, / And send him many years of sunshine days!" (IV, 1). However, the first great passage on forgiveness is found in a subsidiary plot: Aumerle wants to kill the new king, and the father, the duke of York, wants to move against the son, but the duchess begs the king for forgiveness; the word *pardon* occurs sixteen times in a few verses:

Duchess:	Say 'pardon' first, and afterwards 'stand up'.
	An if I were thy nurse, thy tongue to teach,
	'Pardon' should be the first word of thy speech.
	I never long'd to hear a word till now;
	Say 'pardon', king; let pity teach thee how:
	The word is short, but not so short as sweet;
	No word like 'pardon', for kings' mouths so meet.
York:	Speak it in French, king; say *pardonne-moi*.
Duchess:	Dost thou teach pardon pardon to destroy?
	Ah, my sour husband, my hard-hearted lord,
	That set'st the word itself against the word!
	Speak 'pardon' as 'tis current in our land; . . .
	Or in thy piteous heart plant thou thine ear;
	That hearing how our plaints and prayers do pierce,
	Pity may move thee 'pardon' to rehearse.

[4] In addition to Jaques' speech in *As You Like It* (II, 7), cf. *Titus Andronicus* (IV, 1); *All's Well That Ends Well* (Epilogue); *The Merchant of Venice* (I, 1); *Macbeth* (V, 5); *Julius Caesar* (III, 1); *Coriolanus* (IV, 4); *The Tempest* (IV, 1) etc. See on this whole issue A. Righter, *Shakespeare and the Idea of the Play*, 2d ed. (London, 1964).

[5] We can leave aside *The Comedy of Errors*, *The Merry Wives of Windsor*, *The Taming of the Shrew*, the fairy-tale plays (*A Midsummer Night's Dream*) and the satires (*Love's Labour's Lost*), which offer no scope for this theme.

Boling:	Good aunt, stand up.
Duchess:	I do not sue to stand;
	Pardon is all the suit I have in hand.
Boling:	I pardon him, as God shall pardon me.
Duchess:	O happy vantage of a kneeling knee!
	Yet I am sick for fear: speak it again;
	Twice saying 'pardon' doth not pardon twain,
	But makes one pardon strong.
Boling:	With all my heart
	I pardon him.
Duchess:	A god on earth thou art (V, 3).

Through a third party *Henry IV* offers the rebels Percy, Worcester and Douglas "pardon absolute for yourself" (part 1, IV, 3). Only when this has been rejected must he send to their deaths those who have survived the slaughter: "Ill-spirited Worcester! did we not send grace, / Pardon, and terms of love to all of you? / And wouldst thou turn our offers contrary?" (V, 5). His son, *Henry V*, finds it impossible to allow mercy to prevail in the case of the traitors Scroop, Cambridge and Grey; the poet motivates this carefully. The king wants to release a man who has scorned him. Scroop: "That's mercy, but too much security: / Let him be punish'd." King Henry: "O, let us yet be merciful." Cambridge: "So may your highness, and yet punish too." Grey says the same. Only at this point does the king confront the three with their treason. "The mercy that was quick in us but late / By your own counsel is suppress'd and kill'd." Each of the guilty men ask separately for "forgiveness". The king: "God quit you in his mercy! . . . Touching our person seek we no revenge"; it is the security of the realm that they were endeavoring to bring down that calls for their deaths, "The taste whereof God of his mercy give you / Patience to endure, and true repentance / Of all your dear offences!" (II, 2). When Harfleur, besieged, is captured, the king orders his uncle, Exeter, to "use mercy to them all" (III, 3); the army is instructed to compel nothing from the villages, not to abuse the French in disdainful language, "for when lenity and cruelty play for a kingdom the gentler gamester is the soonest winner" (III, 5). In the prayer before the battle the king asks God for forgiveness for his weakness ("Though all that I can do is nothing worth") and above all he prays for the removal of the curse laid on his family on account of Richard II (IV 1). After the battle he gives glory to God: "Take it, God, / For it is none but thine" (IV, 8).

The tragic *Henry VI* prays on his deathbed for God to pardon his archenemy, Cardinal Bedford: "Look with a gentle eye upon this

wretch! . . . He dies, and makes no sign. O God, forgive him!"
(part 2, III, 3). He offers forgiveness to the rebellious populace led by
Cade (part 2, IV, 8-9), and ultimately he is the "saint" whose gentle
mercy rendered him unfit to rule (part 3, II, 6). When at last he is
caught, mocked and finally stabbed to death by Gloucester, the future
Richard III, he dies with the words, "O God forgive my sins and
pardon thee!" (part 3, V, 6). *Richard III* only speaks hypocritically of
pardon (III, 7); he does not entertain pleas for forgiveness (I, 1). He is
cursed by all. But even here, after the battle has been won, Richmond
orders: "Proclaim a pardon to the soldiers fled" and declares the white
rose and the red to be united (V, 5).

The histories treat the theme of forgiveness realistically. It has its limits
where it touches on the *raison d'état*, but, in contrast with the latter, is
portrayed as the preeminent quality of kings. In the plays with which
we shall now deal, the agents are mostly not kings; the plots can be
more ideal, more fantastic; where the poet wants to play forgiveness as
his last card, he is little concerned about the psychological motivation
of the conversion and repentance that make it possible. So it is in the
Two Gentlemen of Verona, in which Proteus scandalously betrays his
friend, Valentine, and his betrothed, Julia, and then, out of the blue,
asks for forgiveness in a couple of verses: "My shame and guilt
confound me. / Forgive me, Valentine: if hearty sorrow / Be a sufficient
ransom for offence, I tender it here" (V, 4). Valentine is immediately
satisfied, and Julia's forgiveness is simply taken for granted. The duke,
too, pardons the erstwhile banished Valentine and even the outlaws
whose leader he was (including many of his nobles). These sudden
conversions occur frequently, thus, in *As You Like It*, the completely
unexpected change of the two villains Oliver (the brother of Orlando)
and Frederick (the usurper of his brother, the duke) once they approach
the paradisal, sinless region of the Ardennes forest (V, 4). In *All's Well
That Ends Well*, Bertram, having escaped from the hated Helena, who
was forced upon him and whom he had treated badly, undergoes an
equally rapid conversion. In the final scene he is brought to judgment:
one word suffices: "My high-repented blames, / Dear sovereign,
pardon to me." The king had already said, "I have forgiven and
forgotten all"; Helena's forgiveness is applied for just as briefly (V, 3).
The play feels like a trial piece for *Measure for Measure*, which ends with
not one guilty person facing judgment, but many. Helena is a first draft
for Isabella as for Mariana. We have already discussed *The Merchant of
Venice*: the Jew, Shylock, is represented as the one who will not forgive
(I, 3, v. 46; III, 3, v. 1; IV, 1, v. 6). Christians forgive one another (thus

Bassanio and Portia in the final scene). The question is whether they forgive the Jew; for he will not forgive, because no one forgives him.

Measure for Measure marks the high point of the problem of justice versus mercy. This is a Christian mystery play, no matter whether or not the poet intended it as such, no matter how many comic and tragic elements are mixed in with it. *Shakespeare* creates a highly realistic world and works toward a single final scene that occupies the whole of the fifth act: everyone is brought to judgment, and no one knows how it will end. The prospect of a happy issue is concealed from moment to moment, the scales of justice are handled gravely, and only then can the sentence be uttered: "I find an apt remission in myself" (V, 1) —compare "Pardon's the word to all" (*Cymbeline*, V, 5). The duke of Vienna goes off (in fact he disappears only to reappear in friar's disguise in order to get to know his people more closely) and entrusts the government to the upright Angelo: "Mortality and mercy in Vienna / Live in thy tongue and heart! . . . [E]nforce or qualify the laws / As to your soul seems good" (I, 1). Escalus, the privy counsellor, is appointed to assist Angelo. In his "stricture", Angelo closes down all the brothels. Claudio, who has got Julia (his betrothed, not yet his wife) with child, has to go to prison; he asks his sister, Isabella, in the convent, to intercede for him with Angelo. Like a true puritan, Angelo says that justice must come before everything else; if he were found guilty of the same misdeed, "Let mine own judgment pattern out my death, / And nothing come in partial" (II, 1). Isabella's intercession for her brother once more indicates the possibility of the judge becoming culpable: "If he had been as you, / And you as he, you would have slipp'd like him; / But he, like you, would not have been so stern." She even refers to the redemption of all by Christ:

> Why, all the souls that were were forfeit once;
> And He that might the vantage best have took
> Found out the remedy. How would you be
> If He, which is the top of judgment, should
> But judge you as you are? O, think on that;
> And mercy then will breathe within your lips (II, 2).

Angelo, however, quotes the "law". He shows mercy by being just. Isabella: "O it is excellent / To have a giant's strength; but it is tyrannous / To use it like a giant. . . . We cannot weigh our brother with ourself: / Great men may jest with saints." She appeals to humility and human solidarity. And in fact Angelo is "going to temptation"; dazzled by Isabella's beauty he compares himself to "carrion": "I . . . do . . . as the

carrion does, not as the flower, / Corrupt with virtuous season" (II, 2).
He begins to weary of the state and of his pride in his own "gravity"; he
would free Isabella's brother if she would give herself to him. She is
outraged: "Lawful mercy is / Nothing akin to foul redemption" (II, 4).
In the dungeon, where the duke, disguised as a friar, has prepared
Claudio for death, which solves all riddles, Isabella tells her brother that
she cannot ransom him from death through sin on her own part. The
duke has overheard this conversation and tells Claudio that Angelo
never intended to misuse his sister and that therefore he should prepare
to die. Claudio: "Let me ask my sister pardon" (III, 1), and "He
professes to have received no sinister measure from his judge, but most
willingly humbles himself to the determination of justice" (III, 2). Now
there follows another "bed-trick". At the duke's instigation, Mariana,
to whom Angelo was once betrothed, deserting her when her dowry
was forfeit, is substituted for Isabella. So the guilty Angelo is made to
do the same, by sleeping with his betrothed and thus concluding the
marriage, as Claudio did prematurely with Julia. However, Angelo
does not cancel the sentence the following day; thereupon the duke
orders the provost to execute another prisoner, who is constantly
drunk, instead of Claudio; but the former is "unmeet" for death, and so
in the end they cut the head off a notorious pirate who has just died. The
duke announces his return, and for the present Isabella has to believe
that her brother has been beheaded: "Forbear it, therefore; give your
cause to Heaven" (IV, 3). When the duke returns she throws herself at
his feet (V, 1) and pleads for justice. Angelo says that her mind has
become unhinged; "She hath been a suitor to me for her brother, / Cut
off by course of justice." Lucio, who had decried the duke in conversation with the man he thought was a friar, now tries to intervene on
Isabella's behalf, but he is abruptly rebuffed: "And when you have / A
business for yourself, pray Heaven you then / Be perfect." Now, in the
presence of the duke, he abuses the friar, "a very scurvy fellow". Next,
Mariana is unmasked; she assures everyone that "I had him in mine
arms, / With all the effect of love." Angelo wants to lift the veil from
"this strange abuse". The duke leaves and returns in friar's disguise;
Escalus accuses him of having prompted the women to slander Angelo,
and the "friar" also accuses the duke of injustice for having rejected the
appeal for redress; he also declares that he, the foreign friar, has observed much corruption of the law here in Vienna. Lucio reviles him
again, tears off his friar's hood and recognizes the duke, who now, "like
power divine", appears in majesty; the judgment begins. To Escalus he
says, "What you have spoke I pardon." To Angelo: "Hast thou or

word, or wit, or impudence / That yet can do thee office?" The guilty
man breaks down: "No longer session hold upon my shame, / But let
my trial be mine own confession: / Immediate sentence then, and
sequent death / Is all the grace I beg." He is sent off to marry Mariana.
To Isabella, who asks pardon for having importuned the duke, the latter
says, "You are pardon'd, Isabel"; she is once more comforted over her
brother's death. The married couple return. Now comes the judgment
on Angelo: "*An Angelo for Claudio* . . . and measure still for measure.*"
Mariana's pleading is in vain; she calls Isabella to assist her. Isabella:
"Look, If it please you, on this man condemn'd, / As if my brother
liv'd"; Angelo intended to sin, but did not carry it out. Claudio is
brought in "muffled" and is "unmuffled": since he is still alive, Angelo
can be forgiven. Three couples emerge: Claudio and Julia, Angelo and
Mariana, the duke and Isabella. We have already mentioned Lucio's
fate. The greatness of this play—which shows signs of hurried crafts-
manship, perhaps, in matters of detail—is that all the characters undergo
the whole seriousness of judgment; with a slight exaggeration we can
say that the judge himself experiences this seriousness, for it cannot be a
matter of indifference to him to let Isabella go on thinking for so long
that her brother is dead. Angelo must not entertain the least hope of
escape; he must thoroughly feel the pain of the misdeeds committed
against the others: "I am sorry that such sorrow I procure: / And so deep
sticks it in my penitent heart / That I crave death more willingly than
mercy; / Tis my deserving, and I do entreat it." Claudio too had to
undergo utter mortal fear in the dungeon: "Death is a fearful thing. . . .
Sweet sister, let me live." Everyone, the guilty and the innocent, must
go through judgment in solidarity—*Shakespeare* underlines the fact that
the guilty and the innocent are interchangeable—for only in this way
can they all receive mercy. *Measure for Measure* shows particularly
clearly how inadequate it is to classify the plays into tragedies and
comedies.

In the nature of things the great tragedies of the middle period (ca. 1596–
1608) yield considerably less. *Romeo and Juliet* ends with the reconciliation
of the hostile families over the dead bodies of their children and the
announcement of imminent judgment by the prince: "Some shall be
pardon'd and some punished." *Hamlet*, essentially a tragedy of revenge,
clearly shows its nature in the king's prayer scene. But even here the
emphasis is more on the mind of the culprit, and how it is possible for
him to pray while enjoying the fruits of his crime, than on what is

going on in Hamlet's mind—how he will have to kill the king when he is "about some act / That has no relish of salvation in't" (III, 3). All the same, Hamlet does not avenge himself but carries out a command that comes from the yonder world (like Orestes); and, what is more difficult, he is told to spare his mother. He pays for the difficulty of this task with his own life. The queen dies of the poison intended by the king for Hamlet; Laertes falls wounded by the poisoned rapier, also designed for Hamlet; now he, also wounded by the same weapon, can finally stab the king. But *Shakespeare* cannot leave it at that. Laertes: "Exchange forgiveness with me, noble Hamlet: / Mine and my father's death come not upon thee, / Nor thine on me!" (He dies). Hamlet: "Heaven make thee free of it! I follow thee." He hands the future over to Fortinbras.

Even the gruesome deeds in *King Lear*, in which criminal heartlessness drives the old king mad, are shot through, at the climax, with words of forgiveness. When the blinded Gloucester learns that his son, Edmund, has deceived him, he says: "O my follies! / Then Edgar was abus'd. / Kind gods, forgive me that, and prosper him!" And again, when he is supposedly brought to the Cliffs of Dover by Edgar, before throwing himself over, he says: "If Edgar live, O bless him!" (IV, 6). In the end, when Edgar and Edmund are fighting, the latter falls and says to him: "If thou'rt noble / I do forgive thee." Edgar: "Let's exchange charity." When Lear, now insane, sees Cordelia for the last time before she is taken away to prison and hanged, he says to her: "Come, let's away to prison: / We two will sing like birds i' the cage: / When thou dost ask me blessing I'll kneel down / And ask of thee forgiveness" (V, 3). And even earlier, when he is first reunited with Cordelia (whom he does not recognize): "You must bear with me: / Pray you now, forget and forgive: I am old and foolish" (IV, 7)—recalling the king's final words in *All's Well That Ends Well*.

Julius Caesar, in spite of its fine psychological nuances, is a play of fate and revenge: Caesar's ghost compels his murderers to die by their own swords at Philippi;[6] in the case of Cassius it is the same sword that killed Caesar, and with which Titinius kills himself. Brutus asks four of his men, one after another, to hold his sword so that he may fall on it. The theme of forgiveness only occurs before the murder, when the conspirators, kneeling, beg for the recall of the banished Cimber— "pardon, Caesar, Caesar, pardon!" (III, 1). Caesar arrogantly compares

[6] "O Julius Caesar, thou art mighty yet! / Thy spirit walks abroad, and turns our swords / In our own proper entrails" (V, 3).

himself to the Pole Star, the only immovable point in the universe, and his assassination follows immediately.[7] In *Shakespeare's* most well-constructed play, *Othello*, there is hardly any place for forgiveness in the breathless increase of tragic tension or in Iago's "theology of hell" (II, 3). Othello's jealousy is so blind by the fourth act that he can only forgive her in an unreal world: "What, not a whore? . . . I cry you mercy, then: / I took you for that cunning whore of Venice / That married with Othello" (IV, 2). In the strange bedroom scene Othello (in contrast to Hamlet) insists that his wife pray and repent of each sin she has committed: "I would not kill thy unprepared spirit: / No, —heaven forfend!—I would not kill thy soul" (V, 2), and yet he kills her as a "perjur'd woman". Dying, in the presence of Emilia, she takes her death upon herself: "O, who hath done this deed?" "Nobody; I myself. Farewell"—showing that she loves Othello and forgives him, although he interprets her last words as a confirmation that she is a fallen woman. When ultimately all is revealed and Cassio proves that he never gave the general any cause to be jealous, the latter answers: "I do believe it, and I ask your pardon." In *Macbeth*, when Lady Macbeth, sleepwalking, tries to wipe the blood from her hand, the doctor, watching her, observes: "infected minds / To their deaf pillows will discharge their secrets. / More needs she the divine than the physician. / God, God forgive us all!" (V, 1). In *Antony and Cleopatra* Antony, having cursed the "triple-turned whore" (IV, 10) and wished her dead, forgives his beloved and dies in her arms. It is characteristic of *Shakespeare* that he makes an exception, in *Timon of Athens*. Flavius, his former steward, is acquainted with the Christian commandment (and that at the time of Alcibiades!): "How rarely does it meet with this time's guise, / When man was wish'd to love his enemies! / Grant I may ever love, and rather woo / Those that would mischief me than those that do!" He calls Timon to come out of his cave; the latter initally refuses, but then moderates his hatred: "Had I a steward / So true, so just, and now so comfortable? / It almost turns my dangerous nature mild. . . . And thou redeem'st thyself: but all, save thee, / I fell with curses." After a further attack of suspicion he gives him a gift but sends him away (IV, 3). Finally there is *Coriolanus*, the tragedy of the great man on the borderline between magnanimity and pride. He is the battlefield of the conflict between his self-evaluation, which places him above the political arena, and his mother's wish for him to attain the consulate. He goes over to the enemy in order to take revenge on Rome, and rejects every compromise until in the end he succumbs to

[7] We should also mention the quarrel between Brutus and Cassius in IV, 3, which ends with them being reconciled.

his mother's urgent persuasion and agrees to a reconciliation between the warring cities (V, 3). This leads to his being the target of the Volscians' daggers, "by his own alms empoison'd, / And with his charity slain" (V, 6).

The late "romances" are closely interrelated. For the most part they begin with a puzzling blindness (*Cymbeline, The Winter's Tale*), a crying injustice (*The Tempest*) or an unnatural crime (*Pericles*), and in this they link up with *King Lear*, whose attitude in the first scene is psychologically incomprehensible and is only the presupposition for the ensuing horrors. The romances, however, rise above the tragic sphere; they look down from the highest level of a divine providence onto the earthly confusions and culs-de-sac, unravelling the tangles with fingers of grace. Sooner or later the evildoers repent; but what is significant is not that they ask for forgiveness but that they are given an overflowing abundance of the grace of forgiveness.

In *Cymbeline* four villains determine Imogen's fate: her devilish stepmother, who wants to force her to marry her son Cloten; the weak, moody king, who banishes Posthumus, secretly married to Imogen; her husband himself, who, in Rome, is persuaded by the scoundrel Iachimo that Imogen has been unfaithful and vows to take revenge on her. Imogen, supposedly dead, disappears from court and, dressed in man's clothes, comes across her brothers from Cymbeline's first marriage, who have been brought up in the forest by the outlawed general, Bellarius, in ignorance of their rank and in a Rousseauesque closeness to nature: they will save Cymbeline's decayed kingdom. There are many twists in the story: thus one of the sons has beheaded Cloten, but he was clad in Posthumus' clothes; Imogen thinks it *is* Posthumus and falls prostrate on the corpse. Posthumus, aware of his guilt, goes off to seek death in battle; the queen, dying, confesses her guilt. Then comes the recognition scene: Imogen is alive, has risen from the dead ("Most like I did, for I was dead" [V, 5]) and forgives her husband. The banished Bellarius makes himself known and is accepted as a "brother" by the king; his sons are given back to him. Iachimo repents and receives forgiveness from Posthumus: "The power that I have on you is to spare you; / The malice toward you to forgive you: live, / And deal with others better." Cymbeline: "Nobly doom'd! / We'll learn our freeness of a son-in-law; / Pardon's the word to all."

The Winter's Tale clarifies the composition that is still confused in *Cymbeline*. Once again the play begins with irredeemable, blind folly. Leontes, king of Sicily, is jealous of his friend, King Polyxenes of Bohemia, who is his guest. Polyxenes flees, and Hermione, Leontes' wife, is thrown into prison, where she gives birth to a daughter, Perdita, whom her father at first wants to consign to the flames and then commands to be exposed to the elements in "Bohemia: A desert country near the sea". An oracle pronounces Hermione's innocence, but says that the king will have no descendants until Perdita is found. The king regards the divine oracle as "mere falsehood", Hermione faints and is carried out for dead, to be looked after (as not even the audience knows) by the servant Paulina, and the young heir to the throne dies. The king experiences remorse, begs Apollo for forgiveness and desires to be reconciled with Polyxenes (III, 2). It is sixteen years later, and Perdita has been brought up by shepherds. Polyxenes' son Florizel loves her and the two escape from the old shepherd and go to Sicily. There Leontes has been living a "saintlike" life of penance; he is urged to "Do as the heavens have done, forget your evil; / With them, forgive yourself" (V, 1). These words reveal the innermost motive power of the later plays. Ought the king to remarry? Paulina persuades him to swear not to do so without her consent. The young couple from Bohemia appears before the king. Polyxenes wants to have the escaped son arrested, but then, at last, Perdita's origins come to light. "This news, which is called true, is so like an old tale that the verity of it is in strong suspicion." Yet it is substantiated. Paulina invites the king and the newly betrothed to her house, where she says she has a statue of Hermione. In the final scene the statue comes alive and steps off the pedestal. The king is gradually more and more overwhelmed by the statue's lifelikeness: "No settled senses of the world can match / The pleasure of that madness." Paulina: "[R]esolve you / For more amazement. . . . It is requir'd / You do awake your faith." Perdita kneels to receive her mother's blessing; the latter receives her daughter back. Leontes asks "both your pardons".

The Tempest goes further still. Prospero has been unjustly banished from his dukedom of Milan by his brother, Antonio, with the assistance of the king of Naples and his brother, Sebastian. The guilty parties are shipwrecked along with the faithful Gonzalo on Prospero's island, where the latter lives with his daughter Miranda, who will soon form a couple together with Ferdinand, the son of the king of Naples. The story is embedded in a field of force of cosmic enchantment: like Ariel, the air-spirit, the savage Caliban, son of a witch, is subject to Prospero, who, for the duration of the performance, represents a kind of symbolic, gracious providence vis-à-vis those who would like to be free from him (and who eventually become so). Without going into the action itself we can note that in hardly any other play of *Shakespeare* is there so much to be forgiven and so much pardon actually given.

Prospero forgives the three miscreants: Alonso, who treated Prospero and his daughter most cruelly, and his brother, Antonio, who, together with Sebastian, continued to plot the king's death while on the island (V, 1). Alonso is ready to give back the dukedom, "and do entreat / Thou pardon me my wrongs". Prospero, who cannot bring himself to call him brother, "forgives" him his "rankest fault". The entrance to the cell opens, revealing Ferdinand and Miranda playing chess; Ferdinand kneels before his father, and the latter knows "that I / Must ask my child forgiveness!" Then there is Caliban, who wanted to kill Prospero; the latter advises the coarse savage: "as you look / To have my pardon, trim it handsomely." Caliban: "Ay, that I will; and I'll be wise hereafter, / And seek for grace." He and Ariel are given back their freedom, and now Prospero quits the role of providence and becomes an ordinary man again. Thus (in the epilogue) he is dependent on his guests' kindness to bring him back to Milan. The enchantment has disappeared, but, lest despair gain the upper hand, its place must be taken by prayer, "Which pierces so, that it assaults / Mercy itself, and frees all faults. / As you from crimes would pardon'd be, / Let your indulgence set me free."

This return from an enchanted world order into the real world of human relations where "prayer" and "indulgence" are necessary also marks the turning from "self-alienation" (so common in *Shakespeare*) to human authenticity: all have found themselves: "and all of us ourselves / When no man was his own" (V, 1).[8]

Pericles, Prince of Tyre is an epic succession of entangled adventures, banishments, shipwrecks, loss and rediscovery. Again it is a play of the "kindness" of the gods (V, 3), which punishes the villains (Antiochus, Cleon and Dionyza), brings the lost daughter, Marina, unscathed even through brothels and reunites her with her father; Thaisa, who had been put in a chest and consigned to the stormy waves as dead, is now brought safely to land to become a priestess of Diana; and in the end all are united once more.

Shakespeare does not abandon the order of justice. The epilogue of *Pericles* shows, in an almost moralizing way, that the "music of the

---

[8] Cf. in *Twelfth Night*, the disguised Viola's, "I swear I am not that I play" (I, 5), "I am not what I am" (III, 1), and the clown's "Nothing that is so is so" (IV, 1). The duke to Claudio in *Measure for Measure*: "Thou art not thyself" (III, 1). Iago in *Othello*: "I am not what I am" (I, 1), "Men should be what they seem; / Or those that be not, would they might seem none!" (III, 3). Othello to Iago: "I think my wife be honest, and think she is not; / I think that thou art just, and think thou art not" (III, 3). In the *Comedy of Errors*, the alienation goes to the limit of the loss of identity.

spheres" (V, 1) cannot dispense with it. We have already seen that *Shakespeare*, like the Spanish dramatists, shows no mercy to hired murderers and traitors. The conclusion of *Othello* would be intolerable if the devilish scoundrel Iago, who is alone responsible for all the ills, were not handed over to the severe justice of the new governor of Cyprus, Cassio: "Cassio rules in Cyprus. For this slave, / If there be any cunning cruelty / That can torment him much and hold him long, / It shall be his." To say nothing of *Richard III*. *Shakespeare* can show us the gaping mouth of hell, and he has plenty of colors with which to paint things that are devilish. He is acquainted with the "burning lake" (*Henry VI*, part 2, I, 4), the "sulphurous pit" (*King Lear*, IV, 6); but, more importantly, he knows the dimensions of the realm of evil. For he has an infallible grasp of what constitutes right action. It can be "ethical", or can translate the ethical into a sphere where, behind the moral squalor, the good heart shines through. We see this in so many of his harlot, pimp and trickster characters. The action never lacks orientation. In accordance with the Christian principle of forgiving mercy, the dramatist causes the Good to predominate without feeling it necessary to reduce the totality of world events to some all-embracing formula. Just as, in his central plays, he takes up a position beyond tragedy and comedy, because the world he portrays is a mixture of both elements, so he also rises above justice and mercy by allowing both of them to persist, partly in each other and partly in opposition to each other. But all the time he is utterly certain that the highest good is to be found in forgiveness.

III. TRANSITION:
FROM ROLE TO MISSION

A. "WHO AM I?"

1. The Meaning of the Question

The theme of the "theatre of the world" seems to belong to the
past insofar as it conceives human life as a play that takes place
before the eyes of God, who allots the various tasks and judges
the play. Yet, some time ago a book was published with the
significant title *The Presentation of Self in Everyday Life* by *Erving
Goffman*.[1] The notion of "roles" is more prevalent in psychology
and sociology than ever before. And although this may be a
transitory vogue (perhaps already on the way out, since "role"
is beginning to give way to "function"), the reality behind the
particular image is always there, namely, that dualism—which
everyone experiences, whether fleetingly or constantly, superficially or profoundly—between what I represent and what I am
in reality, between the more or less fortuitous garb I have been
obliged to put on (or have willingly put on) in order to stay alive
and the body that lies beneath and that is not affected by the
change of clothes. This dualism can also retreat to the individual's internal self: one "has" a particular character that is
largely stamped by heredity, but one is not identical with it; *La
Senne* once compared the character with the piano on which the
"I" plays; the music thus played would be the person.[2] In other
words, the acting "I" cannot be, cannot become itself, except
through the medium in which it plays, its instrument, which,
again, cannot be isolated from the environment in which it
lives. This is the problem of every philosophy of the subject. In
his *L'Action*,[3] Blondel asks how the subject can be aligned with
itself: I must will myself, but it is impossible for me to reach
myself directly, for blocking the way is an unbridgeable abyss.
What is done or yearned for always contains less than the one
who performs this doing or yearning.[4] All the same there is no
other starting point but the concrete, the individual thing, for

---

[1] Erving Goffman, *Presentation of Self in Everyday Life* (New York, 1959).
[2] *"Traité du caractère"* (thèse 1930), 11.
[3] *L'Action* (1893), 338.
[4] *Ibid.*, 337.

this is "the echo of the complete world order in a unique being"; action, however, seems to be the mediating function that enables the particular to enter into a relationship with the general, it is "the substantial bond (*vinculum substantiale*) that creates the concrete unity of each particular being by guaranteeing its communion with everything else".[5] In the drama of "action", therefore, the individual would find himself by finding the whole. This leaves it an open question whether the identity of the "I" with itself has its vanishing point within or above the empirical world, whether it can be attained by the subject's own efforts or can only be received as a gift in the process of striving for it.[6] We can take *Blondel's* statement of the question to stand for every appropriate endeavor to discover the coincidence of the "I" with itself; it is a question that must be taken up by all the various anthropological sciences too, each in its own way. However, neither philosophy nor science can pursue the question any farther back; they must begin where, in "the great theatre of the world", naked souls—apparently identical with their essence —step forth to be given their roles and costumes.

This question, whether the naked souls are really identical, is the last to which we shall turn our attention in these prolegomena. It is the question of *who*, in reality, plays the dramatic play of existence. The answer to this question decides the meaning of the play, or whether it has one at all. We shall press the question so far that we shall reach the boundaries of theology; only from here can we get satisfying information about the actor, which will also provide theology with the preconditions for its own distinctive dramatic dimension. To that extent this concluding assessment belongs to the anteroom of the prolegomena but receives its content and its structure by anticipation of what is to come—which reveals, for the first time, the yawning gulf of its negative results.

The question that has to be asked is not "*What* kind of being is man?" but "Who am I?" The first question is asked of Oedipus by the Sphinx; there is something exciting about solving the riddle and, once it is solved, a lightheartedness supervenes.

---

[5] Henri Bouillard, *Blondel et le Christianisme* (Paris: Seuil, 1961), 24.

[6] P. Henrici, *Hegel und Blondel* (Pullach, 1958), 185.

Later, however, when Oedipus inquires about the guilty person who has spread infection to Thebes and all fingers point ever more implacably to him, so that he has to gouge out his eyes and is rejected and completely isolated, the time for lightness of heart is past. This is no "case of" something or other; there can be nothing in common with anything else (except the "Oedipus complex", perhaps, which he shares with others?). He is alone with his fate. And in this loneliness he must ask himself the question "Who am I?"—for himself, not for everyone. All must ask this question, but each person can only ask it as a solitary individual. "No one who does not wonder about himself can be considered to lead a human life."[7] The fact that someone else questions who he is does not help me to solve the problem of my own self. If someone were to say, "You are an instance of the human being"—and all science is bound to answer in this way—I would know that my question either had been misunderstood or was unanswerable. Science turns its back on me: *quia particularium non est scientia nec definitio*.[8] The "individual" (as meant and addressed by *Kierkegaard*, the individual such as he himself wants to be) has his inaccessible secret; he will never surrender it but will take it with him to the grave. Let two examples stand for many:

Jean Paul deliberately held fast this experience of the "I": "One morning, when I was a very young child, I was standing in the doorway of our house and looking to the left toward the wooden bridge, when suddenly, like a flash of lightning from heaven, I had an inner vision: *I am an I!*—which has stayed like a light within me ever since. For the first time, and for eternity, I saw my own 'I'."[9] An entry in his diary shows how persistent was this experience: "On February 18, 1818, I recounted in a dream how, in childhood, I first had the *awareness of the 'I'*, looking into myself while standing in the doorway of the

---

[7] Plato, *Apol.* 38a.

[8] Thomas Aquinas, *S. Th.* Ia q 44, a 3, obj. e. Cf. *In IMeteor* 1, 1 (Marietti, 391): "Manifestum est quod complementum scientiae requirit quod non sistatur in communibus [e.g., "man", "living being"], sed procedatur usque ad species; individua non cadunt sub consideratione artis [i.e., science], non enim eorum est intellectus, sed sensus." Cf. also *I Anal.* 42a–e, 44b.

[9] *Sämtliche Werke*, ed. Berend, p. II (1928–36), 4, 92.

house—but now it was mixed up with other issues that were troubling me; and I observed that the awareness must come all of a sudden."[10]

The same thing was also profoundly felt by *Dickens*:

> A wonderful fact to reflect upon, that every human creature is constituted to be that profound secret and mystery to every other. A solemn consideration, when I enter a great city by night, that every one of those darkly clustered houses encloses its own secret; that every room in every one of them encloses its own secret; that every beating heart in the hundreds and thousands of breasts there, is, in some of its imaginings, a secret to the heart nearest it! Something of the awfulness, even of Death itself, is referable to this. . . . My friend is dead, my neighbour is dead, my love, the darling of my soul, is dead; it is the inexorable consolidation and perpetuation of the secret that was always in that individuality, and which I shall carry in mine to my life's end. In any of the burial places of this city through which I pass, is there a sleeper more inscrutable than its busy inhabitants are, in their innermost personality, to me, or than I am to them?[11]

But the sum of all these mysteries will not reveal to us the secret of the human being. Fine things can be said about the way the mystery of the individual can be lit up in the loving encounter with the mystery of another person: but here too this mystery is affirmed as such, in its uniqueness; it is by no means removed. From the depth of his own uniqueness a person can give something unique to another, but that does not mean that he is thus rid of his uniqueness. It is an illusion to imagine that thinking and philosophizing in "personal" categories can answer the question "Who am I?" At most it can make us more pressingly aware of the question.

Every other question I put—whether it is answered or not— implies and presupposes this particular question; we can never get it within our sights, for it itself holds the rifle. The asking "I", which is always presupposed, is never something unquestioningly self-constituting; rather, it is latent in all other

[10] *Wahrheit aus Jean Pauls Leben*, ed. C. Otto and E. Forster (Breslau, 1828), II, 125. Quoted in Albert Beguin, *Traumwelt und Romantik* (Bern and Munich: Francke, 1972), 218f.

[11] Dickens, *A Tale of Two Cities* (1859), chap. 3.

questions of whatever kind; it is *what* (*who*) asks them. Suicide
—which is sometimes praised as the highest form of human
freedom[12]—shows that people can become so weary of this
eternal questioning that arises from the depths that they reverse
the rifle barrel and point it at the tormenting questioner. This
can be cowardice.[13] But it was simply that no solution could be
found either in immersing oneself in the role one had to play or
in withdrawing from it or by comparing oneself with other
people. On the contrary; if the questioner regards himself as an
individual of the human species, it cannot escape his notice that
every member of this species is bound to ask the same question
—on his own behalf—and that this is of no help to anyone else.
To the person who commits suicide, his lonely, questioning "I"
has become such a problem that there seems to be no point in
asking any further questions. The most aggravating aspect of
this situation (because it is the most inaccessible to our reasoning)
is the hiatus between the serial emergence of "I"s, of which I am
one—we hear this word everywhere; it seems to be the cheapest
and most interchangeable word—and the locked prison of my
own "I", which cannot for a moment be exchanged or left aside.

Of course, this imprisoned "I" can use its senses, can satisfy
its probing mind and its need for social contact, by relating, to
its heart's content, with everything it can reach in the world. In
this way it can enrich and "form" itself, round itself out to a
"personality", expand itself to a monad in which one aspect of
the universe is reflected. But in the day-to-day business of living
with fellow men in the world, the question "Who am I?" is
simply brushed aside. Perhaps rightly so? Is it perhaps more
important to play our part in the web of relationships, to join in
the common task toward realizable goals, than to concern
ourselves with the question that cannot be answered? All the
same, the strange fact is that, once I am forbidden to enquire
about the unanswerable, I lose interest in the answer that allegedly
lies in realizable and attainable projects. It merely floats like a
raft of meaning upon an ocean of meaninglessness. If everyone

[12] "But life, being weary of these worldly bars, / Never lacks power to
dismiss itself" (Cassius in Shakespeare's *Julius Caesar* 1, 3).

[13] "But I do find it cowardly and vile, / For fear of what might fall, so to
prevent / The time of life" (Brutus, in *Julius Caesar*, V, 1).

gives up listening to the question that persists in pressing itself
on their attention, how can they join together in looking for an
answer that explicitly ignores the individual's question? For
everyone who hears that question within himself knows with
certainty that everyone else is destined to hear it too.[14]

The question becomes all the more excruciating in that the
individual is obliged to attribute his existence to the most
fortuitous event in the world: the sexual act between two
individuals he calls his "parents". He owes himself to a chance
occurrence. Thus his existence seems to know no other necessity
but the biological. Like all other individuals, he has risen,
ephemerally, out of this "ground" and knows for certain that he
will shortly return into it—What else? But how strange it is that
he has the ability to enquire about this origin—for no animal, to
be sure, has this ability—and thus he can reflect, he is a spirit, he
can gain a certain distance from the immediacy of his own being
and in this way can actually perceive the question it poses. Not
only does his own, fortuitous, individual being come under
question; the biological origin and "ground" from which he
comes is also questioned; he questions this "ground" about his
own ground. The questioning gaze of the individual who does
not know who he is opens up the whole realm of existence in the
world; it too, like him, constitutes a question to be answered. It
is interwoven with many causal relationships, like the veins of a
body, but a puzzling nonnecessity breaks out from all its individual members and, ultimately, from its totality. It is either
lethargy or self-violation on reason's part when it accepts this
nonnecessity in all its manifestations and treats it as some
unconditioned totality beyond the scope of questioning.

So the question "Who am I?" acquires a dimension stretching
from the inner-worldly up to a more-than-worldly, a "divine"
area. Thus, with *Berdyaev*, we can call the question of a man a
theandric one,[15] as *Soloviev*[16] and *Franz Baader*[17] had already

[14] Cf. the "fourfold difference" discussed at the end of *Herrlichkeit* III, 1;
English edition: *The Glory of the Lord*, vol. 4.
[15] *Versuch einer personalitischen Philosophie* (Darmstadt and Geneva, 1954),
57ff.; cf. *Existentielle Dialektik* (Munich, 1951), 107, 122.
[16] *Vorlesungen über das Gottmenschentum* (Stuttgart, 1921).
[17] Franz von Baader, *Werke*, ed. Carl Selig (Zurich), 12:542; 11:78–80.

done, simply confirming that dimension which *Plato* (and, following him, the Church Fathers) had attributed to the questioning human mind: as a result of that distance from the world, which the question makes possible, man touches on the area of the *theion*, however much he may be governed by worldly principles in other respects. We recall *Plato's* attempt, in defining the individual's role in the theatre of the world, to answer the question "Who am I?" through a combination of elements of personal freedom on the one hand and of destiny on the other. But since this solution was linked with the problem of the transmigration of souls, the answer ultimately got lost in inaccessible origins. And as for *Socrates'* urgent call to submit oneself, no less than others, to scrutiny,[18] in the end it only attains insight into one's own ignorance. It is precisely on account of this ignorance that *Socrates* was pronounced to be the wisest man by the Delphic Oracle; evidently in fulfillment of the original meaning of the inscription on the portico of the Temple in Delphi: *Gnothi Sauton*: Know thyself.

2. The Ambivalence of the "Gnothi Sauton"

In its original meaning, the Delphic Oracle contains an admonition to man to consider God and be aware of his human limitation.[1] This is how the poetic and philosophical literature of Greece, right up to and including the stoics, interpreted the inscription. From the wealth of possible examples, a few must suffice. In the second Pythian Ode of *Pindar*, man is instructed always to recognize his appropriate measure (verse 34). In the *Prometheus* of *Aeschylus*, Okeanos admonishes Titan: "Know thyself, change thyself, adopt new manners. . . . Chafe not thy body against the spur" (309ff.). *Xenophon* (*Hellenica* II, IV, 41)

---

[18] *Apol.* 28e.

[1] See especially the two books by Eliza Gregory Wilkins, *Know Thyself in Greek and Latin Literature* (Diss. Chicago, 1917) and *The Delphic Maxims in Literature* (Univ. Chicago Press, 1929). For the history of the idea cf. the essays by Pierre Courcelle on "Nosce teipsum", in *Annuaire du College de France* 61 (1961): 337–40; 62 (1962): 375–79; 63 (1963): 373–76; 64 (1964): 391f.; 65 (1965): 429. More references in Alois Haas, "Zur Frage der Selbsterkenntnis bei Meister Eckhart", in *Freiburger Zeitschrift für Philosophie und Theologie* 15 (1968): 190–261.

makes Thrasybulos address the Athenians in these terms: "I advise you, men of the city, to know yourselves; and you would do this best by considering what reason you have to think yourselves superior to us." In *Plato's Philebos* (48cff.), Socrates elucidates those attitudes of men that are opposed to the Delphic Oracle, their total lack of knowledge of themselves, the way they overvalue themselves as regards external goods or physical advantages or virtue.[2] The issue in the *Phaidros* (229eff.) is that of recognizing the limits of one's wisdom; it is ignorance to believe mistakenly that one is wise. In *Epictetus* and *Plutarch* man should know what is within his power and not strain after things for which, by nature, he is not equipped.[3] For *Seneca* the beginning of self-knowledge is insight into one's own errors;[4] the Latin poets often cite *Aesop's* fable in which Zeus hangs two sacks around us: one in front containing the errors of others, and one behind containing our own. A lively awareness of one's own mortality is important in self-knowledge (*Pindar, Pyth.* III, 59f., *Sophocles*,[5] *Euripides*),[6] and *Seneca* very explicitly identifies the *Gnothi Sauton* with it in the consolatory address to Marcia on the death of her son: "Know thyself—this is the advice of the Pythian Oracle. What is man? Only a fragile vessel, thrown from here to there . . . : a feeble body, fragile, naked, by nature defenseless, dependent on help from outside, exposed to all the outrages of fate" (11). In *Lucian's* "conversations with the dead", King Philip receives his son with the words: "This time you cannot deny that you are my son; you would not have died if you had been the son of Ammon. . . . Will you not learn to put away this arrogant talk, to know yourself and see at last that you are mortal?"—instead of comparing himself with Hercules and Dionysos. In *Philo*, when Moses expresses the wish to see God, the latter replies with the Delphic Oracle (*De Spec. Leg.* I, 44). In *Juvenal* (XI, 23ff.) it is regarded as having fallen from heaven in order to teach men discretion. But this is precisely what all these

[2] Cf. also Socrates' rebuke to Alcibiades for not following the Delphic Oracle: *Alc.* I, 124ab.

[3] Plutarch, *De tranquill. an.* 12–13; *de EI ap. Delph.* 21.

[4] *Ep. mor.* III, 7, 10.

[5] *Fragm.* 481 Nauck.

[6] *Alcestis* 780f.

(and numerous other) passages have in common: the admonition has come down from heaven, from God, from the Oracle. It is the Absolute that shows man his proper place, his finitude and mortality. In reaching his own truth, he also arrives at a right relationship with God. Pompey, sacrificing to the gods in Athens, happens to read "certain inscriptions. Thus, on the inner side of the door, there was this one: 'Insofar as thou knowest thyself to be a man, thou art a god'."[7]

Here the saying contains a new note; it seems to be establishing an equilibrium between the movement from God to man and that from man to God. In fact, influenced by *Plato*, an admonition is heard in the stoics and Neoplatonists to the effect that man should arise up out of his forgetfulness and the detritus that clogs his spirit and recall his nobility, his relationship with the gods. In *Phaidros*, self-knowledge is knowledge of the spiritual; in *Alcibiades*[8] this is radicalized: the true man is identified with the soul. Later, *Proclus*, in his commentary on this Platonic dialogue, gives the latter pride of place. In this sense the *Gnothi Sauton*, according to *Julian*,[9] is declared by the stoics to be the "first principle of their philosophy", in which, however, the "God-in-us" is Reason (*nous*).[10] So it is with *Epictetus* and, in considerable detail, in *Cicero*.[11] In *Plotinus*, self-knowledge becomes insight into the structure of the soul;[12] the fundamental philsophical act of "turning around" (*epistrophē*) is identified with the *Gnothi Sauton*. For the Neoplatonists, to know oneself means to look back to one's own origin, whence the soul has "descended". It is well known what a longlasting effect this second aspect of the axiom had on the early and middle periods of Christian thought;[13] but we cannot follow this path any

[7] Plutarch, *Pomp.* 27. Juvenal's dictum is often quoted by Christian theologians in the twelfth century.

[8] *Alc.* I, 129a.

[9] *Sixth Discourse* 185D. In Philostratus' life of Apollonius of Thyana, the *Gnothi Sauton* is practiced by the Brahmans, who thus learn of their divine origin. The connection with India is highly significant.

[10] *Ibid.*, 196D.

[11] *De legibus* I, 58–62.

[12] *Enn.* V, 3, 4; VI, 8, 41.

[13] There is a wealth of references in Courcelle, "Nosce teipsum", from Clement of Alexandria and Origen to the Cappadocians, from Minucius Felix

farther here, for with the gospel a fundamentally new element comes into play.

It would be extremely tempting to pursue these two lines of thought farther into philosophical speculation; we should see that they do not become estranged from each other but remain in relation, just as epistemology learns to see more and more clearly that the outward thrust toward things is simultaneous with thought's "return" (re-flection) to itself. Indeed, in this "return", thought must also become an object to itself, so that it can embrace both the known matter and itself as knowing and hence also become aware of its own limits vis-à-vis the knowable. Thus *Plato*, in his *Charmides*, equates the self-knowledge of the Delphic Oracle with the summons to *sophrosunē* (moderation, discretion); the latter is (tentatively) defined as that *one* knowledge "which is knowledge of no other object but itself, and of the other items of knowledge and also of its own ignorance".[14] This path could be followed via *Aristotle* up to *Augustine*[15] and thence to *Thomas*.[16] However, it would contribute nothing to the question "Who am I?" since it is only concerned with the general basic structures of knowledge.

It is also possible to trace the interconnection of the two lines of thought in the metaphysico-religious field. This would show that the two concluding thought forms in the ancient world—stoicism and Neoplatonism—are each acquainted with both lines and use them to promote proper ethical and religious

---

via Arnobius and Ambrose to Augustine, where the "noverim me, noverim Te" becomes the epitome of prayer and entering into oneself becomes the way to God. On this subject: F. M. Sladeczek, "Die Selbsterkenntnis als Grundlage der Philosophie nach dem hl. Augustinus" in *Scholastik* 5 (1930): 329–56; Gerard Verbeke, "Connaissance de soi et connaissance de Dieu chez S. Augustin" in *Augustiniana* IV (1954): 495–515. This approach (through knowledge of one's own soul to knowledge of God) is close to Plotinus, although each attributes a very different significance to alienation from God; "mecum eras et tecum non eram" (*Conf.* X, 27, 38).

[14] *Charmides* 167bc.

[15] *De Trin.* XV, c, 12. Cf. also Max Zepf, "Augustinus und das philosophische Selbstbewusstsein der Antike", in *Zft. f. Religions und Geistesgeschichte* 11 (1959): 105–32.

[16] "In the same act I understand both what I understand and also that I understand" (*I Sent* d 1, q 2, a 2 ad 2).

conduct, though with reversed charges: the stoics stress the individual person's emanation out of the totality (in the theatrical categories we have worked out), that is, the rational performance of the limited role allotted to *me*. The Neoplatonists, on the other hand, put the emphasis on reflection upon the One; here the external role-play—as we saw from the way *Plotinus* uses the metaphor of the theatre—sinks to the level of an almost insubstantial play of shadows. But the difference is only one of nuance; for in *Epictetus* and *Marcus Aurelius*, likewise, the precondition for playing a good life is to keep an inner distance from what is being played and to keep in touch with universal Reason. In their inner relatedness, these two ancient modes of grounding the "I" in its own uniqueness form a single foil to the Christian view, which we start to discern here, albeit in fragmentary beginnings that cannot ultimately be carried through.

Nonetheless it seems to be meaningful, in what follows, to take the stoic and Platonic approach (together with its modern counterparts), in its internal mutual opposition, as a guide for our investigation. It must remain to be seen how far it can bring us toward a solution of our question. But as an initial approach it is indispensable.

B. ROLE AS THE ACCEPTANCE
OF LIMITATION

1. *Man as an Emanation of the Whole*

In attempting to grasp the "I", we begin with the ancient stoics and particularly with *Epictetus*, since he comes closest to the Christian solution.[1] We have already met him and other stoics in our discussion of the playing of roles in the theatre of the world; many and multicolored are his references to the topic: they reflect the stoic tradition.[2] Stoicism presented an opportunity, otherwise unknown in the ancient world, of coming to grips with the uniqueness and irreplaceability of the "I", and this for three reasons: in the first place because of its empiricist epistemology, which knows no *universalia in rebus* but only a world revealed by sense data, containing unique individual things (*idiōs poia*)—which Reason, of course, can subsequently arrange in particular categories. Furthermore, these individual things were held to be emanations of the world's Divine Being (in *Poseidonios*, where this cosmology is worked out on the grandest scale, they are members of the world's life), a finite substance[3] which, at the end of an aeon, will reabsorb in the cosmic fire all that it has brought forth. Finally, man is given a certain participation in the world's divine reason so that he can not only contemplate the divine providence as a whole but also recognize his own, particular emanation from the Divinity. Naturally, the stoics are just as concerned as the Platonists and Aristotelians with the "essence" of man, which is generally characterized by this participation in the Logos and hence by his freedom, which makes him superior to the world; yet stoicism

---

[1] Cf. A. Bonhöffer, *Epiktet und das Neue Testament* (Giessen, 1911; reprinted 1964); M.-J. Lagrange, "La philosophie religieuse d'Ecpitète et le Christianisme", in *Revue Biblique*, new series IX (1912): 5–21; 192–212; M. Spanneut's article on Epictetus in *RAC* (1962).

[2] Thus Ariston of Chios had compared the "Wise Man" to a good actor who could play equally well the role of Thersites and that of Agamemnon (*Diog. Laert.* VII, 160).

[3] This view existed as early as Zenon and as late as Poseidonios.

evinces a special interest in the uniqueness of individuals. Thus it is characteristic that *Epictetus*[4] felt himself personally addressed when a pupil of *Musonius Rufus*: "He spoke in such a way that every one of us who sat before him had the feeling that his faults had been laid bare; so much did he speak to our condition, so clearly did he indicate our faults to each of us."[5] And: "That I and you are not the same—this I know with the utmost certainty."[6] Thus the *Gnothi Sauton*, the call to self-knowledge,[7] also acquires a special hue. *Panaitios* distinguishes four "masks" or "persons" (*prosōpa*) that need to be integrated in the finding and developing of a self.[8] First there is human nature in general, the source of ethical worth for each individual. Secondly there is the particular nature that is allotted to him by his personal physical constitution, which everyone may legitimately develop, provided that, in doing so, he keeps within the limits of human nature as a whole—he should never attempt to imitate anyone else's nature, forgetting his own, but rather should make sure that everything harmonizes with his own distinctive quality. The third "persona" is whatever we have acquired through chance and external circumstances. And the fourth—and this is the most important—is what we make of ourselves by our own decisions: "It is our own will that decides the role we personally wish to play in life." Here *Panaitios* raises the difficult question of the "life choice" that is to be made in one's youth. This fourfold distinction, however, is not meant to obscure the fundamental stoic twofold division with which both *Epictetus' Conversations* and his *Handbook* set out: in every individual human life there is what is provided by providence as the "given" material—and man must manage with this—and there is his reasoning freedom, by means of which he participates in the divine and enables him to use and fashion the "given"

---

[4] "Dialogues" found in J. Souilhé and A. Jagu, eds. *Les Belles Letres, Entretiens*, vols. I–IV (1948–65), referenced in this section by volume number (I–IV) and page number. The "Handbook" is quoted according to the edition by H. Schmidt (Kröner, n.d.), referenced in this section by E.

[5] III, 23, 29.

[6] I, 27, 17. On the uniqueness of each hair and each ear of wheat cf. *Stoicorum Veterum Fragmenta*, ed. J. von Arnim (Leipzig, 1905), II, 113.

[7] I, 18, 17f.; II, 14, 20; II, 24, 18; III, 24, 20.

[8] Cicero, *De officiis* 107–25.

according to the superiority that is his as a human being. *Prohairesis* is the reflecting and evaluating reason,[9] free will and the ground of the ethical person, as well as its capacity for development. Everyone is equipped with these two elements in such a way that the harmony of the world results from the particularity of all.[10] Everyone must possess "the meaning of his own personality [*idion prosopon*]"[11] and thus decide what value he sets on himself, for "people sell themselves at different prices".[12] Everything depends on freely accepting one's own personality, that is, deliberately opting for one's godlike freedom and for the limited life conditions in which one is placed. "Take this role";[13] what is meant here is the role of the wise man, the man who is truly (that is, in action) serious about his role.[14] True philosophy consists in doing, not in talking and speculating.[15] The wise man does not "mix different roles",[16] for that can never produce a character. The proper way to play one's role is this: from the vantage point (and distance) of freedom to affirm the given earthly conditions without becoming entangled in them. "Do you want me to play poverty? Bring it here, and you will see what poverty is when it meets with a good actor."[17] Everything springs from inner freedom; no earthly power can take its citadel.[18] It is God-given but needs to be exercised. Naturally, every being, including man, tends toward self-preservation and self-promotion (*oikeiōsis*), but in the case of man, who has the divine spark within him, his own good coincides with the ethical good as such, "and so my 'I' is where my ethical being [*prohairesis*] is, and only in this way am I the friend, the son, the father I ought to be."[19] Thus, unlike the third-rate actors who can only appear in the chorus, I can actually perform solo.[20]

Now the whole question is this: What is the relationship

[9] The self-awareness (*dynamis logikē*) that distinguishes man from the animals (I, 1, 4), by means of which he can test the ideas that come to him (I, 20, 7).

[10] I, 12, 16.   [11] I, 2, 14.   [12] I, 2, 11; cf. I, 2, 28.

[13] I, 29, 57.   [14] E, no. 29.

[15] A central concern of Epictetus, e.g., I, 26, 3, 17; I, 29, 35; I, 29, 56; II, 9, 17f.; II, 16, 20; in II, 19, 22f. the question is asked whether there is such a person as a real stoic; Epictetus is content if a person at least strives toward the ideal.

[16] IV, 2, 10; E, no. 33.   [17] IV, 7, 13.   [18] I, 29, 11f.

[19] II, 22, 19–20.   [20] III, 14, 1.

between human and divine freedom? Is the kernel of human freedom personal and unique or is it only a composition scored by the divine freedom under the given material limitations? The answer will depend on *what* and *who* this God is who apportions roles and freedoms. According to stoic cosmology and theology, "what is first and most important is the system that consists of God and mankind",[21] to which gods and demons can also belong, but these gods are themselves emanations of the "highest and omnipotent God, who is named in many names, Zeus, the Lord of Nature . . .";[22] when the world is consumed in fire and all the forms that have come into being are dissolved, Zeus will once more be alone.[23] But in this same passage *Epictetus* alternates between the terms "God", "gods" and "Divinity".[24] God is the whole, human beings are parts (*moria*), fragments, *apospasmata*), "closely linked with God",[25] "related" to God (*syngeneia*);[26] they are like members of a body—if such members could think;[27] they can be certain that they are needed for the total condition of the present world.[28] The freedom they are given is an absolute one: "independent" (*autoexousion*) and autonomous (*autonomon*).[29] "What has he (God) reserved to himself?"[30] "Zeus himself cannot overrule my freedom [*prohairesis*]."[31]

Nothing is more strongly urged by *Epictetus* than that I am "God's friend and freeman and obey him of my own accord".[32] For God is my "Creator" (*poietēs*) and "Father",[33] I am his "adopted son";[34] God, who is present in all things,[35] who is particularly present in the human mind.[36] Obeying him and carrying out his commands[37] is the only true use of human freedom. God is like the commander of an army who has

---

[21] I, 9, 4.

[22] The Hymn of Cleanthes in M. Pohlenz, *Stoa und Stoiker* (Zurich, 1950), 103.

[23] III, 13, 4f.　　[24] II, 14, 11.　　[25] I, 14, 5–6.

[26] I, 9, 1; "They share in the divine fellowship" (I, 9, 6).

[27] II, 10, 4.　　[28] II, 1, 18; II, 5, 25.　　[29] IV, 1, 56.　　[30] IV, 1, 100.

[31] I, 1, 23.　　[32] IV, 3, 9.

[33] I, 9, 7. The term "Father" occurs frequently: I, 3, 1; I, 6, 40; I, 9, 7; I, 13, 3; II, 10, 7; III, 24, 16; III, 26, 28. "Creator": II, 14, 25–27; IV, 7, 6.

[34] I, 3, 2.　　[35] I, 14, 9.　　[36] II, 8, 9–12.

[37] III, 5, 10; III, 24, 42–43; IV, 1, 154.

indicated a position that we must hold at all costs.[38] "Whatever position or rank you may allot to me (as *Socrates* says),[39] I would rather die a thousand times than desert it."[40] The man who guards his post worthily thereby becomes a "witness of God [*martus*]",[41] for he is there on the basis of a special "call" (*klēsis*),[42] which may also be a vocation to suffering;[43] he knows that he has been "found worthy to serve Zeus".[44] God has "entrusted him to himself".[45] He is "a messenger, a spy, a herald" in the service of God.[46] He "follows God"[47] by "learning to will everything as it takes place, as the Disposer has disposed it".[48] He "hangs upon God",[49] he "waits upon God".[50] He is totally impartial with regard to God's instructions.[51] He is patient and gives things time to grow.[52] Above all he is grateful for having been admitted to this marvelous world and allowed to participate in the feast of existence.[53] He lives in a constant hymn of praise to God.[54] Nothing meets with more censure from *Epictetus* than grumbling and quarreling with God. Those who cannot stand existence any longer he shows the "open door", suicide.[55] He is acquainted with prayer but regards it as best kept for special situations.[56] Since man is only a part of God, it is natural for the part to let the whole take precedence.[57] All the same he is convinced that God, who sees everything,[58] in his providence also cares for individuals.[59]

This religious atmosphere, so close to that of Christianity that the two can hardly be distinguished, is separated from Christian

---

[38] I, 9, 24; I, 29, 29; III, 24, 95f.; E, no. 22; the image of the soldier: III, 24, 31; of the sailor: III, 33. Reference to Socrates: III, 24, 31.

[39] *Apol.* 30c.   [40] III, 24, 99.

[41] I, 29, 44ff.; III, 24, 110ff.; III, 26, 28; IV, 8, 32.

[42] III, 22, 23ff.; III, 21, 18. The philosopher is called to wisdom as the initiate is to the mysteries (III, 12, 21).

[43] I, 29, 49; II, 1, 39.   [44] IV, 8, 32.   [45] IV, 12, 12.   [46] III, 22, 69.
[47] I, 12, 8; IV, 7, 20.

[48] I, 12, 15; as formulated by Zeno: I, 20, 15.

[49] IV, 1, 98.   [50] I, 9, 16.   [51] I, 6, 37; II, 16, 42.   [52] I, 15, 18.
[53] I, 6, 1; I, 6, 11.

[54] I, 16, 16.21; II, 23, 5; III, 26, 30; IV, 1, 105–6.108.

[55] I, 24, 20; I, 25, 18; II, 1, 19; II, 16, 37; IV, 10, 27.

[56] II, 18, 29; III, 5, 8.   [57] IV, 7, 7.   [58] I, 14, 9.   [59] I, 12, 3.

religiosity by the stoic framework to which it clings. In the first place this teaching, in which spirit and matter are equals, exhibits an acute dualism between the "hinge" of personal, rational freedom and the "swinging door" of all external goods, including one's own "wretched body" (*sōmation*). True, the *adiaphora* can be given a positive hue through ethical conduct, through the use (*chrēsis*) one makes of them,[60] but freedom is not "incarnated" in the physical body; the corporeal is "affected" from without by the unmoved point of freedom. Here we must recall the repeated recommendation of "caution" where it is a case of involving oneself in worldly relationships, including those with our fellow men.[61] We should not grieve at the death of a loved one: we are simply giving back something that did not, in any case, belong to us. But however close stoic and Christian indifference may come, the first aims to prevent sorrow from affecting the innermost regions of the soul (in spite of the many exhortations to endure injustice, mockery and disgrace),[62] whereas the second is prepared to open its deepest self to suffering if God so wills.

Fundamentally, furthermore, *Epictetus'* teaching remains within the great cosmological framework erected principally by *Poseidonios*:[63] the world is a gigantic organism, animated by a single divine breath ("God is a rational and fiery *pneuma*, formless, transforming itself into anything it desires and becoming like everything");[64] its parts are joined by "sympathy" like the organs of the human body. The human races, cultures and national characteristics are emanations of the cosmic organism; the physico-climatic and mental-spiritual are only two sides of the same thing. But just as, in autumn, the leaves fall, so too individuals pass away to make room for others. "Surrender your place to others".[65] "It is good for the parts to make way for the whole."[66] Each individual should retire from life's stage giving thanks to God and without looking for a continuation

---

[60] III, 24, 66ff.; II, 5, 7.

[61] II, 1; III, 16; III, 24, 85; IV, 13; E, no. 16.

[62] III, 10, 10; III, 20, 9; III, 21, 5; IV, 5, 22; IV, 6, 20.

[63] K. Reinhardt, *Poseidonios* (Munich, 1921); also his *Kosmos und Sympathie* (Munich, 1926).

[64] Poseidonios, according to Aetios, in Diels, *Doxogr. graeci* (1879), 302.

[65] IV, 1, 106.   [66] IV, 7, 7.

of life after death. The ancient stoics had no interest in immortality,[67] neither had *Panaitios*[68] or *Poseidonios*.[69] Nor had *Epictetus*; although he can speak of a "return to God",[70] the "true home",[71] it is only in the sense of man's constitutive elements being returned to the cosmic economy.[72] Thus a veil of resignation is laid over his whole religious thought. The divine spark in man must accept a limited role in the great play of the world; he should try to play it well,[73] should know when it is time for him to leave,[74] and above all he must take things as he finds them.[75] For instance, he must accept the fact that he was born of these particular parents as a result of this particular sexual act.[76] "Can you choose the story? You have been given a particular body, particular parents, particular brothers, a particular home and a particular office in it. And now you come and say to me: 'Change the story.' Have you no resources in yourself to make use of what has been given you? . . . Things have deteriorated so far that the actors imagine that their masks, buskins and robes are they themselves. Man, that is your material, your story! Open your mouth and let us see whether you are a serious actor or a buffoon."[77] Play the part you have been given and then disappear, knowing that "the man who does not die is accursed": "Why does the grain sprout, if not to grow and ripen? And when it is ripe, should it not be harvested?"[78]

On quite different presuppositions, modern times[79] saw the reiteration of a vision of the world and man that, astonishingly,

[67] Pohlenz, *Stoa und Stoiker*, 80.   [68] *Ibid.*, 216.

[69] Reinhardt, *Kosmos und Sympathie*, interpreting Poseidonios: "If one were to speak of the danger of death, it would not consist in the danger of the wretched 'I' ceasing to be, which a faith would immortalize, not in the body's transitoriness, but in the limitation of individual existence, in its separateness from the all-embracing whole" (284). Reinhardt urges this in opposition to Pohlenz, who holds fast to a belief in immortality on the part of Poseidonios (Pohlenz, *Stoa and Stoiker*, 330f.).

[70] I, 9, 14.   [71] IV, 1, 154.

[72] II, 5, 13; cf. II, 6; III, 13, 16; III, 24, 94.

[73] III, 22, 26.   [74] IV, 1, 165.   [75] I, 12, 21.   [76] I, 12, 28f.

[77] I, 29, 29ff.   [78] II, 6, 11–13.

[79] Naturally we should take account of the many intermediate links, i.e., in the middle ages, the philosophers of the school of Chartres, primarily Bernhard

took up the view of stoicism and particularly of *Poseidonios*, namely, J. G. *Herder's Ideen zur Geschichte der Menschheit* (1784–1791). It is his central work, and he put his best into it, yet its inconsistency and manifest *aporia* are characteristic. The book came into being at the time of *Herder's* reconciliation with *Goethe*, who at the time was pursuing his research in science and natural philosophy, so he welcomed *Herder's* essay and promoted it. The world-view of the *Ideen* presupposes a "divine nature" on which it is based, closely related to the stoic *physis*. From it, there organically emanates both all living forms right up to man and the forms of the historical. The latter are intimately connected with natural causes: physical, geographical, climatic. In mankind's development there are anthropological, ethnographical and linguistic causes and those causes studied in constitutional history. But all these causes remain tied to the natural, which, having become conscious in man, will not allow even the spiritual to leave its womb. *Herder* hymns nature as the "Mother and Queen" who has given us her mother's heart.[80] Contemplating a glowworm, a "luminous spark of God" that may perhaps be a "banished immortal", he asks: "Do I recognize myself? / So small, so flowing, coming and going / And sprung from the sun—do I recognize myself? . . . In this holy night, this night of magic, / Mother Nature, I adore thee!"[81] In the midst of a naturalistic vision of the history of man, the question of the "I" raises its head. Both questions are intertwined, for "in the totality of the race it (mankind) had no other destiny than it had in the case of individual members, for the whole only exists in individual members."[82] Yet in the *Ideen* the two questions cut across each other: as far as the race is concerned the horizontal

---

Silvestris, and in the Renaissance the natural philosophers from Fracastro, Cardanus, Telesius, Patritius, Campanella, to Giordano Bruno. The very title of Fracastro's "De sympathia et antipathia", and the doctrine of universal ensouling as put forth by those who came after him, remind us of Poseidonios. We also ought to discuss Spinoza and Leibniz with regard to the relation of divinity and the "I", but we must restrict ourselves to considering one typical representative of this approach.

[80] Herder, "Bestimmung der Menschen", in *Sämtl. Werke*, 40 vols. (Cotta, 1852–54), 13:56.

[81] Herder, "St. Johannes-Nacht", in *Sämtl. Werke*, 13:126f.

[82] Herder, *Ideen zur Geschichte der Menschheit*, bk. 15, chap. 5 (in *Sämtl. Werke*, 29:254).

predominates, for "human nature remains always the same",[83] even if it may move toward a certain optimum. For the "I", however, the vertical takes precedence: here, earthly existence becomes a stage on the ascending journey toward the Sun of Spirits; but it is not *Herder's* business to speak of it here; after the intimations of the fifth book he does not return to this ascent. This shows that the influence of *Leibniz*, which was at work in him from an early stage, could not ultimately assert itself once it had been reinterpreted in a vitalist sense. Even less could the influence of *Spinoza* persist. In his book *Gott*, Herder had defended *Spinoza* against *Jacobi's* attack, yet, again, he reinterpreted the former's understanding of the Absolute according to his own naturalistic world-view: "In all human beings, in all his creatures —which are, as it were, thousands of millions of his organs— this God experiences himself, just as, since he is in us, we enjoy his existence in an infinitely intimate manner."[84] At its most individual, *Herder's* own standpoint was neither Leibnizian nor Spinozist but—without his being aware of it—profoundly Poseidonian. For both, the world is the physical and spiritual emanation of a divine life (which, in *Herder's* case, since he had gone through Christianity, has more personal features); for both, the sun is the central organ of life, and the world is maintained by an equable balance of opposed forces; tension (*tonos*) is the fundamental law of life, which differs according to climatic conditions. Both of them admire and hymn the cosmic harmony. Like *Panaitios*, *Herder* sees man's spirituality in the closest connection with his upright carriage, which sets his hands free.[85] Generally stoic is his view that man's dignity lies in his freely obeying the laws of nature that dwell within him; he carries these laws within him, potentially, at birth; they have to be developed through experience and tradition. Stoic too, ultimately, is the emphasis on the instability of all human achievement,[86] conjoined with the lofty optimism regarding "humanity" in its God-relatedness, and the confidence in providence's guiding

---

[83] *Ideen*, bk. 15, Introduction (in *Sämtl. Werke*, 29:213).

[84] Summary by Rudolf Haym, *Herder* (Darmstadt, 1954), II, 309.

[85] Pohlenz, *Stoa und Stoiker*, 209–11; "Ideen", bk. 3, chap. 6. Kant is scornful of this in his review of the first volume of the "Ideen": to him it is standing things on their heads (Weischedel, VI, 793).

[86] *Ideen*, bk. 13, chap. 6 (in *Sämtl. Werke*, 29:91).

hand.[87] Stoic—and this is particularly relevant to us here—is also the *acceptance of limits*, which is required of the individual insofar as, on earth, he is a member of mankind. In the eighth book he introduces the principle of "happiness"; it is immediately distinguished from full blessedness, which cannot be expected on earth.[88] We have already seen that the core of this happiness lies in existence itself: "Every living being rejoices in its life; it does not question and brood about why it exists; its existence is its purpose, and its purpose is existence. . . . This simple, profound, irreplaceable sense of existence, therefore, is happiness, a tiny drop of that infinite ocean of the All-Blessed who is in everything and delights and experiences himself in everything."[89] This is the grateful attitude of *Epictetus*—"poor Epictetus gives commands, mightier than a king"[90]—privileged to participate in life's feast. But the kind Mother of the Universe knows what we need: "training, effort and toil", and holds out to us "the cup of health in the hard hands of toil"; indeed, we see "that Nature has done all she could, not to expand us, but to restrict us and thus accustom us to our circumscribed life. . . . Thus, O Man, your sole art here below is that of moderation: joy, the child of heaven for which you yearn, is all around you, . . . a sister of temperance and contentment with your existence in life and death."[91] So for *Herder*, the acceptance of limitation within the finite form that Nature has produced, in every conceivable nuance, is part of earthly happiness. "All God's works . . . in their particular limits, rest upon the balance of opposing forces which is maintained by an inner power that directs and orders them": this is the "guiding thread" that can lead us through the labyrinth of history, "for whatever can happen, does happen, and whatever can operate, does so."[92] This constantly repeated principle points directly to *Hegel*; in

[87] A supernatural providence is evident in the communication of language to the first human beings, who "held intercourse with their preceptors, the Elohim" (*Ideen*, bk. 10, chap. 6 in *Sämtl. Werke*, 28:431).

[88] "The very word 'happiness' [*Glückseligkeit*— 'hap-bliss'] indicates that man is incapable of pure blessedness [*Seligkeit*], nor can he manufacture it" (*Ideen*, bk. 8, chap. 5 in *Sämtl. Werke*, 28:333).

[89] *Ibid.*, 337.

[90] *Ideen*, bk. 15, chap. 5 (in *Sämtl. Werke*, 29:258).

[91] *Ideen*, bk. 8, chap. 5 (in *Sämtl. Werke*, 28:334–35, 340).

[92] *Ideen*, bk. 15, chap. 5 (in *Sämtl. Werke*, 29:256).

stoic terms, freedom and destiny (*heimarmenē*) coincide. "All that can be, is; all that can come to be, will be, if not today, then tomorrow."[93] This free acceptance of necessity is also the pathos found in *Goethe*. As *W. von Humboldt* will say, "The element in which history moves is the sense of reality. This contains the feeling of the transitoriness of temporal existence, the feeling of dependence on causes, both foregoing and accompanying, but also the awareness of inner, spiritual freedom and reason's recognition that reality, despite its apparent fortuitousness, is bound together by inner necessity."[94] While *Herder* looks forward to a development through history, for "abuse punishes itself" and reason and the sustaining energies will assert themselves (though, in deliberate contrast to *Kant*, he remains opposed to mankind's increasing subjection to technology and state control), he expects the individual cultures to attain only relative *maxima*.

But what, in all this, becomes of the individual "I" whose inner capacities cannot achieve all-around development under the constraints of earthly existence? In the fifth book *Herder* lifts his gaze to immortality, trusting that the soul, which always needs a material organ, will be provided with it by providence. Now he expressly rejects the doctrine of palingenesis he once advocated. But what is this surviving dimension that, as in stoicism, knows itself to be so closely related to God and yet so transitory? Here, influenced no doubt by *Spinoza*, *Herder* distinguishes between the "I", or "personality", and what he sometimes calls the "self". "What is immortal—what alone is immortal—is what lies substantially in the nature and destiny of the human race, . . . the highest possible development of its form."[95] Immortal is that through which we have emerged from the confines of our "I" and poured what is our own into the nameless treasury of humanity: "Let man's life be all in others; / fruitfulness his best reward."[96] "Courage! Thou belong'st not to thyself: / But to the great, good Universe. / From

---

[93] *Ideen*, bk. 12, chap. 6 (in *Sämtl. Werke*, 29:88). "Everything that can happen on earth must happen insofar as it takes place according to rules which possess their own perfection" (29:251).

[94] "Über die Aufgabe des Geschictsschreibers" (a lecture of 1821), *Werke* IV, 40.

[95] "Über die menschliche Unsterblichkeit" in *Sämtl. Werke*, 30:300.

[96] "Die Bestimmung des Menschen" in *Sämtl. Werke*, 13:55.

it thou hast received and dost; / Thou must give, not only all that's thine / But thyself. . . . / Cut off from every living thing that wrapped thee round / And wraps thee still, nourishing and giving life, / What wouldst thou be? Not an 'I' . . . / The 'I' dies that the Whole may be. . . . / Only if, heedless of thy narrow 'I', / Thy spirit lives in others' souls, thy heart / Beats in thousand hearts, then wilt thou be / Eternal, all-accomplishing, a God; / Like him beyond all sight and name." Hence: "Seek'st thou rest, O Friend, then flee / Thy direst foe: personality."[97] Or, in prose: "The purer and more noble some part of our nature is, the more it transcends itself, renounces its narrow confines, becomes communicative, infinite, eternal. . . . In this way all mankind's benefactors have brought their influence to bear." And if we are to make our contribution too, "we must set aside our 'I' . . . all that smacks of personality must be banished to the abyss"; and here, for once, the poet expresses himself more fully on the subject of "the demons, heroes and geniuses of the ancient world".[98] Yet he is not speaking merely of the individual's being absorbed into the race; this account still lacks the vertical dimension, that of the self: "Forget thine 'I', but never lose thy self. . . . / A man who lost himself—what would remain? / Whate'er of us lives in the hearts of others / Is our truest and profoundest self. . . . / What in me lives, is most alive, eternal, / Cannot ever pass away."[99] It is hard to tell whether this "self" is more than the *prohairesis* of *Epictetus*, insofar as it is a spark of the divine fire in the individual, or whether it may be an anticipation of the "self" of *C. G. Jung*, that is, that synthesis of all vital forces that is attainable by the "I" in its self-transcendence into the universal plane. To the extent to which *Herder*, in his *Ideen*, distances himself from notions arising from his Christian background—sometimes engaging in violent polemics[100]—he also loses his hold on the personal, world-reflecting monad of *Leibniz*; nor can he say what this depersonalized self might be, a "self" from which the "I" has been removed, a "self" that comes to its true self through selflessness.

[97] "Das Ich. Ein Fragment" in *Sämtl. Werke*, 13:56–61.
[98] "Über die menschliche Unsterblichkeit" in *Sämtl. Werke*, 30:303ff.
[99] "Das Selbst. Ein Fragment" in *Sämtl. Werke*, 13:61–65.
[100] *Ideen*, bks. 17, 19, 20.

2. Psychology

It may seem unpromising to ask psychology the question "Who am I?" since both classical and modern psychology (insofar as they are a *logy*) are concerned with the human psyche as such, with what is common to all human beings, not with the particularities of the individual. Or, at any rate, psychology seeks to understand the latter from the standpoint of general laws and to apply healing—through analysis or therapy—on that basis. However, modern psychology is prepared to take the individual seriously with all his distinctive characteristics and peculiarities, and particularly in the disparity between his "I" and his social role; consequently it is not inappropriate for us to look for a moment at the main representatives of modern psychotherapy. We have included them under the general heading of "role as the acceptance of limits", in spite of their differences among themselves, because in all cases they see the "I" as resting upon and oriented toward a vital substratum that governs and sustains it; in *Freud*, the relationship of this "I" to the substratum is explicitly that of "surface" to depth,[1] of the "facade" to the building.[2] Each in his own way, therefore, the great leaders of the three major schools of psychology will advocate that man should come to accept what he is; they will see the ultimate goal of therapy as that of integrating man into the totality that embraces him. We begin with *Sigmund Freud*, the first empirical depth-psychologist, for whom the acceptance of limits is a profound personal attitude to life. Then we move on to *C. G. Jung*, who, in spite of the wide panorama of his doctrine of the soul, ultimately leads the individual, having laid aside his "persona", to acceptance. Finally we shall refer to *Alfred Adler*, who brings the neurotic "I" back from its "uniqueness" and "God-likeness" to accept its modest role within society. He forms the transition to sociology.

[1] Sigmund Freud, *Gesammelte Werke* (London, 1940), vol. XIII, 23ff., referenced in this section by volume and page number only. See also the letters, S. Freud, *Briefe* 1873–39, 2d ed., selected and edited by Ernst and Lucie Freud (Zurich, 1960); referenced in this section by B and the page number.

[2] XIV, 423.

a. Sigmund Freud

Freud, who describes himself as "sensitive and irritable",[3] who had a hard life (and who did not make life easy for himself), was "a total unbeliever",[4] without any illusions as to man's abilities;[5] indeed, he was uncertain whether the "unintelligible comedy"[6] of life had any meaning at all. "The moment anyone asks about the meaning and value of life, he is sick, for objectively neither exists",[7] because "the program of the libido principle, which sets the goal of life . . . , simply cannot be implemented."[8] Life's brutality "wounds" the human heart—the word "wound" often recurs in Freud's letters[9]—in particular since "this irrational life"[10] is ended by "the painful riddle of death".[11] But since there is no court of appeal,[12] man is left in "painful loneliness",[13] and the death of a loved one leaves him "disconsolate . . . , and this is only right".[14] In his last decade *Freud* suffered unbearably; "I cannot cope with a terminal existence";[15] his longing for death, for "the peace I yearn for", "the eternal nothingness",[16] increased, he felt "overdue".[17] But, in a strange "obstinacy",[18] he stayed at his post. Sometimes his "dear fellow human beings"

[3] B, 74.   [4] B, 469.

[5] "We human beings stand on the basis of our animal nature; we shall never become like the gods. . . . Some painful renunciation is unavoidable. . . . The obstacles (to any transformation of man's future) lie in man's instinctual constitution and interests" (B, 398).

[6] B, 357.   [7] B, 452.   [8] XIV, 434; cf. 442.

[9] B, 343, 390, 429, 463; XIV, 337.   [10] B, 378.   [11] XIV, 337.

[12] "Since I am most profoundly an unbeliever, I have no one to blame and know that there is nowhere to lodge an accusation" (B, 346). "Where shall we look for justice? We are not asked what our wishes are" (B, 388). "As for our vulnerability to physical and particularly painful suffering, like you I find it desperate. If one could blame anyone for it, I would call it base" (B, 361). If Freud were ever to meet God, "I would have more to reproach him with than he me" (B, 320).

[13] B, 273, 381.   [14] B, 403.   [15] B, 367.

[16] B, 409. "I look forward with a kind of longing to passing over into nonbeing" (B, 444). "It is good for our span of life to be set a timely limit by a compassionate destiny" (B, 440, cf. 418).

[17] B, 476. "It is time for Ahasuerus to come to rest somewhere" (B, 459).

[18] "Even if my defiance is silent, it is still defiance, and—*impavidum ferient runiae*" (B, 454).

seemed like "riff-raff",[19] religion an infantile compulsive neurosis,[20] a "mass illusion"[21] which analysis had to combat and would eventually destroy. He clung to a single value: empirical science, which had demonstrated "that it is not an illusion"[22] and which, at the end of his book against religion and in his last lectures, he extolled in almost hymnic terms.[23] However, science takes only small steps forward, and *Freud* continually emphasizes how uncertain his hypotheses are, how unknown is the substratum from which the psychic phenomena arise. He is also aware of "the limitations of my gifts".[24] The word "submit" comes easily to his pen.[25] *Freud*, with his horror of philosophy, was a doctor who, starting from his studies in hysteria and the practice of hypnosis, felt his way toward his special field, the psychic unconscious. He calls it the "ground floor and basement of the building" and will not ascend to the higher floors "inhabited by such distinguished guests as religion, art and so forth".[26] He is too cautious to be a materialist.[27] He is convinced of the "unity of the world", which he regards as self-evident.[28]

As a doctor, he was concerned with the "I" of his patients, and he regretted that research into this "I" had progressed so little.[29] His purpose was to use "the data of observation to establish initially extreme and clearly contoured types", albeit such types "can only be found in more blurred outline" in the multiplicity of individual life.[30] As a result of his analysis of the

---

[19] B, 407.   [20] XIV, 367; XIV, 431.

[21] XIV, 440. "*Narkotikum*": XIV, 372.

[22] XIV, 378ff. "There is no instance higher than reason" (XIV, 350).

[23] "Über eine Weltanschauung": XV, 108–97.

[24] XIV, 35.

[25] For example, XIV, 373, 379. "Submission to the inevitable" (XIV, 444).

[26] B, 446.

[27] He insists on the "difference between what is of the soul and what is of the body". "Let us respect (nature's) magnificent variety which ascends from the inanimate to the organically animate, and from the bodily animate to the spiritual" (B, 333). Cf. XV, 171, which speaks of "the spirit and the soul" as objects of scientific study. It must be possible to show "how the spiritual energies operate upon inert matter" (XV, 186).

[28] B, 323.   [29] XIII, 57.   [30] VIII, 77.

unconscious, Freud arrived at the assumption that there was an original pregenital state in which the developing human being, like a monad, is a closed-in, worldless, "autoerotic" system governed by the "pleasure principle"; only "by being born" does it take "the step away from absolute, self-satisfied narcissism toward the perception of a changeable external world".[31] This starting point—an, as it were, eternally (timelessly) self-contained and complacent bliss—is of prime importance for all that follows, not only for the drama of the clash with the external world (which Freud portrays in the celebrated oral-cannibalistic, anal-sadistic and phallic phases) but equally for the continual transformation of his teaching.[32] His first task was to explain the clash with the reality of the external world, in which the monad breaks out of its isolation: in the "bliss of sucking", the mother's nipple seemed to be a part of the baby's own system,[33] but it withdraws itself. The "child's pleasure-'I' that can only wish" arrives at a point where it has to acknowledge the "real 'I', which represents the integration of the behavior patterns acquired through concrete experience".[34] If the original monad is "polymorphously perverse",[35] that is, not predetermined by any object, the experience of dependency (hunger, self-preservation versus the pleasure urge) begins to fix the objects of the external world. (In principle Freud does not speak of a "thou", even in the case of the mother, but always of the "object" of a drive.) Thus there is an immediate opposition between the ego drive and the sexual drive:[36] in coming to grips with the perceived environment—the recognition of "true and false",[37] but then the "cathexis" of the objects of desire with

[31] XIII, 146. "The ego, insofar as it is autoerotic, does not need the external world" (X, 228). "Love arises from the ability of the ego to satisfy a part of its instinctual desires autoerotically, through sensual pleasure. In origin it is narcissistic, and then projects onto the objects which are incorporated in the expanded ego" (X, 231). Thus "the social instinct is not primitive and proof against dissection" (XIII, 74).

[32] On many occasions Freud described the phases of his development; they are summarized most briefly in the note, XIII, 66.

[33] XIV, 61.   [34] II–III, 604.

[35] XIV, 64; I, 451; V, 92ff., 134, 136, 141, 156f.; VIII, 419; XI, 213f., 334f.

[36] XIII, 216f.

[37] XV, 184. In 1911, in his "Formulierungen über zwei Prinzipien des

libido energy and the "repression" of the unacceptable into the unconscious—the ego gradually organizes itself as the conscious part of the psyche.[38] When Freud turned more deliberately to an analysis of the "I", it was only logical that he should give up the dualism of ego drive and sexual drive and, in consonance with his original model, explained the ego drives, too, as coming from the same basic libidinal energy as the externally directed sexual drives. The ego (as a representative of the narcissistic primal monad) is "a great libidinal reservoir . . . whence libido is despatched to the objects and which is always ready to receive the libido which streams back from them." Even the drives toward self-preservation "were sexual drives that had adopted the ego itself, instead of external objects, as their object".[39] In view of this turning back to the "I", *Freud* is prepared to replace the expression "sexual drive" by the wider term "eros", the generalized "power of love" that governs everything—as we can read in *Plato*.[40]

However, the conscious "I" is only a fragment[41] of the former monad or totality. First the child projects its love onto its parents, who simultaneously appear as the embodiment of perfect authority—we need not enter here into the details of the drama of the Oedipus complex—and, when "the Oedipus complex dies a natural death",[42] it reassumes this factor of authority, which now becomes the "superego" ("ego-ideal")

---

psychischen Geschehens", Freud distinguished the "pleasure principle" from the "reality principle": VIII, 235ff.

[38] The ego of the little child is still "feeble"; character only becomes firm when it comes to grips with its environment, which is determined on the one hand by nature (primordially) and on the other hand by life experience (secondarily). In this process much must be repressed as "irreconcilable" with the subject's aims and claims, so that the remaining desires "can coalesce into the comprehensive unity of the ego" (XIII, 7), "in an ever wider integration of the personality whereby the individual instinctual drives and goals, which have grown up independently of one another", are brought together in the service of "the unification of the ego" (XIII, 85, note). "In the course of our development we have split our soul's substance into a coherent ego and whatever is left outside it, unconscious and repressed" (XIII, 146). Thus "the character of the ego is a record of the object-occupations it has given up" (XIII, 257).

[39] XIII, 231.   [40] XIII, 99.

[41] Insofar as the ego comes about only through repression: XIII, 146.

[42] XIII, 395–402.

dominating the ego; it becomes the authority behind ethical values, "conscience", but also, as the representative of the unconscious that is opposed to the ego (the "id"), sadistically and aggressively tyrannizes it.[43] What the ego thus "projects beyond it as its ideal is the substitute for the lost narcissism of its childhood, in which it was its own ideal".[44] In order to understand this, we must recall the earlier reference to the polymorphously perverse primary stage and examine it more closely. Indeed, this stage (which will be replaced, in the final version of the theory, by the "id") is envisaged as a *coincidentia oppositorum*: "The rules of logical thought do not apply, particularly that of noncontradiction. Contrary impulses exist side by side without cancelling each other out";[45] "there is no negation in this system",[46] nor does "the passage of time have any effect on the psychic sequence".[47] This fundamental system gives rise to the ambivalence of drives and feelings which *Freud* so strongly emphasizes: love and hate, "good" and "evil",[48] mutually contain each other; at any point they can turn into their opposite. Just as they can be mixed and "alloyed", they can also be "separated out".[49] Hence we have "man's inborn tendency to 'evil', to aggression, destruction and hence also to cruelty". We seem to hear an anticipation of *C. G. Jung* when *Freud* goes on: "The devil provides the best means of exculpating God, taking on the role of the economic safety valve just as the Jew does in the world of the Aryan ideal."[50] Like *Jung* (with his doctrine of the *anima*), *Freud* regards the human being as fundamentally

[43] XIII, 262f., 277. On the aggression of conscience: XIV, 482.

[44] X, 161; cf. V, 398.

[45] XV, 801. Cf. X, 285–86. The unconscious "has no knowledge of anything negative, of any denials. Opposites coincide in the unconscious. Hence too it has no knowledge of its own death" (X, 350).

[46] X, 285.   [47] XV, 80.

[48] X, 332. As far as "good" and "evil" are concerned, this "paradox" means "simply that man's nature, in good and evil, goes far beyond what he himself believes; i.e., far beyond what his ego is acquainted with as a result of conscious apprehension" (XIII, 282). Freud wrote to A. Zweig: "Truly, this world's tenderness is mingled with cruelty" (B, 445). On the ambivalence of love and hate: X, 232, 332; X, 353f.; XII, 176; XIII, 58; XIII, 270f.; XIV, 528f., as well as the whole chapter on the taboo and emotional ambivalence in *Totem and Taboo*: IX, 26–92.

[49] X, 333; XIV, 15, 143; XV, 112.   [50] XIV, 479.

bisexual.[51] Given this primal condition, it follows that the relationship between the superego (conscience, the censor) and the ego can be portrayed as sadistic-masochistic. (We can pass over the whole topic of inheritance here; under the acknowledged influence of *Jung*,[52] he attempts to demonstrate, in the individual of today, the features of the original human society, the "primal herd". He does this first in *Totem and Taboo* but continues to pursue it up to his book against religion, *The Future of an Illusion*, and in his "elucidation" of Jewish characteristics in *The Man Moses and the Monotheistic Religion*. These works, intended to give concrete form to a "vision",[53] describe man's present constitution—which, for *Freud*, is immutable—in a kind of mythological etiology.)

Once the unconscious has been characterized as not only polymorphous but also involving self-contradiction, the final phase of the Freudian "metapsychology" has been reached, namely, the "autoerotic" primal phase. This phase, in which were juxtaposed all the elements that would eventually become differentiated through their relationship to the outside world, a phase that no subsequent "regression"[54] could ever regain, has now become the "id", the "primary system", in which the contradiction is sublated.[55] But it represents not so much the factor of attraction as that of the uncanny, the dangerous and the menacing; this is the root out of which we "live" our ego (*Freud* here adopts *Groddeck's* expression).[56] "After all, the ego is only a part of the id, changed for functional reasons insofar as it comes into contact with the threatening external world";[57] it is not a

[51] V, 44; V, 120, XIII, 260–61. "The individual is a fusion of two symmetrical halves, which many researchers consider to be male and female respectively. It is equally possible that each half was originally hermaphrodite" (XIV, 465). For a reference to Plato and the Brihad-Aranyaka Upanishad: XIV, 62f.

[52] XIV, 92.

[53] XIV, 93. This vision is described as a "fiction" by the irritable commentator: XIV, 491.

[54] On the attempt to return to the womb, because we cannot cope with the world without some respite: XI, 84f.

[55] X, 385; XV, 80.

[56] "[W]hat we call our ego is essentially passive in our life; we ourselves are 'lived', in fact, by powers we do not know and cannot control" (XIII, 251).

[57] XV, 83.

primary phenomenon,[58] but, as the conscious part, it is the exposed upper and outer surface of the id which faces the world;[59] furthermore, above it and against it, it has the projected (and largely unconscious) superego as its inner governing authority —an authority that represents the id.[60] Thus *Freud* portrays the situation of the ego, full of pathos: "Helpless in both directions, the ego vainly defends itself against the suggestions of the murderous id on the one hand and the reproaches of punishing conscience on the other."[61] It is a "poor thing, under a threefold subjection and consequently threatened by dangers of three kinds, from the external world, from the libido of the id and from the severity of the superego. The three kinds of anxiety correspond to these three dangers."[62] Behind these scientifically couched assertions we can hear *Freud*, the suffering human being, who, when death strikes, "cannot complain and brood but is obliged to bow his head beneath the blow, a poor, helpless man, the plaything of higher powers".[63] "In our view an individual is a psychic id, unacknowledged and unconscious, on the surface of which sits the ego, developed as a nucleus out of the perception system."[64] The id is "the nucleus of the ego",[65] merely "a particularly differentiated part of the id",[66] performing its business "as directed by the id".[67]

It is no surprise, then, that the former nostalgia for the lost paradise of "primal narcissism" now becomes a "death wish", and the entire psychic reality is portrayed as an eternal struggle between eros and thanatos, in which ultimately eros, the will to life, self-preservation and self-propagation, appears to be only a complicated, circuitous path to death.[68] Death is the goal of life.[69] However, the death wish also expresses itself as the con-

---

[58] XIII, 243, 251–52; XV, 82.   [59] XIII, 22, 25.

[60] XIII, 264, 267, 278.   [61] XIII, 283.

[62] XIII, 286. "The Ego is the real seat of anxiety" (XIII, 287).

[63] B, 343.   [64] XIII, 251.

[65] XII, 79 (note). "The id is the older; the ego has developed out of it like a skin, under the influence of the external world" (XVI, 203).

[66] XIII, 267.   [67] XV, 82.

[68] XIII, 233, 269, 276. On "[t]he opposition, which is probably irreconcilable, between the primal instincts of eros and death": XIV, 501; cf. XIV, 84; on pleasure in the service of the death instinct; XIII, 69.

tinually erupting and apparently irrational "urge to destroy"[70] —which is why wars cannot be eliminated—and as the apparently amoral "aggressive instinct", which inheres so profoundly in everything related to the psyche.[71] *Freud* observes "that we have inadvertently made landfall in the harbor of the philosophy of *Schopenhauer*, for whom death is 'the ultimate result' of life and, to that extent, its purpose".[72] Now it is "futility" that imparts to earthly things their "rarity value", to which we ought not to cling.[73] But everything that is given the name "culture", for which man is obliged to strive, has the seed of death in it, insofar as it involves an ever-greater distance from the immediacy of eros, requires the latter to be channeled (in a way that is psychically impossible) into a "generalized love of one's fellow men" and calls for an inhuman renunciation of instinctual drives and the restriction (going as far as the extinction) of the sexual function.[74] Technologized man becomes "the artificial god"; his artificiality and the "grandiose inflation of love" that results from its stereotyping elicit the urge to destroy. Consequently *Freud* rejects both the hopes and the methods of communism as illusory.

In presenting his theory to *Roman Rolland*, *Freud* described the goal of his analysis as "simply that of the higher harmony of the 'ego' " and its task as that of "mediating successfully between the demands of the instinctual life (the 'id') and those of the external world, that is, between inner and outer reality";[75] but this is to put it in euphemistic terms. The "poor ego" is doomed to be the locus of anxiety, caught between the three superior and sinister powers that conspire against it: the id, the superego and the external world. In this world, for the rationalist *Freud*, there are only "objects", there is no "thou" that could form a bridge leading out of the lonely isolation.

[69] XIII, 40.

[70] XIII, 59, 269, 271.

[71] On "[t]he descendant and chief representative of the death instinct": XIV, 481.

[72] XIII, 53.   [73] X, 358–61.

[74] "Das Unbehagen in der Kultur", XIV, 419–506.

[75] B, 410f.

b. C. G. Jung

We can risk setting foot in the labyrinthine work of C. G. Jung[1] only if we take with us, as our Ariadne's thread, our approach to the problem of the "I" and the "role"; this will permit us to limit ourselves to four of his constantly recurring main topics: the "I", the persona, the process of individuation and the self. (He often equates the concept "personality" with that of the persona or the mask, but his terminology varies,[2] just as he circles around and approaches the four main concepts from continually new perspectives.) This means excluding the whole area of the conscious-unconscious (in the personal and collective senses), the ego-shadow, the *anima* (*animus*) and the archetypes. At the same time it must be borne in mind that, for *Jung* (and here he differs from *Freud*), the vast world that confronts the tiny ego-consciousness, the gigantic world of the unconscious (primarily the collective unconscious), the stream of life on which individuals are carried along, acquires a weight which will compel the ego to find its meaning and its equipoise in an ever-deeper coexistence with this stream out of which it has raised its head.

---

[1] Here we are primarily concerned with these works: C. G. Jung, *Erinnerungen, Träume, Gedanken. Aufgezeichnet und herausgegeben von Aniela Jaffé* (Zurich: Ex Libris, n.d.), referenced here as E [*Memories, Dreams, Reflections*, London, 1963]; *Die Beziehungen zwischen dem Ich und dem Unbewussten*, 4th ed. (Zurich: Rascher, 1945), referenced here as Bz; *Psychologie und Religion* (Rascher, 1962), referenced here as PR [*Psychology and Religion*, New York, 1938]; *Die Beziehungen der Psychotherapie zur Seelsorge* (Rascher, 1932), referenced here as S; *Aion. Untersuchungen zur Symbolgeschichte* (Rascher, 1941), referenced here as A [*Aion: Researches into the Phenomenon of the Self*, London, 1959]; *Psychologie und Alchemie* (Rascher, 1944), referenced here as Al [*Psychology and Alchemy*, London, 1953]; in collaboration with R. Wilhem, *Das Geheimnis der Goldenen Blüte* (Rascher, 1944), referenced here as G; *Zur Psychologie westlicher und östlicher Religion* (Rascher, 1963), containing among other things an "attempt at a psychological explanation of the dogma of the Trinity" and "The symbol of transubstantiation in the Mass", referenced here as WO [*Psychology and Religion: West and East*, London, 1958]; *Antwort auf Hiob* (Rascher, 1952), referenced here as H [*Answer to Job*]. There are introductions by Jolan Jacobi, *Die Psychologie C. G. Jungs*, 2d ed. (Rascher, 1945) [Jolande Jacobi, *The Psychology of C. G. Jung*, London, 1968] and Frieda Fordham, *Eine Einführung in die Psychologie C. G. Jungs* (Rascher, 1959) [Frieda Fordham, *An Introduction to Jung's Psychology*, Penguin, 1973].

[2] In E, 248, for instance, the "ego", as the "conscious person", the "total personality", is equated with the "self".

In terms of *Weltanschauung*, the unconscious, with its own rationality that expresses itself in compensatory attitudes vis-à-vis the one-sidedness of the ego, takes the place of the stoic *physis* (that is, of the *logos* or *nous*). Certainly, *Jung* intends to pursue a strictly empirical psychology and—in a Kantian manner[3] —renounces recourse to anything lying outside the psyche,[4] but at the same time he believes that he is bringing to life again the lost treasures of the mythico-religious world of symbols (which is indispensable for human civilization), as a psychic experience or as the latter's unconscious precondition, in place of a metaphysics,[5] which is now dead, and an ecclesiastical dogma and liturgy,[6] which have become empty and ineffectual. Modern man's psyche carries a vast prehistory within it and is nourished by its treasures;[7] therefore a psychotherapy that wishes to heal man of the modern demons of rationalism and utilitarianism must know about these treasures and win them back for the individual, insofar as he needs them.[8] The help the therapist

---

[3] It is very significant that Jung emphasizes the great "illumination" that came to him through Kant's theory of knowledge (E, 75). In his "Later reflections" we read: "In attempting to demonstrate the limitation of the psyche, I do not mean to suggest that there is only the psyche. It is simply that we cannot look out beyond the psyche where perception and knowledge are concerned. Science is tacitly convinced that there is a nonpsychical, transcendental object" (E, 353).

[4] "In fact the only form of existence of which we have direct knowledge is psychic existence. . . . The psyche is existent; indeed, it *is* existence" (PR, 16–17).

[5] A, 60.

[6] There are numerous instances: "The present time is a time when God is dead and is vanishing" (PR, 106). "The very words uttered from the pulpit are unintelligible and cry out for explanation: How can the death of Christ have redeemed us, if no one feels redeemed?" (A, 60f.). "The Christian Church has shown itself frighteningly empty: it has an external polish, but the inner man is untouched and hence untransformed by it. The condition of the soul does not correspond to the externals of belief" (Al, 24). For Jung, church life became a "torment" very early on (E, 51), a "place I could no longer visit" (E, 61); the religion of the Christian nations today is "asleep" (E, 334). Dogma's inner tensions and paradoxes are no longer bearable (Al, 30–31).

[7] Jung is convinced that the archetypes were acquired in mankind's history. Even primitive consciousness is predominantly collective (Bz, 50); the differentiation of consciousness between individuals only develops gradually (Bz, 50, 149; PR, 62).

[8] "Nowadays the psychological approach alone can provide an *understanding*

provides, in *Jung's* view, is not a mere technique: it calls for a venture on the part of a whole person,[9] not unlike the "spiritual father" of former times.

Who then is this individual with whom *Jung* is concerned? Before attempting an answer, we must emphasize *Jung's* reverence in the face of the mystery of being: he has "come to see that the greatest and most important problems of life are all insoluble, indeed, they must be. . . . We can never solve them but only grow beyond them."[10] "At this point we come up against ultimate questions: From where does consciousness come? What is this thing called the soul? Here our entire science has reached its limits."[11] From the midst of this not-knowing, man asks about his "I". As a small boy, *Jung* sits on a stone: "The stone could also say 'I'. . . . That raises the question 'Am I the one sitting on the stone, or am I the stone on which *he* is sitting?' "[12] Later, on the way to school, he has "the overpowering feeling", "the consciousness that now *I* am. . . . At that moment *I happened to myself*."[13] Later again, in a dream, while carrying a candle through a storm, he is followed by a big black figure. On waking he knows that it was "my own shadow . . . produced by the little candle I was carrying before me. I also knew that the candle was my consciousness, the only light I have. While my own knowledge is infinitely small and fragile compared to the

---

of religious things" (PR, 105). But in fact practically all patients have religious problems (S, 12), which means that "we physicians of the soul (must) concern ourselves with problems which, properly speaking, belong in the faculty of theology" (S, 26). Methodologically it is quite correct of Jung, as a psychologist, to use the psychically available material—the archetypes—in "explaining" the dogmas. His religious psychology could be regarded as completing the theological *méthode d'immanence* of the end of the nineteenth century, which, in its best proponents (like Blondel), had no intention of dissolving the objective mystery into a subjective one. However, the psychological method necessarily restricts the dogma—e.g., the Trinity or the figure of the God-man, Christ—and reduces it to one respresentation, among others, of a (perhaps privileged) universal human archetype. Jung's increasing fondness for using gnostic and alchemistic symbols to illuminate the psyche is a trait of his which need not concern us here.

[9] E, 138f.   [10] G, 14.

[11] S, 27. "We do not even know the essence of a simple thought, let alone the ultimate principles of psychic reality" (PR, 103).

[12] E, 26.   [13] E, 38–39.

powers of the darkness, yet it is a light, my only light."[14] The conscious "I", the "resultant" of a particular configuration of numerous collective elements of the stream of life—and their possible combinations are infinitely varied[15]—emerges like an "island in the ocean",[16] "embedded in an indefinably vast, unconscious psyche": hence man is far more than his consciousness.[17] *Jung's* endeavor was "totally to renounce the super-ordination of the ego" and to allow himself "to be carried along with the stream" for years in order to be receptive to the utterances of the unconscious;[18] his aim was to bring this underwater world, which is connected to the "I" as its "shadow" and ultimately as the whole world of the archetypes, into a correct relationship with extruded consciousness. The individual "I" can only be defined formally; "every other way of looking at it would have to take account of the individuality that adheres to the ego as a major quality of it".[19] But here *Jung* is concerned not so much with the factor of the *individuum ineffabile* as with the fact that the "real individual", the problem of his "identity", can only be defined by a process, namely, the process of "individuation", the result of which (if it were fully realized) is the "self". This, of course, is completely paradoxical, as *Jung* readily admits in his discussion of the "self". For the point of destination will be distinguished from the point of departure by its uniqueness: whereas the "ego" initially seems to exist only as a variation of the collective,[20] uniqueness will be the mode in which the elements are integrated into the totality. But in this case how can this mode be distinguished from any other, except by the element of uniqueness of each ego, a uniqueness that was always there right from the beginning anyway and which science cannot grasp?

The doctrine of the "persona"—which can mean both "mask"

---

[14] E, 92–93.

[15] A, 19. It is "variability that makes individuality possible" (Bz, 92); consequently the individual, "as a living unity", is "composed of nothing but universal factors" and to that extent "totally collective" (*ibid.*, 92–93). Hence no individual is "so differentiated as to be absolutely unique" (PR, 62).

[16] PR, 100.   [17] PR, 97.   [18] E, 200.   [19] A, 19.

[20] "Both our soul and our body are made up of individual parts which were already at hand in the ancestral line. What is 'new' in the individual psyche is an infinitely varied recombination of ancient constituents" (E, 239).

and "role"—exhibits clear contours. It is the mode in which the ego presents itself in the collective. It is "only a mask of the collective psyche, a mask giving the illusion of individuality . . . , while in fact it is only a role-playing, . . . a compromise between individual and society, . . . an illusion".[21] So it is, for instance, when a man is totally absorbed in his profession and prestige, while behind this "shell", this "get-up", there is only "a pitiful little man".[22] Here *Jung* speaks of "inflation"; it is something that could reappear once the illusion of the "persona" was shattered and the ego was able to reach out, unhampered, for the "great truth" in order to identify itself with it. "Personality" (in the restricted sense of persona) "is a more or less arbitrary slice of the collective psyche".[23] We must ask whether he is not underestimating the positive relationship between the "I" and the social role here, in what is evidently a polemical stance against *Alfred Adler*; the whole dialogical plane, the realm of becoming-a-self in the context of one's fellow human beings, is something that *Jung*, while he does not simply ignore it, passes quickly through to get to the totality of the "self", which alone really interests him.

It is completely legitimate for *Jung* the psychologist to set forth a grandly conceived doctrine of psychological types (1921), his first major book after *Psychology of the Unconscious* (1912), which marked the parting of the ways between himself and *Freud*; here the reality of the psyche's energy is generalized "beyond the bounds of the sexual" and is illustrated in its most significant expressions (archetypes). The doctrine of types develops according to the governing categories of tension, polarity and complementarity. "A great part of my life's work [consisted in] research into the problem of opposing features",[24] not only the conscious-unconscious, the ego and the shadow, the person and the *anima* (*animus*), but also "good and evil, spirit and matter, light and darkness".[25] The good-and-evil polarity

---

[21] Bz, 61, 64, cf. 124.   [22] Bz, 41f.   [23] Bz, 62.

[24] E, 237. The problem of opposites is discussed most fully in the late work *Mysterium Conjunctionis*, 3 vols. (Rascher, 1956) [*Mysterium Coniunctionis: An Inquiry into the Separation and Synthesis of Psychic Opposites in Alchemy*, London, 1963].

[25] E, 239.

must not be extrapolated from the weft and woof of the psyche, because "it is only in the field of human willing and acting that the opposition between them is brought to a head morally";[26] the man who cannot come to terms with his dark shadow, his latent evil, and integrate it is doomed to become a religious spectre. The horizon onto which the ego projects itself and is thereby "individualized", that is, the "self", whose symbols are not distinct from those of the divine,[27] is thus, for *Jung*, consistently quaternary. The Christian Trinity is one-sidedly masculine, lacking *sophia*, the female principle;[28] and on the other hand, it is exclusively light, it lacks the shadow, evil; beside Christ, the good Son, it needs the devil, the son who has gone astray. For, confronted with the world as it is, who can take refuge in the excuse that God did not will the evil in it?[29] *Jung's* book *Answer to Job* (1952) puts forward a defense (an "emotionally laden" defense, as *Jung* himself says) of this doctrine of polarity as the ultimate horizon; here, suffering man, having "discerned the opposites in the divine nature",[30] appeals from a nonintegrated God to an integrated God—which ultimately means a God who has become man. For *Jung*, psychologically speaking, it is contradictory to speak of an "absolute" God, that is, "cut loose" from relationship with the world; only where the totality (the "self") is incarnated in the ego and thus initiates individuation, the decisive *mysterium conjunctionis*, does it become alive. If, today, it seems that "the place of the Divinity . . . is being taken over by the totality of the human",[31] this can mean two things: it can signify modern man's loss of God and of himself, but it can also imply that, through God's becoming man, Christ has become a historical archetype.[32] The first version could be interpreted along the

[26] A, 380.   [27] Bz, 203; A, 56 WO, 207.

[28] Hence Jung's hearty concurrence with the dogma of Mary's Assumption into Heaven: E, 205, n. 2, 334.

[29] On "quaternity": G, 21ff.; Bz, 184ff.; A, 321–78; WO, 179–204; Al; Jung, *Mysterium Conjunctionis* I, 5ff., 229ff.

[30] H, 31. On the problem of evil in God cf. the memoirs E, 61–65; also PR, 72f.; Al, 36. He correctly recognizes that the full notion of the devil only emerges with Christianity, as a counterreality to Christ: E, 105.

[31] PR, 97.

[32] As stated in the interpretation of Gerhard Zacharias, *Psyche und Mysterium*.

lines of *E. Bloch*; the second is assuredly nearer to *Jung's* inner-most attitude.[33] However, we are still left with the question whether this projection onto God of a polarity structure that is typical of the creature (adducing the *coincidentia oppositorum* of *Cusanus* and the split Divinity of *Böhme*) can lead conditioned man beyond himself to the unconditioned, to that which con-ditions him.

Jung is acquainted with a transcendence of the empirical ego (in the process of individuation) toward the superordinate[34] self, a totality that can only be reached in an approximate manner. But he also speaks of an a priori on the part of the self; initially seeming to be abstract, it incarnates itself, of itself, in the ego.[35] In this apriority, the self (which can only be ap-proached in symbols)[36] can also appear and manifest itself in personal images.[37] Thus (in a Kantian manner, and similarly to *Freud*) he can say that "the individuated ego experiences itself as the object of an unknown and superordinate subject", an ex-travagant idea, since the "notion of the self is already a transcendent postulate".[38] In this context we frequently come across the word "grace" or "voice";[39] however, prayer never becomes a foundational act.

Die Bedeutung der Psychologie C. G. Jungs für die christliche Theologie und Liturgie. Studien aus dem C. G. Jung-Institut V (Rascher, 1954), 22ff.

[33] "At that time I suddenly realized that, for me at least, God was one of the most certain and direct experiences" (E, 67). Cf. also *Wirklichkeit der Seele*, 3d ed. (Rascher, 1939), 23.

[34] Bz, 98f.; A, 18.   [35] WO, 203f.; A, 55.   [36] WO, 171.

[37] Bz, 207. Cf. E, 325–27: "I am projected by the magic lantern as C. G. Jung. But who is operating it?" Jung dreams of a yogi who meditates *him*: "I knew that when he wakes up, I shall be no more." But what is doing this projecting, this thinking, is once again understood as an "unconscious totality", which, as such, is "the actual *spiritus rector* of all biological and psychic events". In spite of this, however, he speaks of the "influence of the greater personality, the 'inward human being', on the life of everyone"; cf. *Von den Wurzeln des Bewusstseins* (1954).

[38] For example, E, 338.

[39] "Since the contents of the soul are only conscious and perceptible to the extent that they are associated with an ego, the phenomenon of the voice" (he means an interior voice, inwardly addressing us) "with its markedly personal character, could possibly also originate in an *ego-center* that is not identical with the conscious ego. This conclusion is permissible if we view the ego as subordinate to, and contained in, a superordinate self which is the center of the entire, unlimited and undefinable psychic personality" (PR, 51). In this tentative

Thus we come back to the ultimate question of this "individuation", the process of becoming a "self". *Jung* places these two concepts at the heart of his reflections.[40] He calls this self "individual, in the strictest opposition to the Freudian superego".[41] He calls it the "central point of the personality", not of course residing in the empirical ego, but "situated in the middle between consciousness and the unconscious",[42] as the highest "synthesis"[43] of the two; thus it is two things at once: subjectively it is rendered "most intimately and extremely solitary", but objectively it has "the totality of the universe for its background".[44] Only in this paradox can *homo totus*[45] be grasped; he is self-realization or a process of "selving" (*Verselbstung*), "insofar as we understand individuality to mean our innermost, ultimate and incomparable uniqueness",[46] leading into that complete loneliness to which *Jung* refers, at the beginning and end of his memoirs, as his destiny.[47] But this is also an incarnation of that totality into which he has transcended himself and to which he has surrendered himself. Christ and Buddha are continually mentioned at this point: Christ as the "highest symbol of the self",[48] an "embodiment of the archetype of the self".[49] Thus we should not "follow" him externally but, as his "mystical members", allow him to live in us.[50] Christ must necessarily be history and myth (archetype) at one and the same time, so that he can be both a unique incarnation and an event

---

formulation the *ego-center* (my italics) would have to be something different from the mere "unconscious totality" in note 37 above.

[40] "At the center of my psychological discoveries stands . . . individuation" (E, 206; cf. 213: the "central concept of my psychology: the process of individuation"). "At that time, in my reflections, I reached the central point of my psychology, namely, the idea of the self" (E, 211).

[41] WO, 282.   [42] Bz, 175f.   [43] Al, 36; WO, 206.

[44] WO, 207.

[45] Al, 17.   [46] Bz, 91.

[47] E, 47 (on his youth: "an almost unbearable loneliness"; "[a]nd today I am still lonely"). On his old age: E, 397–98. Here we meet the view which is found elsewhere too, e.g., "The solitary person does not experience fellowship, and fellowship blossoms only where each individual is aware of his distinctive nature and does not identify himself with the others" (Bz, 59, note). During the period of almost ten years when Jung devoted himself to the influence of the archetypes, he was totally alone in all his decisive experiences. The same is true of the decades he spent on gnostic and alchemistic studies.

[48] Al, 35.   [49] A, 64.   [50] Al, 19.

taking place everywhere;[51] but Buddha is "the more complete human being".[52] Buddha also is a better embodiment of quaternity, the symbol of totality—for *Jung* the Christian idea of the Trinity is basically deficient. But whether man is conceived according to one model or the other, and even if he attains the greatest possible completeness, he retains the profound ambiguity we have already mentioned, which springs ultimately from the fact that his fundamental "I" is envisaged as a phenomenon of the collective. Thus "the self is not only indeterminate but—paradoxically—has a character of determinateness, indeed of uniqueness."[53] Or again: "Knowing myself to be unique in my personal combination . . . I can also become aware of that which has no limits. . . . Uniqueness and limitation are synonyms."[54]

This expression shows that the acceptance of limitation is *Jung's* last word too. This is not an acceptance of the role or the mask (persona), for *Jung* regards the latter as a mere wanting to appear other than one is—it is something that must be put aside and transcended. It is an acceptance of the insight that our attempt to embrace totality can never succeed in such a way that we can identify ourselves with it, that is, with the divine. It may be that the divine has to incarnate itself "in order to be all in all", but we ourselves never represent this incarnation. At most, we move among symbols of the totality, and they take effect in us. The greatest danger we have to avoid is that of "mana personality", becoming identified with the absolute hero or the wisest sage.[55] We should avoid the "arrogance of the ego" and strive for "that intermediate degree of modesty that is necessary if we are to maintain a condition of balance".[56] "We do not know what life is. . . . Man's life is ambivalent and tentative."[57] "The human being is a part and cannot grasp the whole."[58] "We can spend our entire lives thinking that we are following our own plans, never discovering that, for the most part, we are supernumeraries on the world stage."[59]

---

[51] PR, 104–5. From this standpoint Jung can describe Christ as the Lord of the (present) aeon: A and E, 224.

[52] E, 283. [53] Al, 35. [54] E, 328. [55] Bz, 184ff. [56] A, 47.

[57] E, 11. [58] E, 356. [59] E, 96.

c. Alfred Adler

Adler[1] distanced himself from *Freud* at an early stage (1904), although the final break only occurred in 1911. His initial studies concerned organ inferiority and its compensation and over-compensation by the organ itself or by other organs;[2] subsequently he transposed this model into the existential realm[3] and found that it applied to both the normal and the pathological mind—the difference between them being only one of degree.[4] Quite early on we find his approach being called "individual psychology" (1908); this means that each individual has his unique psychic constellation and is an "indivisible individuality".[5] Speaking of "types" is only a rule of thumb; "it can never explain the individual case" but only serves to "throw light on a general area, where the individual case must be discovered in its uniqueness".[6] Consequently the doctor needs to have a positively divinatory gift for grasping each particular individual totality, "best of all through artistic contemplation, intuiting the nature

---

[1] Adler's works quoted here: *Studie über Minderwertigkeit von Organen* (1907, new printing 1965), referenced here as O; *Über den nervösen Charakter* (1912, reprint by Fischer in 1972 with intro. by Wolfgang Metzger), referenced here as N; *Heilen und Bilden* (with Carl Furtmüller, 1914, containing the early essays since 1904), referenced here as H; *Praxis und Theorie der Individual-psychologie* (1920, edition of 1930 reprinted in Darmstadt, 1965), referenced here as P [*The Practice and Theory of Individual Psychology*, London, 1940]; *Menschenkenntnis* (1927, reprint by Fischer in 1966 with intro. by O. Brachfeld), referenced here as M; *Individualpsychologie in der Schule* (1929, reprint by Fischer in 1973 with intro. by W. Metzger), referenced here as S; *Der Sinn des Lebens* (1933, reprint by Fischer in 1973 with intro. by W. Metzger), referenced here as L [*What Life Should Mean to You*, London, 1933].

[2] O, 11ff.

[3] Cf. "Der Aggressionstrieb im Leben und in der Neurose" (1908), in: H, 23ff., esp. 27. "Über neurotische Disposition" (1909), in: H, 56ff., esp. 59f.

[4] H, 50; N, 36; M, 21.   [5] P, 16.

[6] L, 30. This is continually emphasized: "What is unique about an individual cannot be encapsulated in a short formula" (L, 30); the human being is an "indivisible whole" (L, 33); "The path to mastery is different for each individual, with nuances a thousandfold. Consequently we have no words to do anything more than describe what is typical" (L, 56f.); "And it is precisely each individual's differentness that manifests the unique creation which is the child" (L, 70); "We are in the presence of the millionfold differences . . . and now the difficult task begins—to discover that which is individual" (L, 117f.); "Each instance (manifests) itself differently" (L, 167).

of the patient".[7] What is unique expresses itself in a life's freely chosen "law of movement"; movement, in turn, "becomes a movement with a shape, it becomes form". Thus "the human being can be recognized on the basis of such form";[8] finally, the form is seen to be a "frozen movement"[9] and can be described as a *Gestalt*[10]—here is the link with *Gestalt* psychology—provided that the law of movement inherent in the form is able to manifest itself in the latter.[11] For *Adler*, however, the law of movement of a human being is always a matter of his correct or incorrect attitude toward his social environment; this "individual psychology" can equally be called "social psychology";[12] hence, too, for *Adler*, psychology and ethics increasingly converge.

The issue here is explicitly one of renewing the *Gnothi Sauton*[13] (against the background of the Freudian insights but developing away from them), of pedagogically "awakening self-knowledge".[14] This is all the more necessary since, according to *Adler's* basic insight, man (and particularly neurotic man) conceals from himself his deepest ambition, the blueprint of his understanding of life and corresponding law of action.[15] "Nothing in man's life and development is pursued with such secrecy as the erection of his personality ideal."[16] One can speak of man's being "unaware", but with a proviso:[17] "The human being knows more than he understands."[18] He becomes the

---

[7] P, 29. "Good guesswork also helps us to master the task set before us" (L, 33). "Artistic guesswork" (L, 167).

[8] L, 67.   [9] L, 71.   [10] L, 107.   [11] L, 163.

[12] S, 121. Cf. the expression "*Positionspsychologie*" and Metzger's explanation of it: N, 18ff.

[13] N, 92.

[14] S, 43. "We always have the 'Know thyself' as the sovereign educational method; it enables us to furnish the child with a complete understanding of its mistakes." This "is no easy task" (S, 93).

[15] Adler is fond of adducing Nietzsche's dictum at this point: You did it, says memory. I cannot have done it, says man. "Ultimately the memory gives in" (N, 71). In general he bases himself on Nietzsche's "will to seem": N, 32, 54, whereas the expression "fiction" comes from Vaihinger.

[16] N, 82.

[17] Cf. P, 157f. "In consciousness there is only a pale reflection of it (the life plan), and sometimes even its opposite" (M, 95f.).

[18] L, 156. "We cannot even speak of a repressed unconscious here, but rather of an unconscious that is not understood, that is withdrawn from understanding" (L, 25); cf. P, 22 (note).

victim of the "artistic achievement"[19] of the fiction he has created.[20]

To understand this, we need to grasp two of *Adler's* basic presuppositions: man's initial situation, one of tension between individuality and community, and his free, goal-seeking behavior that leads to the building up of "character".

The categories "sense of personality"[21] and "sense of community"[22] are viewed partly as poles of tension in life (particularly in *Adler's* later attempts to construct a metaphysics of life) and partly as negative and positive poles (this chiefly at the beginning, corresponding to his point of departure: organ inferiority). The sense of community is "inborn". The sense of personality, however, arises as "a striving toward personal superiority", that is, as (over-)compensation for the child's original situation of inferiority; thus it is "acquired by experience, a general temptation, ceaselessly attempting to exploit the community for its own prestige."[23] In explanation of this shift of perspective—from proper, healthy self-love and self-affirmation to neurotic "aggression"[24] toward society in compensation for the experience of inferiority—*Adler* asserts that man is born more helpless than any animal;[25] "in fact every child is inferior over against life".[26] He generalizes this inferiority: "to be human means to feel inferior".[27] The child's "great insecurity",[28] its "restlessness which looks for compensation",[29] is the basis for the human being's teachability.[30] *Adler* can actually speak of man's "primal anxiety"[31] of not being able to

[19] L, 96.

[20] Sartre, an avid reader of Adler, has developed this further. Cf. J. Ratter, *Alfred Adler* (Rowohlt, 1972), 76, 80; Brachfeld, in M, 13.

[21] N, 63.

[22] The ubiquitous, chief category, developed particularly in L.

[23] P, V. Thus he can speak of "the pair of opposites: the feeling of inferiority and the personality ideal" (N, 93).

[24] Adler's starting point is the Freudian aggressive instinct ("Der Aggressionstrieb im Leben und in der Neurose" [1908], in H, 23ff.), but then he increasingly distances himself from Freud and interprets aggression as a neurotic, antisocial ego-emphasis: N, 33–34; M, 170–204; L, 71.

[25] "From the point of view of nature, man is an inferior being" (M, 39). This view is evidently related to the basic ideas of A. Portmann.

[26] M, 71. The child "begins its life with suffering and difficulties" (S, 39).

[27] L, 67.   [28] N, 47.   [29] M, 150.

[30] P, 10; M, 44; N, 66: *Bildsamkeit*.   [31] M, 239; S, 83.

cope with life's superior power. And insofar as man's ultimate goal, of mastering life, is "larger than life",[32] and he therefore strives for an "unattainable, ideal perfection",[33] and since the fulfillment of his sense of community is likewise "an unattainable ideal",[34] it is only too easy for him to embrace neurotic goals,[35] the "masculine protest"[36] or the "will to power",[37] and so forth. On the other hand, the "sense of community"—a "biological inheritance"[38]—is assured, since it is "inborn";[39] with a certain pathos he describes it as the "immortal" sense;[40] it is "the absolute truth"[41] of human existence, indeed, it is even "absolute logic".[42] It expresses itself in the child's need for caresses and must meet with a correct response from the mother's love (which determines practically everything): she must not be cold, nor yet must she spoil the child.[43] The sense of community must be developed in such a way that the child accepts "his role as a fellow human being",[44] learns how to be an "actor" ("player") like others,[45] to forget himself,[46] to think of others,[47] to understand that it is more blessed to give than to receive[48] and "that unjustified wishes must be recognized as infringing the sense of community".[49] A certain unease remains (and it has been underlined by *Wolfgang Metzger*): Has the social sense (phylogenetically and in the individual) arisen only out of the weakness of the isolated individual,[50] or is not man's entire constitution (even at the level of the senses) oriented to "solidarity"?[51]

---

[32] P, 6.   [33] L, 35.   [34] S, 29.

[35] M, 43. "God-likeness": N, 84, P, 20 and frequently elsewhere. Hence he rejects the religious ideal of man as the "image of God" (M, 189).

[36] Adler recognizes the historical conditioning involved in the overvaluing of the male sex (with its wanting to be "on top", corresponding to the position in the sexual act): prior to the male society—still dominant—there was matriliny (M, 117ff.). Adler often stresses the importance of the women's movement and its fight for completely equal rights, cf. M, 136.

[37] N, 77.   [38] L, 17.   [39] N, 66.   [40] N, 26; P, 7, 19.

[41] M, 37. "Through the degree of the sense of community . . . we acquire a firm standpoint from which we can judge what is right and what is not" (L, 72). "Absolute truth . . . eternal rightness" (L, 171).

[42] N, 27. "A thing is only logical if it is universally valid" (with regard to the human community) (M, 40).

[43] This point of view dominates in the late work *Der Sinn des Lebens*.

[44] M, 114.   [45] L, 33; cf. P, 45.   [46] L, 48.   [47] S, 30.

[48] N, 72.   [49] L, 175.   [50] S, 34.   [51] S, 34, 55.

And what of the individual's cultural achievements? Are they the product of a biological urge for superiority or rather an interest in something that is of value for all?[52]

In the difficult situation in which the child is feeling its way in a world that initially it cannot master, *Adler's* second thrust becomes dominant: the Freudian orientation to causality is overthrown by an orientation to finality. We cannot think, feel, will or act "without having some goal before us. . . . The life of the human psyche, like the character created by a good dramatist, takes its bearing from the fifth act."[53] Reason becomes an essentially "foreseeing", planning organ[54] that attempts "to hold fast, in fixed forms, through unreal assumptions and fictions, what is chaotic, fluid, never-graspable;[55] it "runs on ahead of" reality and becomes an "organ of defense and attack" against reality.[56] "It tends to make for security."[57] It draws up a "life plan",[58] adopts and rehearses a "role" that, in its fixedness, can become fatal.[59] The most contrary modes of behavior can be used to implement this role, depending on the situation; this results in the meaning of "ambivalence" as found in *Freud* and *Jung* being completely reversed.[60] "A person may pursue two

[52] Metzger refers to Adler's little treatise (1928) "Kurze Bemerkungen über Vernunft, Intelligenz und Schwachsinn", in which Adler casts "his eyes over these borders, like Moses, without stepping over them" (S, 11). Cf.: "Accordingly it would be a prime task of education to prevent people falling from the healthy feeling of 'I can't yet' into the feeling of inferiority in the second [harmful] sense" (S, 13). In this treatise the idea emerges that effort can and should be directed "not toward one's own perfection, but toward the perfection of the work" (L, 21).

[53] P, 2–3. "Thus the life of the human soul is determined by a goal" (M, 31). In this connection Adler evinces his fundamental agreement with William Stern's (supracausal) theory of the person presented in Stern's great work *Person and Thing*, 3 vols. (1906–23): P, 1; N, 31, 36.

[54] S, 36.   [55] N, 58.   [56] N, 66.

[57] N, 64. It creates "stereotypes" by the "fiction of abstraction" (N, 63).

[58] L, 18. On "building into the empty future": N, 69.

[59] S, 33: If a child "is set a task that is no part of its role, we see what it can do. It is like the theatre: someone who has always played comic roles suddenly has to appear in a tragedy, and everyone laughs. Every child steps out into life equipped with its own role-consciousness and always acts according to it." The "role-consciousness" can also be a "role-unconscious". "Then, after a time, it becomes mechanical" (S, 43).

[60] N, 104; cf. M, 82, 155. In this connection Adler discusses the problem of

contrary purposes and yet will one and the same thing",[61] now attacking and now retreating, in an "attitude of hesitation",[62] a weakness that tyrannizes those around him. We need to examine all behavior with regard to its "whither". Two things result from this: in the first place, a high assessment of man's original, constructive freedom right from childhood,[63] which employs all the material of the psyche as "means"; furthermore, the denial of any predetermined and fixed "character".[64] "Character is man's spiritual approach, the way he stands over against his environment; it is the path along which his sense of personal worth asserts itself together with this sense of community. . . . Consequently, traits of character are only the external manifestations of a person's line of movement", they are not inborn but "acquired" and must always "be seen teleologically".[65] Thus, along a different path, *Adler* approaches the "persona" of *Jung*. He is of the opinion "that a particular characteristic of this line of movement must be an indestructible unity. This is what enables us to grasp a human being as a unitary personality."[66] "Thus the person bears the character traits required by his fictitious goal, just as the character-mask—the persona—of the actor in ancient tragedy had to be appropriate to the tragedy's finale."[67]

Here we must protest, and for two reasons: if man, in a freedom which is his birthright, attributes an "indestructible unity" to himself, is this only his mask ("persona", in the Jungian sense) or is it his irreplaceable individuality, which was so strongly emphasized at the beginning? Surely, however, the role of the physician is to bring the neurotic, "through the conscious development of the sense of community . . . consciously to abandon the striving for power",[68] that is, to demonstrate the nonnecessity of his persona and reach back to that original freedom according to which he can fashion himself teleologically. But this leads to the second question: If every human being finds

---

hermaphroditism (P, 14f., 23; N, 95–96) and finally of homosexuality.

[61] P, 40.   [62] P, 70.

[63] Strongly emphasized in M, 27, 29 ("free will" in the context of the organism's "free mobility"), M, 32 (free commitment to the chosen goal).

[64] N, 37; M, 146ff.   [65] M, 146–47.   [66] M, 82.

[67] B, 81.   [68] P, 10.

his "truth" (predominantly) in cultivating his sense of community, in fitting into the play of human society, what has happened to his "uniqueness"? Does it lie merely in the status allotted to him by society, which he is free to affirm? Is this where the "unity of the ego",[69] the "unity of the personality",[70] the "unity of the individuality"[71] is to be found? If this were the final result, "individual psychology" would really and truly dissolve into the sociology of roles. And in fact this is what happens in *Adler*, although in his last works he manifests the ambition to offer something more, namely, "a piece of metaphysics".[72]

The person-society system is extrapolated into the cosmic realm: there is a tendency even at the atomic and cellular level "to be a whole",[73] "partly through the processes of rounding out and setting limits, partly through the addition of further parts". The whole is an "evolution", a "constant development",[74] with the "creative energy that is found in every living being".[75] But this goal of the being's own perfection is portrayed as both attainable and unattainable. What is attainable is that—as *Adler* frequently repeats—everyone can feel himself "a part of the whole" and can act as such with increasing success.[76] Consequently it is "our task to fashion the child into an instrument of social progress. That is the heart of individual psychology as a world-view."[77] For then, socialized man feels himself "to be a reflection of the interrelatedness of all cosmic reality".[78] In glaring contrast to and criticism of *Freud*, fellow humanity is praised as the highest value. "Consequently it is the way a man acts in the place appointed to him by the community's distribution of labor that establishes his value."[79] Seen in this light, even the constitutive sense of inferiority appears "a blessing",[80] since it enables man to get in tune with humanity's infinite striving. Individual psychology trains man in the attitude "that can be

---

[69] L, 125.   [70] L, 155.   [71] P, 1.   [72] S, 166.   [73] L, 53.
[74] S, 35.   [75] L, 163.
[76] S, 35–36, 55; L, 23. We ought to "approach a situation in which there is more contribution, greater cooperation, and in which each individual acts—more than heretofore—as a part of the whole" (L, 168).
[77] S, 35–36. Cf. N, 26.   [78] M, 65.   [79] M, 114.
[80] L, 69.

taken as valid for the most remote future",[81] for "our idea—
according to which the sense of community is the ultimate form
of humanity, a condition in which we envisage all questions of
life, of our relation to the external world as being solved"[82]—
carries within it "the goal of an ideal community" in which
"man will radiate a sense of community just as naturally as he
breathes".[83] However, such passages, which clearly show that
Adler considers this ideal to be within reach,[84] are contradicted
by others which portray it as unattainable, "man's yearning to
raise himself, to fly, to achieve the impossible".[85] "Every new
idea lies beyond immediate experience",[86] and so the development cannot come to a conclusion.[87] We are to be those "who
feel at home on this poor earth's crust",[88] yet with an insatiable
"upward urge", which is nothing other than the urge of life
itself. In this contradiction *Adler* has reached his limit; it is the
authentically Jewish limit, and he cannot get beyond it. The
Christian *Rudolf Allers*,[89] pursuing *Adler's* path, will try to solve
the contradiction. *Adler's* neurotic is striving to be "unique", to
be "like God",[90] and the physician's task is to drive out these
notions, the best projection of which is "the concept of God
itself".[91] Religion is mainly seen as neurotic[92] and egoistic.[93] At
this point *Adler* does not have the breadth of *Jung*. In *Adler's*
context the idea that the individual's authentic uniqueness might
be guaranteed by God cannot occur; indeed, even in *Jung*, as in
the whole internal realm of psychology, it could not occur.
Adler's man must *accept his limits* and become one with his social
role. All the same *Adler*, in a way that is different from that of

---

[81] L, 164.   [82] L, 167.

[83] L, 172. Earlier, Adler liked to speak of the "compulsion" exercised by life
in society, to which the individual must yield, e.g., P, 18.

[84] "Personally I have no doubt that this stage will be reached, albeit perhaps
at a very remote time"; then the sense of community will "operate automatically,
like breathing and walking upright" (L, 39).

[85] N, 56.   [86] L, 166.

[87] Already quoted: P, 6; S, 29; L, 35.

[88] L, 101.

[89] *Die Erziehung der sittlichen Person. Wesen und Erziehung des Charakters*
(Herder, 1929).

[90] P, 20.   [91] L, 165.   [92] M, 207; cf. N, 61.   [93] M, 231.

Jung and possibly more direct, has centered on those human values that lie in the approaches to the Christian world-view and that could not have been discerned apart from it. In *Adler's* very first essay (1904) we read: "Love is the most important resource in education."[94]

3. *Sociology*

By its very nature sociology is concerned, not with the question "Who am I?" (in contrast with everyone else), but with what is common to all human subjects, with their socialization. If we assume, however, that each of these subjects is a unique "I" and ask how this unique subject can participate in the universally accessible (and, indeed, obligatory) form or role of common humanity in such a way that it persists through the latter (or perhaps only comes into being as a result of it), we are bound to confront this fundamental question after all. It is precisely the difference between the "I" and his social role, his "alienation" (*Hegel*) from himself in generality and his subsequent self-revindication, that has produced a wealth of role-sociology in recent decades. We must take a brief look at this sociology, not least because it continually and explicitly uses the analogy of the theatre, both with regard to the difference between person and role in the actor and also with regard to the dramatic process as a whole.

It has a manifold prehistory with many branches,[1] partly in sociology itself (*E. Durkheim* and his theory of the objective facticity of social realities; *G. Simmel*), and partly in social psychology,[2] where *William James* had already distinguished the

[94] H, 5.

[1] Most fully described in Biddle and Thomas, *Role Theory, Concepts and Research* (New York, London, Sydney, 1966), which gives 34 antecedents for the "theatre" analogy and includes a bibliography of 1400 titles. Cf. also the large bibliography in Uta Gerhardt, *Rollenanalyse als kritische Soziologie*, Soziol. Texte 72 (Luchterhand, 1971), referenced here as G. This work assembles and critically assesses all the nuances of a widely ranging research.

[2] Cf. Manfred Sander, "Rollentheorie", in *Handbuch der Psychologie*, vol. 7,

pure "I" from the social self which lives in the role-expectations of its environment,[3] and *C. H. Cooley* described the self as a mirror-reflex, reflected from the environment back onto the "I",[4] up to *G. H. Mead*, in whose posthumous work *Mind, Self and Society*,[5] is portrayed the integration of the "I" (the positing consciousness) and the "me" (the consciousness posited in the context of one's fellow human beings, which reflects back upon the "I") in the identity of the "self". (Note that this self, as an end product, has been mediated by society far more than in *C. G. Jung.*) In 1936 *Ralf Linton*[6] laid the foundation of an explicit role-sociology with his distinction between "status" (the sum of the individual's diverse positions in society) and "role" (the dynamic aspect in the living-out of status, soon to be termed "position").

Ralf Dahrendorf, with his *Homo sociologicus* (1958), was the spokesman for role-psychology in Germany, basing himself primarily on *Talcott Parsons*. Quoting the chapter in *E. R. Curtius*, he once again traced[7] the theatrical origin of the concept, where "role" can alternate with "mask, person, character". He lists the points of analogy: (1) role as something allotted to the actor; (2) role as a complex of behavior patterns which (3) form part of the totality of behavior occurring in the play—hence the role is termed a "part"; (4) the role is something that must be learned but (5) is not exhaustive as far as the actor is concerned, for he can learn and play many roles and is not inwardly affected by them.[8] This last point is the really characteristic one in Dahrendorf's view. If the common starting point of all role-sociology is the dualism between the "I" and the role ("me"), and if role is fundamentally a socially prescribed "behavior-expectation"[9]—or more precisely, "a bundle of behavior norms"

"Sozialpsychologie", pt. 1: "Theorie und Methode" (1969), 204–31 (with bibliography).

[3] *Psychology* (New York, 1892), 177ff.

[4] *Human Nature and Social Order* (New York, 1902).

[5] G. H. Mead, *Mind, Self and Society* (Chicago, 1934).

[6] *The Study of Man* (New York, 1936).

[7] Ralf Dahrendorf, *Ein Versuch zur Geschichte, Bedeutung und Kritik der Kategorie der sozialen Rolle* (quoted according to the 12th printing, Obladen, 1973), referenced here as *Der sozialen Rolle*.

[8] *Ibid.*, 21–23.   [9] *Ibid.*, 63.

(*Heinrich Popitz*)[10]—we are faced with this crucial question: "Does the man Smith begin where his roles come to an end? Does he live in his roles?"[11] Here two anthropologies confront each other. One is based on *Kant*[12] and is represented by *Dahrendorf*; according to it, man, entering into the role offered him by society, becomes alienated, a scientific statistic: "The unique becomes an instance, the individual becomes a member of a class, the free, autonomous creature becomes a product of his alienated characters";[13] consequently he must return, through reflection, from his empirical character to his "intelligible character", and from this position "the individual can assert himself against the claims of society".[14] The other anthropology is based on *Hegel* and advocated by numerous opponents of *Dahrendorf* (for instance, *F. H. Tenbruck*[15] and *Helmuth Plessner*);[16] according to this, "man does not and cannot exist within roles";[17] the theory that work is "self-alienation" is an ideology that is compromised by idealism's identity thesis and fails to take account of man's eternal dual nature.[18] We

[10] Heinrich Popitz, "Der Begriff der sozialen Rolle als Element der soziologischen Theorie", in *Recht und Staat* 331/332 (Tübingen, 1967), 21; referenced here as "Der Begriff der sozialen Rolle".

[11] Dahrendorf, *Der sozialen Rolle*, 79–80.

[12] *Ibid.*, 86. Contrary to the German view: "We cannot understand Kant apart from Hegel" (113).

[13] *Ibid.*, 81.   [14] *Ibid.*, 113.

[15] F. T. Tenbruck, "Zur deutschen Rezeption der Rollentheorie", in *Kölner Zeitschrift für Soziologie und Sozialpsychologie* 12 (1961): 1ff.

[16] "Soziale Rolle und menschliche Natur", in *Erkenntnis und Verantwortung. Festschrift für Th. Litt* (Düsseldorf, 1960), 105–15.

[17] Tenbruck, *"Zur deutschen Rezeption der Rollentheorie"*, 31. Jurgen Ristert argues (on the basis of Kant) against Dahrendorf and related theories: "If by freedom over against society we really mean those factors which allow men to raise themselves even above social determinants, we must not forget that Kant, in his third antinomy, had already seen that it was not sufficient to posit man as somehow lifted above such determinants, but that it was necessary critically to deduce a law of freedom referring to concrete acts and geared to the interrelatedness of rational beings" (*Handlungstheorie und Freiheitsautonomie* [Berlin, 1966], 134).

[18] "Renunciation [*Entäusserung*] does imply self-alienation [*Entfremdung seiner selbst*] . . . , it is an opportunity for man to be totally himself" (Plessner, "Soziale Rolle und menschliche Natur", 112). "Freedom must be able to play its part, and it cannot do this if the individuals see their social function as a mere

should note that each of these positions puts a foot into philosophical anthropology in order to justify its particular sociological thesis: one position does it to defend the individual's noumenal freedom against the superior strength of planning and manipulation;[19] the other to assure man, as he takes the risk of self-alienation that the role implies, that he will not lose his self.[20] The first sees man in a "situation that is not free of contradiction",[21] indeed in a situation of "genuine tragedy";[22] the second transcends this tragedy by assuming that man has an original "ex-centric" vantage point (for he both *is* and *has* a body and similarly both *is* and *has* a social role).[23] The first would like at all costs to prevent the transition from the sociological thought form—the *homo sociologicus* as a working hypothesis—into concrete reality but sees that this transition has already occurred in people's unscientific everyday understanding. Consequently it retreats to the scientifically unassailable ground of intelligible freedom. The second sees the human condition, in no less realistic terms, in man's irreversibly exposed situation in the midst of the world: "Thrust into life, man, a living organism, must himself create the conditions for life. . . . The fact that man is hidden from himself—*homo*

---

masquerade in which everyone is in disguise." Indeed: "Each person's ability to identify himself with something that, of himself, he is not, is the sole constant factor in the fundamental relationship between social role and human nature" (114–15). H. Plessner conducts a vigorous campaign against the Hegelian-Marxist concept of alienation in his Rectoral Address of 1960, *Das Problem der Öffentlichkeit und die Idee der Entfremdung* (Göttingen, 1960): "That element of the role which irks me, the compulsion it exercises upon my behavior, simultaneously guarantees the order I need if I am to achieve and maintain contact with others. The distance which the role creates . . . is the detour, characteristic of the human being, by which he arrives at his fellow man; it is the means whereby he attains immediacy" (18).

[19] "A nonresigned, political anthropology of protest against the alienation of society" (Dahrendorf, *Der sozialen Rolle*, 117).

[20] Cf. note 17.

[21] Dahrendorf, *Der sozialen Rolle*, 118.

[22] This is a reference to Max Weber's strict (Kantian) separation of science and value judgment, which had such tragic consequences, contrary to Weber's intentions and yet arising logically out of his position. For this separation produced a "value-free sociology" in which man disappeared "in the dignity of his freedom and individuality" (92–93).

[23] H. Plessner, *Die Stufen des Organischen und der Mensch* (Berlin, 1928).

absconditus—coincides with his openness to the world. He can never recognize himself fully in his deeds, only his shadow, which runs ahead of him and remains behind him."[24]

If one tries to translate *Plessner's* philosophically substantiated position into the terms of empirical sociology, his "man the *doppelganger*" soon becomes a being whose identity is threatened through a plethora of roles, reflections and masks. The path taken by *George H. Mead* in his chief work (1934)[25] leads from an "I" that projects itself as a "me"—both are "parts of the self"[26] —to an empirical integration or identity: "The 'I' reacts to the self which arises through the taking of the attitudes of others. Through taking those attitudes we have introduced the 'me', and we react to it as an 'I'."[27] "The basic relevance structures referring to everyday life are presented to me ready-made by the social stock of knowledge itself."[28] If self-identity depends on social processes—and we have seen that role was defined as normative social expectation—we are also faced with the disturbing question of the historical changes in these expectations, as *Jürgen Habermas*, among others, points out;[29] the individual who has submerged himself in a role must lose his identity (partially or wholly) if the expectations change. Should role theory presuppose a relative stability of the forms of alienation of the laborer in society and—in the face of today's "contractual world", which is structured in purely functional terms—be an ideology—of "middle-class culture", for instance—clinging to the past for reasons of power politics, as *Dieter Claassens* insinuates?[30] This also raises the question of whether "role" is an

[24] H. Plessner, "Homo absconditus", in *Philosophische Anthropologie heute*, ed. R. Rocek and O. Schatz (Munich, 1972), 40f., 43.

[25] German edition: G. H. Mead, *Geist, Identität und Gesellschaft aus der Sicht des Sozialbehaviorismus* (Suhrkamp, 1968); English edition: *Mind, Self and Society* (Chicago, 1963).

[26] G. H. Mead, *Mind, Self and Society*, 174.

[27] *Ibid.*, 174.

[28] Peter L. Berger and Thomas Luckmann, *The Social Construction of Reality* (Garden City, N.Y., 1966), 60. It is easy to see how an approach such as Mead's can be combined with Freud's genesis of the ego.

[29] *Theorie und Praxis* (Neuwied and Berlin, 1963), 174f.

[30] Dieter Claessens, "Rollentheorie als bildungsbürgerliche Verschleierungs-ideologie", in *Spätkapitalismus oder Industriegesellschaft? Verhandlungen des 16.*

"elementary category"[31] in understanding all sociological conditions or a secondary and "deducible"[32] one; whether it betrays
its historical origin in American society, which "is far more
familiar than we are with people changing their professions and
occupations", and sees itself "both practically and ideologically
as a totality of functions that give each person his position, his
role and his social prestige";[33] or whether "role" belonged more
to "traditional society", where everyone ("peasant" or "knight")
identified himself as a matter of course with the role in society
which fell to him.[34] In the latter case the concept of "role"
would be anachronistic in the context of today's dichotomy
between the role a person plays in society and his private sphere.
Would it not be better, therefore, to speak of "function",[35]
which can more easily be developed from the "expectation
ambivalence" and the corresponding "role conflicts" which
form man's normal situation for action?[36] Yet is not this very
dichotomy between the "I" and its changing social roles the
most apt starting point for every sociology of roles? Each of the

---

deutschen Soziologentages, Th. W. Adorno, ed. (Stuttgart, 1969); also the same
author's "Rolle und Macht", in Grundfragen der Soziologie, D. Claessens, ed., 2d
ed., vol. 6 (Munich, 1970).

[31] Dahrendorf, Der sozialen Rolle, 19.

[32] Popitz, "Der Begriff der sozialen Rolle", 8.

[33] Plessner, "Soziale Rolle und menschliche Natur", 106f.

[34] Claessens, in "Rolle und Macht", 45, adduces some very significant
quotations from Hegel's Rechtsphilosophie (sections 146, 147, 151) in which the
"laws and powers" of "ethical substance" in a society of this kind are "not
something alien" to the subject: "Spirit bears witness to them, that they are its own
nature, in which it possesses its sense of itself [Selbstegefühl], living in them as in an
element not distinct from itself—a relationship that is even more immediate and
identical than faith and trust."

[35] Claessens, "Rolle und Macht", 66: " 'Genuine' roles only existed in
traditional society. . . . It can be questioned whether 'role' implies anything
more than 'function'."

[36] According to R. K. Merton, Social Theory and Social Structure (Glencoe,
Ill., 1957), role conflict embodies the basic context of human behavior (380).
U. Gerhardt indicates three paths pursued by research with the aim of eliminating
role conflict: (1) Role conflict is eliminated by the effect of social mechanisms.
(2) Internalized values mediate between antagonistic normative expectations.
(3) The personality is seen as responsible for the individual's selecting an
appropriate strategy of behavior in a situation of conflict (G, 73). Only the third
path is of interest to us here.

approaches we have mentioned can be substantiated: the concept of "role" leaves room for every kind of notion of the self,[37]
particularly when "role" is understood in purely instrumental
terms.[38] But it is not the task of sociology to guarantee the
philosophical identity of the person who plays the role. Such
identity appears—in varying degrees—as the *result* of the role-
playing. This is so whether, on the basis of the modern dichotomy,
one discerns an entirely new "breadth of a sense of identity"[39]
arising behind the "role distance" and the willingness to "change
roles" (which could be nothing more, however, than arbitrariness in the "I"); or whether, with *T. W. Adorno*, one disclaims
any clinging either to the concept of role or to its stubborn
antithesis, the "firm selfhood of the 'I' ", and instead strives for
"the liberated 'I' which is no longer imprisoned in its identity".[40]
It applies equally if, logically following up *Mead's* line of thought
(like *Anselm Strauss*), we "even ask questions about the 'core of
the self' ", "that self which I assume to be behind or at the root
of all my actions".[41] And it applies if we take the ability to
distance oneself as the mark of individual identity (*E. H. Erikson*)[42]
or regard it as a product of the high-level detachment of the ego
image from particular roles (*H. P. Dreitzel*)[43] so that a distinction
can be drawn between "personal identity" (the self as the plane
of integration of diverging roles) and "social identity" (the self
as the representation of a particular role) (*E. Goffman*).[44] In this
way the reciprocal interplay of the two forms of identity can be
pointed out (*Oevermann* and others).[45] Provided one remained

[37] Popitz, "Der Begriff der sozialen Rolle", 16–17.

[38] *Ibid.*, 7.

[39] Claessens, *Rolle und Macht*, 178.

[40] *Negative Dialektik* (Frankfurt, 1966), 272f.

[41] *Mirrors and Masks. The Search for Identity* (New York, 1959).

[42] "The Problem of Ego-Identity", in *Identity and Anxiety*, Stein, Vidich,
White, eds. (New York and London, 1960).

[43] *Die gesellschaftlichen Leiden und das Leiden an der Gesellschaft: Vorstudien zu
einer Pathologie des Rollenverhaltens* (Stuttgart, 1968).

[44] *Stigma: Über Techniken der Bewältigung beschädigter Identität* (Frankfurt,
1967).

[45] Cf. G, 107 and the references to Simmel (*Soziologie* [1908], 413) and to
Popitz ("Soziale Normen", in *Europ. Archiv f. Soziologie* 2 [1961], 192), who
considers the possibility that there is "a link between the degree of unhomogeneity

aware of the methodological limitations of such an empirically developed "I" (which, to a certain extent, could also be dismantled), the totality could be held together under a philosophico-sociological umbrella. P. L. *Berger* and T. *Luckmann* also approach the borderline where the "I" becomes problematical, yet they do not step over it. In their "sociology of knowledge", they recognize the necessity of a legitimating instance for the " 'correctness' of the individual's subjective identity. By the very nature of socialization, subjective identity is a precarious entity." In the words of symbolic meaning (with religion at the peak), man creates the ultimate legitimation of his identity: "Mythologically speaking, the individual's 'real' name is the one given to him by his god. The individual may thus 'know who he is' by anchoring his identity in a cosmic reality protected from both the contingencies of socialization and the malevolent self-transformations of marginal experience."[46]

In this "sociology of knowledge" these two authors have created a method, free from all suspicion of ideology, that is able to unite the most opposed approaches. They do this by taking as their object the reality of the "everyday world"—which is always structured in social terms and equipped with a modicum of intersubjective knowledge[47]—and reflecting upon it as the "highest reality". This reveals the fundamental and irreducible circle: society is a human product.[48] Society is an objective

---

of the different social obligations and the degree in which the individual is conscious of himself as an individual existence. There is a latent conflict and competition between the norm-structures which intersect in the individual, and it may be that these have to become manifest before we can grasp the social bonds as a dimension of human life and gain that distance from ourselves which is specific to individual reflection." An assessment such as this is by no means totally nullified by the evidence of a (middle-)class bond and the analysis of "class-specific world models".

[46] Berger and Luckmann, *The Social Construction of Reality*, 118. On the religious problems involved, cf. the two works by P. L. Berger: *A Rumor of Angels, Modern Society and the Rediscovery of the Supernatural* (1969), and *Zur Dialektik von Religion und Gesellschaft: Elemente einer soziologischen Theorie* (Fischer, 1973).

[47] In this they follow Alfred Schütz in *Der sinnhafte Aufbau der sozialen Welt*, 2d ed. (Vienna, 1932, 1960), who translated the approach of his teacher, Edmund Husserl, from the "Lebenswelt" into the realm of sociology.

[48] "Similar modes of behavior . . . are not something invented by sociology,

reality. Man is the product of society.[49] Thus society is first of all the objectivization of reciprocal human behavior, institutionalizing it and legitimizing it in order to render it ultimately meaningful. Behavior is typified here in terms of roles that represent the social order; the individual, through his action, enters into these roles with a part of his self. This part is his actual "social self", which is experienced subjectively as distinct from his total self, indeed as "confronting the self in its totality".[50]

> First, performance of the role represents itself. For instance, to engage in judging is to represent the role of judge. . . . Second, the role represents an entire institutional nexus of conduct. The role of judge stands in relationship to other roles, the totality of which comprises the institution of law. . . . The institution, with its assemblage of "programmed" actions, is like the unwritten libretto of a drama. The realization of the drama depends upon the reiterated performances of its prescribed roles by living actors. The actors embody the roles and actualize the drama by representing it on the given stage [that is, in the—sociologized—everyday world].[51]

P. L. Berger will have to modify what he says here, as we shall show. First, however, we must reflect on the second step of his project, the "internalizing" of the legitimated, objective societal reality. This is something *Dahrendorf* was also aware of: "Just as an actor must learn his part, so must man as a social being. . . . Here we encounter a second basic mechanism of society, the process of socialization through the internalizing of norms of behavior."[52] For him this process, seen from the standpoint of society, was one of "depersonalization"; seen from the angle of the individual, however, it was the adoption of the given into his own interiority: he "makes it part of his own individual

---

but by society" and ultimately by human beings who founded society in the first place. Popitz, "Der Begriff der sozialen Rolle", 19. This process is necessary as a result of man's openness to the world; the "artificial" nature of social reality is indispensable to him and to that extent natural (Berger and Luckmann, *The Social Construction of Reality*, 65, referring to Plessner and Durkheim: *Les formes élémentaires de la vie religieuse* [Paris, 1912]).

[49] Berger and Luckmann, *The Social Construction of Reality*, 79.

[50] *Ibid.*, 91, with mention of Mead and of Durkheim's *Homo duplex*.

[51] *Ibid.*, 92.

[52] Dahrendorf, *Der sozialen Rolle*, 48.

personality".[53] At this point, however, *Berger* and *Luckmann* introduce a major distinction, namely, between primary and secondary socialization. Primary socialization takes place through "significant others" (*Mead*), first and foremost through the mother, and it lays the foundations for understanding one's context among fellow human beings and for "grasping the world as a meaningful and social reality". As a result of these "others", the child becomes able to identify with itself too, in a dialectical process "between identification through others and self-identification, between an identity objectively allotted to it and an identity which it subjectively makes its own".[54] This is followed by the step from the "significant" other to the "generalized" other (*Mead*). The child's identity is now no longer an identity vis-à-vis this or that significant other but has attained identity as such, corresponding to its openness to the world. At the same time "there are always elements of subjective reality", for instance, the sense of being in one's own body, "which do not have their roots in socialization"—as G. *Simmel* had already noted.[55] Only after this primary discovery of self comes the secondary socialization, "the internalization of institutional or institution-based 'subworlds' ", such as the growing child experiences in school and later in training for a career. Only here can there be the possibility of that "role distance" which a man can set between his self and his role-specific partial self. "This important feat is only possible after primary socialization has taken place"[56]—which relegates the problem discussed above, namely, where the role-system

[53] *Ibid.*, 58. Basing himself on Freud, he says that the social sanctions too are internalized as the "superego" and "conscience".

[54] Berger and Luckmann, *The Social Construction of Reality*, 158.

[55] *Soziologie*, 4th ed. (Berlin, 1958), 21–30. For Simmel, pure knowledge of individuality is impossible; if social knowledge is to exist at all, it must perceive types. But socialized man knows "that every element of a group is not only a part of society but something else as well", an "extrasocial being" which manifests a "different nuance each time" and whose "social image is shot through with *extrasocial* imponderabilia". This is certainly a sociological observation. Yet it is questionable whether, with U. Gerhardt, we can conclude that (in Simmel) "there is no extrasocial realm of the individual" (G, 31).

[56] Berger and Luckmann, *The Social Construction of Reality*, 162.

is really applicable, to a position of secondary significance. E. *Goffmann* sees this role distance as the only way in which human beings can maintain their dignity, at least in their own eyes.[57] However, "Since subjective reality is never totally socialized, it cannot be totally transformed by social processes";[58] this means that, in the healthy person, the transformations possible on the basis of this distance affect only the sphere of secondary internalization. Naturally it is possible for a child to be introduced into different worlds even in its primary socialization (for example, the parents introduce it to a middle-class world and the nurse to a proletarian world). Here there is the possibility of an "option", of choosing one identity rather than another, which involves one's being a "traitor to oneself" in a certain respect. "Individualism" can be used to describe the phenomenon whereby, as a result of unsuccessful primary socialization, the person is able to (and must) choose between different realities and identities; the individualist "has at least the potential to migrate between a number of available worlds and

[57] In his book *The Presentation of Self in Everyday Life* (New York, 1959), E. Goffman has followed the theatre metaphor as a model for everyday life in every detail. Not only is there the role in which a person wishes to be seen, there is also the self-contained ensemble of actors, with all that goes on behind the scenes. There are the audience, the front stage on which the action takes place and the back stage, which the spectator may not see, where, however, many important things are enacted. There is the person's belief in his own role, as well as his lack of belief in it, and frequently a "middle position that can be maintained with the help of a little self-deception". Goffman consistently follows up this "dramaturgic approach" as "an ultimate principle of organization", but places it as the fifth beside four others: the technical, political, structural and cultural principles. For him, the dramaturgic principle elucidates "the techniques of manipulative impression", and it is also indispensable to the other four principles. He does not go into the relationship between the (role-)self which "the actor puts forward during the performance" and which the spectators are inclined to accept, and the "person" giving this performance—who is something else; the person, with his body, only provides the temporary peg on which to hang what has been produced by a cooperative effort. The means of producing and affirming a self do not lie with the peg on which it is hung. In the end Goffman relativizes the system of concepts he has borrowed from the world of the stage; the theatrical action is an artificial illusion, unlike the structures of social encounter, which, in Goffman's terms, constitute a montage.

[58] Berger and Luckmann, *The Social Construction of Reality*, 176.

. . . has deliberately and consciously constructed a self out of the 'material' provided by a number of available identities".[59]

The "phenomenological" reference to the "option" concludes this sociology of knowledge, which consists of two departments: objectivization (institutionalization) and subjectivization (internalization). Empirical sociology can go no farther.

However, just as *Dahrendorf* kept hold of the Kantian postulate of freedom, a citadel that could not be invaded by a sociology intent on total planning, a freedom that alone can inform the whole social scene with human meaning, so *Peter L. Berger*, in his *Invitation to Sociology*, has complemented his first two aspects —"man in society" and "society in man"—by a third, in which he takes the liberty of leaving strict sociology behind and venturing into the "forbidden" philosophical area of freedom. He wants to see what happens to the sociological determinants when they are viewed in this perspective.[60] The first aspect ("man in society", that is, in the objective institution) is summed up in the image of "imprisonment":[61] man is at the center of concentric circles in a political and legal system that raises taxes and conscripts him into the armed forces, he is situated in a morality, an ethical code, accepted ways of behavior, career pressures; finally he is part of the control system of family and friends. . . . Whereas the animal is guided by its instincts, human activity—according to *Arnold Gehlen*[62]—is regulated by institutions whose imperatives seem inescapable. The second aspect ("society in man", internalization) seems to liberate him from imprisonment, since human beings generally accept the part allotted to them voluntarily. "The individual actors, therefore, need but slip into the roles already assigned to them before the curtain goes up."[63] "Each role has its inner discipline. . . .

---

[59] *Ibid.*, 191. More precise analyses in Gerhardt.

[60] Peter L. Burger, *Invitation to Sociology* (Garden City, N.Y., 1963). In fact this book should not have been called "Invitation to Sociology" but "an invitation to sociology to see itself in the context of an all-embracing anthropology".

[61] *Ibid.*, 109.

[62] *Urmensch und Spätkultur* (Bonn, 1956), which draws the sociological conclusions from his chief work, *DerMensch, seine Natur und seine Stellung in der Welt* (Frankfurt and Bonn, 1940).

[63] Berger, *Invitation to Sociology*, 112.

The role forms, shapes, patterns both action and actor."[64] Deviations from it are foreseen and sociologically staged; the whole is legitimated by comprehensive, internalized systems. What formerly appeared as imprisonment, since it was enforced from without, now seems to be laid upon us from within, by our own selves, just as much as by the influence of external forces: "A more adequate representation of social reality now would be the puppet theatre, with the curtain rising on the little puppets jumping about on the ends of their invisible strings, cheerfully acting out the little parts that have been assigned to them in the tragi-comedy to be enacted."[65]

Thus far sociology is authorized to go, and that is why we have included our consideration of it under the heading "Role as the Acceptance of Limitation"—notwithstanding all "internalization". Once again the role arises out of the grand totality; now, however, the latter is no longer the stoic cosmos-logos, no longer the Freudian or Jungian unconscious or Adler's sense of community and its ontic anticipation, but human social existence.

But for *P. L. Berger* this role-playing results in a mere puppet theatre. It is only the presupposition of freedom—in his "third sociological perspective"—that gives us "society as drama". Only when men involve themselves freely does their common action acquire a human "meaning". World history is substantially governed by the free creation of meaning on the part of great individuals (*Max Weber's* doctrine of "charisma"). Here role distance becomes possible, that is, the opportunity of freely choosing a life-role, of laying aside a role and transforming its meaning. " 'Role distance' marks the point at which the marionette clown becomes Bajaccio—the puppet theatre is transformed into a living stage."[66] "This third picture does not obliterate the previous two, but it is more adequate. . . ." Now, social reality suddenly becomes relatively dependent on "the cooperation of many individual actors. . . . Stage, theatre, circus and even carnival—here we have the imagery of our dramatic model, with a conception of society as precarious, uncertain, often unpredictable." "In this way, the dramatic

[64] *Ibid.*, 115.   [65] *Ibid.*, 140.   [66] *Ibid.*, 157.

model opens up a passage out of the rigid determinism into which sociological thought originally led us."[67]

Our question is "Who am I?" The reply that we are an emanation of the whole is unable to guarantee the personal uniqueness of individuals. No doubt, the acceptance of limitation will have to be one element of human existence, but it cannot be an end in itself, nor can it be the key to the whole picture. This being the case, should not man be emboldened to anchor his uniqueness where—in the phenomenology of ascending orders, according to their wider grasp of meaning—religious thought has already indicated, namely, in God? But if man takes his stand in eternity, does not all secular being and doing, that is, the role he has to play here below, turn into mere alienation?

[67] *Ibid.*, 159–60.

C. ROLE AS ALIENATION

1. *The Return to Man's Essence*

The stoics saw man as essentially active, freely and responsibly sharing in the activity of the entire Logos from his particular point in the cosmos. Late Neoplatonism saw man as essentially contemplative: in the fragility of the temporal he anchors his identity and dignity by looking backward and upward to the divine. As we have already said, both these attitudes are closely related; only within this close relationship are they opposed to one another. But the stoic has the divine behind him, so to speak, and maintains contact with it in that way, whereas the Neoplatonist has it before him and strives toward it, hoping to find his authentic self (*Eigentlichkeit*: this controversial word is unavoidable here). For the "many" is and remains ambiguous and preliminary: while it can also be regarded as a representation of the fullness of the "One" (as in stoic thought), at a more essential level it veils the latter, it is a decline, an alienation from it. The Platonic concept of the *regio dissimilitudinis*[1] becomes, in Neoplatonism, the epitome of all being outside the One; everything that can be subsumed scientifically under concepts is lacking in essence; *Fichte*, summing up the ethos of the Neoplatonic upward gaze, will describe the One as the tomb of all concepts. The concluding words of *Plotinus'* Enneads, *monos pro monon*, "the solitary before the solitary", is not so much an ideal of seclusion as the fundamental expectation of finding one's own uniqueness in the confrontation with the uniquely One. Thus everyone who desires to respond to the demands of the *Gnothi Sauton* will meet with an unexpected, albeit paradoxical, answer. Everyone will discover, in the uniquely One, his own inalienable uniqueness, a discovery that can coincide only with the loss of individual selfhood.

Proclus develops the Plotinian idea that that which generates

---

[1] The prime source for *regio dissimilitudinis* is Plato, *Politikos* 273D; the concept migrates via Plotinus to Augustine (*Conf.* VII, 10, n. 16) and Bernard. Cf. E. Gilson, *La théologie de S. Bernard* (Paris, 1947), 57, 63, 223.

is at a higher level and embraces more than that which is generated,[2] which means that the latter has a higher authenticity (*Eigentlichkeit*) in its origin than in itself, and that the caused is fulfilled by returning into its cause. This is also the basic movement in the system of *Scotus Eriugena*. The idea, however, is bound to crop up wherever God's absoluteness and nonnecessitous totality are taken seriously;[3] it seems that the conclusion must be drawn that, to the extent that creatures are, were or will be in God, they participate more in being and are more true there than in themselves. In spite of all the attempts to counterbalance it in Christian thought, this particular line persists; it is supported by that well-known punctuation of a verse from the Prologue of John's Gospel: "Quod factum est in ipso vita erat",[4] which seems to affirm that all creatures, including nonliving things, receive their original life in God. The idea is often repeated in *Augustine* in connection with his exposition of Platonic ideas, but he emphasizes that the "life" which creatures always had in God from all time is the life of God himself, the *vita creatrix*.[5] Thus, as it were incidentally and as a matter of course, the idea arises that, in God, things are "better and truer, because they are

---

[2] *Institutio Theologica*, prop. 7.

[3] The idea of this totality is put forward most impressively and tirelessly by Gregory the Great. Cf. Michael Frickel, *Deus totus ubique simul. Untersuchungen zur allgemeinene Gottegegenwart im Rahmen der Gotteslehre Gregors des Grossen* (Herder, 1956). What Gregory regarded as the Creator's "support" and "maintenance" (*sustenare*), his "containing" (*continere*) of the creature, was, in Neoplatonism, the "embracing" (*perioche̅*, *ambitus*) of the cause vis-à-vis the effect.

[4] The comma can be placed after *est* or after *ipso*. On the spread of this incorrect punctuation (Tertullian, Origen, Cyril, Ambrose, Augustine, Bede, Rupert, Albert, Bonaventure, Thomas) see J. Knabenbauer, *Evang. sec. Joh., Cursus S. Scripturae* (1898), 70ff.

[5] *De Gen. ad Litt*. II, 6, 12 (PL 34, 268): the creature's two modes of being are clearly distinguished: being in itself, but contained by God, and being in God; "in illo sunt ea quae ipse est". Thus stones etc. live not in themselves but in God, since God is eternal life (*De Gen. ad Litt*. V, c 14, 31). What in itself is distinct and separate is a living unity in God; "omnia vita sunt et omnia unum sunt, et magis unum est et vita est" (*De Trin*., lib. 4, c 1, 3). "In its finished form a wooden chest is not life, but in its design and execution [*in arte*] it is life, because the soul of the craftsman is alive" (*In Joan*. tr. 3, 4). On the doctrine of ideas: *De div. quaest*. q. 46 (PL 40, 29–31).

eternal and unchangeable".[6] Later on this will be underlined; when the *Summa* of *Alexander* quotes *Augustine*, it adds, by way of interpretation: since creatures are in God according to the unchanging idea he has of them, "magis sunt vita in ipso quam in seipsis".[7] *Anselm* repeats *Augustine*,[8] only adding that the changeable beings "are all the more true and noble" the more they approach the absolute mode of being that they have in God.[9] However, the *Summa* of *Alexander* insists that things have one being in the life and Spirit of God, and one in themselves; yet their life in themselves adds nothing to the absolute life of God.[10] *Rupert of Deutz* expresses himself similarly.[11] The question crops up all the time in scholasticism; the view that, in God, existents possess "not only a true and genuine being but . . . a far higher [*superius*], more noble [*nobilius*], more sublime [*sublimius*], more eminent [*eminentius*] and more excellent [*excellentius*] being than they possess in themselves" is "one of the standard teachings of ancient and medieval philosophy".[12] *Bonaventure* distinguishes between the being of things "in the eternal prototype", "in the created reason" and "in the world itself"; if we ask whether things have a truer being in God or in themselves, the initial answer is: in themselves as existing beings. Only then is the

---

[6] "Priusquam fierent, erant in notitia facientis. Et utique ibi meliora, ubi veriora, ubi aeterna et incommutabilia" (*De Gen. ad Litt.* V, 5, 15, 33).

[7] Ed. Quaracchi II no. 13.

[8] "Quidquid factum est, sive vivat sive non vivat aut quocumque modo in se sit, in Illo est ipsa vita et veritas" (*Monolog.* c 35).

[9] *Ibid.*, c 34. An objection in the *Summa* of Alexander (I, no. 175 V) mistakenly says that this passage is "very close to the heresy that all things are God". This is refuted at 3.

[10] "[N]on quod sit nobilius esse in proprio genere quam esse causae quo sunt causata in ipsa causa" (*Summa* of Alexander, II, no. 13 ad 3). Existing things can be said to live "pluribus rationibus", but not "magis, quia non est ponere excellentiorem vitam illa quae Deus est vel secundum quod sunt in illo vita".

[11] If souls do indeed bear their ideas within them, so much the more do they bear the divine insight "quae non est formata, sed ipsa forma" (*In Joan.* [PL 169, 210]). Like music in the soul of the artist, so the whole world is music playing in the Logos, the wisdom of God (PL 212).

[12] Klaus Kremer, *Gott und Welt in der klassichen Metaphysik* (Kohlhammer, 1969), 13. On the teaching of other scholastics cf. Bonaventure, *In I dist.* 36, scholia to qq. 1 and 2.

question asked, *which* being is *verius* and *nobilius*, that of the thing in itself or that of its prototype, and here the answer is given in favor of the second.[13] *Thomas* also takes that passage of the Prologue of John's Gospel as his starting point, listens to what *Augustine* and *Anselm* have to say and concludes that nothing can be in God's essence but himself; thus, insofar as things are perceived or created by him, they are the *causatrix essentia*. If we compare the being of the creature in itself with the being it has in God, in God it possesses a "truer being", existing as "uncreated", whereas in itself it exists as "created".[14] In the *De Veritate* the whole emphasis seems initially to fall on the existence of the creature: it may possess a *nobilius esse* in God, yet it is "truer in itself" where it is "real" and "possesses its own activity". Strangely enough, the decision is given from the perspective of the Platonic principle that "caused things are defective [*deficiunt*] in their imitation of their causes" and that therefore, "because of the gap between cause and effect", true statements can be made about the latter without being appropriate to the former. If the modes of being (*res*) are compared, the truth in the divine prototype is naturally greater. But if the "truth of the utterance" (*veritas praedicationis*) is compared, man is truer in his own nature than in the divine Word, and not because of some lack in the latter but because of the latter's excessive sublimity.[15] The Platonic principle, which here, on the basis of the gap between the creature and God, gives the creature the opportunity of having its own truth, has such weight in the

---

[13] *I dist.* 26, q 2. The proof by analogy: the thing perceived by the human mind is more, as perceived, than it is in itself as unperceived, according to Augustine, *De Trin.* 9, 44 and 9, 11, 16. Bonaventure goes beyond the line of thought that concerns us here when he moves in the direction of trinitarian doctrine and Christology, in discussing the relationship of things to the "exemplar exprimens" (*I dist.* 26, q. 1).

[14] In *I Sent. dist.* 36, q 1, a 3 ad 2; once more it is added that, if a material thing is compared with itself as perceived by a creaturely mind, the mode of being of the latter ranks higher than that of the former. Thus (in ad 3) the same can be said *a fortiori* of the image of things in the divine intellect, since God as totality is "life" and "light".

[15] *De Ver.* q 4, a 6. *S. Th.* Ia, q 18, a 4 ad 3 is entirely Platonic when it says that man's *esse hoc* is truer in his own nature than in the divine intellect, because "it belongs to man's truth to be in *matter*, which, in the divine intellect, he is not". But in that case how do things stand with the angels?

works of *Aquinas* that he continually emphasizes the superiority of the mode of being in God. In fact he shows considerable influence from the idea of the *Areopagite* (and, behind him, of *Proclus*), namely, that things which are "manifold and opposed" in themselves (*diversa et opposita in seipsis*) are one and joined (indeed, they interpenetrate) in God. Moreover—and this is specific to *Thomas'* thought—being (*esse*), since it is the highest perfection, includes within it all individual forms of being, which can only share in it. Hence all the perfections of things preexist *secundum eminentiorem modum* in God.[16] This is illustrated by quotations from *Dionysius*. The same can be found in the *Commentary on Dionysius*.[17]

It is well known how *Thomas Aquinas* waged a fierce battle, as a Christian fighting for the value of the individual, against a league of non-Christian opponents. Thus he passionately defended the view that divine providence extends not only to genera and species but also to the individual members which God created as such.[18] Correspondingly he represented the view that the higher the intellect, the more concrete individual things (at a lower level than itself) it could embrace with a single concept.[19] But statements such as these somehow ran contrary to a powerful trend from which Christian scholasticism could not entirely extricate itself. Two currents of thought, a weaker, Aristotelian one and a stronger, Neoplatonic, had joined together in Arabic philosophy, which was to have such a seminal and lasting influence on Western thought.

From *Aristotle* we have the idea that active reason is "always in

---

[16] *S. Th.* I, q 4, a 2 c et ad 1.

[17] Ed. Pera no. 641: "In seipsis enim omnia causata sunt finita, in Deo autem sunt infinita, quia in Deo sunt ipsa divina essentia. . . . Iterum in seipsis oppositionem habent et diversitatem, in Deo autem coniunguntur simul." Cf. also nos. 661–62, 50–51. The sentence in "De Substantiis separatis" (c 14) could have been written by Proclus himself: "Sicut causa est quodammodo in effectu per sui similtudinem participatem, ita omnis effectus est in sua causa excellentiori modo secundum virtutem eius." Similarly in the commentary on the "Liber de Causis". In the Lectura Super Joannem (lib II, 3), Thomas gives a historically nuanced interpretation of the particular verse of the Prologue. Here too, in continuity with Augustine: "Unde creatura in Deo est creatrix essentia".

[18] *De Ver.* q 3, a 8; *S. Th.* Ia, q 15, a 3; *De Div. Nom.* c 5, lib 3.

[19] *S. Th.* Ia, q 57, a 2; Ia, q 89, a 4; *De Ver.* q 8, a 9.

act". *Alexander of Aphrodisias* had equated this *intellectus agens* with the divine intellect that enters into us "from outside" (*thyrathen*). The Arabs take up this point; many passages also show the influence of *Proclus* (whose views were edited in the famous *Liber de Causis* ca. 850 A.D.). *Kindi* takes up the idea that the individual's passive reason receives knowledge of reality from its superordinate active reason; *Farabi* says that the passive creaturely spirits are so illuminated by the active cosmic Spirit that the latter provides them with the universal concepts that— similarly originating in God—are universal natures applying to individual things. *Avicenna* is similar; he may put forward an Aristotelian theory of abstraction, but he holds fast to the view that the forms of knowledge are stamped upon the human reason by the active intellect, an emanation of the *intelligentia prima* (which is God's sole direct product). *Averroes* gives the doctrine its final shape: the active intellect is a substance absolutely separate from individual souls; it is common to all men; their passive reason can be affected by contact with the active reason. The burning problem for *Averroes* is the individual's continuance after death: what continues is not an individual substance but the nous that is common to man as a whole, insofar as it has once touched the individual and been absorbed by him. The philosophical thrust in Islam is paralleled by the mystical; superficially the two often seem in conflict, yet at a deeper level they are one: the individual has to be united with and dissolve in the One, Absolute Subject (*Al Hallaj*). The Averroists of Paris (later of Padua) abandoned all individual immortality, as well as providence in the area of the contingent and the freedom of the will; *Thomas* opposed them in many writings and in an impassioned university sermon.[20] All the same it is well known what a place of honor *Dante* accorded, in his paradise, to the leading Averroist, *Siger of Brabant*.

One can ask, however, whether *Thomas*, who essentially adopted the ontology of *Avicenna*—God as *actus purus*, the intelligences (angels in *Thomas*) combined of *esse* and *essentia*, and man of form and matter—was in a position to lead the battle

---

[20] Ed. Vivès, vol. 32:676. Cf. M. Grabmann, *Mittelalterliches Geistesleben* (Munich, 1926), 294f.

for the Christian dignity of the individual to a triumphant conclusion. For here the human person becomes an individual *ratione materiae*, and an entity is more intelligible the more it is abstracted from matter and generalized. We know how difficult *Thomas* found it to substantiate the spiritual and intellectual activity of a soul separated from the body.

The great efforts which *Thomas* made seem to have been totally thrown to the winds in the mysticism of *Meister Eckhart*. The latter's ultimate aim—if we follow him through a confusing welter of terminological masquerades—seems to be to obliterate the difference between the ("ideal") being of the creature in God and its ("real") being-in-itself.[21] Since, for *Eckhart*, God is simply Being, there can be nothing outside God (not even a Neoplatonic "emanation"); thus the creation must coincide with the generation of the Son.[22] Insofar as God, as Being, is also the One, he is "the least different from the totality of creatures and from each of them. For if something is distinguished precisely by its nondifference, the more it is nondifferent, the more it will be distinct, and vice versa." And what applies to God applies also to every created entity and also to pluralities, since they always consist of nothing but single entities.[23] Thus the idea of the "I" becomes necessarily dialectical. On the one hand *Eckhart* likes to speak in entirely personal terms at crucial points in his argument (God "gives birth to *me* as his Son");[24] on the other hand this same individual "I" must be renounced, lest it should be in any way opposed to the sole Unity: "*abnegare personale, abnegare proprium*".[25] The doctrine of the existing

[21] Pierre Duhem, *Le Système du Monde*, vol. 6 (Paris, 1954), at the end of the chapter "La doctrine de Proclus et les dominicains allemands", 216–17.

[22] "Simul enim et semel quo deus fuit, quo filium sibi coaeternum per omnia coaequalem deum genuit, etiam mundum creavit" (Eckhart, *Expos. libri Genesis* c 1, v 1; vol. 1 of the Latin works (referenced hereafter as LW), 190.

[23] LW, II b 154.

[24] Eckhart, *Deutsche Werke* I, 218 (*Deutsche Werke*, referenced hereafter as DW). Other examples in Shizuteru Ueda, *Die Gottesgeburt in der Seele und der Durchbruch zur Gottheit. Die mystische Anthropologie Meister Eckharts und ihre Konfrontation mit der Mystik des Zen-Buddhismus* (Marburg, 1965); this work by Ueda is abbreviated in this section to *Die Gottesgeburt*.

[25] LW, III; *Joh* n. 290. Cf. also Quint, *Meister Eckhart, Deutsche Predigten und*

creature's immanence in God's Logos is substantiated more profoundly in *Eckhart's* teaching on the Incarnation. Here he clearly states that the Logos did not adopt any individual human nature but that human nature that is common to all men and that has no existence of its own as such: "The nature adopted is that which is common to all men without distinction; hence it has been given to every man to become Son of God."[26] The existential conclusion follows immediately: "Empty yourself, therefore, of all things; then all that remains will be what Christ took to himself, and so you will have put on Christ."[27] This self-emptying, alienation, applies to all man's individual and personal qualities, which are nothing but accidentals (*zuoval* = *Zufall*);[28] only in this way can man put on Christ, whose person is not human but divine.[29] But if "the soul leaves its ground, in

---

Traktate (1955), 171. "All creatures are pure nothing. . . . Their being depends upon the presence of God. . . . If a man were to add the whole world to God, he would have no more than if he had God alone" (LW, IV, 437).

[26] Cf. *Von abgescheidenheit*: "Know this: when Christ became man, he did not take unto himself a single human being, but human nature" (DW, V, 430 and the numerous parallel passages, e.g., 458, note).

[27] DW, V, 546.

[28] "For man is an accident of nature, and so all that is accidental must pass away" (Pfeiffer, *Meister Eckhart* [1924], 158, 1.12ff.).

[29] For the spread of this view in late medieval mysticism cf. Alois Haas, "Nim din selbes war. Studien zur Lehre von der Selbsterkenntnis bei Meister Eckhart, Johannes Tauler und Heinrich Seuse" (*Dokimion* 3 [Fribourg, 1971], 29). A prime expert on Eckhart, Nicholas Cusanus, turned Eckhart's concept of incarnation in such a way that it could be seen as orthodox, in spite of the vehement hostility meted out to him on this account during his lifetime by Johannes Wenk and later—in 1889—by M. Glossner. Cf. Rudolf Haubst, *Die Christologie des Nikolaus von Kues* (Herder, 1956), 220. According to Cusanus, too, Christ coincides with the nature of humanity itself, his humanity is "universal". He explains it like this: Christ contains the whole human nature in *contractio* within himself; with regard to human beings, within the limitations imposed by human nature, he has the same relationship that God has vis-à-vis all that exists (*Doct. Ignor.* III, 3; *De vis. Dei* c 20). Cusanus is strongly influenced by Proclus, as the following text shows: "Who could understand the infinite Unity, which is infinitely beyond all oppositions, where everything is enfolded in the simplicity of unity without being organized in combinations, where there is nothing that is other or different, where the human being is not distinguished from the lion nor heaven from the earth, and yet they are at their most true there, not in their finitude, but folded together in the highest unity?" (*Doct. Ignor.* I, 24).

which it has more unity with God than with itself, . . . it becomes enclosed in itself, clinging to itself in its self-identity". This introverted self-identity of the soul is its characteristic selfhood, "*Eigen-schaft*", the "I",[30] and it "imprisons everything in images, divides and apportions everything, as its own possession [*Eigen-tum*]".[31] Self-knowledge is the abandonment of this "self": "Apprehend yourself, and wherever you find yourself, leave yourself there."[32] "*Debet igitur anima se exuere omnibus, ut nuda nudum quaerat deum.*"[33] Thus the soul will arrive at the place where "there are no longer any oppositions",[34] the place of "matutinal knowledge".[35] Over against the concept of selfhood (*Eigenschaft*) there is that of the "authentic self" (*Eigentlichkeit*): man, as the image of God, possesses his essence most authentically (*aller eigentlîchest*) not in himself (as a mirror of God), but in the original, God: "The image is more original in the origin from whence it comes."[36] Here the mystical summons, "O man, embrace your nature" ("*Mensch, werde wesentlich*"), acquires an antipersonal hue. For *Eckhart*, man's nature is "more interior to him than his person": "*natura humana est cuilibet homini interior quam ille sibi*".[37] The purpose of this depersonalization, however, is simply to enable man to enter into the Divine Person of Christ and thus into the free, creative life of the Trinity. Here the "I" is resurrected in a power of willing and knowing that is divine. "God made all things through me when I stood in the unfathomable ground of God."[38] "Thus the soul works with the Father in all his works."[39] Compare the statement that provoked censure: "*Humilis homo non indiget quod deum roget, ipse potest deo*

[30] Ueda, *Die Gottesgeburt*, 69.

[31] *Ibid.*, 71.

[32] DW, V, 196. Cf. Pfeiffer, *Meister Eckhart*, 509, 17ff.: "The soul must be utterly annihilated to itself, so that nothing remains but God".

[33] *Serm.* n. 246 (LW, IV).

[34] Pfeiffer, *Meister Eckhart*, 264, 28. Love and suffering, black and white coincide.

[35] Pfeiffer, *Meister Eckhart*, 111, 4, i.e., the Augustinian *cognitio matutina*, an intuition of things in the being of God.

[36] DW, I, 154.

[37] *John* n. 289, cf. 290.

[38] Pfeiffer, *Meister Eckhart*, 581, 1.

[39] Pfeiffer, *Meister Eckhart*, 161, 27f.

inperare."[40] Moreover: "In my (eternal) birth all things were born. I was the cause of myself and of all things. And if I did not will it so, neither I nor all things would exist; if I did not exist, God would not exist either." Located in the First Cause, "I was the cause of myself."[41] *Angelus Silesius* will say the same thing.

Insofar as he is "created", man is pure passivity, so that he may receive into himself the Son whom the Father generates ("*Imago dei capax dei, cujus totum est esse ad aliud*").[42] But he is genuinely man only by having the divine power—which is pure activity—implanted in him, enabling him to give birth to the Son in him and so return him to the Father;[43] to that extent he is not "created", nor can he be grasped in any way in the categories of "created" and "uncreated".[44] However, in its absolute activity (compare the *intellectus agens* of the Arabian philosophers)[45] the soul is able to break through to the "ground" of God himself; this is the soul's response to God's having infused his whole activity into it and awakened the soul's own "ground". Here it is clear that *Eckhart* regards the personal trinitarian process as something penultimate in God (analogously to his anthropology, where "nature", "essence", is more interior than the personal "I"); it is only "relational" and secondary compared with the "substantial" reality of the primal ground,[46] the "silent desert" —"into which nothing differentiated has ever looked, neither Father, Son nor Holy Spirit".[47] The primal ground of God, an eternal darkness, is impenetrable even to the perceptual light of

---

[40] Cf. DW, I, 236.

[41] Quint, *Meister Eckhart, Deutsche Predigten und Traktate*, 304, 308.

[42] *Serm.* n. 152.

[43] DW, I, 383.

[44] On the impossibility of applying this category (and that of nature and grace) to Eckhart's concept of the *homo divinus*, cf. Ueda, *Die Gottesgeburt*, 90, 92, 131, 134.

[45] Cf. J. Koch, "Meister Eckhart und die jüdische Religionsphilosophie des Mittelalters", in *Jahresbericht der Schlesischen Gesellschaft für vaterländische Kultur* (special issue 1928), where the influence of Avencebrois and Maimonides is particularly demonstrated.

[46] "In Deo substantia sua non habet rationem relationis" (LW, II, Exod, n. 72; cf. n. 65). Eckhart sees this "relational" aspect as being both interior to the Godhead and characteristic of God's relationship with his creature. Thus he can say: "Before creatures existed, God was not God" (Pfeiffer, *Meister Eckhart*, 281, 27).

[47] Quint, *Deutsche Predigten und Traktate*, 206, 316.

the Trinity: "God abides there unknown in himself, and while the light of the eternal Father has eternally shone in upon it, the darkness has not comprehended the light."[48] Thus it is clear that the preservation of the human "I" in the idea (where it is identical with the Son) cannot be *Eckhart's* last word. God himself has his personless ground, which logically is identical with man's ground (which similarly lacks an "I"): "Here God's ground is my ground, and my ground is God's ground",[49] and "prior to" being eternally begotten in the eternal Son we "rested and slept eternally in pristine purity".[50] Here, for *Eckhart*, the highest poverty (*armuot*)[51] has been attained, possessing neither itself nor God. So two barriers appear between the "I" and its "authentic self" (*Eigentlichkeit*), namely, human nature, which is already more interior to the "I" than the "I" is to itself; and the personal God, who "according to Augustine is more interior to the soul than the soul to itself".[52] But even God's "I" refers to his mere "substance",[53] beyond all quality and form, beyond the trinitarian process. Individuation is understood as a negation, self-renunciation: "All creatures have (reciprocally) an inherent renunciation. The one renounces being the other."[54]

However, there is an aspect of *Eckhart's* teaching that seems to contradict all this: his doctrine of internal and external works (extolling the *vita activa*) as found in the astonishing sermon on Martha and Mary[55] and in a number of texts tending in the same direction.[56] It is plain from what has been said that *Eckhart* has already overstepped the opposition between passivity (absolute, contemplative) and activity (absolute and cooperating with God). Thus the radical Christian is fruitful in his entire life in God, his existence coincides with his "internal work" and the external works he is bound to perform have a Christian meaning insofar as they flow from the internal works and embody

---

[48] DW, I, 389. Quint, *Deutsche Predigten und Traktate*, 164.

[49] DW, I, 90; cf. Pfeiffer, *Meister Eckhart*, 467, 15.

[50] DW, I, 382 with Quint's note.

[51] Pfeiffer, *Meister Eckhart*, 283, 17.

[52] *Serm.* n. 452.

[53] *Exod.* n. 14.

[54] Pfeiffer, *Meister Eckhart*, 322, 18.

[55] Quint, *Deutsche Predigten and Traktate*, 28, 280 ff.

[56] Esp. Pfeiffer, *Meister Eckhart*, Sermon III.

them.[57] *Eckhart* desires the external work to be "orderly" ("corresponding to the Highest in all points"), "full of insight" ("beyond which nothing better can be envisaged at the present time") and "quietly deliberate" ("as when, in good works, one senses the living truth with its blissful presence"). In fact it is a matter of obediently fulfilling the will of God at any one time ("then the soul says: 'Lord, inspire me to know your eternal will' "). It would be an exaggeration to call these aspects of *Eckhart's* teaching "exoteric"; it would also be questionable to speak—with *Rudolph Otto*—of the "theistic foundation" of his doctrine (of which this teaching would then be a part) and go on to distinguish it from a monistic superstructure,[58] for *Eckhart* intends unequivocally to be a Christian in all his utterances. Yet we *can* ask whether the radical dying of the "I" in God, indeed, in the ineffable depths of God's primal ground, is not bound to cause its existence in time and space to seem inauthentic and alienated. Is it still an "I", distinguishable from God? "*Ego*, the word 'I', truly belongs to no one but God alone in his unity."[59] Can we speak, in this context, of a personal, Christian vocation in the sense of salvation history? "In Eckhart, salvation history shrinks from its cosmic dimensions to that point (lacking all location) at which man's union with God is dynamically articulated as an ever-new event."[60] But the Christian in *Eckhart* pushes back the aspect of alienation that is inherent in his presuppositions and prevents it from taking effect. There can be no doubt that this whole metaphysical theology is conceived as a theology of grace, a theology of the unimaginable intimacy between man "born of God" and the Divinity; yet it uses intellectual components that come from the Platonist realm (in part fashioned by Arabian philosophers) and cause nature, and hence man's personal freedom, to dissolve in the supernatural.

---

[57] On this whole topic: Dietmar Mieth, *Die Einheit von Vita activa und Vita contemplativa in den dt. Predigten und Traktaten Meister Eckharts und bei Johannes Tauler* (Pustet, 1969), 119–233.

[58] *Mysticism: East and West* (London, 1932).

[59] Quint, *Deutsche Predigten und Traktate*, 302.

[60] Alois Haas, "Meister Eckharts mystische Bildrede", in *Miscellanea Mediaevalia* vol. 8 (1971): 126. B. Weiss, *Die Heilsgeschichte bei Meister Eckhart* (Mainz, 1965).

No wonder, then, that there have continually been attempts to build a bridge from *Meister Eckhart* to Indian and Japanese (Zen Buddhist) mystical metaphysics, where what we have called the personal "role" appears even more clearly as "alienation". Here Eckhart can be entirely assimilated to the idea of Zen Buddhism (for example, in *Daisez Suzuki*),[61] or, as in the balanced work of *Shizuteru Ueda*,[62] it is shown how *Eckhart's* Christianity prevents him from drawing the final Zen Buddhist conclusions.[63] In Zen, the Platonic doctrine of ideas practically disappears: the "authentic being" of the finite in the infinite is made absolute, as is the annihilation of the divine in its "un-ground". All that remains, in fact, is the complete paradox of the world's reality, arising out of sheer nothingness and affected by it through and through. The "simple affirmation of everyday life as such" is not grounded in its being in the Logos of God; hence the mediation of language also disappears, and the dumb human being can only point to "that there"—and no reason of any kind can be given for its existence. God's disappearance in the void can turn into pure secularity: "Cold ashes catch fire." Later we shall show that there are paths from both *Eckhart* and Zen Buddhism to German idealism.[64]

First, however, we must turn to *Rudolph Otto's* nuanced analyses in *West-Östliche Mystik*,[65] which draws the parallels between the Master of the Vedanta, Šankara, and *Eckhart*, highlighting both the similarities and the significant dissimilarities. As a result of the equation of the Absolute with Being, apart from which nothing can be, both have to ponder the meaning of the individual being as such. As we saw, *Eckhart* traces his essentiality or authentic being back to the Divine Being; it is the

[61] *Mysticism Christian and Buddhist* (1957).

[62] See note 24 above.

[63] *Ibid.*, 145–69. Cf. also Minoru Nambara, "Die Idee des absoluten Nichts in der deutschen Mystik und seine Entsprechung im Buddhismus", in *Archiv für Begriffsgeschichte* vol. VI (Bonn, 1960: 143–277.

[64] The Japanese philosopher Kitaro Nishida has endeavored to fertilize specifically Eastern thought by contact with German idealism (self-renunciation = discovery of one's true self by calling upon the Absolute).

[65] Rudolf Otto, *West-Ostliche Mystik* (Gotha, 1929) [*Mysticism: East and West*, London, 1932]. By the same author: *India's Religion of Grace and Christianity Compared and Contrasted* (London, 1930).

latter's *ebullitio* in himself. Šankara says almost the same thing in his commentary on the Chāndogya Upanishad: "This entire manifold of created being which exists in name and form is true *insofar* as it is Being itself. Of itself, however, it is untrue."[66] Maya is the "magical power" of Being (Brahma) whereby it causes multiplicity to appear; but the relationship between Brahma and Maya remains indefinable,[67] indeed, the question as to the nothingness of things is not even asked; it is unanswerable.[68] Equally, the question of the relationship between the "I" as soul (âtman) and the Brahma is ultimately insoluble; according to *Otto* their equation is covertly a "synthetic judgment": it forms the content of the theory and practice of the Vedanta. The path leads from the "I" to the Absolute, in which (as in *Eckhart*) *esse* and *intelligere* are identical.

2. Idealism

Stress has often been laid on the fact that *Eckhart*—whose writings *Cusanus* preserved and interpreted—was one of the most important mediators between the Neoplatonic thought of the ancient world and modern idealism.[1] The connection interests us only in regard to the question of the "I". In varying degrees and forms, from *Fichte*, via *Schelling*, to *Hegel*, we encounter the same tendency to dissolve the empirical, personal "I" in the "essential", the "ideal". Here too, therefore, we must speak of "alienation". This is all the more strange since the idealists, even more than *Eckhart*, are characterized by that underlying pathos of nobility of soul that seeks to attain to what is highest and most profound in man by thought and in free ethical conduct. "He who strives for noble things is noble", said *Eckhart*,[2] and for *Fichte* it is a case of "fanning into flame the

---

[66] Otto, *Mysticism: East and West*.

[67] *Ibid*.   [68] *Ibid*.

[1] Ernst von Bracken in *Meister Eckhart und Fichte* (Würzburg, 1943) gives a survey of the literature (632–37). On Schelling: Walter Heinrich, *Verklärung und Erlösung im Vedanta, bei Meister Eckhart und bei Schelling* (Munich, 1962).

[2] Pfeiffer, *Meister Eckhart*, 168; the example of Peter, who "goes through" iron doors and walks on the water (25).

spark of higher genius that has been quenched".[3] None of the idealists are engaged in a flight from the world: on the contrary, they seek to penetrate and master it (and no more consistent and titanic plans have ever been put forward). The end result is all the more remarkable, namely, the—almost inadvertent—loss of the individual as a person. The process has often been elucidated: we shall only recall it briefly here. We shall take no account of *Kant's* postulate of the immortality of the soul, which he interprets as "an infinitely prolonged existence and personality of the rational being", supporting his view of an infinite approximation to the goal of sanctity,[4] since it points back to *Leibniz* and the Enlightenment (*Lessing*), although the idea of "infinite progress" does point to the future.

a. Fichte

Fichte is well acquainted with our question: "Who am I really? What kind of an individual? And what is the reason for my being this particular one?" He asks this in the 1798 *System der Sittenlehre*.[5] *Fichte's* answer contains his whole system in a nutshell: "From the moment I have attained consciousness *I am the person I freely make myself to be; I am this person because I make myself such.*—At each moment of my existence, my being is what it is as a result of freedom, not insofar as it is conditioned, but with regard to its *ultimate* character." "The root of my individuality" is the fact that there is at least one individual apart from me who can influence me: this is evidently not the result of my freedom but arises "from my connection" with other rational beings; "but what I shall become, or shall not become, from now on depends purely and entirely on myself alone".[6] Negatively this means that the answer sought can in no way be found in psychological data,[7] the "particular features of your personality";[8] "a particular material 'I' or a person", together

---

[3] Fichte, *Werke*, ed. Medicus, 7 vols. (Leipzig, 1909–19), I, 220 (*Werke* referenced in this section by volume and page only).

[4] In the *Critique of Practical Reason*.

[5] II, 616.   [6] II, 616–17.

[7] "The *Wissenschaftslehre* is not psychology" (III, 589).

[8] III, 588.

with his exclusive sphere of possible free actions, is to be seen only as a limitation of the "naked 'I' " (*der blossen Ichheit*).[9] The true point of departure is this "I", this clear and complete self-consciousness, "just as you, I and all of us are conscious of ourselves";[10] from this vantage point we look toward the infinitely distant goal where the original "act" (*Tathandlung*), in which the "I" posits itself as continuous through the sphere of the empirical, has become identical with itself in perfect ethical action. At the beginning there is the "I", in self-contemplation, in which "only the form of the 'I' resides", and at the end "the full materiality of the 'I' " (*Materie der Ichheit*), which, however, philosophy (since it takes that *beginning* as its starting point) can only "establish as an idea", as "the highest goal for which reason strives". The latter "cannot be distinctly envisaged, nor will it ever be; it is an infinite idea, to be approached asymptotically".[11] Since, according to *Fichte*, thought's origin and point of reference are in the primal act and the contemplation of it, and the sphere of the will is the embracing medium, the same thing can be put this way: "Man should be what he is, simply because he is. In other words, all that he is should be referred to his pure 'I', his mere 'I'-ness [*Ichheit*]. . . . Man himself is the goal. . . . The empirical 'I' should be attuned in such a way that it could remain so eternally. . . . Act in such a way that you could take the maxim of your will as an eternal law for yourself."[12] Hence come the ruthless demands—presented right at the beginning, logically enough, and which only later appear transfigured as a result of a religious atmosphere—namely, "that the person needs to be sacrificed to the idea, and that . . . the individual shall not exist, being of no importance, but shall perish".[13] The idea, which is what is really alive, can present itself to people in different "material" forms, in art, law, science, religion; but in each case man, limited as he is, must plunge into and dissolve in their spiritual fullness, with a self-forgetfulness that is concerned only about the totality; for ultimately even the indirect egoism of the family, of friendship, is just as reprehensible as direct self-love.[14] The ideal is "humanity", which is described

9 II, 61.   10 III, 585.   11 III, 101.   12 I, 224f.   13 IV, 431f.
14 IV, 429–30.

as "the one, external, powerful, living and self-dependent life of God",[15] but which, like the "species", can be contrasted with the individual: "Thus the rational life consists in the person forgetting himself in the species."[16] When protests are raised at this by certain "aesthetes" (the romantics) in the name of "dear, sweet individuality", *Fichte* is prepared to grant "that the one eternal idea manifests itself in a new and previously unknown form in each particular individual through whom it thrusts its way to life";[17] but on closer inspection this only means that the idea, as it descends to the level of realization, makes a "breakthrough" to a new concrete form in a particular human being. It does not involve the personal individuality of this human being being taken up, in its distinctness, into the idea. Thus the limits of the concept of "interpersonality" in *Fichte* are staked out in advance. True, in deducing the self-limitation of the "I" as an individual, it is borne in mind that it must also be limited in its free activity, which is only possible if it encounters another's free activity;[18] but in the end, the idea of another (or of others) besides me can be none other than my own. Thus, in natural constitutional law as in the system of ethics, all forms of social coexistence are bound to tend (in infinite approximation) toward an overcoming of genuine "dialogue" in favor of an ethical autonomy that is the same in everyone. The conscience which dwells in each individual is superindividual. "We should all act in the same way."[19] "The object of the ethical law in me as an individual is not myself alone but the whole realm of reason. I am its object only insofar as I am one of the instruments bringing about its realization in the world of the senses."[20] The distinct quality of this tool is ultimately of no account.[21]

[15] IV, 582. "Motionless I stand in awe. I hear the summons: Here is *humanity!*" (II, 619). "The concept of man is thus in no way the concept of an individual, which is unthinkable, but of the race" (II, 43).

[16] IV, 429.   [17] IV, 463.

[18] II, 612. "It is a condition of self-consciousness, of the 'I', that it is receptive to a real, rational being outside itself" (II, 615).

[19] II, 627.   [20] II, 630.

[21] "It is in the nature of the 'I' that each 'I' is individual; but only individual in an overall sense, not the particular individual A, B or C. . . . Since, therefore, as far as 'I-ness' is concerned, it is entirely fortuitous that I, the individual A, am A, and since the instinct of autonomy is an instinct of 'I-ness' as such, it is not a

After the atheism controversy, *Fichte* gradually transformed his system in the direction of a religious pantheism. In the *Versuch einer neuen Darstellung* (1798) the primal contemplation of the "I" is already asking the question how such contemplation is possible without the "I" splitting into subject and object; the answer points to the original unity of the two, which is the first step toward an identity that relativizes the "I" (as subject). In the *Sonnenklarer Bericht* (1797) we encounter the concept of "life", upon which the theory of knowledge only reflects.[22] Reflection, which arises by stages from sense experience to reason, swims against the current of descending life. This concept of life is then expanded, becoming the Absolute, which is prior to the primal "I" (as its root and ground) and cannot be grasped in concepts (*interior intimo*); it is "pure Being" (the *Wissenschaftslehre* of 1801), the conjunction and interplay of life and light that has no awareness of itself, comparable with the "One" of Plotinus. In the face of this, the whole realm of the "I", of reflection (subject-object) is something nonabsolute, existent nonbeing; it sinks to the level of a merely schematic representation of the inconceivable and uniquely real. The theory of knowledge is a "reconstruction" of it, and "since to reconstruct is to conceptualize, and since here such (per se legitimate) conceptualizing explicitly renounces itself, what we have is a grasp of what is utterly inconceivable *qua* inconceivable".[23] Earlier, the empirical-personal "I" surrendered to " 'I'-ness pure and simple" (*Ichheit überhaupt*); now a further step is taken: the entire "I"-ness is to suspend itself—albeit, in order to suspend itself, it must also continually posit itself. The ungraspable is "posited by annihilating the absolute concept, which is only posited so that it can be annihilated".[24] And "this ungraspability [*Unbegreiflichkeit*] itself arises from the concept [*Begriff*] and from direct inner evidence", which gives the theory of knowledge its essentially intermediate position between "God" and the world.[25] For it

---

question of the autonomy of A, but of the autonomy of reason in general" (II, 625).

[22] "The *Wissenschaftslehre* is offered merely as a model of life; by no means does it claim to be real life" (III, 620).

[23] *Wissenschaftslehre* (1804) in *Werke*, IV, 193.

[24] IV, 195.   [25] IV, 199, 211.

also mediates in the direction of Light/Life, in the "unity of reciprocity" (of the poles), as a genuine a priori synthesis, from which springs the realm of being as well as the realm of the subject and of his self-realization. The *Anweisung zum seligen Leben* (1806) is concerned with the "longing for the eternal"; we are to leave behind the "life of appearances", the "ceaseless dying", the "distractedness" that is "our actual nature", and attain to the contemplation of God. This is something each person must carry out for himself, for "religion consists in this: everyone is to behold, have and possess God directly, in his own person and not in the person of someone else, with his own spiritual eyes and not through those of another. This is only possible, however, as a result of pure and self-reliant thought; for only through such thought does anyone *become* a distinct and authentic person."[26] All the same we would not be justified in understanding this concept of "person" in any way but as at the beginning: as an (approximating) realization of the idea, which is superempirical. *Fichte* likes to quote the "Johannine Christ"[27] in support of religious intuition, which he calls the "Kingdom of heaven". Even in his latest lectures (1813) *Fichte* attributes direct intellectual contemplation to Jesus; it constitutes his vocation "to institute the Kingdom of heaven": "He was, in his *being*, what he desired to *make* all men to be."[28] "The *content* of this vocation manifested to him its *form*: he understood (and was the first to do so) that he was a native citizen of the Kingdom of heaven."[29] However, we should not take him as a "model": rather, we should "reconstruct the necessary concept he formed of himself",[30] in order—according to the *Reden an die deutsche Nation*—"to find heaven on earth, letting what is everlasting flow into (our) daily work on earth".[31] *Fichte's* concern is always to render eternal what is present and temporal; he is never interested in a post-mortem immortality in the sense of the Kantian postulate.

This emphasis on the immanence of the eternal in the temporal, or, in other words, the immanence of secular activity in the

---

[26] V, 130, cf. 150.   [27] V, 136.   [28] VI, 577.

[29] VI, 578. Cf. the sixth lecture in the "Anweisung zum seligen Leben" in *Werke*, V, 187ff.

[30] VI, 575.   [31] V, 490.

contemplative surrender to the divine, is also found in the
Anweisung zum seligen Leben. On the one hand, we are required
"to be profoundly convinced of our nonbeing and that we have
our being solely in God and through God"[32] (observe the
similarity to *Eckhart*); that we must "annihilate"[33] ourselves in
the face of absolute existence; that there is only "the appearance
of multiplicity in thought"—"partly as a result of there being, as
there must be [!], diverse thinking subjects and partly because of
the infinite series of objects upon which the thought of these
subjects is destined to play for all eternity [!]." Thought cannot
remove this "appearance", but it does not believe in it, does not
love it, nor does it take delight in it.[34] On the other hand, too,
we face no less of a challenge: as a result of the self-suspension of
the all-embracing concept and our rising above the prismatic
splitting[35] of unity into multiplicity through reflection—which
causes the light to "split and dissipate and . . . become alienated
from itself and its original source"[36]—and by grounding our
being in God, even to the extent of seeming to become alienated
from ourselves,[37] we are to experience God as that which works
in and through us: God "*is* that which the one who is devoted to
him and inspired by him *does*".[38] Nor does he do this in order to
succeed or fail, but solely "because it is the will of God in him,
because it is his own, authentic share in Being".[39] Here *Fichte*
deliberately lifts his *Sittenlehre* (in accord with the earlier form of
his *Wissenschaftslehre*) onto a higher plane. He may identify this
perspective with the Johannine teaching on the Logos (as "word",
"reason" or "wisdom")—the Logos who was in the beginning
with God and was God (the complementary opposites of primal
life and "existence", as the reciprocal interpenetration of thought
and being), the Logos who becomes flesh, that is, enters into an
individual "personally human and sensory existence".[40] Moreover, *Fichte* may separate what is historical and dogmatic in the
Christian faith from what is perennial and metaphysical ("there
is salvation only in the metaphysical, not in the historical"),[41]

---

32 V, 161. "Everything else that we regard as existence—things, bodies,
souls, we ourselves insofar as we ascribe autonomous and independent being to
ourselves—does not exist, truly and in itself" (dashes altered for the sake of
clarity) (V, 160).

33 V, 153.   34 V, 153.   35 V, 170.   36 V, 173.   37 V, 183.

38 V, 184.   39 V, 187.   40 V, 194.   41 V, 197.

although the metaphysical owes its unique breakthrough in history to the "great phenomenon" of Jesus of Nazareth. Consequently he may appropriate John's "realized eschatology" for his own purposes. But when he says that the Christian should "only reiterate Jesus in his personality" (instead of "merely imitating him as an unattainable model"),[42] we see that an abyss separates him from the Bible. His vehement rejection of the concept of creation[43] means that the world is nothing more than a necessary "infinite splintering": this is how "the Divine Being within it . . . fashions itself",[44] returning to itself in a series of possible forms graspable by the human mind: "It is not as if it creates a freedom outside itself; it *is* itself, in this part of the form, its own freedom outside itself."[45] This is made clear in the way *Fichte* gets beyond a morality of indifference. According to the latter, an "I" with its own limited will attempts to transcend itself in the direction of a divine law that lies above him (the Kantian view): "Through this indifference of its own will, the other (divine) will becomes an alien will that it represents to itself as a law, a law that its own will naturally does not wish to accept."[46] In transcending this position, the "two wills" of Christ are, as it were, erased, so that the human being and God coincide in a way that is Monotheletic (and hence ultimately Monophysite): Thus

the former "I" is absorbed into the pure divine existence, with the result that, strictly speaking, one cannot even say that . . . the love and will of this divine existence become its own. For there are no longer two at all, but only one; no longer two wills, but only one and the same will, all in all. So long as man still desires to be something else, God will not come to him, for no man can become God. But as soon as he annihilates himself purely, totally and to his very roots, all that is left is God and is all in all. Man cannot produce a God for himself; but what he can do is annihilate himself, *for he is the real negation*, and then he will sink into God.[47]

Naturally, the greatest riddle of the 1794 *Wissenschaftslehre* remains that of the "deduction" of interpersonality. This would

[42] V, 200–201.   [43] V, 191.   [44] V, 223.   [45] V, 224.
[46] V, 230.
[47] V, 230 (my italics). On characterizing it as Monotheletic cf. Schelling, *Sämtliche Werke*, 14 vols. (1856–61), VII, 372.

be acceptable provided the "fundamental 'I'" (*Ich überhaupt*) were taken as a purely methodological starting point for reflection, and provided the reciprocal limitation of persons and their freedoms were understood as purely descriptive. But *Fichte* means more than this. Even in the last revision of the *Wissenschaftslehre* (1810), knowing is "God's being outside his being . . . as a direct consequence of his being",[48] and once it "became an 'I' as a result of self-contemplation", it "necessarily split into a world of 'I's".[49] In the terms of Christian philosophy it could be said that God the Father beholds in the one Logos the infinite possibilities (*possibilia*) of his own imitability. But for *Fichte*—since everything takes place in thought—these possibilities, while "real" as such, are real according to a reality that suspends itself in the face of the unique reality of God.

b. Schelling

Here we do not have to present the whole of *Schelling's*[1] very considerable contribution to theodramatic theory, but only that small section that is relevant to the question at issue. *Fichte* had addressed himself passionately to individuals among those who heard his lectures, challenging them to carry out the operations of thought and hence of moral conviction and action. He wanted to confront the individual, even if the latter could be designated only as "a dart, a longing" in the direction of something superindividual—whether the "nation" or "humanity". *Schelling* did not possess this personal pathos. As his thought unfolded, he strove—in deliberate contrast to *Fichte* and *Hegel*—to work out an ever-clearer definition of "person" or "personality",[2] but only of the essence of the person, not of the individual as such. *Schelling* arrives at the very threshold of the

---

[48] V, 615.

[49] V, 622. The links in this reasoning are omitted; nonetheless, in the text itself, the leap of thought remains unbridged.

[1] Schelling, *Sämtliche Werke*, 14 vols. (1856–61). Unless otherwise stated, the volume number refers to the first series (vols. 1–10) and in this section only the volume and page number are given.

[2] The two words are used without any concern for consistency of meaning. Cf. e.g., "Nothing results from universal laws, but God, i.e., the person of

gospel, acknowledges the significance of the person of Christ, and of faith too, but for him "revelation's aspect of word and summons"[3] remains in obscurity. We can divide *Schelling's* intellectual path into three phases—not without a certain arbitrariness: the first would be his exposition of *Fichte's* system and his transcending of it in his philosophy of nature and of art (1795–1802/1803). The second, extending roughly from *Bruno* (1802) and *Philosophie und Religion* (1804) to the *Essay on Freedom* (1809), his Stuttgart private lectures, *Clara* (1810/1811) and the *Anti-Jacobi* (1812), effects the transition to religious thought and the concentration on the themes of freedom and personality. The third is heralded by his *Weltalter*, with the late Berlin lectures at its heart; in its own way it takes Christian theology as the object of its philosophical reflection. Of these three only the second, middle phase concerns us here. The first, generally speaking, does not really reach the problem of the person,[4] and the third, by virtue of its subject matter, goes beyond the field of philosophy.

We shall begin with a few references to the first period by way of introduction. In the essay "*Vom Ich*" ("On the 'I' ") of 1795, he says, with *Fichte*, "that the essence of man consists solely in absolute freedom; according to his authentic being . . . man is in no way an object";[5] the same thing is affirmed, however, of the absolute "I" (it is that "which simply cannot ever become an object"),[6] with the result that this "I", which cannot be a subjective "I", must be regarded as "the essence of man". The "I" is "neither species, nor genera, nor individual",[7] so that the appearance that "there are several 'I's, reciprocally being 'I' and 'non-I' for each other",[8] is decidedly dependent on the idea that the "I"—beyond the "moral law"—necessarily determines itself in perfect (absolute) freedom.[9] The *Essay on Freedom* will return

God, is the universal law, and all that takes place does so by the power of God's personality" (7:396).

[3] Walter Kasper, *Das Absolute in der Geschichte, Philosophie und Theologie der Geschichte in der Spätphilosophie Schellings* (Mainz, 1965), 174.

[4] Even in the (posthumous) *Philosophy of Art* of 1802–5, the individual artists are only treated as representatives of the particular genre under consideration, and in *Bruno* we have only "the" artist confronting "the" philosopher.

[5] 1:157.   [6] 1:167.   [7] 1:184.   [8] 1:183.   [9] 1:236–37.

to this topic. More radically than in *Fichte*, however, the freedom of the empirical subject is understood purely "vertically", that is, *Schelling* expects no influence from the mutual relation of subjects to one another. —In the *Philosophische Briefe über Dogmatismus und Kritizismus* (1795) the one-sided, Spinozist objectivism ("dogmatism") of the Absolute—and the corresponding ethical demand that man shall surrender his "I" in God[10]—is overcome by the "intellectual contemplation" of the absolute "I" ("criticism"): "For we are all indwelt by a secret, wonderful ability to withdraw from the vicissitudes of time into our innermost self, stripped of everything extrinsic to it, there to contemplate the eternal in us under the form of the unchangeable." Here alone is *being*, whereas everything else merely *appears*; here alone is freedom, whereas elsewhere we are "overwhelmed by the intrusive power of objects".[11] This is what, deceiving himself, *Spinoza* really meant and experienced: he did not envisage the loss of the "I", but "only the expansion of his personality to the dimensions of the 'I' ";[12] the less the "I" has an object over against it, however, "the nearer it is to disappearing".[13] *Schelling* praises the honesty of the Chinese sage ("Zen") in "asserting that the highest good, absolute blessedness, consists in—nothing".[14] Life that is human and self-conscious can exist only in the infinite approximation toward this condition (which abolishes it); it requires the resistance of the objective, the necessary, the fated, in order to persist.

It is from this perspective that the young *Schelling* elucidates the paradoxes of Greek tragedy:

> It has often been asked how Greek rationality could endure the contradictions of Greek tragedy. Here is a mortal, destined by fate to be a criminal; he himself fights *against* this fate and yet is punished terribly for the crime that was fate's work! The reason for this contradiction, and what made it bearable, lay at a deeper level than that at which it was sought: it lay in the struggle of human freedom with the power of the objective world. In this struggle, the mortal, confronted with a superior objective power

---

[10] "We must return back to the Godhead, the primal source of all existence; we must be united with the Absolute and annihilate ourselves" (1:317).

[11] 1:318.   [12] 1:321f.   [13] 1:325.   [14] 1:326.

—a *fatum*—must *necessarily* succumb, yet, because he did not succumb *without a struggle*, he must be *punished* for it. The fact that the guilty man, who only succumbed because of the superior power of fate, was nonetheless *punished* was a recognition of human freedom; it was a due *honor* paid to freedom. Greek tragedy honored human freedom by causing its heroes to fight against the superior power of fate. . . . [15]

In the first period the pathos *Schelling* sees in the tragedy of existence is softened by the idea of the Fichtean "realm of spirits", whose "intelligences" are "the eternal sustainers of the universe", "so many indestructible mirrors of the objective world",[16] experiencing "a never-ceasing mutual influence".[17] Thus, too, the abolition of consciousness in intellectual contemplation is also moderated: it is designated the return of the "I" to itself from the "prison of the objective world".[18]

Meanwhile, although the Absolute will be defined more and more clearly as the nondifference of subject and object[19]—and here *Fichte* will follow *Schelling*—it can still be described (in the *Methode des akademischen Studiums* of 1802/1803) as a "knowing that is in itself unconditioned", "that, dividing into branches only at different levels of the phenomenal ideal world, expands to form the entire and immeasurable tree of knowledge". All branches of knowledge, each of which is an "organic part" of the whole, together constitute "a symbol of that eternal knowing".[20] In this ideal world of knowledge, which is the "concern of the race", the individual plays a purely instrumental role: "Knowledge is involved in time only insofar as it expresses itself through the individual. In itself, knowing is as little a

---

[15] 1:336. This is one possible presentation of the abiding tragic dimension of all human existence, since "criticism" can "only regard the ultimate goal as the object of an infinite endeavor" (1:331). "There is only an infinite approximation to this ultimate goal—hence the infinite duration of the 'I', immortality" (1:201). Later, it is true, Schelling relativized the Greek tragic dimension when he came to divide history into periods. Cf. 3:603f.; 5:225.

[16] Schelling, *System des transzendentalen Idealismus* (1800) in *Sämtliche Werke*, 3:556, 3:540ff.

[17] 3:557.   [18] 1:321.

[19] Schelling, *Darstellung meines Systems der Philosophie* (1801), in *Sämtliche Werke*, 4:107ff.

[20] 5:215–17.

question of individuality as action is".[21] In a way that has never been surpassed, *Schelling's* formally most complete work, *Bruno* (1802), depicts the pantheistic God/Nature at rest and in total harmony with itself: that-which-knows-no-opposition stands, as such, in opposition to the oppositions found in the world; in order to overcome all oppositions, therefore, it must encompass them in itself. *Philosophie und Religion* (1804) claims to be a continuation of *Bruno*,[22] but in fact it breathes a totally new atmosphere. Although it still speaks of the process of "separation", or of "finite things having their origin in the Absolute",[23] this genesis is now described as a "remove", a "fall from the Absolute",[24] recalling the soul's decline from primal bliss in *Plato*. We are instructed "to envisage the origin of the world of the senses not, as in popular religion, in *creation*, as a positive coming-forth from the Absolute, but as a fall from it". This means "that no finite thing can arise directly out of the Absolute and be brought back to it". We can anticipate that, as far as eschatology is concerned, the soul will be redeemed from its self-preoccupied existence in the body and—speaking in *Eckhart's* terms—will be "essentialized" or "unfashioned": "The true essence, or 'in-itself', of the merely phenomenal soul is the idea or the eternal concept of it which is in God; the two combined form the principle of eternal knowledge. . . . Hence it is clearly mistaken to think of the soul discarding the body in death and yet continuing to exist as an individual." "Individuality", however, "the interlacing of the soul with the body", is "the result of a negation in the soul itself; it is a punishment"; consequently the religious attitude is "the love of death" and "the freeing of the *daimōn*" (that is, the eternal idea in oneself).[25]

This denial of individual immortality in favor of a "realm of spirits" consisting of mere ideas in God disappears after the death of *Schelling's* wife Caroline (in September 1809). This change, which is evident in the Stuttgart lectures (1810) and in *Clara* (1810/1811), *Schelling's* monument to Caroline, is already anticipated in the *Essay on Freedom* (1809).[26] We must briefly turn to the latter's concept of "person".

---

[21] 5:224.   [22] 6:28.   [23] 6:28.   [24] 6:38.

[25] 6:39, 41, 60–64.

[26] This essay is put forward expressly as a continuation of *Philosophie und*

First *Schelling* defends himself against the accusation that the central concept of idealist philosophy, that is, freedom, is incompatible with what he calls the "identity system" or pantheism, the being of things in God. Even in a simple sentence with its subject, predicate and copula, identity is a synthesis, not a mere coincidence. The fact that things are dependent "does not eliminate independence, or even freedom", otherwise it would be impossible for a son to be free and independent of his father.[27] "God is not a God of the dead, but of the living"; what God appoints to be cannot be other than independent, otherwise the world would not be the "self-revelation" of the independent God. "God can be manifest only in what is like him, that is, in free, independently acting beings."[28] *Schelling* shows that he is serious about this momentous statement by understanding the freedom of the nondivine spirit as a freedom for both good and evil; the central section of his treatise discusses first the possibility, and then the reality, of evil. The possibility of evil is deduced in the same way as man is deduced as a person; at this point we must see whether *Schelling's* categories are sufficient to create the concept of a free person who is not God himself.

In 1806, when *Schelling* was still speaking of "the eternal nonbeing of the finite",[29] conceiving it as a mere "reflection",[30] and was ceaselessly circling around the relationship of infinite and finite, he encountered a new thought. It was to take root in his system and ultimately burst it apart: "Mere existence, without regard to its manner and form, is bound to strike anyone who sees it in this way as a miracle. . . . It is existence itself, in every individual instance of the real, that is unfathomable, infinite and can only be grasped from within itself."[31] The stimulus may have come from *Fichte*, but the idea has a new ring to it: existence cannot be deduced from anything else. From now on, in the *Essay on Freedom* and right up to Schelling's later philosophy, God himself is understood as the unification and interpenetration (only in "synthetic" identity) of two principles:

Religion: what remained "unclear" in the latter is "to be presented in perfect definition" here (7:334).

[27] 7:346.   [28] 7:346–47.   [29] 7:159.
[30] 7:164; i.e., expressly including man himself: 168.
[31] 7:198.

of his "essence" and of the ground of his existence. Nature and man have this ground outside themselves; but since "there is nothing prior to or outside God . . . he must have the ground of his existence within himself. All philosophies say this; but they speak of this ground as a mere concept, without making it something concrete and real. . . . This ground is *nature*—in God; a being that, while it is inseparable from him, is yet distinct from him."[32] One page later on, the word "distinct" is replaced by "different". Certainly there is no priority in God, neither in terms of the ground nor in terms of the existing being: each reciprocally produces the other in a "circle". But everything depends on the various concepts used to elucidate this "ground". "Humanly" speaking, it is "the yearning of the eternally One to give birth to itself", "thus, considered in itself, it is also will, but a will in which there is no ratiocination, . . . an intuitive will." From the perspective of the existing world, in which restraint constitutes form, the "ground" appears as "that which knows no rule", chaos, always liable to break out. Here, clinching the matter, comes the twofold description: "the incomprehensible basis of reality, the residuum that is never absorbed"[33]—and on the other hand "selfhood and the nonbeing"[34] into which God launches the general and essential ideas. Here it seems that two quite different intuitions concerning the relation of essence and being are forcibly made to coincide.[35] What is important for us is the interchangeability of "selfhood" (*Selbstheit*) and "nonbeing" (*das Nichtseiende*), sometimes called "the shadowy" (*das Dunkle*)[36] or "the dark principle",[37] to use an enigmatic term beloved by the romantics. The process of becoming a human being, that is, the coming-to-be of nondivine freedom, is portrayed in such a way that "things have their ground in that in God which is not *he himself*", in the ground of his existence; God's Spirit works upon this ground ("like a heaving, rolling

[32] 7:357–58.   [33] 7:359–60.   [34] 7:404.

[35] In the *Stuttgarter Privatvorlesungen*, the relationship of the two principles in God is described as that of the existent (*des Seienden*) and of being (*des Seins*)—or of those which have being (*der Seienden*) and that which has not (*des Nichtseienden*) (7:436).

[36] "Deep night" (7:360).   [37] 7:363.

sea, similar to Plato's matter"),[38] distinguishing the energies in order to unfold the "hidden unity or idea" that inheres in the chaos. These separated energies produce the corporal reality; "but the living bond that comes about in this process of separation, that is, emerges from the depths of the natural ground —the central point of these energies—is the soul." The more the soul-principle informs ("transfigures") the corporal, the higher is the level of the natural organism; in man, however, the soul, in the form of self-consciousness, breaks through into the light of the universal. Thus the shaping activity of the divine Spirit on the "ground" has reached its goal, and "the innermost center is opened up". The product, man in his freedom, is thus the point of encounter of two principles: "The principle, insofar as it arises from the ground and is shadowy, is the creature's own will", the will of the human being, "individual" and "particular"; "over against the creature's particular will there is reason, the universal will, which employs the former and subordinates it to itself as a mere tool".[39] "Selfhood *as* such is spirit; man, as a particular being distinct from God, is self-ish; the connection between them constitutes the personality."[40] Whereas in God the two principles totally interpenetrate and the ground/will is always only the carrier of the Spirit (as love), in man the connection remains unstable; man is able freely to determine the relationship of the two principles. Thus he can exalt his own particular will over the universal—which constitutes evil. This is how a "false life" comes about, which is different from the mere *malum metaphysicum* of *Leibniz*. Man has to decide between the two principles that meet in him, and the fact that there are two of them is crucial: "The will of love and the will of the ground are two different wills; each exists for itself. But the will of love cannot resist the will of the ground, nor can it abolish it, for in doing so it would be resisting itself. For the ground must operate if love is to be, and it must operate independently of love so that love may exist in concrete reality." So the human being is like a person "seized by vertigo on a high and sheer peak": he experiences "life's *angst*"[41] as a result of the "solicitation" of the

[38] 7:360.   [39] 7:363–64.   [40] 7:364.   [41] 7:381.

ground[42] in him—and no devil is called for here. The "Fall" is the preference accorded to our own, particular will over the divine "supercreaturely" will of love.

This explains the possibility of evil: it comes from the "dark principle" in all being: the higher the begins ascend, the more it manifests itself as what is selfish. However, for the reality of evil, *Schelling* returns to a theory that, as we saw, he had developed in his first treatise; after all, idealism was the doctrine of that intelligible, superempirical freedom that embraces and determines man's entire life. Man is the being who determines himself, he is *"his own deed"*—*Fichte* is named here explicitly[43]— and this is necessarily the result of a decision that takes place "outside all time and hence coincident with original creation. . . . The act that determines his life in time belongs . . . to eternity; . . . hence man too, as a result of this act, is outside created reality; he is free, he himself is an eternal origin." The way he determines his life, whether for good or for evil, is already given in his primal decision, through which he "laid hold of himself in a particular form in the original creation".[44] This leads us back not only to *Eckhart's* prior decision of the will in the un-ground, but also to *Plato's* myth at the end of the *Republic* and to the intelligible decision on the part of the characters in *Hofmannsthal's Das Salzburger grosse Welttheater*. On this basis it is hard to explain any person's conversion during the course of his temporal life.[45]

These two aspects could mutually complement each other if the first constituted the human being as "selfhood pure and simple" and the second (self-determination) made him this particular self. As in *Fichte*, the question "Who am I?" is solved by saying: "I am who I make myself to be." But somehow this answer does not fit into the totality of the construction of freedom, for, in order to be good, man would have to subordinate his own will entirely to the universal will; in order to be able to live in God, who "is a devouring fire to every particular will", "man must die to all particularity on his own part";[46] consequently it is not clear how human beings who choose the good can be distinguished from one another. Finally

Schelling tries to bring the two principles that are opposed in God back to an "un-ground", an "absolute indifference",[47] retracing *Eckhart's* path, who sought to penetrate to the "silent desert" behind the divine tri-personality. Since "in the un-ground or the indifference there is no personality",[48] the latter remains a kind of epiphenomenon.

The atmosphere of the *Stuttgarter Privatvorlesungen* is close to that of the *Essay on Freedom*. "In his loftiest dignity, God is the universal being of all things", but he is not some general essence hovering over things; he has his own individual basis, "self-hood, egoism in God":[49] only "through this" can he be concrete love. The development of man and his freedom is similarly portrayed, but then *Schelling* presents a strange anthropology that is more relevant to us. Man attains his freedom only "along a religious path"; to do this, he must be acquainted with the constitution of his spirit. It has three potencies or sides: the side turned toward the material world is *feeling*, *Gemüt* (the spirit's "dark principle", its inner "gravity" (*Schwerkraft*), "melancholy" (*Schwermut*), but also the "yearning for being" and "sensitivity"; in general, the materially real); the *spirit* in the narrower sense, *"l'esprit*, what is really *personal* in man and thus also his own potential for consciousness", in his "own will" and "reason" (where "the highest level is that of the most activated and yet subordinate individual will", attained through freedom's "point of indifference"); the "highest and third potency is the *soul*. It is what is really divine in man, that is, it is the *nonpersonal* element, what really has being, to which what is personal (since it is nonbeing) should be subordinated." So again we have the relegation of the personal in favor of an ecstatic vision of impersonality in the divine: "to 'act in harmony with the soul' means to act, not as a personal being, but entirely impersonally: do not allow your personality to interfere with the soul's influences within you."[50] Death is necessary if this is to be fully realized, and, through death, the "passing over into the realm of spirits". Then *Schelling* offers a description of this latter realm, showing how the human being can establish rapport with it, even while still on earth.

[47] 7:406.   [48] 7:412.   [49] 7:438.   [50] 7:473.

This theme is taken up by the closely related dialogue, *Clara* (1810/1811), which, like the *Privatvorlesungen*, was written under the profound effect of Caroline's death. Here the issue is man's process of perfection: he takes himself out of the potentialities of this life and into the higher possibilities of the beyond; thus he is "redeemed from transitoriness"[51] ("the whole earth is one great ruin"). Looking back to the *Privatvorlesungen*, it is clear what the "immortality of the soul" means here: the soul is a "divine bond" between body and spirit, "what is really human in man",[52] yet it only exists as the "living intercourse" between the three parts. The soul is "what I myself have always been from the beginning", that which others have loved in me through all the various transformations, "my real self, which was neither body nor spirit, but the unifying consciousness of both, that is: soul". The soul passes over to the beyond, and with it goes the spiritual body that has already germinated on this side of the grave, so that the tension or difference between being (*Sein*, the ground) and that which has being (*das Seiende*) "might entirely disappear".[53] As a matter of fact, however, this implies the annihilation of consciousness, which, in idealism, always presupposes an object; yet the state of the dead is described poetically as an "intimate consciousness" (*Innigkeit des Bewusstseins*), uniting the two dimensions, "for, to me, death always seemed a gathering rather than a scattering, a producing of intimate bonds [*verinnigend*] rather than of alienation [*veräussernd*]".[54] In this life we must "regard ourselves as persons, distinct from everything else"; on the very ground of our consciousness we feel "something dark, as it were supporting the personality" and clouding "our being's essential purity". All the same—and this is the answer, in *Clara*, to our question—this dark, selfish substratum "cannot be eliminated"; "but it is to be transformed, to be made luminous: it is to become the silent bearer of the higher light, retaining its own distinctness only for that purpose; having root and ground, but not for its own sake."[55] Thus, even when we are in God, there is still a part of us "which was not God". It is nature, which belongs to God and is God outside of God. "It is something like the flower: it can only bloom through the animating power of the sun, and yet it shoots up as a result of a drive coming from within itself, from dark regions independent of the sun. Ultimately it transfigures its native darkness into light yet remains something distinct from light and sun."[56] In the end, therefore, *Schelling* can speak of the "perfect secularity of heaven" insofar as "nature" or "earth" is taken up into the eternal and is transfigured.[57] Once again we hear the word "essence"; it is "the most refined extraction, as it were, the spice and the perfume" of the earthly: "Yonder we shall have to do with the essence [*Wesen*] of things." We also come across the phrase "composure and tranquility" (*Gelassenheit und Ruhe*): this is the frame of mind in which we are to allow the divine to operate.[58]

Here, within his own system, *Schelling* has finally found a word that can lend credibility to the "essentializing" (*Verwesentlichung*) of the individual (in the language of German mysticism) without his being annihilated in the divine. However, there is still something negative attached to the words "person" and "personality"; this understood as self-will, which has to subordinate itself absolutely, as an instrument. To that extent, as we said at the beginning, an ultimate factor remains unexpressed, namely, the word which God addresses to the individual as such, not in the dark, but in the light. And this in spite of the fact that, in all the last-mentioned works, *Schelling* explicitly reflects on the work of Christ as a reconciliation between God and the world and regards Christianity less and less as a mere speculative truth—"an incarnation from all eternity"[59]—but attempts to grasp revelation as a historical religion that must contain more "than is to be found in reason", otherwise "it would be of no interest whatsoever".[60]

---

[56] 9:75.   [57] 9:99.   [58] 9:100, 105.   [59] 5:298.

[60] 13:142f. Cf. on this topic the essay by W. Kasper, "Krise und Neuanfang der Christologie im Denken Schellings", in *Evangelische Theologie*, vol. 33 (1973): 366–84.

c. Hegel

Hegel[1] is by no means uninterested (as one might think) in the question of who the individual is; but from the outset his interest runs in a particular direction. In indicating what it is, we must once again restrict ourselves to a few excerpts from his entire works, placing his *Phänomenologie des Geistes* (1807) (*The Phenomenology of Mind* [London, 1910]) at the center—though this whole study only forms the introduction to his main work, the *Logik* (*Science of Logic* [London, 1929]). In the latter, however, there is no role for the individual in his distinctness, but only (in the third part) for "subjectivity".

The third part of the *Encyclopaedia*, its *Philosophie des Geistes*, begins with the Delphic Oracle, "Know thyself", immediately observing:

> Neither in itself nor in its historical applications does this absolute command simply mean self-knowledge in terms of the individual's particular abilities, character, inclinations and weaknesses. Rather, it signifies knowledge of what is true of man, what is true in itself—knowledge of the nature of spirit itself. . . . Thus the challenge issued to the Greeks by the Delphic Apollo, to know themselves, is not to be understood as a commandment addressed to the human spirit by some power from outside; the God who urges man to know himself is in fact nothing other than the absolute law of his own spirit. All that the spirit does is consequently only a mode of grasping itself, and the purpose of all genuine pursuit of knowledge is only that the spirit should recognize itself in everything that is in heaven and on earth.

However, the Greeks did not manage to arrive at an absolutely free relationship between the human and divine spirits; "only Christianity, through its teaching of God's becoming man and of the presence of the Holy Spirit in the believing community, was able to give human consciousness a perfectly free relation to the infinite and so facilitate the spirit's understanding grasp in its absolute infinitude."[2] Thus self-knowledge can only come about

[1] Hegel, *Werke*, vols. 1–18 (1832–40), referenced in this section by volume and page number only. Hegel, *Theologische Jugendschriften*, ed. H. Nohl (1907), referenced in this section as N.

[2] 7/2, 3–4.

in a perfect integration—to be progressively demonstrated in thought—of the particular individual into the totality of the spirit (as his truth); for *Hegel*, the step-by-step journey toward this is a ruthless process whereby all that is particular is stripped of its illusion of being able to reach truth in and for itself; in the entire literature of asceticism, this is the most rigorous course of self-transcendence for a "personality that clings to itself".

This can already be seen in the fact that *Hegel* puts the nation, "the generalized individual", at the center of his thought, to which anything "particular" is a contrasting element: "The particular individual is the imperfect spirit, a concrete figure in whose whole existence *one* partial aspect dominates, and in which the others are only present in blurred features." In the generalized individual "the inferior concrete existence has dwindled to an element of minimal significance; what was previously the entire issue is now only a trace; its form is enveloped in the whole and becomes a mere shaded contour."[3] "Nations are ethical totalities and constitute themselves as individuals";[4] only from this point on does the *Phänomenologie* embark on its doctrine of "spirit". The great sections on "consciousness", "self-consciousness" and "reason", in which the individual is given a thorough drilling, are preliminaries; reason becomes "spirit only when the certainty of being the whole of reality is raised to the level of truth and when it becomes conscious of itself as its world and of the world as itself".[5] This is the very goal of the young *Hegel's* very first endeavors (1792–1793), on the subject of "popular religion and Christianity".[6] "The lofty ideal erected by Christ, while it was capable of governing the development of individual men, could not be implemented in a society", and instead of the "Kingdom of God" there had arisen a superficial cult of the Church. "Only when the private religion of Christ is refashioned into a popular religion can it become the bearer of a healthy ethic."[7] The Greek ideal, which enabled individuals and gods to meet on the level of

---

[3] 2:22.   [4] 1:372.   [5] 2:327.   [6] N, 3–71.

[7] Summary by W. Dilthey in *Die Jugendgeschichte Hegels*, *Schriften* IV (1921), 15f. His concern is thus to mediate "between a pure religion of reason" and "fetishist faith": "How popular religion should be organized in order, (a) negatively, to give as little opportunity as possible for people to get stuck at the level

the *polis*, only survives in the form of a painful yearning:[8] it awaits its reimplementation in Christian terms. *Hegel* puts forward a *Life of Jesus* (1795)[9] as the foundation stone for a popular religion of this kind; here we only need point out that it is seen as ending with the burial of Jesus.[10] Even at this early stage *Hegel* regards individual immortality as presumption, a refusal of the "incomplete spirit" to be integrated into that totality in which alone it can become concrete spirit: man can only be eternalized in the vertical axis that arises from the interior of time and history and reaches up into the all-embracing totality. Here, unlike *Schelling* in his middle and late periods, *Hegel* takes up the more primitive demands of *Fichte's* popular addresses, that is, that in all our actions we should have the "nation" or simply "the race" in mind.

This does not mean that *Hegel* did not attend to the particularity of the individual. He speaks of the "genius", which we should "understand as that decisive particularity that determines a man's actions and destiny in all his situations and relationships"; "this internal particularity of mind constitutes my fate; for it is the oracle on whose utterance depend all the individual's decisions; it is the objective element, asserting itself from the innermost core of the character." *Hegel* is clearly moving in the direction of *Plato's* and *Schelling's* intelligible, free self-choosing when he says that "on the one hand, the genius is . . . a selfish 'other' over against the individual, and, on the other hand, it unites with the individual to form a unity as inseparable as that of the

---

of the letter and usages, and (b) positively, to lead them toward the religion of reason and help them to acquire a receptivity for it" (N, 17).

[8] N, 29.   [9] N, 73–136.

[10] Nor will Hegel speak any differently later on. In the *Phänomenologie*, similarly, he passes straight from the "death of the divine Man" to the philosophical event of Pentecost: "Death is elevated from its immediate meaning, i.e., the nonbeing of this particular individual, and transfigured into the universality of the Spirit, who lives in his community, dying and rising daily therein" (2:589). In *Philosophie der Religion* a clear line is drawn between Christ's death seen as "the death of death", as "negation of the negation" (which is the essential), and the statement: "The Resurrection belongs essentially to the realm of faith: after his Resurrection Christ only appeared to his friends", i.e., it is only a dimension of faith (12:249–50).

psyche and the world of its dreams."[11] But this particularity is only the product of a "special, fortuitous amalgam of external conditions with the internal state of individuals"; it is not even significant enough to be allotted a place in the process of the *Phänomenologie des Geistes*: it is not to be found at the beginning, where the (apparently absolute) uniqueness of "this" and "here" is simultaneously the absolutely universal (hence: "when I say 'I', this individual 'I', I also say 'I' as such, all 'I's; every 'I' is that which I say"[12]—nor is it to be found at the conclusion, with the "spirit that has become certain of itself". The most one could say is that "the unhappy, so-called 'beautiful' soul" is a "dying ember" as it reflects on its own geniality.[13] Like *Fichte*, *Hegel* also engages in polemics against *Schleiermacher* when he says:

> When the individual casts off its subjectivity . . . , this subject-objectivity that contemplates the *Universum* is still supposed to remain something particular and subjective. The virtuosity of the religious artist is supposed to be permitted to mix its subjectivity into the tragic seriousness of religion. . . . If the priest can only be an instrument and servant, sacrificing the community and himself, for it and for himself, performing the limiting and objective aspects of religious contemplation; if he is only a representative of the community-come-of-age (from which all his power comes), is the community then to disenfranchise itself and have some virtuoso of edification and fervor practise this inner contemplation within it? . . . A person is an idiot [*idios*: particular, peculiar—Tr.] insofar as he manifests peculiarities.[14]

To the extent that the normative is the "generalized individual", in whose substantial ethical world particular individuals have their true freedom (provided each of them is integrated into it), the problem of intersubjectivity that so tormented *Husserl* does not bother *Hegel*; it is a fundamental fact of that "experience" that is recapitulated in the *Phänomenologie des Geistes*. Only here "are we presented with the concept of spirit", for it is "that absolute substance that, in the perfect freedom and independence of its opposite, namely, diverse and self-subsistent self-consciousness, constitutes their unity. Thus the 'I' is the

[11] 7/2, 161–62.   [12] 2:78.   [13] 2:496.   [14] 1:113–14.

'We'; the 'We' is the 'I'."[15] There is a living and reciprocal relationship between the "We" and the "I's". The I's "are aware that they are individual and self-subsistent beings by virtue of surrendering their individuality; this generalized substance is their soul and essence. Conversely, the general is what they as individuals do; it is their achievement."[16] The spirit consists in the conscious performance of this interpenetration. Thus it is characteristic of *Hegel* that he begins to discuss what we call the I-thou relationship only when he has reached this stage; for him, man and woman encounter each other with a view to the family, which is the basic cell of the community of the nation; this can lead to the tragic tension between family law and common law, which *Hegel* likes to illustrate by referring to the *Oresteia* and *Antigone*. In both cases, though differently, the issue is one of "sacrificing existence"[17] in view of the all-embracing reality; in the case of Orestes the two conflicting commandments—of blood-kinship and of God—are reconciled in the Athenian institution of the national code of law.

"Hence the spirit is the self-subsistent, absolute, concrete being. All previous configurations of consciousness are abstractions of it",[18] because in them the individual confronts true reality while being yet unintegrated into it; he does not recognize his own essence in the objective realm. We must hasten through the initial stages: the certainty of the senses, in which what is most concrete is revealed as what is most empty and most general; the perception of things, where the thing's being-in-itself deceives through the multiplicity of its modes of appearance (for it is "one thing for itself, but something different for others");[19] the penetration to the ground of the object, which is posited as the power (perceptible in its apparent qualities) holding together the utterances of this ground; but the

---

[15] 2:139. At the level of reason: "Reason is present like a fluid, universal substance, manifesting itself in a multitude of completely separate beings, just as light is disseminated in the stars, in countless, individually shining points" (2:265).

[16] 2:265.

[17] A reference to the *Antigone* (2:341f.) and the *Oresteia* (2:344ff., 1:387; 2:381).

[18] 2:329.   [19] 2:94.

"power" (*Kraft*)—"the supersensible", "nature's inner realm"—remains an empty concept, whose truth is "appearance *qua* appearance":[20] "We find that there is nothing to be seen behind the so-called 'curtain' that is supposed to conceal the inner realm unless we ourselves go behind it, both in order to see anything at all and to see what is to be seen." But, *Hegel* goes on, the possibility of thus "going behind" is itself the "result of an involved movement through which the modes of consciousness, of thinking, perception and reasoning all disappear", making room for self-consciousness.[21] At this level, consciousness is life and desire; it experiences the self-subsistence of its object, which is another "self".[22] The first way in which two self-subsistents acknowledge each other is by each affirming and proving itself to the ultimate: in a struggle, a conflict, that ends in death. "The individual who has not risked his life, while he may indeed be recognized as a person, has not attained to the truth of his being recognized as a self-subsistent self-consciousness."[23] And just as "life is the natural position of consciousness, self-subsistence without absolute negativity, death is the natural negation of it, negation without self-subsistence, that is, lacking the required significance of recognition."[24] There are two significant things here. *Hegel* takes struggle or conflict as the primal fact of conscious life—and he will always represent war as an indispensable factor in the life of nations[25]—and he accords death an absolutely fundamental function in his entire system: death alone is the criterion of truth, from this primal struggle and through all stages, right up to the constantly resounding cry: "God is dead!" ("This is the most terrible thought, that everything that is eternal, everything that is true, *is not*, and that negation itself is in God; this is the ultimate pain, the feeling of utter hopelessness.")[26] In the *Preface* we read: "Death . . . is the

---

[20] 2:111. [21] 2:130. [22] 2:138. [23] 2:143-44. [24] 2:144.

[25] 1:373. "War is necessary for the ethical totality." At the risk of totally destroying the nation "it upholds the ethical soundness of nations in its indifference to their fixed and habituated institutions, just as the movement of the winds protects the oceans from the corruption which would result from a permanent calm. So too an enduring peace, let alone 'an eternal peace', would corrupt nations." Similarly at 2:339.

[26] 12:249 and 2:590.

most terrible reality, and to hold fast to what is dead demands the greatest possible strength." We must look death "in the eye", we must spend time with it.[27] Even the life of God would be nothing but "a playing with love", mere insipid edification, "if it lacked the seriousness, the pain, the patience and the labor of the negative".[28] In connection with the relationship between vassal and sovereign he says: "The only true self-sacrifice of one's existence-for-oneself is . . . that which is as thoroughgoing as death; yet in this self-emptying it preserves itself, only in this way really becoming what, in itself, it is." This is the only way that loyalty and honor can prove themselves to be serious.[29] We must constantly remember that the individual can look forward to no other immortality than that of service to the nation or the state; so we shall grasp the full meaning of the "sacrifice of one's existence" in *Hegel's* sense: "The individual as such is nothing",[30] but since he can raise himself up above every external compulsion, "his individual being . . . is an absolute individuality that has been elevated and adopted into the concept; it is negatively absolute infinitude, pure freedom. This negative absolute, pure freedom, appears in the form of death; and it is through the ability to die [!] that the subject shows itself to be free and above all compulsion."[31]

These observations arose from the portrayal of self-consciousness as proving itself in a "life and death struggle".[32] One of its primary forms, however (arising directly out of the preceding), is the duality of rank in the *polis*—freemen and slaves: "individuals of an absolute ethic (whose organs the various individuals are)", who relish the totality and therefore also expose themselves to death—and individuals whose "labor is directed to particularity and thus does not involve the danger of death"(!), and who are thus by nature "another's".[33] In the *Phänomenologie*, *Hegel* laid down the principles of this historically oriented portrayal of the two forms of self-consciousness, in terms of the master/servant relationship;[34] only here it is revealed in all its radicality. The servant's labor is decisive for the relationship; it is productive not only for the master but also for the servant himself, who shows himself to be genuinely free in giving himself to and for the task. The "freedom of self-consciousness"[35] is presented in the three forms in which the latter has not yet attained "reason", namely, stoicism—the purely negative freedom from desire, that being-present-to-oneself that "has no content of itself" and ends in "boredom"; scepticism—a "confused self-consciousness" that eternally "goes around in circles in a world of chance", self-contradictory in word and deed; and the unity of both, the "unhappy consciousness that is split within itself"—a mischievous designation of the Christian consciousness, which regards what is unchangeable in it as something extrinsic to it (*Feuerbach* and *Marx* will speak of "projection" here) and holds on to what is changeable as "its own nothingness". "In attempting to reach its own essence, it only attains its own split reality", and thus it has no choice but to posit the other side (God) as a "beyond" that "cannot be reached". *Kierkegaard* will later apply this distortion to *Hegel* himself. Initially it is a mere feeling of this opposition in the form of "devotion"—*Andacht*—("the unthinking droning of the bells"), but it is a painful, broken feeling because, as the active, hither side (the "servant"), it is powerless compared with the "absolute might" of the beyond; all it can do is surrender itself and "ascribe the essence of all action to the beyond, not to itself". (Thus God has to take the initiative in the process of reconciliation.) Where such action is posited as the overcoming of opposed aspects, "conscious selfhood" is once again "overthrown by the attitude of thanksgiving". The situation is most acute where "finitude . . . , in its outermost extreme, constitutes evil",[36] which results in the unhappy consciousness "seeing itself as always besmirched"; at the same time the "content of its striving, instead of being some essential thing, is the lowest; instead of being universal, it is the most individual"; consequently "we see nothing but a personality that is as unhappy as it is wretched, limited to itself and its petty activity and brooding upon itself".[37] Through renunciations—surrendering its own independence (obedience), giving up ex-

---

[35] 2:150–73.

[36] 12:250. Cf.: "This finitude, in its self-sufficient resistance to God, is evil, alien to him" (12:251).

[37] 2:170.

ternal possessions (poverty) and renouncing pleasure (in "fasting and mortification")—it tries to respond to God's deed. This is *Hegel's* final characterization of Christianity in its historical development, which is therefore allotted a place among the preliminary stages of spirit. In the end, in his *Offenbare Religion*, he will present a purified picture of the relationship between finite and infinite spirit, but there too he will say: "The unhappy consciousness has the painful feeling that God himself has died"—explaining it thus: "This harsh dictum expresses the most intimate knowledge (simply and immediately present to itself), the return of consciousness to the deep night of the 'I' = 'I', . . . the loss of substance" (this is *Fichte's* view), "but simultaneously (!) it is the pure subjectivity of the substance . . . , the bespiriting [*Begeistung*] whereby the substance has become subject (its abstractness and lifelessness having died) and has *really* become a simple and universal self-consciousness."[38]

In other words, the death of God that is represented (in the death of Christ) as the form of reconciliation and the self-revelation of the infinite spirit is, in its truth, the form of inner self-reconciliation, not for the "unhappy" consciousness, but for the consciousness that has realized itself as spirit. If this is correct, the center of the *Phänomenologie* is the end of the section concerning the spirit that is certain of itself,[39] whereas the following chapter on "religion" is only the unfolding of this dimension, and the final chapter on "absolute knowledge" is simply reflection upon it. All paths lead to this center, constituting an education toward perfect ethical behavior: the overcoming of the point of view of one's immediate happiness[40] (since "individuality's absolute brittleness is shattered to dust against the equally hard but perduring reality");[41] the overcoming of the point of view of insane self-conceit, which undertakes to improve the world according to the "law of one's own undisciplined heart" and ends by discrediting all law and order as "repression";[42] the overcoming of the point of view of private virtue, which is "conquered by the world's onward course".[43] But even where an individuality has been attained

---

[38] 2:590.   [39] 2:451–508.   [40] 2:267.   [41] 2:274.   [42] 2:282.
[43] 2:290.

that is "real in and for itself" (*an und für sich selbst reel*) and that has integrated itself into the common totality, there are yet more unmaskings in store: the illusion that one has devoted oneself to "the issue", whereas in reality one has placed one's own interest, "one's *own* actions and endeavors" at the center and desired the recognition of others; the perverse attempt to master concrete ethical behavior through abstract laws or imperatives (for it can never be trapped in a net of this kind);[44] and finally the "hypocrisy" that arises when "conscience" is made absolute (for conscience is in fact "concrete moral spirit"), obliterating the separation between the "in-itself"—*Ansich*—(of pure duty) and the "self"—*Selbst*—(that "nature and sense-existence that is opposed to the pure pursuit of aims").[45] "Conscience has its own truth in its immediate certainty of itself"; here "its own immediate individuality" is the content of moral conduct, and the latter's form is "this very self as pure motion": "personal conviction". But here too there is a subjective one-sidedness: if conscience takes itself as its ultimate norm, it becomes "arbitrary", "out of step with the universal" and, finally, "hypocrisy". At this point *Hegel* discusses language in some detail as the mediating "existence of spirit", compared with which the "moral consciousness is as yet dumb, enclosed within its inner self", and the consciousness that evaluates the individual is "another mode of being evil": the "hard heart". The final possibility of achieving the necessary reconciliation of the particular and the universal, in which a true ethical approach reaches its perfection—the center of the *Phänomenologie* to which we have already referred —lies in the word of recognition (*Bekenntnis*, acknowledgment, confession) and the responding word of forgiveness (which includes the religious attitude of looking up to the all-embracing gesture of reconciliation on the part of the absolute spirit): "The

---

[44] We are passing over those chapters that practically sum up the dialectic of modern history: feudalism and absolutism; "the language of division" (embodied, for instance, in the intellectual world of the Encyclopedists); Christianity as "positive faith" in opposition to the Enlightenment; the Enlightenment's injustice to Christianity (and, at a deeper level, its justice); the French Revolution ("absolute freedom coupled with terror"); Kantian ethics ("self-conscious spirit; morality"); romanticism ("the beautiful soul"), which brings us up to Hegel.
[45] 2:478.

word of reconciliation is the existent spirit [*der daseiende Geist*] who beholds the pure knowledge of himself as a *universal* being in his opposite, in the pure knowledge of himself as absolute, self-existent *individuality*;—this reciprocal recognition is *absolute spirit*";[46] it is "the reconciling Yes in which both 'I's relinquish their opposed existences".[47]

It is clear that the "generalized individual", the community of the nation, which, for *Hegel*, acquires its organization in the state, is ultimately fashioned after the model of a Christian community; the spirit who, being absolute, opens up individuals into a genuinely self-subsistent community, is understood in the sense of the *pneuma hagion*, the Holy Spirit of the Church of Jesus Christ. But whereas in the granting of individual charisms the ecclesial Spirit's effect is both personalizing and universalizing (since he is the Spirit of the risen and pneumatically universalized Jesus Christ), *Hegel's* spirit is one-sidedly universalizing, for no personalizing vocation is imparted to the individual; here too, universalization is not based on a personal rising from the dead. Hence we find in *Hegel* the all-permeating pathos of death, which, in fact or potentially, represents the highest deed through which the individual can manifest his solidarity with the nation. Thus he continually speaks of sacrifice, even of the "shattering of individuality".[48] This shows, against all appearances to the contrary, that we are ultimately right in placing *Hegel's* understanding of the "I" in the category of "alienation": for, in its sacrifice for the sake of the whole, the "I" as such is not sustained, in fact it declines to the level of "an element of minimal significance", as we have seen. And so, by a different path, we have arrived at the same conclusion as in the chapter on *Hegel* at the beginning of this volume, where, in the context of dramatic theory, we noted a missing dimension in *Hegel's* understanding of Christianity.

Symptomatic of this obstinate one-sidedness is the total lack, in the entire realm of German idealism, of the reality of prayer. *Hegel* can admit prayer as an expression of religion, but it is only a penultimate stage of the spirit's absolute self-knowledge, which renders all prayer obsolete. No living God is needed to

---

[46] 2:506.   [47] 2:508.   [48] 2:275.

render intelligible the highest ethical act, that is, reciprocal recognition through the word of acknowledgment and reconciliation. The path from *Fichte's* concept of the "race" (or "humanity") and *Hegel's* universal self-consciousness, which has raised itself above the dialectic of freeman and slave, master and servant, leads directly to Marxism, where (quite logically) the individual is practically reduced to the level of material in the common cause, even if this cause is seen in terms of *Hegel's* model of the "generalized individual", in which individuals allegedly find both freedom and fulfillment.

The inner logic that leads from *Hegel* to *Marx* is so strong that all attempts to reinterpret *Hegel* in a personalist sense were doomed to have no effect on history—thus, for instance, the theism and teaching on immortality of the young *I. H. Fichte* or the Christian metaphysics of *C. H. Weisse* or the attempts of *Anton Günther* and *Martin Deutinger* to find a theological way out. (We have excluded Christian theology from our prolegomena.) Of all the attempts to mediate between a philosophy of accepting one's limits and a philosophy of alienation, it is at best the last of them, *dialogics*, that is able to enter upon a serious debate with *dialectics*.

D. ATTEMPTS AT MEDIATION

1. *Representation: The King*

The previous two attempts to answer the question "Who am I?" have failed because in each case the personal "I" has had to surrender itself to some all-embracing life or essence, and no necessary connection has been demonstrated between the life/essence and this particular "I".

In the history of ideas, however, there have been attempts to avoid this fiasco and reach a positive answer. Here, deliberately excluding the Christian period, we shall present four of them in outline, two pre-Christian and two post-Christian. The most important ones are pre-Christian, they have an "advent" character; they must be mentioned at this point because, unlike anything else, they represent a kind of "hollow mold" of biblical and Christian revelation and to that extent are an instance of "negative Christology". Indeed, it is "negative" in many ways: not only is it timebound and forever past, it is also internally defective, either too exclusive or too vague. All the same, it manifests the closest possible approach to Christianity. It is also important to note that the transition from this "negative" Christology to "positive" Christology (which alone, as we shall show, can answer the question at issue) is not a direct one. The Old Testament lies between the two, separating them; there is no correspondence between question and answer, between the expectant "hollow mold" and the fulfillment.

As far as all the peoples of the Near East are concerned —Egyptians, Sumerians, Assyrians, Babylonians, Hittites, Phoenicians, Canaanites—there is at least one person who is able to answer with some precision the question "Who am I?" namely, the king.[1] This is a feature common to them all, in spite

[1] I. G. Frazer, *The Magical Origin of Kings* (London, 1920); I. Engnell, *Studies in Divine Kingship in the Ancient East* (Uppsala, 1943); H. Frankfort, *Kingship and the Gods* (Chicago, 1948); C. G. Gadd, *Ideas of the Divine Rule in the Ancient East* (Oxford Univ. Press, 1948), esp. Lecture II: "The King" (33–62); text hereafter abbreviated as *Ideas of Divine Rule*. Full bibliography in Karl-Heinz Bernhardt, "Das Problem der altorientalischen Königsideologie im Alten Testament", *Vet.*

of considerable variation in concepts. The answer is revealed by a god who is understood in personal terms, who by his own power either begets or adopts this particular human being. The answer has not a merely private significance, for the king is not only a representative of the god to the people but also, in his own person, lends shape to the individuals of his people and represents them before the deity. "It is the king who gives man whatever position he has in the state and in society", insofar as he "is the representative of his subjects before the heavenly powers . . . , but conversely he is responsible to the gods for the transgressions and failures of his subjects. Thus we can hardly describe this figure better than by using the image of the mediator between the world of the gods and the world of men."[2]

Here we can quote only a few examples from a tremendous wealth and variety of material. The Egyptian pharaoh[3] is god incarnate. This conception has two variants. In one, the most high god is present in him as in a cultic image or a sacred animal, an indwelling that comes about through the king's enthronement. From this moment the king bears the name of the god as well as his own: he is called "Horus NN". This is the more ancient version, but it is not extinguished with the emergence of the second. According to this, the pharaoh is (from very early times)[4] the son of the king of heaven, sharing in his nature and power; from the beginning of the religion of Osiris he is "Horus", as the latter's "coessential" son,[5] "the living image of the father on earth"; naturally enough, this is not something that begins with his anointing as king: it is already so "in the

---

Test. Suppl. VII (Leiden: Brill, 1961); abbreviated hereafter as "Der altorient. Königs. im A.T."

[2] Bernhardt, "Der Altorient. Königs. im A.T.", 70ff. "The kingship understood as a balance and channel between gods and men" (Gadd, Ideas of Divine Rule, 38).

[3] The article "König" in Bonnet, Reallexikon d. ägypt. Rel. Gesch. (Berlin, 1952), 380ff.; A. Erman, Die Religion der Ägypter (Berlin and Leipzig, 1934), 123ff.; A. Moret, Du caractère religieux de la royauté pharaonique (Paris, 1902).

[4] K. Sethe, Urgeschichte und älteste Religion der Ägypter (Leipzig, 1930, §132ff.).

[5] "For the son is like the father (i.e., Osiris) that begat him": Breasted, Ancient Records of Egypt III (1906), §269.

egg". In the most ancient texts this birth is traced back to primeval times, "when neither heaven nor earth nor mankind existed, before the gods had been born".[6] This view makes sense only if Egypt's first ruling generations were gods, followed by human kings. All the same, each dawn can be interpreted as an instance of the ceaseless coming-to-birth of the glorious son from the (Sun-)god.[7] Only in Egypt is this birth seen as a physical act: Re, in the form of the ruling king, begets his successor from the queen. At other times (as Aton) he penetrates her with his rays;[8] this whole theme must not be forced, otherwise it would threaten the hereditary legitimacy of the successor. On the other hand this notion of the begetting of the son places a certain distance between him and his father; it sets him in a relationship of obedience; he has been begotten "to carry out what he (his father) commands"[9]—but the latter's will is always "righteousness" (*Maat*), not the arbitrary will of a despot. This distancing means that the pharaoh, although in essence divine, is still a human being; he has two natures in one person, as it were, and hence is "both subject and object of the cult".[10] He stands before his divine Ka in order to be blessed by him, while at the same time he is the one who, as the chief priest, blesses the people. Ramses II is depicted in human form, hand in hand with "the great god Ramses" (with the falcon's head

---

[6] K. Sethe, *Die altägyptischen Pyramidentexte* I–IV (1908–22), 1466.

[7] Davies, *The Rock Tombs of El Amarna* I–VI (1903–8), IV, pl 33, 8.

[8] One example is the decree of the god Ptah to King Ramses II (in *Urkunden zur Religion des Alten Ägypten*, translated, with an introduction, by Günther Roeder, 2d ed. [Jena, 1923], 159–63). The god addresses the king: "I am thy father and have begotten thee as God, to reign on thy throne as King of Upper and Lower Egypt. . . . I am thy father; I begot thee among the Gods, so that all thy members are Gods. . . . I cause thy heart to be divine, like my own, I choose thee, I appoint thee, I prepare thee." Finally the king answers: "I am thy son whom thou hast set upon thy throne. . . . Thou hast fashioned me in thy form and appearance, and hast given into my hands all that thou hast created. I am the one who again and again rejoices thy heart by being the sole lord, as thou wert, in order to conduct the affairs of the land."

[9] A. Erman, *Die Literatur der Ägypter* (Leipzig, 1933), 80.

[10] Bernhardt, "Der altorient. Königs. im A.T.", 77. Cf.: "The king is always upon the point of stepping over into the god, and yet is always subordinate" (Gadd, *Ideas of Divine Rule*, 47).

surmounted by the sun disk). While the outer walls of the temple illustrate the king's great deeds, the inner walls and pillars depict his familiar intercourse with the divine world: the god embraces him, teaches him archery, promises him years without number, and so on. Few pharaohs erected temples for themselves; people prayed only to statues of the king (if we set aside the religious impact of court ceremonial); only the dead pharaoh is given unlimited divine status. But the way he is portrayed in bas-reliefs and paintings—towering larger than life over the other figures—shows that he is "The Man".

This is how the king is seen in the other cultures of the Near East too, although, almost invariably, they do not attribute to him a physical equality of nature with the Divinity. The king of Ugarit is "the Man of Ugarit"; in Sumer he is Lugal, "the Great Man". In Mesopotamia, too, he is the (albeit adopted) "son of god".[11] More than in Egypt he is the governor appointed by god, responsible on earth for the country's entire well-being;[12] consequently he must be more expressly concerned for physical and moral order. In its long prologue and epilogue, the Code of Hammurabi explains that the king has been chosen by Marduk "in order to cause righteousness to arise in the land and to destroy perverse and wicked men, so that the strong shall not oppress the weak". But Egyptian wisdom literature,[13] in par-

---

[11] R. Labat, *Le caractère religieux de la royauté assyro-babylonienne* (Paris, 1939), 166ff. Engnell, *Studies in Divine Kingship in the Ancient East*, 16f.; Frankfort, *Kingship and the Gods*, 273ff. References to Ugarit in Bernhardt, "Der altorient. Königs. im A.T.", 76.

[12] The extreme case is in Sumer, where the entire land and its produce belong to the god, and the king must give account to him of his stewardship. He is aware of the weight of the responsibility: "I am the King, the Cherished One, of good seed from the very womb, / Lipit-Ishtar, Enlil's son . . . who carries the tall Shepherd's staff; I am the life of the land of Sumer, / the Husbandman who pours out the (great) heaps of grain, / the Herdsman who multiplies the herd's milk and fat, / who causes fish and fowl to grow in the swamp, / who makes an abundance of water to run in the water-courses, / I am he who increases the bountiful yield of the great mountain." / "It is sweet to hymn my praises" (*Sumerische und akkadische Hymnen und Gebete*, introduced and translated by A. Falkenstein and W. v. Soden [Zurich and Stuttgart, 1953], 126–30). Cf. H. Zimmern, "Konig Lipit-Istars Vergöttlichung", *Berichte . . . der sächs. Ak. d. Wiss, phil-hist. Kl.* (1916), 68, 5.

[13] *Altägyptische Lebensweisheit*, intro. and trans. Fr. v. Bissing (Zurich, 1955).

ticular the instructions of a king to his son, Merikere,[14] mani-fests similar ideas.

Kingship was introduced late in Assyria; in Babylon it was strangely precarious, the king laying his power aside at each New Year festival and being reinvested with it by the priest (who could actually refuse). In Egypt the periodical repetition of the investiture at the feast of Sed was purely ceremonial. In both countries, less markedly in Egypt and more markedly in Assyria, kingship is a drama played between heaven and earth; in Babylon it also involves a symbolic battle on the part of the king with the powers of the Abyss. The world order, in its prevalently static form in Egypt and its prevalently dynamic form in Babylon, is epitomized by the king. He is quite simply "The Man",[15] which includes his function as "shepherd"—the chief title of the Mesopotamian kings; the people he pastures, which he represents before the gods, only attain real personality in him. In Egypt, "only the divine Ka of the king is a representa-tional 'double'. By contrast, the Ka of the subject is *impersonal*."[16] Thus we have the bold, striking Akkadic dictum: "The shadow of God is the 'Man', and men are shadows of the 'Man'. The 'Man' is the king, the image of God."[17] In Egypt, men receive their Ka from the king. "My-Ka-comes-from-the-king" is one of the names in the ancient Empire.[18] The king alone is the fixed "I", as such representing the divine world; his subjects represent nothing—except insofar as they reflect the king. And all this in spite of the profound wisdom teachings in which the ethical

[14] *Ibid.*, 54ff. Cf. also J. M. Breasted, *The Dawn of Conscience* (New York, 1934).

[15] Which caused Aage Bentzen, in *Messias, Moses redivivus, Menschensohn* (Zurich, 1948), to place him beyond the particular concepts of king, priest, prophet, miracle worker—all of which he embodies—and equate him with the "primal man" (of the later apocalyptic and gnosticism), and to understand him as *schema Christi*. Cf. 37–42. S. Mowinckel has resisted this extreme view in "Urmensch und 'Königsideologie' ", in *Studia Theologica, Lund* I (1948): 71ff.

[16] Bernhardt, "Der altorient. Königs. im A.T.", 75, with examples. My emphasis.

[17] F. T. M. Böhl, "Der babylonische Fürtenspiegel", in *Mitteil. d. Altorient. Gesellschaft* XI, 3 (Leipzig, 1937): 49.

[18] Frankfort, *Kingship and the Gods*, 60; H. Jacobson, "Die symbolische Bedeutung des göttlichen Pharaonentums für den ägyptischen Menschen", in *Atti dell' VIII congresso internazionale di storia delle religioni* (Florence, 1956), 70.

conduct of the individual is taken very seriously and which
regards human beings as God's "images, come forth from his
members. . . . God knows the name of each of them."[19]

Here we must make brief mention of kingship in Israel in the
context of the Near East. In recent times it has been moved into
the center of the debate by the "divine kingship" and "ritual
pattern" school. There is nothing surprising about the considerable
influence exerted by the surrounding countries on the theology
of kingship. The Phoenician-Canaanite area, in which Israel
lived, was no exception here. It is not strange that images,
concepts and titles were borrowed from surrounding nations
when it came to founding the Israelite kingdom with its court
and temple ceremonial. The question is whether Israel submitted
to the common "pattern" or whether it filtered and as it were
sterilized what it adopted into its own unique religion. We can
show most easily that the latter is the case by pointing out that,
in Israel, the king is not a representative of Yahweh, let alone an
"incarnation" of him (S. Mowinckel). It is unanimously accepted
that, of the surrounding ideologies, the pharaohs' physical
divine sonship and divine identity cannot have had any influence
on Israel[20] and that the most we can speak of is an analogy to the
adoptive divine sonship found in Babylon and the surrounding

[19] "Lehre für Merikare", in *Altägypt. Lebensweisheit*, Bissing, trans., 56.
[20] G. Widengren, *Sakrales Konigtum im Alten Testament und im Judentum*
(Stuttgart, 1955) suggests that there was an almost total adoption of the
Canaanite kingship ideology—in the "syncretistic cult in Jerusalem". Cf. his
article in S. H. Hooke, *Myth, Ritual and Kingship, Essays on the Theory and
Practice of Kingship in the Ancient Near East and in Israel* (Oxford, 1958). One of
the major texts he uses as a basis is Ps 110:3—"The dew of thy birth is of the
womb of the morning"—which he regards as more than adoptionist; he sees it as
indicating physical generation (from a female deity, cf. Is 14:12). He finds
evidence in the Old Testament of the veneration of female deities (Jer 44:17—
Queen of Heaven = Anat), temple prostitution connected with the *hieros gamos*,
the addressing of the king as God (Ps 44) and an "erotic sphere of concepts"
(Hos, Ezek, Song). Widengren's extreme position has been rejected by, among
others, S. Mowinckel: even this text contains "nothing more than a 'mythopoetic'
expression of the idea of covenant and election and of the close relation between
the king and the god which election establishes" (*He That Cometh* [Oxford,
1956], 56). Similarly Gerald Cooke, in his "The Israelite King as Son of God", in
ZAW 73 (1961): 202–205 (following his fuller dissertation, *The Problem of Divine
Kingship. The Divine Sonship of the Hebrew King* [Yale, 1958]) campaigns for a

area. But here again there is a parting of the ways. The assumption of the Swedish school, that is, that the Babylonian New Year festival—with its cultic drama of the king's descent into the underworld, overcoming the powers of chaos and being reinvested with royal status—had been taken over in Israel would impart a far more mythical note to its kingship; but the existence of a dramatic ritual of this kind, which has always been deduced in a purely indirect way, seems increasingly dubious and difficult to establish on the basis of straightforward exegesis.[21] Those who lay stress on a king who "suffers" (and perhaps even atones on behalf of his people?) in his struggle with chaos, reminiscent of the Tammuz literature and pointing forward to the "Suffering Servant",[22] are engaging in wayward speculations. The position of the king was always contested in Israel, fiercely at the beginning and below the surface subsequently;[23] Isaiah recognized it only as an "office" in the titles he applied to it (9:6), whereas the royal name was kept for Yahweh alone (6:5).[24]

---

thoroughgoing adoptionism, referring to Martin Noth, "Gott, Konig und Volk im AT", in *ZTK* 47 (1950): 148ff., and C. R. North, "The Religious Aspect of Hebrew Kingship", in *ZAW* (1932): 8ff. According to him, Ps 110 is to be interpreted in the context of the investiture of the king: "The notion of begetting is transformed to a metaphor by the emphasis on the immediate occasion on which the king has become God's son"—i.e., "this day I have begotten thee". Widengren's rendering of Ps 110:3 (like LXX and Vulgate) is at least questionable; even if it were valid, the dawn need not be any mythical figure but simply an indication of time. J. Gray, in "Canaanite Kingship in Theory and Practice", *Vet. Test.* 2 (1952): 193–20, endeavors to contrast the Canaanite version with that of Egypt and of Babylon and thus to diminish the distance between it and Israel, but his view does not fully convince.

[21] Cf. H.-J. Kraus, *Psalmen* II (Neukirchner Verlag, 1961), 590–91 and 351f., 503f., 590f., 617f., where he takes up a position against S. Mowinckel, I. Engnell, G. Widengren, A. Bentzen and others.

[22] Helmer Ringgren, "König und Messias", in *ZAW* 64 (1952): 120–47. Aberrant, too, is the version by Aubrey R. Johnson, *Sacred Kingship of Ancient Israel* (Univ. of Wales Press, Cardiff, 1955), who envisages a complicated synthetic ritual drama—first come Yahweh's battle with the waters of chaos, his victory and enthroning, then follows a drama of the humiliated king or messiah (who is also the "Suffering Servant"), who is ultimately lifted up again by Yahweh.

[23] Bernhardt, "Der altorient. Königs. im A.T.", 91–117.

[24] This is referred to by A. Alt, "Das Königtum in den Reichen Israels und Juda", in *Kleinschriften zur Geschichte des Volkes Israel* II (Munich, 1933), 116–34,

Representing God is one form of asserting an "I"; but it is an extraordinary and superhuman form that leaves the other members of the nation indeterminate. This form practically dies out with Roman antiquity—if we exclude its echo in the Christian middle ages[25]—not without clashing violently with Christianity.

2. *Authenticated Status: The Genius*

It is going too far to say that what the divinity of the oriental king does for him (and, in him, for the people), namely, affirming the "I", the *genius*, in the Italic view, it does for everyone. For this *genius* has a will-o'-the-wisp character; qualitatively it tends to become obscured and quantitatively it tends to splinter and scatter. For not only has every living human being his *genius*; every town, people, every region, every neighborhood, every house, stable and tree has its own *genius* too. The notion of the *genius* is so diffuse that, while it espies from afar its goal of providing a basis for the individuality of each human being, it cannot reach it. The concept of the *genius* has its origin in the most ancient elements of Italic religion; subsequently aspects of the late Greek idea of the *daimōn* flow into it. (As we shall show, the latter had its own, different, origin, which contained little in common with the Italic *genius*, but then it broadened and diffused and in that form manifested some affinity with the Roman understanding.)[1]

---

esp. 133. Alt places the ritual of the enthroning of the king in Judah (by contrast with the Northern kingdom) in the context of the dynastic bond of this Davidic kingdom: according to him, the ritual shows that Yahweh's free decision consecrates each successor in office, and thus the distance between God and king is maintained. "It is all the more difficult to imagine that the divine kingship so often assumed nowadays to have been universal in the ancient Near East, should have found acceptance in this milieu, unless it had been sufficiently remodeled to fit with the strict subordination to Yahweh of even the kings of the House of David" (134). Cf. Alt's 1930 essay, "Die Staatenbildung der Israeliten in Palästina" (now in *Kleineschriften* II, 1–65).

[25] E. Eichmann, *Die Kaiserkrönung im Abendlande*, 2 vols. (Würzburg, 1942); P. E. Schramm, *Das Herrscherbild in der Kunst des frühen Mittelalters, Vorträge der Bibl. Warburg* 1922–23 (Leipzig and Berlin, 1924).

[1] Cf. chiefly F. W. Otto, article "Genius", in *RE* by Pauly-Wissowa-Kroll 13 (1913), which corrects the very full, older article by Birt in Roscher, *Lexikon*

The *genius* is a god, given to man as a companion (*comes*)[2] and protection (*tutela*).[3] Every man has a protecting spirit of this kind, equal in birth to the gods; in the case of women this spirit is often called their Juno.[4] *F. W. Otto* raised weighty objections to the view that *genius* was originally man's generative potency and then became extended to all his determining drives ("it was the personality, the character, which emerged from the human being and was made into a god");[5] according to Otto the *genius*, (that is, *g. natalis*) is the *daimōn* of the birthday,[6] celebrated on that day; offerings are brought to him as to a Divine Being. He accompanies the human being all his life long,[7] and after the latter's death he is venerated and invoked, partly as *manes* and partly still as "*genius*". Inscriptions often mention the two together: *manibus et genio*. From the very outset, therefore, the *genius* is a principle that in dignity goes beyond the mortal being of the individual. "This doctrine can only be understood from the vantage point of a belief in immortality";[8] the *manes* of the dead are also called gods (*di manes*). Strangely enough, the *genius* does not exist prior to the human being, but "*quodammodo cum homine gignitur*", as *Apuleius* says.[9] He was clearly influenced by the Greek teaching on the *daimōn*, particularly in the form it

---

der griechischen und römischen Mythologie (1886–90). See also the article "Daimōn" in both works. Also F. Altheim, *Röm. Rel. Geschichte* (1931) I, 60f.; (1932), II, 78f. U. v. Wilamowitz, *Der Glaube der Hellenen* (1931), I, 362ff.; W. Foerster, article "Daimōn" in *ThWNT* II (1935): 1ff.

[2] Horace, *Ep.* II, 2, 187.

[3] Censorinus, *De die natali* 3, 1; Ammianus Marcellinus, *Rer. gest.* 21, 14, 3.

[4] Pliny, *Nat. hist.* II, 16.

[5] Birt in Roscher, *Lexikon der griechischen und römischen Mythologie*, 1615.

[6] *Ibid.*, 1159.

[7] Horace, *Ep.* II, 2, 187–89: "Scit Genius, natale comes qui temperat astrum, / naturae deus humanae mortalis, in unum / quodque caput voltu mutabilis, albus et ater." Whence comes inequality, even among brothers? [Ask the genius who lives with us, who rules the stars at the hour of our birth; the divine in man, which with him falls prey to death, changing his appearance in each individual being, now full of gravity, now cheerful.] The fact that the genius is here described as "a mortal god" does not negate its survival beyond death (which is attested at an early date), but refers to the severing of its connection with the mortal human being, whom Cicero, in *De fin.* II, 40, speaks of as "quasi mortalem deum". The assertion that the genius "temperat astrum" rules the horoscope, implies that it is not itself this given configuration, but only guides it.

[8] Birt in Roschen, *Lexikon der griechischen und römischen Mythologie*, 1617.

[9] *De Deo Socratis* 151.

acquired in stoic philosophy, according to which the *daimōn* is the divine in the human spirit itself.[10]

Let us take a brief look, then, at the historical origin of the *daimōn*. In *Homer* the gods (*theoi*) can also be called *daimōnes*, not in the context of the cult or when uttering their names, but to the extent that, as "formless personality", they apportion destiny. In the *Iliad* (book 3, verse 182) Agamemnon, the fortunate son of Atreus, is addressed as *moirogenes olbiodaimōn*: "thou who hast received a *daimōn* of good fortune at birth"—which comes close to the Italic *genius*. But in general the Greek *daimōn* is more remote from man; the term *daimōnie*, used in astonishment or fright, implies that someone has done or said something that is inexplicable on the basis of his usual nature; he must have been under the influence of a good or evil god. In *Hesiod* the theme of the tutelary *geniuses*[11] is more a passing one; in the *Alcestis* the dead woman can be venerated at her graveside as a "holy *daimōn*"[12] but for the most part the *daimōn* is destiny, indispensable and incalculable, which the individual feels to be his own, yet without being able to give it a name: *daimōn* is moving in the direction of *tyche*. Philosophically the concept is not a unitary one: the two occurrences of *daimōn* in *Heraclitus* are divergent: "his distinct character [*ēthos*] is man's *daimōn*" (that is, his destiny: Fragm. 119), and "man is called childish in the presence of the *daimōn* (that is, the deity), just as the boy in the presence of the man" (Fragm. 79): the former idea tends toward immanence, the latter toward transcendence. In *Plato* the tension is even greater. In one place he testifies to the *daimōn* of Socrates, that "voice which always forbids but never commands me to do anything which I am going to do"[13]—something between conscience and divine guidance and inspiration. But elsewhere he speaks in terms of hallowed tradition, describing lesser gods as *daimōnes* and calling the *daimōn* eros a mediator between us

[10] The whole passage: "Quodam significatu et animus humanus etiamnunc in corpore situs daemon nuncupatur, eum nostra lingua . . . poteris genium vocare, quod is deus qui est animus sui cuique, quamquam sit immortalis tamen quodammodo cum homine gignitur."

[11] *Erga* 121ff. After death, the men of the Golden Gate are appointed by Zeus as (good) geniuses of the earth, guardians of mortals, bestowers of wealth: "This royal honor is allotted to them."

[12] *Alcestis* V, 1002.

[13] *Apol* 31d.

and God; he is already acquainted, however, with the division of gods, *daimōnes* and heroes,[14] which will become dominant later. Thus the development can continue to diverge, with, on the one hand, the stoic line rendering the *daimōn* immanent as the most noble part of the soul and, on the other, the doctrine of "demons" put forward by *Xenocrates*, the disciple of Plato, in which the evil demons take responsibility for the immoral acts ascribed to the gods, and the good demons become tutelary spirits watching over men—which provides a link with the Italic *genius*.

However, as the religion of antiquity proceeds, a dynamic concept of power becomes established at its center,[15] interpreting both the objective spectrum (of gods, *daimōnes* and heroes) and the subjective potential of the human soul as graded emanations of a primal, divine power. This relativizes the opposition between objective, quasipersonal entities and the subjective layers and dispositions of the soul. As early as *Plutarch* and *Apuleius* (in their writings on the *daimōn* of *Socrates*) we can detect this ambivalence;[16] it becomes quite evident in the mystical and theurgic forms of Neoplatonism. Here, as in the Hermetic writings, the soul hardly clings at all to its individuality, but, ascending through the planetary stages, is able to divest itself of its human qualities in order, at the highest stage, to pass over into pure energy and sink into God.[17] Both *daimōn* and individuality belong to a preliminary state.[18]

[14] *Pol* 3, 392a; 4 427b; *Nom* 4, 717 ab: here mention is also made of the household gods (*lares*).

[15] M. P. Nilsson, *Greichischer Glaube* (Bern, 1950), 117ff.

[16] Examples from the stoics: Zeller, *Philosophie der Griechen*, 4th ed., III/1, 328f. Cf. my *Herrlichkeit* III/1, 177f. English edition: *The Glory of the Lord*, vol. 4. Even Plato (*Tim* 90a) had described the rational soul as a guardian spirit, a *daimōn*, given to man.

[17] *Poimandres*, *Tr* I, 24–26 (ed. Festugière, *Corpus Hermeticum* I, 15–16). Strangely enough this ascent begins thus: after the dissolution of the body, the henceforward unactive *ēthos* (Festugière translates this as *moi habituel*) is left to the *daimōn* ("sans doute ici le *daimōn* personnel de chaque homme"); as it ascends to each successive level it loses something of the aberrant, earthly posturing which had attracted the soul in its descent, and thus ultimately it can become divine (*theōthēnai*). Festugière gives a commentary on this passage in *La Révélation d'Hermès Trismégisthe II, La Doctrine de l'Ame* (Vrin, 1953), 123–52.

[18] The passage quoted in the previous note gives rise to two mutually irreconcilable eschatologies. Either the moral "I" is handed over to the *daimōn*,

Here we can see clearly that ambivalence that characterized the doctrine of *genius* from the very first. Neither *genius* nor *daimōn* can be fully identified with the human "I", nor can they be set against it as something completely other, as another "I". In either case they would forfeit their intended function. They are "what is personally divine in our person"—which cannot be reasoned out in the categories of antiquity. The *genius* is not personal enough to attract an attitude of genuine religious, self-surrendering trust;[19] and, on the other hand, it is not identical with the "I" such that the latter could describe it as its possession. As far as philosophy is concerned, it is predominantly that part of the soul that is "divine" or "akin to the divine", the *hegemonikon*, that governs by attending to the divine *Logos*; for popular religion it is primarily the tutelary spirit, given to the individual by the Most High God, which becomes an expression of the individual's worth before God.

Even in Hellenistic interscriptions *daimones* are occasionally called *angeloi*, messengers of the divine world. The Septuagint adopts the word and applies it to the good spirits who are obedient to God; in the Old Testament we already find them being sent to protect men (Gen 24:7; Dan 6:23; Tob; and in a more general sense, Ps 91:11). (The idea of a permanent guardian angel for each person is a late development.) But in a certain regard this notion, which continues in the New Testament, has no longer anything to do with the *genius* of the ancient world: now the angel is a personal being clearly distinct from the human being. The same thing is true in the case of the *daimones*: in the Bible they are always understood as evil spirits.[20]

---

to be led by the latter to its deserved place of reward or punishment (Plato, *Phaed.* 107d; *Pol* 620 de; Virgil, *Aeneid* VI, 743: "Quisquis suos patimur manes", which Norden retranslates as "ton haeutou hekastos tis daimona paschomen"; according to Servius' commentary on the *Aeneid*, each man has from birth two *daimons*, a good and an evil one, and when he dies one or the other of them will give him his deserts), or else there is the eschatology of the ascent through the spheres, in which the soul, relieved of *daimons*, is also totally depersonalized.

[19] For the Romans, the genius is primarily the life-sustaining spirit, who, in the comedies of Plautus and Terence, is regularly entertained with good food. "Genium indemnatum habeo" means, "I enjoy my life unmolested" (Juvenal 6, 562). While this can be combined with the religious dimension, it shows that the genius is not primarily, let alone exclusively, a religious potency.

[20] On the transition from a pagan to a Judaeo-Christian concept of angels cf.

The ancient world's concept of *genius* and *daimōn* does still flare up in the context of the Christian world, in the baroque drama, for instance (*Bidermann's Philemon, Masen's Jovinianus*), when the angel plays the part of the human being he is guarding. But more typical is *Novalis*, who describes inspiration in these terms: "Man feels that he is taking part in a conversation in which some unknown spiritual being is mysteriously guiding him to develop the most evident ideas. . . . It must be a homogeneous being. . . . This superior 'I' is related to man as man is to nature, or as the sage to the child. Man yearns to be like this 'I'."[21] *Franz von Baader*, summing up a long theosophical tradition (which includes *Schelling*), resurrects the doctrine of *genius*: for him it expresses both the tutelary spirit that is given to us[22] and "the spiritual essence of sonship that is given and entrusted to us"[23] as well as the ideal it signifies, namely, "not some perfected creature existing prior to and apart from man, since this *genius* accompanies the naturally created human being in a creaturely personality. Yet this does not stop us acknowledging it as a personal and tangible influence making its presence felt even in our earthly existence", for it is a "spirit that is given to us both as a gift and as a task".[24] *Goethe's* many-layered concept of the "demonic" is at a far remove from the world of Christianity; its indifference to the moral side puts it close to early Greek thought; but its primary reference is quite un-Greek, namely, the geniality that impels the great creative artist, bringing him both bliss and danger. Here there is no longer any trace of the

J. Michl's article "Engel" (I–X) in *RAC* V (1962), which gives copious references, p. 256. Also W. Foerster's article "Daimon" in *ThWNT* II (1935).

[21] *Fragmente des Jahres 1798*, Franz von Baader, *Werke*, ed. Carl Selig (Zurich), vol. III, 20, no. 800, cf. vol. I, 264, no. 2890.

[22] F. v. Baader, *Werke* XIII, 129.

[23] F. v. Baader, *Werke* IV, 351–52.

[24] *Ibid.*; cf. *Werke* IX, 200. Cf. on this topic Hegel's remarks in the *Enzyklopädie* §405, 3 and 406 "The relationship of the individual to his genius" (vol. 7/2, 161–98), and the teaching of the speculative theists who follow Hegel, in particular Christian Hermann Weisse, who in his aesthetics develops a full theory of genius, not only of what is genial, but also of sexual love and ethics. For contemporary works, cf. R. Guardini's reflections on the myth of the *Folgegeist*: "He is different from the man he follows, yet somehow he is this man, but higher in form and power." For Guardini this myth is a help toward understanding the doctrine of the guardian angel. *Engel, Drei Meditationen* (privately published 1964).

central notion of Italic genius. In the celebrated passage in the last book of *Poetry and Truth*, the *Goethe* of the Egmont period discerns something "that manifested itself only in contradictions and thus could not be held fast in any concept, let alone in any word. It was not divine, for it seemed irrational; not human, for it had no reason; not devilish, for it was beneficent; not angelic, for it often evinced malicious delight. It was like chance, for it was not the product of a chain of events; like providence, for it indicated connections. . . . It seemed to take pleasure only in the impossible. . . . I endeavored to escape from this terrible being." Further on he says that the demonic constitutes "a power that, while it is not opposed to the moral world order, nevertheless cuts across it, as if the two are warp and woof". This reflection culminates in the "monstrous utterance" that already stood as the motto of the fourth book: *Nemo contra deum nisi deus ipse*.

We let this passage stand as it is, without further commentary, to form a mysterious upbeat to our next section. But it is well to remember it when reading Goethe's harmonious syntheses, such as the conclusion of *Faust* and the mysticism of the *Wanderjahre*. It is clear from the context that Goethe did not experience the demonic primarily as a world principle that could be objectified, but as something that operated in his person and life, placing him above and beyond identifiable categories.

One last name has been awakened, as it were, by the "monstrous utterance": that of *C. G. Jung*. His "unconscious" similarly sublates the contradiction between God and anti-God; he is aware that, where the "unconscious" is concerned, he "could speak just as well of 'God' or 'demon' "; "the great advantage of the terms 'demon' and 'God' is that they . . . facilitate personification. . . . The whole human being is challenged and, with the whole of reality, enters the battle."[25] Here the "self" is that which—in a gnostic mode—rises again from its prison, as "spirit, demon, spark".[26]

---

[25] *Memories, Dreams, Reflections* (London, 1963).
[26] *Psychology and Religion* (New York, 1938).

3. The Individual Law

a. Today these diverse observations on *genius* and *daimōn* no longer correspond to any living cultural awareness. But there is one thinker, at the end of the Christian and idealist periods, whose whole oeuvre was a struggle for a new and contemporary expression of individuality (in the sense of what-is-always-unique) and deserves special mention among the various attempts to answer the question "Who am I?" namely, *Georg Simmel*.[1] We have already encountered him in connection with the problem of the actor,[2] which concerns him as a mode of artistic existence in its individuality. *Simmel* is aware of the debt that he owes to the Christian era, and to that extent he is an expressly post-Christian thinker. For him, the fixed content, the Church's

[1] The following works of Simmel are quoted: "Über sociale Differenzierung. Sociologische und psychologische Untersuchungen", in *Staats- und socialwissenschaftliche Forschungen* 10, 1 (Leipzig, 1890), referenced here as D. *Die Probleme der Geschichtsphilosophie* (Leipzig, 1892; quoted from 4th ed., 1922, unless otherwise noted), referenced here as PG. *Philosophie des Geldes* (Leipzig, 1900; quoted from 4th ed., 1922), referenced here as Gd. *Kant*. 16 lectures (Leipzig, 1904; quoted from 2d ed., 1905), referenced here as K. *Kant und Goethe* (Berlin, 1906; quoted from 4th ed., Leipzig, 1918), referenced here as KG. "Die Religion" in *Die Gesellschaft. Sammlung sozialpsych. Monographien*, ed. Martin Buber, 2 vols. (Frankfurt, 1906; quoted from 2d ed., 1912), referenced here as R. *Schopenhauer und Nietzsche* (Leipzig, 1907; quoted from 3d ed., 1923), referenced here as SchN. *Soziologie. Untersuchungen über die Formen der Vergesellschaftung* (Leipzig, 1908), referenced here as S. *Hauptprobleme der Philosophie* (Leipzig, 1910; quoted from 4th ed., 1917), referenced here as HPh. *Philosophische Kultur* (Leipzig, 1911; quoted from 3d ed., 1923), referenced here as PhK. *Goethe* (Leipzig, 1913; quoted from 1917 ed.), referenced here as G. *Rembrandt* (Leipzig, 1916; quoted from 1923 Munich ed.), referenced here as Rt. *Grundfragen der Soziologie (Individuum und Gesellschaft)* (Berlin and Leipzig, 1917), referenced here as GrS. *Lebensanschauung. Vier metaphysische Kapitel* (Munich and Leipzig, 1918), referenced here as L. Posthumous works: *Zur Philosophie der Kunst*, ed. Gertrud Simmel (Potsdam, 1922), referenced here as PhKu. *Brücke und Tür, Essays des Philosophen zur Geschichte, Religion, Kuntst und Gesellschaft*, together with M. Susman, ed. M. Landmann (Stuttgart, 1922), referenced here as BrT. "Das individuelle Gesetz. Philosophische Exkurse", in *Theorie* I, ed. M. Landmann (Suhrkamp, 1968), referenced here as IG. "Aus Georg Simmels nachgelassenem Tagebuch", in *Logos. Zft. f. Philos. d.Kultur* VIII (1919/20): 121–51.

[2] This problem was a central concern of his. The early essay, "Zur Philosophie des Schauspielers", in *Morgen* 2 (1908): 1685–89, is not identical with the one

dogma, is gone forever.[3] But burned into the post-Christian
world like a brand is the knowledge that, in former times, the
soul's salvation and the Kingdom of God had been presented to
man "as an unconditional value, a definitive goal beyond everything in life that was individual, fragmentary and meaningless",
and that nations had lived by it. When *Schopenhauer* equates the
will's absoluteness with life, saying that it cannot rest in anything outside itself, *Simmel* asserts that "this yearning . . . [is]
the inheritance of Christianity", which "persists as an empty
striving toward a goal that has become intangible".[4] *Simmel*
knows that the personality of the Christian God was something
entirely new in the history of human ideas.[5] He knows that this
God thus became not only the "object of all searching"[6] but also
the basis for the "most fundamental unity among Christians",
"substantial peace",[7] to such an extent, ultimately, that the
"overarching unity of the God of the Christians exploded . . .
sociological restrictions". So "Christianity must therefore be
tolerant of the diverse ways to the one and only God" but
"intolerant with regard to what is definitive in religion".[8] The
personal uniqueness of the Christian God created the sense of
the here-and-now uniqueness of his image, the human person.[9]
"The special quality of existence, the feeling of having been
called to do something that no one else can do, of standing on a
spot that has been waiting for us, so to speak", the demand "that
everyone make profit with *his* particular pound"[10]—this elicits
from *Simmel* something that has the ring of a confession of faith:
"I see the deepest, meta-ethical core of Christianity in the soul's

---

published later in *Logos* IX (1920/21) and also in *Fragmente und Aufsätze aus dem
Nachlass*, ed. Gertrud Kantorowicz (Munich, 1923). An independent, preliminary
stage of the latter is "Der Schauspieler und die Wirklichkeit", *Berliner Tageblatt*
of Jan. 7, 1912 (reprinted in BrT, 168–75). Here, similarly to Gouhier, the
actor's art is seen in the sensory presentation of the poetic work, not in making it
into reality; the acted Hamlet is a "true" king but not a "real" one, although the
actor must plunge into the same depth of reality as the poet if he is actively to
create the figure out of it.

[3] PhK, 217.   [4] SchN, 3.

[5] R, 51. "It was Christianity that first created the all-embracing God who is
at the same time a person"; in fact this universality is affirmed contrary to the
God of the Old Covenant.

[6] R, 50.   [7] R, 59.   [8] R, 93, 92.   [9] D, 11.   [10] R, 80–81.

absolute responsibility for itself, standing naked before its God, at every moment of life. Gone is all righteousness through the law, all solidarity of the race or of anything else, gone is all obscuring of the ultimate nucleus of personality, whether through the opinions of the world or one's own past life history: all that is left are the soul and God. This responsibility for itself, undiminished by any factor, nowhere else attaining such inward and personal dimensions, is, however"—*Simmel* adds the qualification—"evidently an unbearable burden for the majority of souls";[11] it is eased by objective means of grace. We can leave aside the question whether the personal structure of Christian reality can be envisaged at all apart from its objective content,[12] and hence whether the soul's aloneness with God really is the absolute center of Christianity; even for *Simmel*, individuality is only *one* pole of an irreducible tension, the other being that of objective values and society. What is important here is simply the fact that he is aware of the origin of his "individual law". Hence, for him, Christianity also really vanquishes that death that he regards as inherent in every moment of life; every such moment gives the Christian direct access to eternal life.[13]

Simmel is also aware of the historical inheritance lying behind his idea. After the Enlightenment and *Kant*, with whom he is locked in a fierce argument because both have substituted the idea of universal humanity with its universal law (as the categorical imperative) for metaphysical personality, there were a few great figures who knew about individuality. He mentions *"Lessing, Herder, Lavater"* and *Goethe*,[14] but the latter only with

---

[11] L, 138.

[12] "Catholicism discovered religion's objectivity, of which Jesus knew nothing" (T, 49).

[13] L, 107.

[14] GrS, 97. Simmel took too little account of F. H. Jacobi's efforts to elucidate individuality, particularly as he opposes the basic concept of "life" to the spirit (reason) and applies the same criticism to Kant's imperative. At this point we do not need to go into the philosophical origins of the concept of individuality in the Christian realm (starting with Duns Scotus, via nominalism, to Cusanus, and via Renaissance philosophy to Descartes and especially Leibniz, with an echo in Shaftesbury and extending to Herder and the romantics). Evidently Simmel also adopts Fichte's individualizing tendency in the ethical field; Fichte was already familiar with something like an "individual law".

reservations. Again and again, however, and without any reservations, he mentions *Schleiermacher*: "For him, the ethical task is precisely that each individual represents humanity in a special way . . . , each one shapes this material, common to all, into an entirely individual form." Thus "Schleiermacher becomes the fulcrum of a *Weltanschauung* with his view that the absolute only lives in the form of the individual, that individuality is not a limitation of the infinite but its expression and mirror."[15] Consequently he is always referred to as the critic of the Kantian imperative.[16]

Simmel's fundamental problem is announced on the second page of his first publication, *Über sociale Differenzierung* (1890), and, unchanged, accompanies all the transformations of his thought. "That the world is ultimately absolutely unitary and that all individualizing, all difference, is only an illusory appearance—this can be rendered as plausible as the belief in the absolute individuality of every part of the world, where not a single leaf is identical with any other, and all apparent unity is only a subjective contribution on the part of our intellect, not objectively demonstrable."[17] "Our thought operates in such a way", he stresses in the *Philosophie des Geldes* (1900), "that it must strain toward both of these ideas in search of a definitive conclusion, without ever being able to reach this conclusion in

[15] GrS. Cf. HPh, 61: "It was probably Schleiermacher who most perfectly carried out this transformation." For him, "the One, the Absolute" presents itself "in the form of what is individual and incomparable. . . . But it is not that each individual egoistically tears itself away from all the others, with nothing to restrain it; rather, each particular form is only a special realization of the universe's totality of power." Cf. L, 235. On romanticism in general: G, 143. In addition SchN, 149: "Schleiermacher alone got beyond this dichotomy (between God and 'I'), by not entertaining the assumption. Particularity and divine universality do not mutually exclude each other. In fact, the reverse is the case: particularity is the sole form in which divine universality presents itself." In "Das individuelle Gesetz" (1913, in IG, 224) he can even put it like this: "We can even posit it as a law of universal application that every one should behave absolutely differently from every other. Schleiermacher's ethics, and that of the romantics in general, takes this line." Schleiermacher and Goethe are mentioned together: they "not only repulsed" the Enlightenment view, "but put forward a different ethics to complement it or compete with it. The crucial difference lies in the abolition of the ideal of equality" (K, 178).

[16] KG, 88; IG, 184; L, 220.   [17] D, 4.

either. . . . As a result, the development of philosophy, like that of individual thought, goes from multiplicity to unity and from unity to multiplicity. The history of thought shows it to be futile to try to hold fast to one of these standpoints as the definitive one; rather, the structure of our reason in relation to its object calls for equal rights for both points of view."[18] This shows us where his front line is drawn up: he is opposed to all forms of the *arbor porphyriana*, according to which what is individual is deduced ontically and noetically from the universal by the addition of a *differentia specifica*: "But it is precisely the *differentia specifica* that permit us to establish ultimate causal relationships in the genuine and strict sense. Without them, the concept does not attain the real, individual, clearly delineated content."[19] Again, however, it must be remembered that the two opposed tendencies exist simultaneously. In religious terms this means that it is "man's *yearning* to stand on his own feet and find the meaning of life in himself alone—even over against the highest authority of existence—which collides with the other yearning, namely, to be involved in the divine world plan and to draw some of the latter's greatness and beauty upon himself and thus acquire value. This can be done only by a selfless dedication and by integrating oneself into the divine plan as an element of it."[20]

A first and chiefly sociological method of holding onto the divergent interpretations of existence was so-called "differentiation", which consisted in taking an originally medial state of affairs and tracing its simultaneous divergence into its extremes. In *Simmel's* great *Soziologie* (1908), this method is briefly recapitulated but then retires into the background. In a constricted social milieu the individual elements remain relatively undifferentiated, and even where a differentiated milieu clashes with others, their competitive struggle reveals tendencies toward unification; however, this very process also allows the individuals

[18] Gd, 74.

[19] PG (1st ed.), 27; PhK, 31.

[20] R, 66; cf. IG, 206: "Thus life manifests the greatest continuity, upheld by or expressing itself in the greatest discontinuity. It is a unity . . . consisting entirely of beings whose existence centers on themselves—all the more so, the higher and more mature the level of life they have attained."

more room for their own differentiation, whereas, as a part of this whole, they retain less individuality. In short, "the elements of the differentiated milieu are undifferentiated, and those of the undifferentiated milieu are differentiated."[21] This formula—which is meant to apply not only to sociologico-historical developments but also on a universal scale—is illuminating at least to the extent that it renders untenable the recurring attempt of monism (*Plotinus*, *Spinoza*, *Kant* and the idealists) to deduce the particular from the universal. Although *Simmel* continues to exert himself on behalf of the balance of opposed formulas, his interest is clearly in individuality. The universal, culture, can actually be regarded as a means to the end of individual development: "Man cultivates himself only insofar as culture is significant for, or actually is, the development of undefinable, personal unity. . . . Culture is the path from closed unity through developed multiplicity to developed unity"; this latter is already "germinally present in the personality; its own ideal plan is etched upon it, so to speak".[22] To that extent "even universality is something singular, insofar as individuality is set over against it"; where individuality is lost, universality becomes a "party violation".[23] "My problem is the desubjectivization of what is individual".[24] "What is specific to human beings is objectivity; not the interest in the subject (in however lowly or lofty a sense), but interest in the thing itself. . . . This is the practical working-out of the purely spiritual-intellectual fact that man can make himself into his own object."[25] *Simmel's* concern here, to which we shall have to return, shows that the pole of individuality, "the uniqueness of which is not a formal *accidens*, arising out of being compared with something else, but a specific, inner quality, sustained by the center of the whole",[26] must be regarded as a central metaphysical principle. This is particularly evident in art, which is concerned with the significance a thing "possesses in its individuality and in contrast to everything else". Like *Claudel*, *Simmel* says that "beauty is attributed to this very distance per se".[27] So much so that, in early times, the universal—the "truth" common to things—is

---

[21] S, 715.   [22] PhK, 238.

[23] *Das individuelle Gesetz* (1913) in IG, 179.

[24] T, 122.   [25] T, 135.   [26] PG, 47.

[27] *Soziologische Ästhetik* (1896) in IG, 72–73.

seen primarily in their reciprocal relations and interactions. It is inevitable, however, that such relationships will become more and more universal, resulting in opposition between the universal formula (now become independent) and the mere individual. "A clear example" of this is provided by "the stoic doctrine"[28] (the dominance of which *Simmel* most obstinately opposed), whether in the form of the "universal human nature" of the Enlightenment or of *Kant's* doctrine to which it gave rise or, finally, in socialism and Marxism, which likewise sprang from idealism. The Enlightenment lays aside the ossified class forms and thinks that, in doing so—in liberating the original human "nature"—it can achieve both freedom and equality. Here, however, what is distinctive and individual becomes of no consequence in the face of a "fiction of isolated and uniform individuals", just as, in idealism, even the empirical "I", "the psychological, subjective, contingent human being", becomes a kind of mask covering the real "I"—which is now purely formally such.[29] *Simmel's* campaign against the Kantian categorical imperative intends to show that the latter's aspect of law remains heteronomous as far as the individual is concerned and that autonomy can only be brought in by the back door, by splitting the concrete human being into a spiritual "I" (which prescribes conduct) and a sensible "I" (which fulfills the prescription as a duty).[30] His rejection of German idealism in its entirety—though he acknowledges the gigantic achievements of *Kant*[31] and *Hegel*[32] —is fundamental: it sacrifices individuality[33] and to that extent is nothing but the link between the premises of the Enlightenment and the conclusions of socialism. For *Simmel* the sociologist is no friend of socialism. Right from the start he applauds the individual's resistance to being commandeered by society under

---

[28] D, 55.   [29] K, 171, 173.

[30] Thus in the two treatises on the individual law, 1913 (in IG, 174–230) and 1918 (in L, 154–245). See below.

[31] He speaks of "Kant's gigantic achievement" whereby he was able to combine the "lofty self-concept of the 'I', and its irreducibility to matter" with the "firmness and significance of the objective world" (KG, 11–12). His "book is the only one in the vast literature on Kant which really brings out the inner structure of the problems with which Kant is dealing, revealing this apparently most sober, and even pedantic, of all philosophers as an artist of the fugue", Erich Przywara, *In und Gegen* (1955), 36.

[32] HPh, 74–83.   [33] Cf. D, 56f.; GrS, 83–86; L, 178.

the pretext of the distribution of labor (which would emphasize each person's particular place in it).[34] He regards socialization as possible only in the lower value-strata, which all acknowledge, whereas the higher strata are normally accessible only to the few, to individuals.[35] "The socialist dogma" has a "leveling" tendency, a "radical indifference to the individuality of psycho-spiritual realities",[36] "making the individual into the mere point of intersection of the threads that society has spun around him, the mere vessel of social influences, the particular content and hue of his existence to be deduced from varying admixtures of these influences".[37] It emerges that it is impossible to have both freedom and equality at the same time; hence extreme socialism is likewise impossible.[38] The social dimension is meaningful only in terms of relationship between individuals of intrinsic value; true, what is most inwardly unique in them is incom-municable, but the higher their degree of uniqueness, the higher are the forms of society they render possible.[39] A most pro-found loneliness is the lot of everyone, particularly the man who is conscious of himself.[40] He knows that "he cannot share his deepest layer of personality . . . with anyone, cannot com-municate it to anyone; there is a qualitative loneliness of personal

[34] Initially the principle of the division of labor seemed positive in its opposition to abstract notions of leveling (K, 179, IG, 186 and GrS, 99). But if we look more closely there is a great danger, on this view, of the individual being sucked up into the social process: HPh, 62. Here Simmel sees the division of labor in the same perspective as the organism; whereas (Schleiermacher's) "doctrine of individuality has a different metaphysical nerve". In R, 64, where, similarly, society is viewed as an organic whole of which the individual becomes a function, we read: "But this role is resisted by the individual's urge for unity and totality." See also GrS, 72.

[35] Cf. the entire fourth chapter of D. Cf. also (in S, 47ff.) the leveling tendencies in the group, and its attraction to simple ideas which operate one-sidedly and recklessly; socialism is compelled by external forces, politically, to water down its radicalism. Similarly see chap. 2 ("The social and the individual level") in GrS (34–50), where this same doctrine is presented some-what heavily. "What we have here could be termed the sociological tragic dimension as such" (41). He quotes Heine, among many others: "Seldom did you understand me, / Seldom, either, did I you. / But when in the mire we lay, / Understanding came our way."

[36] HPh, 130f.   [37] G, 144.   [38] GrS, 82, 89ff.

[39] The excursus on the nobility (S, 732ff.) is to be read in this context.

[40] S, 77ff. Loneliness as a sociological concept. Cf. PhKu, 14; IG, 14; L. 179.

life, and self-reflection intensifies the realization that it cannot be bridged".[41]

Of course it would be perverse simply to brand *Simmel* as an individualist; he is emphasizing the one pole of life's polarity so strongly because everywhere there is the tendency for society to take the individual over and treat him as a mere function. Here, however, for the first time, we encounter *Simmel's* profoundly pessimistic view of history. In *Der Begriff und die Tragödie der Kultur* (1911), he takes his metaphysics of life (which we have yet to set forth)—which necessarily gives rise, out of itself, to obsolescent, rigid forms and then, as it develops, contradicts and destroys them—and applies it to the technological civilization of our times: technological production, having become "fatefully" self-justifying and "mass-oriented", leads with "demonic pitilessness" into a "cul-de-sac": that which is produced by the increasingly more specialized individual (and this specialization only *seems* to individualize him) becomes in fact his master; with its "ability to amass goods unorganically", it becomes "profoundly incommensurate with the form of personal life". "This is civilization's real tragedy. For what we mean by a tragic fate—as opposed to a pathetic fate or one that is thrust on us from outside—is that the destructive forces that are directed against a particular being in fact arise from its own deepest levels; that its destruction is a fate inherent in it, a logical development, so to speak, of the very structure with which the being has constructed its own positivity."[42]

[41] IG, 223. According to Simmel, Nietzsche went further than Kant in trying to prevent the pure socialization of the individual: GrS, 76f.; K, 180.

[42] PhK, 263. Again: "We can perhaps define the essence of the tragic thus: some destiny is on a course that is contrary to nature's life will and that will destroy the meaning and value of an existence, while at the same time we sense that this destiny comes forth from the depths and necessity of this very existence" (T, 146). Similarly in "Die Zukunft unserer Kultur" in BrT, 95f., where he speaks of "tragic discrepancy". See also "Der Konflikt der modernen Kultur" (1918, later included in IG, 148ff.), where, at the end of the First World War, he attempts to draw up a balance sheet; the will to overcome all opposing elements by the pure life (an impossible project, 171) is something that, at a deeper and more universal level, "contradicts the essence of life itself". Indeed "this contradiction becomes all the more crass and irreconcilable, the more that inwardness which we can only call simply 'life' asserts itself in its unformed strength" (172). These are "manifestations of the most profound, inner self-contradiction on the part of spirit, once it develops into culture" (173). Cf. the

b. This anticipates the conclusion of a second look at *Simmel's* works, designed to provide a philosophical elucidation of the initial tension between the unity of the whole and the unity of the individual. Our starting point here is a pair of terms that are fundamental to *Simmel*, though at first sight they do not seem to promise to shed much light on the subject, namely, the "absolutely basic opposition between the life principle and the form principle".[43] Employing these categories, which acquire greater precision after his discovery of *Bergson*[44] (although it will be necessary to go beyond him),[45] *Simmel* moves from a pure philosophy of life—life seen as a power that crystallizes in forms and overflows these dead, constricted habitations,[46] where these transitory forms can also be particular individuals[47]—into a philosophy of "form". This philosophy of "form" (as "validity", "value", "ought") approaches the Neo-Kantianism of the Baden school without reaching it; for *Simmel*, this "form", even in its suprapsychological,[48] factual objectivity, remains a protuberance of life.[49] But the values are "self-sufficient",[50] both for the

---

analysis of decadence in SchN, 142–69.

[43] L, 161.   [44] PhK, 126ff.

[45] Cf. e.g., T, 123: "The Bergsonian difficulty, namely, how is the intellect to grasp life, when it is itself an emanation of life, is resolved thus: this retro-action, this understanding oneself, is the very essence of living spirit."

[46] Thus in chap. 1 of his last work "Lebensanschauung" (1918), which, taken on its own, signals an earlier stage of his thought and needs to be seen in a broader context.

[47] "By flowing through—or, more properly, in the form of—these individuals, the stream of life is contained in each of them and becomes a form with a fixed outline" (L, 12).

[48] Gd, 62ff.; chap. 2, "Die Wendung zur Idee" in L.

[49] Thus objective religion is always "the becoming operative of certain fundamental powers and impulses of the soul", of man's "religious nature. The significance of its object . . . is only the significance of the functions themselves" (R, 40). That applies equally to all areas of material value: science, art, economics, etc. Simmel's concern throughout is to "create an organic relationship between psychology and logic" (L, 96), however much he wants to distinguish the former from the latter. Consequently, for him, the Kantian categories are also one historically conditioned "form" (a "philosophical attitude") among others. Simmel can complement them by new questions and categories ("How is historical knowledge possible?"): PG, Preface to 3d ed., V–VII. In this context the celebrated essay "Der Henkel" (PhK, 126–34) should be read: where two spheres materially divide, there is a uniting element.

[50] HPh, 112. So much so that the objective form actually dominates life and

ATTEMPTS AT MEDIATION 615

individual and for society; yet it is life itself, to whose inner form it belongs, that has this value, this "ought", above it. This can only be expressed by the paradox that life, in its positive, is "already its own comparative";[51] that, as life, it is "more life", and that, as spiritual life, it is "more than life".[52] He emphasizes that an "irreconcilable opposition" lies at the heart of this essential self-transcendence, a "contradiction" with which life remains "encumbered".[53]

The next step in bringing the fundamental principles (individual and totalitarian unity—life and form) closer to one another is to interpret the highest stage of life, conscious spirit, by means of reflection, that is, self-positing as subject and object.[54] Here *Simmel's* early notion of truth—as relation, relationship, reciprocal influence—has "reached, as it were, its absolute shape".[55] Spirit is what is alive absolutely,[56] the "highest and most concentrated form of life";[57] it guarantees that everything that is objectified, on the basis of the structure of spirit, can be understood as rooted in life and coming from it.[58] This could be interpreted in a Kantian or Fichtean sense, but it is meant quite differently, as the increasingly emphatic references to *Goethe* show. (*Goethe* finally has the upper hand over *Kant*.) What appears here as the subject-object relationship is an intimate reciprocal influence, a mutual "fitting-in", based on their continual coming-forth, together, from life's ground.[59] Only from this perspective can the unity of the individual spirit and its world (and world-view) be intelligibly conceived as individuated from the outset—however open it may be to the universal.[60] At this point the closest thinker to *Simmel* must be *Poseidonios*, but

---

draws it into itself (L, 89, 94).

[51] L, 27.   [52] L, 21, 23.   [53] L, 18, 22.   [54] PhK, 211.   [55] PhK, 212.

[56] L, 7.

[57] *Einleitung in die Moralwissenschaft*, 2 vols. (Berlin, 1893) I, 22.

[58] "Der Konflikt der modernen Kultur" in IG, 148ff. "Therefore . . . all objectivity, too, the object of knowledge, had to be transformed into life, so that the process of knowing (seen as a function of life itself) should be guaranteed an object that is entirely penetrable because it is of the same nature as itself" (164).

[59] G, 3 (and the whole of chap. 1); KG, 41, 91f.

[60] "The terrible conflict between the whole and the part is resolved, in principle, as far as spirit is concerned, in that the latter has the ability to represent the whole in its form. . . . It is immaterial whether this possibility is realized completely or only in the slightest approximation" (T, 127).

there are also links with *C. G. Jung* insofar as everything that has a spiritual dimension is already present in archetypal form (uniting contradictions). For *Simmel*, initially, the possible aspects of the world (scientific, artistic, religious, practical, and so forth) are thoroughly individuated and cannot be synthesized;[61] this is the foundation of his doctrine of the various *Weltanschauung* "attitudes". He is also aware of the governing ideas (*Leitideen*)[62] that change with the changing epochs of history, ideas that concentrate on a particular aspect of the whole. Here, however (as with *Jung*), individuation only gets as far as a concept of "type"; it raises problems that we shall have to consider in the next section on the "individual law". The great monographs[63] on *Kant, Goethe, Schopenhauer und Nietzsche* and—his masterpiece—*Rembrandt* constitute a doctrine of attitudes or a philosophical typology in this sense, particularly since they contain a theory (analogous to *Wölfflin's*) of the opposition of romance and Germanic attitudes to the world, the latter epitomized by *Rembrandt*. All the same it would be unjust to excise *Simmel's* basic concern, individuality, from these works; he succeeds in setting before us, in figures of unique creativity whose works characterize a whole epoch, an unrepeatable world panorama. Each of the figures he selects is incomparable, and his interpretative art comes so close to them, examines them with such subtle instruments, that their singularity really shines through what is communicable and to that extent universal. What is individual does not reside in the special, the minute detail: "These things are precisely what is general, what is common to a large number of phenomena; it is only by looking beyond all this, to the unity of the phenomenon that is not dissected into details, that one can grasp its individual essentiality and uniqueness."[64] "The fewer self-subsistent boundaries an

---

[61] For example, L, 28ff.

[62] IG, 152ff.: Being (Greek), God (medieval), nature (Renaissance and, in a different sense, in the Enlightenment), the "I" (idealism); for the nineteenth century, possibly, "society", and for the present day, according to Simmel, "life".

[63] For an excellent evaluation of these monographs see Ernst Troeltsch, *Der Historismus und seine Probleme* (Tübingen, 1922), 587.

[64] IG, 111.

individual exhibits between himself and others, the more tangible that individual life becomes."[65]

However, even great, normative individuality cannot escape the contradiction at the heart of the phenomenon of life. It is not only that it puts forward a one-sided attitude, the opposite of which is represented with equal validity by another individual; thus we have *Schopenhauer's* horror of life and *Nietzsche's* exultation[66] (*Ionesco* experienced both at the same time), or world mastery in *Kant* and surrender to the world in *Goethe*—Goethe, who, in his own way, also embraces the former. Rather, it is that life's contradiction, with "its ubiquitous, constant rhythm, its simplest symbol being that of our breathing in and out", pulsates in every living being, for it is "the essence of life to produce that which contradicts the content of every moment; the opposite produces what it posits and is complemented by it".[67] "The conflict between the whole and the part that itself wants to be a whole", which was our starting point, is "a contradiction in principle; it is an inner contradiction, radically irreconcilable".[68] The positions are "so opposed that we would have to speak of hostility if the realm of highest spirituality did not conclude a truce between even the most irreconcilable parties. No one, to be sure, will undertake to decide whether some ultimate unity of all spiritual life lies beneath these polarities."[69] Beneath, not above! In his diary he puts it pointedly: "For men of the more profound sort there is only one way of coping with life, namely, with a certain degree of superficiality. . . . Below a certain depth, the lines of being, of the will and of the 'ought' collide so radically and violently that they would tear us to pieces. Only by stopping them from going

[65] IG, 112; cf. T, 142–43: "The student of human nature, because he sees the whole, will always have individuals as his object, since a spiritual form always takes the form of the individual. Only when it is dissected into elements can each element appear like a section through many individuals; only then can what is common to all emerge. Thus the student of human nature has an entirely different object of study from the psychologist."

[66] HPh, 59.

[67] KG, 115–16. "If we look at an isolated piece of existence, we find fragmentary realizations, traces of simultaneity of the most opposed fundamental concepts" (HPh, 42).

[68] R, 70.   [69] KG, 56.

below that boundary can we keep them sufficiently far apart so that life may be possible. It is quite the reverse of monist optimism, which says that if we trace the oppositions down deeply enough, we shall arrive at their reconciliation."[70]

Simmel would not be a philosopher if he did not tackle the problem of the unity of the as yet irreconcilable contradictions; here, as he knows, he is bound to come up against the *Logos* of *Heraclitus*. In connection with *Rembrandt* he discusses "human destiny and the Heraclitean cosmos".[71] In particular he experiences the art of *Rodin* as a "modern Heraclitism".[72] He puts the principle thus: "Even if the mutual hostility of things were to emerge as a metaphysical interpretation of the world, it would appear as a unitary character of the whole, realized by the reciprocal relationships of the elements."[73] Hence the attempts to bridge the oppositions, albeit with a concept that is shadowy and hinted at. When *Goethe* says, "Necessary conditions of existence are bound up with both the true and the false", *Simmel* comments: "This concept of the true is so lofty, so comprehensive, what it refers to is so absolute, so to speak, that it includes equally the true and the false, insofar as they are related opposites."[74] And when the young *Goethe* asks impatiently, "Then is good not evil, and evil not good?"—*Simmel* refers to the doctrine of reverence in the *Wanderjahre*, according to which what is abhorrent, hated and repellent is also to be held in reverence. "Good and evil may be at opposite poles in the same plane, but above them there is something higher, a spiritual and cosmic perfection, the totality of being."[75] In his aesthetics, the dualism between utility and beauty is overcome by "that higher beauty, which the theory of art hardly mentions, of which all beauty in the narrower sense is only one element", namely, a "supraaesthetic beauty . . . of the very highest authority".[76]

---

[70] T, 130. In his *Einleitung in die Moralwissenschaft. Eine Kritik der ethischen Grundbegriffe* (1892–93), Simmel gave a penetrating portrayal of the difficulties involved in the "ought". He did the same in the last chapter of his *Hauptprobleme der Philosophie* (1910), 153ff.

[71] Rt, 130–40. On Heraclitus: HPh, 66f.

[72] Rt, 134; in BrT, 195, he compares him with Proteus ("Erinnerung an Rodin").

[73] HPh, 34.   [74] G, 23–24.   [75] G, 33–34.   [76] PhK, 132–33.

And true life is a unity of life and death.[77] Embracing everything, at the profoundest level, is "life, inwardly coursing through" the opposites.[78] At the end of a section, *Simmel* often quietly lifts the veil on the mystery and leaves us with it: "Thus is fulfilled what life genuinely shows us, namely, that it is a struggle in the absolute sense, embracing the relative opposition of war and peace; whereas absolute peace, which may perhaps equally embrace this opposition, remains the divine mystery."[79] Or: "This is the greatness and glory of the human soul, that at every moment its pulsating life, its unity that cannot be conceptualized, causes those energies to operate in it that, in themselves, flow from totally irreconcilable sources toward totally irreconcilable confluences."[80]

No wonder, then, that the word "tragic" is everywhere. We have already discussed the nature of tragedy:[81] that which builds up is necessarily and simultaneously that which pulls down. This structure is already present within the organism[82] insofar as it is centered in itself and related to something beyond itself. It is a structure that impresses itself first and foremost on the life of the spirit (*Geist*): there is the "tragedy of the spirit" (*Geist*),[83] the "tragedy of intellectual culture" (*Geisteskultur*),[84] the "tragedy of thought"[85] and the most acute ethical tragedy of the clash of duties.[86] In spite of existence being so extremely exposed in this way, *Simmel* is working toward an affirmation that will embrace the whole of everyday life, with its divine and nondivine aspects, in a single, religious attitude.[87]

c. This being so, how is the question of the "individual law" to be formulated? Taking the subject–object structure of self-reflecting spirit, which is individual in each case, *Simmel* demands

[77] Rt, 89ff.; "Life and death on one and the same rung of being, as thesis and antithesis. But this implies something higher above both", in which "life really comes to its full self-realization, attains its highest self-meaning" (L, 111).

[78] HPh, 152.

[79] The concl. of "Der Konflikt der modernen Kultur", IG, 173.

[80] The concl. of "Soziologische Ethik", IG, 74.

[81] Cf. note 42, p. 613 above.

[82] "The typical tragedy of the organism" (IG, 206).

[83] L, 98.   [84] L, 160; PhK, 236ff.   [85] HPh, 85.

[86] HPh, 153–55.   [87] IG, 168; Rt, 144f., 150.

that the essential (that is, not contingent, not psychological) ideal image that it puts forth should be predicated of it as its very own, sprung from its very self.[88] The idea is "unreal", yet "present";[89] it is one dimension of life, and the other is the real.[90] Everyone carries his "ought" within him; it does not come to him from outside, from "metaphysical realities in the beyond", or from the "law of reason", but is "woven into this individual with ideal lines [*mit ideellen Linien*], following the fundamental uniqueness of his life's meaning".[91] The objectivizing of ethical norms, making them into an authority independent of life, is a form of the dying and hardening of life products,[92] whether such law takes the form of a "decalogue"[93] imposed from above, or of a state law[94] that commands the citizen from outside or of the categorical imperative, whose law-quality, according to Kant, comes from the sphere of natural science.[95] All the same it really *is* a "law"[96] on the basis of the "individual objectivity"; "even his ideal 'ought' is present as something objectively valid",[97] indeed, it is much more deeply rooted in the real than any externally imposed law can be. "Insofar as life's flowing and fashioning appears as an 'ought', insofar as the absolute nature of the demand becomes, in this sense, absolutely historical, the severity of the norm goes far deeper than the level at which, up to now, ethics has exclusively addressed human responsibility."[98] Above all, it is no longer possible to speak of any "utility", however lofty, for ethical conduct.[99] The good has its "meaning" in itself, in the self-actualization of personal life;[100] the "good will" is a quality of man's being.[101] Certainly,

---

[88] "Above every human-spiritual existence, or in it, written with invisible lines, there is its own ideal, an 'ought-to-be-thus' " (IG, 201). "It belongs to the universal structure of the conscious spirit to be simultaneously subject and object. It is in this context that life manifests itself as an 'ought' " (L, 157).

[89] PhK, 237.   [90] L, 156.   [91] L, 160.   [92] L, 162.

[93] IG, 199; L, 167.   [94] IG, 183.   [95] IG, 182; L, 199, 207.

[96] L, 228.   [97] IG, 217.   [98] IG, 228.

[99] IG, 213; on the proof that all ethical "goals" are always one-sided and contradict others: HPh, 150.

[100] L, 164.

[101] HPh, 164. An illustration: "Logically speaking, truthfulness only seems to apply to the relationship between the thought and its utterance. But it has a deeper meaning beyond this dualistic relationship, namely, the peaceful, self-

the world is constituted in such a way that the individual can never fully realize the powers and ideals that are within him, and this provides a rationale for the postulate of immortality.[102] Things do not fulfill the "I",[103] which must remain incomplete on earth;[104] yet the promise of being is inscribed upon it, namely, that it is to "fulfill itself into a totality",[105] its development into an "I" is to reach perfection,[106] the "total-I" (*Gesamt-Ich*)[107] is to realize itself, if only asymptotically.[108] *Simmel's* aristocratism causes him to applaud *Goethe's* view that the higher and more unique an individual is, the greater prospects he has of personal immortality.[109] Precisely because higher life is more mortal, it has more claim to immortality.[110]

However, *Simmel* speaks of different types of individuation, chiefly two, which he sees as romance and Germanic.[111] Rightly, he recalls his presupposition, that individuality is one-sidedly and self-sufficiently centered in itself and yet has a relationship to the world and thus has a need to be complemented. The romance type represents the individual as the particular representation of the universal type, man, in such a way that "the type and the supraindividual idea of this individual" irradiate each other. The Germanic type,[112] by contrast, causes the entire validity of the world to arise out of the inner, personal unity. But this typology, which was developed primarily with *Rembrandt* in mind, fails when it comes to both *Kant* and *Goethe*, who mediate between the two types: the former is influenced by the (French) Enlightenment, the latter by Italy and the ancient world. This would

---

contained and unitary quality of the soul which expresses itself necessarily (it can do no other) in this adequacy of the thought to the word" (T, 124).

[102] "Tod und Unsterblichkeit" in L, 99–153.

[103] L, 113.   [104] PhK, 206.   [105] PhK, 237.

[106] L, 116–17.   [107] PhK, 247.

[108] L, 117, 181; cf. "Zur Metaphysik des Todes" in BrT, 29–36: "that the 'I' can perform it completely" (35).

[109] L, 137.

[110] L, 132; Rt, 89ff. He quotes Rilke on "one's own death": Rt, 99.

[111] Fully treated in "Rembrandt", chap. 2, "Die Individualisierung und das Allgemeine". See in addition the many preliminary studies and the summary, "Individualismus", in *Marsyas* I (1917), now in BrT, 251–59.

[112] In addition to Rembrandt and Beethoven he mentions Herder, Schleiermacher, Kierkegaard, Ibsen, Lagerlöf.

imply that the purely "individual law" is actually a borderline case and that the element of the universal, which is necessarily transcendent in what is partial, is bound at least to limit and relativize the apodictic demand for something solely self-determining.

Of course, this would not substantially threaten the idea of the individual law. Yet in *Simmel's* total plan there are several lines of thought that put a serious question mark over the Christian legacy he has inherited, namely, the absolute uniqueness of every spiritual being.

First of all there is the strangely problematical concept of God[113] that interprets God's personality as the absolute reciprocity (in terms of "reflection") of the things in the world. This gives him independence vis-à-vis any particular "other" and thus (since he naturally includes all that is single and individual) secures his distinctness from all beings that exist only in relationship. Thus, for *Simmel*, the idealist axiom is reversed: it had stated that God cannot be personality because the latter always presupposes limitation; but the contrary is the case: "A being that is part of a whole, like man, can never be a complete personality."[114] But what God gains in this formulation, man loses. For, if it is true, the perfection of the "I" of which the doctrine of immortality spoke must consist in the overcoming of every "other". Certainly, "by putting forth the perceived world, including its own self-perception, as emanations of itself, it is also, as seen from within, an absolute reality. Recognizing itself, it integrates itself into its phenomenal world as a part of it. However, since it is the being *that* appears to itself, both borne and bearer, both object and its absolute subject, content and the activity that forms the content—we have, at this sole point, something 'behind', something 'in-itself', apart from the appearance: we have this something because we *are* it."[115] But here we must ask, does "its own self-perception" (that is, reflection) belong to the "perceived world" that it puts forth?

[113] Chiefly in "Die Personlichkeit Gottes" (PhK, 198–216). It is clearly only an academic convention when Simmel here (as in R, 20) asserts that he is only engaging in phenomenological scanning, not attempting to say anything about reality.

[114] PhK, 205.   [115] SchN, 21.

If so, this "absolute subject" would still be on the hither side of the subject-object opposition ("below" it, in the terminology of *Lebensphilosophie*), and so completion would have to consist in the removal of this opposition. In fact, immortality is understood as a condition of the soul "in which it no longer experiences anything, that is, in which its meaning is no longer fulfilled by a content in some way external to it".[116] "The feelings of homelessness, of having lost one's way, of being cast hither and thither" are removed, because "the entire duality of the elements of existence" is "abolished".[117] These Indian ideas are brought to a conclusion with *Simmel's* speculation on the possible meaning of the notion of the transmigration of souls,[118] which ultimately (and logically) leads to the dissolution of the person. Only the constellation, not the substratum, would be individual.[119] "The life of the beyond has retreated to pure function; it no longer has any object but is simply the self", with the result that "this 'I' *is* the universe".[120]

Naturally, the creaturely distance separating man from God is here thought of as annihilated; for *Simmel* this boundary never existed. Just as he saw all objective religion as a product of a living religiosity, he traces it so deeply into its vital matrix that, as pure being, it coincides with life: "Only subsequently, as it were, does this fundamental religious being separate out into need and fulfillment", creating a second-order objectivity.[121] "Religious being" is "totally independent of the content that faith seizes and produces".[122] Here life—both its neediness and its superabundance![123]—is felt to be "such an absolute value" that it no longer needs the transcendent content of any religion;[124] God no longer needs to be "substantialized",[125] since the absolute resides in life itself.[126] Once more, at this point, the idea

---

[116] L, 117.   [117] L, 122.   [118] L, 143–53.

[119] "If we wish to reach down deeper to the individual's point of uniqueness . . . we must examine the mode of functional relationships of the individual elements, for this constitutes what is *universal to this individual*, the law of *its* nature." This could be thought of as timeless, as "the ideal form of the individual reality"; "in that case, what survives death would be, not the soul in its historically concrete substantiality, but a timeless essence, manifesting itself now in this, now in that reality-complex" (L, 149).

[120] L, 118.   [121] PhK, 221.   [122] PhK, 224.   [123] PhK, 233.   [124] PhK, 231.

[125] R, 49.   [126] R, 49–52.

of individuality has been eroded: it dissolves in the pure self-actualization of life as such.

Finally we must advert to the fact that, just where he should have held fast to the uniqueness of the personal, *Simmel*, in his monographs, slips unobserved (in the guise of "aesthetic considerations") into the categories of the typical. Now it is "not a question of uniqueness [*Einzigkeit*], but of authenticity [*Eigenheit*]";[127] "what is unique and incomparable in an individual" would be incomprehensible to others, so there must be "some third thing" in man (beyond uniqueness and universality) that is "the bedrock of philosophy": "the stratum of typical spiritual being" (*der typischen Geistigkeit*).[128] This is described—in an illegitimate shift of terms—as "the inwardly objective dimension of a personality that obeys no law but its own".[129] Typology may well be the only way to delimit and approach what is individual, but it must be in no way equated with it. Nor can this be justified by saying that "the most perfect poetic figures we possess, in Dante and Cervantes, Shakespeare and Goethe, Balzac and C. F. Meyer", constitute a unity "that we can only characterize as the simultaneity of the opposed directions here suggested. On the one hand, they are something utterly general, as if the individual were liberated from itself and sublimated into a typical outline . . . , and, on the other hand, they are deepened to such an extent that the human being is nothing but himself, at the source whence his life springs in absolute and irreplaceable self-responsibility."[130] For here the concept of the typical acquires a different coloring from that given above: here the unique, as such, becomes the norm, the point of orientation for what is diffusely present throughout mankind.

In conclusion we can say that *Simmel's* initial problem, that is, the thrust toward integration into the whole and the contrary thrust toward centering in the individual, suffers from an abstractness that prevents the interpersonal dimension from really expressing itself. The "thou" disappears in the world of objects (things are not very different in *Kant*), and so it is understandable that no attention whatsoever is paid, in the transcendent perfecting of the "I", to interpersonal relationships.

---

[127] Ig, 222. Similarly, L, 233.
[128] HPh, 25.   [129] HPh, 27.   [130] L, 80.

The fact, however, that a lone individual is unlike any other is not enough to give the person his due dignity and guarantee his personal significance.[131] And none of the great men to whom *Simmel* devoted a monograph regarded this element as primary. As a result, the last word of this tremendous endeavor of thought is one of tragedy. "To that extent Schopenhauer . . . is, on the whole, right."[132] The somber tone of his posthumous diary reveals the depths of this Heraclitean heart: "What is decisive and characteristic of man is to be found at those points where he despairs."[133] "Dogmatism, in which the elderly become fixed, is often no doubt an indispensable support, since, the older one becomes, the more problematical, confused and incomprehensible life appears."[134] "The strange thing is that everyone knows himself a thousand times better, knows a thousand times more about himself than about anyone else, even the person closest to him; and yet no other person ever seems as fragmentary, as incomplete, as little an integrated whole as we seem to ourselves."[135] "The human soul is the greatest cosmic endeavor, undertaken with worthless means."[136] "Man can only exist in an intermediate area between spiritual limitation and spiritual breadth. . . . Illusion is an intermediate thing between ignorance and knowledge; in practical terms it is an 'as if'. . . . But knowing that one *could* know more than one does—that is authentically human. This despair on man's part is what makes him a human being."[137]

[131] At this point Simmel's relationship to the person and work of Stefan George is significant, cf. the Simmel bibliography in *Buch des Dankes, Briefe, Erinnerung, Bibliographie*, ed. K. Gassen and M. Landmann (Berlin, 1958): essays nos. 62 (1898), 87 (1901 = PhKu, 29ff.), 154 (1909 = PhKu, 74ff.). In saying this, we have not forgotten the great chapter on "Zweierverbindung" in the "Soziologie", which is put forward as the foundation for all further socialization. All the same, this category hardly has any further influence in Simmel's work.

[132] E. Troeltsch, *Der Historismus und seine Probleme*, 583. Similarly the conclusion of Simmel's "Hauptprobleme der Philosophie": "Optimism is on the defensive right from the start. The sum total of evil, of suffering, of imperfections and conflicting ideals in the world is so overwhelming that the burden of proof lies with the person who seeks to defend the 'best of all possible worlds', whereas all the pessimist has to do is to point, without uttering a word, to that sum total" (HPh, 167–68).

[133] T, 130.   [134] T, 140.   [135] T, 144.   [136] T, 127.

[137] T, 127–28. The fact that he speaks openly of "illusion" here sheds light on

4. The Dialogue Principle

One final step will bring us to the threshold of the answer we have been seeking to the question "Who am I?"; and if the exhortation to seek it originated from the Temple of Delphi, the answer will ring out from quite different temple precincts.

It is not insignificant that, in 1918, the year *Simmel* died, and in the following year, one of the strangest phenomena of "acausal contemporaneity" in the history of the intellect took place. This was the simultaneous emergence of the "dialogue principle" in thinkers who could not be farther apart.[1] Altogether there were four of them: three were isolated individuals, namely, the solitary primary school teacher *Ferdinand Ebner*[2] in Wiener Neustadt; *Martin Buber* in Frankfurt, who acknowledged the influence of *Ebner* on the third and last part of his *I and Thou* but who arrived as his central insights from much earlier reflections of his own; and *Gabriel Marcel* in France, who had edited his *Journal métaphysique*[3] since 1914 and who in 1918, precisely, came to almost identical formulations. Finally there was the circle associated with *Franz Rosenzweig*. He had been a pupil of *Hermann Cohen* and had read, in manuscript, the latter's last work, *Religion der Vernunft aus den Quellen des Judentums* (1917–1918), where he found that "it is the 'thou', the discovery of the 'thou', that brings me to the awareness of my 'I' ". In September 1917, from the trenches of Macedonia, *Rosenzweig* wrote that long letter to *Rudolf Ehrenberg*, which he later described as the

---

Simmel's frequent use of the concept of the (right) "distance" that is necessary if an object or an idea is to appear "properly" (HPh, 36ff.).

[1] Cf. Michael Theunissen's foundational work, *Der Andere: Studien zur Sozialontologie der Gegenwart* (Berlin: De Gruyter, 1965), 46; hereafter this work is abbreviated as *Der Andere*. Also Martin Buber's unique presentation of the issues in his "Zur Geschichte des Dialogischen Prinzips" (first published as an epilogue to L. Schneider's *Schriften über das dialogische Prinzip* [Heidelberg, 1954]; now in Buber's *Werke* I [Kösel and L. Schneider, 1962], 293–305). Cf. also Bernhard Casper, *Das dialogische Denken, Franz Rosenzweig, Ferdinand Ebner, Martin Buber* (Herder, 1967).

[2] F. Ebner, *Das Wort und die geistigen Realitäten. Pneumatologische Fragmente* (Regensburg: Pustet, 1921).

[3] G. Marcel, *Journal Métaphysique*. (Gallimard, 1927). *Être et avoir* (Aubier, 1935) is the continuation of this [English ed.: *Being and Having*, London, 1949].

"very germ of the *Star of Redemption*".[4] (He completed the *Star* itself in 1921.)[5] But as early as 1913 *Rosenzweig*, a student in Leipzig, had met *Eugen Rosenstock-Huessy*, and from 1916 onward they wrote to each other on the subject of Judaism and Christianity.[6] *Rosenstock* sent his friend the preliminary draft of his linguistic theory, which seems to have had a substantial influence on the development of the *Star*, as did *Hans Ehrenberg*, *Rosenzweig's* cousin, with whom he had corresponded since 1906. *Rosenzweig* and *Buber* only began to collaborate after their respective programs had appeared in print.

The first thing that strikes us is that, apart from the Christian *Ebner*, all those mentioned are Jews. Doubtless this means that the "discovery" of the "dialogue principle" has something to do with reflection on the Bible of the Old and New Covenants. Nor is this undermined by the fact that many Neo-Kantians and the leading proponents of *Lebensphilosophie* (*Bergson*, *Scheler*, *Simmel*) were also Jews and, on the other hand, that the "dialogue principle" also had non-Jewish antecedents, whom *Ebner* frequently cites: *Hamann*, *Kierkegaard*, *Wilhelm von Humboldt*, *W. Grimm*, whereas *Buber* is more concerned with *Jacobi* and *Feuerbach*, and *Hans Ehrenberg*—in his *Disputation I* (1923)—engages in a debate with *Fichte*. On the whole it is clear that the first period of "dialogism" exhibits a prevalently theological character; not until years later is it replaced by a prevalently philosophical current of thought.[7] This philosophical shift began with *Karl Löwith's* inaugural dissertation, *Das Individuum in der Rolle des Mitmenschen* (1928), a critique of Heidegger's *Sein und Zeit* (1927) (*Being and Time* [London, 1962]), which, together with *Buber*, forms the starting point for *Ludwig Binswanger's Grundformen und Erkenntnis menschlichen Daseins* (written ca. 1930, but not published until 1942), flanked by *Eberhard*

[4] Franz Rosenzweig, in *Kleinere Schriften* (Berlin, 1937), 357–72.

[5] Quoted from the 3d ed: *Der Stern der Erlösung* (Heidelberg, 1954).

[6] F. Rosenzweig, *Briefe* (Berlin, 1935), nos. 641–720.

[7] Exceptions are Dietrich von Hildebrand's *Metaphysik der Gemeinschaft* (1930, 1955), Karl Barth's theological teaching on *"Mitmenschlichkeit"* in *Church Dogmatics*, III/2 (Edinburgh, 1936), F. Gogarten's *Ich glaube an den dreieinigen Gott* (1926) and *Glaube und Wirklichkeit* (1928) and Emil Brunner's *The Divine-Human Encounter* (London, 1944).

Grisebach's Gegenwart (1928); the period comes to an end with *Karl Jaspers' Philosophie II: Existenzerhellung* (1932).[8] *Buber's* settling of accounts with *Jaspers*[9] can be taken as representative of the whole relationship between the first and second period of "dialogism", "in which the so-called 'free' philosophy masters the new discovery in a reductionist manner. Reductionist, I say, because the link between transcendence and concrete reality, which distinguished this discovery, is treated as being arbitrary; the thrust toward the limitlessness of the 'thou' is, as it were, rendered null and void. . . . The biblical view saw the love of God and the love of man in a sisterly relationship in the twofold commandment, directing our gaze to the transparence of the finite 'thou', but also to the grace of the infinite 'Thou', manifesting itself wherever and however it will": but of these two intersecting axes, philosophy has only held onto the horizontal.

Here an acute embarrassment arises as we seek, in this short chapter, and after so many culs-de-sac, to bring the question "Who am I?" to a positive destination. On the basis of many indications in what has gone before, and from *Simmel's* references to Christian Tradition, it is unavoidably clear that a positive answer can only be expected from the vertical axis of biblical revelation. This rings out most clearly in *Rosenzweig*, clearly too in *Ebner* and the later *Buber* (veiled in the early *Buber*): only through the "name" that God uses to address the individual human being is he validly and definitively distinct from every other human being; only thus is he no longer simply an individual of a species but a unique person. Neither pre-Christian thought nor mysticism and idealism; neither psychology nor sociology were equipped, or even authorized, to give this answer.

This means that, however much philosophical dialogism exerts itself to understand how the "I" becomes a person through the "thou", it simply cannot give that precise answer. For however much a genuinely fulfilling encounter with a "thou" may seem, to the individual, to have a quality of "destiny", it remains

---

[8] Prior to Löwith, Theodor Litt's *Individuum und Gemeinschaft* (1919, 1924, 1926) had appeared, giving a thorough discussion of the topic "I and thou" (17–55).

[9] Buber, *Werke* I, 300ff.

ultimately fortuitous and is at most transitory. For one exclusive "I-thou" relationship can be followed by a second . . . and a tenth. In each of these, the "I" is endowed with a new and different name and nature: Who am I, then, in the end? *Buber* had a sober grasp of the finitude, and the inherent disappointment, in every relationship between human beings; for him it is only the eternal Thou which—as *Jaspers* says—does not allow communication to be broken off. In practice, all that the philosophers can do is either take up residence in this precarious, interhuman area or reserve the place that, in *Buber*, is occupied by God for certain human relationships, which will then become archetypal.

Löwith seems to build on *Buber's* foundation: "I" and "thou", in their "original conjoining", "signify their entire world to each other"[10] directly and not mediated by the world. Yet they do so as individuals, as his title indicates (that is, as separate, incommunicable substances), adopting the role (persona) of a fellow man, appearing as a "thou" in a relationship that is constitutive of the "I",[11] enabling the "I" to be "constituted as a first person".[12] Now, however, this reciprocal relationship shows itself to be more and more ambiguous as far as *Löwith* is concerned, insofar as the "I" and the "thou" relate to each other, not of themselves, but through their relationship, that is, from the perspective of the other and of the response that the other expects. The only way out of this vicious circle, which can be a concealing just as well as a revealing, is to go behind the persona to the "I myself" and the "thou thyself" (the "individual"), which show themselves, on the basis of the "relationship", to be genuine freedom: "But if the other were not already 'mine' beforehand, his independent existence could not concretely demonstrate itself to me."[13] As in the case of *Simmel*, we find in *Löwith* the idea of the mutual immediacy of individuals in the relationship itself, "but the more the aspect of relationship comes to the fore, the more individuality diminishes".[14] For it is precisely the "thou", turned entirely toward the "I", which is "not itself"; there is an egoism operating even in altruism, and

---

[10] Löwith, *Das Individuum in der Rolle des Mitmenschen* (reprinted 1969), 57.
[11] *Ibid.*, 62.   [12] *Ibid.*, 169.   [13] *Ibid.*, 138.
[14] Theunissen, *Der Andere*, 431–32.

only "by acknowledging their nonrelational existence"[15] can the two individuals maintain authentic, independent existence even within their relationship. Then, however, the latter becomes a medium that distances the one from the other and ultimately renders reciprocal influence impossible.

In *Grisebach*, the "I-thou" relationship is reduced to the "contradiction"[16] that the "thou" presents to the "I", limiting it and its claims. This vetoing of the attempt of the "I" to "appropriate it" is the conclusive indication of transcendence. Faced with this, all the "I" can do is passively to "listen", which makes it, in its turn, the passive "object" of the more powerful "thou", leading to the opposite of dialogue, namely, the "separation of human beings who are ultimately eternally alien to each other".[17] The only relationship left—as in *Sartre*—is that of "conflict". It is clear that the question "Who am I?" cannot be answered from the perspective of the "other".

In his *Existenzerhellung*[18] Karl Jaspers does not speak of the "thou" at all, but of the "other self". In "existential communication", "unique in each instance", "the one self reciprocally creates the other self", since both "are only *these* selves, not representatives, and hence they cannot be represented".[19] All the same, the main accent lies on the limits of such communication, not least since, to reach it, we must "go through the early, painful experience of loneliness, proving ourselves and learning how to wait". I must learn that, even in relationships, I am to remain "an independent, self-subsistent self", not losing myself in the other;[20] all relationship involves a "loving struggle", in

[15] Löwith, *Das Individuum in der Rolle des Mitmenschen*, 71.

[16] Grisebach, *Gegenwart: Eine kritische Ethik* (Halle, 1928), 71f., 83, 139ff., 151ff.

[17] *Ibid.*, 317.

[18] Karl Jaspers, *Philosophie*, 2d ed., I–III (1948).

[19] *Ibid.*, 345. Cf. 355f.: "Thus, becoming a self through communication seems like a creation *ex nihilo*. It is as if, in the polarities of isolation and unification . . . it became possible to fight a battle having no recognizable origin, in order to produce self-being [*um aus sich das Selbstsein hervorgehen zu lassen*]. In fact we must confront all assertions that attempt to fixate a self-subsistent individual being [*Einzelsein*] as a closed monad, and oppose to them the dialectic of a process of becoming in which the members are only what they produce together with others, namely, their self-being [*Selbstsein*]."

[20] *Ibid.*, 347. Cf. 363: "In communication, loneliness is the irreducible pole

sincerity, for truth, and ultimately it may be necessary sometimes to "break off communication"[21]—which no one has
described as compellingly as *Jaspers*. However, a contradiction
is thus introduced into this theory of communication, according
to which the "I" is described, on the one hand, as the product
of a being-together and, on the other hand, as existing outside
it. So this being-together cannot be located in the same transcendence[22] either, nor can the latter be understood (as in *Buber*)
as the divine substratum that supports each "I-thou". Here too,
therefore, the "I" lacks a real name.

Ludwig Binswanger[23] tries the opposite path to the three
thinkers we have mentioned. He takes *Buber's* "between" (I and
thou) and places it prior to the partners-in-relationship, as a
radical "we-ness" (*Wirheit*). This he understands as springing
straight from what they have in common, which in turn is
experienced as a "soaring above" (*Überschwung*) the world (the
divine ground). The passage in Buber from which he develops
his theory is as follows:

> I see a symbol in those human beings who are so transported, in
> the passion of fulfilled eros, by the miracle of their embrace, that
> their awareness of "I" and "thou" dissolves in the feeling of a
> oneness that does not, and cannot, exist. What the ecstatic calls
> "union" is the transporting dynamism of the relationship; it is not
> a unity that has come to be at this particular moment of world
> time, dissolving "I" and "thou", but the dynamism of the relation-
> ship itself. . . . What we have here is a peripheral heightening of
> the act of relationship; the relationship itself, its vital unity, is felt
> so strongly that its members seem [!] to pale in its presence; *their*
> life causes them to forget the "I" and the "thou" between which it
> has been created.[24]

Binswanger leaves out this "seems" and replaces it with being
itself: the erotic "soaring above" (*Überschwung*) the world as a

---

without which there can be no communication."

[21] *Ibid.*, 365–74.

[22] *Ibid.*, 356f. Full analysis in Theunissen, *Der Andere*, 476–82.

[23] Ludwig Binswanger, *Grundformen und Erkenntnis menschlichen Daseins*, 3d
ed. (Munich and Basle, 1962).

[24] Martin Buber, *I and Thou* [87]. [Quotations from *I and Thou* appear in my
own translation. Page numbers in square brackets refer to R. G. Smith's
published translation (T & T Clark, 1984)—Tr.].

result of the rapture (*Überschwang*) of love is, for him, the ontic primal reality (the "dual we-ness") out of which the "I" and "thou" subsequently crystallize.[25] Union, which (seen from below) seems to be the act of two individuals—man and woman —is (seen from above) the supramundane ground of unity, the "eternity" and "homeland" that is beyond speech, which actually puts forth the two partners from within itself insofar as they are temporal beings in the (Heideggerian) world of *Zuhandenheit* and *Besorgen von Zeug*. *Binswanger's* erotic metaphysics thus splits man into two spheres (which allegedly constitute each other reciprocally, since, of course, transcendence is also manufactured from below in the soaring love of the couple); neither sphere will allow man to be authentically a person, for in the upper sphere he is beyond personality (and here this philosophy is moving toward *Timothy Leary*), and in the lower sphere he remains this-worldly, "a particular someone" in *Buber's* "it"-world.

Martin Buber's sketch *Ich und Du* (*I and Thou* [Edinburgh, 1937]) occupies a special place[26] in the transition to a theology of dialogics, insofar as his approach claims initially to be entirely philosophical, but is progressively filled with theological light, although it never becomes clear what kind of theology it is—to what extent it implies a biblical faith or a belief in universal humanity. Nor could we expect it to become clear, for at this particular time *Buber* had been intensively occupied with the phenomenon of Hasidism, which can be interpreted equally well in the sense of Jewish faith or in the sense of a universally human, "practical" mysticism that is "open to the world". At this point, therefore, I must abandon *Theunissen's* interpretation of *Buber*, insofar as he explains *Buber's Eternal Thou* as an absolutizing of the dimension of shared humanity,[27] and con-

---

[25] The "we" (*Wirheit*) in love is "not a bridge between two existential abysses . . . but an independent and original mode of human existence; it is this that gives rise to the 'I' and the 'thou' " (Binswanger, *Grundformen und Erkenntnis Menschlichen Daseins*, 481).

[26] A similar position could be attributed to Gabriel Marcel, for analogous reasons, since his philosophy operates with a more or less explicit theological a priori.

[27] Theunissen, *Der Andere*, 340f.

centrate on the other ambiguity that lies in the concept of revelation.

Buber can speak of the "I-thou" encounter and the encounter with God that is given through it—as grace—in these terms: "This is the eternal revelation, present in the here-and-now. I know of no revelation that would not be identical in that primal phenomenon; nor do I believe in any such thing. I do not believe in God giving himself a name or giving a self-portrayal before men. . . . The eternal source of power flows. . . ."[28] Here he denies that revelation fundamentally has a content. Nonetheless the latter will not go away; it will constitute a danger to all religion, which is permanently bound to try to get back from the "object of faith" that I "have" to the divine life that "has me". According to *Buber* the human "I" exists fundamentally in the two modes of the "I-thou" and the "I-it", the originally vital relationship (*Marcel's* "being") and the distanced, objectivizing affirmation (*Marcel's* "having"). These basic attitudes could be compared to *Augustine's frui* and *uti*: both belong essentially to existence; the "I-it" attitude "is not evil—no more than matter is evil", it only becomes evil when man allows the "ceaselessly growing 'it'-world" to "become overgrown".[29] The state, economics, politics—these are not evil so long as they are fashioned and restrained by the source of personal responsibility in the "I-thou".[30] And it is "the lofty pathos of our fate that every 'thou' in our world must become an 'it' ";[31] the direct relationship must become "latent"; "it is impossible to live in the naked present—it would devour us".[32] Where the direct relationship embraces the world within itself, it appears "as an injustice to the world",[33] whereas, where the "I" becomes an "it", retreating into the world, this is felt to be an injustice to the inner "exclusivity"[34] of the "thou"-relationship.

Here we become suddenly aware how close *Buber's* central perspective is to *Simmel's*: the "pathos" informing the relationship between "thou" and "it" corresponds exactly to the tragic relationship between the "lifestream" and the "form" (ossified content). In both cases this "twofold nature" is most profoundly

[28] *I and Thou* [111–12].
[30] *I and Thou* [47–51].
[32] *I and Thou* [34].
[34] *I and Thou* [78].

[29] *I and Thou* [46].
[31] *I and Thou* [16].
[33] *I and Thou* [78].

determining and most profoundly disconcerting. True, *Rosenzweig* is right in his polemics against *Simmel*: "He does not think in secret dialogue with his partner",[35] but in a monologue. The difference between them shows itself in that *Simmel* presses forward out of the tragic and into a "life" that comprehends the dualism, whereas for *Buber*: "Man's sense of 'thou', which, on the basis of its relationships with all individual 'thou's, is disappointed to find that each of them becomes an 'it', exerts itself to get beyond them and yet cannot reach its eternal 'Thou'."[36] For the "I-thou", rooted in the relationship, in the "between",[37] is real, whereas the "I-it" is the unreal, the defective, "diminution".[38]

The "between" is not constituted by "I" and "thou" in separation but is always the prior place of encounter where both of them become themselves for each other. With a view to this constitutive "between" it is possible to speak of a "relational a priori" in man, that is, of an "inborn thou", designed to realize itself in the encounter with a "thou";[39] but this realization takes place in the "between". What is it? At this point *Buber's* oscillation between philosophy and theology is at its clearest. For he begins explaining it by referring to the primitive "*mana or orenda*", "whence a path leads to the Brahman in its original meaning and on to the *dynamis* and *charis* of the magical papyri and the Apostolic Letters".[40] Another term for it is "spirit", evidently in the sense of the Old Testament *ruach* ("spirit is not in the 'I' but between 'I' and 'thou' "),[41] and finally—no doubt under the initial influence of *F. Ebner*—he can also call it "word": "spirit is word".[42] His mention of the Apostolic Letters points to the (personal/apersonal) *pneuma* of the New Testament, which is the soul and, as it were, the substance of the community of the Church. *Buber* wishes to include everything, from *mana* to *pneuma*, that can be regarded as a personalizing medium of the "I-thou" relationship; its final name, then, must necessarily be presence (or revelation) of God in the relationship that has been created.

---

[35] Rosenzweig, *Briefe*, no. 155. Other references in Theunissen, *Der Andere*, 256.

[36] *I and Thou* [131].   [37] *I and Thou* [15].
[38] *I and Thou* [43].   [39] *I and Thou* [27, 70].
[40] *I and Thou* [20].   [41] *I and Thou* [39].
[42] *I and Thou* [39, 95].

Here we stand at the crossroads: Is this God the eternal aspect of the "I-thou", which, on the human side, will decline into the "it"? Or is he not only the one who creates relationships but himself one pole of a relationship? *Buber* decides unequivocally for the latter. God is the eternal Thou that the human "thou" cannot reach of its own accord; but every "I" has a direct relationship with this Thou:[43] "The inborn 'thou' . . . can only become complete in direct relationship with that Thou which, of its own nature, cannot become an 'it'."[44] The "latency" of our relation to God, our "distance from God", the "pain of dryness"—these do not indicate that God is no longer there "but that we are not always there".[45] It is the creature who must learn, through the "I-thou" relationship and "through the grace of its comings and the pain of its departures",[46] to practice the presence of God, who is always there. Tentatively, *Buber* elicits from this a "metacosmic" law according to which the twofold "I-thou" and "I-it" would express a twofold movement of the universe: "Both a turning-away from the primal ground, by means of which the universe maintains itself in a process of becoming, and a turning-toward the primal ground, by means of which the universe redeems itself in being. Both movements unfold in time according to their destiny, whereas according to grace they are enclosed in (timeless) creation, which is simultaneously—and incomprehensibly—a letting go and a preserving, a setting free and a binding."[47] Each individual human being, in his entirety, is summoned to enter into this rhythm; the influence he puts forth[48] is at the same time a participation in the medium of influence,[49] and so it takes place beyond activity and passivity.[50] "Man's 'religious' situation, his existence in this presence, is characterized by essential and insoluble antinomies. . . . I know that 'I am in the hands of someone (something) else', and . . . yet I know 'that it all depends on me'."[51]

However, this totality evinces two characteristics, namely,

---

[43] *I and Thou* [134–37]. The attribution of personality to God is indispensable for anyone for whom God is not a mere "principle", or "idea".

[44] *I and Thou* [75].

[45] *I and Thou* [99].

[46] *I and Thou* [33].

[47] *I and Thou* [101].

[48] *I and Thou* [14, 15, 21].

[49] *I and Thou* [63].

[50] *I and Thou* [76–77].

[51] *I and Thou* [95–96].

the aforementioned tendency[52] to turn the entire content of
revelation and religion into human acts[53] and, following from
it—as *Buber's* Hasidism might lead one to expect—the view that
God is encountered as "Thou" only within the human "I-thou"
relationship (albeit *also* in the "pain of its departures"). This is
the thrust of *Buber's* cosmic mysticism, in its openness to the
world and its aim of bringing the world to God. Thus it is
important that he concludes his work with the prospect that
each new religion will be more world-inclusive. True, the
weight of ill destiny increases throughout history (as in *Simmel*
and his "tragedy of culture"), and the world of the "it" increasingly
overthrows the world of the "thou": "Each succeeding aeon
finds destiny more baneful and reversals more explosive. And
the theophany comes *closer* and *closer*; more and more it focuses
on the sphere *between beings*, approaching the realm that is in our
midst, in the 'between'."[54]

Now we should be able to get a clearer picture of *Buber's* place
in our problem. His central concern is the encounter with God
in (and thus also beyond) the "I-thou" relationship. Only
incidentally, in his last pages, evidently influenced by *Ebner*,
does he say that "all revelation is vocation and mission".[55] *Buber*
certainly emphasized that he was familiar with these categories
—of what takes place between God and man, the one-who-
calls and the one-who-is-called[56]—from his youth; but there is
strikingly little of this in his introductions to the Hasidic books.
Clearly, *I and Thou* lacks the very category we are looking for,
namely, man's being directly addressed, summoned, called and
sent by God. This is the only satisfying reply to the question
"Who am I in my particularity?" This is the reply *Franz
Rosenzweig* gives us.

Rosenzweig's thought matures as he distances himself from
German idealism. (As is well known, it was *Rosenzweig* who
discovered the latter's "earliest program of a system".)[57] In the

---

[52] This cannot be more than a tendency (cf. Simmel), since the "it"—and
hence the aspect of content and form—is necessary to everything in the world.

[53] *I and Thou* [111–12]. Cf. the distinction between the form (*Gestalt*), which
confronts man, and the work (*Gebilde*), which is wrought by man [9, 41].

[54] *I and Thou* [119–20].   [55] *I and Thou* [115].

[56] Buber, "Zur Geschichte des dialogsichen Prinzips", in *Werke* I, 297.

[57] Franz Rosenzweig, *Kleinere Schriften* (Berlin, 1937), 230–77.

"germ" of the *Star of Redemption* he discovers his "philosophical Archimedean point"[58] by means of which he aims to lift the idealist system from its hinges. How can revelation be protected from the incursions of thought? "The trait of 'repugnance' " (*das Merkmal des "Ungerne"*)—of its running counter to the human—was not enough; *Rosenstock's* concept of "orientation", which creates an "upper and a lower level in nature ('heaven' and 'earth') . . . and a real, firm 'earlier' and 'later' in time (complementarities that cannot be relativized)"—was much better. But does this really come to grips with idealism (*Hegel* and *Goethe*)? Here, like *Kierkegaard*, *Rosenzweig* comes up against the facticity of the individual human being, which survives all system-building. "I, the mere private subject; I, with my first and second names; I, who am but dust and ashes—I am still there, . . . and now, suddenly, I come, as if nothing had happened to me, and (like Grabbe in the final act) shed light on the whole. *Individuum ineffabile triumphans*."[59] This is illustrated in more detail in connection with the concept of facticity in the later *Schelling* (where *Rosenzweig* proceeds from *Schelling's* construction of God as the eternal "There", with which God's essence identifies itself as personal, and moves over to God's relationship to the created world): there is the God-world relationship that thought includes in the system and the other God-world relationship in which "the free personality" resists being absorbed into the system. In the system, all relationships "take place only between third persons; the system is the world in the form of the third person"; even man, distancing himself from himself in reflection, enters into the third person. "Spinoza —supported by Goethe—writes of this man that no one who loves God should ask God to love him in return", for this is "a love in the third person; the 'he' surrenders to the 'it'; no 'thou' is uttered." Here A = B (i.e., God = nature) can be "the governing world-formula".[60] However, "Man as 'I' may and must desire God to love him in return. Indeed, he must actually desire God to love him first. For his 'I' is dull and inarticulate and waits for the liberating word from the mouth of God. 'Adam, where art thou?' . . . In the 'I' of revelation and in the 'thou' of conscience or of the commandment and the responding

[58] *Ibid.*, 357.   [59] *Ibid.*, 359.   [60] *Ibid.*, 363.

'I' of Adam's sense of shame and of Abraham's readiness for obedience; and then, again, in the 'I' of repentance and the 'thou' of prayer and the 'I' of redemption". Now it is a "trumpet voice", addressing, not the human being who luxuriates in his ideals, but summoning "the deaf 'I', sunk in the depths of its 'I'-ness", "this 'I' of which nothing can be presupposed except that it loves *itself*". Only insofar as he is addressed by God can this "I" recognize "his brother", recognize "that he is *not a 'he-she-it'*, *but an 'I'*, an 'I' like me, not a coinhabitant of the same, directionless and centerless place, not a fellow traveller on a journey through time without beginning or end, but my brother, the companion of my destiny". The one addressed by God does not love the other person as someone who "shares the same nature" (like the stoic and the Spinozist) but as someone who is likewise addressed by God in "what is most individual to him". And the issue is not the world's beginning or ending but this very center—"a circumscribed dwelling, a piece of earth between four tent posts" (like *Heidegger's* "foursome" [*Geviert*]), because revelation is something that "happens to the *point*, the rigid, deaf, immovable point, the stubborn 'I' that 'I just am' ".[61] The system "leads back" ("reduction"), whereas revelation creates a "reciprocal relationship between 'I' and 'Thou' " ("correlation").[62]

This is the "germ" from which *Rosenzweig* can develop the ample system of the *Star of Redemption*. Here, in place of abstract logic, we find the three-dimensional language with its "I", "thou" and "he" ("she", "it");[63] the irreducible facticity of the death experience,[64] of love and of action provides the locus of development in each case. Once again, at the center, there is the question that heaven puts to the earth. "But where is there to be found an independent 'thou' of this kind, freely standing over against the hidden God, a 'thou' in whom God can recognize himself as 'I'? . . . Where is there a 'thou'? Where? This is what

[61] *Ibid.*, 364–66.

[62] "Hermann Cohens Nachlasswerk", in *Kleinere Schriften*, 297; "Hermann Cohens jüdische Schriften", *ibid.*, 334.

[63] Rosenzweig, *Der Stern der Erlösung* (1954) II, 27ff., passim.

[64] The opening sentence of the book is: "All knowledge of the universe begins with death and the fear of death."

God asks too." Man hides from the question "Where art thou?" Then comes the vocative, the summons, "and man is denied every escape route through objectivization". "The personal name. The personal name, which is not a name personally adopted by someone of his own volition but the name which God himself has created for him; it is only personal to him because it is created as such by the Creator." At this point "the stubborn and hardened self" emerges: "Here I am. Here is the 'I'. The individual, human 'I'. It is as yet entirely receptive, open, as yet empty, without content, without being, pure readiness, pure obedience, all ears."[65] Into this empty vessel the commandment drops, calling for love, here and now. Then comes the horizontal dimension: "The personal name calls for other names outside itself." "For, truly, the name is not mere 'sound and smoke', as unbelief would continually suggest in its hardened obstinacy, but word and fire."[66]

Ferdinand Ebner's path is more toilsome, pursued in total isolation. Yet the change takes place earliest in him, for in 1912 his notes and diaries reveal traces of the dialogue principle: "This is the most difficult problem for ethics: the recognition of the 'I' in the other, which actually constitutes the 'thou'; thus the 'thou' is posited as an ethical demand."[67] And at the beginning of 1913: "We should look for an 'objectivization' of the 'I' in the ethical positing of the 'thou'."[68] Initially his thoughts circle around language. Language is both the given medium in which alone the human being can become, and be, spirit; and it is also the medium in which man himself is (linguistically) creative; here, as one-who-speaks, he is ethically involved. This anticipates the second phase, "the jump into dialogue",[69] leading to a grasp of the way man receives the word and is endowed with gifts, that is, grace.[70]

---

[65] Rosenzweig, *Der Stern der Erlösung*, II, 112–14.

[66] *Ibid.*, II, 127–29.

[67] Ferdinand Ebner, *Schriften*, ed. Franz Seyr, I–III (Munich, 1963) II, 94; hereafter this work referenced as W.

[68] W, II, 103.

[69] B. Casper, *Das dialogische Denken, Franz Rosenzweig, Ferdinand Ebner, Martin Buber*, 210ff.

[70] W, II, 293: "The existential implied in an 'is' sentence, namely, 'there is'

In his chief work, *Das Wort und die geistigen Realitäten. Pneumatoligische Fragmente*,[71] the first thing to be explained is the title. "The word" (*das Wort*) is the way the "I" addresses the "thou", and since God is man's "sole Thou",[72] the basis for all instances of "thou" between human beings,[73] all language has its origin in him; as far as man is concerned, language is "given". For the Christian, *Ebner*, however, continually meditating upon the Prologue of John's Gospel, this Word has become flesh "in order to express itself, in order to speak to man",[74] to give us "the true object and content of faith",[75] "to tear man away from the danger of spiritual 'disintegration' and to reveal the meaning of his existence".[76] "Disintegration" (*Entwerdung*) is that unreal dream existence of the man who is enclosed in himself, the dream existence that philosophy—still "living on the basis of idealism"[77]—constructs as its own realm.[78] Over against this there is "reality": what is real is solely what takes place in the genuine word between "I" and "thou": " 'I' and 'thou'—these are life's spiritual realities", for "the 'I' only exists in its relation to the 'thou', not apart from it".[79] But what does "spiritual" mean here? It means the same as "pneumatological" in the Pauline sense, and in *Ebner*, the Christian, it corresponds to the "medium" or the "between" that *Buber*, the Jew, viewed as a spectrum from *mana* to *dynamis* and the *charis* of the New Testament. It is what is divinely "given" along with the reality of the word that comes from God; in it and with it—"sharing in it as cocreator"[80]—man can live in the reality of the love of God and of neighbor.[81]

From this explanation of the work's title we can already glimpse its main burden. First it consists in the indivisibility of word and love: "Word and love belong together: word as the 'objective' and love as the 'subjective vehicle' of the relationship between the 'I' and the 'thou'."[82] The *pneuma* is "the spiritual

---

[*es gibt*], is not without a deep meaning: it grasps all being as a gift, i.e., ultimately as grace."

[71] *Das Wort und die geistigen Realitäten Pneumatologische Fragment Ebner*, quoted from the 1st ed. (Pustet, Regensburg, 1921), referenced here as GR.

[72] GR, 24.   [73] GR, 184–85.   [74] W, I, 630.   [75] GR, 155.
[76] GR, 179; cf. W, I, 529.   [77] GR, 112.   [78] GR, 57, 133, passim.
[79] GR, 15.   [80] GR, 59.   [81] GR, 116, 180ff.
[82] GR, 51; similarly, 77, 116.

atmosphere . . . in which the word breathes and lives",[83] and if word, language and grammar (which, as in *Rosenzweig*, must be a "pneumatological" grammar)[84] are examined with regard to their foundation and origin, *pneuma* really is the *"hagion pneuma* of the New Testament, in which man is reborn and is named a child of God".[85] Word-Spirit is originally God's mode of address to man, in which the latter is constituted as an "I" and is enabled to grasp God as his true "Thou". Thus, as *Hamann* rightly says, language comes from God;[86] man can seize upon it and develop it only as something already given.[87] Thus *psyche* and *pneuma*, the psychological and the pneumatological, are continually opposed to one another;[88] a purely psychological humanity could only exist as a race, a species—"its individuals swim in the river of life, the strength whereby they hold themselves above the water gradually fails, until the selfsame stream that gave them birth swallows them up"[89]—but a humanity of this kind would not be a "natural" one; it would be one that had sunk from reality into "dreaming", an "ego-enclosed" humanity. However, if man lives in the reality of God's address to him, he is always "an individual before God".[90] And if the incarnate Word of God, "the Christ . . . is not a mere type but the 'absolute', unique instance",[91] *Ebner* is not afraid to attribute the very same to the human being to whom God has spoken in Christ:

> In the real meaning of the statement ("I am"), to exist means being not only a physical individual but primarily a spiritual individual; it means being an "absolute, unique existence". . . . To other men, however, a man is never an absolute, unique instance. Nor is he in the "ego-loneliness" of his existence. But before God he is and is meant to be. . . . Of himself, man never becomes an absolute, unique instance, not even in his relation to God. Only through Christ does he become such, through Christ's

[83] GR, 25.   [84] GR, 52, 98.   [85] GR, 170.   [86] GR, 20f.

[87] GR, 17: "on the one hand it is something presupposed, on the other, something that is produced."

[88] "We can never understand 'psychologically', but 'pneumatologically' ", how the "I-thou" relationship is presupposed if an "I" is to attain self-understanding (GR, 21). The concrete "I" and its thoughts are to be understood "either as *psyche* or as *pneuma*" (GR, 41). What is spiritual in man "can never be grasped psychologically, but only pneumatologically" (GR, 97).

[89] GR, 226.   [90] GR, 184.   [91] W, I, 625.

demand for faith and through his faith. He is an absolute, unique instance in the personal actuality of the Word which was in the beginning and *in the presence of* this actuality. Christ is the absolute, unique instance, not only—as in man's case—in the presence of God; in summoning man's faith, he claims to be such in the presence of men too.[92]

From this perspective we can understand his criticism—in spite of his recognition of the "astonishing" closeness—of the "lyrical mystic", *Buber*.[93] The latter ascends from the human "I-thou" to the divine "Thou", whereas *Ebner* resolutely follows the opposite path: everything has its roots in the God-relationship and its solitariness, in a fundamental faith[94] that becomes a full faith only when confronted with Christ's cry of dereliction[95] and that, originating in God and Christ, makes Christian love of neighbor possible. Now it can be affirmed that only the "thou" is divine (since God in Christ is present in it), never the "I"; all the "I" can do is humbly admit its frail humanity and refrain from making itself into a "thou"; yet, as the "thou" of some other "I", it can receive this quality of Divinity.[96] Here the "individual before God" has become the opposite pole of the "individual in his ego-loneliness"; he cannot come before God "without praying in fellowship with all human beings".[97] Just as firmly as *Buber*, *Ebner* rejects that mysticism which turns its back on the world in order to find God. "Shifting the center of gravity of the spiritual life from the Kingdom of God", which is among us in the human "I-thou", "to one's own soul", which ultimately leads back to "ego-loneliness", seems to

[92] W, I, 482.

[93] W, I, 584; a mention of Rosenzweig at 582.

[94] Faith in the word: GR, 28; faith versus understanding: GR, 49; faith does not require proofs of God's existence: GR, 27; faith as the total commitment of one's existence: GR, 55.

[95] GR, 206, and the whole essay "Das Kreuz und die Glaubensforderung" in W, I, 383–401. "God's becoming man absolutely in the last moment of the life of Jesus makes the inner man free for faith; it exposes man's 'inwardness' ", i.e., his own Godforsakenness (395). This must be seen in the whole context of Ebner's teaching on the Fall and on language, which he sees as originating in man's crying out for God when he finds himself far away from him (GR, 86f., 157ff., 165).

[96] GR, 185.   [97] GR, 184.

Ebner the most dangerous perversion of Christianity into sterile churchiness or mysticism: "All mystics either want to avoid this reality (of the Kingdom of God among us) or else they fail to reach it."[98] *Ebner* sees what is really Christian as the essential turning toward one's fellow men. That is why he speaks so positively of *Alfred Adler* and especially of *Rudolf Allers*.[99] Thus, too, he sees "the fundamental propositions in Feuerbach's *Philosophie der Zukunft*" as leading "directly to the Prologue of Saint John's Gospel".[100] Ultimately for him, however, everything depends on the scandal of the Cross, which cannot be domesticated in any "Christian culture".[101] This is what happens in the idealist philosophy (with its roots in Christianity)[102] and its ultimate formalization, mathematics;[103] it is a refusal to take account of faith in the scandal of the Cross, and thus it is inevitably surrendered to (unbelieving) Judaism.[104] *Ebner's* final diagnosis and prognosis are like *Kierkegaard's*, but even bleaker:

Did Western civilization founder—and it has already foundered—on anything other than the stylizing of the Cross, on its Platonic misunderstanding of Christianity? Let us not deceive ourselves: it is this and nothing else that has brought forth the unbelief and the godlessness of our time. In the end, whether the Americanization of life or Bolshevism will finally clear a path for the Mongols to take over in Europe is a matter of indifference.[105]

[98] W, I, 626. [99] W, I, 618ff. [100] W, I, 622. [101] GR, 232. [102] GR, 99f.
[103] GR, 154.
[104] W, I, 608. "Modern man's life was and is a negation of Christianity. Thus, however anti-Semitic it may seem at present, and however enthusiastically, in our country, it may swear allegiance to the Christian-German ideals of beauty and culture, it has been handed over, body and soul, to Judaism" (W, I, 398).
[105] GR, 234; cf. W, I, 399.

E. CONCLUDING REMARKS

Our aim here is not to recapitulate the wealth of material offered in this book and bring it into a synthesis—we can only see how it hangs together once we have carried through this theodramatic program—or to give a preliminary sketch of the work that will have to be undertaken. Suffice it to say that the circuitous paths of this "transition" have actually brought us where we hoped, namely, "from role to mission". Our path's direction gave us the question "Who am I?": we needed to get away from the arbitrariness of a "role" that was simply thrown over a colorless "I" like some coat that happened to be to hand and could at any time be exchanged for another and to arrive at an "I" that was irreplaceable as such and thus could be enabled to take on a genuinely dramatic role in the realm, not of the theatre, but of life. If we had not discovered this unique "name" (*Rosenzweig*) of the individual addressed by God and endowed with his personal name, the irreplaceable human being, the "absolute, unique instance" (*Ebner*), we would not have been justified in attempting a theory of theo-drama, for the unique God would have lacked a partner. The fact that this partner came to light in the field of biblical theology, transcending all the approaches made by mysticism, philosophy, psychology and sociology, is no surprise, since from the outset he himself is a product and an element of that dramatic tension that unfolds exclusively, in our view, in the realm of the Bible. Moreover, the man who is a serious co-actor with God will be able, for his part, to contribute to the unfolding of this dramatic tension.

It only remains for us to indicate why, in that biblical realm in which *Rosenstock*, *Rosenzweig*, the *Ehrenbergs* and *Buber* have achieved so much of lasting validity, the transition from the Old Covenant to the New appears necessary. In the *Star of Redemption* we attain to the "name", that is, the individual's perfect definition as assigned by God. In *I and Thou* we also glimpse the world-fullness of the man who has been signed with a name. But only in Jesus Christ does it become clear how profoundly this definitive "I"-name signifies vocation, mission. In him the "I" and the role become uniquely and ineffably one in the reality of his mission, far beyond anything attainable by earthly means. *Theodor Haecker* saw this:

> By and large the actor's nature and person do not coincide with the role he has to play, and this is true not only of the stage play that, on the basis of an inborn instinct, human beings creatively set forth in image and speech, but also of the *theatrum mundi* itself. In the play that takes place on the world stage, the author, director and producer is—in an absolute sense—God himself. True, he allows freedom to act its own part according to its nature—and this is the greatest mystery of creation and of God's direct creative power—yet ultimately the play he plays is his own. In this play there can be a tragic or comic dichotomy between the actor and the role; and this produces the comedies and tragedies of world history—and its farces too, of which we today are both spectators and actors, as we have always been. Only in the drama of the God-Man do we find identity between the sublime actor and the role he has to play.[1]

Thomas Aquinas describes this identity by saying that in Christ the *processio* within the godhead, which constitutes the Son as the Father's dialogue partner, is identical, in God's going-out-from-himself toward the world, with the *missio*, the sending of the Son to mankind. (This *missio* is completed by the sending of the Spirit into the world, proceeding from both Father and Son.)[2] Once and for all, the duality of "being" and "seeming", which goes through man's entire structure, is absolutely overcome in the identity of person and mission in Christ. But this duality is not cast off as something ambiguous and inferior: its two aspects are brought together in the humanity of Jesus, who, as the "Suffering Servant", does the will of his Father. Since, however, the Spirit who mediates between God and the incarnate Son prevents any "heteronomy", the same Spirit, given to men to enable them to be and act in a God-ward manner, can close the tragic breach between person and role in mission. And the Spirit is two things: he is most interior to the "I", making the person a son and causing him to cry "Abba,

---

[1] Theodor Haecker, *Was ist der Mensch?* 2d ed. (Hegner, Leipzig, 1934), 128f.
[2] *Summa Theol.* Ia q 43, a 1–8.

Father"; and he is the socializing "between", rooting human fellowship in a (trinitarian) personal depth that cannot be realized by purely earthly means. Both dimensions, the aloneness of the "I" with God and its subsequent opening-up to the world in its entirety, are inseparable in the biblical event of mission: the two can be seen in the call of the prophets, which is completed in the mission of the Son, who, as the Only-begotten, is in the bosom of the Father and can "make him known", "interpret" him to us (Jn 1:18); he passes on the mission to Christians, who hold themselves ready to be appointed and sent out in this way. However, since the call of the individual Christian always takes place within the context of the community of those who are in Christ, that is, in the Church, the individual cannot in any way reflect upon himself—in the sense of the *Gnothi Sauton*—without encountering the Church and his fellowship in her with others. The stage erected before the world's eyes, to which he is sent as an actor, is always occupied by an ensemble of fellow actors; he is inserted into the ensemble. We cannot at this point go into the fluid relationship between this ensemble of the Church community and the total human community.

From this vantage point we can anticipate how the two triads we presented in "Resources" will find their blueprint in Christian theo-drama, how seriously—more seriously than in any other *Weltanschauung*—finitude and death are part of the action and how the battle for the good is waged at a more profound level here than anywhere else; for here man's freedom is established by God's freedom, and the doctrine of the *imago Dei* in man is taken to its ultimate conclusion.[3] As a result the "aesthetic" picture becomes dramatically three-dimensional.

It follows quite naturally that if, obedient to his mission, a person goes out into a world that is not only ungodly but hostile to God, he will be led to the experience of Godforsakenness. And this will take place—as *Ebner* warned us—in the fifth act, where events converge on the final action, which becomes a passion: in death. The question here will be this: How, in

[3] Cf., by way of anticipation: Robert Javelet, *Image et Ressemblance au 12e siècle. De St. Anselme à Alai Lille*, 2 vols. (Letouzey et Ané, 1967), which recapitulates the whole history of the problem since Plato.

Christian terms, can the highest tragic action be reconciled with a tragedy that in fact has been overcome? And how can the highest reality of earthly existence point to an existence in God, from the perspective of whose transcendent reality, nonetheless, "Life's a dream"? "And death shall be no more, neither shall there be mourning nor crying nor pain any more, for the former things have passed away" (Rev 21:4).

INDEX OF AUTHORS' NAMES